FOUR CENTURIES OF MUSICAL INSTRUMENTS

ALBERT R. RICE THE MARLOWE A. SIGAL COLLECTION

PHOTOGRAPHS BY MARLOWE A. SIGAL

Schiffer Publishing Ltd®

4880 Lower Valley Road • Atglen, PA 19310

Other Schiffer Books on Related Subjects:

Antique Brass Wind Instruments: Identification and Value Guide
978-0-7643-0027-1

Antique Woodwind Instruments: An Identification and Price Guide
978-0-7643-2224-2

Library of Congress Control Number: 2014955459

Designed by Justin Watkinson
Type set in Univers LT Std/Minion Pro

ISBN: 978-0-7643-4712-2
Printed in China

Published by Schiffer Publishing, Ltd.
4880 Lower Valley Road
Atglen, PA 19310
Phone: (610) 593-1777; Fax: (610) 593-2002
E-mail: Info@schifferbooks.com

For our complete selection of fine books on this and related subjects, please visit our website at www.schifferbooks.com.
You may also write for a free catalog.

This book may be purchased from the publisher.
Please try your bookstore first.

We are always looking for people to write books on new and related subjects. If you have an idea for a book, please contact us at proposals@schifferbooks.com.

Schiffer Publishing's titles are available at special discounts for bulk purchases for sales promotions or premiums. Special editions, including personalized covers, corporate imprints, and excerpts can be created in large quantities for special needs. For more information, contact the publisher.

CONTENTS

PREFACE

Visitors to the collection of musical instruments usually ask me the following questions: When did you start collecting? How long did it take? Where do you find instruments for the collection? Here are the answers.

When did I start collecting musical instruments? How long did it take?

When I was in junior high school, the Wilson High School, Easton, Pennsylvania, marching band needed a tenor saxophone player. I wanted to join the band. My father bought me a Buescher tenor sax (number 1943.01). After a few lessons by high-school music teacher Paul Filer, followed by serious instruction by Ken Brader in Easton, I joined the band. Throughout high school, college, and graduate school, I played this sax in marching bands and continue to do so. In fact, I've never attended a football game without this horn. A clarinet (1944.01, see page 224) followed soon after.

A year later, my father found and bought an Estey reed organ (1960.01, see page 278). It needed considerable repairs. He told me that if I could repair this organ, I could have it. I repaired it, and it still plays well. He gave it to me in 1960, when my wife and I moved into our first home in Newtonville, Massachusetts.

My interest in keyboard instruments really started in the second grade, when I began piano lessons. My teacher, Paul Shocker, quickly pointed me in the direction of early classical composers, and I was playing selections from Bach's *Anna Magdalena Workbook* within several months. Music 1 at Harvard with Archibald Davidson introduced me to the history of music, which has been very valuable as I have collected musical instruments over the years.

For my birthday in 1964, my father asked me what I'd like to receive as a present. At that time, Zuckermann harpsichord kits were quite popular, and I told him I'd like to have and build one. He very wisely suggested that I find and purchase a real antique harpsichord rather than building a modern replica. I should mention that my parents, Arthur and Serena Sigal, were both avid collectors. Dad collected antique motorcycles — he was one of the founders of the Antique Motorcycle Club of America, and Mother collected "Pennsylvania Dutch stuff."

The following year, I found an 1834 Broadwood square piano in a local antiques shop. It wasn't a harpsichord, but it was an antique keyboard instrument. I bought it (1965.01, see page 40). Two years later, a very early New York square piano was offered for auction in Cambridge, Massachusetts, and I bought it (1967.01, see page 40). This was followed by two antique grand pianos in the following year. Finally in 1969, an antique Shudi harpsichord was advertised in *ANTIQUES* magazine by a dealer in Glasgow, and I bought it (1969.02, see page 11). At that point, I was hooked, and many antique keyboards were added to the collection in the following years.

By 1974, it was clear that we would need a much larger house to contain this growing collection. Happily, at that time, a large Victorian house in Newton Centre came on the market. It contained a built-in, 19-rank, tracker-action organ. Not only was this another keyboard instrument for the collection, but it solved the space problem. We bought this house and have lived in it ever since.

Despite the large size of this second home, collecting keyboard instruments is a self-limiting hobby. They do take a lot of room. Since I had played saxophone and clarinet since I was a kid, I decided to turn the focus of my still-growing keyboard collection toward woodwind instruments. Obviously, they take up much less space. With the help and encouragement of Philip Young, I purchased an August Grenser bassoon (1993.02, see page 176) and several other interesting and important woodwinds. Over the past two decades, I have added hundreds of other woodwinds to my collection.

While searching for keyboard and woodwind instruments, I inevitably saw many other types of musical instruments. Occasionally, I would buy some of them, if I found them interesting, beautiful, or from important makers.

Where did I find instruments?

Many sources. Auctions, ads in newspapers and magazines, dealers, eBay, the Internet, referrals from friends. After many years of collecting, it became widely known that I bought antique musical instruments, and many owners contacted me with offers to sell.

I must acknowledge with warm and sincere thanks the following persons who helped me build the collection over the years:

Family members. My father who got me started and my wife, Elise, and children, Erica and Andrew, who put up with my strange hobby and resigned themselves to living in a museum all these years.

Dealers. Tony Bingham in London and Jean Michel Renard in Bellenaves, France, were especially helpful. I could not have made many acquisitions without them.

Auctioneers. Graham Wells at Sotheby's, London, and Kerry Keane, first at Skinners, Boston, and then at Christie's, London and New York. Alas, Sotheby's and Christie's have abandoned musical instrument sales.

Musical instrument museum directors and curators. André Larson and Peggy Banks at the National Music Museum, Darcy Kuronen, Sam Quigley, and Barbara Lambert at the Boston Museum of Fine Arts, Laury Libin at the Metropolitan Museum of Art, and Gerhard Stradner at the Sammlung alter Musikinstrumente, Vienna.

Experts. John Koster at the National Music Museum, keyboard scholar, who has probably forgotten more about early keyboard instruments than anyone else knows. Frank Hubbard, pioneer in the renaissance of the harpsichord, who was especially sharing in his knowledge of this instrument. Phil Young, author of woodwind directories. Eric Hoeprich, clarinet performer, author, and maker.

Restorers. In the beginning, I restored several keyboards myself. As the collection grew and other activities demanded my time and attention, other highly skilled instrument restoration professionals made important improvements to instruments in the collection. Especially Tim Hamilton, first in London, now in Boston, and David Winston, Biddenden, England.

Fellow collectors. Even though we sometimes competed for the acquisition of certain instruments, the following friends were very sharing in their knowledge. Bill Waterhouse, bassoons and other woodwinds. Sir Nicholas Shackleton, clarinets. Douglas Koeppe, American woodwind instruments, and Peter Thresh, London salerooms.

Associations. Over the years, I have gained much knowledge and many friends as the result of my membership in the American Musical Instrument Society, the Galpin Society in England, and CIMCIM (International Committee for Museums and Collections of Musical Instruments). I highly recommend that anyone interested in musical instruments join all of these organizations.

Finally, to Al Rice, author of this catalog, I owe a great debt of thanks for his friendship, expert knowledge of all musical instruments, help and encouragement as I assembled this collection over these many years.

Marlowe A. Sigal
Newton Centre, Massachusetts

ACKNOWLEDGMENTS

The author would like to thank Marlowe and Elise Sigal for the gracious hospitality they showed during a visit to their home in Newton Centre, Massachusetts. The experience was enjoyable, and Marlowe is a great source of knowledge and wisdom regarding his extensive collection. For their expert suggestions and guidance regarding cataloging conventions and specific instruments, the author thanks: James Kopp (bassoons), Michael Finkelman (English horns), Geoffrey Burgess (oboes), René Pierre (Roulleau flute), Robert Bigio (Rose and Rudall flute), David Thomas (Rose and Rudall flute), Doug Koeppe (American-made instruments), Bruno Kampmann (Leblanc alto saxophone), James Westbrook (Stradivari guitar), Andrew Dipper (Stradivari guitar), Daniel Sinier de Ridder (Stradivari guitar), Gianpaolo Gregori (Stradivari guitar), James Westbrook (Stradivari guitar), Thierry Maniguet (Erard grand piano), Michael Latcham (Stein and Walther pianos), Francesco Carreras (Cromametro and Pelitti's contrabassoon), Michael Cwach (Dudelsack), Panagiotis Poulopoulos (English guitars), Tony Bingham (pitch pipes), and Rick Wilson (Swanee-whistle).

Lastly and most importantly, I am indebted to my wife, Eleanor Montague, for her editing and optimistic and challenging work ethic.

FOR **ELISE SIGAL**

INTRODUCTION

Every musical instrument collection is unique. Some are stronger in certain areas than others, but all of them reflect the collecting interests of the founding collector or institution. Marlowe A. Sigal started seriously collecting keyboard instruments during the late 1960s and since that time has developed a vast knowledge about the finest and most important makers, and in the process, honed his observational skills. After a few years of filling up a large home with harpsichords, clavichords, and early pianos, he also focused his attention on obtaining high-quality woodwind instruments and several fine plucked and bowed instruments. The result is a connoisseur's collection of more than 600 instruments that is the envy of collectors and curators.

Sigal's collection has been widely recognized as an important collection by members of the American Musical Instrument Society, the Galpin Society, CIMCIM (the International Committee for Museums and Collections of Musical Instruments), scholars, collectors, and players. The purpose of this catalog is briefly to describe these instruments illustrated by photographs taken by Marlowe Sigal, refer to relevant literature about the instruments in a large bibliography; and make the contents of this important collection known to the public. The author's cataloging work was carried out from September 2012 to December 2013, including a visit of five days to Sigal's home.

The Sigal Collection offers a wide selection of keyboards dating from the sixteenth to the twentieth centuries: harpsichords, virginals, spinets, clavichords, a variety of pianos, chamber organs, and other types of keyboards. Among the keyboard instruments is a superb example of Pascal Taskin's 1769 double-manual harpsichord with a dark olive varnished case decorated with gold floral borders and grotesqueries, painted vermillion in the interior, underside of the lid, and on the lid stick. The keyboard surround is painted red and decorated with gold flowers. Extra fine workmanship is displayed on the 1761 Kirkman double-manual harpsichord with a detailed marquetry of scrolling foliage, birds, and trumpet-playing angels. This exquisite instrument is believed to have been one of the instruments owned by Queen Charlotte, wife of George III of England.

The historically most important piano in the collection is the grand piano by Johann Andreas Stein of Augsburg made in 1784. Stein was a gifted and inventive maker, and Mozart, during a visit to Augsburg in 1777, praised his grand piano's fine touch, dynamic flexibility, knee-lift dampers, and its escapement. The Sigal Stein is classically designed with walnut veneer, four tapered legs, and brass medallion in ovals on the bentside. It was owned for many years by the Museum of Art in Toledo, Ohio, and served as the model for the Zuckermann and Hubbard fortepiano kits, from which many modern replicas were built. The elegant beauty of the 1817 Erard grand piano shines with a satinwood nameboard and richly hued mahogany veneered case with gilded brass decorations on the bent side and two coiled and winged serpents on either side of the keyboard. Exceptionally rare instruments include examples from the Broadwood collection, such as a "transposing" 1808 Broadwood square piano that allows the player to transpose the part to fit a singer's vocal range by sliding the keyboard laterally. Among the earliest extant upright pianos are two beautifully decorated Hawkins uprights, both dated about 1805. The keyboards of both may be folded upward to make the instrument appear as a bureau. Unusual designs of pianos include William Southwell's spectacular 1785 piano made in a half round shape. Its case consists of mahogany, kingwood, and satinwood cross banding, burr yew stringing, marquetry of amaranth, and a satinwood nameboard, keywell, and sides designed as a console table when the lid is closed. Another highly attractive and important instrument is a grand piano by Anton Walter made in Vienna about 1815. Its walnut veneered case has five legs supported by five Nubian males with cloaks, and the keywell is decorated with black panels inlaid with red classical imagery.

Since several of the keyboard instruments are in playing condition, including a few instruments that have been used in several recordings, it is possible to hear the sound of individual examples, although the sound produced cannot be the same as heard during the eighteenth and nineteenth centuries. This is because the players bring their approach and experience to the instrument, the acoustics of the rooms are different, and some modern materials are used for strings, hammers, dampers, and other parts of the pianos. Nevertheless, recreating music with early instruments is a unique and rewarding process for both players and listeners.

The flutes and whistle instruments date from the eighteenth through the twentieth centuries. Recorders include breathtaking examples of highly decorated instruments by Gahn (ca. 1710) in ivory with a fish head mouthpiece and carved floral designs by Staub (ca. 1710) in ivory with an intricate wave pattern on the head and the foot. Rare examples include recorders by J.H. Eichentopf (ca. 1725), Rippert (ca. 1715), Wilhelm Beukers (ca. 1750), Bernhard (ca. 1720), and Oberlender (ca. 1730). Flutes are quite diverse with important early examples by Naust (two, ca. 1720, ca. 1730), G. H. Scherer (ca. 1750), M. Lot (ca. 1760), Villars (ca. 1770), August Grenser (ca.

1760), Delusse (ca. 1775), Crone (ca. 1780), Richard Potter (1782), Prudent (two, ca. 1785, ca. 1785), Fornari (1794), Heinrich Grenser (ca. 1800), and others. Nineteenth-century flutes include examples by Badger (two, ca. 1865, ca. 1880), Boehm & Mendler (ca. 1875), Bonneville (ca. 1884), Drouet (ca. 1820), C. Godfroy (two, ca. 1840, ca. 1864), P. Godfroy (ca. 1835), J. C. Haynes (two, ca. 1845, ca. 1870), Kauffman (ca. 1820), Koch (ca. 1825), Laurent (1818), Monzani (three, 1815, ca. 1815, ca. 1820), Rudall & Rose (ca. 1847), C. Sax (ca. 1840), and others. Piccolos include instruments by Clapisson (ca. 1790), Klemm (ca. 1820), Wrede (ca. 1820), Tulou (ca. 1845), and Bélisaire (ca. 1850).

The double-reed instruments represent a wide variety of wooden and metal instruments. Many oboes are of the highest quality workmanship and later examples include some important advances in mechanisms. These include instruments attributed to Dupuis (ca. 1700), by Hans Richters (two, ca. 1720, one highly carved), J.H. Rottenburgh (ca. 1720), Bizey (ca. 1740), Vincent (ca. 1750), Panormo (ca. 1760), August Grenser (two, ca. 1760, 1778), Sattler (ca. 1770), Porthaux (ca. 1780), Crone (ca. 1790), Fornari (1795), Astor (ca. 1800), Savary (ca. 1800), Küss (ca. 1820), Koch (ca. 1825), Triebert (three, ca. 1835, ca. 1860, ca. 1890), Tulou (ca. 1835), Golde (ca. 1840), Ziegler (ca. 1840), L.A. Buffet (1843), and Lorée (ca. 1885). English horns include examples by Adler (ca. 1820), Koch (ca. 1825), Triebert (ca. 1830), Nechwalsky (ca. 1840), and Lorée (1893). Other large-size double-reed instruments are a rackett (eighteenth century), oboe da caccia attributed to Weigel (ca. 1740), basse de musette attributed to Jeanneret (ca. 1770), vox humana or tenor oboe by Thomas Key (ca. 1810), baritone oboe by Brod (ca. 1835), and musette de cour by Esprit Philippe or Nicolas Chédeville (ca. 1730).

The bassoons encompass the most well-known makers of the eighteenth and nineteenth centuries: August Grenser (1773), Prudent (ca. 1770), Huittl (ca. 1790), Milhouse (ca. 1790), Porthaux (ca. 1790), Astor (two, ca. 1798 with a brass bell and ca. 1800), Baumann (ca. 1800), Catlin (ca. 1805), Merklein (ca. 1810), Parker (ca. 1810), Savary (two, ca. 1810, 1830), Bühner & Keller (ca. 1815), Cuvillier (ca. 1820), C. Doke (ca. 1820), Koch (ca. 1820), Küss (ca. 1825), Pezé (ca. 1825), Winnen (two, ca. 1825, ca. 1835), Hirschbrunner (ca. 1825), C. Sax (ca. 1826), Savary jeune (1830), Tabard (ca. 1835), Wiesner (ca. 1840), A. Sax (ca. 1845), Heckel (ca. 1887), and Mahillon (ca. 1910). Small-size bassoons are by G.A. Rottenburgh (ca. 1760), Astor & Horwood (ca. 1815), and Tauber (ca. 1815); contrabassoons are by Schölnast (ca. 1810), Schemmel (ca. 1830), a contrabassophon attributed to Haseneier (ca. 1860), contrabassoons by Pelitti (ca. 1880) in metal, and by Buffet-Crampon (ca. 1930) in wood. Double-reed instruments in metal include an alto Sarrusophone by Rampone e Cazzani (ca. 1920), tenor and bass Sarrusophones by Gautrot-Marquet (ca. 1880), and a tenor Rothphone by Bottali (ca. 1915).

Single-reed instruments comprise a large and fine selection of clarinets and saxophones. The clarinets include examples by Payne (ca. 1780), Cahusac (ca. 1785), Porthaux (ca. 1790), Keller frères (ca. 1794), August Grenser (1796), Bernard (ca. 1800), Tuerlinckx (ca. 1800), Heinrich Grenser in D (ca. 1807) and in B♭ with a corps de rechange in A (1810), Jouve (ca. 1810), Savary (ca. 1815), Simiot (ca. 1815), Amelingue (ca. 1820), Küss (ca. 1820), Millhouse (ca. 1820), Whiteley (two ca. 1820, ca. 1825), Charles Sax (ca. 1825), Koch (ca. 1830), Graves & Co. (ca. 1835), Tabard (ca. 1835), Schöllnast (ca. 1840), Thomas Key (1847), Adolphe Sax (ca. 1850) in C and A, Stehle (ca. 1850), Wernicke (ca. 1860), C. Godfroy (ca. 1865), and Oehler (ca. 1910). Others represent unusual clarinets or unusual systems such as B♭ and A seven-key clarinets by Baumann (ca. 1815) with specially designed keys invented by C.H. Felix in 1813, a left-handed five-key clarinet by Pezé (ca. 1815), sets of C, B♭, and A by Bühner & Keller (ca. 1815), Golde (ca. 1850), and Kruspe (ca. 1875), an ivory clarinet by John Pfaff (ca. 1865), a double-wall clarinet with silver-plated metal over wood by Mahillon (ca. 1890), a combination clarinet in C or B♭ by Clinton (ca. 1890), and a Grafton acrylic plastic clarinet (1953). Large-size clarinets include clarinets d'amour by Collin (ca. 1810) and Heckel (ca. 1880), alto clarinet by Simiot & Brelet, basset horn by Harrach (ca. 1815), and bass clarinets by L.A. Buffet (ca. 1835), Moritz (ca. 1865), and Adolphe Sax (ca. 1870).

There is one of the few quintets of saxophones, all by Adolphe Sax: soprano (ca. 1859), alto (ca. 1860), tenor (ca. 1865), baritone (ca. 1864), and bass (ca. 1870). Other saxophones are a sopranino in B♭ by Adolphe Sax fils, a soprano by Sudre, a soprano by Henri Sax (ca. 1905), a Leblanc, semi-rationnel model alto (ca. 1935), and a Grafton alto by Dallas (ca. 1955). An unusual Dudelsack or bagpipe was made near Pilsen in Bohemia (ca. 1850) with single reeds in the chanter and drone.

Free Reed instruments consist of a symphonium (ca. 1830) by Wheatstone, accordions, bagpipes, and rocking melodeons, a bible reed organ, and reed organs. Cup-mouthpiece instruments are a bass horn by Stiegler (ca. 1810) and a Russian bassoon by Dupré (ca. 1820). Percussion instruments are a doubled-headed cylindrical drum from Africa, two small and one large double-head drum from China, a long drum from Haiti, and a cromametro or piano tuning device by Ricordi (ca. 1828).

The bowed and plucked string instruments include fine examples of a viola d'amour by Jacques Pierre Michelot (ca. 1775), a rare mandora in original condition by Antonio Monzino (ca. 1790), a pochette attributed to Mathias Wörle (1686), a vielle à roue by Claude Bas (ca. 1860), guitars by Gennaro Fabricatore (1826), by Dubois (ca. 1840), by C.F. Martin (ca. 1870), by John C. Haynes with William Tilton's improvements (ca. 1870), English guitars by Preston (ca. 1770), and an English guitar attributed to Longman and Broderip (1780s).

This collection has several great strengths. One is a collection of nine early harpsichords and one virginal by Baffo (ca. 1575), two anonymous Italian harpsichords from Trentino (ca. 1625) and Bologna (ca. 1660), Dulcken (Antwerp, 1745), Kirkman (1761), Taskin (1769), Shudi (1767), Bull (1778), Shudi and Broadwood (1781); spinets by Joseph Harris (ca. 1750) and William Harris (1765); and two anonymous clavichords of Spanish origin (ca. 1780), and Austrian origin (ca. 1790), several of which are extensively decorated. The breadth and depth of the seventy-seven pianos are notable for the grand, upright, square, and other unusual types. Researchers have a great advantage because of the multiple types of instruments made by the same maker that can easily be compared. For example, Broadwood is represented by a harpsichord, a grand piano, an upright piano, and three square pianos; Clementi by an upright piano and three square pianos. Four types of woodwinds are represented by Klemm: piccolo, flute, clarinet, and bassoon. Three types are represented by Tulou (piccolo, flute, oboe), Küss (clarinet, oboe, bassoon), Adler (flute, oboe, English horn), Koch (flute, clarinet, English horn), William Milhouse (flute, oboe, clarinet), Bühner & Keller (flute, clarinet, bassoon), Baumann (flageolet, clarinet, bassoon), August Grenser (flute, clarinet, bassoon), Prudent (flageolet, flute, bassoon), and Charles Sax (flute, clarinet, bassoon). Among the rarest woodwinds are two flutes by Naust of Paris (ca. 1720); a bassoon and a clarinet attributed to Nathan Curtiss of Woodbury, Connecticut (ca. 1800); and a bassoon by George Catlin of Hartford, Connecticut (ca. 1805). Many instruments are rare and fine examples, several of which are unique to this collection.

Marlowe Sigal continues his discriminating collecting, calling it an addiction. By gathering these stellar examples into one collection, he is providing a unique opportunity for organologists, players, makers, fellow collectors, researchers, and curators to study and enjoy a collection painstakingly and intelligently assembled.

Each chapter presents a short description of each instrument with a photograph; within each section they are arranged by accession number. The descriptions include identification of the material used, technical details, and basic measurements in millimeters. For each instrument, historical information, provenance, and specific bibliographical citations are given when appropriate. Measurements of bassoons and other wind instruments with U-shaped bores are not provided.

Albert R. Rice
Claremont, California

ABBREVIATIONS, CONVENTIONS & GLOSSARY

Some definitions were adopted from the glossaries in Koster 1994 and Clinkscale 1999. All measurements are in millimeters.

/ one line below in a stamp or inscription

// several lines below in a stamp or inscription; upper and lower sections of both sides of a bassoon

Action for piano: system of levers, hammers, keys, and other moving parts by which the movement of the finger on the key is transmitted to the hammer which sounds the string; for harpsichord: registers, or a set of jacks controlled by a stop

Barret action a single side key for R1 on the oboe produces c^2 or $b\flat^1$; on the clarinet it produces c^3 or $b\flat^2$, and in the lower register, f^1 or $e\flat^1$

ca. circa, around

Check in grand and mid-nineteenth century square pianos with a single action (Stoßmechanik); a small bit of leather attached to a short wire, its purpose being to catch the hammer and prevent its rebounding against the string

Crank damper an individual wooden damper with cloth underneath and above strings, attached by wire to a short wood lever above the end of piano key

Cranked kink of about 60 degrees on the F♯/C♯ lever of a clarinet

D depth (keyboards), diameter (percussion, stringed instruments)

Damper rack narrow box in which over dampers are held over the strings

D.R.G.M. Deutsche Reichs Gebrauchmuster

Découpage a collage of colored engravings cut out in silhouette, glued to a painted ground on a harpsichord or piano case, and covered with varnish

Dolly damper individual damper made of small cloth-covered blocks, which resemble dolls and are lifted at the ends of the keys by wire stems

Escapement any piano mechanism engaging the hammer in its forward thrust, allowing it to fall away from the strings

GSJ *Galpin Society Journal*

H height

Harpischord registers a set of strings usually described by a particular octave or tonal characteristic, such as "4' register," "lute register," or "back 8' register." Many harpischords have two 8' registers and one 4' register, abbreviated to 2X8', 1X4'.

Irish damper a dolly damper with its wire stem attached directly to the key lever

Journal of American Instrument Society *Journal of the American Musical Instrument Society*

Keyboard surround nameboard and perpendicular sides of a keyboard

L length, on upright piano from left to right

L1 first finger left hand

LT left thumb

Long-tenon mouthpiece a long wooden tenon on clarinet mouthpieces primarily made in Great Britain and the United States

NAMIS *Newsletter of the American Musical Instrument Society*

No(s). number(s)

Patent C♯ mechanism on a simple-system clarinet, a lever positioned above the F/C key head so that when the E/B touch is closed alone, it produces $f\sharp$ or $c\sharp^2$

Peau de buffle a buff stop made of thick, soft, oil-tanned leather, or plectra

Prellmechanik piano action in which the hammer has its head facing the player and resting on the key lever or a small attached block. It is hinged near the lever's distal end or often to a forked-shaped piece joined to it

R1 first finger right hand

RT right thumb

Ravelement the process of enlarging a harpsichord to extend its compass

S.G.D.G. sans garantie du gouvernement

Satellite key a small key head pad attached to a movable ring on woodwinds

Scale the length of the longest c^2 string used in designing a harpsichord

Spurs small projections on eighteenth- and nineteenth-century woodwind keys mounted in a ring or a block

Sticker action upright action in which the key and jack reach the hammer by means of a long, slender sticker or wooden rod

Stock-bell one clarinet joint combining the stock below the right-hand finger joint and the bell

Stoßmechanik piano action in which the hammer is hinged to a rail and pushed upward by a jack

Three-octave measure measurement of three octaves on a keyboard

Trompe l'oeil a style of painting that creates an illusion of photographic reality

Viennese action a Prellmechanik with an escapement

Vol(s.) volume(s)

W width, on upright piano from front to back

W, W2, W3 wing keys on a bassoon

Waisted barrel an incurved barrel on clarinets primarily made in Great Britian or the United States

CHAPTER 1
KEYBOARD INSTRUMENTS

Harpsichord, one-manual, Burkat Shudi, London, 1767.

Walnut veneered; cross banded with stringing of lighter wood; matched figured burr walnut keywell. Trestle stand, four round and square legs ending in wooden ball casters. Three large decorative hooks on cheek and bent side. Action: 2X8', 1X4'; 3 hand stops; compass: 5 octaves, FF, GG-f^3. Three-octave measure: 488; natural coverings: ivory with two scribe lines including head/tail seam; sharps: ebony; key fronts: molded boxwood. L=2,320; W=934; D=265; H=630.

Name batten inscription on boxwood cartouche in black with swirls: "Burkat Shudi N°. 540 Fecit Londini 1767".

Boalch 1995, 618-619.

1969.02

Harpsichord, one-manual, Burkat Shudi, London, 1767, and inscription.

Harpsichord, one-manual, Anonymous, attributed to Trentino, Italy, seventeenth century.

Inner-outer construction. Outer case cheek, bent side panels, and lid painted with découpaged figures (animals, birds, people, trees). Large carved trestle stand. Inner case, cypress. Soundboard with an ornately carved rose. Action: 2X8', 1X4'; three hand stops inside the case; compass: 4 octaves, GG, CC-c^4. Three-octave measure: 489; natural coverings: boxwood with two scribe lines including head/tail seam; sharps: black stained wood with ebony tops; key fronts: arcaded boxwood, blue cloth. L=2,230; W=882; D=252; H=885.

No inscription.

1984.01

Harpsichord, one-manual, Anonymous, attributed to Trentino, Italy, seventeenth century.

Harpsichord, two-manual, Burkat Shudi and John Broadwood, London, 1781.

Mahogany; satinwood cross banding and stringing. Brass butt hinges on lid with three S hooks. Stand, four square tapered legs ending in brass casters; carved music desk. Stringing: 2X8', 1X4'. Action: keyboard I: front 8' (quill), back 8' (leather), 4' (quill); keyboard II: front 8' (quill), lute 8' (quill). Buff stop; two pedals (Venetian swell, machine stop); six hand stops; compass: 5 octaves, FF-f^3. Three-octave measure: 488; natural coverings: ivory with two scribe lines including head/tail seam; sharps: ebony; key fronts: molded boxwood; scale: 330. L=2,457; W=953; D=326; H=613.

Name batten inscription in black with swirls: "Burkat Shudi et Johannes Broadwood / N°. 899, Londini Fecerunt 1781 Great Pultney Street Golden Square. // Patent."

Boalch 1995, 623. Tsalka 2013, Türk sonata nos. 1 and 6 recorded.

1986.09

Harpsichord, two-manual, Burkat Shudi and John Broadwood, London, 1781, and name batten inscription.

Close-up of keywell.

Close-up of name batten.

Harpsichord, two-manual, Joseph Kirkman, London, 1761.

Harpsichord, two-manual, Joseph Kirkman, London, 1761.

Panels veneered with figured burr walnut; walnut cross banded including spine. Detailed marquetry on keywell, interior, and jack rail with scrolling foliage, birds, angels playing trumpets, trophy of instruments on keywell. Panels under lid, borders of decorative white squares. Solid walnut trestle stand, carved acanthus leaves; four cabriole claw and ball feet, "Jackendale" lower legs; prop stick. Gilt brass soundboard rose with carved, seated harpist between initials "I" and "K." Stringing: 2X8', 1X4'. Action: keyboard I: front 8' (quill), lute 8' (quill); keyboard II: front 8' (quill), back 8' (quill), 4' (quill). Four hand stops, two on each side; no swell; no harp stop; compass: five octaves, FF, GG-f^3. Scale: 331. Three-octave measure: 485; natural coverings: ivory with two scribe lines including head/tail seam; sharps: ebony; key fronts: molded boxwood. L=2,330; W=931; D=302; H=600.

Name batten inscription on oval in black with swirling decoration: "Jacobus Kirckman Londini Fecit 1761".

According to Germann: "No more magnificent British harpsichord survives than this 1761 Jacob Kirkman, which was formerly Queen Charlotte's, and was probably played by the nine-year-old Mozart for the royal family at Buckingham House in 1764."

Boalch 1995, 430; Germann 2002, 186, fig. 5.21 (full harpsichord); 188, fig. 5.24 (rose); 5.27 (hinges); 5.28 (hook).

1987.07

Harpsichord, one-manual, Johann Daniel Dulcken, Antwerp, 1745, and inscription.

Harpsichord, one-manual, Johann Daniel Dulcken, Antwerp, 1745.

Poplar painted gray with brown cross banding on cheek, bent side, and lid; stand, five cabriole legs painted dark green. Decorated soundboard, flowers, gilt lead rose with monogram "ID." Lock and key on cheek. Stringing: 2X8'; 2 genouillères (knee pedals) inoperative. 2 hand stops. Action: front set of double-sided jacks (quill and leather); back side of jacks (leather); compass: originally BB-d^3 after ravalement, 5 octaves + 7, AA-e^3. Three-octave measure: 490; natural coverings: ebony with four scribe lines including head/tail seam; sharps: black stained fruit wood, bone tops; key fronts: paper, vermillion rectangle on white ground. L=2,243; W=835; D=257; H=630.

Name batten inscription in black: "IOANNES DANIEL DULCKEN ME FÆCIT ANTWERPIÆ 1745".

Sotheby's 1992, 224-225; Boalch 1995, 301-302; Germann 2002, 132, fig. 2.95 (plan view), fig. 2.96 (detail of rose); Kottick 2003, 284-287.

1992.12

Harpsichord, two-manual, Pascal Taskin, Paris, 1769.

Wood; painted and varnished dark olive; gold floral borders and grotesqueries; interior, underside of lid, and lid stick painted vermillion. Red painted keyboard surround, gold flowers. Soundboard decorated with massive wreaths of mixed flowers and bird, large wreath around gilt rose of angel playing harp in between the initals "P T." Soundboard dated "1769." "Asseman," the name of a twentieth-century Parisian restorer, stamped on tuning plank. Gold-plated hinges on lid. Louis XV-style stand, six cabriole legs, floral design on skirt; keyboards, modern replacements. Taskin's card on instrument reads: "Pascal Taskin Facteur de clavessins du Roi, elève et successeur de M. Blanchet, demeure même maison Rue de le Verrerie vis-à-vis la petite porte de St Merry à Paris." Stringing: 2X8', 1X4'; compass: 5 octaves, FF-f^3. Two hand stops, left side; one hand stop, right side. One genouillère operates back 8' jacks. Three-octave measure: 485; natural coverings: ebony with three scribe lines including head/tail seam; sharps: ebony, ivory tops; key fronts: gilt semicircles. L=2,333; W=985; D=290; H=700.

Name batten inscription on gold-stained wood in black: "PASCAL TASKIN." Inscription on the border around the rose: "PASCAL TASKIN ELEVE DE BLANCHET".

Dowd 1984, 84-85; Germann 2002, 158, fig. 3.44 (plan view), fig. 3.45 (close-up of rose).

1997.07

Harpsichord, two-manual, Pascal Taskin, Paris, 1769, and inscription.

Harpsichord, two-manual, Johannes Petrus Bull, Antwerp, 1778.

Brown-stained poplar, varnish finish; gilt panels; one-piece lock on cheek; interior painted sea green; beechwood stand, six square tapered legs decorated with gilt fluting; two drawers; gilded rose with floral designs. Compass: 5 octaves, FF-f^3; action: 2X8', 1X4'. Four hand stops including lute and harp, two genouillères (knee levers). Right knee lever (absent), left knee lever dampens both 8' choirs simultaneously. Three-octave measure: 490; natural coverings: ivory with two scribe lines including head/tail seam; sharps: ebony with rounded fronts; key fronts: incised rectangles punched with floral design. L=2,585; W=950; D=270; H=680.

Name batten inscription in gilt: "JOANNES PETRUS BULL ME FECIT ANTVERPIÆ ANNO 1778".

Boalch, 1995, 261-262; Kottick 2003, 289.

2001.03

Harpsichord, two-manual, Johannes Petrus Bull, Antwerp, 1778, and inscription.

Harpsichord, one-manual, of Italian origin, possibly Bologna, ca. 1660.

Inner-outer construction, outer painted dark green; large lock on cheek. Two round floral designs on front lower corners of outer case, two round designs on front part of lid when closed. Inner case unpainted, square tail. Under lid and inside of removable lockboard is a seventeenth-century Italian landscape painting. Nameboard decorated with gilt and polychrome painted lines, three inlaid ivory diamonds in two ebony rectangles. Compass: 4 octaves, EE-e^3; action: 1X8', 1X4'. Three-octave measure: 482; natural coverings: ivory with two scribe lines including head/tail seam; sharps: ebony, triangular inlay of ivory; key fronts: molded ivory. L=2,055; W=795; D=295; H=640.

No inscription.

2009.04

Harpsichord, one-manual, of Italian origin, possibly Bologna, ca. 1660, and lid painting.

Virginals, attributed to Giovanni Antonio Baffo, of Italian origin, ca. 1575.

Inner-outer case of cypress and spruce. Outer case probably original with nineteenth-century decoration. Decorated with groups of flowers in golden borders on side cheeks, bucolic scene in center of underside of lid. Probably nineteenth-century stand, six cabriole legs, stretchers decorated with leaves and flowers. Moldings on inner instrument outline all edges and scrolled key cheeks; moldings and cheeks decorated with ivory buttons, two ivory buttons secure removable name batten. Rose is intricately carved. Compass: 4½ octaves, C/E- f³; action: 2x8'. Three-octave measure: 540; natural coverings: boxwood with two scribe lines including head/tail seam; sharps: dark stained wood; key fronts: semicircles carved in wood. L=1,770; W=580; D=200; H=630.

No inscription.

1974.03

Virginals, attributed to Giovanni Antonio Baffo, of Italian origin, ca. 1575.

Octave virginals, Arnold Dolmetsch, Chickering Co., Boston, 1907.

Inner-outer construction. Outer case painted dark green. Mahogany triangular shaped inner case; tuning pins in front, five pins in right back corner, without stand. Compass: 4 octaves, C-c³; action: 1x8'. Three-octave measure: 475; natural coverings: boxwood with four scribe lines including head/tail seam; sharps: dark stained wood; key fronts: semicircles carved in wood. L=780; W=520; D=175.

Inscription on right side above keyboard, in a scroll in black: "Made – by – Chickering - & - Sons / under - the - direction – of / Arnold Dolmetsch / Boston, U.S.A. / MCMVII / Nº 42".

2008.08

Octave virginals, Arnold Dolmetsch, Chickering Co., Boston, 1907, and inscription.

Spinet, Joseph Harris, London, ca. 1750.

Walnut veneer; satinwood cross banding; double-curved bent side; chased brass strap hinges; stand, turned legs; stretchers. Nameboard, mahogany (?) rectangular inlay bordered with light brown wood; sides, mahogany (?) right-triangle inlay bordered with light wood. Carved black-stained scrolls, both sides; brass bracket for candle sconce, right side. Compass: 5 octaves, GG-g^3; action: 1X8'. Three-octave measure: 480; natural coverings: ivory with three scribe lines including head/tail seam; sharps: ebony, ivory stripe down middle; key fronts: ivory, gilded semicircle. L=1,820; D=600; H=740.

Name batten inscription on paper label in black, cut out to look like an inlaid boxwood cartouche: "Jofevhus Harris Londini Fecit."

Boalch 1995, 360.

1976.01

Spinet, Joseph Harris, London, ca. 1750.

Spinet, William Harris, London, 1765.

Mahogany veneer; holly cross banding; mahogany stand; stretcher; four cabriole legs. Bottom key signed with maker's name and date; candle sconce, left side. Compass: 5 octaves, GG-g^3; action: 1X8'. Three-octave measure: 488; natural coverings: ivory, no scribe lines; sharps: ebony, ivory strip down middle (known as "skunk-tail" sharps); key fronts: molded boxwood. L=1,275; W=870; D=210; H=580.

Name batten inscription boxwood cartouche in black: "Gulielmus Harris Londini Fecit 1765".

Boalch 1995, 360.

1996.12

Spinet, William Harris, London, 1765, and inscription.

Clavichord, of Spanish origin, possibly Avila, ca. 1780.

Mahogany; four slightly tapered turned legs; tuning pins on right; angled bridge. Compass: 4 octaves + 2, C-d^3. Three-octave measure: 490; natural coverings: ivory, no scribe lines; sharps: ebony, one inlaid ivory dot on front, three ivory dots on top, triangle at back of sharp; key fronts: ebony, with pairs of ivory triangles on adjacent key fronts forming a diamond pattern. Straight key levers. Unfretted: C to a; fretted: b to d^3. Stringing: C to E♭, twisted brass wire. Double strung throughout. L=1,064; W=360; H=590.

No inscription.

Formerly in the Monastery of Santa Ana, Avila, Spain.

Kenyon de Pascual 1991, 97, pl. XVI (a); Brauchli 1998, 187-188, 188, pl. 5.39; Kenyon de Pascual 2003, 145-146.

1978.03

Clavichord, of Spanish origin, ca. 1780, and soundboard.

Clavichord, of Austrian origin, the Tyrol, ca. 1790.

Wood; no decorations or stand; tuning pins on right. Compass: 4 octaves and one note, EE-f^3. Three-octave measure: 476; natural coverings: walnut (?) with three scribe lines including head/tail seam; sharps: wood, light brown stained tops; key fronts: wood. L=1,194; W=363; D=127.

No inscription.

2008.02

Clavichord, of Austrian origin, the Tyrol, ca. 1790.

Grand piano, John Broadwood, London, 1805.

Mahogany; cross banding and light wood stringing; trestle stand, four square tapered legs and casters; brass hinges, round hooks on bent side. Two wooden pedals: keyboard shift, dampers. Adjustable music desk. Serial no. 3206. "MARSHALL" on action frame. Compass: 5½ octaves, FF-c[4]. Three-octave measure: 490; natural coverings: ivory, with two scribe lines including head/tail seam; sharps: solid ebony; key fronts: molded light hard wood. L=2,270; W=1,050; D=290; H=600.

Nameboard inscription in oval: "1805 / John Broadwood and Son, / Makers to his Majesty / and the Princefses / Great Pulteney Street, Golden Square / London."

Clinkscale 1993, 47, no. 43; Clinkscale Online, CEP no. 517.

1968.01

Grand piano, John Broadwood, London, 1805, and inscription.

Grand piano, Erard Frères, Paris, 1817.

Mahogany veneer; side panels; on bent side, gilded bronze decorations, two swans, scrolls and leaves. Two gilded and coiled winged snakes on tops of both sides of keyboard. Satinwood nameboard, mahogany double line inlay and border. Folding mahogany music desk in double cross pattern. Interior sycamore veneer with stringing. Three round and tapered legs, gilded collar and casters, mahogany prop stick. Six metal pedals: bassoon, buff, dampers, jeu de buffle (moderator), keyboard shift, janissary. "1816" on soundboard; serial no. 398. Compass: 6 octaves, FF-ff^4. Three-octave measure: 490; natural coverings: ivory, no scribe lines; sharps: solid ebony; key fronts: molded light hard wood. L=2,095; W=1,090; D=265; H=648.

Nameboard inscription in black among swirls: "Par Brevet d'Invention N°. 398. / Erard Frères. / Facteurs de Forté-Piano & de Harpes du Roi, / de ses menus plaisirs, / & de la Cour Impériale de Russie. / Rue du Mail N°. 13 & 21. à Paris 1817." This piano includes Erard's first repetition action of 1808.

Clinkscale 1993, 100, no. 11; Clinkscale Online, CEP no. 1331; Cole 1998; Maniguet 2009, 97.

1968.02

Grand piano, Erard Frères, Paris, 1817, and inscription.

Grand piano, of German origin, School of Johann Andreas Stein, Augsburg, ca. 1780.

Mahogany; fallboard and lid diamond pattern inlay; ivory key lock; four carved and tapered legs; large music desk; two hooks on bent side. Two knee levers: damper, moderator; compass: 5 octaves, FF-f^3. Three-octave measure: 466; natural coverings: ebony with two scribe lines including head/tail seam; sharps: stained wood, ivory tops; key fronts: stained wood. L=2,130; W=212.7; D=240; H=595.

No inscription.

Clinkscale Online, CEP no. 3754.

1981.01

Grand piano, of German origin, School of Johann Andreas Stein, Augsburg, ca. 1780.

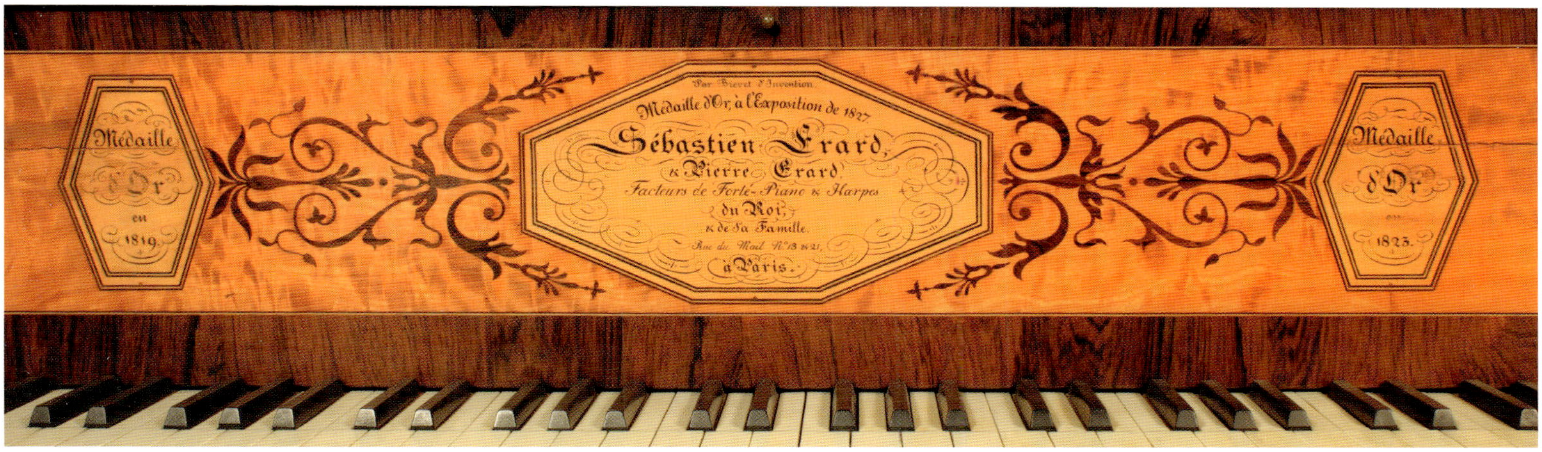

Grand piano, Sébastien and Pierre Erard, Paris, 1830.

Flame satinwood veneer; stylized ship's wheel both keyboard sides; large dust cover inside. Three reeded, baluster legs in urn shape; large triangular wooden base, decorated edge. Folding music desk; satinwood nameboard, rosewood border. Serial no. 12964. Compass: 6½ octaves, CC-f^4; two metal pedals: damper and keyboard shift; floral decorated pedal lyre. Three-octave measure: 490; natural coverings: ivory, no scribe lines; sharps: ebony; key fronts: ivory. L=2,350; W=1,250; D=310; H=630.

Nameboard inscription on light wood inside two rhombi in lighter wood, next to floral rosewood inlay, on both sides of an octagon: "Médaille / d'Or / en / 1819 // Par Brevet d'Invention. / Médaille d'Or, à l'Exposition de 1827. / Sébastien Erard, / & Pierre Erard, / Facteurs de Forté-Piano & Harpes / du Roi, / & de Sa Famille. / Rue du Mail N°.13 & 21, / à Paris. // Médaille / d'Or / en 1823."

Date of 1830 from a list of Erard pianos in Musée de la Musique, Paris. Watercolor by Henry Hawkins (1820-1881), sold at Lempertz auctions, May 16, 2009, entitled "Portrait des jungen Eduard Hummel," dated 1838, depicts a similar Erard piano with stylized ship's wheels at keyboard sides, large pedal lyre, similar carving at movable panels next to music desk, decoration around skirt. Hawkins was a British portraitist, landscapist, and figure painter.

Clinkscale 1999, 120; Clinkscale Online, CEP no. 1318; Cole 1998; Maniguet 2009, 97.

1983.02

Grand piano, Sébastien and Pierre Erard, Paris, 1830, and inscription.

Grand piano, Thomas Tomkison, London, ca. 1802.

Mahogany veneer; inlaid maple stringing; side panels. Trestle stand, four square legs, casters; solid mahogany lid. Maple veneer keyboard surround, rosewood binding. Nameboard inscription between two groups of painted instruments and sheet music; the right group with actor's mask. Serial no. 210. Compass: 5½ octaves, FF-c^4; two wooden pedals attached diagonally to front legs: damper, una corda. Three-octave measure: 490; natural coverings: ivory, no scribe lines; sharps: ebony; key fronts: molded boxwood. L=2,250; W=1,045; D=288; H=635.

Inscription on nameboard in decorated oval, within a wreath: "THO^S. TOMKISON / GRAND AND SQUARE / Piano Forte / Manufacturer / Dean Street, Soho LONDON".

Formerly in Luttrelstown Castle, near Dublin, Ireland.

Clinkscale 1993, 299, no. 1; Clinkscale Online, CEP no. 3379.

1983.15

Grand piano, Thomas Tomkison, London, ca. 1802, and inscription.

Grand piano, Anton Walter and Son, Vienna, ca. 1815.

Walnut veneer; rosewood skirt; five walnut square tapering legs supported by five gold-painted Nubian males with cloaks; four black panels inlaid with monochrome red classical imagery on left side, one on right side; keywell black panels inlaid with monochrome red line painting of classical imagery covered with layers of clear lacquer; folding music desk. Oval inscription on nameboard is surrounded by a wreath of flowers; both sides of inscription are a red-line painting of semi-nude female angels playing natural trumpets facing each other. Four black-stained wooden pedals: keyboard shift, bassoon, dampers, moderator. Compass: 6 octaves, FF-f^4, Viennese action with check. Three-octave measure: 480; natural coverings: ivory, no scribe lines; sharps: stained-brown wood, ebony tops; key fronts: ivory. L=2,160; W=1,150; D=280; H=555.

Inscription on nameboard on a porcelain plaque in black: "Anton Walter u Sohn / in Wien (cursive)".

Clinkscale 1993, 315, no. 14; Clinkscale Online, CEP no. 3935.

1986.07

Grand piano, Anton Walter and Son, Vienna, ca. 1815, and inscription.

Grand piano, Robert Wornum, London, 1850-1852.

Mahogany veneer; three turned, tapered hexagonal legs, cuffs, casters; square tail; large folding music desk. Compass: 6¾ octaves, CC-a^4; down striking action, two large wooden pedals; serial nos. 9542, 840. Three-octave measure: 492; natural coverings: ivory, no scribe lines; sharps: ebony; key fronts: ivory. L=1,905; W=1,275.

Inscription on nameboard on a dark rectangle in gold: "Royal Patent SEMI ALBION GRAND Piano Forte, / Patented and Manufactured by / Robert Wornum, / MUSIC HALL, Store Street, Bedford Square, LONDON".

The patent probably referred to Wornum's tapecheck action of 1842, British patent no. 9262.

Harding 1933, 246-247; Clinkscale 1999, 405; Clinkscale Online, CEP no. 4062.

1987.06

Grand piano, Robert Wornum, London, 1850-1852, and inscription.

Grand piano, Johann Andreas Stein, Augsburg, 1784.

Walnut veneer; brass medallions in ovals on bent side; four round, tapered fluted legs; spruce soundboard. Compass: 5 octaves, FF-f^3, FF-$d\sharp^2$ bichord, e^2-f^3 trichord; Prellmechanik; solid wooden hammers with leather covering; two knee levers; dampers. Three-octave measure: 475; natural coverings: ebony with two scribe lines including head/tail seam; sharps: solid ebony; key fronts: flat brown veneer. L=2,122; W=965; D=218; H=604.

The Toledo Museum of Art's collection record states: "The maker's plate was stolen from the instrument during the period of Mrs. Ketcham's ownership." Thus, the paper label on the instrument was a later addition. When Philip Belt restored the piano for the Toledo Museum of Art, he found an ink inscription on the bottom board inside the case: "Joh. Andreas Stein Augsburg 1784".

Formerly in the Toledo Museum of Art, Toledo, Ohio. This piano was the model for Zuckermann and Hubbard fortepiano kits, from which many modern replicas were constructed.

Clinkscale 1993, 275, no. 13; Latcham 1998, 123, 141 n 42, 147; Clinkscale Online, CEP no. 3011. Türk sonata nos. 2 and 3 recorded, Tsalka 2013.

1996.25

Grand piano, Johann Andreas Stein, Augsburg, 1784, and inscription.

Grand piano, James Longman and Francis Broderip, London, ca. 1780.

Mahogany veneer; holly and stained fruitwood stringing; satinwood keyboard surround, king wood cross banding; square tail; large brass rings on bent side and cheek; trestle stand, four square legs, casters; no music desk. "218" stamped on stiffening bar glued to the top front of the wrest plank; prop stick attached inside case. Compass: 5 octaves, FF/GG-f³. Three-octave measure: 490; English grand action, one pedal, una corda (no damper mechanism); natural coverings: ivory with two scribe lines including head/tail seam; sharps: solid ebony; key fronts: molded light hard wood. L=1,755; W=920; D=215; H=634.

Inscription on nameboard in black on enameled oval plaque bordered by metal frame: "BY ROYAL PATENT / LONGMAN & BRODERIP / MUSICAL INSTRUMENT MAKERS / N°. 26 CHEAPSIDE & N°. 13 HAYMARKET / LONDON".

Grand pianos made to a reduced length were advertised by Longman and Broderip in their *Complete Catalogues* of 1789 and 1793 as: "Portable Grand Piano Fortes, on a new Improvement, reduced in Size and Price considerably under the original Grand Piano Fortes, and universally admired for their peculiar Brilliancy of Tone, and excellent Quality of standing long in Tune."

Clinkscale Online, CEP no. 5336.

1997.08

Grand piano, James Longman and Francis Broderip, London, ca. 1780, and inscription.

Grand piano, Vincenzo Sodi, Florence, 1786.

Walnut veneer; decorative stringing in holly and boxwood; curved tail; keywell sides; front rosewood veneered; two paintings in gilt frames attached to fallboard and underside of lid. Painting under first lid section has four nude nymphs under a tree in an idyllic setting; painting under lid has nymphs in water, both possibly added during the nineteenth century. Four round, tapered stop-fluted legs. Compass: 5 octaves, FF-f^3; the lowest eight notes are double-strung, the rest are triple-strung; Viennese action; two knee levers, dampers. Three-octave measure: 486; natural coverings: ebony with two scribe lines including head/tail seam; sharps: ebony with ivory tops; key fronts: flat black stained. L=1,720; W=990; D=220; H=650.

Inscription on name batten on an ivory cartouche in black: "VINCENTIUS SODI FLORENTINUS FECIT ANNO DOMINI MDCCLXXXV. 166".

One of two known Sodi grand pianos.

Clinkscale Online, CEP no. 6428. Türk sonatas nos. 3, 4, and 5 recorded, Tsalka 2013.

1998.07

Grand piano, Vincenzo Sodi, Florence, 1786, and inscription.

Nameboard.

Upright (Giraffe) piano, Anton Martin Thym, Vienna, ca. 1815.

Rosewood; strings arranged obliquely. Upright back curved on right side to form shell connected to diagonal side. Decorated, gilded horn from which pour gilded vines, berries, and dark green leaves, all mounted on light blue silk. Two small drawers on either side of keyboard, small brass ring handles, light wood ledge for music. Four carved, black-painted Nubian males at top of each tapered leg ending with foot, clothed in long, gilt turbans wearing gold crosses. Three metal pedals: dampers, moderator, bassoon on a gilded pedal stand, two gilded winged goddesses attached to rosewood stretcher between front legs. Keywell painted black against brown background with sylvan scene. Small metal pedestals on top of either side of keyboard. Serial no. 82. Compass: 6 octaves, FF to f^4. Three-octave measure: 480; natural coverings: ivory, no scribe lines; sharps: stained-brown wood, ebony strip on top; key fronts: ivory. L=1,315; W=565; H=1,710.

Nameboard inscription middle, right in black: "Ant: Martin / Thÿm. / à Vienne. / Nº 82." (cursive)

Fomerly in the George F. Harding Jr. Collection, Chicago.

Clinkscale 1993, 298, no. 1; Clinkscale Online, CEP no. 3369.

1976.03

Inscription

Upright (Giraffe) piano, Anton Martin Thym, Vienna, ca. 1815.

Upright piano, John Isaac Hawkins, London, ca. 1805.

Mahogany; two gilt ornaments of two winged lions between lyres; two gilt ornaments of two putti back to back playing straight trumpets (one trumpet missing); two grooved brass ormolu castings on upper case or gallery at each side (one missing on left); two small busts of Egyptian pharaohs in headdresses at top of each side, two gilt feet at bottom of stylized legs; gilt lock in center, two lower panels. Keyboard may be folded back by pressing down ivory locks on keyboard, making it appear as a bureau. Iron bar braces behind independent soundboard; folding music desk (absent). Compass: 5½ octaves, FF-c^4; front striking Stoßmechanik action with escapement. Tuning plank at top; strings descend almost to floor. Unison strings attached to "carriage" with watch key screw mechanism for tuning, following Hawkin's British patent of November 13, 1800 (no. 2,446). Below added gallery, small lid may be lifted to amplify sound. Three-octave measure: 481; natural coverings: ivory, no scribe lines; sharps: ebony; key fronts: molded wood. L=975; W=620; H=1060, 1380 (with upper gallery).

Inscription on light brown figured center panel, rectangle bordered by brown wood, encircled with two flower wreaths, on a gray pedestal: "(crowned Royal Coat of Arms, lion on left, unicorn on right)", attached by green ribbon below to black oval bordered by red pearls, inscription in gilt: "John I. Hawkins / Inventor & Patentee / Dalby Terrace, City-Road / LONDON."

Exhibited at the International Inventions Exhibition 1885, London in group XXXIV, historic collections of class 179, musical instruments and appliances.

This piano may have been made in Philadelphia and taken by Hawkins to London when he returned. Formerly Broadwood Collection, London, no. xvii.

International Inventions Exhibition 1885, 316, no. 3577; Harding 1973, photo of inscription before 221, 222, 224, 225; before 225, pl. III; Mann 1977, 113-114, 117; Cole 1998, pl. 21; Clinkscale Online, CEP no. 1648.

1985.01

Upright piano, John Isaac Hawkins, London, ca. 1805, and inscription.

Upright lyre piano, attributed to Johann Christian Schleip, Berlin, ca. 1825.

Mahogany; in shape of large lyre; upper case backed by yellow silk; removable frame; seven gilt dowels representing lyre strings; four rounded and tapered mahogany veneer legs. Light wood nameboard stringing, unmarked rectangle on nameboard. Compass: 6 octaves, FF-f^4; upright single Stoßmechanik action with check; two knee levers. Three-octave measure: 480; natural coverings: ivory, no scribe lines; sharps: black wood; key fronts: ivory. L=1,120; W=580; H=2,120.

No inscription.

Clinkscale 1993, 327; Clinkscale Online, CEP no. 3157.

1990.02

Pianino or small upright piano, Samuel Chappell and Co., London, ca. 1815, and inscription.

Upright lyre piano, attributed to Johann Christian Schleip, Berlin, ca. 1825.

Pianino or small upright piano, Samuel Chappell and Co., London, ca. 1815.

Mahogany veneer; satinwood sides, keywell; two foliate vents on either side of nameboard. Pedal-shaped stand, five splayed legs, casters; folding music desk used as lid prop. Down striking action strikes glass rods. Compass: 3 octaves, c-c^3. Three-octave measure: 513; natural coverings: ivory, no scribe lines; sharps: ebony; key fronts: molded light hard wood. L=564; W=560; D=165; H=610.

Inscription on nameboard on white oval in black: "Patent / CHAPPELL & C°. / No. 124, New Bond Street, / London."

Jourdain 1922, 222, fig. 336 (described as conductor's piano); Yorke 1986, 53; Clinkscale 1993, 66, no. 3; Clinkscale Online, CEP no. 4984.

1993.03

Plaque inscription.

Upright piano, John Isaac Hawkins, London, ca. 1805.

Upright piano, John Isaac Hawkins, London, ca. 1805.

Mahogany; inlaid dark and light stringing; intricately carved panels on top; light wood borders with white cloth underneath; metal prop stick on right; two brass handles on either side. Iron frame. Keyboard may be folded back into case making it appear as a bureau; white casters. Stoßmechanik action. Vertical strings extend to floor; music desk is missing. Compass: 5½ octaves, FF-c^4; FF-D♯ bichord overspun (E could not be determined); F-A♯ bichord; B-c^4 trichord. Three-octave measure: 483; natural coverings: ivory, no scribe lines; sharps: solid ebony; key fronts: molded light hard wood. L=1,014; W=144; H=1,049.

Inscription on light brown figured wooden rectangle bordered by light wood, encircled with two flower wreaths, on gray pedestal: "(crowned United Kingdom coat of arms, lion on left, unicorn on right)"; attached by a ribbon below to red oval bordered by blue pearls, inscription in gilt among swirls: "John I. Hawkins / Inventor & Patentee / LONDON."

On center, underside of mahogany lid, engraved on silver plaque attached by four screws: "This Ancient Piano / was made by Thomas Sheraton in 1790 / and became the property of / Lord Byron when at Newstead Abbey; / where it remained until his demise in / 1824."

Clinkscale 1993, 138, no. 2; Good 2001, 143; Clinkscale Online, CEP no. 5581.

1998.06

Inscription.

Cabinet (upright) piano, Erard, Paris, ca. 1840.

Rosewood (?) veneer; candle brackets; double candle holders above keyboard. Decorative beaded skirt below lid below keyboard and at bottom. Two brass side handles; two spiral-turned legs. Early tape check action; compass: 6½ octaves, CC-g^4; single-strung, close-wound, CC-EE; double-strung, close-wound FF-f♯; remainder triple-strung; two metal pedals: damper, moderator; serial no. 16624; "A DuFour" on action rail. Three-octave measure: 496; natural coverings: ivory, no scribe lines; sharps: solid ebony; key fronts: ivory. L=1,262; W=510; H=1,130.

Inscription on nameboard in rectangle boarded by gilt inlay, in gilt: "Par Brevet Erard à Paris." (cursive)

Clinkscale Online, CEP no. 1341.

2000.12

Cabinet (upright) piano, Erard, Paris, ca. 1840, and inscription.

Cottage (upright) piano, John Broadwood and Sons, London, 1825.

Mahogany; pleated red silk front, probably not original; two rounded, tapered legs, casters; folding music desk. Satinwood nameboard, sides, blocks. Compass: 6 octaves, $FF\text{-}f^4$; double-strung throughout, overspun FF-G (15 notes). Serial no. 268. Two wooden pedals; action: sticker. Three-octave measure: 490; natural coverings: ivory, no scribe lines; sharps: solid ebony; key fronts: molded boxwood. L=1,135; W=596; H=1,285.

Inscription on nameboard in dark wood bordered rectangle, in brown with swirls: "John Broadwood & Sons / Maker to His Majesty & the Princesses / Great Pulteney Street Golden Square / London".

Clinkscale Online, CEP no. 6051.

2002.51

Cottage (upright) piano, John Broadwood and Sons, London, 1825, and inscription.

Upright piano, Louis Benoit, Paris, ca. 1870.

Black-stained wood; marquety decoration of red tortoiseshell with ornate inlaid brass, in the manner of André-Charles Boulle, on lid, upper and lower front panels, and folding keyboard cover. Gilt decorations on sides, handles, upper and lower parts of both legs. Gilt decorative skirt borders lid sides, two gilt skirts on front and sides and around bottom. Two metal pedals for damper and moderator. Three-octave measure: 490; natural coverings: ivory, no scribe lines; sharps: ebony; key fronts: ivory. L=1,346; W=660; H=1,200.

Inscription on nameboard on a white rectangular plaque bordered in gilded bronze, in black: "1$^{ER.}$ PRIX À L'EXPOSITION DE SYDENHAM DE 1865 / LOUIS BENOIT / 38, RUE DES ÉCLUSES S^{T}. MARTIN, 38 / PASSAGE FEUILLET, 4 / Paris."

Clinkscale Online, CEP no. 6429.

2003.04

Upright piano, Louis Benoit, Paris, ca. 1870, and inscription

Upright piano, Steinbeck and Petersen, Copenhagen, ca. 1855.

Walnut veneer; upper section, two decoratively carved panels; two candle holders, two brass candle sconces. The keyboard folds upward and instrument could have been used on a ship. Partial metal plate; straight strung; one metal pedal, dampers. Two front legs, carved; missing lower panel. Compass: 6¾ octaves, CC-g^4; single-strung CC-AA♯, close overspun; double-strung BB-A♯, close overspun, remainder double-strung. Three-octave measure: 489; natural coverings: ivory, no scribe lines; sharps: solid ebony; key fronts: molded light hard wood. L=1,281; W=583; H=1,158.

Inscription on nameboard on either side of floral engraving: "STEINBECK & PETERSEN / PATENT / KJÖBENHAVN."

Clinkscale Online, CEP no. 6055.

2003.13

Upright piano, Steinbeck and Petersen, Copenhagen, ca. 1855.

Cottage (upright) piano, Clementi and Co., London, 1830-1832.

Plain solid mahogany; solid mahogany lid; thumb molding; double-curved keyboard cover, attached wooden lip for music, two knobs; upper case, removable panel backed with cream-colored silk moiré, two turned baluster legs, casters, lower case, two panels. Two wooden pedals: una corda, damper; the una corda shifting affects only hammers. Compass: 6 octaves, FF-f^4; double-strung throughout; scale 282; FF-C tight overspun; sticker action; serial no. 25346; "614" stamped on tuning plank; "750 & RENDELL" stamped on hitch pin rail; "Collard & Collard, late Clementi, Collard & Collard No. 26, Cheapside, & 195, Tottenham Court Road, London" stamped on damper action. Three-octave measure: 490; natural coverings: ivory, no scribe lines; sharps: ebony; key fronts: molded wood. L=1,148; W=623; H=1,131.

Nameboard inscription on black background in gold letters among swirls: "Clementi & Comp^{y}. London."

Clinkscale Online, CEP no. 1016.

2004.03

Cottage (upright) piano, Clementi and Co., London, 1830-1832, and inscription.

Upright grand piano, André Stein, Vienna, ca. 1820, and inscription.

Upright grand piano, André Stein, Vienna, ca. 1820.

Mahogany veneer; ormolu rosettes on keyboard sides, on upper part of case, and on two curved black varnished ornamental pieces taking the position of legs; floral decoration around black nameboard, large lyre below keyboard. Wide ormolu skirt below lid, cloth front cover not original, ormolu lock in front. Compass: 6 octaves, FF-f^4; double-strung, FF-BB (close overspun); triple-strung bass (next six notes); remainder triple-strung iron. Hanging Viennese action; four metal pedals: damper, partial moderator, full moderator, action shift. Three-octave measure: 480; natural coverings: ivory, no scribe lines; sharps: ebony topped dark-stained wood; key fronts: ivory. L=1,145; W=558; H=1,950.

Nameboard inscription on paper label behind glass in rectangular gilt metal frame: "ANDRÉ (lyre) STEIN / d'Augsbourg / à / VIENNE."

Clinkscale Online, CEP no. 6299. Türk sonatas nos. 4 and 5 recorded, Tsalka 2013.

2005.09

Square piano, John Broadwood and Sons, London, 1835.

Mahogany (?) veneer; four turned baluster legs, casters; rounded front corners; keyboard surround curved over keys at bass and treble ends; two fretwork vents on either side of nameboard, yellow cloth backing; one wooden pedal, dampers. Cast-iron string plate with several holes, one black-stained bar along spine at rear; tuning pins at back; fretwork triangle, back right corner; internal folding music desk and prop stick; second folding music desk above lid flap; prop stick on right. Four turned and bulbous legs, cups and casters; serial no. 45450. "OCT 6, 1834" in pencil on right action bed. Compass: 6 octaves, FF-f^4. Three-octave measure: 493; natural coverings: ivory, no scribe lines; sharps: solid ebony; key fronts: molded light hard wood. L=1,710; W=650; H=493.

Nameboard inscription on rectangular ivory plaque, in black with swirls: "John Broadwood & Sons, / Makers to their Majesty & the Princesses / Great Pulteney Street Golden Square, / London."

Clinkscale 1999, 52; Clinkscale Online, CEP no. 218.

1965.01

Square piano, John Broadwood and Sons, London, 1835, and inscription.

Square piano, Archibald Whaites and George Charters, New York, ca. 1795, and inscription.

Square piano, Archibald Whaites and George Charters, New York, ca. 1795.

Mahogany; light wood stringing; light wood keyboard surround, pink and white painted flowers on either side of inscription. Stand, four square tapering legs, with stringing, brass medallions on each corner, casters. Tuning pins on right; crank dampers; prop stick on left. Compass: 5 octaves, FF-f^3. One hand stop, damper, English single-action. Three-octave measure: 485; natural coverings: ivory, no scribe lines; sharps: ebony; key fronts: molded light wood. L=1,565; W=580; D=215.

Nameboard inscription within floral wreath in black: "Whaites and Charters. / N°. 19 / Barclay Street. / LONDON." (19 Barclay Street was located in New York, the city location of London was used for stronger marketing).

Libin 1985, 163; Groce 1991, 171-172; Clinkscale 1993, 320, no. 1; Clinkscale Online, CEP no. 3980.

1967.01

Square piano, Alickham T. Robb and Edward Mundy, New York, ca. 1825, and inscription.

Square piano, Alickham T. Robb and Edward Mundy, New York, ca. 1825.

Rosewood; mahogany panels; rosewood stringing; two drawers with pulls (absent), either side below keyboard; tuning pins to right. Stand, two large pedestals, two curved legs each with casters, partially decorated, floral carving, connected by stretcher holding wooden pedal and pedal lyre. Curved rosewood keyboard surround; brass stringing; floral gilt decoration around rectangular name plate. Tuning pins on right; prop stick on left. Missing carved triangular vent in right corner. Compass: 6 octaves, FF-f^4; one pedal (absent), damper; serial no. 1000. Three-octave measure: 485; natural coverings: ivory, no scribe lines; sharps: ebony; key fronts: molded wood. L=1,720; W=640; D=320.

Nameboard inscription on gilt rectangle in black: "NEW PATENT / ROBB & MUNDY / NEW YORK."

Groce 1991, 132; Clinkscale Online, CEP no. 2734.

1969.01

Square piano, Alpheus Babcock, Boston, ca. 1826.

Mahogany veneer; rosewood cross banding; mahogany stringing; gilt cast-lead molding. Rosewood veneer nameboard; brass stringing; foliate vent on both sides of inscription, red cloth backing. Six reeded legs, brass collars, casters; three drawers with brass bail-type pulls; short soundboard with tuning pins at back, folding music desk. Dust board painted light green, decorated with three lines on the borders and a long slit for wire-mounted dampers. English double action, crank dampers from FF-c^3, strings: double-strung throughout; scale: 255. Two pedals on round reeded legs: damper, harmonic swell. Serial no. 205. Three-octave measure: 486; natural coverings: ivory, no scribe lines; sharps: ebony; key fronts: molded dark hardwood. L=1,683; W=650; D=239; H=530.

Formerly owned by John J. Enneking (1840-1916), a Boston artist.

Engraved on nameboard on brass plaque among swirls: "MADE BY / A. Babcock. (cursive) / for J.A. Dickson. (cursive) / Boston. (cursive)."

Clinkscale 1993, 14, no. 4; Koster 1994, 244; Clinkscale Online, CEP no. 379.

1969.03

Square piano, Alpheus Babcock, Boston, ca. 1826, and inscription.

Square piano, Michael Schuster junior, Neukirchen, ca. 1830, and inscription.

Square piano, Michael Schuster junior, Neukirchen, ca. 1830.

Mahogany veneer keywell; two nameboard rectangles of light wood and two floral ormolu decorations of a woman's face in the center; ormolu floral decoration on both sides; ormolu helmet on both end blocks. Stand, two splayed legs, gilt metal lion's paws, gilt floral figures on both sides below, man on the middle of the legs; folding music desk with platforms on each side for candle holders. No metal inside; tuning pins at front; missing metal lock on front. Compass: 6 octaves + 1, EE-f^4. Two metal pedals on decorative lyre with ormolu decoration of man holding a wreath leaning on decorated post. Three-octave measure: 480; natural coverings: ivory, no scribe lines; sharps: ebony; key fronts: ivory. L=1,770; W=790; D=330; H=490.

Nameboard inscription on paper label with decorative gilt brass border, in black among swirls: "M. Schuster jun. (cursive) / à NEUKIRCHEN prés d'ADORF / en Saxe."

Clinkscale 1993, 259; Weller 2004, 250; Clinkscale Online, CEP no. 2920.

1971.02

Square piano, William Dubois and Adam Stodart, New York, 1831.

Rosewood; rounded corners; light wood, rounded keyboard surround; two intricately carved vents in dark wood on both sides of inscription, white cloth backing. Four intricately carved, tapered, reeded legs, casters. Tuning pins in back; four oval-shaped metal frame sound holes on right side. Carved beading skirt below keyboard. Folding music desk and prop stick, prop sticks on both sides. Compass: 6 octaves, FF-f^4; one pedal, damper; serial no. 290. Three-octave measure: 490; natural coverings: ivory, no scribe line; sharps: ebony; key fronts: molded boxwood. L=1,725; W=655; D=310.

Nameboard inscription in gilt rectangle bordered by floral gilt inlay in black: "DUBOIS & STODART, / Manufacturers, / No. 167 Broadway / NEW YORK."

Clinkscale 1999, 108; Clinkscale Online, CEP no. 1050.

1972.01

Square piano, William Dubois and Adam Stodart, New York, 1831, and inscription.

Square piano, George Astor, London, ca. 1797.

Mahogany; wide light wood banding; case painted with green leaves with red stems, on right; with woman's face and urn with cover, on left. Light wood keyboard surround, two intricately carved vents on either side of inscription, red cloth backing, paintings of floral wreaths on both sides. Tuning pins on right; prop stick on left; key in lock. Four square tapered legs, light wood inlay; music shelf painted, designs in red, orange, black. Compass: 5½ octave, FF-c^4; one pedal (absent), damper; serial no. 2380. Three-octave measure: 480; natural coverings: ivory, no scribe lines; sharps: ebony; key fronts: molded wood. L=1,670; W=572; D=210.

Nameboard inscription in center of enamel plaque, with gilt brass ring border, in black: "New Patent / G. ASTOR & C°. / N°. 79 CORNHILL / London."

Clinkscale 1993, 8, no. 13; Clinkscale Online, CEP no. 340.

1972.07

Square piano, George Astor, London, ca. 1797, and inscription.

Square piano, Anonymous, of American origin, probably New England, ca. 1790.

Square piano, Anonymous, of American origin, probably New England, ca. 1790.

Stained eastern white pine case and lid; four slightly tapered square legs; door lock on front. Compass: 4 octaves and 2 notes, C (dummy D♯) to d^3. Three-octave measure: 476; natural coverings: ivory, no scribe lines; sharps: black wood; key fronts: dark stained wood. L=1,170; W=407; D=194; H=535.

No inscription.

Exhibited at Museum of Fine Arts, Boston, at the Exhibition *Music in Colonial Massachusetts*, May 16–September 2, 1973.

Lambert 1985, Vol. 2, 801; Clinkscale Online, CEP no. 3441.

1972.09

Square piano, Alpheus Babcock, Boston, ca. 1824.

Mahogany veneer; rosewood cross banding, mahogany stringing; rosewood veneer nameboard, brass stringing; foliate fretwork vents on both sides of nameboard; white cloth backing. Rounded front corners; keyboard surround curves over keys; brass stringing; prop sticks on both sides. Three drawers under keyboard, brass handles; internal folding music desk; tuning pins at back, crank dampers. Six turned, reeded legs, casters. Two pedals on two reeded legs: damper, harmonic swell; serial no. 440. Compass: 6 octaves, FF-f^4. Three-octave measure: 483; natural coverings: ivory, no scribe lines; sharps: solid ebony; key fronts: molded light hard wood. L=1,679; W=655; D= 317.

Nameboard inscription engraved on gilt brass plaque, among swirls: "A BABCOCK, / Boston."

Clinkscale 1999, 18; Clinkscale Online, CEP no. 6050.

1973.01

Square piano, Alpheus Babcock, Boston, ca. 1824, and inscription.

Square piano, Clementi and Co., London, ca. 1808.

Mahogany; chevron stringing, banding; two fretwork vents on either side of nameboard, dark-colored cloth underneath; flowers and wreath encircle inscription. Four brass medallions cover large screws on stand corners; four turned tapered legs, casters. Tuning pins at right; serial no. 7374 stamped on tuning plank; other numbers stamped: "06472", "163"; green silk-covered dust cover; folding music desk. Compass: 5½ octaves, FF–c^4; one wooden pedal, damper. Left side storage compartment has advertisement: "(Prince of Wales feathers; Royal Coat of Arms, crowned lion on a pedestal) / Clementi, Banger, Hyde, Collard & Co. / Manufacturers of / Upright & Horizontal Grand & Small / Piano-Fortes. / ORGANIZED PIANO FORTES, CHURCH & / Barrel Organs &c &c. / and / Music Sellers to their Majesties, / His Royal Highneſs the Prince of Wales / and all the / ROYAL FAMILY, / N°.26, Cheapside & Tottenham Court Rd. / LONDON. / NB. Clementi & Comp^{y}. Having observed that Piano Fortes &c. / constructed in the usual way for this Country are not calculated to resist / the effects of warmer Climates: have Manufactured the above Instruments / for Exportation, of solid materials. upon such an Improved and Secure plan / as to remove all doubts of their durability." Three-octave measure: 485; natural coverings: ivory, no scribe lines; sharps: ebony; key fronts: molded light hard wood. L=1,675; W=590; D=220; H=580.

Nameboard inscription on black oval in gilt: "New Patent / Muzio Clementi & Co- / Cheapside, London."

Clinkscale 1993, 69, no. 14; Clinkscale Online, CEP no. 866.

1973.02

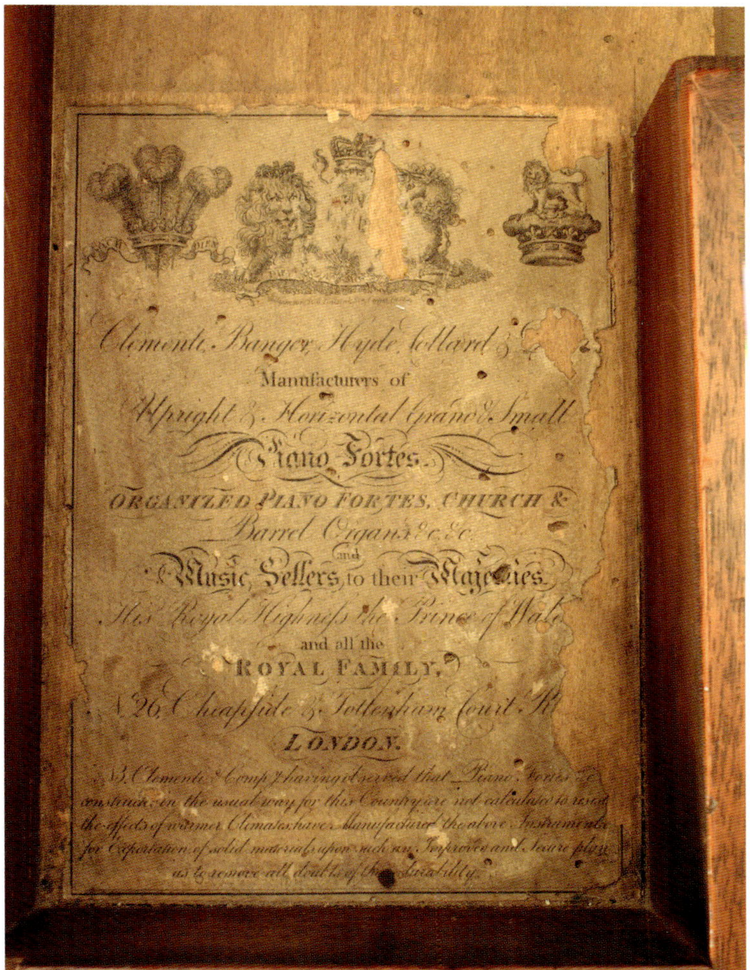

Advertisement

Square piano, Clementi and Co., London, ca. 1808.

Inscription.

Square piano, Joseph Dale and Son, London, ca. 1805.

Mahogany; cross banding; satinwood nameboard; two carved vents on either side of nameboard; dark cloth backing. Four square tapering legs, light wood inlay, casters, shelf underneath. Brass hooks, front and sides; triangular carved vent, right-hand rear corner. Internal folding music stand; prop sticks on both sides; single action; under dampers attached to metal arms, FF to b$\flat^2$. Compass: 5½ octaves, FF-c^4. Three-octave measure: 490; natural coverings: ivory, no scribe lines; sharps: stained wood with ebony tops; key fronts: molded wood. L=1,600; W=590; D=215; H=570.

Nameboard inscription in oval, bordered by three inlayed dark lines, in black among swirls: "Joseph Dale & Son, (cursive) / MAKERS & MUSIC SELLERS / to the Royal Family. / Cornhill, Oxford Street & New Bond Street, / London".

Brass under dampers first appear in John Broadwood's British patent of July 17, 1783 (no. 1,379).

Harding 1973, 57; Cole 2005, 42-43; Clinkscale 1993, 82; Clinkscale Online, CEP no. 1061.

1973.03

Square piano, Joseph Dale and Son, London, ca. 1805, and inscription.

Square piano, Thomas Culliford, William Rolfe, and Barrow, London, ca. 1795, and inscription.

Square piano, Thomas Culliford, William Rolfe, and Barrow, London, ca. 1795.

Mahogany; light wood stringing; stand, four tapered square legs, casters, brass bolt covers above front legs; spruce soundboard; tuning pins on right side. Rectangular chevron inlay on satinwood keyboard surround; missing vent cover in right-hand corner; shelf below keyboard; prop stick, left side; serial no. 3807. Compass: 5½ octaves, FF-c^4; one pedal, damper (missing). Three-octave measure: 482; natural coverings: ivory with two scribe lines including head/tail seam; sharps: ebony; key fronts: molded wood. L=1,670; W=605; D=230.

Nameboard inscription in brown among swirls; penciled on reverse: "Culliford, Rolfe and Barrow / 112 Cheapside, / London".

Clinkscale 1993, 81, no. 3; Clinkscale Online, CEP no. 889.

1973.04

Square piano, John Broadwood and Sons, London, ca. 1815, and inscription.

Square piano, John Broadwood and Sons, London, ca. 1815.

Mahogany; rosewood cross banding; two foliate carved vents on either side of satinwood nameboard; inlaid squares on keyboard sides; black inlaid decorative lines around rectangular inscription. Six round tapered, reeded, carved legs, casters; folding music desk; carved vent in right-hand corner; prop sticks on both sides. Compass: 5½ octaves, FF-c^4; one pedal (missing), damper, English double action with mop-stick dampers; painted dust cover, dark wood inlay; serial no. 18643. Three-octave measure: 490; natural coverings: ivory with two scribe lines including head/tail seam; sharps: ebony; key fronts: molded wood. L=1,660; W=630; D=245.

Nameboard inscription in black bordered rectangle, in black among swirls: "John Broadwood and Sons. / Makers to His Majesty, & the Princefses. / Great Pulteney Street. Golden Square. / London."

Clinkscale 1993, 39, no. 81; Clinkscale Online, CEP no. 686.

1973.05

Square piano, George Wilkinson, London, ca. 1815, and inscription.

Square piano, George Wilkinson, London, ca. 1815.

Mahogany; rosewood nameboard; two fret work openings on either side of nameboard; red cloth backing; tuning pins at back; prop stick on left; four round reeded and tapered legs, casters. Compass: 5½ octaves, FF-c^4; one pedal, dampers (missing); serial no. 328. Three-octave measure: 487; natural coverings: ivory, no scribe lines; sharps: solid ebony; key fronts: ivory. L=1,675; W=635; H=605.

Nameboard inscription on gilt brass rectangle, gilt brass border, in raised letters: "GEORGE WILKINSON / 315 Oxford Street LONDON".

Clinkscale 1993, 322, no. 1; Clinkscale Online, CEP no. 3991.

1973.06

Square piano, Christopher Ganer, London, 1781, and inscription.

Square piano, Christopher Ganer, London, 1781.

Mahogany; black and white stringing; curly sycamore nameboard; prop stick on left; mahogany trestle stand; four square legs. Compass: 5 octaves, FF/GG-f^3; tuning pins on right with crank dampers, three hand stops: bass dampers (to c^1), treble dampers, buff. Three-octave measure: 485; natural coverings: ivory with two scribe lines including head/tail seam; sharps: ebony; key fronts: molded wood. L=1,510; W=500; D=150; H=630.

Nameboard inscription on light wood oval, in black among swirls: "Christopher Ganer, Londini, Fecit 1781 / Broad Street Soho."

Clinkscale 1993, 114, no. 12; Clinkscale Online, CEP no. 1360.

1974.01

Square piano, Charles Lemme, Paris, 1803.

Red mahogany; two gilt brass female trumpeters both sides of front; beaded gilt metal decoration on ledge below keyboard; four dark wood round tapering legs. Satinwood keyboard surround with rosewood borders; tuning pegs on right side, dampers absent. Wide folding music desk, prop sticks on both sides. Compass: 6 octaves, FF-f^4; three wooden pedals: damper, buff, moderator. Three-octave measure: 480; natural coverings: ivory, no scribe lines; sharps: ebony; key fronts: boxwood with stripe. L=1,555; W=590; D=225.

Nameboard inscription in black among swirls: "Charles Lemme. / Rue d'Orléans N°. 7 au Marais. / à Paris."

Clinkscale 1993, 180; Clinkscale Online, CEP no. 2119.

1975.01

Square piano, Charles Lemme, Paris, 1803, and inscription.

Square piano, Johannes Pohlman, London, ca. 1780.

Mahogany; satinwood nameboard; rosewood banding; mahogany trestle stand; square tapering legs. Tuning pins on right; overhead dampers; prop stick on left. Compass: 5 octaves, FF-f^3; "149" on underside of key lever for f^3; three hand stops: bass dampers (to c^1), treble dampers, buff. Three-octave measure: 485; natural coverings: ivory with three scribe lines including head/tail seam; sharps: ebony; key fronts: molded wood. L=1,520; W=555; D=190.

Nameboard inscription on light wood cartouche, in black among swirls: "Johannes Pohlman Londini Fecit."

Clinkscale 1993, 220, no. 14; Clinkscale Online, CEP no. 2510.

1976.02

Square piano, Johannes Pohlman, London, ca. 1780, and inscription.

Square piano, George Astor, London, ca. 1805, and inscription.

Square piano, George Astor, London, ca. 1805.

Mahogany and satinwood; banding of double lines and chevrons; satinwood nameboard; carved vents on either side of nameboard, right vent missing; nameboard painted blue and green flowers with green leaves around inscription; carved vent in right-hand corner; green material covering dust cover. Internal folding music desk, prop stick; shelf underneath case; four square tapered legs, casters; pedal leg without pedal. Compass: 5½ octaves, FF-c^4; one pedal, damper; serial nos. 3356, 158. Three-octave measure: 480; natural coverings: ivory, no scribe lines; sharps: ebony; key fronts: molded wood. L=1,645; W=590; D=220.

Nameboard inscription in black oval surrounded by red beads, in gilt letters among swirls: "New Patent / Astor & Comp^y / 79 Cornhill, London".

Clinkscale 1993, 10, no. 24; Clinkscale Online, CEP no. 336

1977.01

Square piano, John Zumpe and Gabriel Buntebart, London, 1770.

Mahogany; rectangular chain pattern inlay on front; leaf decorations in each corner. Tuning pins on right; overhead dampers; prop stick on left. Dark mahogany trestle stand (replacement). Compass: 5 octaves, FF/GG-f^3; three hand stops: dampers (to c^1), treble dampers, buff. Three-octave measure: 484; natural coverings: ivory with two scribe lines including head/tail seam; sharps: solid ebony; key fronts: molded light hard wood. L=1,449; W=502; D=171; H=628.

Nameboard inscription on light wood cartouche, in black among swirls: "Johannes Zumpe / et Buntebart / Londini Fecit 1770, / Princes' Street Hanover Square." (Note, "fecit" should read "fecerunt".)

Clinkscale 1993, 332, no. 19; Clinkscale Online, CEP no. 4113.

1977.02

Square piano, John Zumpe and Gabriel Buntebart, London, 1770, and inscription.

Square piano, James Longman and Francis Broderip, London, ca. 1791.

Mahogany; light wood stringing; satinwood keyboard surround; flowers and wreath around nameboard plaque. Four square tapered legs, collars and cuffs; shelf underneath; tuning pins on right; overhead dampers in rack, prop stick on left. Three hand stops: bass dampers, treble dampers, buff. Compass: 5 octaves, FF-f^3. Three-octave measure: 485; natural coverings: ivory with two scribe lines including head/tail seam; sharps: ebony; key fronts: molded wood. L=1,555; W=560; D=215.

Nameboard inscription on oval enamel plaque surrounded by a beaded brass oval, in black: "BY ROYAL PATENT / LONGMAN & BRODERIP / MUSICAL INSTRUMENT MAKERS / N°. 26 CHEAPSIDE & N°. 13 HAYMARKET / LONDON".

Clinkscale 1993, 187, no. 37; Clinkscale Online, CEP no. 2150.

1978.01

Square piano, James Longman and Francis Broderip, London, ca. 1791, and inscription.

Square piano, Jacques Goermans, Paris, 1782, and inscription.

Square piano, Jacques Goermans, Paris, 1782.

Wood originally painted white or cream and varnish that has darkened, probably nineteenth-century decoration with classically inspired scenes. On lid, various colors of balls or gems, border of entwined leaves. Within gold-bordered oval: seated angel at table conversing with woman, holding drum or tambourine, accompanied by three putti. On fallboard in center: instrument group of lyre, panpipes, tambourine, cymbals, bagpipes, and woodwinds. Two gold-bordered ovals on fallboard (left) and front (right): seated woman playing aulos or double pipe and seated woman playing clarinet. Two gold-bordered ovals on each side; on left side, seated woman playing harp; on right side, seated woman playing lyre, both accompanied with single sprays of flowers. Tuning pins to right; overhead dampers in rack; prop stick on left. Four square tapered legs, front two, painted flowers and leaves. Two wooden pedals on stretcher, between two legs for dampers and buff stop. Compass: 5 octaves, FF-f^3; three-octave measure: 490; natural coverings: ivory with two scribe lines including head/tail seam; sharps: ebony; key fronts: molded wood. L=1,510; W=535; D=200; H=625.

Inscription on nameboard on light wood cartouche in black: "(symbol) Fecit Goermans dit Germain. à Paris. 1782. (symbol) / (symbol) Rue des Fosses S^t. Germain des Pres Faubourg S^t. Germain (symbol)".

Clinkscale 1993, 123; Clinkscale Online, CEP no. 1430.

1978.04

Square piano, John Geib, Adam Geib, and William Geib, New York, ca. 1820, and inscription.

Square piano, John Geib, Adam Geib, and William Geib, New York, ca. 1820.

Mahogany; rosewood binding; satinwood keyboard surround; two simulated vents; verre eglomisé (gilt under glass), with white decoration on either side of nameboard. Brass gilt decoration on lower ledge. Six round tapered, carved reeded legs, gilt brass collars, casters. Four gilt brass medallions on upper part of stand next to two drawers, round pulls; four small brass medallions, center of stand. Compass: 6 octaves, FF-f^4; round tapered, reeded pedal leg; wooden pedal, damper; crank dampers; prop sticks on both sides; missing carved vent in right-hand corner; serial no. 5740. Three-octave measure: 490; natural coverings: ivory, no scribe lines; sharps: ebony; key fronts: molded wood. L=1,670; W=723; D=225.

Nameboard inscription in oval surrounded by floral engravings on verre eglomisé (gold material under glass), in white: "New Patent, / J. A. & W. Geib / NEW YORK."

Clinkscale 1993, 119, no. 10; Clinkscale Online, CEP no. 1408.

1978.05

Square piano, George Astor and Horwood, London, ca. 1820, and inscription.

Square piano, George Astor and Horwood, London, ca. 1820.

Mahogany; dark stringing; light wood keyboard surround; two carved vents, either side of nameboard; on either side of inscription, a wreath around a lute and a wreath around a tambourine. Small internal folding music desk; prop sticks on both sides; green painted dust cover; line border in gilt; tuning pins on right. Six round carved and tapered legs, gilt collars, casters. Compass: 5½ octaves, FF-c^4; one pedal, damper (missing); serial nos. 5286, 186. Three-octave measure: 483; natural coverings: ivory, contiguous heads and tails (replacements); sharps: ebony; key fronts: molded wood. L=1,697; W=620; D=220.

Nameboard inscription in white rectangle surrounded by symbols, in black: "New Patent / (line designs) / Astor & Horwood, / 79 Cornhill, London."

Clinkscale 1993, 11, no. 7; Clinkscale Online, CEP no. 346.

1979.01

Square piano, John Joseph Merlin, London, 1783.

Mahogany; ebony, holly, and elm chevron stringing and cross banding; keyboard surround in burr walnut; light wood stringing; tuning pins to right, dampers in rack; stand, four tapered legs, brass medallions over screws at stand corners. Compass: 5 octaves, FF/GG-f^3; double-strung; two hand stops: dampers, buff. Three-octave measure: 486; natural coverings: ivory with two scribe lines including head/tail seam; sharps: solid ebony; key fronts: molded light hard wood. L=1500; W=508; H=760.

Nameboard inscription on oval boxwood plaque, in black among swirls: "Josephus Merlin Londini FECIT 1783 / No. 2 Princes Street Hanover Square."

Exhibited at *John Joseph Merlin, the Ingenious Mechanick*. Kenwood, London, July 19 to August 26, 1985.

Clinkscale 1993, 198, no. 3; Clinkscale Online, CEP no. 2277; Palmer, 103-105.

1979.02

Square piano, John Joseph Merlin, London, 1783, and inscription.

Square piano, attributed to Christopher Ganer, London, ca. 1790.

Mahogany; curved sides; wide light wood banding; chevron stringing on lid. Tuning pins at back; light wood keyboard surround; sides, painted scenes or applied on cards (découpage); rectangle of rosewood surrounds inscription. Dark wood trestle stand, curved sides. Compass: 5 octaves, FF-f^3; no hand stops or pedals. Three-octave measure: 480; natural coverings: ivory, no scribe lines; sharps: ebony; key fronts: molded wood. L=1,233; W=650; D=186; H=510.

Nameboard inscription in light wood oval in black among swirls: "Ganer / BROAD STREET, GOLDEN SQUARE / London".

Clinkscale Online, CEP no. 1374.

1979.03

Square piano, attributed to Christopher Ganer, London, ca. 1790, and inscription.

Square transposing piano, John Broadwood and Son, London, 1808.

Rosewood veneer; dark wood stringing. Boxwood and rosewood keyboard surround; carved vents on both sides of nameboard; boxwood inlay below keyboard; internal folding music desk; carved vent in right-hand corner; tuning pins in back; prop sticks on both sides; four carved, reeded legs, brass collars, casters. Compass: 5½ octaves, FF-c^4; with two wooden pegs that operate a spring catch, keyboard may be moved laterally downward or upward as much as the interval of a sixth. Ivory-capped pin placed in a wooden rack of eleven numbered holes on left side, below keyboard, regulating the lateral movement. Fifteen additional notes available with transposition slide, making use of keyboard notes from DD to f^4. One wooden damper pedal; crank dampers from GG♯ to d^2; serial no. 11,406. A chromatic scale from e^1 to e^2 is written one step lower above the keys for d^1 to d^2 in order to show a transposition possibility. Three-octave measure: 490; natural coverings: ivory with two scribe lines including head/tail seam; sharps: solid ebony; key fronts: molded light hard wood. L=1,655; W=615; D=245; H=565.

Square transposing piano, John Broadwood and Son, London, 1808, and inscription.

Nameboard inscription in cartouche in black: "PATENT TRANSPOSING PIANO FORTE / John Broadwood and Son. / Makers to his Majesty / & the Princefses, / Great Pulteney Street. / London. 1808."

Harding 1933, 278, pl. XV; Cole 2005, 95, 181; Clinkscale 1993, 37, no. 63; Clinkscale Online, CEP no. 585.

A British patent for a transposing piano was taken out by Edward Ryley, titled "Movable keys for pianofortes, organs, and all other instruments which are performed upon by keys" (no. 2,562), November 28, 1801. Broadwood is said to have purchased the patent shortly after it was approved. This piano was exhibited in 1885 at the International Inventions Exhibition, London, group XXXIV, historic collections, class 179.

Formerly Broadwood Collection, London.

International Inventions Exhibition 1885, 316, no. 3577.

1980.01

Square piano, Jonas Chickering, Boston, 1827, and inscription.

Square piano, Jonas Chickering, Boston, 1827.

Rosewood veneer; Sheraton style; rounded corners; brass inlay in keyboard surround; three drawers below keyboard; wide gilt brass skirt below keyboard; four round reeded and tapered legs, carved capitals, brass collars, casters; folding music desk on top of lid; inscription on brass plaque bordered by inlaid brass rectangle. Tuning pins in back; crank dampers; one wooden damper pedal in pedal lyre; full-width soundboard; prop sticks on both sides. Compass: 5½ octaves, FF-c^4; stringing: single-strung FF-D; double strung D♯-c^4; English double action, serial no. 529. Three-octave measure: 490; natural coverings: ivory, no scribe lines; sharps: ebony; key fronts: flat light wood. L=1,775; W=711; D=298; H=857.

Nameboard engraving on brass plaque among swirls: "PATENT / J. CHICKERING, Maker, / N°. 20 Common Street, / Boston."

Chickering adopted James Stewart's 1827 US patent (no. 5,475) indicated by strings looping around hitch pins.

Haupert 1989, 79, 117-133; Clinkscale 1999, 74, 357; Clinkscale Online, CEP no. 935.

1983.01

Square piano, John Osborne, Boston, 1822-1824.

Mahogany; rosewood banding; rosewood nameboard; round corners; two carved vents on both sides of nameboard; red cloth backing; two stylized white- and brown-colored lyres inlaid on both sides of inscription plaque; brass inlay around vents, lyres, and inscription plaque. Two drawers below keyboard; wide silver-plated brass decoration on ledge; six turned dark wood legs with gilt brass collars, casters; slim carved pedal lyre; brass rectangle inlay and redwood inlay bordering plaque. Tuning pins at back, with dolly crank dampers. Large folding music desk, and prop. Compass: 5½ octaves, FF-c^4; one wooden pedal, damper; serial no. 308. Three-octave measure: 489; natural coverings: ivory with no scribe lines; sharps: ebony; key fronts: molded wood. L=1,685; W=625; D=326.

Nameboard engraved on brass rectangle with swirls: "PATENT. / John Osborne, / Boylston Market, / Boston."

Clinkscale 1999, 275; Clinkscale Online, CEP no. 2456.

1983.14

Square piano, John Osborne, Boston, 1822-1824, and inscription.

Square piano, Adam Beyer, London, ca. 1775, and inscription.

Square piano, Adam Beyer, London, ca. 1775.

Mahogany; dark wood stringing; keyboard surround; dark wood inlay on trestle stand; four square legs; tuning pins on right; English single action; dampers in rack; lid string on right. Compass: 5 octaves -2, GG, AA-f^3; three hand stops: bass damper to b^1, treble damper, buff. Three-octave measure: 486; natural coverings: ivory with two scribe lines including head/tail seam; sharps: black wood; key fronts: molded light hardwood. L=1,444; W=480; D=170.

Nameboard inscription on light wood cartouche in black: "Adam Beyer Londini Fecit 1775".

Clinkscale 1993, 22, no. 4; Clinkscale Online, CEP no. 439.

1986.08

Square piano, Clementi and Co., London, ca. 1803.

Mahogany veneer (faded); light and dark wood stringing; satinwood nameboard; two carved vents on either side of nameboard; right vent damaged; nameboard painted with blue and red flowers, green leaves around inscription. Mahogany stand, square tapered legs, light wood collars, casters; brass medallions covering screws on stand; carved vent in right-hand corner; dolly crank dampers. Compass: 5½ octaves, FF-c^4; one pedal (absent), dampers; serial nos, 3468, 3312, 35, 3468. Three-octave measure: 482; natural coverings: ivory, no scribe lines; sharps: ebony; key fronts: molded light hardwood. L=1,667; W=587; H=590.

Nameboard inscription on black oval, in white among swirls: "New Patent / Muzio Clementi & Co. / Cheapside London."

Clinkscale 1993, 68, no. 10; Clinkscale Online, CEP no. 855.

1988.01

Square piano, Clementi and Co., London, ca. 1803, and inscription.

Square piano, Joseph Kirkman, London, 1798.

Mahogany; chevron stringing; satinwood keyboard surround; mahogany stand; light wood stringing; tuning pins on right; prop stick on left; dampers in rack; four square tapered legs, cuffs, casters. Compass: 5½ octaves, FF-c[4]; two hand stops: damper, buff. Three-octave measure: 480; natural coverings: ivory, no scribe lines; sharps: ebony; key fronts: molded light hard wood. L=1,635; W=580; D=210.

Nameboard inscription in an oval, in black among swirls: "Jofephus Kirckman Londini Fecit 1798 / N°. 19, Broad Street Soho."

Clinkscale 1993, 167, no. 5; Clinkscale Online, CEP no. 1966.

1990.01

Square piano, Joseph Kirkman, London, 1798, and inscription.

Square piano, Clementi and Co., London, ca. 1818, and inscription.

Square piano, Clementi and Co., London, ca. 1818.

Mahogany; rosewood cross banding; brass floral skirt around ledge; brass inlay on nameboard; two carved vents on either side of nameboard; two gilt and painted decorations on both sides of inscription; fretwork vent in right-hand corner. Inscription bordered in gilt, orange, and red painted striping. Internal folding music desk; dust cover painted green; prop stick on left; six tapered, round, and reeded legs, brass collars, casters. Compass: 5½ octaves, FF-c[4]; one wooden pedal on carved leg, damper; serial nos. "15536" in ink; "12351" stamped. Three-octave measure: 485; natural coverings: ivory, no scribe lines; sharps: ebony; key fronts: molded wood. L=1,710; W=620; H=590.

Nameboard inscription in gilt rectangle, in black among swirls: "New Patent / Clementi & Co, / Cheapside, London".

Clinkscale Online, CEP no. 6049.

1992.13

Square piano, James Stewart and Jonas Chickering, Boston, 1826.

Mahogany; brass stringing; rosewood keyboard surround; tuning pins in back; crank dampers; prop sticks on both sides; carved and bulbous legs, casters; metal pedal and probably later pedal lyre; serial no. 411. Compass: 5½ octaves, FF-c^4; double action. Three-octave measure: 490; natural coverings: ivory, no scribe lines; sharps: black wood; key fronts: boxwood. L=1,765; W=690; H=605.

Nameboard engraving on brass plaque bordered by wooden inlay, with swirls: "PATENT. / Stewart & Chickering. / Makers, Tremont Street, / Boston."

Clinkscale 1999, 358; Clinkscale Online, CEP no. 4640.

1993.01

Square piano, James Stewart and Jonas Chickering, Boston, 1826, and inscription.

Square piano, Alpheus Babcock, Boston, ca. 1825, and inscription.

Square piano, Alpheus Babcock, Boston, ca. 1825.

Rosewood; mahogany panels, brass inlay; mahogany nameboard, brass inlay; two wide, gilt cast-lead moldings below keyboard; two foliate vents on both sides of nameboard; mahogany dust board; internal folding music desk; three drawers with gilt brass pulls; prop stick on both sides; six round, reeded, tapered carved legs on casters, gilt brass collars; two wooden pedals on reeded legs, casters. Tuning pins in back; serial no. 176. Compass: 5½ octaves, FF-c^4; double-action; three-octave measure: 379; natural coverings: ivory, no scribe lines; sharps: ebony; key fronts: molded boxwood. L=1,675; W=650; D=320; H=615.

Nameboard inscription on brass plaque, with swirls: "MADE BY / A. Babcock, / for J.A. Dickson, Boston."

Koster 1994, 244. Clinkscale 1993, 358; Clinkscale Online, CEP no. 4461.

1993.05

Square piano, Christian Frederick Louis Albrecht, Philadelphia, ca. 1825, and inscription.

Square piano, Christian Frederick Louis Albrecht, Philadelphia, ca. 1825.

Mahogany; rounded corners with gilt brass decoration on both corners; rosewood cross banding; gilt brass floral molding below keyboard; two drawers (no middle drawer); four gilt brass knobs; four gilt brass medallions above legs. Two foliate vents, both sides of inscription; left vent with yellow cloth backing; inlaid brass floral patterns on either side of inscription; folding music desk with prop; prop sticks on both sides. Six turned, tapered, bulbous legs, carved leaves, embossed brass collars, brass casters; full-width soundboard, tuning pins on right. Compass: 6 octaves, FF-f^4; double strung FF-E; overspun; modified English action with back checks, overhead dampers in rack; wood pedal, damper; serial no. 169. Three-octave measure: 485; natural coverings: ivory, no scribe lines; sharps: ebony; key fronts: flat rosewood. L=1,685; W=690; D=310; H=520.

Nameboard engraving on gilt brass rectangle with decorative border and swirls: "C.F.L. Albrecht. (gothic) / PHILADELPHIA."

Clinkscale 1999, 5; Clinkscale Online, CEP no. 4983.

1994.09

Square piano, André Stein, Vienna, ca. 1835, and inscription.

Square piano, André Stein, Vienna, ca. 1835.

Figured, book-matched mahogany veneer; two hexagonal pillars; stretcher; two splayed legs. Black-stained wood below keyboard; music desk damaged; tuning pins in front; prop sticks on both sides. Two metal pedals below lyre: damper, moderator. Compass: 6 octaves, FF-f^4; single-strung, close overspun FF-BB; C-F double-strung, close overspun; remainder double-strung. Three-octave measure: 482; natural coverings: ivory, no scribe lines; sharps: solid ebony; key fronts: ivory. L=1,748; W=743; H=550.

Nameboard inscription on cast brass oval plaque bordered by serpent swallowing its tail: "ANDRÉ STEIN / d'Augsbourg / a / VIENNE".

Clinkscale Online, CEP no. 6053.

2003.20

Square piano, Christian Baumann, Deuxponts (Zweibrücken), ca. 1800, and inscription.

Square piano, Christian Baumann, Deuxponts (Zweibrücken), ca. 1800.

Walnut; inlaid cross-grain panels in lid; wide rosewood banding; four round tapered, and fluted legs; tuning pins on right; prop stick on left. Compass: 5 octaves, FF-f^3. Three hand stops, buff, two dampers at each side of keyboard. Three-octave measure: 470; natural coverings: ebony with two scribe lines including head/tail seam; sharps: ivory topped ebony; key fronts: flat dark stained wood. L=1,497; W=525; H=615.

Inscription on paper label inside right corner: "CHRISTIAN BAUMANN, / Facteur d'Orgues & d'Instruments / à Deuxponts."

Clinkscale Online, CEP no. 6297.

2005.15

Square piano, attributed to Juan del Mármol, Seville, ca. 1785.

Mahogany; light and dark stringing; white and dark stringing on nameboard in rectangle; tuning pins on right side; dampers in rack; missing stand. Three hand stops: bass damper, buff, treble damper; single-action with overhead dampers. Compass: 5 octaves, GG-g^3; double-strung throughout, bass strings twisted. Three-octave measure: 484; natural coverings: ivory with two scribe lines including head/tail seam; sharps: black-stained mahogany; key fronts: ivory. L=1,415; W=486; D=166.

No inscription.

Clinkscale Online, CEP no. 6298.

2006.01

Square piano, attributed to Juan del Mármol, Seville, ca. 1785.

Square piano, James Stewart and Jonas Chickering, Boston, ca. 1824.

Rosewood; inlaid light brass stringing; inlaid brass stringing on light wood nameboard; light wood key slip; mahogany dust cover; tubular bar in front; tuning pins at back; internal folding music desk; round bulbous legs, with black-stained trim, casters; two brass inlaid borders around inscription. Serial no. 309. Compass: 5½ octaves, FF-c^4; double-strung throughout, FF-BB close overspun. One wooden pedal: damper; ornately carved lyre. Three-octave measure: 490; natural coverings: ivory, no scribe lines; sharps: ebony; key fronts: flat wood. L=1,755; W=695; H=490.

Nameboard engraved on rectangular brass plaque, with swirls: "PATENT. / STEWART & CHICKERING, / Makers, Tremont Street, / Boston."

Clinkscale Online, CEP no. 6300.

2006.05

Square piano, James Stewart and Jonas Chickering, Boston, ca. 1824, and inscription.

Square piano, John Haberacker, Reading, Pennsylvania, ca. 1800.

Mahogany; dark wood stringing; light wood keyboard surround; tuning pins to right; folding music desk with prop stick; prop stick on right; stand with four square tapering legs, light wood inlay, casters; brass medallions at each corner covering screws; shelf under case; inscription surrounded by flowers and berries. Compass: 5 octaves, FF to f^3; one pedal, dampers. Three-octave measure: 481; natural coverings: ivory, no scribe lines; sharps: ebony; key fronts: molded light hard wood. L=1,596; W=565; H=545.

Nameboard inscription in wreath of leaves, in black: "John Haberacker / READING".

Clinkscale Online, CEP no. 7157.

2011.03

Square piano, John Haberacker, Reading, Pennsylvania, ca. 1800, and inscription.

Square piano, William Bent, Boston, 1807-1809.

Mahogany; chevron stringing; light wood banding; light wood skirt on bottom of stand; stand with four square tapering legs, casters; tuning pins on right; prop stick on left. Light wood nameboard, painted wreath and five blue flowers. Compass, 5½ octaves, FF to c^4; bichord, wound bass strings; pedal missing, no hand stops; English double action with captive (Irish) dampers. Three-octave measure: 487; natural coverings: ivory, no scribe lines; sharps: ebony; key fronts: molded wood. L=1,683; W=595; D=230; H=500.

Nameboard inscription on black oval, in gold: "Willm Bent, / BOSTON."

Formerly in the Los Angeles County Museum of Art.

Clinkscale Online, CEP no. 424.

2011.07

Square piano, William Bent, Boston, 1807-1809, and inscription.

Square piano, Benjamin Crehore and Alpheus Babcock, Milton, Massachusetts, ca. 1805, and inscription.

Square piano, Benjamin Crehore and Alpheus Babcock, Milton, Massachusetts, ca. 1805.

Mahogany; rosewood cross banding; alternate light and dark wood stringing; tuning pins on right; stand, four square tapered legs inlaid with rosewood, brass cups, missing casters; folding music desk; satinwood keyboard surround; prop stick on left. Under fallboard a ledge for holding music; internal folding music desk. Case attributed to John and Thomas Seymour, Boston, with nameboard, floral polychrome decoration of roses attributed to the shop of John Ritto Penniman. Compass: 5 octaves, FF-f^3; bichord with English double action, one hand stop, dampers. Three-octave measure: 485; natural coverings: ivory, no scribe lines; sharps: stained wood with ebony tops; key fronts: molded light hard wood. L=1,610; W=568; D=215; H=600.

Nameboard inscription between bouquets of roses, in black with swirls: "Crehore & Babcock. / MILTON."

This is the only example of a square piano by both of these makers.

Clinkscale Online, CEP no. 7128.

Kuronen 1992, 55-56, 64-74.

2011.08

Square piano, John Crang Hancock, London, 1777, and inscription.

Square piano, John Crang Hancock, London, 1777.

Mahogany; holly or boxwood stringing; concave sides similar to bentside spinet; trestle stand, four legs, casters. Satinwood nameboard; tuning pins in front; removable prop stick on right; lid crack repaired with three wood inserts. Three-octave measure: 490; compass: 5 octaves, F (no F♯)-f^3; bichord with maker's unique action, no hand stops or pedals, natural coverings: ivory with two scribe lines including head/tail seam; sharps: ebony; key fronts: flat brown wood. L=1,675; W=620; H=620.

Name batten inscription in light wood cartouche in black: "Crang Hancock London Fecit 1777 / Tavistock Street."

Harding 1933, 59-60, 318; Cole 1998, 112.

2013.04

Lying harp piano, attributed to Johann Matthäus Schmahl, Ulm, ca. 1780.

Lying harp piano, attributed to Johann Matthäus Schmahl, Ulm, ca. 1780.

Cherry (?) or walnut (?); interior of lid carved with three geometrical designs; scrolled key cheeks in dark wood at both sides of keyboard; two hand stops at either side of keyboard; no dampers; tuning pins on right side; no legs or stand. Soundboard decorated with découpage and rose hole. Compass: 4½ octaves, C-f^3; Stoßmechanik, hammer heads facing player, single action. Three-octave measure: 476; natural coverings: walnut (?) with two scribe lines including head/tail seam; sharps: black wood, ivory diamond in center; key fronts: gilt cardboard. L=125; W=490; D=120.

No inscription.

Clinkscale 1993, 251, no. 19; Clinkscale Online, CEP no. 2880.

1972.02

Desk piano, James Semple, Glasgow, ca. 1860.

Mahogany, in form of a desk; lip for music desk with two movable metal arms; four turned and tapered legs; two knee levers: damper (right), moderator (left, inserts strip of felt between hammers and strings). Compass: four octaves, F-f^3; down striking action. Serial nos. S. 157, 36. Three-octave measure: 487; natural coverings: ivory, contiguous heads and tails; sharps: ebony; key fronts: ivory. L=790; W=670; D=235; H=560.

Two inscriptions, underside of lid in black rectangle bordered in white, in white: "JAMES SEMPLE, / Manufacturer, / 7 STIRLING ROAD, / GLASGOW."; "SEMPLE'S / PATENT / NON-BLOCKING / CHECK ACTION."

Clinkscale 1999, 340; Clinkscale Online, CEP no. 3197.

Semple was active as a piano manufacturer in Glasgow from 1850 to 1875.

Eileen Joyce Studio, Historical instrument collection, the University of Western Australia, www.music.uwa.edu/au/community/historic-instrument-collection.

1986.02

First inscription.

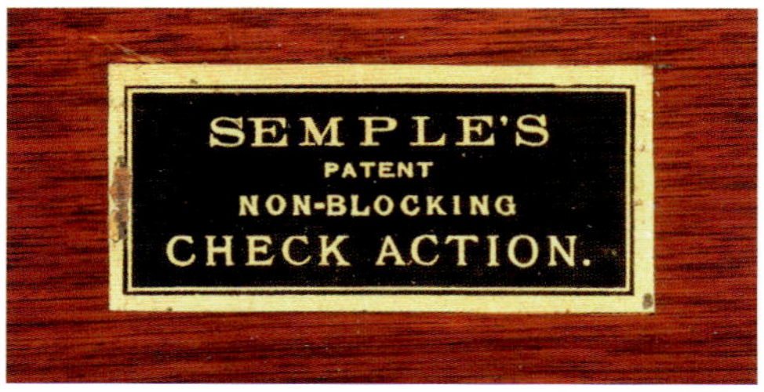

Second inscription.

Desk piano, James Semple, Glasgow, ca. 1860.

Keyboard carillon, Henry Godden, London, ca. 1810.

Mahogany; front above keyboard covered in pleated red silk; decorated wood border; trestle stand, four molded square legs, casters. Mechanism strikes bells. Ivory capped lever on right. Compass: 1 octave, c^2-c^3. Two-octave measure: 353; natural coverings: ivory, no scribe lines; sharps: ebony; key fronts: molded wood. L=474; W=560; H=610, D=820 (with stand).

Nameboard inscription on ivory rectangle, in black: "H[y] Godden, MAKER."

This keyboard instrument is quite unusual and possibly unique. It was thought this instrument could have been the "istromento d'acciaio" (keyboard glockenspiel) required by Mozart in *Die Zauberflöte* (1791) in Papageno's second act aria, "Ein Mädchen oder ein Weichen" ("A child or a woman"). However, this aria requires an instrument with a compass of three octaves and one note, c to d^3.

Baines 1992, "Glockenspiel," 130-131; Montagu 2002, 94-95.

1987.04

Keyboard carillon, Henry Godden, London, ca. 1810, and inscription.

Piano in half round shape, William Southwell, Dublin, ca. 1785, and inscription.

Piano in half round shape, William Southwell, Dublin, ca. 1785.

Mahogany; king wood and satinwood cross banding; burr yew stringing; amaranth marquetry; satinwood keywell surround; lower part of satinwood nameboard painted with alternating red roses and green leaves; ribbon inlay on bottom ledge. With lid closed, appears as a demi-lune console table; one knee lever for swell (raising louvers on right). Music desk folds away when lid closed. Four square tapered amboyna wood legs, satinwood inlay, decorative cuffs, lower part of legs. Compass: 5 octaves, FF/GG-f^3; Prellmechanik, brass lever over-dampers end in form of a small bird, wooden kapsels; hammer heads face player. Three-octave measure: 490, natural coverings: ivory, no scribe lines; sharps: solid ebony; key fronts: molded light hard wood. L=1,594; W=590; D=150; H=630.

Nameboard inscription on lower part of nameboard on green bordered scroll, in black: "SOUTHWELL.FECIT".

Clinkscale 1993, 269, no. 1A; Clinkscale Online, CEP no. 2963.

1994.10

Piano-harp or claviharpe, Christian Dietz, Paris, ca. 1884, and inscription.

Piano-harp or claviharpe, Christian Dietz, Paris, ca. 1884.

Upright piano with harp placed on upper section. Dietz's action uses small leather-covered hooks for plucking strings. Tan-painted wood with flower motifs and trompe l'oeil depictions; leaf motif on both sides of nameboard. Compass: 6 octaves, FF-f^4; two metal pedals with ornate decoration: left raises pitch one octave (FF to f'); right, damper. Three-octave measure: 505; natural coverings: ivory, no scribe lines; sharps: solid ebony; key fronts: molded light hard wood. L=1,130; W=441; H=2,180.

Inscription on nameboard in gold leaf: "Dietz."

2001.04.

Orphica, attributed to Joseph Klein, Vienna, ca. 1820.

Orphica, attributed to Joseph Klein, Vienna, ca. 1820.

Portable piano played as a guitar set on table or stand, or resting on the performer's lap. Wood stained black; harp-shaped open frame at performer's left; small sound box; tuning pins at right. Strings placed transversely across the sound box; single-strung; missing decorative scroll at left end. Compass: 4 octaves, C-c^3; Viennese action; over-dampers missing. Three-octave measure: 379; natural coverings: ivory, no scribe lines; sharps: ebony; key fronts: ivory. L=1,170; W=390; D=155.

No inscription.

Style of stringing was intended to imitate the ancient lyre.

Ripin and Koster 2013; Clinkscale Online, CEP no. 5919.

2001.16

Dulcitone, Thomas Machell and Sons, Glasgow, ca. 1890, and inscription.

Dulcitone, Thomas Machell and Sons, Glasgow, ca. 1890.

Mahogany; small shelf for sheet music on underside of lid; four square tapering legs; wooden pedal on right, sustain. Pitches produced by steel tuning forks struck by hammers. Compass: 5 octaves, AA-a^3. Three-octave measure: 500; natural coverings: ivory, contiguous heads and tails; sharps: ebony; key fronts: ivory. L=945; W=375; D=270; H=540.

Nameboard inscription on rectangular label, in gold stencil: "DULCITONE / REG^D. / PATENTEES AND SOLE MAKERS / Thomas Machell & Sons / GLASGOW, SCOTLAND."

International Inventions Exhibition 1885, 314, no. 3534, Thomas Machell address, 35 & 39 Great Western Road, Glasgow.

2002.64

Bell Piano, Johann Baptist Cramer and Co., London, ca. 1870.

Rectangular keyboard; mahogany veneered; hammers strike rectangular metal bars; ledge for sheet music on inside of fallboard; without stand. Compass: 4 octaves, A-a^3. Three-octave measure: 488; natural coverings: ivory, no scribe lines; sharps: ebony; key fronts: ivory. L=750; W=428; D=210.

Nameboard inscription on stained black wood within white oval, in white: "J. B. CRAMER & Co."

2003.24

Bell Piano, Johann Baptist Cramer and Co., London, ca. 1870, and inscription.

Monochorde à clavier (keyed monochord), Joseph Poussot, Pierre-la-Treiche, ca. 1890.

Monochorde à clavier (keyed monochord), Joseph Poussot, Pierre-la-Treiche, ca. 1890.

Brown wood; upward pointing scroll, left; downward pointing scroll, right. Single thick, gut string tied to screw, left; attached to end of large single peg, right. String placed under keyboard of two octaves plus ten notes, d to c^2 (the lowest C is missing), above pear-shaped viol body with two C-holes, over bridge. Stand, two double-splayed legs; folding music desk above keyboard. Each key stops string at a different note while performer bows, producing vibrato by moving finger on key. Unmarked bow. Three-octave measure: 490; natural coverings: ivory, no scribe lines; sharps: ebony; key fronts: stained flat wood. L=1,360.

Stamped in wood on front and top of left side of case: "POUSSOT".

Joseph Poussot (1861–1891) worked with his uncle, the Abbot, Charles Tihay, on a French patent (no. 174,615) for a "polycorde," approved on March 8, 1886. Single-string monochords were manufactured in Poussot's shop in Pierre-la-Treiche from 1886 to 1896. He also wrote a *Méthode* using a special notation for playing the instrument.

Ravenel 1992, 3-14.

2006.20

Inscription.

Stop knobs.

Bureau pipe organ, Adam Geib and William Geib, New York, ca. 1825.

Mahogany; in form of large upright piano; upper section, red pleated cloth cover; painted depictions of three organ pipes on each side; folding music desk and ledge on inside of fallboard; two ornate candle holders above keyboard; rosewood veneered lower section; metal pedal for operating bellows; blue cloth tell tale indicates amount of air pressure. Brass inlay on rosewood nameboard, inscription flanked by gilt inlay of two groups of flowers and leaves; three ranks of metal and wooden pipes. Compass: 5 octaves, CC to c[3]; three hand stops on left with ivory plaques marked: "Open Diapason Treble; Stop Diapason Treble; Stop Diapason Bafs." Three-octave measure: 460; natural coverings: ivory, no scribe lines; sharps: ebony; key fronts: molded boxwood. L=1,270; W=455; H=1,730.

Nameboard inscription on gilt-bordered cartouche, in black with swirls: "A. & W. Geib. / 23, Maiden Lane / New York".

Bureau pipe organs were made for use in churches or homes.

Cranmer et. al. 2013.

2000.11.

Bureau pipe organ, Adam Geib and William Geib, New York, ca. 1825

Chamber pipe organ, Edward Pistor and John Pistor, London, ca. 1790.

Mahogany veneer; with top closed the instrument appears as a desk with three drawers (center) and two cabinets (one on each side). Fretwork top, brown cloth backing; shelf for holding music; ivory-capped telltale bracket, one rank of 33 wooden pipes, wood and metal pedal, bellows. Compass: 4 octaves + 4, C-e^3. Three-octave measure: 485; natural coverings: ivory with two scribe lines including head/tail seam; sharps: ebony; key fronts: molded wood. L=885; W=495; H=1,010.

Inscription: fragment of paper label inside contains name: "Edw[d] Piftor".

Wilson 1968, 87-88.

2004.19

Chamber pipe organ, Edward Pistor and John Pistor, London, ca. 1790.

Practice keyboard, Oliver Ditson Co., Boston, ca. 1908.

Black-stained wood in black carrying case with handle, two latches; brass lever for holding the top open; two swiveling wooden tabs for holding music. Compass: 4 octaves, C to c^3. Three-octave measure: 490; natural coverings: white plastic, contiguous heads and tails; sharps: ebony; key fronts: ivory. L=747; W=213; D=114.

Inscription inside case, gilt stencil: "Oliver Ditson Co. / New York – Boston / Philadelphia".

"History of Oliver Ditson Company" 1915, 8; Adams 2009, vol. 1, p. 188.

1996.15

Practice keyboard, Oliver Ditson Co., Boston, ca. 1908, and inscription.

Practice keyboard, Neely-Forse Manufacturing Co., Anderson, Indiana, ca. 1930.

Brown wood in folding case; simple metal music desk. Compass: 4 octaves, C to c^3. Three-octave measure: 488; natural coverings: wood painted white, contiguous heads and tails; sharps: ebony; key fronts: ivory. L=718; W=210; D=680.

Inscription inside case on brass engraved plaque with black infill: "PATS. PEND. / Neely (cursive) / FORSE MFG. CO. / ANDERSON, IND. U.S.A."

2001.42

Practice keyboard, Neely-Forse Manufacturing Co., Anderson, Indiana, ca. 1930, and inscription.

Practice keyboard, Virgil Piano School Co., New York, ca. 1900.

Brown-stained wood in black carrying case with handle; three latches; two movable metal arms to hold music. Compass: 4 octaves, C to c^3. Three-octave measure: 499; natural coverings: ivory, no scribe line; sharps: ebony; key fronts: ivory. L=715; W=215.

Nameboard inscription inside case, gilt stencil above keyboard: "VIRGIL PIANO SCHOOL CO. / NEW YORK".

Nahm and Sheldon 1996, 429-432.

2002.57

Practice keyboard, Virgil Piano School Co., New York, ca. 1900, and inscription.

Practice keyboard, Virgil Piano Co., New York, 1904.

Practice keyboard, Virgil Piano Co., New York, ca. 1904, and inscription.

Mahogany; rectangular form; four square tapered legs that fold. Keyboard is used to strengthen the student's fingers. With the use of lead weights suspended a few millimeters over rear end of keys, keyboard simulates the faint impact of a jack slipping over the hammer knuckle, followed by an immediate stronger impact of the key front contacting its felt. Weight-of-touch control from two to twenty ounces controlled by moving a handle positioned on nameboard, operating a machine screw moving a leather-faced wooden batten against coiled springs mounted vertically on rear of keys. Clicking sound available on down and/or up strokes of each key develops proper timing and key release. Audible clicks are set by moving levers at either end of the keyboard. Nameboard has scale with a dial from two to twenty ounces, stating underneath "Do not use the up clicks beyond 5 ounces." Compass: 7⅓ octaves, AAA-c^5, serial no. 7303. Three-octave measure: 496; natural coverings: ivory, contiguous heads and tails; sharps: ebony; key fronts: ivory. L=1,675; W=650; H=615.

Nameboard inscription on right side, in gold stencil: "VIRGIL / PERFECTED / Practice Clavier. / NEW YORK".

Almon Kincaid Virgil (1842–1921) devised his first practice keyboard in 1883. US patent dates for his sixth, seventh, and eighth patents are listed on this instrument's nameboard as: "June 29, 1888, Oct. 23, 1888, and July 19, 1892." Two paper notices are pasted underneath the lid: "Directions for Regulating Clavier" and "Warrantee" indicating May 26, 1904 as completion date for this instrument.

Nahm and Sheldon 1996, 429-432.

2003.25

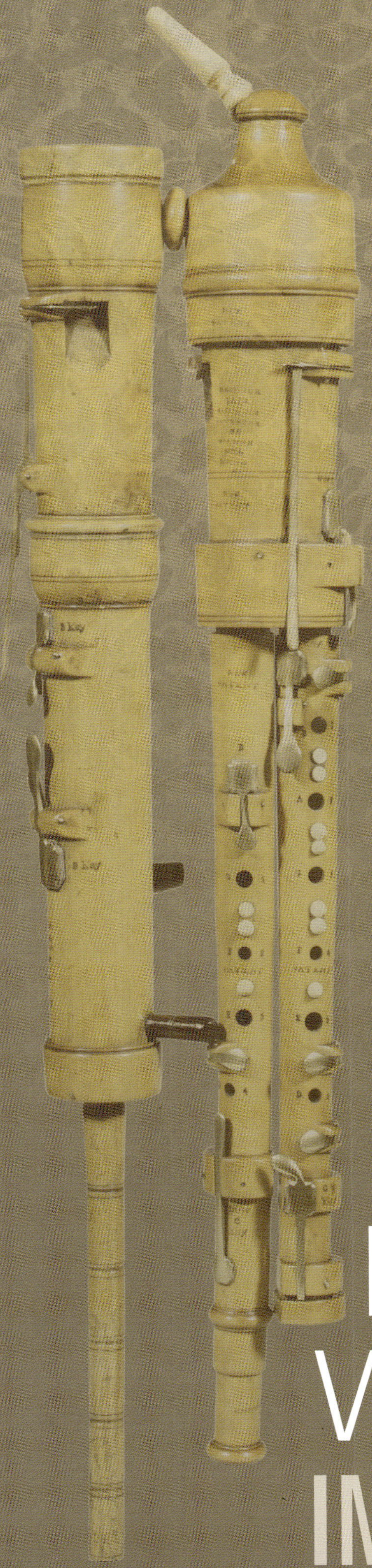

CHAPTER 2
FLUTE & WHISTLE INSTRUMENTS

Thomas Gibson (ca. 1680-1751), portrait of Lewis Christian Granom (1722-1763) holding a 1-key flute, London, 1743.

Alto recorder, Johann Heinrich Eichentopf, Leipzig, ca. 1725.

Boxwood; boxwood ferrules; multiple beading. Three sections: head, body, bell. L=485.

Stamped on mouthpiece, body, bell: "(flower pot with two oak leaf sprays bearing acorns) / I•H•EICHENTOPF / (star)."

1997.13

LEFT: *Alto recorder,* Johann Heinrich Eichentopf, Leipzig, ca. 1725.

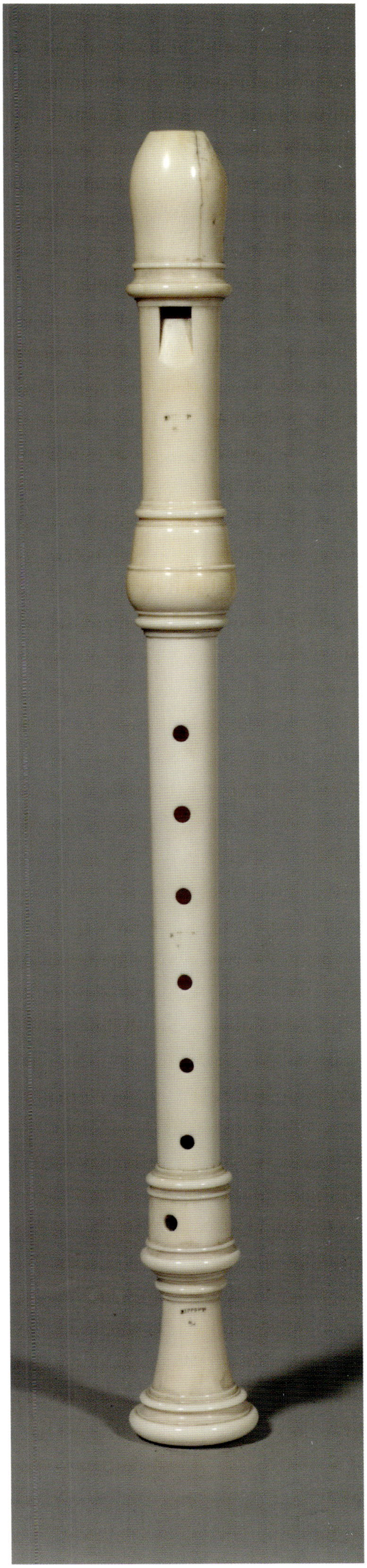

Alto recorder, Jean Jacques Rippert, Paris, ca. 1715.

Ivory; multiple beadings. Three sections: head, body, foot. Head cracked and repaired. L=460.

Stamped on head, body, foot: "RIPPERT / (shield bearing six lozenges)."

1998.09

RIGHT: Alto recorder, Jean Jacques Rippert, Paris, ca. 1715.

Soprano recorder, attributed to Johann Benedict Gahn, Nuremberg, ca. 1710.

Ivory; highly intricate carving on head of acanthus leaves and mask, a motif linked to Nuremberg. The entire foot is highly carved with acanthus leaves. Three sections: head, body, foot. L=436.

Stamped on the upper part of the body with a decorative monogram similar to a monogram on a Gahn ivory recorder at the Germanisches Nationalmuseum in Nuremberg, no. MIR 204. This recorder is also similar to an ivory recorder attributed to Johann Wilhelm Oberlender I of Nuremberg in the Musée de la Musique, E.98 C.390. Both Oberlender and Gahn made recorders of boxwood and ivory with similar carving.

Ex Barons Nathaniel and Albert von Rothschild Collection.

Kirnbauer 1994, 24-25; Christies London Auction 1999.

1999.16

LEFT: *Soprano recorder,* attributed to Johann Benedict Gahn, Nuremberg, ca. 1710.

Soprano recorder in C, Nikolaus Staub, Nuremberg, ca. 1710.

Ivory; decorated with carved undulations highlighted in black on the head and bell. Three sections: head, body, bell. L=500.

Faintly stamped on body: "N. STAVB (in a scroll with rolled ends) / NS (monogram)". This is similar to a stamp on a Staub ivory recorder in the Germanisches Nationalmuseum, no. MI 211.

Kirnbauer 1994, 32-34.

Reported to be tuned at A=415 hertz.

Hôtel des ventes de Vichy, 2005.

2005.17

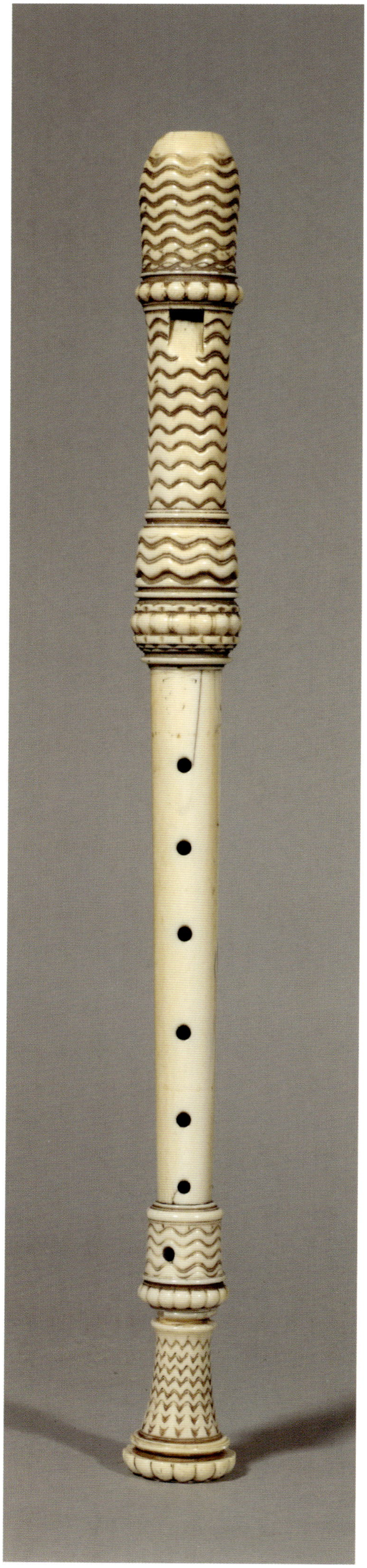

RIGHT: *Soprano recorder in C*, Nikolaus Staub, Nuremberg, ca. 1710.

Alto recorder in F, Friedrich von Huene, Boston, copy of recorder by Engelbert Terton, Amsterdam, ca. 1980.

Boxwood; boxwood beading; detailed decorative silver ferrules around the end of the head joint socket and lower portion of the bell. Three sections: head, body, bell. L=342.

Stamped on head, body: "(crown) / E.TERTON / (striding lion)".

Copy of Terton soprano recorder in the Gemeentemuseum, The Hague, no. Ea 1974-1933.

Van Acht, Van der Ende, Schimmel 1991, 128-135.

2007.07

Soprano recorder, Wilhelm Beukers I, Amsterdam, ca. 1720.

Stained boxwood; multiple beading; second finger hole for R4 filled on foot. Three sections: head, body, foot. L=349.

Stamped on head, body: "W:BEUKERS / (iris flowers)".

Van Acht, Van der Ende, Schimmel 1991, 82-85; Bouterse 2005, 59.

2007.17

Alto recorder, Johann Heinrich Bernhart, Nordhausen, ca. 1720.

Boxwood; multiple beading. Three sections: head, body, foot. L=469.

Stamped on head: "BERNHART / 1".

Offered at *Vichy Enchères* 2011; Dullat 2010a, 77.

2011.05

Alto recorder in F, Friedrich von Huene, Boston, ca. 1980.

Soprano recorder, Wilhelm Beukers I, Amsterdam, ca. 1720.

Alto recorder, Johann Heinrich Bernhart, Nordhausen, ca. 1720.

Soprano recorder, Johann Oberlender I, Nuremberg, ca. 1730.

Ivory; multiple beading. Three sections: head, body, foot. Second foot joint of different diameter and slighter larger length, possibly from another Oberlender ivory recorder. Head cracked and repaired. L=346; L of second foot joint=70.

Stamped on head: "OBERLENDER (in scroll) / O".

2012.02

Soprano recorder, Johann Oberlender I, Nuremberg, ca. 1730, with details of two foot sections.

1-key flageolet in D, George Cloos, New York, ca. 1880.

Rosewood; nickel-silver ferrules, one missing on the lower part of the head. Five sections: mouthpiece (missing), cap, wind cap, head, pipe. One pillar-mounted nickel-silver-key with a modern key head. Seven finger holes for LT, L1, L2, L3, R1, R2, R3, R4. D♯. Serial no. 6375. L=436.

Stamped on wind cap, pipe: "GEO. CLOOS / CG (monogram) / 6375".

1986.04

1-key flageolet in D, Jabez McCall Camp, Litchfield, Connecticut, ca. 1830.

Boxwood; ivory ferrules; single beading. Four sections: ivory mouthpiece, wind cap, head, pipe. One thumb hole, seven finger holes for L1, L2, L3, R1, R2, R3, R4, separated by five ivory knobs, except R4, one ivory knob below thumb hole. One ring-mounted silver key, round, flat key head, bulge turned out above the C tone hole. D♯. L=405 (with mouthpiece).

Stamped on wind cap, head: "J.M.CAMP (curved) / LITCHFIELD/ CONN".

1991.02

1-key flageolet in D, Anonymous, of United States origin, ca. 1850.

Black-stained boxwood; ivory ferrules; single beadings; incised lines. Four sections: ivory mouthpiece, wind cap, head, pipe. One thumb hole, first hole partially plugged, seven finger holes for L1, L2, L3, R1, R2, R3, R4, separated by five ivory knobs. One ring-mounted silver key with flat, round key head, bulge turned out above the C tone hole. D♯. L=400 (with mouthpiece).

No inscription.

1995.12

1-key flageolet in D, George Cloos, New York, ca. 1880.

1-key flageolet in D, Jabez McCall Camp, Litchfield, Connecticut, ca. 1830.

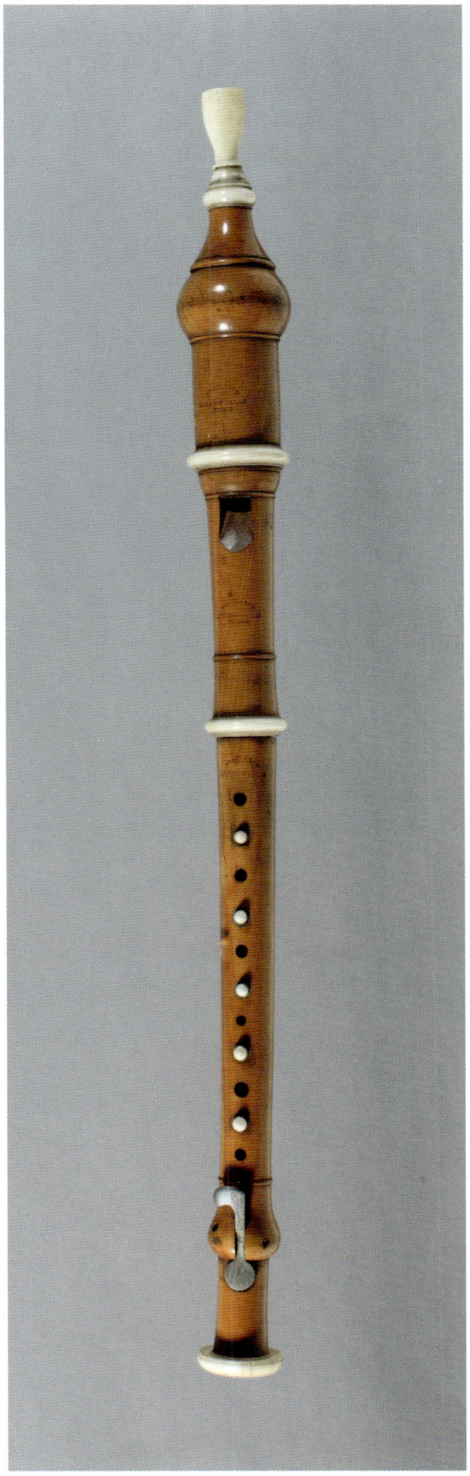

1-key flageolet in D, Anonymous, of United States origin, ca 1850.

Double tenor flageolet in D, Allyn Bacon and Abraham Hart, Philadelphia, ca. 1820.

Boxwood; ivory ferrules; single beading; dark lines. Six sections: ivory mouthpiece, cap (missing ivory ferrule), wind cap, stock, l.h. pipe, r.h. pipe. Seven block and ring-mounted silver keys, bevel edge square key heads, two wind cutter keys mounted on stock. From player's viewpoint, l.h. pipe: six finger holes for L2, L3, R1, R2, R3, R4, each, except the lowest, separated by four double ivory knobs and one single knob. First finger hole plugged and used as a speaker hole. Wind cutter (L1) allows rests while a continuous sound is played on the r.h. pipe. D^1 (octave), D♯, bulge turned out above the C tone hole, r.h. pipe: one thumb hole (L1), five finger holes for L2, L3, R1, R2, R3, each, except the lowest, separated by two double ivory knobs and one single knob. Wind cutter (LT) closes air to the r.h. pipe so l.h. pipe is played as a solo flageolet. D^1(octave), C^1 (LT), D♯ (R4), bulge turned out above C tone hole. Melodies are played in thirds and sixths, lowest note for both pipes is C. L=485 (with mouthpiece).

Stamped on stock: "BACON & HART / PHILA. / (lyre)".

MacMillan 2013, 142-147.

1996.21

LEFT: *Double tenor flageolet in D*, Allyn Bacon and Abraham Hart, Philadelphia, ca. 1820.

Flûte d'accord or double flageolet, Hentz Jouve, Paris, ca. 1815.

Fruitwood; two pipes joined in one body from mouthpiece to edge at base of window. Each pipe has a separate window, the right pipe placed higher than the left. Both pipes are separated by a cut at the wind way at the right pipe, and reinforced against further cracking with a brass band. Right pipe has thumb hole and six finger holes of varying diameters; left pipe or solo pipe has thumb hole and seven finger holes of varying diameters. The lowest note is C. L=325.

Stamped on upper part of body: "(five-pointed star) / JOUVE. / A PARIS / (five-pointed star)".

2001.37

RIGHT: *Flûte d'accord or double flageolet*, Hentz Jouve, Paris, ca. 1815

5-key flageolet, Anonymous, of French origin, ca. 1880.

Rosewood; nickel-silver ferrules; single beading. Five sections: ivory mouthpiece, wind cap, sponge chamber, head, pipe. Six holes for LT, L1, L2, R1, RT, R2. Six pillar and saddle-mounted keys with modern key heads, bulge cut straight above the B♭ key head. E♭-F trill (R1), E-F trill (R1), F (L2), D♯ (LT), B♭ (L4). L=505 (with mouthpiece).

No inscription.

2001.38

5-key flageolet, Anonymous, of French origin, ca. 1880.

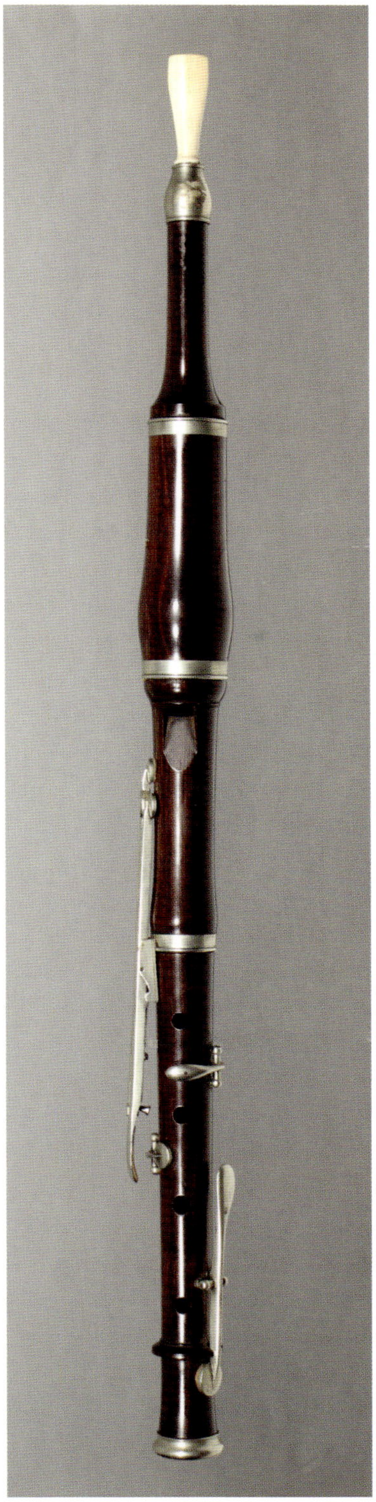

3-key flageolet in A, A. Guerin, Marseille, ca. 1885.

Fruitwood; brass ferrules; single beading. Five sections: ivory mouthpiece, wind cap, sponge chamber, head, pipe. Six holes for LT, L1, L2, R1, RT, R2. Three pillar-mounted keys, modern key heads, bulge cut straight above the B♭ key head. F (R1), D♯ (LT), B♭ (L4). L=375 (with mouthpiece).

Stamped on wind cap; head: "A GUERIN / BREVETÉ / A MARSEILLE (in an oval of points)".

Rousselet and Watel 2012, 83.

2001.39

3-key flageolet in A, A. Guerin, Marseille, ca. 1885.

Walking-stick flageolet, Anonymous, Unknown, ca. 1830.

Fruitwood; decorated with several parallel lines. Body, one thumb hole, and seven finger holes. L=791.

No inscription.

2001.40

Walking-stick flageolet, Anonymous, Unknown, ca. 1830, front and back views.

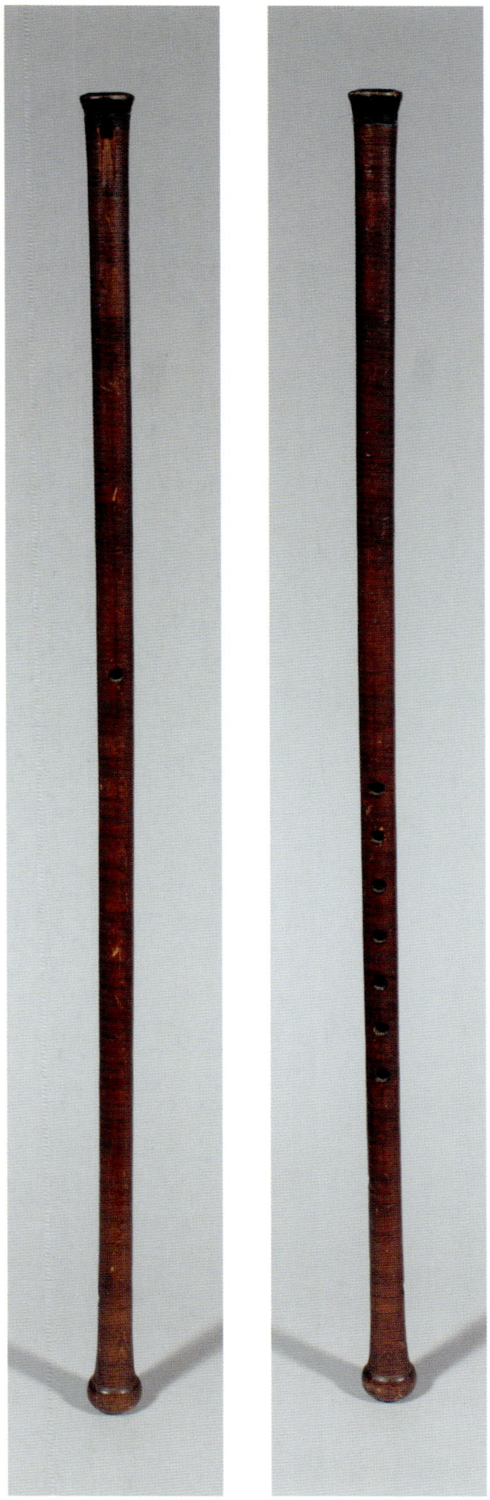

1-key flageolet in B♭, William Hall and Son, New York, ca. 1850.

Boxwood; ivory ferrules. Five sections: ivory mouthpiece, cap, wind cap, head, pipe. One ring-mounted brass key with a flat, circular key head, in a bulge cut down above the D key. D♯ (R4). One thumb hole, seven finger holes. L=479 (with mouthpiece).

Stamped on wind cap: "WILLIAM HALL & SON / N-YORK"; head: "WILLIAM HALL & SON / N-YORK / B"; pipe: "WILLIAM HALL & SON / 239 BROADWAY / N-YORK".

2002.41

2-key flageolet, Jean-François Thierriot Prudent, Paris, ca. 1820.

Ebony; ivory ferrules; single beading. Five sections: ivory mouthpiece, wind cap, sponge chamber, head, pipe. Six holes for LT, L1, L2, R1, RT, R2. Two pillar-mounted silver keys, flat, round key heads, bulge cut straight above the B♭ key head. D♯ (LT), B♭ (L4). L=470 (with mouthpiece).

Stamped on head, pipe: "PRUDENT / A PARIS".

Jeltsch 1997, 139, 152.

2002.46

4-key flageolet, Thomas Isidor Lot, La Couture, ca. 1870.

Dark-stained cocus wood; nickel-silver ferrules. Five sections: ivory mouthpiece, wind cap, sponge chamber, head, pipe. Six holes for LT, L1, L2, R1, RT, R2. Four pillar and saddle-mounted nickel-silver keys, modern key heads, bulge cut straight above the B♭ key head. E-F trill (R1), E♭-F trill (R1), D♯ (LT), B♭ (L4). L=508 (with mouthpiece).

Stamped on head: "(lyre) / ISIDOR / LOT (cursive) (in an oval) / IL (monogram)"; pipe: "ISIDOR / LOT (cursive) (in an oval) // IL (monogram)."

Rousselet and Watel 2012, 111.

2002.47

1-key flageolet in B♭, William Hall and Son, New York, ca. 1850.

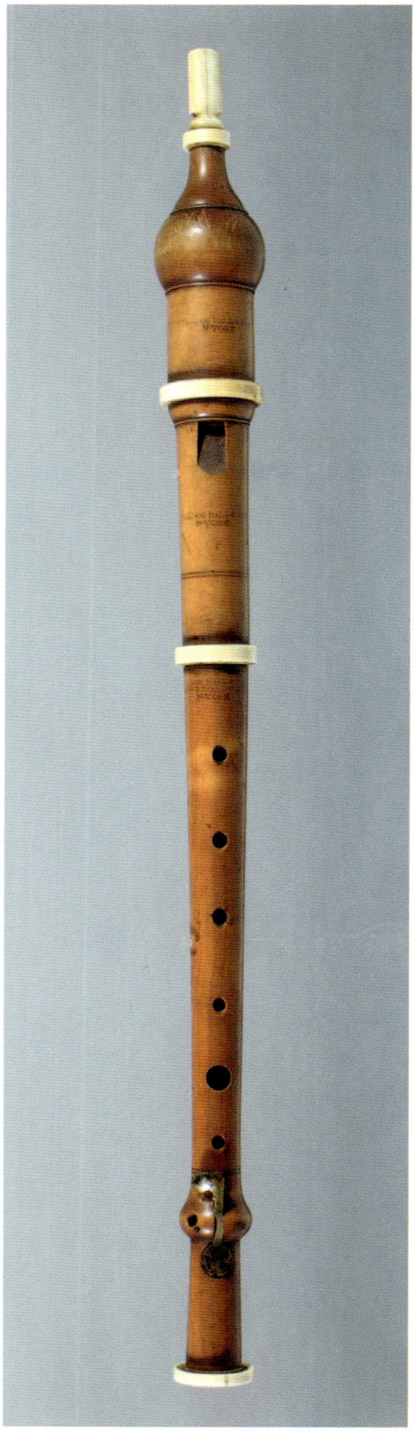

2-key flageolet, Jean-François Thierriot Prudent, Paris, ca. 1820.

4-key flageolet, Thomas Isidor Lot, La Couture, ca. 1870.

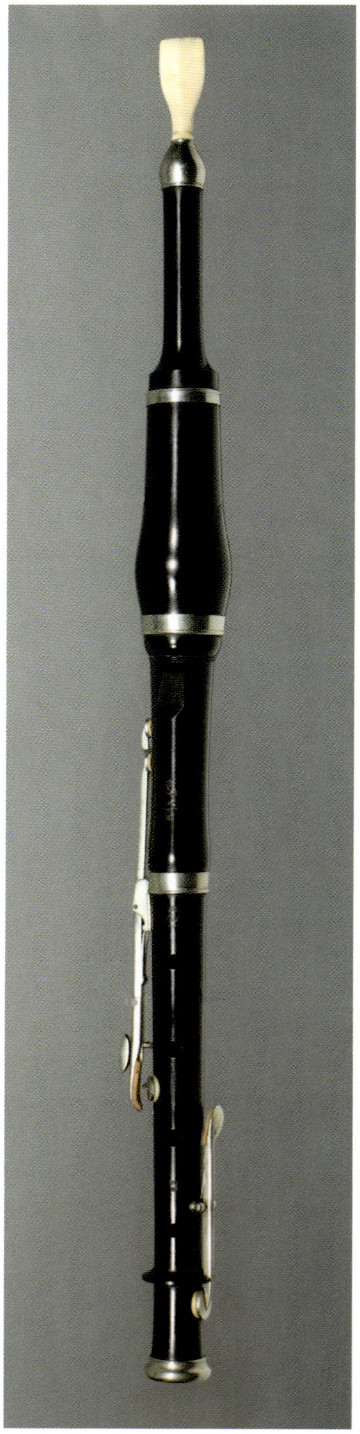

5-key flageolet, Margueritat, Paris, ca. 1890.

Ebony; nickel-silver ferrules; single beading. Five sections: ivory mouthpiece, wind cap, sponge chamber, head, pipe. Six holes for LT, L1, L2, R1, RT, R2. Five pillar and saddle-mounted nickel-silver keys, modern key heads, bulge cut straight above the B♭ key head. G♯ (R1), F (L2), D♯ (LT), C♯ (R2), B♭ (L4). L=390 (with mouthpiece).

Stamped on head: "MARGUERITAT / 21 Bd BONNE NOUVELLE / PARIS (in an oval of points)".

Rousselet and Watel 2012, 115.

2003.12

4-key flageolet, Frédéric Eléanor Godfroy, Paris, ca. 1835.

Dark-stained rosewood; ivory ferrules; single beading. Five sections: large ivory mouthpiece, wind cap, sponge chamber, head, pipe. Six holes for LT, L1, L2, R1, RT, R2. Four pillar and saddle-mounted nickel-silver keys, modern key heads, bulge cut straight above the B♭ key head. G♯ (R1), F (L2), D♯ (LT), B♭ (L4). L=365 (with mouthpiece).

Stamped on head: "FE (monogram) / GODFROY / AINÉ, (in oval of points) / (star)".

Rousselet and Watel 2012, 80.

2003.57

6-key flageolet in G, Keith, Prowse & Co., London, ca. 1840.

Stained cocus wood; nickel-silver ferrules decorated with lines. Four sections: ivory mouthpiece, wind cap, head, pipe. Five block-mounted nickel-silver keys, with salt-spoon key heads, six finger holes. D♯ (R1), long F, short F, G♯, F (LT), C (LT). Serial no. 103. L=400 (with mouthpiece).

Stamped on pipe: "KEITH. PROWSE & Co / 48 CHEAPSIDE / LONDON / 103".

2003.63

5-key flageolet, Margueritat, Paris, ca. 1890.

4-key flageolet, Frédéric Eléanor Godfroy, Paris, ca. 1835.

6-key flageolet in G, Keith, Prowse & Co., London, ca. 1840.

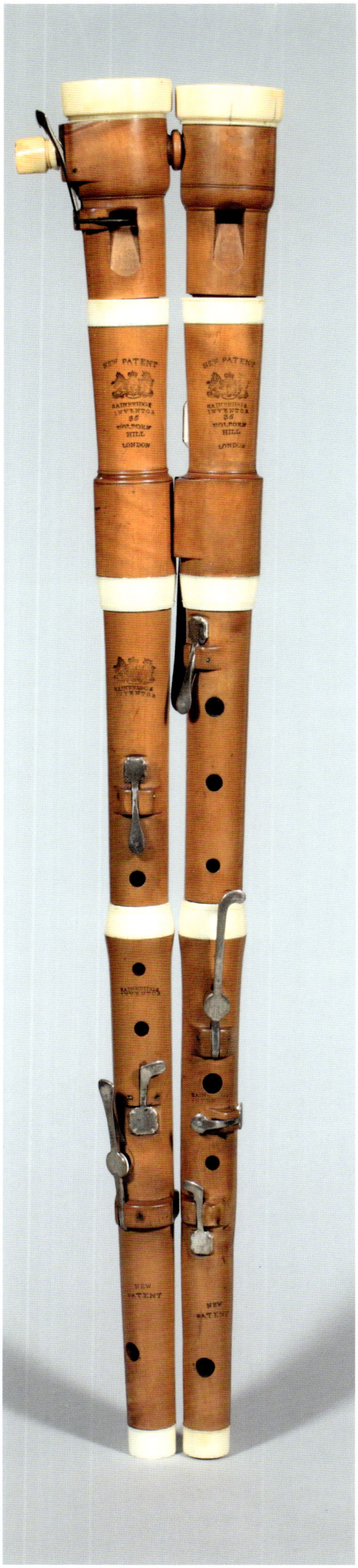

Double flute-flageolet, William Bainbridge, London, ca. 1825.

Boxwood; ivory ferrules; single beading. Four sections each for flute and flageolet: wind cap with large ivory screw-on caps, head, l.h. joint, r.h. joint. Block-mounted silver keys, round and octagonal or chamfered key heads. Ivory mouthpiece on right side of the flageolet connects to flute by a junction piece, to the right of flageolet. Wind cutter operates by pressing lips against the flageolet side opening a wind passage to the flute. Left pipe (flute), five keys: C on head (LT), octave D (L1), F♯ (L3 or R1), F (cross, R3), D♯ (R4); finger holes for L1, L2, L3, R2, R3; right pipe (flageolet), four keys: D (octave, LT), B (L1), F (R3), D (R4); finger holes for L2, R1, R2. L of right pipe (flageolet)=581; L of left pipe (flute)=571. Resonance holes at the ends of the r.h. joints for flageolet and flute. This example is one of seven extant double flute-flageolets.

Stamped on heads of flute and flageolet: "NEW PATENT / (United Kingdom coat of arms with lion, unicorn) / BAINBRIDGE / INVENTOR 35/ HOLBORN / HILL / LONDON"; l.h. joint of flageolet: "(United Kingdom coat of arms with lion, unicorn) / BAINBRIDGE / INVENTOR"; r.h. joints of flageolet and flute: "BAINBRIDGE / INVENTOR / BAINBRIDGE / INVENTOR // NEW PATENT".

Accompanying this instrument is *Bainbridge's Preceptor for the Patent Double Flute & Double Flageolet*, London, after 1819.

See Waterhouse 1999, 172-181; MacMillan 2013, 176-177, 387.

2005.14

LEFT: *Double flute-flageolet*, William Bainbridge, London, ca. 1825.

3-key flageolet, Jean Jacques Baumann, Paris, ca. 1810.

Ebony; ivory ferrules; single beading. Five sections: large ivory mouthpiece, wind cap, sponge chamber, head, pipe. Six holes for LT, L1, L2, R1, RT, R2. Three pillar-mounted silver keys, round, flat key heads, bulge cut straight above the B♭ key head. G♯ (R1), D♯ (RT), B♭ (L4). L=354 (with mouthpiece).

Stamped on head: "(star) / BAUMANN / A PARIS / (star)".

2005.16

RIGHT: *3-key flageolet*, Jean Jacques Baumann, Paris, ca. 1810.

Tenor triple flageolet in D, Henry Hastrick, London, ca. 1840.

Boxwood; boxwood ferrules; single beading; dark lines. Six sections of double flageolet on left side: ivory mouthpiece (placed at 45° angle), cap, wind cap, stock, l.h. pipe, r.h. pipe. L.h. pipe: six finger holes, three separated by two ivory knobs, fourth by one knob. Each hole has pitch letter and number, each key has letter name. Six ring and block-mounted brass keys, bevel edge square key heads. New C (on head, L1), E♭ (L1), D (L1), F (R2), D♯ (R3), C♯ (R4). Two block-mounted wind cutters on front and back of head directing air into either pipe. R.h. pipe: five finger holes, one separated by two ivory knobs, one by one knob, r.h. pipe has extended foot. Five block-mounted silver keys: C (back, LT), B (L2), D♯ (R2), low C (R4), low B (LT). Third pipe, three sections: head, pipe, screw-in strut or support. Four block-mounted brass keys: A (back), B, C^1 (back), D^1 (LT). Block-mounted wind cutter on head closes air to third pipe. Flageolet can be played with l.h. alone, l.h. and r.h. together, or using one or both melody pipes and third pipe. L of r.h. pipe=490 (without mouthpiece); L of l.h. pipe=430 (without mouthpiece); L of third pipe=530.

Stamped on double flageolet wind cap: "NEW PATENT"; stock: "HASTRICK / LATE / BAINBRIDGE / INVENTOR / 35 / HOLBORN / HILL / LONDON / NEW PATENT"; l.h. pipe: "NEW PATENT //PATENT"; r.h. pipe: "PATENT".

This example is one of ten extant triple flageolets.

MacMillan 2013, 162, 164, 165-167, 328.

2007.23

LEFT: *Tenor triple flageolet in D*, Henry Hastrick, London, ca. 1840.

Keyless flageolet in F, John Parker, London, ca. 1805.

Dark-stained boxwood; thin boxwood ferrules. Four sections: ivory mouthpiece, wind cap, head, pipe. Thumb hole, seven finger holes marked with pitch names: B (with an ivory insert), A, G, F, E, D, and C. L=344 (with mouthpiece).

Stamped on head: "(F in circle of fire) / PARKER / LONDON"; pipe: "PARKER // PARKER".

2009.01

RIGHT: *Keyless flageolet in F*, John Parker, London, ca. 1805.

6-key fife in B♭, George Cloos, New York, ca. 1880.

Dark-stained cocus wood; wide nickel-silver ferrules decorated with hatching and lines. Two sections: head, body. Large oval embouchure, six pillar-mounted nickel-silver keys, modern key heads. C[1], B♭, G♯, F (long), F (short), D♯. Serial no. 9410. L=388.

Stamped on head: "GEO. CLOOS / CG (monogram) / 9410"; body: "B♭ // 9410".

1986.05

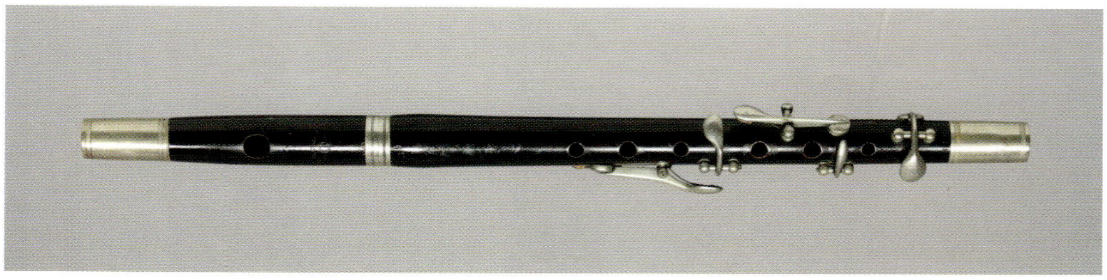

6-key fife in B♭, George Cloos, New York, ca. 1880.

Fife, Meacham & Co., Albany, New York, ca. 1827.

Fruitwood; long brass ferrules decorated with incised lines. Body, large oval embouchure, six finger holes. L=437.

Stamped on body: "MEACHAM & CO. / ALBANY".

Eliason (1979-1980), 64.

2001.10

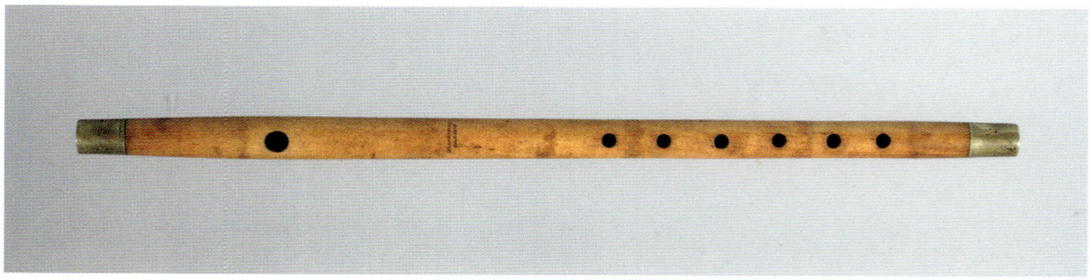

Fife, Meacham & Co., Albany, New York, ca. 1827.

Fife in B♭, John Firth, Sylvanus Pond, and Co., New York, ca. 1845.

Stained rosewood body; wide nickel-silver ferrules decorated with incised lines. Body, large oval embouchure, six finger holes. L=422.

Stamped on body: "FIRTH POND & CO. / BROADWAY / N-YORK / B".

2001.46

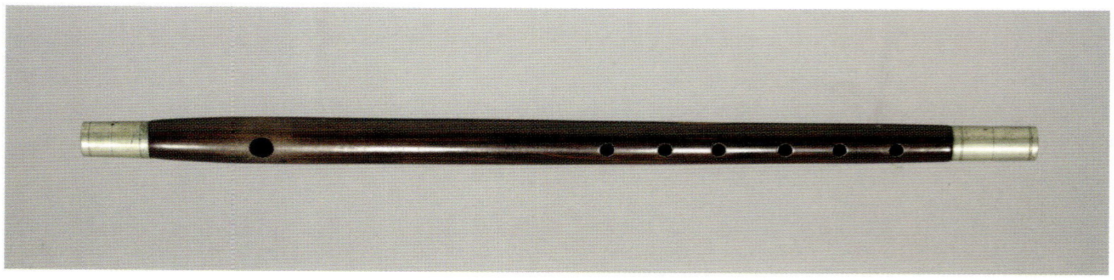

Fife in B♭, John Firth, Sylvanus Pond, and Co., New York, ca. 1845.

Fife, George Cloos, Brooklyn, New York, ca. 1920.

Stained rosewood; wide nickel-silver ferrules decorated with incised lines. Body, large oval embouchure, six finger holes. L=392.

Stamped on body: "GEO. CLOOS / CG (monogram) / BROOKLYN, NY".

2002.02

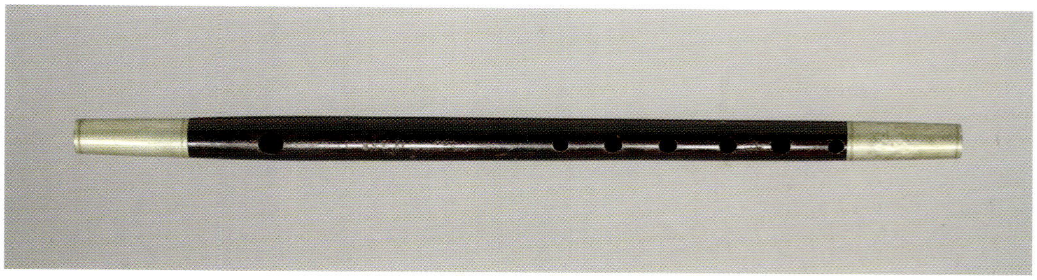

Fife, George Cloos, Brooklyn, New York, ca. 1920.

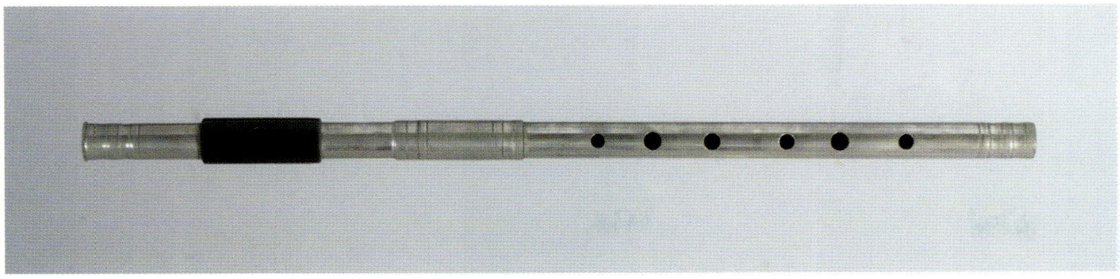

Fife, Penzel-Müller Co., New York, George Cloos model, ca. 1950

Fife, Penzel-Müller Co., New York, George Cloos model, ca. 1950.

Nickel-silver decorated with incised lines; ebonite embouchure. Two sections: head, body. Oval embouchure hole, body has six finger holes. In bag. L=414.

Stamped on body: "GEO. CLOOS".

Farrar (1995), 99.

2002.11

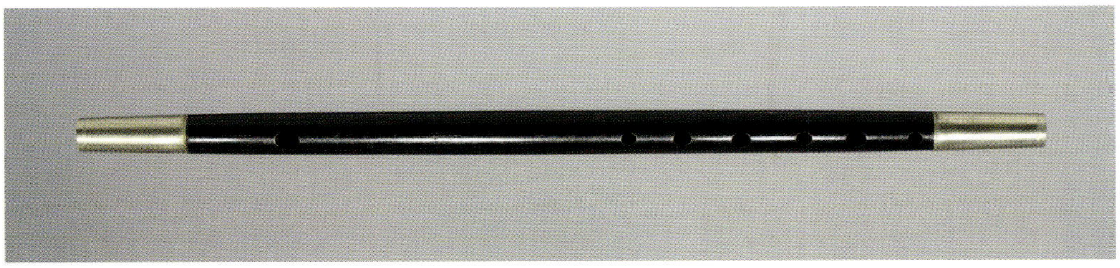

Fife, Penzel-Müller Co., New York, Crosby model, ca. 1950.

Fife, Penzel-Müller Co., New York, Crosby model, ca. 1950.

Stained cocus wood; wide nickel-silver ferrules decorated with incised lines. Body, large oval embouchure, six finger holes. L=434.

Stamped on body: "CROSBY / <CG> (monogram)".

Farrar (1995), 99.

2002.14

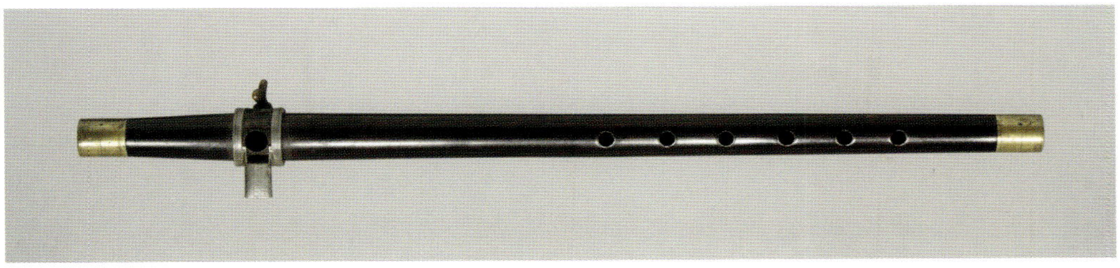

B♭ *fife*, Anonymous, of United States origin, ca. 1880.

B♭ *fife*, Anonymous, of United States origin, ca. 1880.

Stained fruitwood; wide brass ferrules; incised lines. Body, six finger holes. Nickel-silver "cheater" with brass screw directs air across a slightly oval embouchure hole. L=422.

No inscription.

2002.15

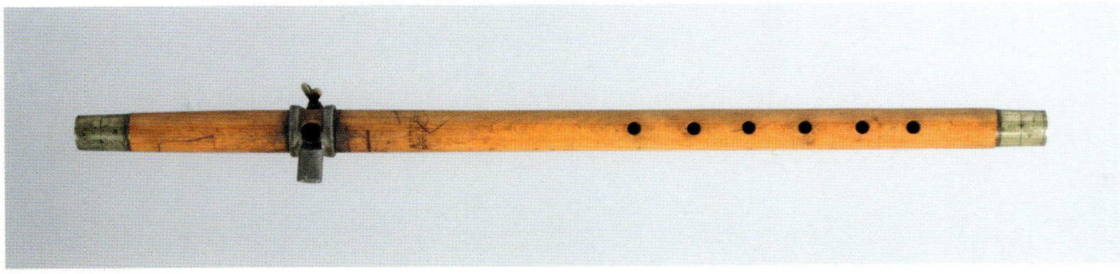

Fife, Edward Riley, New York, ca. 1825.

Fife, Edward Riley, New York, ca. 1825.

Fruitwood; wide brass ferrules; incised lines. Body, six finger holes. Nickel-silver "cheater" with brass screw directs air across a slightly oval embouchure hole. L=470.

Stamped on body: "E. RILEY / 29 CHATHAM ST / N-YORK".

2002.69

Fife, Leopold Mitsching, Düsseldorf, ca. 1910.

Stained cocus wood; nickel-silver ferrules. Body, oval embouchure hole, nickel-silver cap with nickel-silver screw-cork indicator, six finger holes. In a leather case with brass cap cover and brass ferrules. L=375.

Stamped on body: "LEO MITSCHING / ELBERFELD / HOFLIEFERANT".

2002.84

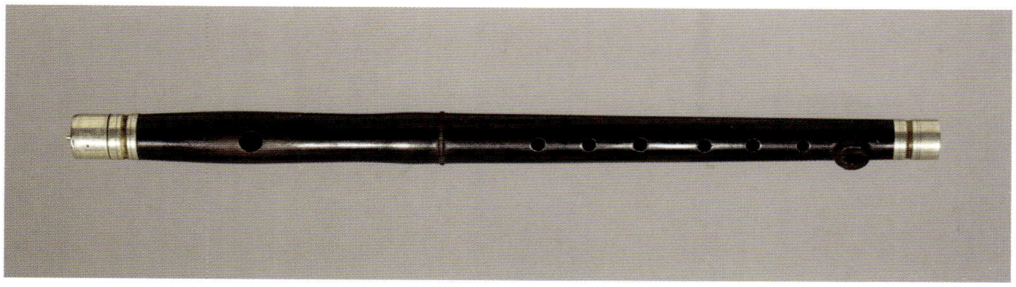

Fife, Leopold Mitsching, Düsseldorf, ca. 1910, without and with case.

Fife, Franz Lauter, New York, ca. 1860.

Stained cocus wood; nickel-silver ferrules. Two sections: head, body. TV screen embouchure hole, one nickel-silver pillar-mounted key with flat, round key head, D♯ (R4). L=405.

Stamped on head: "F. LAUTER / NEW YORK".

2003.10

Fife, Franz Lauter, New York, ca. 1860.

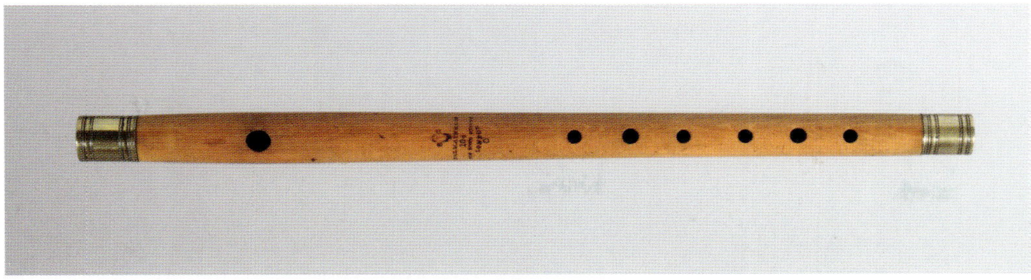

Fife, D'Almaine and Co., London, ca. 1860.

Fife, D'Almaine and Co., London, ca. 1860.

Fruitwood; brass ferrules; incised lines. Body, oval embouchure hole, six finger holes. L=370.

Stamped on body: "(Prince of Wales feathers) / D'ALMAINE & C^{O} / 104 / NEW BOND STREET / LONDON / O".

2003.41

Fife in B♭, Barnett Samuel, London, ca. 1850.

Fife in B♭, Barnett Samuel, London, ca. 1850.

Rosewood; nickel-silver ferrules; incised lines. Two sections: head, body. Oval embouchure hole, six finger holes. Pillar-mounted key for D♯ (missing). L=380.

Stamped on head: "B.S. (within a triangle) / Patented (cursive) / IMPROVED / B♭".

2003.42

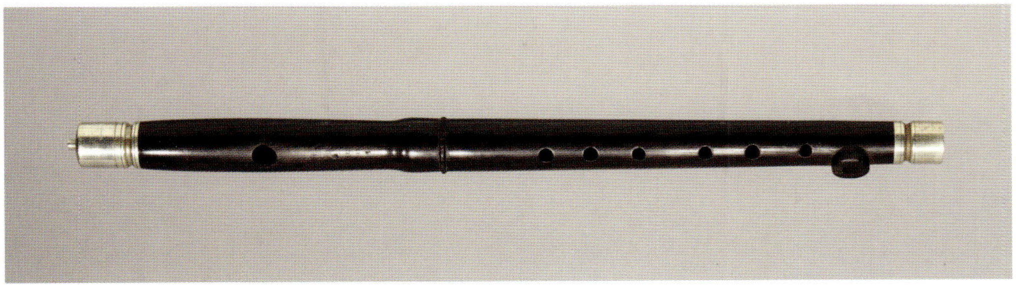

Fife, Gebrüder Alexander, Mainz, ca. 1880.

Fife, Gebrüder Alexander, Mainz, ca. 1880.

Stained cocus wood; nickel-silver ferrules decorated with incised lines. Body, seven finger holes, the seventh on raised platform, oval embouchure hole. Serial no. 1978. L=375.

Stamped on body: "ALEXANDER / MAINZ / 1978".

2003.56

6-key piccolo, H.F. Meyer, nach, Hannover, probably Markneukirchen, ca. 1900.

Stained cocus wood; nickel-silver decorated ferrules. Three sections: head, barrel, body. Nickel-silver cap, nickel-silver screw-cork indicator. Large oval embouchure, six finger holes, six pillar-mounted nickel-silver keys, modern key heads. C[1], B♭, G♯, F (long), F (short), D♯. Missing lowest ferrule of barrel. L=333.

Stamped on head: "NACH / H.F. MEYER / HANNOVER."

1986.06

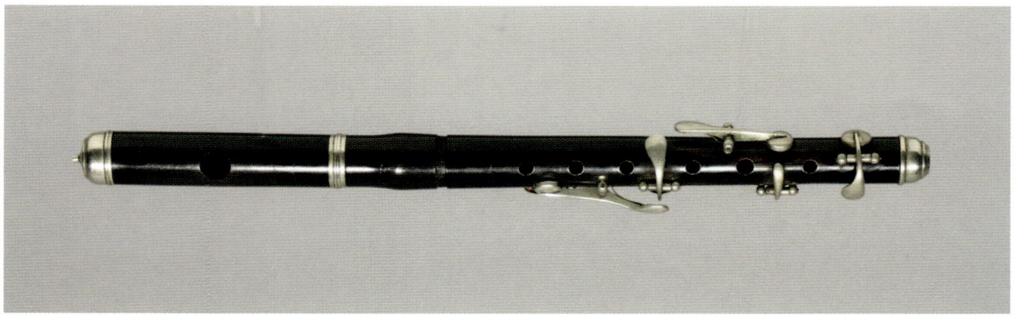

6-key piccolo, H.F. Meyer, nach, Hannover, probably Markneukirchen, ca. 1900.

1-key piccolo in B♭, Klemm, Philadelphia, probably Markneukirchen, ca. 1820.

Boxwood; ivory ferrules; single beading. Three sections: head, l.h. joint, r.h. joint-foot. Oval embouchure, six finger holes, one ring-mounted brass key in rounded bulge. D♯. L=377.

Stamped on head: "B♭"; l.h. joint: "KLEMM / PHILAD[A]".

1992.10

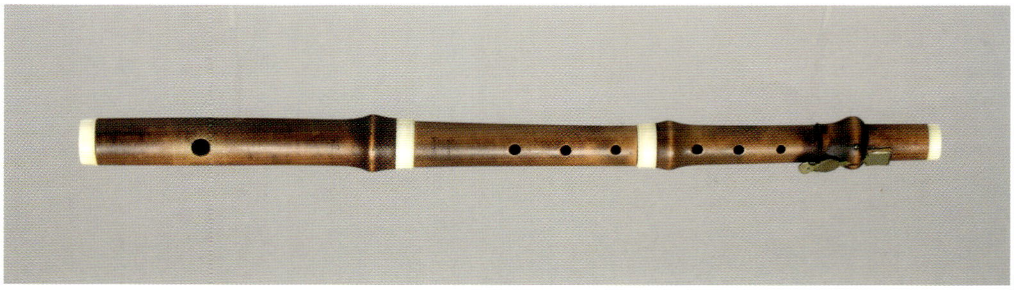

1-key piccolo in B♭, Klemm, Philadelphia, probably Markneukirchen, ca. 1820.

1-key piccolo in B♭, Herman Wrede, London, ca. 1820.

Boxwood; decorative rings incised on head, r.h. joint-foot, brown stained wooden head cap. Three sections: head, l.h. joint, r.h. joint-foot. Large oval embouchure, six finger holes, one ring-mounted brass key, square key head, in a bulge. D♯. L=395.

Stamped on head: "H • WREDE (curved) / LONDON / B"; l.h. joint, r.h. joint-foot: "H • WREDE (curved) / LONDON".

1996.19

1-key piccolo in B♭, Herman Wrede, London, ca. 1820.

4-key piccolo (left-handed), George Potter and Co., London, ca. 1890.

Stained cocus wood; nickel-silver ferrules; decorative lines. Two sections: head, body. Oval embouchure hole, six finger holes. Four nickel-silver pillar-mounted keys, modern key heads made for left-handed player. B♭ (R2), G♯ (R4), F (L3), D♯ (L4). L=380.

Stamped on head, body: "POTTER & C[o] / LONDON (in an oval of points)".

2002.63

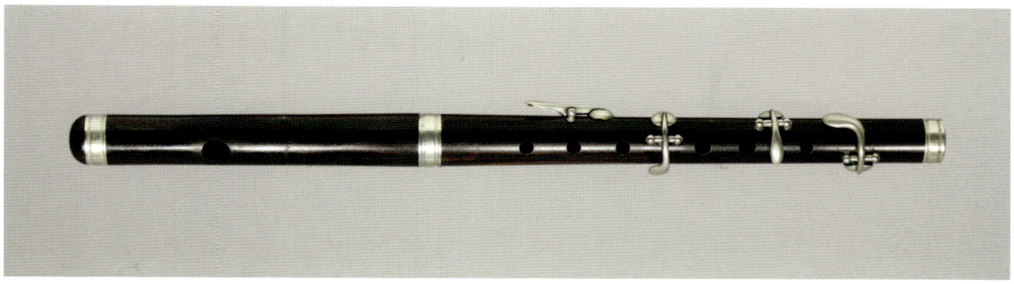

4-key piccolo (left-handed), George Potter and Co., London, ca. 1890.

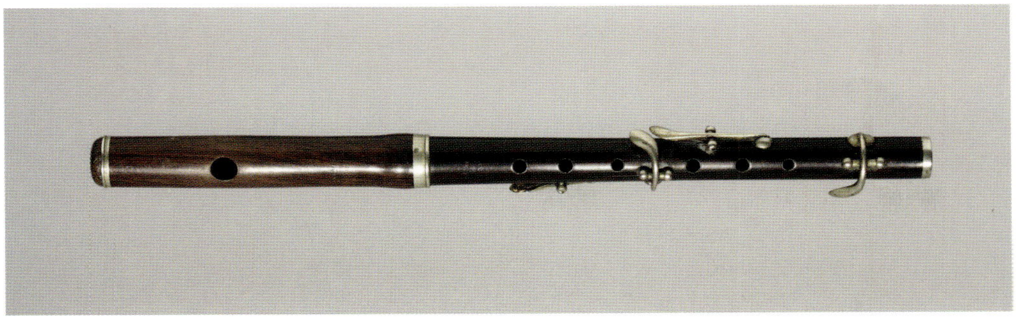

4-key piccolo, Claire Bélizaire, Paris, ca. 1850.

4-key piccolo, Claire Bélizaire, Paris, ca. 1850.

Stained cocus wood; nickel-silver ferrules; single beading. Two sections: head, body. Oval embouchure hole, six finger holes. Four nickel-silver pillar-mounted keys, salt-spoon key heads. B♭ (LT), G♯ (L4), long F (L4), D♯ (R4). L=300.

Stamped on head, body: "CLAIRE / Bélizaire (cursive) / A PARIS".

Rousselet and Watel 2012, 23.

2003.30

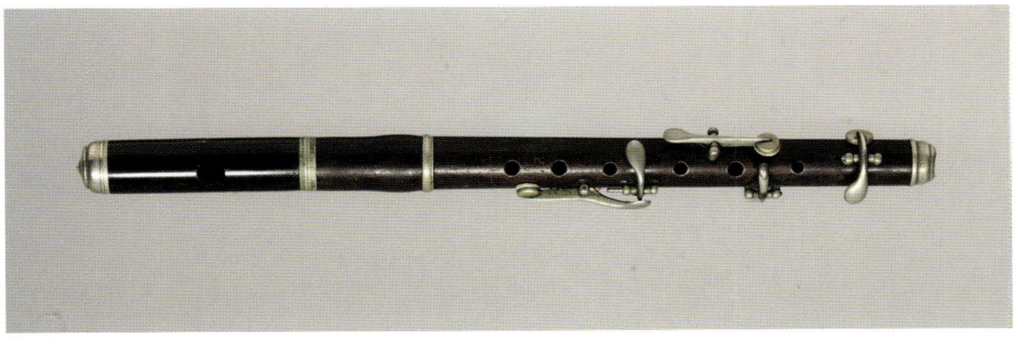

6-key piccolo, H. F. Meyer, nach, Hannover, probably Markneukirchen, ca. 1900.

6-key piccolo, H. F. Meyer, nach, Hannover, probably Markneukirchen, ca. 1900.

Stained cocus wood; nickel-silver ferrules; single beading. Three sections: head, barrel, body. Oval embouchure hole, six finger holes. Six nickel-silver pillar-mounted keys, modern key heads. C^1 (R1), B♭ (LT), G♯ (L4), long F (L4), F (R3), D♯ (R4). L=313.

Stamped on barrel: "NACH H.F. MEYER / C / L.P."; body: "C / L.P."

2003.34

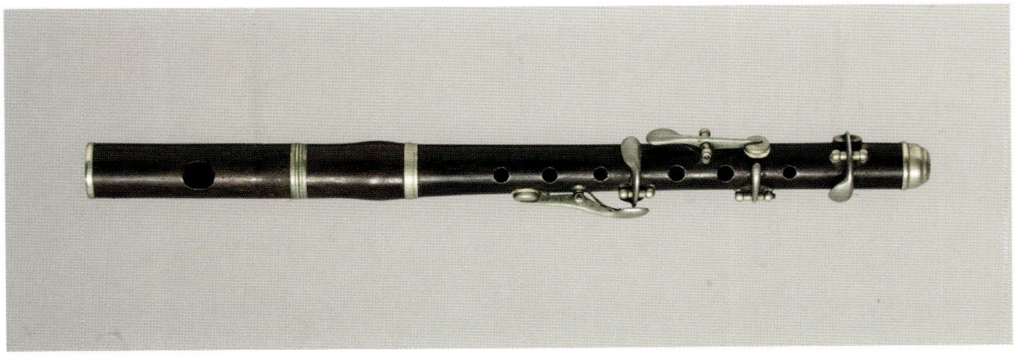

6-key piccolo, Charles Bruno, New York, ca. 1900.

6-key piccolo, Charles Bruno, New York, ca. 1900.

Stained cocus wood; nickel-silver ferrules; single beading. Three sections: head, barrel, body. Oval embouchure hole, six finger holes. Six nickel-silver pillar-mounted keys, modern key heads. C^1 (R1), B♭ (LT), G♯ (L4), long F (L4), F (R3), D♯ (R4). L=292.

Stamped on head: "BRUNO / NEW YORK".

Bruno was a dealer.

2003.35

Boehm-system piccolo, Auguste Bonneville, Paris, ca. 1890.

Boehm-system piccolo, Auguste Bonneville, Paris, ca. 1890.

Stained cocus wood; nickel-silver ferrules. Two sections: head, body. Oval embouchure, nickel-silver, Boehm-system pillar-mounted keys, plateau keys for L1, L3, rings for L2, R1, R2, R3, lowest note, D♯. Serial no. 4161. L=306.

Stamped on head, body: "AB (monogram) / A$^{\underline{TE}}$ / BONNEVILLE / A PARIS (in an oval) / 4161".

2004.13

5-key piccolo, Jean-Louis Tulou, Paris, ca. 1845.

Rosewood; thin nickel-silver ferrules. Two sections: head, body. Oval embouchure, six finger holes. Five nickel-silver pillar-mounted keys, round, flat key heads. C[1], B♭, G♯, F, D♯. L=315.

Stamped on head, body: "(nightingale) / TULOU / PARIS".

Giannini 1993, 71 (d).

2007.06

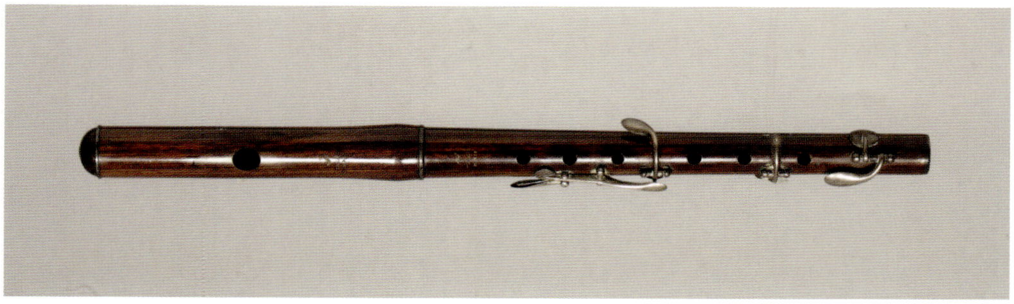

5-key piccolo, Jean-Louis Tulou, Paris, ca. 1845.

1-key piccolo, Léonard Clapisson, Lyon, ca. 1790.

Ebony; ivory ferrules; single beading. Three sections: head, body, foot. Ebony cap with ebony screw-cork indicator, six finger holes. One block-mounted silver key, square key head. D♯. L=320.

Stamped on head, body: "CLAPISSON".

Rousselet and Watel 2012, 47.

2010.06

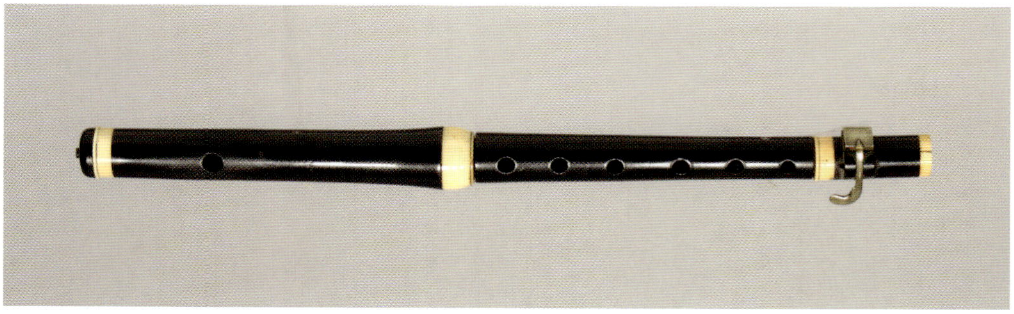

1-key piccolo, Léonard Clapisson, Lyon, ca. 1790.

4-key piccolo, Michel Rivet, Lyon, ca. 1860.

Stained rosewood; nickel-silver ferrules. Four sections: head, barrel, body, foot. Oval embouchure, six finger holes. Four pillar-mounted silver-plated keys, modern key heads. B♭, C♯, F, D♯. L=325.

Stamped on head: "(five-pointed star) / RIVET / A LYON / (five-pointed star)"; body: "RIVET / A LYON".

2010.07

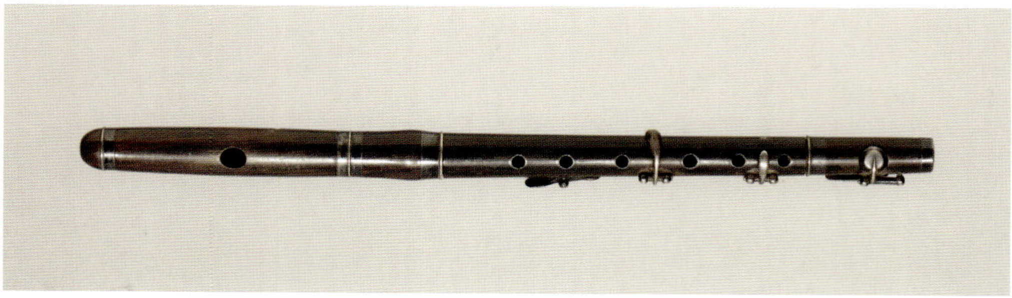

4-key piccolo, Michel Rivet, Lyon, ca. 1860.

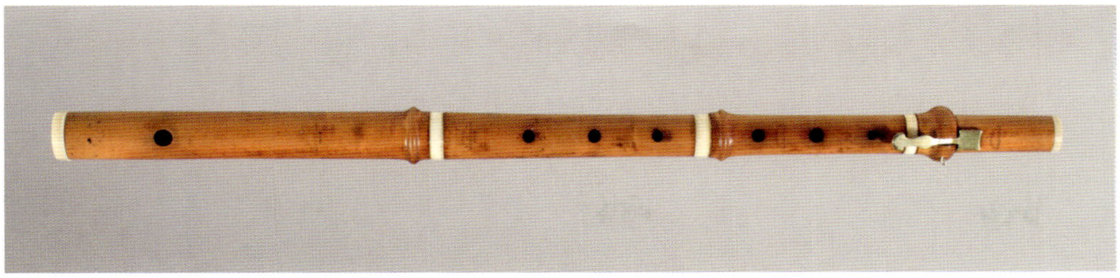

1-key flute, Asa Hopkins, Litchfield, Connecticut, ca. 1810.

1-key flute, Asa Hopkins, Litchfield, Connecticut, ca. 1810.

Boxwood; ivory ferrules; single beading; ornamental rings near end of head and upper part of lower joint. Four sections: head, upper joint, lower joint, foot. Oval embouchure hole, one ring-mounted brass key, square key head. D♯. L=599.

Stamped on head, upper joint: "A HOPKINS (curved) / LITCHFIELD / CONN"; lower joint, foot: "A HOPKINS (curved) / LITCHFIELD".

1991.03

4-key flute, Thomas J. Weygandt, Philadelphia, ca. 1845.

4-key flute, Thomas J. Weygandt, Philadelphia, ca. 1845.

Boxwood; ivory ferrules; single beading with a dark line. Four sections: head, l.h. joint, r.h. joint, foot. Ivory cap with ivory screw-cork indicator. Oval embouchure hole, four silver block and ring-mounted keys, flat, round key heads. B♭, G♯, F, D♯. L=613.

Stamped on head, l.h. joint, r.h. joint, foot: "T.J.WEYGANDT / PHILA. / (statue)".

1992.01

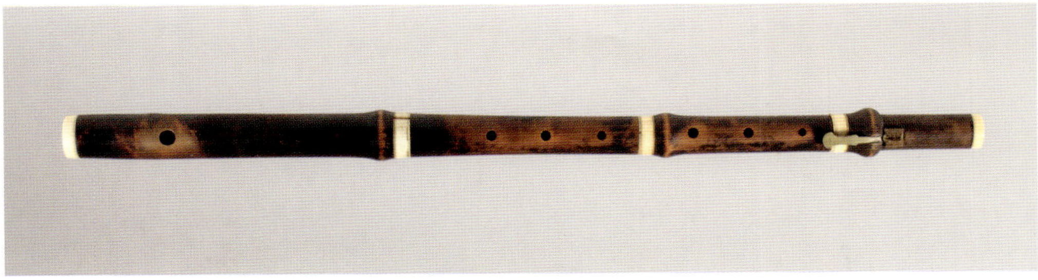

1-key flute, John Geib, Adam Geib, and William Geib, New York, ca. 1820.

1-key flute, John Geib, Adam Geib, and William Geib, New York, ca. 1820.

Stained boxwood; ivory ferrules; single beading with dark line. Four sections: head, upper joint, lower joint, foot. Oval embouchure hole, one silver ring-mounted key, square key head. D♯. L=598.

Stamped on head: "J.A. & W. GEIB / 23 / MAIDEN LANE / NEW – YORK".

An English imported flute.

1992.02

1-key flute in G, John C. Haynes and Co., Boston, ca. 1865.

1-key flute in G, John C. Haynes and Co., Boston, ca. 1865.

Boxwood; boxwood ferrules; single beading. Four sections: head, upper joint, lower joint, foot. Oval embouchure hole, one brass ring-mounted key, flat, round key head. D♯. L=453.

Stamped on head: "J.C. HAYNES & C^{O} / BOSTON – MASS. / G"; upper joint: "J.C. HAYNES & C^{O} / 33 COURT S^{T} / BOSTON – MASS."; lower joint, foot: "J.C. HAYNES & C^{O} / BOSTON – MASS."

1993.07

1-key flute, Meacham and Co., Albany, New York, ca. 1827.

Boxwood; ivory ferrules; single beading. Four sections: head, upper joint, lower joint, foot. Oval embouchure hole, one silver key, square key head. D♯. L=606.

Stamped on head, upper joint, lower joint, foot: "MEACHAM & CO. (curved) / ALBANY".

Eliason (1979-1980), 64.

1994.07

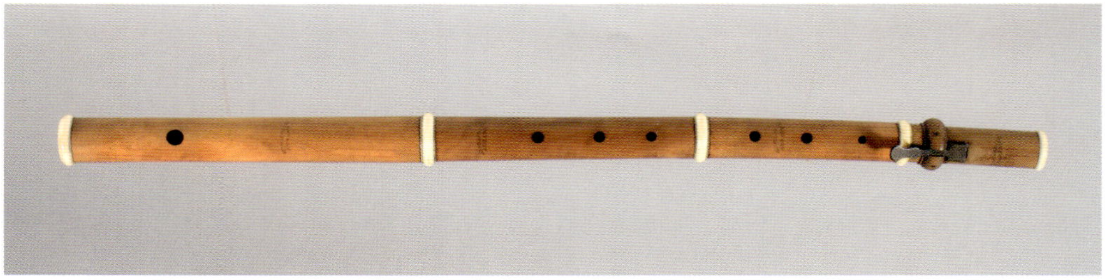

1-key flute, Meacham and Co., Albany, New York, ca. 1827.

1-key flute, Willam A. Pond and Co., New York, ca. 1840.

Stained rosewood; nickel-silver ferrules; single and double beading. Four sections: head (cracked), upper joint, lower joint, foot. Oval embouchure hole, one ring-mounted nickel-silver key, flat, round key head, missing ferrule on foot. D♯. L=610.

Stamped on upper joint: "WM A. POND / 547 BROADWAY / N-YORK".

1994.14

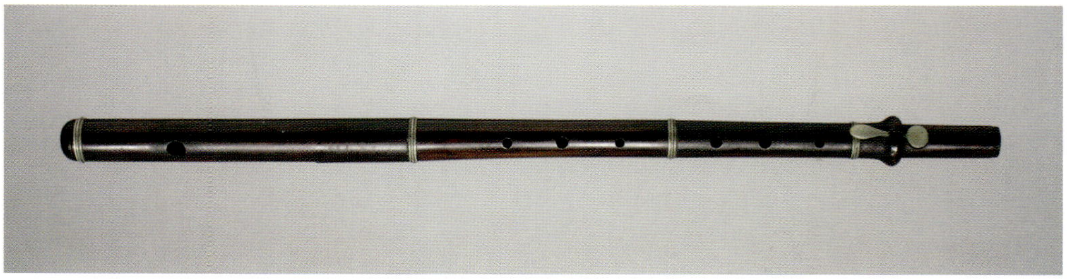

1-key flute, Willam A. Pond and Co., New York, ca. 1840.

1-key flute d'amour, Andrea Fornari, Venice, 1794.

Boxwood; boxwood ferrules. Four sections: head (cracked), upper joint, lower joint, foot. Oval embouchure hole, one brass key, square key head mounted in bulge; ivory cap on head. D♯. L=743.

Stamped on upper joint: "(star) / FORNARI / (star)"; lower joint: "(star) / FORNARI / (star) // A VENEZIA"; foot: "(star) / FORNARI / (star) / 1794 / (star)".

1995.01

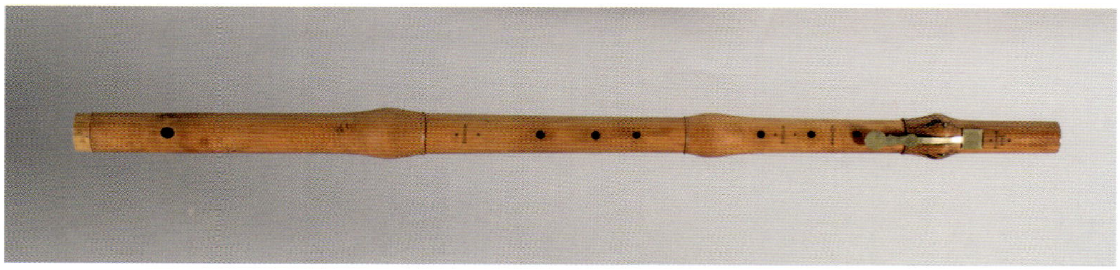

1-key flute d'amour, Andrea Fornari, Venice, 1794.

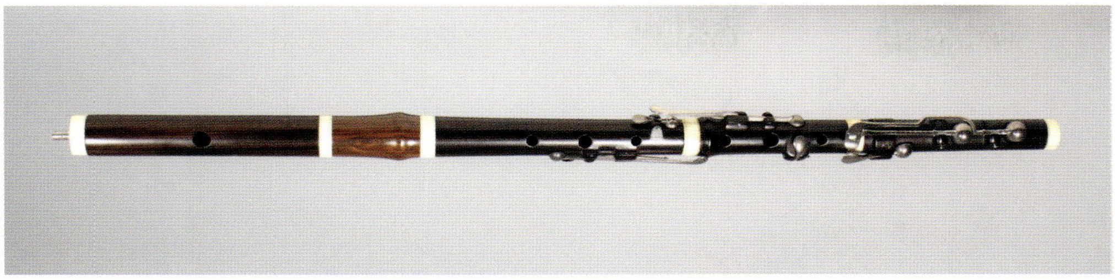

8-key flute, John Firth, William Hall, and Sylvanus Pond, New York, ca. 1840.

8-key flute, John Firth, William Hall, and Sylvanus Pond, New York, ca. 1840.

Stained rosewood; ivory ferrules; single beading. Five sections: head, barrel, l.h. joint, r.h. joint, foot. Metal-lined head with nickel-silver tenon. Ivory cap, nickel-silver screw cork indicator. Oval embouchure hole, eight block and ring-mounted nickel-silver keys, salt-spoon key heads. Large Nicholson-type finger holes for L1, L2, R1, R2. C^1 (R1), B♭, G♯, F (L4, long), F (short), D♯, C♯, C (the latter two, overlapping touches). Serial no. 676. L=675.

Stamped on head, r.h. joint: "FIRTH HALL & POND / FRANKLIN SQ$^{\underline{E}}$ / N-YORK"; l.h. joint: "676 / FIRTH HALL & POND / FRANKLIN SQ$^{\underline{E}}$ / N-YORK".

1995.02

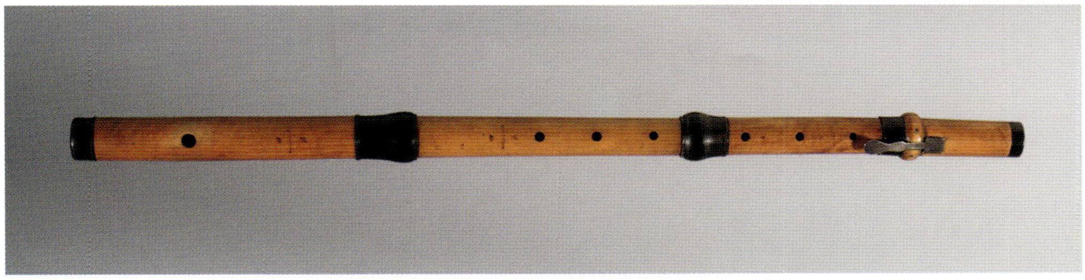

1-key flute, Carl Augustin Grenser, Dresden, ca. 1760.

1-key flute, Carl Augustin Grenser, Dresden, ca. 1760.

Boxwood; large horn ferrules; single beading. Four sections: head, upper joint, lower joint, foot. Round embouchure hole, one ring-mounted silver key, square key head. D♯. L=625 (with longest corps); L of three unnumbered upper joints or corps de rechange=172, 163, 151.

Stamped on head, upper joint, lower joint: "(three-pointed crown) / GRENTZER / (crossed swords)."

1996.06

4-key flute, John C. Haynes and Co., Boston, ca. 1870.

4-key flute, John C. Haynes and Co., Boston, ca. 1870.

Stained rosewood; nickel silver ferrules. Four sections: head, l.h. joint, r.h. joint, foot. Oval embouchure hole, four block and ring-mounted nickel-silver keys, round, flat key heads. B♭, G♯, F, D♯. L=605.

Stamped on l.h. joint: "J.C. HAYNES & C^{O}. / 33 COURT S$^{\underline{T}}$ / BOSTON – MASS. / GERMAN SILVER"; head, r.h. joint, foot: "J.C. HAYNES & C^{O}. / BOSTON – MASS."

1996.07

1-key flute, Johann Gotlieb Freyer, Potsdam, ca. 1780.

Ebony; ivory ferrules; single beading. Four sections: head, upper joint, lower joint, foot. Ivory cap, metal screw-cork indicator. Oval embouchure hole, one block-mounted silver key, square key head. D♯. L=615.

Stamped on head, lower joint, foot: "(Prussian eagle) / I.G. FREYER"; upper joint: "(Prussian eagle) / I.G. FREYER /4".

1996.10

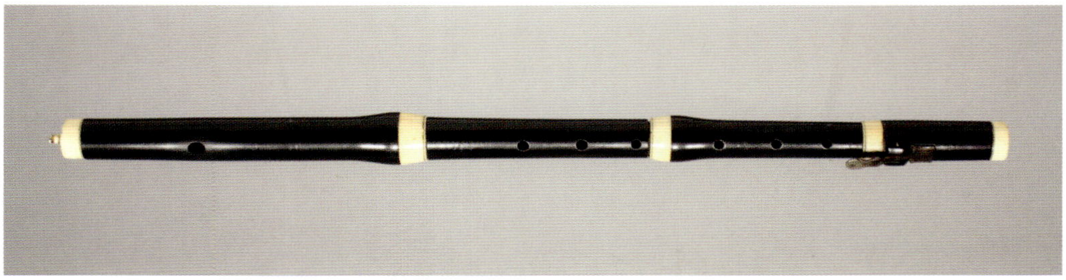

1-key flute, Johann Gotlieb Freyer, Potsdam, ca. 1780.

1-key flute in F, Henry Starck, London, ca. 1880.

Rosewood; rosewood ferrules. Three sections: head, upper joint, lower joint-foot. Oval embouchure hole, one ring-mounted brass key, round, flat key head. D♯. L=493.

Stamped on head: "(crown) / STARCK / London (cursive) / IMPROVED / F".

1996.13

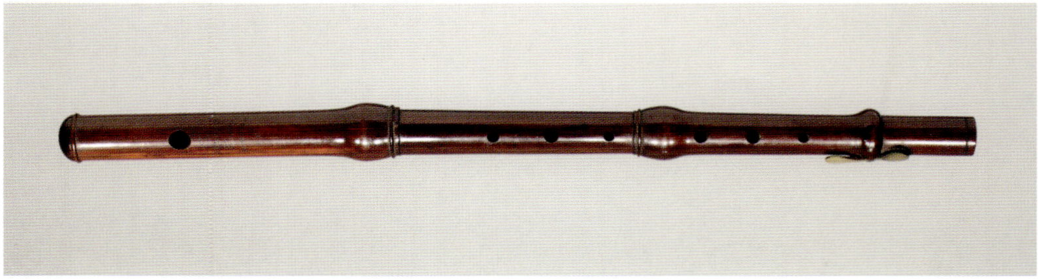

1-key flute in F, Henry Starck, London, ca. 1880.

8-key flute, Andrew Kauffman, London, ca. 1820.

Ivory; silver ferrules. Five sections: head, barrel, l.h. joint, r.h. joint, foot. Round embouchure hole, eight block-mounted silver keys, salt-spoon key heads. C^1 (R1), B♭, G♯, F (L4, long), F (short), D♯, C♯, C. L=673. Large block mountings for G♯, C♯, and C are unusual.

Stamped on head, barrel, l.h. joint, r.h. joint, foot: "A•KAUFFMANN / LONDON".

1996.18

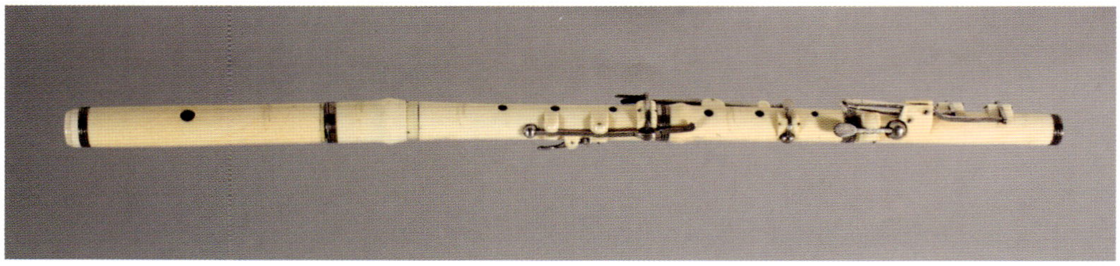

8-key flute, Andrew Kauffman, London, ca. 1820.

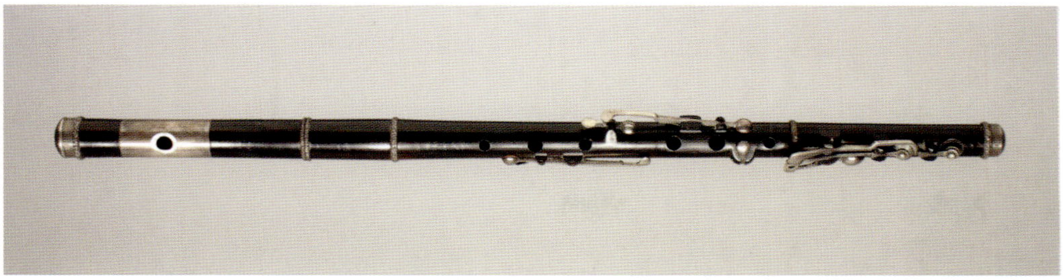

8-key flute, Joseph Prowse, London, Nicholson model, ca. 1825.

8-key flute, Joseph Prowse, London, Nicholson model, ca. 1825.

Black-stained rosewood; silver ferrules ornamented with flowers and leaves; silver lip plate with ivory embouchure bushing. Four sections: head, barrel, body, foot. Oval embouchure hole, eight block-mounted silver keys, salt-spoon key heads, pewter plug heads for C♯ and C, oversized finger holes. C[1] (R1), B♭, G♯, F (L4, long), F (short), D♯, C♯, C. Serial no. 1309. L=661.

Stamped on head, barrel, foot: "Nicholson / Improved (cursive)"; body: "C. Nicholson's / Improved / 1309 / J. Prowse / Hannover Street / London (cursive)".

1996.23

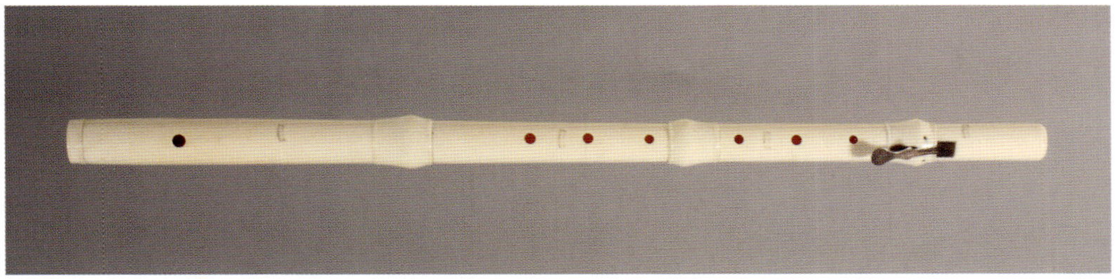

1-key flute, Benjamin Hallett, London, ca. 1730.

1-key flute, Benjamin Hallett, London, ca. 1730.

Ivory; large ivory ferrules. Four sections: head, upper joint, lower joint, foot. Round embouchure hole, one silver key, square key head. Key mounted in bulge. D♯. L=613.

Stamped on head, upper joint, lower joint, foot: "BENJAMIN / HALLETT (slightly curved)".

An incomplete ivory 1-key flute by Hallet is in the Miller Collection, Library of Congress, no. DM1044.

Seyfrit 1982, 178.

1996.26

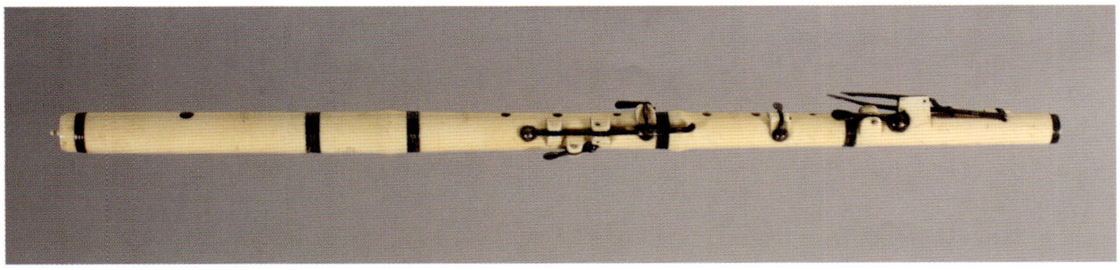

8-key flute, Louis Drouet, London, ca. 1820.

8-key flute, Louis Drouet, London, ca. 1820.

Ivory; silver ferrules. Five sections: head, barrel, l.h. joint, r.h. joint, foot. Ivory cap with ivory screw-cork indicator, slightly oval embouchure hole. Eight block-mounted silver keys, salt-spoon key heads. C[1] (R1), B♭, G♯, F (L4, long), F (short), D♯, C♯, C. L=665. Large block mountings for G♯, C♯, and C are unusual.

Stamped on head, barrel, l.h. joint, r.h. joint, foot: "DROUET / LONDON".

This flute is very similar in construction and key mountings to the ivory flute by Andrew Kauffman (no. 1996.18), and it seems likely this example was made in Kauffman's shop.

1997.03

5-key flute in F, Monzani and Co., London, 1815.

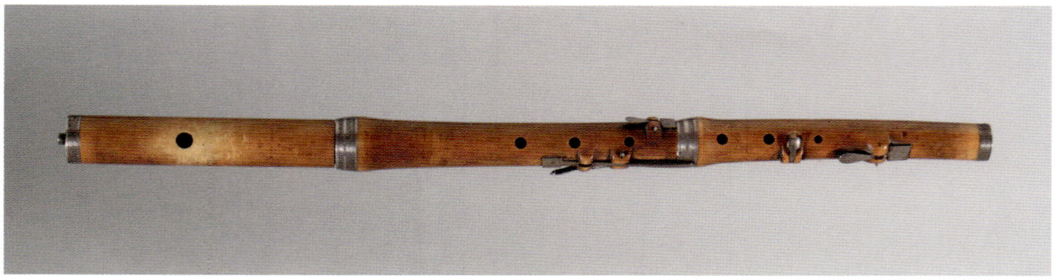

5-key flute in F, Monzani and Co., London, 1815.

Boxwood; silver ferrules; multiple grooves. Three sections: head, l.h joint, r.h. joint-foot. Silver cap, silver screw-cork indicator. Oval embouchure hole, five block-mounted silver keys, square key heads; each key head stamped with a crown on the upper side. C^1 (R1), B♭, G♯, F, D♯. L=510.

Ferrules on l.h. and r.h. joints stamped with hallmarks indicating a date of 1815. Serial no. 1872.

Stamped on head: "(crown) / MONZANI & Cº / F"; l.h. joint: "PATENT / (crown) / MONZANI & Cº / 24 DOVER ST / 1872"; r.h. joint: "PATENT / (crown) / MONZANI & Cº".

1998.12

4-key flute, John Firth, William Hall, and Sylvanus Pond, New York, ca. 1840.

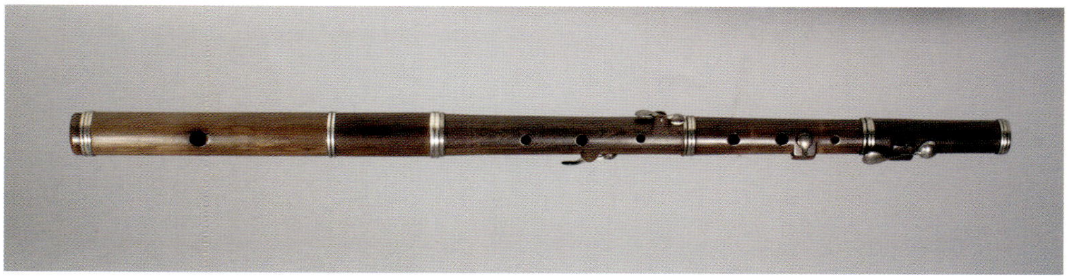

4-key flute, John Firth, William Hall, and Sylvanus Pond, New York, ca. 1840.

Rosewood; nickel-silver ferrules; multiple grooves. Five sections: head, barrel, l.h. joint, r.h. joint, foot. Metal-lined head, oval embouchure hole, four block-mounted nickel-silver keys, salt-spoon key heads. B♭, G♯, F, D♯. L=613.

Stamped on head, barrel, r.h. joint, foot: "FIRTH HALL & POND / N-YORK"; l.h. joint: "FIRTH HALL & POND / FRANKLIN SQE / N-YORK".

1999.06

4-key flute, John Firth, William Hall, and Sylvanus Pond, New York, ca. 1855.

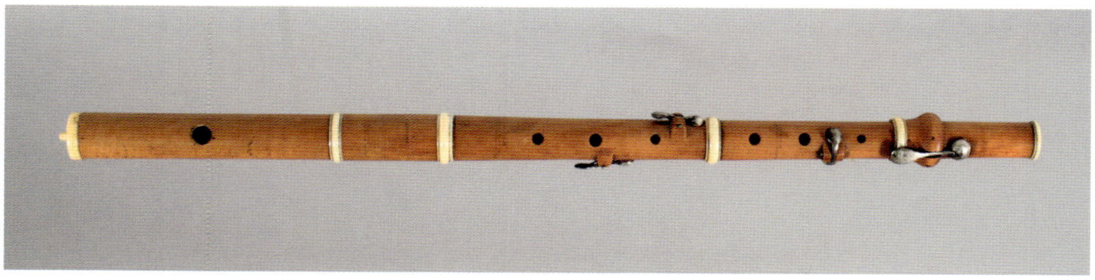

4-key flute, John Firth, William Hall, and Sylvanus Pond, New York, ca. 1855.

Boxwood; ivory ferrules; single beading; dark lines. Five sections: head, barrel, l.h. joint, r.h. joint, foot. Ivory cap, ivory screw-cork indicator. Partially metal lined barrel and tenon with two lines as guide for tuning. Slightly oval embouchure hole, four block and ring-mounted silver keys, salt-spoon key heads. B♭, G♯, F, D♯. L=605.

Stamped on head, r.h. joint, foot: "FIRTH HALL & POND / N-YORK"; barrel: "FIRTH HALL & POND / N-YORK / PATENT"; l.h. joint: "FIRTH HALL & POND / FRANKLIN SQE / N-YORK".

1999.07

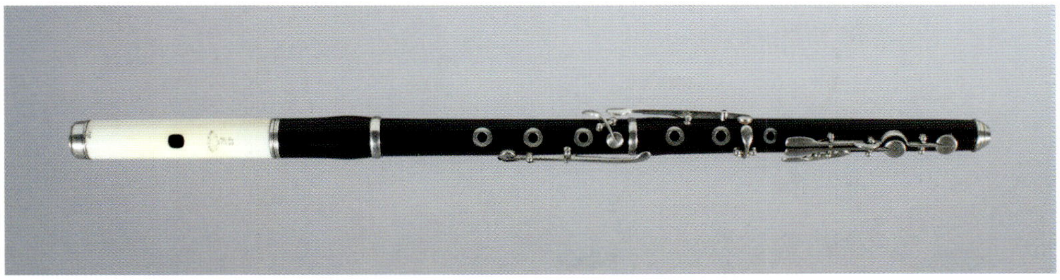

8-key flute in D♭, George Cloos, New York, ca. 1885

8-key flute in D♭, George Cloos, New York, ca. 1885.

Black-stained African black wood; nickel-silver ferrules. Five sections: ivory head, barrel, l.h. joint, r.h. joint, foot. Brass lined head with tenon and two lines for tuning, silver inserts around six finger holes. Slightly rectangular embouchure hole, eight pillar-mounted nickel-silver keys, modern key heads. C[1] (R1), B♭, G♯, F (L4, long), F (short), D♯, C♯, C. Serial no. 9800. L=660.

Stamped on head: "GEO CLOOS (curved) / < CG (monogram) > / D♭ / LP"; back of barrel: "9800".

The arrangement of "foot" keys for D♯, C♯, and C is the same as found on the popular Meyer system flute. Low pitch (LP) flutes tuned to about A=435 hertz were introduced to the United States during the last two decades of the nineteenth century.

1999.08

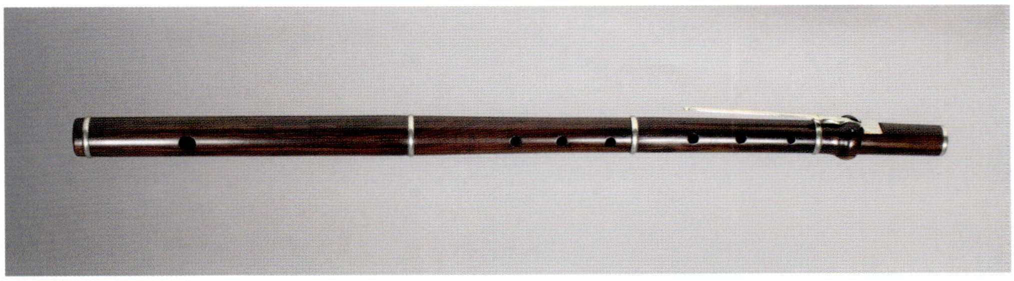

1-key flute, Edward Baack, New York, ca. 1850.

1-key flute, Edward Baack, New York, ca. 1850.

Rosewood; nickel-silver ferrules. Four sections: head, l.h. joint, r.h. joint, foot. Oval embouchure hole, one ring-mounted nickel-silver key, square key head. D♯ (long lever, R1). Unusually long lever for D♯ key with round touch. L=604.

Stamped on head, l.h joint, r.h. joint, foot: "E. BAACK / N-YORK".

1999.09

1-key flute, Edward Baack, New York, ca. 1850.

1-key flute, Edward Baack, New York, ca. 1850.

Boxwood; boxwood ferrules; single beading. Four sections: head, l.h. joint, r.h. joint, foot. Oval embouchure hole, one ring-mounted brass key, square key head. D♯. L=600.

Stamped on head, l.h. joint, r.h. joint, foot: "E. BAACK / N-YORK".

1999.10

Boehm-system flute, Rudall, Carte, and Co., London, "Old system" model, 1903.

Stained rosewood; nickel-silver ferrules. Three sections: head, body, foot. Oval embouchure hole. Old system employs eight-key flute fingerings using cylindrical body with conical head. All finger holes are covered by plateau keys except for a perforated key for L1 with a ring mechanism closed by L2. F may be played by fingering E and opening either the F natural key (LT) with R3, or the long F key with L3. B♭ (LT); C^1 is produced by fingering B and using R1, the small trill key above it. The keys for C^1 (R1) and B♭ (LT) are retained. Serial no. 3505. L=655.

Stamped on head, foot: "(crown) / RUDALL / CARTE & Co. / LONDON"; body: "RUDALL / CARTE & Co. / 23, BERNERS STREET / OXFORD STREET / LONDON / 3505".

According to the Sales Records of Rudall, Carte & Co., this flute was made by a Mr. Reid, who completed it March 20, 1903. It was sold to G.J. Huth of Putney on March 23, 1903.

Bigio 2012, 183.

1999.11

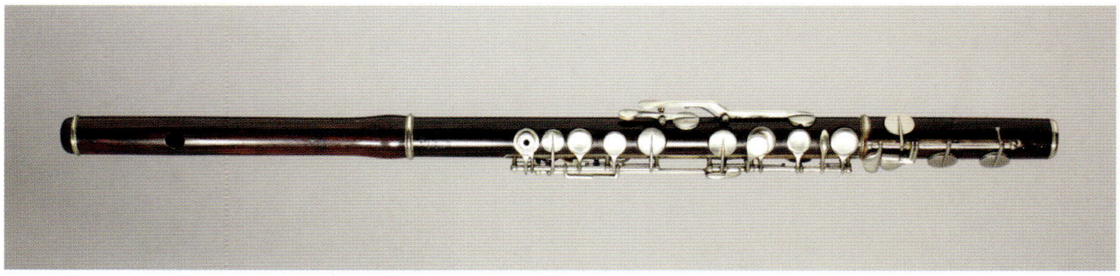

Boehm-system flute, Rudall, Carte, and Co., London, "Old system" model, 1903.

1-key flute, Anonymous, Dresden, probably made in Vogtland, ca. 1800.

Boxwood; ivory ferrules; single beading. Four sections: head, upper joint, lower joint, foot. Oval embouchure hole, one block-mounted brass key. D♯. L=610.

Stamped on head, upper joint, lower joint, foot: "(crown) / DRESDEN / 1D".

1999.12

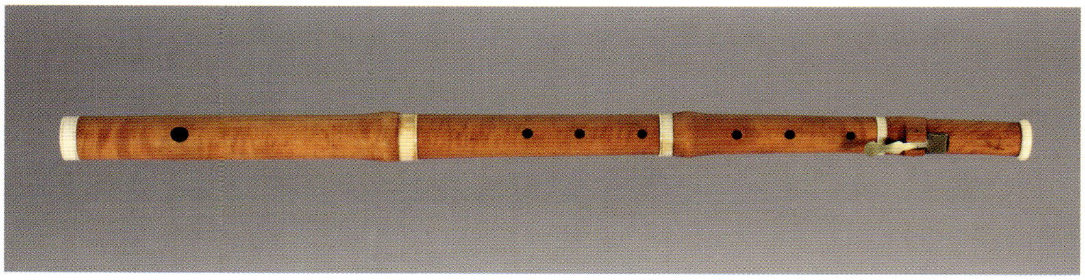

1-key flute, Anonymous, Dresden, probably made in Vogtland, ca. 1800.

1-key flute, Thomas Cahusac senior, London, ca. 1790.

Boxwood; ivory ferrules; multiple beading. Four sections: head, upper joint, lower joint, foot.

Oval embouchure hole, one block-mounted brass key in a bulge. D♯ (long lever, L4). L=611.

Stamped on head: "CAHUSAC (curved) / STRAND / LONDON (curved)"; upper joint, lower joint, foot: "CAHUSAC (curved) / LONDON (curved)".

It is possible that this long D♯ lever was made for a player who didn't have, or couldn't use, his right-hand pinkie finger (R4).

1999.17

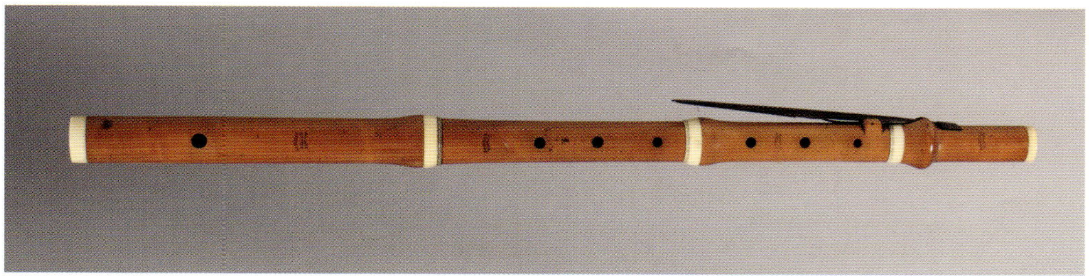

1-key flute, Thomas Cahusac senior, London, ca. 1790.

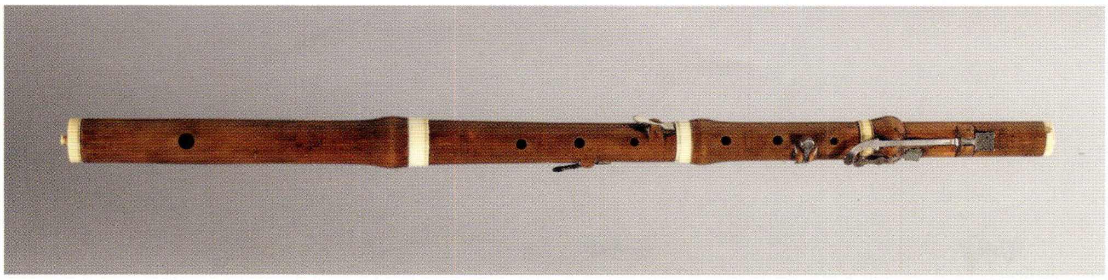

5-key flute, Richard Potter, London, 1782.

5-key flute, Richard Potter, London, 1782.

Boxwood; ivory ferrules; single beading; dark lines. Four sections: head, l.h. joint, r.h. joint, foot. Ivory cap, ivory screw-cork indicator. Round embouchure hole, five block and ring-mounted silver keys, square key heads. B♭, G♯, F, D♯, C. L=640.

Stamped on head, l.h. joint, r.h. joint: "POTTER / LONDON"; foot: "POTTER / LONDON / 1782".

Dated flutes by Richard Potter are known from 1776 to 1782 according to Ardal Powell's list of dated historic flutes, www.flutehistory.com/Resources/Lists/Dated_Instruments.php3.

1999.18

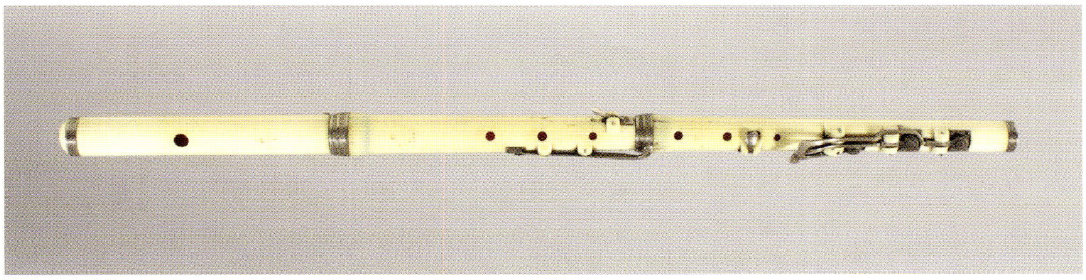

7-key flute, Monzani and Co., London, ca. 1815; shown below with second head joint in case.

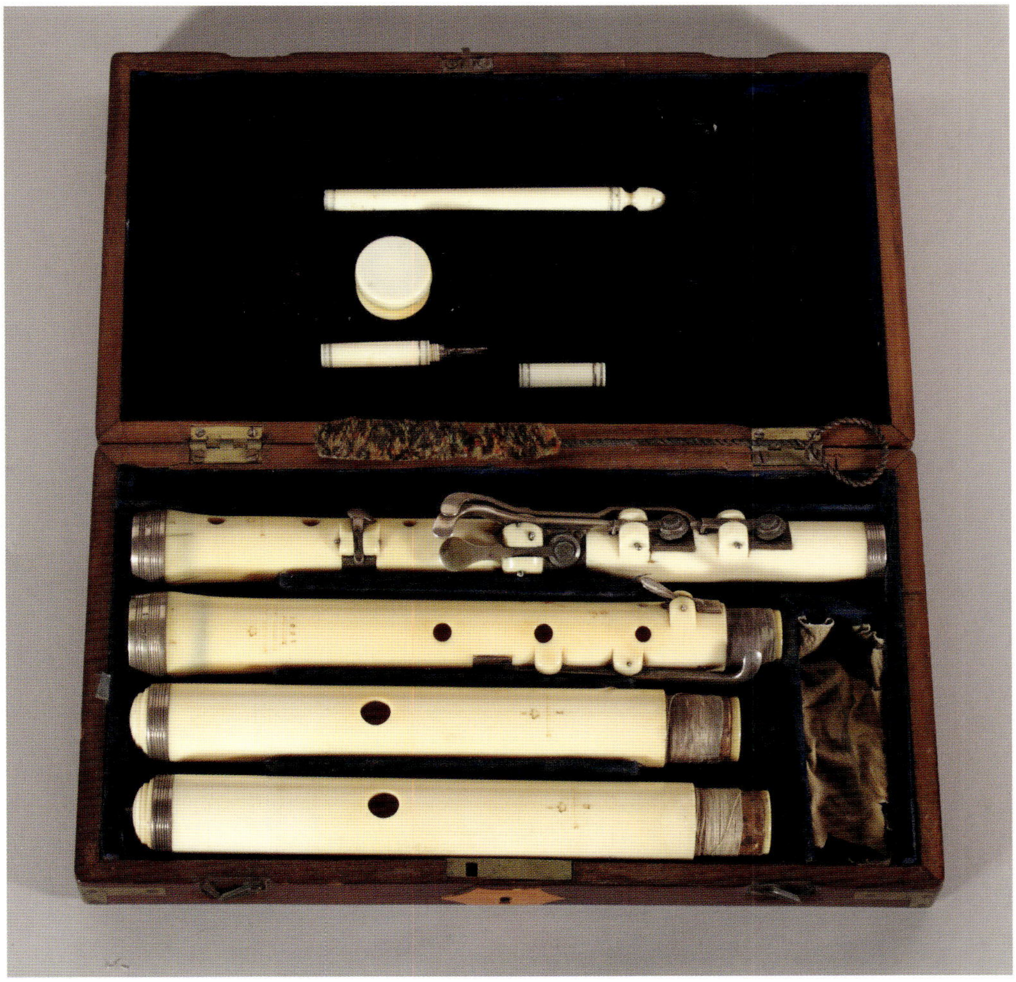

7-key flute, Monzani and Co., London, ca. 1815.

Ivory; silver ferrules; multiple grooves. Three sections: head, l.h. joint, r.h. joint-foot. Ivory cap, silver screw-cork indicator, hallmarks on l.h. and r.h. ferrules, second ivory head joint marked "2". Oval embouchure hole, seven block-mounted silver keys, flat key heads, pewter plug key heads for D♯, C♯, C, C[1], B♭, G♯, F, D♯, C♯, C. In original blue felt-lined wooden case with ivory cleaning rod, round grease container for corked tenons, ivory handle screwdriver with ivory cap, cleaning brush on metal rod. Serial no. 1608. L=682 (no. 2); L=675 (no. 1).

Stamped on head: "(crown) /MONZANI & Co. / 1"; l.h. joint: "PATENT / (crown) / MONZANI & Co. / 3 OLD BOND ST. / LONDON / 1608"; r.h. joint-foot: "PATENT / (crown) / MONZANI & Co."

1999.19

1-key flute, Jean-Baptiste Prudent Thierriot, Paris, ca. 1785.

Boxwood; ivory ferrules; single beading. Four sections: head, upper joint, lower joint, foot. Oval embouchure hole, one block-mounted silver key, square key head. D♯. L=590.

Stamped on head, upper joint, lower joint, foot: "(flower on a stem) / PRUDENT / APARIS".

Giannini 1993, 39 (c); Jeltsch 1997, 136, 152; Rousselet and Watel 2012, 144.

1999.25

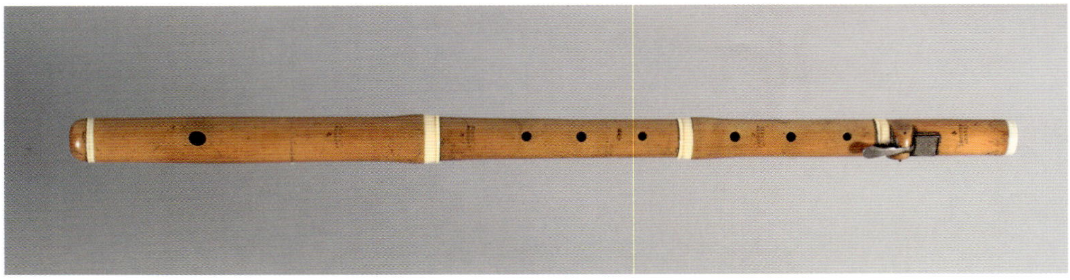

1-key flute, Jean-Baptiste Prudent Thierriot, Paris, ca. 1785.

1-key flute, Friedrich Erdmann Grimm, Brunndöbra, ca. 1800.

Boxwood; horn ferrules; single beading. Four sections: head, upper joint, lower joint, foot. Round embouchure hole, one ring-mounted brass key with square head, three upper joints. D♯. Stored in a paper box. L=615 (with longest joint); L of three unnumbered upper joints or corps de rechange=160, 184, 138.

Stamped on head: "(star) / (star) GRIMM (star) / (star)".

Dullat 2010, 180.

1999.26

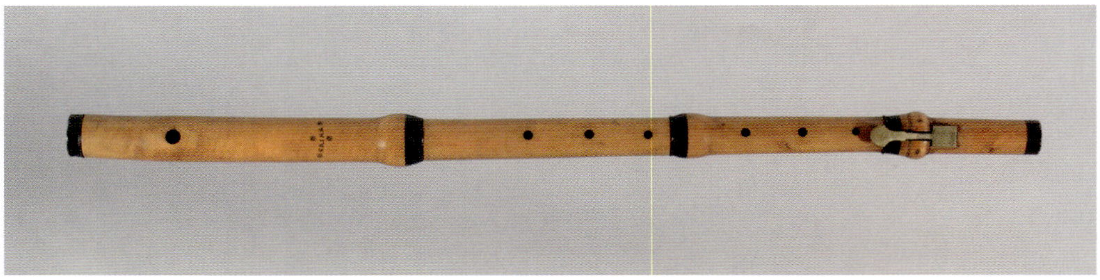

1-key flute, Friedrich Erdmann Grimm, Brunndöbra, ca. 1800.

Boehm-system flute, Vincent Hipolyte Godfroy, Paris, ca. 1851–1852.

Cocus wood; nickel-silver ferrules. Three sections: head, body, foot. Oval embouchure, nickel-silver plate below the embouchure hole, conical body. Plateau key for R1, ring keys for R2, R3, L1, L2, L3; Dorus G♯, D♯, C♯ (roller), C. Serial no. 122. L=665.

Stamped on head: "(head of Medusa) / CLAIR / Godfroy ainé / A PARIS (in oval) / CG (monogram) / BREVETÉ / 122"; body: "(head of Medusa) / CLAIR / Godfroy ainé / A PARIS (in oval) / CG (monogram)".

Lenski and Ventske (1992), 170; Giannini (1993), 107 (b), 167; Rousselet and Watel 2012, 80.

1999.27

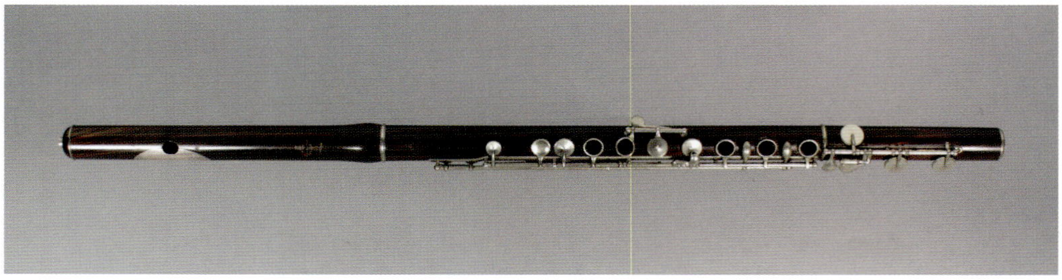

Boehm-system flute, Vincent Hipolyte Godfroy, Paris, ca. 1851–1852.

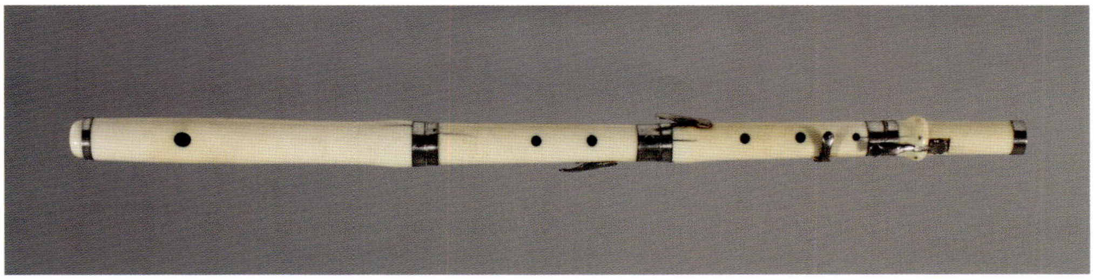

4-key flute, Heinrich Christian Eisenbrandt, Philadelphia, ca. 1814.

4-key flute, Heinrich Christian Eisenbrandt, Philadelphia, ca. 1814.

Ivory; silver ferrules. Four sections: head, l.h. joint, r.h. joint, foot. Third finger hole bored through a silver ferrule. Oval embouchure, four silver keys, bevel edge square key heads, three attached to plates, one ring-mounted. B♭, G♯, F, D♯. L=605.

Stamped on head, l.h. joint, r.h. joint, foot: "(crown) / EISENBRANDT / PHILAD$^{\underline{A}}$ (curved)".

2000.02

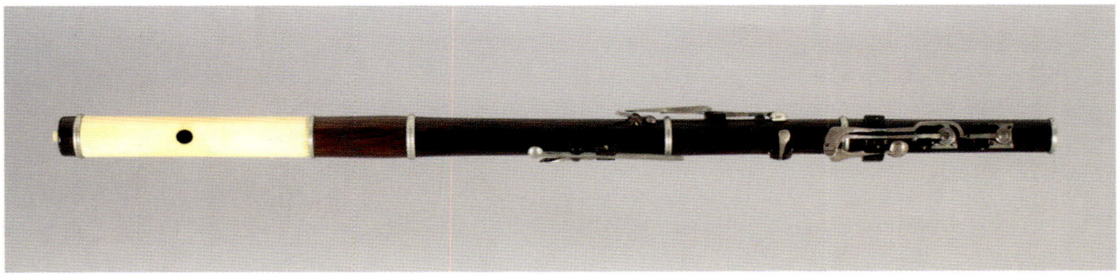

8-key flute, Dollard, Dublin, ca. 1830, with ivory head by George Catlin, Philadelphia.

8-key flute, Dollard, Dublin, ca. 1830, with ivory head by George Catlin, Philadelphia.

Stained cocus wood; silver ferrules. Five sections: ivory head, barrel, l.h. joint, r.h. joint, foot. Cocus wood cap, ivory screw-cork indicator. Oval embouchure, eight block and ring-mounted nickel-silver keys with salt-spoon key heads, C♯ and C with pewter plug keys. C^1 (R1), B♭, G♯, F (L4, long), F (short), D♯, C♯, C. The C♯ and C have overlapping touches. In case. L=667.

Stamped on head: "CATLIN / PHILAD^{A}"; l.h. joint, r.h. joint, foot: "DOLLARD / DUBLIN / (unicorn head)".

2000.06

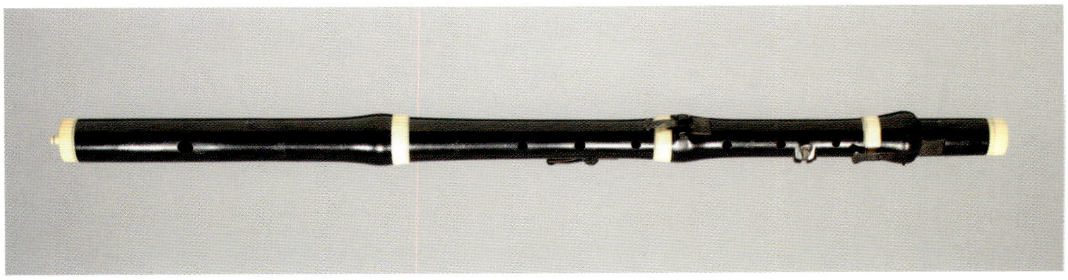

4-key flute, Heinrich Grenser, Dresden, ca. 1800.

4-key flute, Heinrich Grenser, Dresden, ca. 1800.

Ebony; ivory ferrules; multiple beading. Four sections: head, l.h. joint, r.h. joint, foot. Ivory cap, ivory screw-cork indicator. Oval embouchure, four block and ring-mounted silver keys. B♭, G♯, F, D♯. L=617. Unusual placement of G♯ key on r.h. joint.

Stamped on head, foot: "(crossed swords) / H.GRENSER / DRESDEN"; l.h. joint: "(crossed swords) / H.GRENSER / 2"; r.h. joint: "(crossed swords) / H.GRENSER".

2000.08

1-key flute, Roulleau, Paris, ca. 1740.

Boxwood; ivory ferrules; single beading. Four sections: head, upper joint, lower joint, foot. Slightly oval embouchure, one ring-mounted silver key, square key head. D♯. L=630.

Stamped on head, upper joint, lower joint, foot: "(five-pointed star) / ROULLAV / (lyre)".

A vielle à roué signed "Roullau-Denis-Saint-Jeans-De Latreans-A-Paris-1739" is in the Musée de la Musique, E.2054.

2000.13

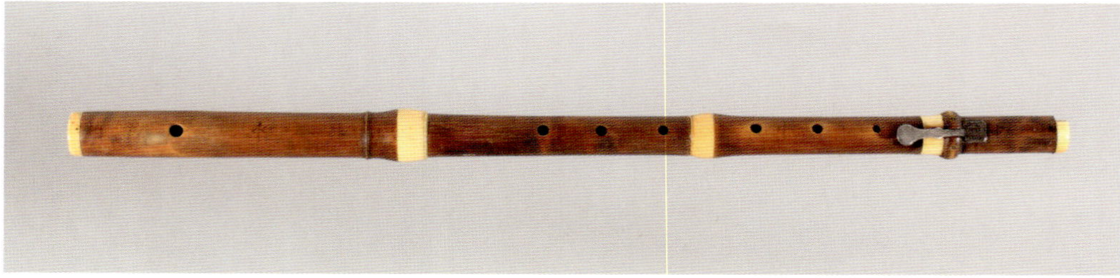

1-key flute, Roulleau, Paris, ca. 1740.

1-key flute, Pierre Naust, Paris, ca. 1720.

Ebony; ivory ferrules; single beading and dark line; one silver ferrule with grooves, probably a repair. Four sections: head, upper joint, lower joint, foot. Round embouchure, one block-mounted silver key with square key head, three upper joints. D♯. L=660; L of three unmarked upper joints or corps de rechange=198, 181, 170. Missing embouchure cap and foot ferrule, cracked head and foot.

Stamped on upper joint, lower joint, foot: "NAUST / (striding lion)".

Giannini 1993, 4-6; Powell 2002, 67, 74-75, 80.

2000.14

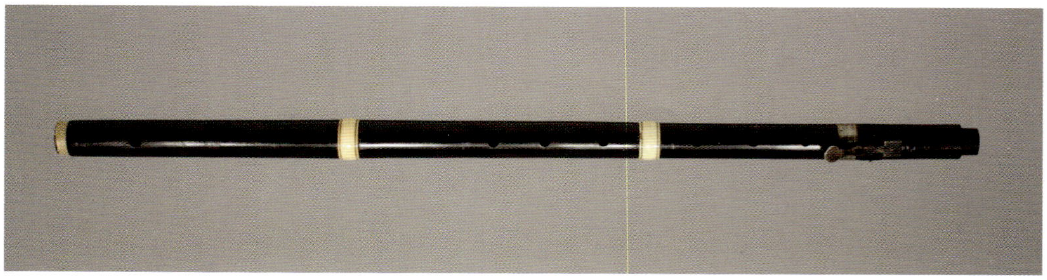

1-key flute, Pierre Naust, Paris, ca. 1720.

Boehm-system flute, Boehm and Mendler, Munich, ca. 1875.

Stained cocus wood; nickel-silver ferrules. Three sections: head, body, foot. Rectangular embouchure hole, Boehm-system, nickel-silver keys, lowest note, C. L=660.

Stamped on upper metal tenon of the body: "BOEHM & MENDLER / MÜNCHEN" (in small font).

2001.02

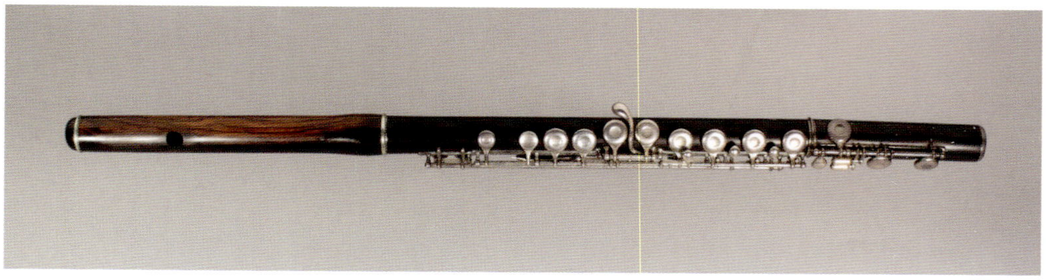

Boehm-system flute, Boehm and Mendler, Munich, ca. 1875.

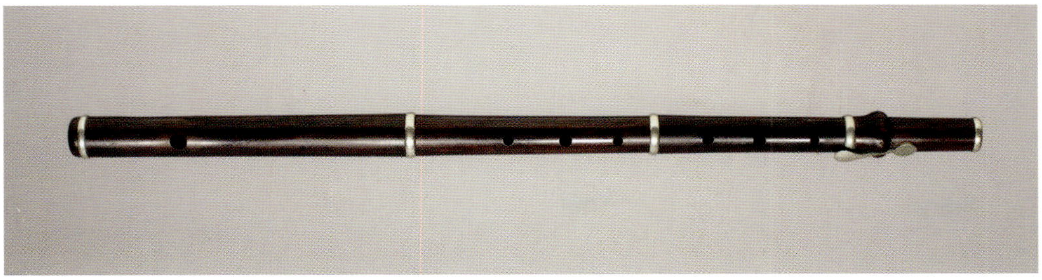

1-key flute, Chabrier Peloubet, New York, ca. 1840.

1-key flute, Chabrier Peloubet, New York, ca. 1840.

Stained rosewood; nickel-silver ferrules. Four sections: head, upper joint, lower joint, foot. Oval embouchure, one ring-mounted nickel-silver key. D♯. In paper box. L=600.

Stamped on head, upper joint, lower joint: "C.PELOUBET / NEW-YORK"; foot: "C.PELOUBET / NEW-YORK / FACTORY IN / BLOOMFLD NJ".

2001.08

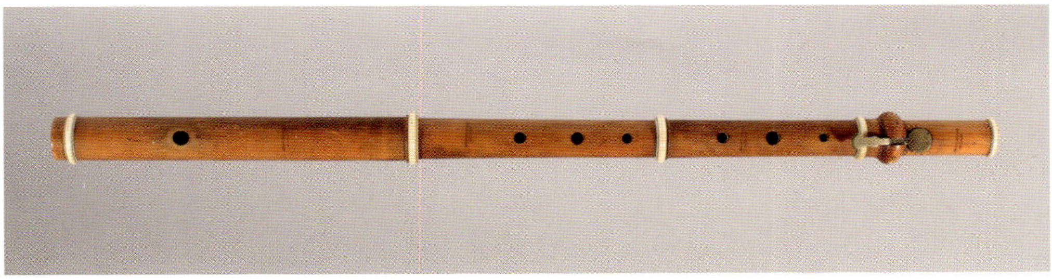

1-key flute, Meacham and Co., Albany, New York, ca. 1827.

1-key flute, Meacham and Co., Albany, New York, ca. 1827.

Boxwood; thick ivory ferrules; single beading; dark lines. Four sections: head, upper joint, lower joint, foot. Oval embouchure, one ring-mounted brass key, flat, round key head. D♯. L=618.

Stamped on head, upper joint, lower joint, foot: "MEACHAM & C^{O} / ALBANY".

Eliason (1979-1980), 64.

2001.34

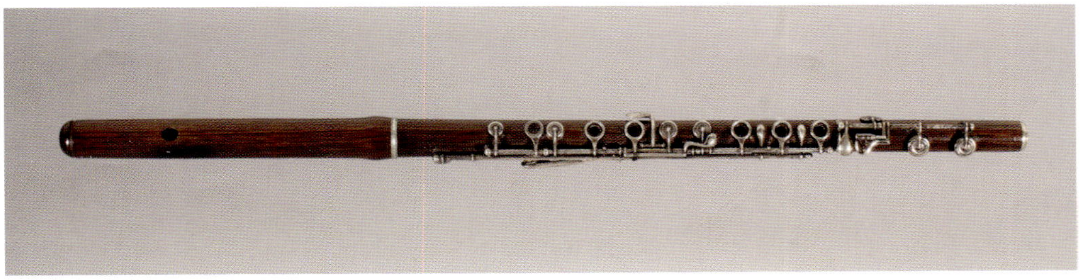

Boehm-system flute, Florentin Barbier, Paris, ca. 1875.

Boehm-system flute, Florentin Barbier, Paris, ca. 1875.

Palisander; nickel-silver ferrules. Three sections: head, body, foot. Oval embouchure, Boehm-system, plateau key (L1), ring keys for L2, L3, R1, R2, R3, low C. Ferrule on upper part of head missing. L=675.

Stamped on head: "F.BARBIER / PARIS".

2001.36

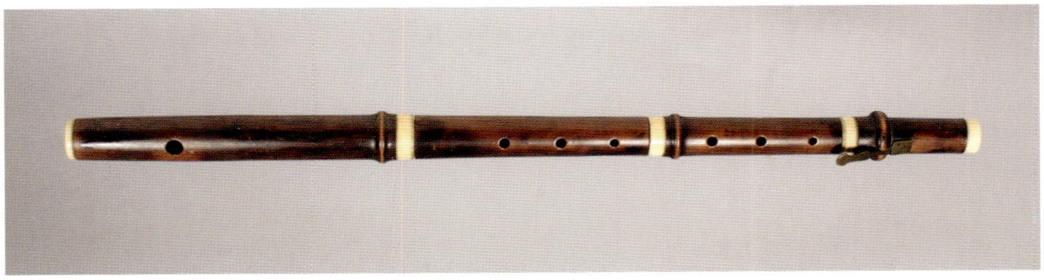

1-key flute, Edward Riley, New York, ca. 1825.

1-key flute, Edward Riley, New York, ca. 1825.

Stained boxwood; ivory ferrules; single beading; dark lines. Four sections: head, upper joint, lower joint, foot. Oval embouchure, one ring-mounted brass key, square key head. Ornamental rings on lower section of head, upper section of lower joint. D♯. L=601.

Stamped on head: "E.RILEY / 23 CHATHAM / N-YORK"; upper joint, lower joint: "E.RILEY / N-YORK".

2001.48

8-key flute, H. F. Meyer, Nach, Hannover, probably Markneukirchen, ca. 1890.

Stained cocus wood; nickel-silver ferrules. Five sections: head, barrel, l.h. joint, r.h. joint, foot. Eight nickel-silver pillar-mounted keys, modern key heads. C^1 (R1), B♭, G♯, F (L4, long), F (short), D♯, C♯, C. L=665.

On barrel: "NACH / H.F. MEYER (cursive) / HANNOVER."

2002.01

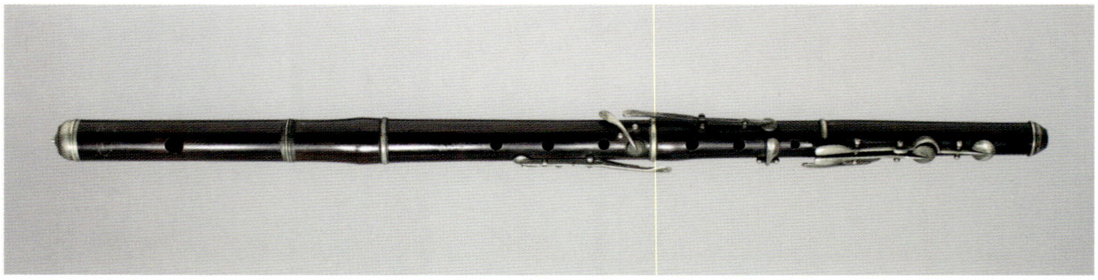

8-key flute, "Nach H. F. Meyer, Hannover," probably Markneukirchen, ca. 1890.

4-key flute, James W. Hoey, New York, ca. 1840.

Rosewood; nickel-silver ferrules. Five sections: head, barrel, l.h. joint, r.h. joint, foot. Rosewood cap, nickel-silver screw-cork indicator, metal-lined head with long tenon, metal lined barrel with tenon. Oval embouchure, four block-mounted nickel-silver keys, flat, round key heads. B♭, G♯, F, D♯. L=611.

Stamped on l.h. joint, r.h. joint, foot: "HOEY / NEW YORK".

2002.04

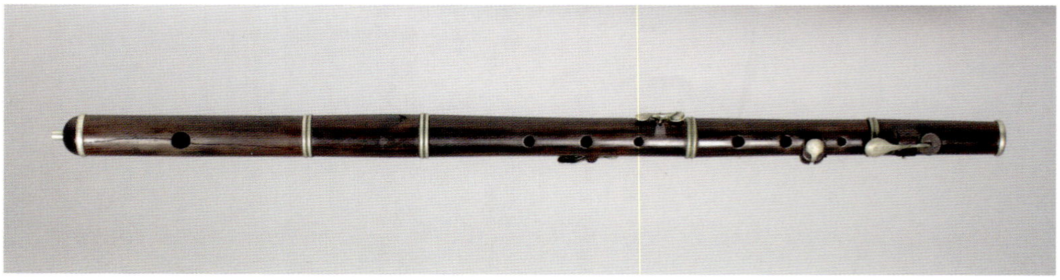

4-key flute, James W. Hoey, New York, ca. 1840.

1-key flute, John Firth, William Hall, and Sylvanus Pond, New York, ca. 1835.

Boxwood; ivory ferrules; single beading; dark lines. Four sections: head, upper joint, lower joint, foot. Oval embouchure, one ring-mounted brass key, square key head. D♯. L=596.

Stamped on head, lower joint, foot: "FIRTH HALL & POND / N-YORK"; upper joint: "FIRTH HALL & POND / FRANKLIN SQ[E] / N-YORK".

2002.07

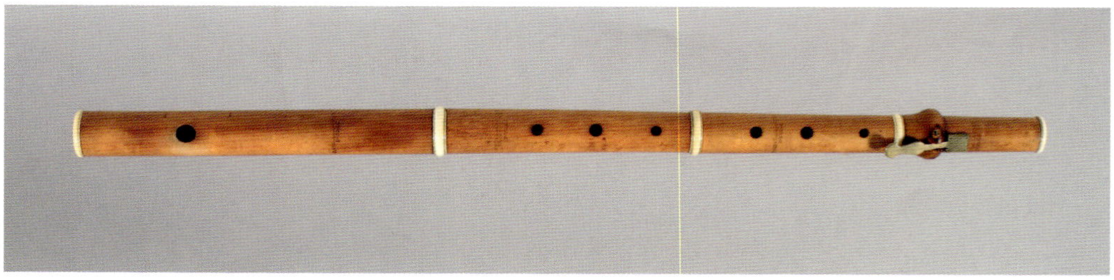

1-key flute, John Firth, William Hall, and Sylvanus Pond, New York, ca. 1835.

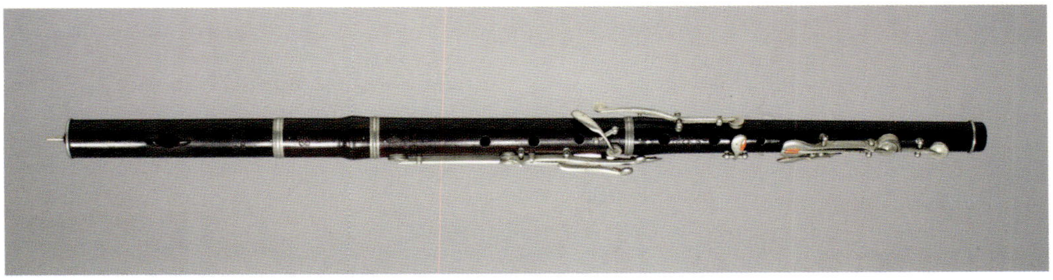

10-key flute, Franz Carl Kruspe, Erfurt, ca. 1890.

10-key flute, Franz Carl Kruspe, Erfurt, ca. 1890.

Stained cocus wood; nickel-silver ferrules. Four sections: head, barrel, l.h. joint, r.h. joint-foot. Oval embouchure with raised cups on either side, ten pillar-mounted nickel-silver keys. E-D trill, C^1 (R1), B♭ (LT), B♭ (R1), G♯, F (L4, long), F (short), D♯, C♯, C. Orange rollers on short F and C♯ key touches. L=665.

Stamped on head: "CKRUSPE / ERFURT"; barrel: "CK (initials on wings of butterfly) / C"; l.h. joint, r.h. joint-foot: "CK (initials on wings of butterfly) / CKRUPSE / ERFURT / C".

2002.08

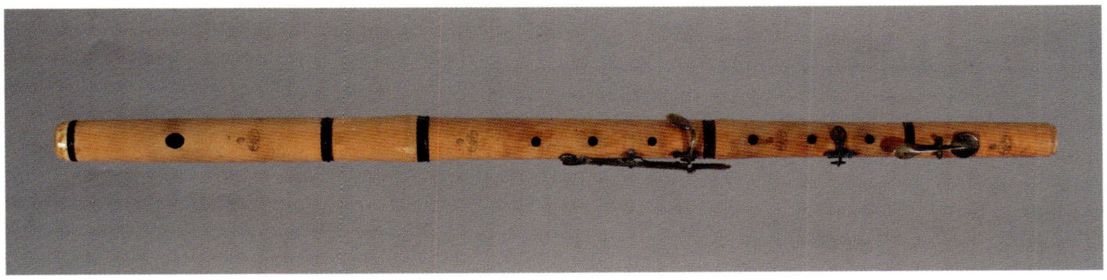

5-key flute, Denis Noblet ainé, La Couture, ca. 1860.

5-key flute, Denis Noblet ainé, La Couture, ca. 1860.

Boxwood; horn ferrules. Five sections: head, barrel, l.h. joint, r.h. joint, foot. Oval embouchure, five pillar-mounted nickel-silver keys. C^1 (R1), B♭ (LT), G♯, F, D♯. L=620.

Stamped on head, l.h. joint, r.h. joint, foot: "(face in the sun) / D. Noblet (cursive) / AINÉ / (star) (in an oval)".

Rousselet and Watel 2012, 130.

2002.20

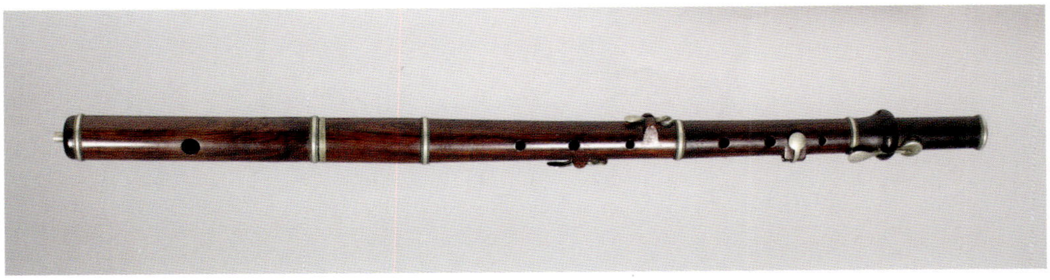

4-key flute, William Hall & Son, New York, ca. 1860.

4-key flute, William Hall & Son, New York, ca. 1860.

Rosewood; nickel-silver ferrules. Five sections: head, barrel, l.h. joint, r.h. joint, foot. Rosewood cap, nickel-silver screw-cork indicator, metal lined head, metal lined barrel. Oval embouchure, four pillar-mounted nickel-silver keys. B♭ (LT), G♯, F, D♯. L=610.

Stamped on head, r.h. joint: "WILLIAM HALL & SON / BROADWAY / NEW-YORK"; barrel: "WILLIAM HALL & SON / NEW-YORK"; l.h. joint: "WILLIAM HALL & SON / BROADWAY / NEW-YORK / GERMAN SILVER".

2002.21

8-key flute, Abel Siccama, London, Siccama system, ca. 1860.

Rosewood; nickel-silver ferrules. Four sections: head, barrel, body, foot. Rosewood cap with nickel-silver screw-cork indicator, metal lined head, four finger holes. Oval embouchure, eight pillar-mounted nickel-silver keys. C[1] (R1), B♭, G♯, F (L4, long), F (short), D♯, C♯, C; two pillar-mounted plateau keys for L3 and R3. Touches for C♯ and C are overlapping, key heads are pewter plugs. Serial no. 775. L=645.

Stamped on barrel, upper part of body: "(crown) / SICCAMA. / PATENTEE. / LONDON. / 775"; foot: "(crown) / SICCAMA. / LONDON."

Probably made by John Hudson, London.

Waterhouse 1993, 185; Bigio 2011, 96.

2002.22

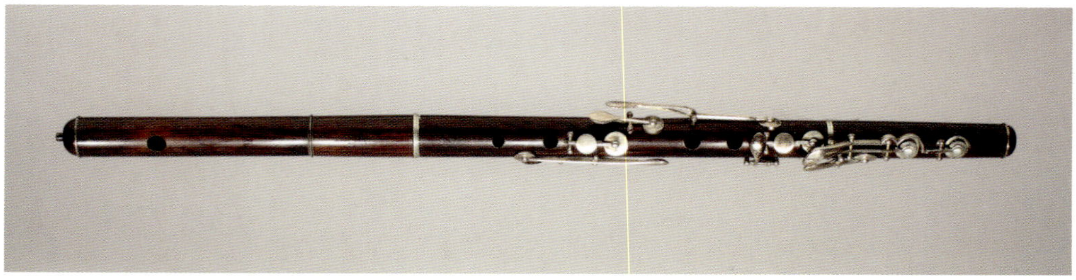

8-key flute, Abel Siccama, London, Siccama system, ca. 1860.

5-key flute, Jean Winnen, Paris, ca. 1840.

Ebony; ivory ferrules; single beading. Four sections: head, l.h. joint, r.h. joint, foot. Oval embouchure, five pillar-mounted silver keys on silver plates, flat, round, and oval key heads. Three l.h. joints. C[1], B♭, G♯, F, D♯. L=632; L of three unnumbered l.h. joints or corps de rechange=175, 170, 162.

Stamped on head, l.h. joint, r.h. joint: "(face in sun) / VIENNEN / CADET / A PARIS (curved)".

Rousselet and Watel 2012, 182, 184.

2002.24

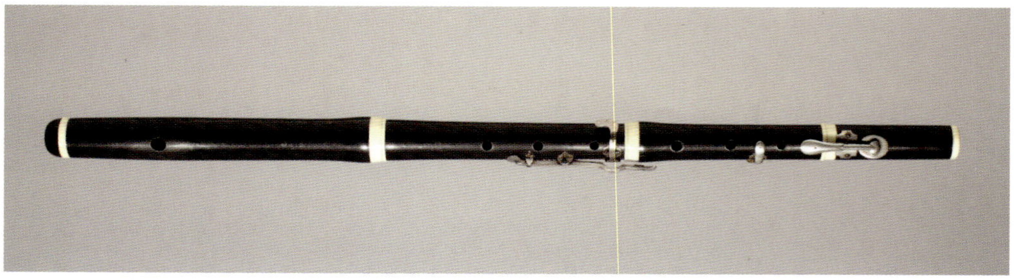

5-key flute, Jean Winnen, Paris, ca. 1840.

1-key flute in F, John Firth, William Hall, and Sylvanus Pond, New York, ca. 1840.

Boxwood; boxwood ferrules; single beading. Four sections: head, upper joint, lower joint, foot. Oval embouchure, one ring-mounted brass key, flat, round key head. D♯. L=520.

Stamped on head, lower joint, foot: "FIRTH HALL & POND / N-YORK"; upper joint: "FIRTH HALL & POND / FRANKLIN SQ[E] / N-YORK / F".

2002.25

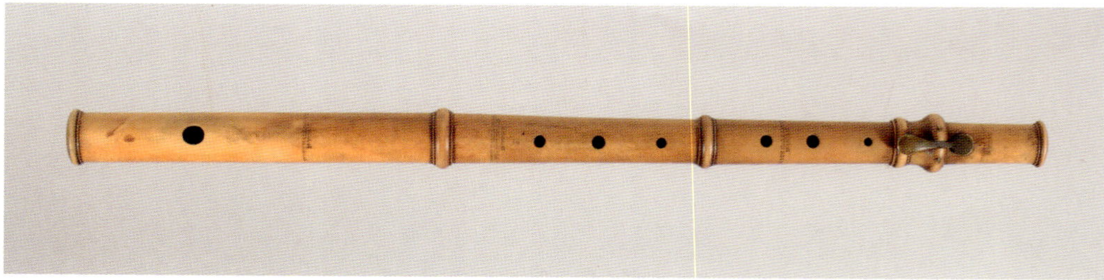

1-key flute in F, John Firth, William Hall, and Sylvanus Pond, New York, ca. 1840.

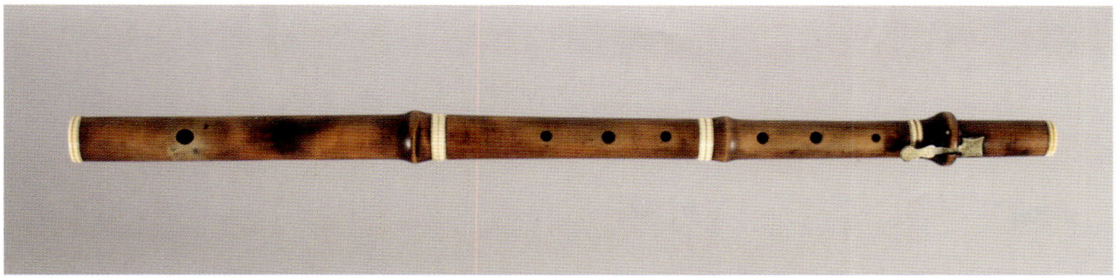

1-key flute, Chabrier Peloubet, New York, ca. 1840.

1-key flute, Chabrier Peloubet, New York, ca. 1840.

Stained boxwood; ivory ferrules; single beading; dark lines. Four sections: head, upper joint, lower joint, foot. Oval embouchure, one ring-mounted brass key, square key head. Ornamental rings on lower section of head, upper section of lower joint. D♯. L=600.

Stamped on upper joint: "C.PELOUBET / NEW-YORK"; foot: "C.PELOUBET / NEW-YORK / FACTORY IN / BLOOMFLD NJ".

2002.27

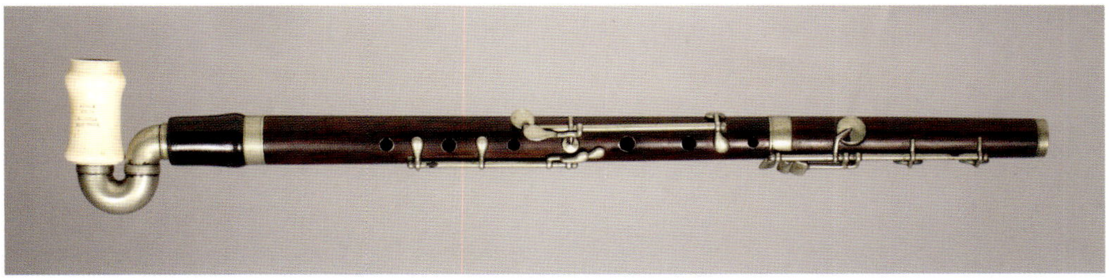

8-key flute, John Pfaff, Philadelphia, ca. 1865.

8-key flute, John Pfaff, Philadelphia, ca. 1865.

Stained cocus wood; nickel-silver ferrules. Five sections: ivory head (right-angled with embouchure hole on top for playing vertically), crook (nickel-silver), barrel, body, foot. Oval embouchure, eight nickel-silver pillar-mounted keys, flat, round key heads, thumb hole. C^1 (duplicate lever, R1), B♭ (duplicate lever, R1), G♯, F (L4, long), F (short), D♯, C♯, C. L=625.

Stamped on head: "J.PFAFF / PHIL^A. / PATENTED / NOV.29.64."

Pfaff's 1864 U.S. patent (no. 45,270) is for a fife with ridges around the embouchure hole on the head joint for easily adjusting the embouchure. Pfaff's design of a flute with a mouthpiece placed at a right angle was to avoid "the distortion of arms, fingers, and neck required in playing upon flutes of the ordinary construction" and patented on April 14, 1857 (no. 17,054). The incorrect date stamp on the head may have been due to Pfaff's forgetfulness.

Waterhouse 1993, 301; Dullat 2010b, 103, 200.

2002.29

8-key flute, Charles Christman, New York, ca. 1845.

Rosewood; nickel-silver ferrules. Five sections: head, barrel, l.h. joint, r.h. joint, foot. Rosewood cap, rosewood screw-cork indicator, metal lined head, barrel with metal tenon for tuning. Oval embouchure, eight block-mounted nickel-silver keys, salt-spoon key heads, missing ferrule at end of foot. C^1, B♭, G♯, F (long), F (short), D♯, C♯, C. The C♯ and C keys have overlapping touches, key heads are pewter plugs. L=673.

Stamped on head, barrel, l.h. joint, r.h. joint: "(unicorn head) / C. G. CHRISTMAN / 404 / PEARL ST. / NEW-YORK"; foot: "C. G CHRISTMAN / 404 / PEARL ST. / NEW-YORK / (unicorn head)".

See Eliason (2001).

2002.34

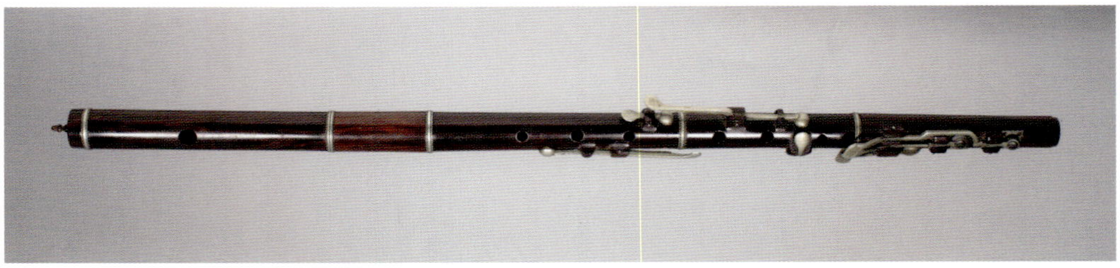

8-key flute, Charles Christman, New York, ca. 1845.

1-key flute, Georg Heinrich Scherer, Butzbach, ca. 1750.

Ivory; ivory ferrules; multiple beading. Four sections: head, upper joint, lower joint, foot. Oval embouchure, one ring-mounted silver key, square key head. D♯. In case. L=650.

Stamped on head, upper joint, lower joint, foot: "(two dots) / SCHERER / (striding lion)".

2002.35

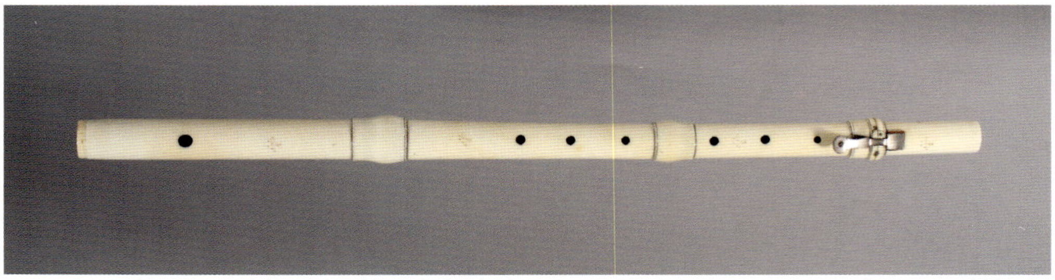

1-key flute, Georg Heinrich Scherer, Butzbach, ca. 1750.

6-key flute, Clair Godfroy ainé, Paris, ca. 1830.

Stained cocus wood; silver ferrules; single beading. Five sections: head, barrel, l.h. joint, r.h. joint, foot. Rosewood cap, silver screw-cork indicator. Oval embouchure, six pillar-mounted silver keys on silver oval and half-plates, round, flat key heads. C^1, B♭, G♯, F (long), F (short), D♯. L=620.

Stamped on head; r.h. joint: "(portrait head) / CLAIR / Godfroy ainé / A PARIS (in oval) / CG (monogram)"; l.h. joint: "(portrait head) / CLAIR / Godfroy ainé / A PARIS (in oval) / CG (monogram) // CG (monogram)"; foot: "CLAIR / Godfroy ainé / A PARIS (in oval)".

2002.40

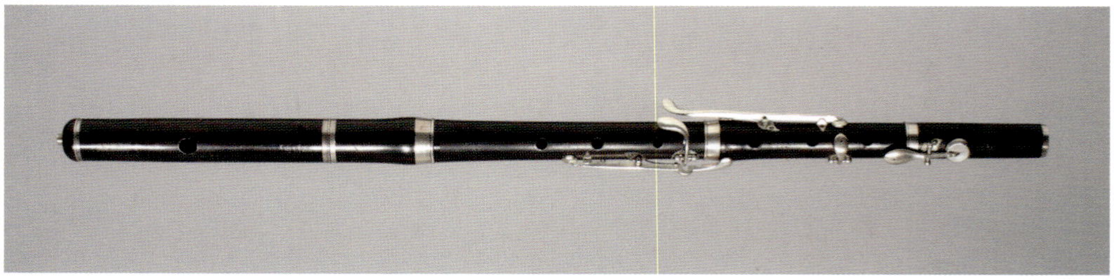

6-key flute, Clair Godfroy ainé, Paris, ca. 1830.

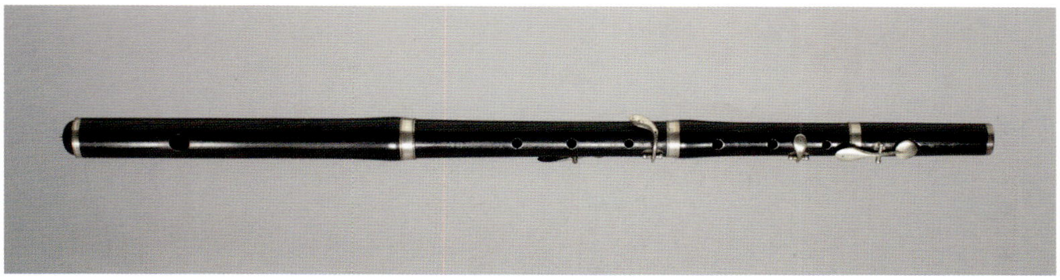

1-key flute, Jean-Louis Tulou, Paris, ca. 1840.

1-key flute, Jean-Louis Tulou, Paris, ca. 1840.

Ebony; silver ferrules; single beading. Four sections: head, l.h. joint, r.h. joint, foot. Ebony cap, silver screw-cork indicator, cracked head. Oval embouchure, four pillar-mounted silver keys on oval plates, round, flat key heads. B♭, G♯, F, D♯. L=610.

Stamped on head, l.h. joint, r.h. joint, foot: "(nightingale) / TULOU / PARIS".

2002.44

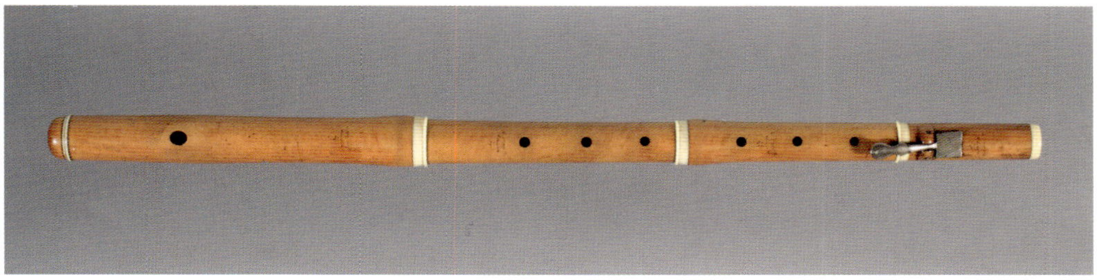

1-key flute, Louis Raver, Bordeaux, ca. 1860.

1-key flute, Louis Raver, Bordeaux, ca. 1860.

Boxwood; ivory ferrules; single beading. Four sections: head, upper joint, lower joint, foot. Oval embouchure, one block-mounted silver key. D♯. L=630.

Stamped on head, upper joint, lower joint: "(five-pointed star) / RAVER / A BORDEAUX (curved)"; foot: "(five-pointed star) / RAVER / A BORDEAUX".

2002.48

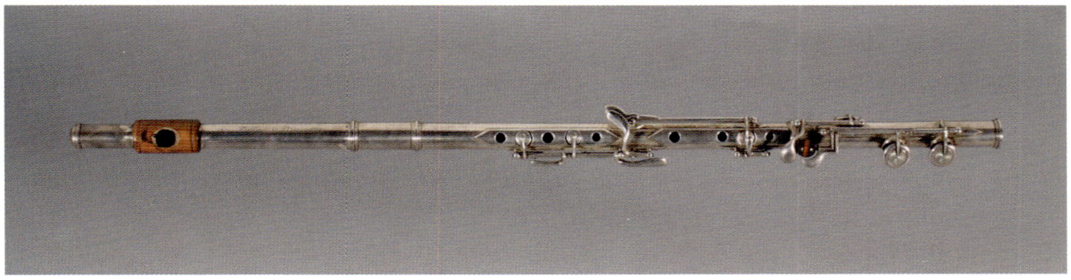

8-key flute, Charles Sax, Brussels, ca. 1840.

8-key flute, Charles Sax, Brussels, ca. 1840.

Silver; silver ferrules. Four sections: head, barrel, body, foot. Wooden barrel embouchure on head, altered oval hole, eight pillar-mounted silver keys, modern key heads. C^1, B♭, G♯, F (long), F (short), D♯, C♯, C. The finger holes and keys are mounted on a raised metal strap. Touch for C♯ key is a round, polished piece of wood. In cloth case. L=670.

Engraved on head: "C. Sax in Bruxelles (cursive)".

2002.52

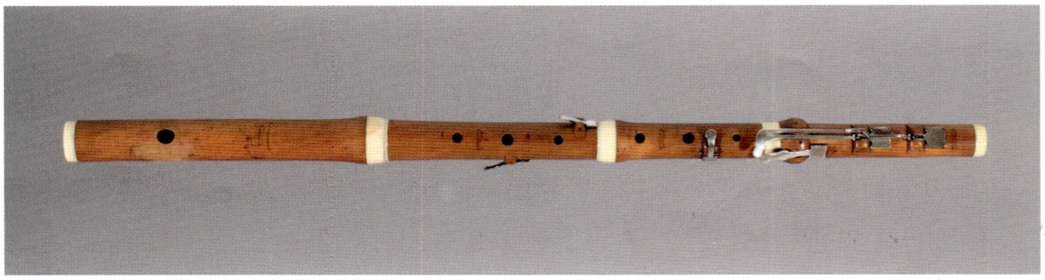

6-key flute, William Milhouse, London, ca. 1815.

6-key flute, William Milhouse, London, ca. 1815.

Boxwood; ivory ferrules; single beading. Four sections: head, l.h. joint, r.h. joint, foot. Oval embouchure, six block-mounted silver keys, square key heads. B♭, G♯, F, D♯, C♯, C. The C lever vaults over the C♯ key head. L=663.

Stamped on head: "W MILHOUSE / LONDON / 337 OXFORD ST^{T}"; l.h joint: "WMILHOUSE / LONDON / 6"; r.h. joint, foot: "WMILHOUSE / LONDON".

2002.53

12-key flute, Theodore Berteling, New York, ca. 1900.

Stained African black wood; nickel-silver ferrules. Four sections: head, barrel, l.h. joint, r.h. joint-foot. Oval and partially rectangular embouchure, thirteen pillar-mounted nickel-silver keys, modern key heads. E-D trill, B-C trill, C[1], B♭ (L3), B♭ (R1), G♯, F (long), F (short), D♯, C♯, C, B (long, L4). Case includes an extra unstamped ivory head. L=700; L=710 (with ivory head).

Barrel, owner's mark on nickel-silver oval: "Giacomo Sforza. (cursive)"; l.h. joint: on nickel-silver plate: "BERTELING / NEW . YORK".

"Berteling's Concert Flutes" (1893).

2002.70

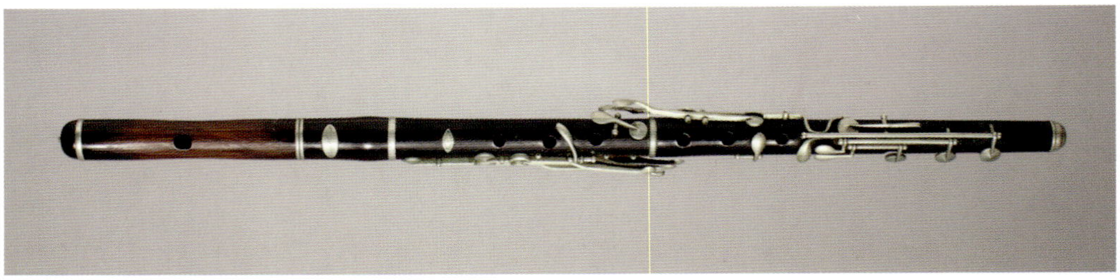

12-key flute, Theodore Berteling, New York, ca. 1900.

1-key flute in F (third flute), D'Almaine & Co., London, ca. 1830.

Boxwood; single and double beading. Four sections: head, upper joint, lower joint, foot. Oval embouchure, one ring-mounted brass key, square key head. Warped body. D♯. L=500.

Stamped on head: "(Prince of Wales feathers) / D'ALMAINE & C^{O}. / LATE / GOULDING & D'ALMAINE (curved) / SOHO SQUARE / LONDON / 3"; upper joint, lower joint, foot: "(Prince of Wales feathers) / D'ALMAINE & C^{O}."

2002.76

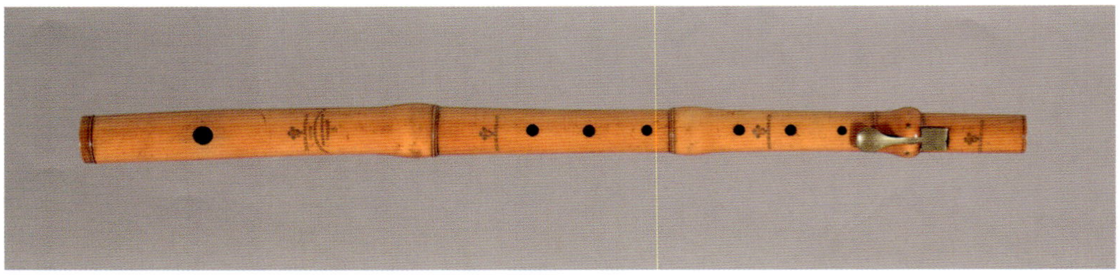

1-key flute in F (third flute), D'Almaine & Co., London, ca. 1830.

Boehm-system flute, attributed to George Rudall and John Mitchell Rose, London, ca. 1850-1870.

Silver; barrel embouchure; oval hole. Four sections: head, barrel, body, foot. Boehm-system, plateau key (L1), ring keys for L2, L3, R1, R2, R3, low C. L=660.

Engraving on head: "Rudall & Rose London (cursive)".

This flute is not typical of Rudall & Rose metal flutes in the shape of its G♯ key, unusually shaped key heads, a red stone set at the end of the head, and unique engraved name on the head. It also includes a silver-plated screwdriver, a grease box with a decorated silver lid, and a silver rod with swabs at both ends. It may have been a specially made flute by Rudall and Rose for a wealthy client, or could possibly be a very well-made counterfeit.

Bigio 2011, 110-113.

2002.77

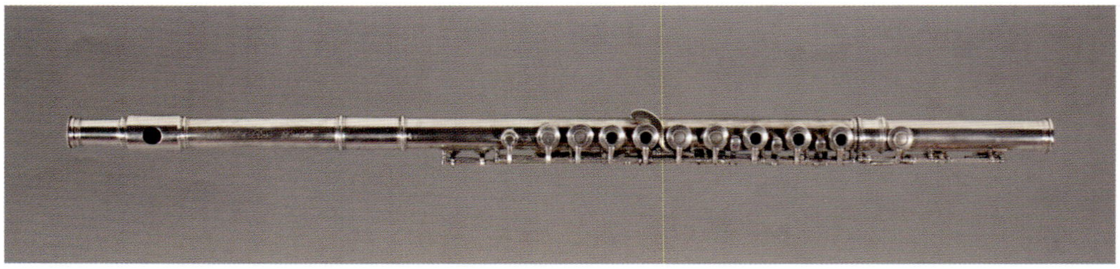

Boehm-system flute, attributed to George Rudall and John Mitchell Rose, London, ca. 1850-1870.

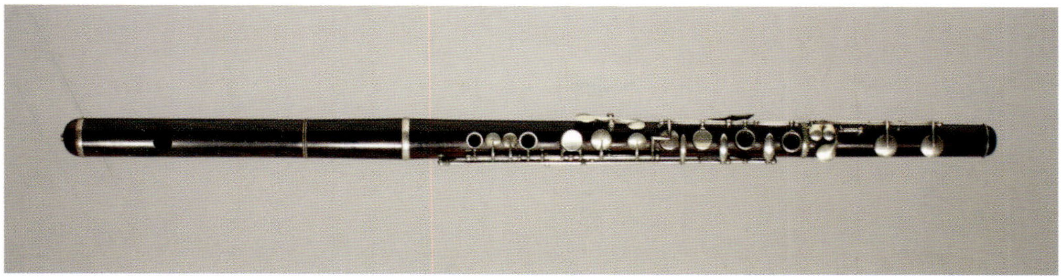

Clinton-system flute, Clinton and Co., London, Equisonant model, ca. 1860.

Clinton-system flute, Clinton and Co., London, Equisonant model, ca. 1860.

Stained cocus wood; nickel-silver ferrules. Four sections: head, barrel, body, foot. Cocus wood cap, nickel-silver screw-cork indicator. Oval embouchure, Clinton key system, nickel-silver pillar-mounted keys. Rings for L1, L2, R2, R3; plateau keys for L3 and R1. In case. Serial no. 653. L=650.

Stamped on barrel: "CLINTON & CO. / LONDON"; body: "No. 653 / CLINTON & C^{O}. / EQUISONANT / 35 PERCY ST. / BEDFORD S^{QRE}. / LONDON".

Bigio 2011, 98-100.

2002.78

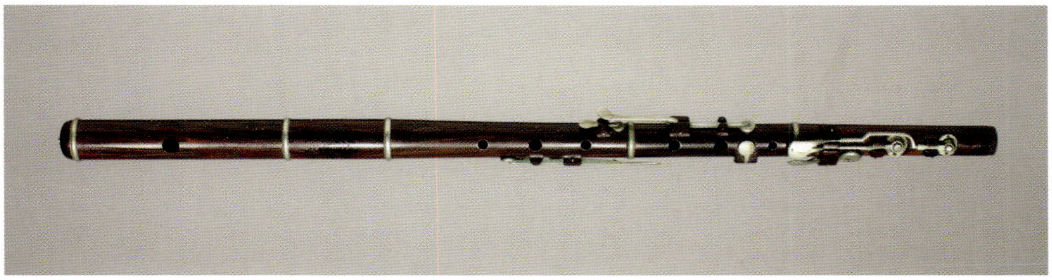

8-key flute, William A. Pond and Co., New York, ca. 1870.

8-key flute, William A. Pond and Co., New York, ca. 1870.

Stained cocus wood; nickel-silver ferrules. Five sections: head, barrel, l.h. joint, r.h. joint, foot. Cocus wood cap, nickel-silver screw-cork indicator, head cracked, head has metal liner, missing ferrule at end of foot. Oval embouchure, eight block-mounted nickel-silver keys, pewter plug key heads for C♯ and C. C^{1}, B♭, G♯, F (long), F (short), D♯, C♯, C. The touches of the C♯ and C are interlocking. L=665

Stamped on barrel, l.h. joint: "POND & Co. / NEW YORK".

2002.85

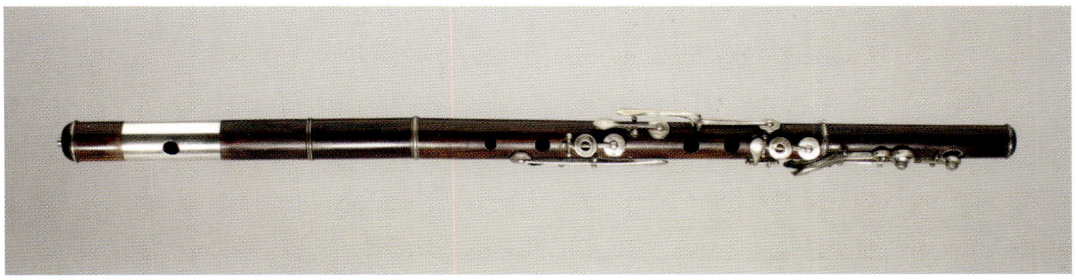

8-key flute, William Hall and Son, New York, Siccama system, ca. 1850.

8-key flute, William Hall and Son, New York, Siccama system, ca. 1850.

Stained cocus wood; nickel-silver ferrules. Four sections: head, barrel, body, foot. Cocus wood cap, nickel-silver screw-cork indicator. Oval embouchure, nickel-silver embouchure plate, eight pillar-mounted nickel-silver keys with an open ring plateau key for L3 and L4, pewter plug key heads for C♯ and C. The touches of the C♯ and C are overlapping, four finger holes are very large. C^{1}, B♭, G♯, F (long), F (short), D♯, C♯, C. Serial no. 6009. L=645.

Stamped on head, foot: "WILLIAM HALL / & SON / NEW YORK"; body: "WILLIAM HALL & SON / 547 N. BROADWAY / NEW YORK / 6009".

2002.86

4-key flute, Armand Ferry, Mirecourt, ca. 1845.

Stained cocus wood; nickel-silver ferrules. Four sections: head, barrel, body, foot. Cocus wood cap, nickel-silver screw-cork indicator, ferrule missing at end of foot. Oval embouchure, four pillar-mounted nickel-silver keys, round, flat key heads. C[1], G♯, F, D♯. L=620.

Stamped on head: "AF (monogram) / A. FERRY / BRÉVETÉ / AF (monogram)".

Rousselet and Watel 2012, 70.

2002.87

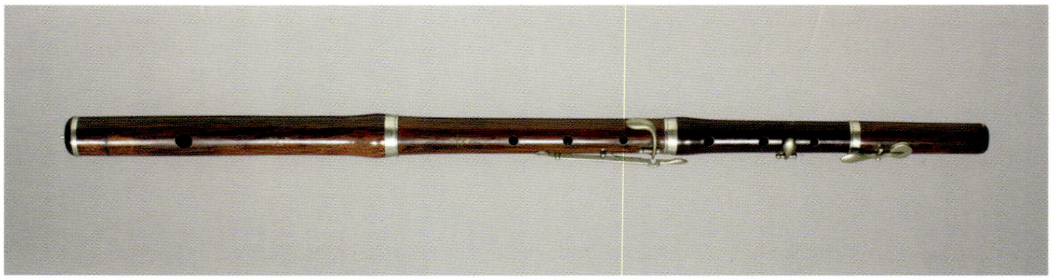

4-key flute, Armand Ferry, Mirecourt, ca. 1845.

1-key flute, Jacques Delusse, Paris, ca. 1775.

Boxwood; ivory ferrules; single beading. Four sections: head, upper joint, lower joint, foot. Oval embouchure, one ring-mounted silver key, square key head. D♯. L=633.

Stamped on head: "(crown) / C / DELUSSE / APARIS / (sun)"; upper joint: "(crown) / C / DELUSSE / (star) / I"; lower joint, foot: "(crown) / C / DELUSSE / (star)".

Giannini 1993, 39 (d).

2002.88

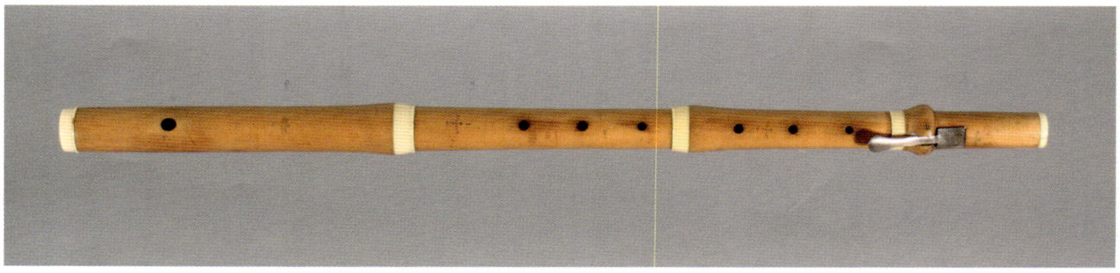

1-key flute, Jacques Delusse, Paris, ca. 1775.

1-key flute in F, Frédéric Guillaume Adler, Paris, ca. 1830.

Stained boxwood; ivory ferrules; single beading. Four sections: head, upper joint, lower joint, foot. Ivory insert at end of cap head. Oval embouchure, one block-mounted silver key, square key head. D♯. L=440.

Stamped on head, lower joint, foot: "(crown) / ADLER / A PARIS"; upper joint: "(crown) / ADLER / A PARIS / 2".

2002.95

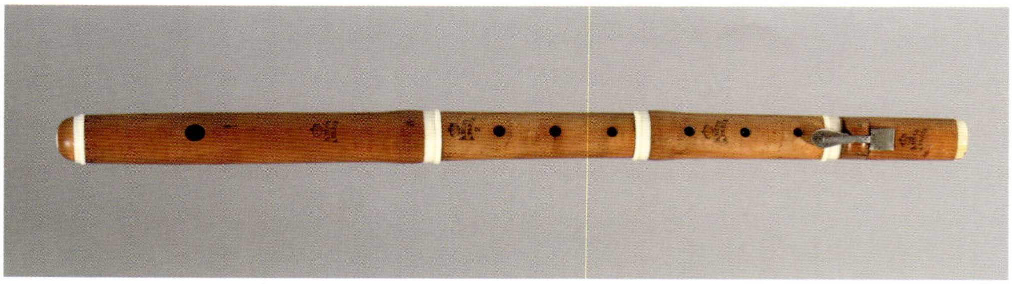

1-key flute in F, Frédéric Guillaume Adler, Paris, ca. 1830.

10-key flute, Gustav Ludwig Penzel and Gustav Frederick Penzel, New York, ca. 1895.

Stained cocus wood; nickel-silver ferrules; multiple rings. Four sections: head, barrel, l.h. joint, r.h. joint-foot. Oval embouchure, ten pillar-mounted nickel-silver keys, modern key heads, cracked head. E-D trill, C[1], B♭ (R1), G♯, F (long), F (short), D♯, C♯, C, B (long, L4). L=710.

Stamped on l.h. joint: "PENZEL / & BRO. / NEW YORK".

2002.96

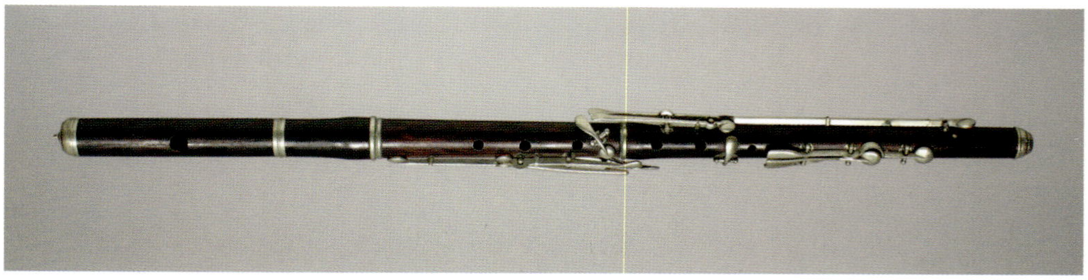

10-key flute, Gustav Ludwig Penzel and Gustav Frederick Penzel, New York, ca. 1895.

1-key flute, Thomas Cahusac senior, London, ca. 1790.

1-key flute, Thomas Cahusac senior, London, ca. 1790.

Boxwood; boxwood ferrules; double beading. Four sections: head, upper joint, lower joint, foot. Oval embouchure, one silver key, square key head, missing head cap. D♯. L=595.

Stamped on head: "CAHUSAC / 196 / STRAND / LONDON (curved)"; upper joint, lower joint, foot: "CAHUSAC / LONDON (curved)".

2003.02

12-key flute, Augustin Rorarius, Vienna, ca. 1840.

12-key flute, Augustin Rorarius, Vienna, ca. 1840.

Boxwood; ivory ferrules; multiple beading. Four sections: head, barrel, l.h. joint, r.h. joint-foot. Boxwood cap with ivory screw-cork indicator, one horn ferrule with one beading, metal-lined head, cracked head. Semi-rectangular embouchure, twelve block and ring-mounted brass keys, all with pewter plug key heads. C^1 (short, L2), B♭ (LT), B♭ (R1), G♯, F (long), F (short), D♯, C♯ (brass roller), C (brass roller), B (R4), B♭ (L4), A (L4). L=785.

Stamped on head, barrel, l.h. joint: "(crown) / RORARIUS / WIEN / (star)"; r.h. joint: "(crown) / RORARIUS / WIEN / (star) // (crown) / RORARIUS / WIEN / (star)".

2003.15

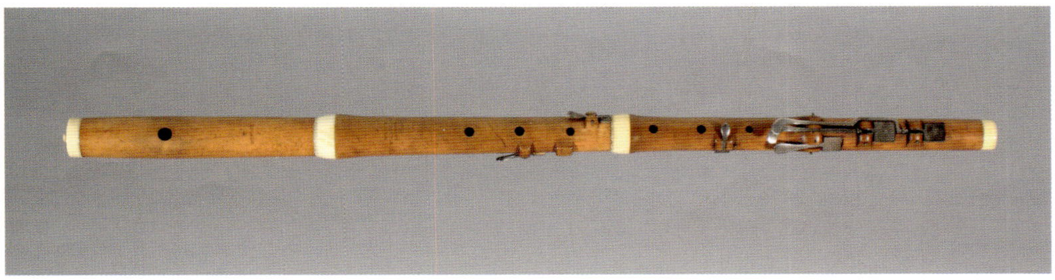

6-key flute, Monzani and Co., London, ca. 1820.

6-key flute, Monzani and Co., London, ca. 1820.

Boxwood; ivory ferrules; single beading. Three sections: head, l.h. joint, r.h. joint-foot. Ivory cap, ivory screw-cork indicator. Oval embouchure, six block and ring-mounted silver keys, square key heads. B♭, G♯, F, D♯, C♯, C. C key touch is overlapping the C♯ touch; the shaft of the C goes around the key head of the C♯. Unused block for a C^1 key that was not added. L=670.

Stamped on head: "(crown) / MONZANI / 1"; l.h. joint: "(crown) / MONZANI / N°2 4 DOVER ST / LONDON"; r.h. joint-foot: "(crown) / MONZANI" // "(crown) / MONZANI / LONDON".

2003.19

5-key flute, Charles Sax, Brussels, ca. 1840.

Cocus wood; nickel-silver ferrules; single beading. Five sections: head, barrel, l.h. joint, r.h. joint, foot. Cocus wood cap, nickel-silver screw-cork indicator. Oval embouchure, five pillar-mounted nickel-silver keys on oval plates, round, flat key heads. C^1, B♭, G♯, F, D♯. In case. L=543.

Stamped on l.h. joint, r.h. joint, foot: "(star) / SAX / BRUXELLES / (star)".

2003.21

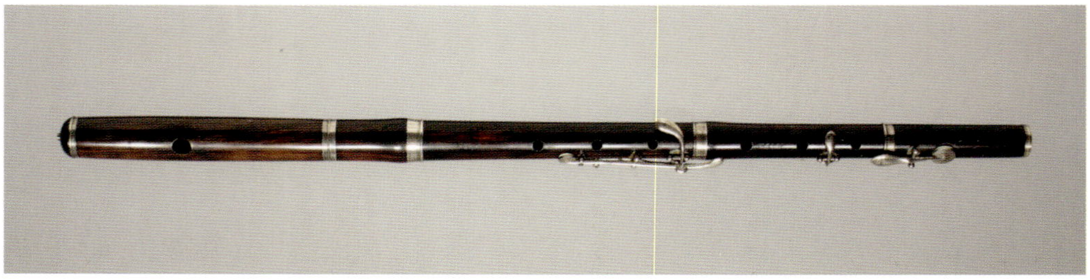

5-key flute, Charles Sax, Brussels, ca. 1840.

1-key flute, John George Klemm and Frederick August Klemm, Philadelphia, probably Markneukirchen, ca. 1850.

Dark stained cocus wood; ivory ferrules; single beading. Four sections: head, upper joint, lower joint, foot. Oval embouchure, one ring-mounted nickel-silver key; round key head. D♯. L=595.

Stamped on upper joint: "KLEMM & BRO. / PHILA".

This flute was likely imported from the Klemm family in Markneukirchen.

2003.22

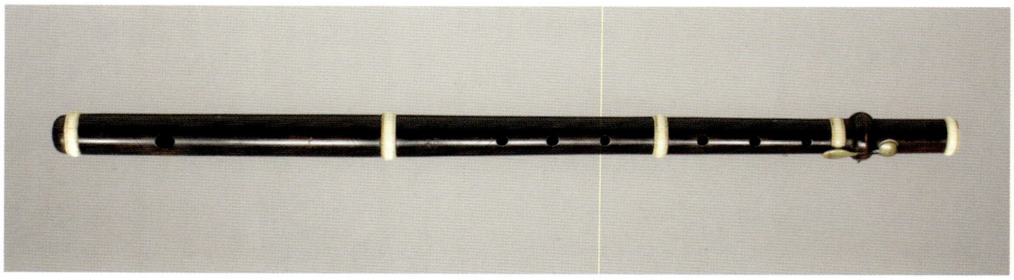

1-key flute, John George Klemm and Frederick August Klemm, Philadelphia, probably Markneukirchen, ca. 1850.

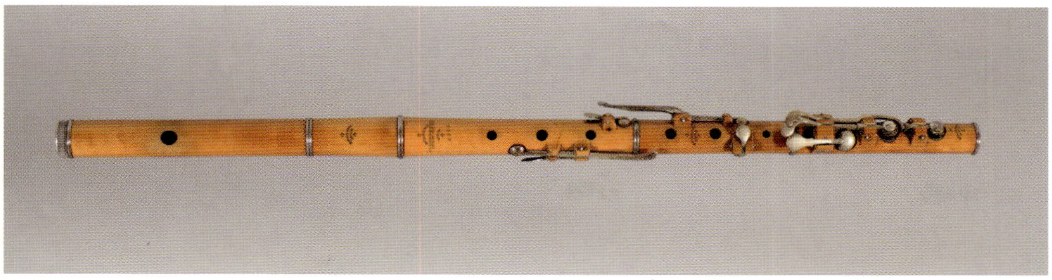

8-key flute, George Rudall and John Mitchell Rose, London, ca. 1847, shown also in ca. 1847 case with printed notice.

8-key flute, George Rudall and John Mitchell Rose, London, ca. 1847.

Boxwood; thin silver ferrules. Four sections: head, barrel, l.h. joint, r.h. joint-foot. Oval embouchure, eight block-mounted silver keys, salt-spoon key heads, leather covered pewter plug key heads for C♯ and C. Silver head cap decorated with serrations. C^1, B♭, G♯, F (long), F (short), D♯, C♯, C. In case. Metal grease case, round, black, wooden top. Serial no. 5209. L=670.

Raised words and an embossed design on top of silver head cap: "RUDALL & ROSE / (Royal Coat of Arms of the United Kingdom) / DIEU (in scroll) / ET MON (in scroll) / DROIT (in scroll) / PATENTEES"; stamped on barrel: "(four-petalled flower) / RUDALL & ROSE (curved) / LONDON"; l.h. joint: "(four-petalled flower) / RUDALL & ROSE (curved) / No 1 TAVISTOCK STREET / COVENT GARDEN / LONDON (curved) / (four-petalled flower) / 5209"; r.h. joint-foot: "(four-petalled flower) / RUDALL & ROSE (curved) / LONDON (curved) / (four-petalled flower) // (four-petalled flower) / RUDALL & ROSE (curved) / LONDON (curved) / (four-petalled flower)".

Rudall and Rose's British patent for a headjoint in 1832 (no. 6,338) links the end cap or crown and a tuning slide. When the end cap is rotated, it simultaneously extends the barrel with the use of a four-start screw, moving the cork stopper to a predetermined position, altering the pitch.

Original case with printed notice inside: "Rudall & Rose, having discovered that Flutes are offered for Sale, bearing their names & address, which have not been made by them, are determined to guard the Public against such imposition, by not sending out in future any Flute from their Manufactory, without This Notice affixed to the top of the Case. George Rudall, John M. Rose (signatures). Flute no. 5209."

Bigio 2011, 70-71.

2003.23

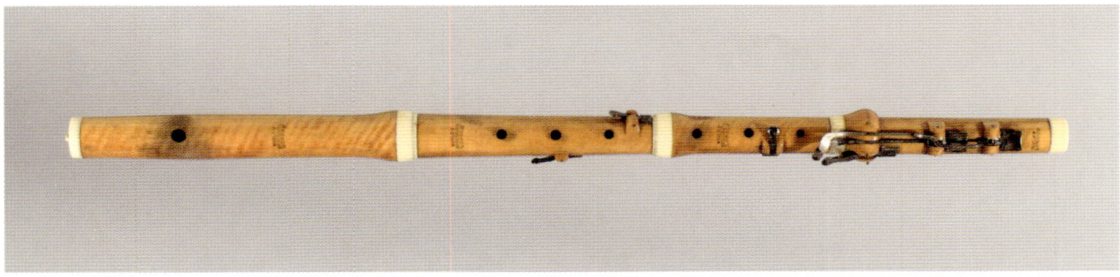

6-key flute, Charles Wigley, London, ca. 1805.

6-key flute, Charles Wigley, London, ca. 1805.

Boxwood; ivory ferrules; multiple beading. Four sections: head, l.h. joint, r.h. joint, foot. Ivory cap, ivory screw-cork indicator. Oval embouchure, six block and ring-mounted silver keys, square key heads. The C key lever is over the C♯ key head. B♭, G♯, F, D♯, C♯, C. In wooden case. L=670.

Stamped on head, l.h. joint, r.h. joint: "WIGLEY / 204STRAND / LONDON"; foot: "WIGLEY / LONDON".

2003.26

Boehm-system flute, Auguste Bonneville, Paris, ca. 1884.

Silver; silver pillar-mounted Boehm-system keys. Four sections: head, barrel, body, foot. Semi-rectangular embouchure, open holes, L2, L3, R1, R2, R3, low C. Serial no. 1728. L=679.

Stamped on head: "AB (monogram) / A^{TE} / BONNEVILLE / PARIS (gothic)"; barrel: "AB (monogram)"; body: "AB (monogram) / BONNEVILLE / PARIS (gothic) / 1728".

Lenski and Ventske (1992), 208; Giannini 1993, 163 (b).

2003.29

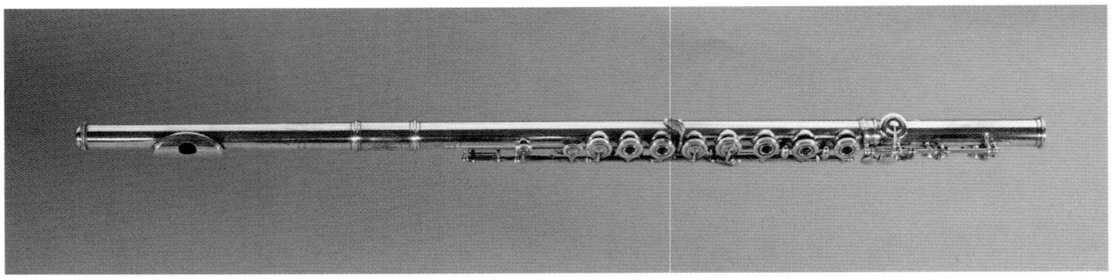

Boehm-system flute, Auguste Bonneville, Paris, ca. 1884.

11-key flute, Rampone, Milan, ca. 1900.

Stained cocus wood; nickel-silver ferrules. Four sections: head, barrel, l.h. joint, r.h. joint-foot. Cocus wood cap, nickel-silver screw-cork indicator. Oval embouchure, eleven pillar-mounted nickel-silver keys, modern key heads. E-D trill, C^1 (short), C^1 (R1), G♯, B♭ (R1), F (long), F (short), D♯, C♯ (with roller), C, B (L4). In case. L=710.

Stamped on head, barrel, l.h. joint, r.h. joint-foot: "(tuning fork with leaves) / RAMPONE / MILANO / BREVETTATO / ER (monogram)".

2003.33

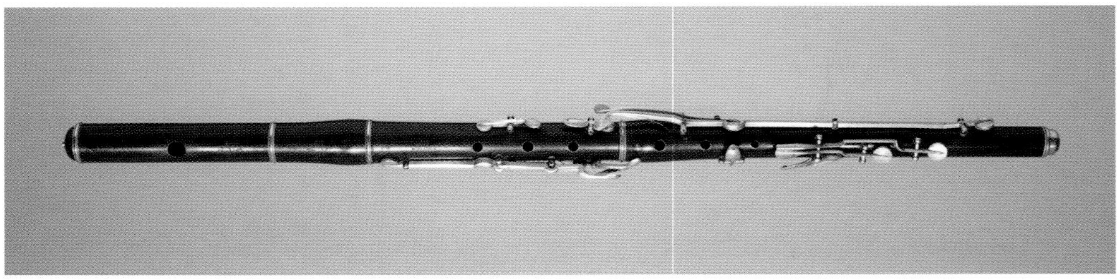

11-key flute, Rampone, Milan, ca. 1900.

10-key flute, Lecomte Co., Paris; Calvo, Buenos Aires, ca. 1890.

Silver; silver ferrules; triple beading. Four sections: head, barrel, body, foot. Oval embouchure, ten pillar-mounted silver keys, modern key heads. E-D trill, C^1 (R1), B♭ (R1), G♯, F♯, F (long), F (short), D♯, C♯ (roller), C. In case. L=665.

Stamped on head: "LECOMTE CO. (curved)/ CALVO / BUENOS - AIRES (curved)".

2003.38

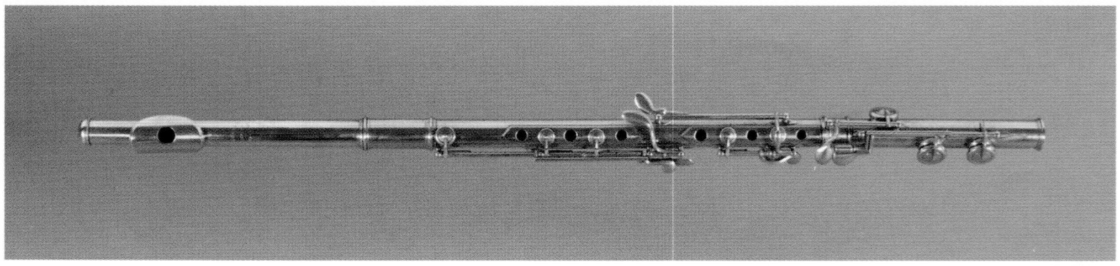

10-key flute, Lecomte Co., Paris; Calvo, Buenos Aires, ca. 1890.

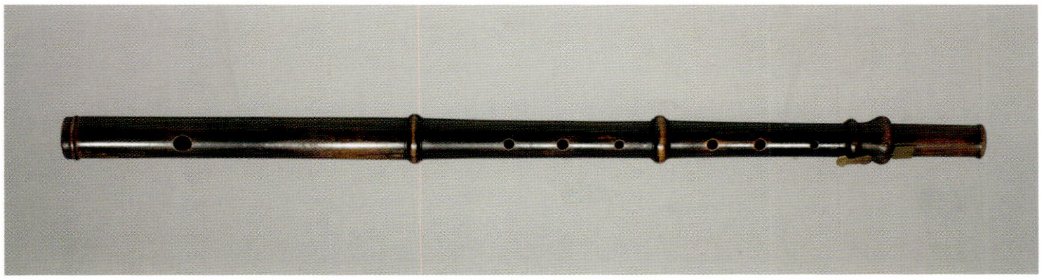

1-key flute, Johann Friedrich Floth, Dresden, ca. 1805.

1-key flute, Johann Friedrich Floth, Dresden, ca. 1805.

Boxwood; boxwood ferrules; single beading. Four sections: head, upper joint, lower joint, foot. Oval embouchure, one ring-mounted brass key, square key head. D♯. L=660.

Stamped on head: "(crossed swords) / FLOTH".

2003.39

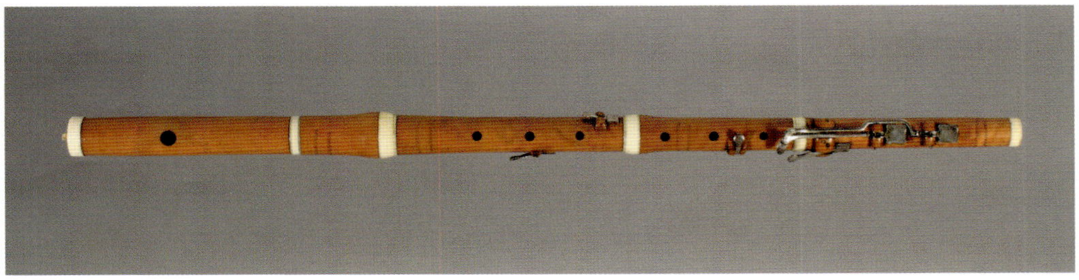

6-key flute, Paine and Hopkins, London, ca. 1830.

6-key flute, Paine and Hopkins, London, ca. 1830.

Boxwood; ivory ferrules; single beading; black lines. Five sections: head, barrel, l.h. joint, r.h. joint, foot. Ivory cap, ivory screw-cork indicator. Slightly oval embouchure, six block-mounted silver keys, square key heads. B♭, G♯, F, D♯, C♯, C. L=675.

Stamped on barrel, l.h. joint, r.h. joint, foot: "PAINE&HOPKINS / N° 69 CORNHILL".

2003.40

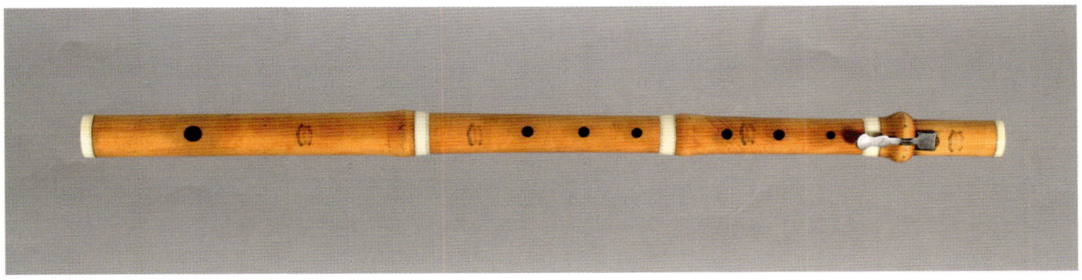

1-key flute, John Meacham, Horace Meacham, and Sylvanus Pond, Albany, New York, ca. 1830.

1-key flute, John Meacham, Horace Meacham, and Sylvanus Pond, Albany, New York, ca. 1830.

Boxwood; ivory ferrules; single beading. Four sections: head, upper joint, lower joint, foot. Oval embouchure, one ring-mounted silver key, square key head. D♯. L=600.

Stamped on head, upper joint, lower joint, foot: "MEACHAM (curved) / & POND / ALBANY (curved)".

Eliason (1979-1980), 67-68, 73.

2003.46

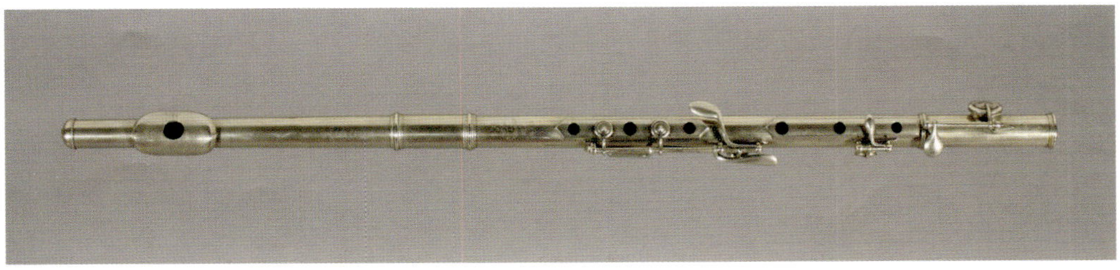

5-key flute, P. Gautié et Cie, Toulouse, ca. 1890.

5-key flute, P. Gautié et Cie, Toulouse, ca. 1890.

Silver-plated; silver-plated ferrules. Four sections: head, barrel, body, foot. Oval embouchure on lip plate, five pillar-mounted silver keys, modern key heads. C^1, B♭, G♯, F, D♯. Serial no. 4858. L=600.

Stamped on head, foot: "G (lyre) D / P. GAUTIÉ & CIE / (star) / TOULOUSE (in an oval of dashes) / (star)"; body: "G (lyre) D / P. GAUTIÉ & CIE / (star) / TOULOUSE (in an oval of dashes) / (star) / 4858".

Rousselet and Watel 2012, 76.

2003.47

1-key flute, William Whiteley, Utica, New York, ca. 1830.

Boxwood; ivory ferrules; single beading. Four sections: head, upper joint, lower joint, foot. Ivory cap, ivory screw-cork indicator. Oval embouchure, one ring-mounted silver key, square key head. D♯. In case. L=602.

Stamped on head, upper joint: "WHITELEY / UTICA".

2003.51

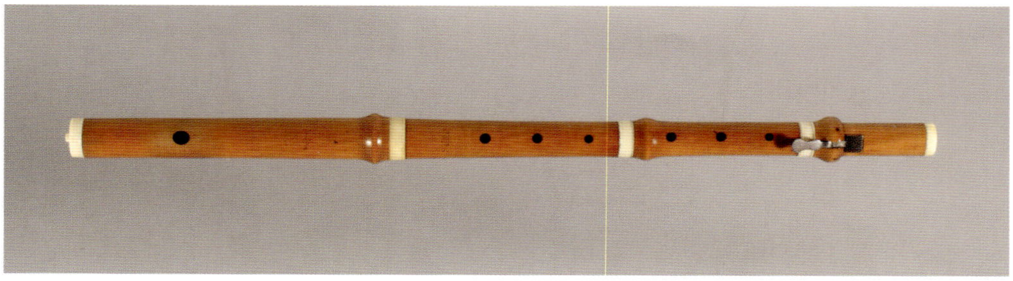

1-key flute, William Whiteley, Utica, New York, ca. 1830.

1-key flute, William Cotton, London, ca. 1770.

Ivory; ivory ferrules. Four sections: head, barrel, body, foot. Round embouchure, one silver ring-mounted key, square key head. D♯. L=650.

Stamped on head, barrel, body, foot: "COTTON".

Lasocki (2010), 103-104.

2003.52

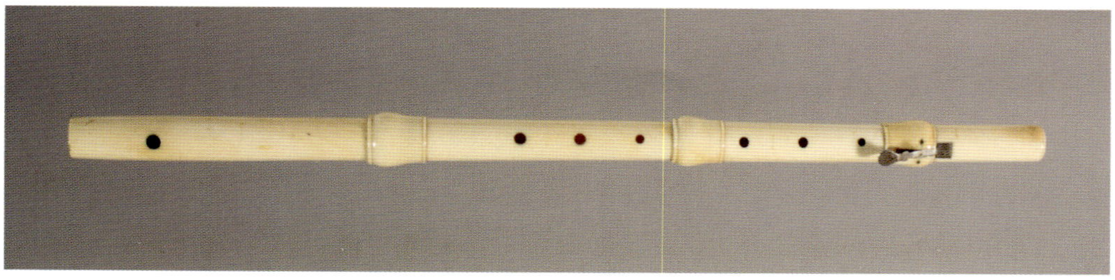

1-key flute, William Cotton, London, ca. 1770.

Boehm-system flute, Julius Max Bürger, Carl Rinkel successor, Strasbourg, ca. 1930.

Rosewood; nickel-silver ferrules. Three sections: head, body, foot. Rosewood cap, nickel-silver screw-cork indicator. Slightly rectangular embouchure, Boehm-system pillar-mounted nickel-silver keys, modern key heads. Ring keys for L2, R1-R3, low C. In case. L=677.

Stamped on body: "(angel playing trumpet) / J.M. BÜRGER / C.RINKEL-NACHF / STRASBURG / (flower)".

2003.53

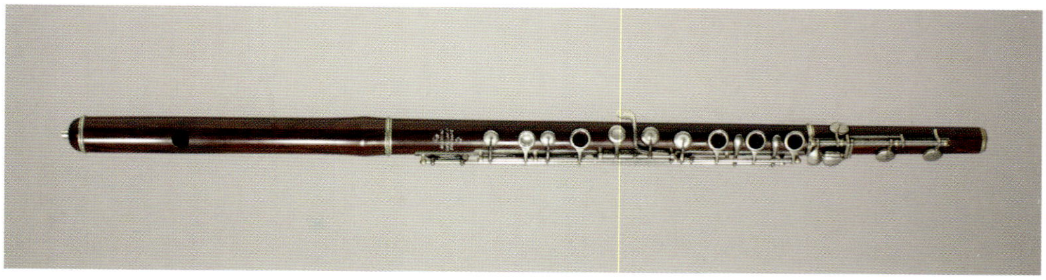

Boehm-system flute, Julius Max Bürger, Carl Rinkel successor, Strasbourg, ca. 1930.

9-key flute, Ubaldo Luvoni, Milan, ca. 1835.

Boxwood; ivory ferrules; single beading. Four sections: head (cracked), barrel, l.h. joint, r.h. joint-foot. Square embouchure, nine block and ring-mounted brass keys, all pewter plug key heads. C[1], B♭, G♯, F (long), F (short), D♯, C♯ (roller), C (roller), B (L4). In case. L=790.

Stamped on head, barrel, l.h. joint: "(faun) / U. LUVONI / (star) / A MILANO"; r.h. joint-foot: "U. LUVONI / (star) / A MILANO".

2003.54

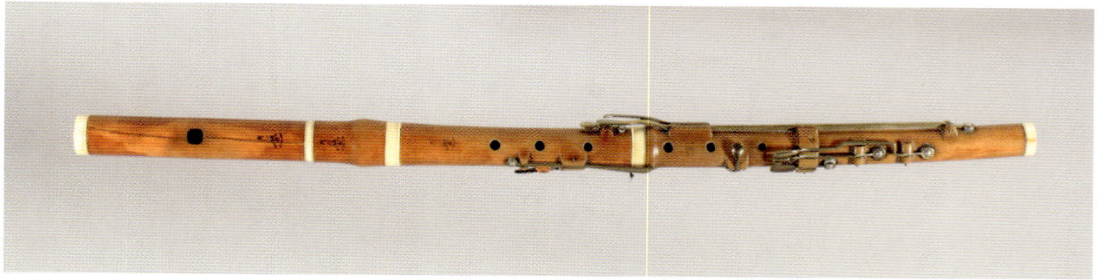

9-key flute, Ubaldo Luvoni, Milan, ca. 1835.

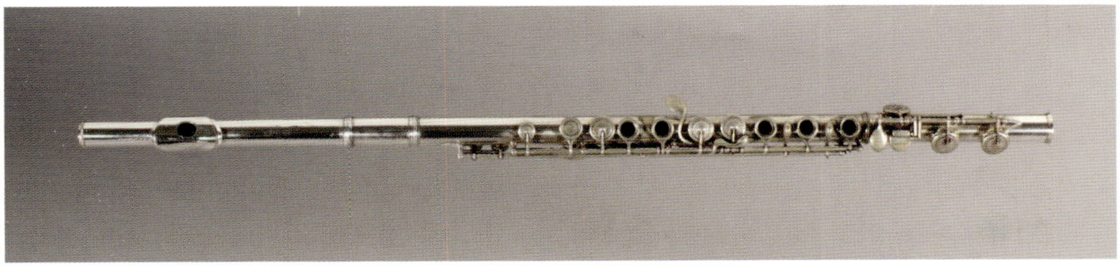

Boehm-system flute, Thomas Isidor Lot, La Couture, ca. 1875.

Boehm-system flute, Thomas Isidor Lot, La Couture, ca. 1875.

Silver-plated; silver-plated ferrules; multiple beading. Four sections: head, barrel, body, foot. Oval embouchure on lip plate, Boehm-system, ring keys for L2, L3, R1-R3, low C. In case. L=670.

Stamped on head: "(lyre) / I. LOT / IL (monogram)".

2003.58

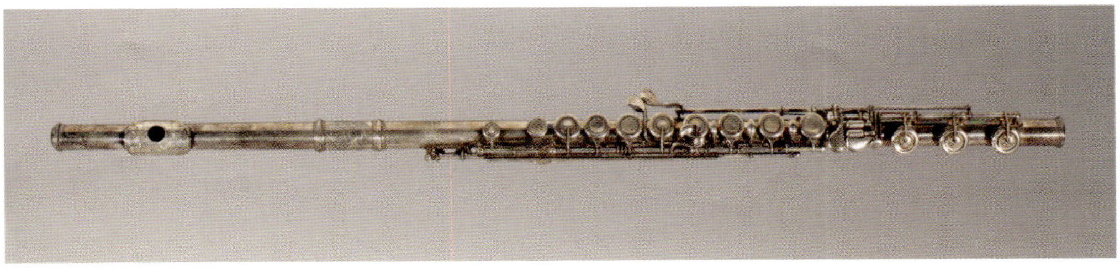

Boehm-system flute, Rampone, Milan, ca. 1910.

Boehm-system flute, Rampone, Milan, ca. 1910.

Silver; silver ferrules; multiple beading. Four sections: head, barrel, body, foot. Oval embouchure on engraved lip plate, Boehm-system, plateau keys, low B (R4), low B (L4). L=715.

Stamped on barrel: "RAMPONE MILANO (in a circle) / 2205 (in the center of the circle) / BREVETTATO (all within a floral engraving)".

2003.59

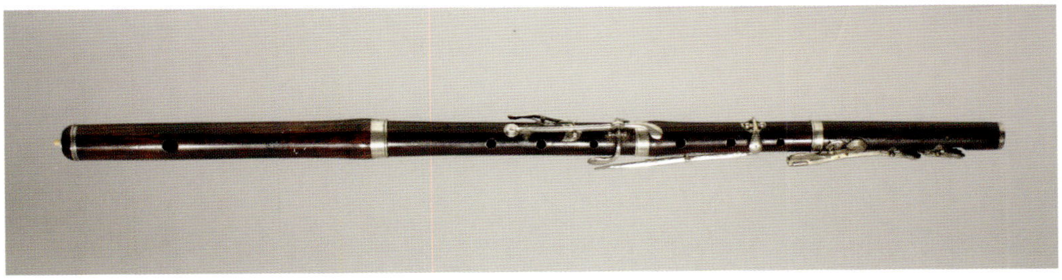

8-key flute (left-hand), Pierre Godfroy, Paris, ca. 1835.

8-key flute (left-hand), Pierre Godfroy, Paris, ca. 1835.

Stained cocus wood; nickel-silver ferrules. Four sections: head, r.h. joint, l.h. joint, foot. Oval embouchure, eight pillar-mounted nickel-silver keys on oval plates. C^1, B♭, G♯, F (long), F (short), D♯, C♯, C. L=670.

Stamped on head, r.h. joint: "(sun) / PIERRE / Godfroy jeune / A PARIS (in an oval of points) / PG (monogram)"; l.h. joint, foot: "PIERRE / Godfroy jeune / A PARIS (in an oval of points)".

Rousselet and Watel 2012, 81.

2003.60

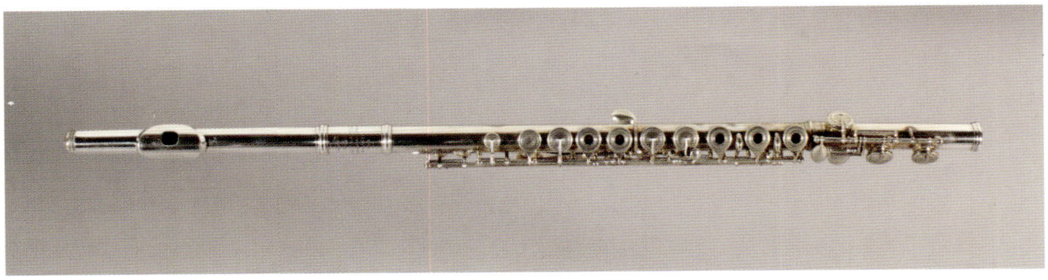

Boehm-system flute, Fils de P. Gautié, Toulouse, ca. 1920.

Boehm-system flute, Fils de P. Gautié, Toulouse, ca. 1920.

Silver-plated; silver-plated ferrules; multiple beading. Four sections: head, l.h. joint, r.h. joint, foot. Rectangular embouchure on lip plate, Boehm-system, ring keys for L2, L3, R1, R2, R3, low C. In case. L=673.

Stamped on barrel: "SGDG (in banner) / G (lyre) F / Fils de P. GAUTIÉ / médaille speciale certificate (cursive) / TOULOUSE / PARIS / (star)".

Rousselet and Watel 2012, 76.

2003.65

4-key flute, John Geib, Adam Geib, and William Geib, New York, ca. 1820.

Stained boxwood; ivory ferrules; multiple beading; dark lines. Five sections: head, barrel, l.h. joint, r.h. joint, foot. Ivory cap, ivory screw-cork indicator. Oval embouchure, four block and ring-mounted brass keys, salt-spoon key heads. B♭, G♯, F, D♯. L=610.

Stamped on head, r.h. joint, foot: "GEIB / 23 / MAIDEN LANE / LONDON".

An English imported flute.

2003.66

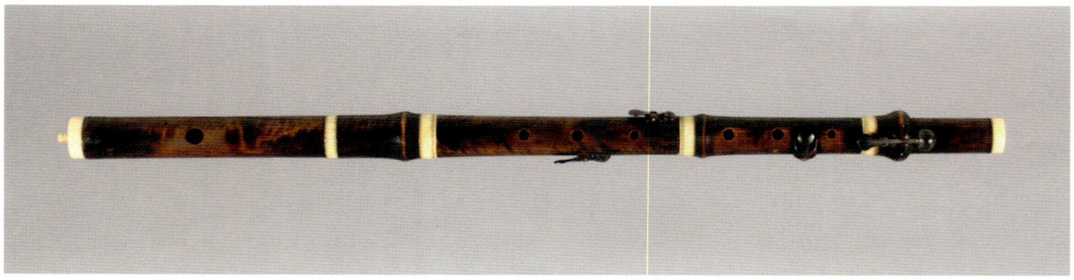

4-key flute, John Geib, Adam Geib, and William Geib, New York, ca. 1820.

4-key flute, Jérôme Thibouville-Lamy, Paris, ca. 1890.

Rosewood; nickel-silver ferrules. Five sections: head, barrel, l.h. joint, r.h. joint, foot. Oval embouchure, four pillar-mounted nickel-silver keys, flat, round key heads. B♭, G♯, F, D♯. L=612.

Stamped on head: "(lyre in aureole) / J.T.L. / (exhibition awards) / JÉRÔME / THIBOUVILLE / LAMY / PARIS / 69 / RÉAUMUR"; l.h. joint: "(lyre in aureole) / J.T.L. / PARIS / 69"; r.h. joint: "PARIS / 69 RÉAUMUR".

2003.67

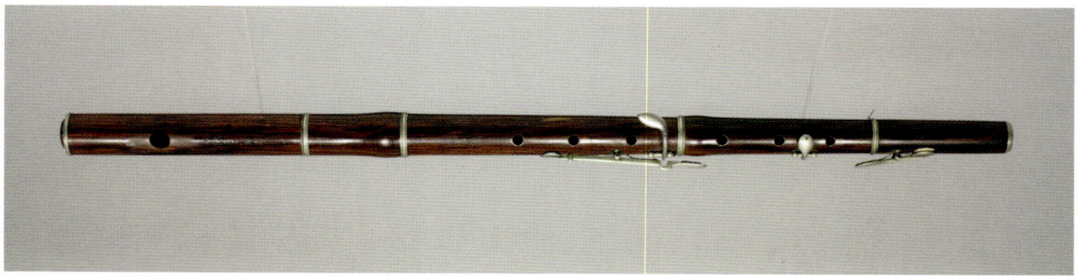

4-key flute, Jérôme Thibouville-Lamy, Paris, ca. 1890.

1-key flute in B♭, John Meacham, Horace Meacham, and Sylvanus Pond, Albany, New York, ca. 1830.

Boxwood; ivory ferrules; multiple beading. Three sections: head, l.h. joint, r.h. joint-foot. Oval embouchure, one ring-mounted key, with bulge cut straight above D♯ key. D♯. L=355.

Stamped on head: "PATENT // MEACHAM / & POND (curved) / ALBANY (curved)"; l.h. joint, r.h. joint-foot: "MEACHAM / & POND (curved) / ALBANY (curved)".

The word "Patent" may refer to the use of pewter plug keys for low C♯ and C on this firm's flutes.

Eliason (1979-1980), 67-68, 73.

2004.06

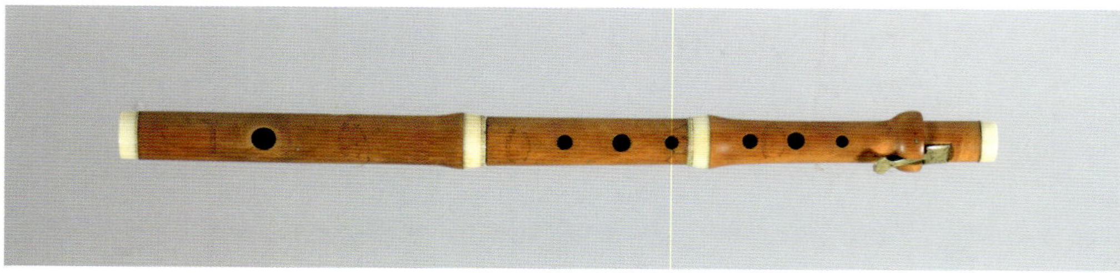

1-key flute in B♭, John Meacham, Horace Meacham, and Sylvanus Pond, Albany, New York, ca. 1830.

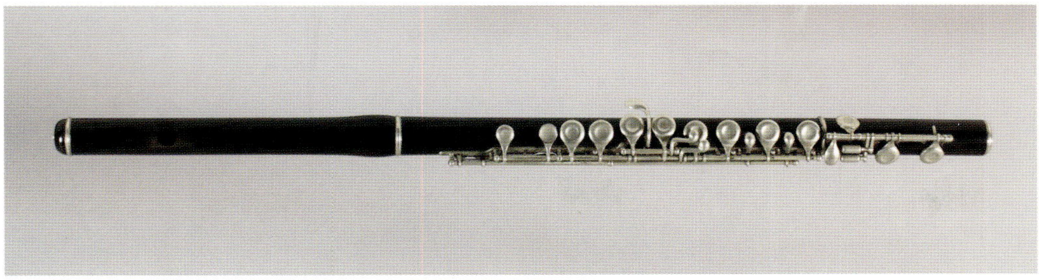

Boehm-system flute, Penzel-Müller Co., New York, ca. 1910.

Boehm-system flute, Penzel-Müller Co., New York, ca. 1910.

Stained African black wood; nickel-silver ferrules. Three sections: head, body, foot. Oval embouchure, Boehm-system, nickel-silver pillar-mounted plateau keys, to low C. In case. L=676.

Stamped on head, body: "(American eagle) / PENZEL / MÜLLER / NEW-YORK (in oval of dots)".

2004.07

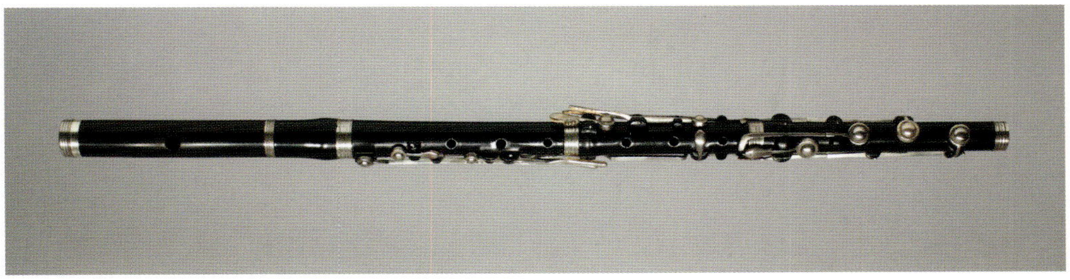

11-key flute, Niels Christensen Thorsen, Copenhagen, ca. 1830.

11-key flute, Niels Christensen Thorsen, Copenhagen, ca. 1830.

Ebony; silver ferrules; multiple grooves. Five sections: head, barrel, l.h. joint, r.h. joint, foot. Oval embouchure, ten block-mounted silver keys, all key heads have leather pads. E-D trill, D-C trill (L1), B♭, G♯, G♯ (RT), F (long), F (short), D♯, C♯, C (L4), B (RT). L=702.

Stamped on l.h. joint, r.h. joint: "(star) / THORSEN / (star)".

2004.09

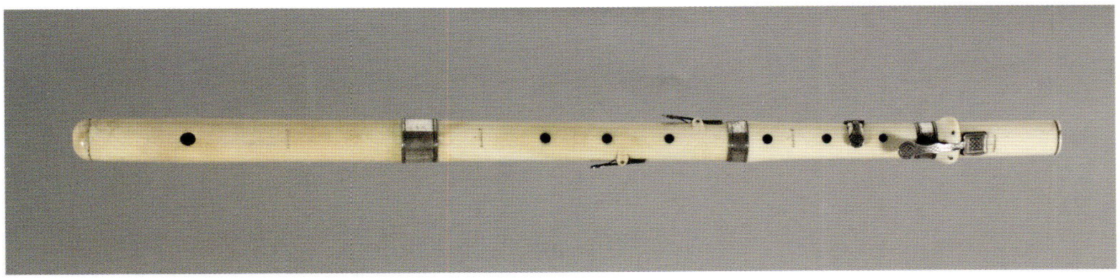

4-key flute, Jean-Baptiste Prudent Thierriot, Paris, ca. 1785.

4-key flute, Jean-Baptiste Prudent Thierriot, Paris, ca. 1785.

Ivory; large silver ferrules; two decorative lines. Four sections: head, l.h. joint, r.h. joint, foot. Oval embouchure, four block and ring-mounted silver keys, square key heads; all key touches, shanks, heads have checkerboard pattern. B♭, G♯, F, D♯. L=618.

Stamped on head, l.h. joint, r.h. joint, foot: "(fleur-de-lis) / PRUDENT".

Rousselet and Watel 2012, 144.

2004.12

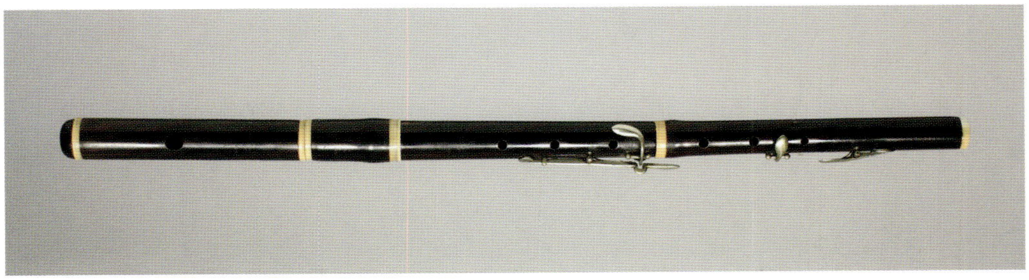

4-key flute, Gabriel Bühner and Jean Keller IV, Strasbourg, ca. 1820.

4-key flute, Gabriel Bühner and Jean Keller IV, Strasbourg, ca. 1820.

Stained African black wood; ivory ferrules; single beading. Four sections: head, barrel, l.h. joint, r.h. joint-foot. Oval embouchure, four pillar-mounted nickel-silver keys, flat, round key heads. C^1, G♯, F, D♯. In case. L=613.

Stamped on head, foot: "(angel trumpeter) / BÜHNER / & / KELLER / A STRASBOURG"; barrel: "(angel trumpeter) / BÜHNER / & / KELLER / A STRASBOURG / (angel trumpeter)"; l.h. joint: "BÜHNER / & / KELLER / A STRASBOURG / (angel trumpeter)".

2004.14

4-key flute, Claude Laurent, Paris, 1818.

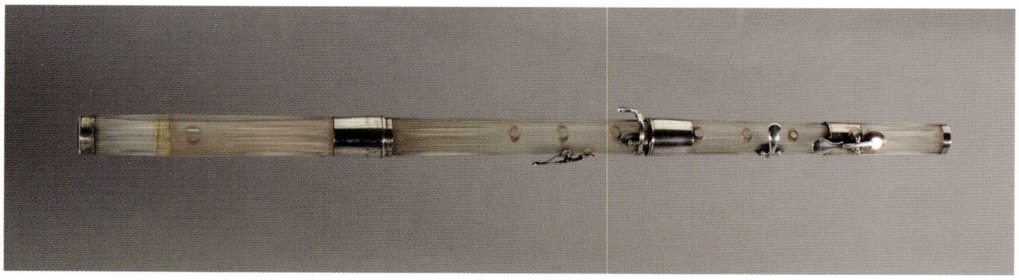

4-key flute, Claude Laurent, Paris, 1818.

Crystal glass with ribs; wide silver ferrules; beading. Four sections: head, l.h. joint, r.h. joint, foot. Tuning head may be pulled out its entire length and then latched. Oval embouchure, four pillar-mounted silver keys attached to oval plates, round key heads. B♭, G♯, F, D♯. In case. Dated 1818. L=622.

Engraved on large ferrule of l.h. joint: "LAURENT A PARIS / Brevete (cursive) 1818".

2004.15

6-key flute, William Milhouse, London, ca. 1820.

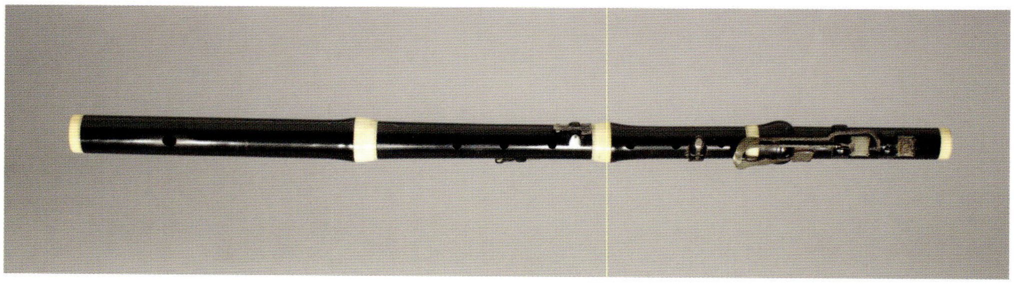

Ebony; ivory ferrules; single beading. Four sections: head, l.h. joint, r.h. joint, foot. Oval embouchure, six block and ring-mounted silver keys, square key heads. B♭, G♯, F, D♯, C, C♯. L of flute with four l.h. joints or corps de rechange=677 (stamped "4"), 670 (stamped "5"), 661 (stamped "6"), 662 (unnumbered, four block-mounted silver keys). In a two-tier wooden case.

Stamped on head: "W•MILHOUSE / LONDON / 337 OXFORD ST^{T}"; l.h. joint: "W•MILHOUSE / LONDON / 4"; r.h. joint, foot: "W•MILHOUSE / LONDON".

The original box has six spaces for all joints, lined with green felt, and two l.h. joints stamped "5" and "6." Inside the top of the case attached to green felt is the maker's label: "William Milhouse, / MUSICAL INSTRUMENT MANUFACTURER, To their Royal Highneſses the Dukes of Kent & Cumberland / No. 337 Oxford Street / Facing Great Portland Street, / London. Wholesale & for / Exportation / (United Kingdom coat of arms with lion, unicorn, bassoon, natural trumpet, tenor drum, banner) / Muſic Seller".

2004.16

6-key flute, William Milhouse, London, ca. 1820; the second image shows the flute in case; the third shows the maker's label.

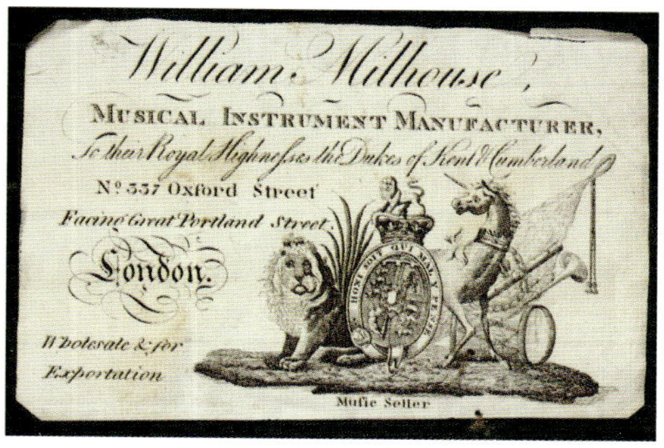

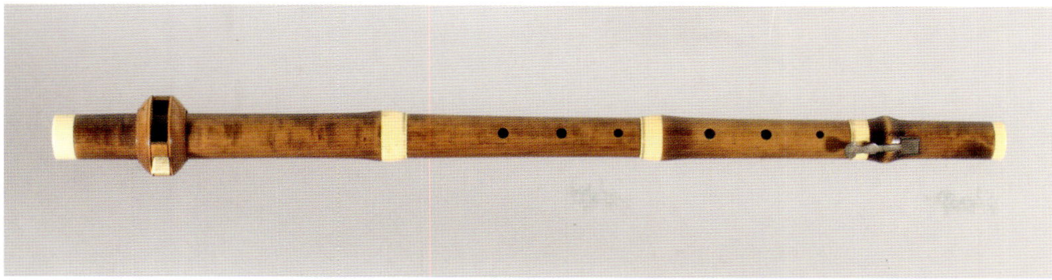

1-key flute, Haystrom, Great Britain, ca. 1770.

1-key flute, Haystrom, Great Britain, ca. 1770.

Boxwood; ivory ferrules; double dark lines. Four sections: head, l.h. joint, r.h. joint, foot. Large wooden circular ring with an adjustable knob and ivory mouthpiece or "cheater" may be attached over the embouchure hole. One ring-mounted silver key, square key head. The instrument is stored in a form-fitting case that resembles a book marked on the spine: "GERMAN / FLUTE / INSTRUMENT". D♯. L=610.

Stamped on head, l.h. joint, r.h. joint, foot: "HAYSTROM".

2004.17

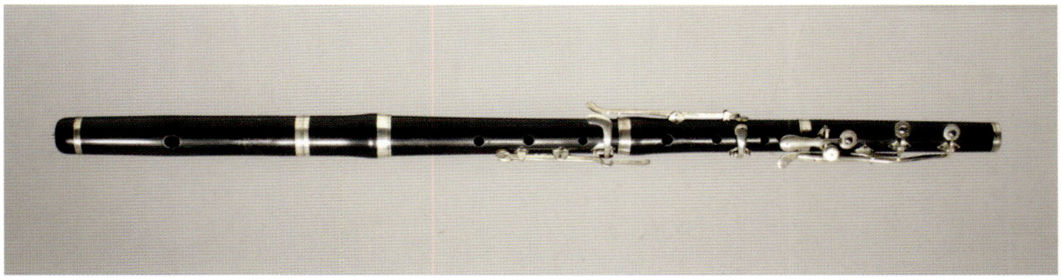

8-key flute, Jean Daniel Holtzapffel, Strasbourg, ca. 1820.

8-key flute, Jean Daniel Holtzapffel, Strasbourg, ca. 1820.

Ebony; silver ferrules; single beading. Five sections: head, barrel, l.h. joint, r.h. joint, foot. Oval embouchure, eight saddle and pillar-mounted nickel-silver keys on nickel-silver plates, round, flat key heads. C^1, B♭, G♯, F (long), F (short), D♯ (with adjusting screw), C♯, C. Adjustment screw on the C♯ and C keys. In case. L=673.

Stamped on head, barrel, l.h. joint, r.h. joint, foot: "(five-pointed star) / HOLTZAPFFEL / A Paris / (five-pointed star)".

2004.20

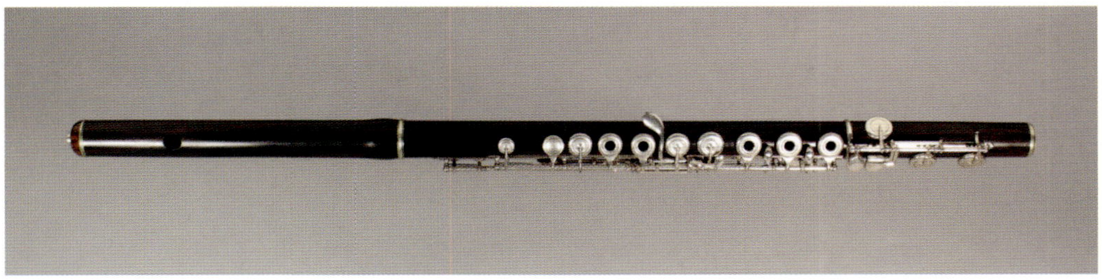

Boehm-system flute, Louis Lot, Paris, ca. 1883.

Boehm-system flute, Louis Lot, Paris, ca. 1883.

Stained rosewood; nickel-silver ferrules; double beading. Three sections: head, body, foot. Wooden cap, nickel-silver screw-cork indicator. Oval embouchure, Boehm-system, pillar-mounted mechanism, low C. Serial no. 3575. L=675.

Stamped on head: "L.L. / LOUIS - LOT / PARIS"; body: "L.L. / LOUIS - LOT / PARIS 3575 / BREVETÉ".

2005.05

8-key flute, Stephan Koch, Vienna, ca. 1825.

Ebony with silver tenons; ivory ferrules; single beading. Five sections: head, barrel, l.h. joint, r.h. joint, foot. Ivory cap, ivory screw-cork indicator. Semi-square embouchure, eight block and ring-mounted silver keys, all pewter plug key heads. C^1 (L2), B♭ (R1 or LT), G♯, F (long), F (short), D♯, C♯, C. The short and long F touches share the same key head. In case. L=712.

Stamped on barrel, l.h. joint, foot: "(Hapsburg eagle) / S.KOCH /WIEN".

2005.12

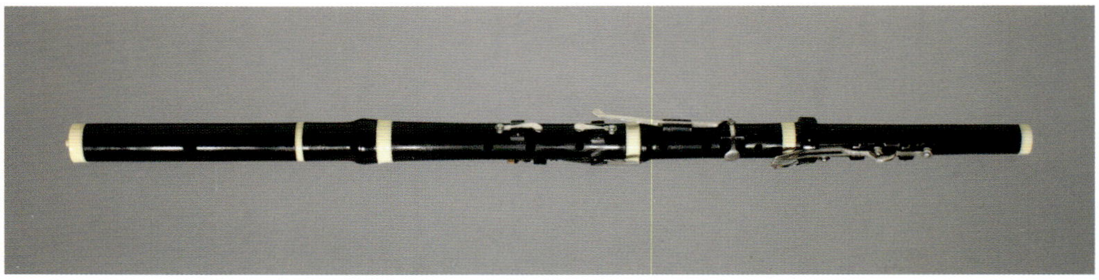

8-key flute, Stephan Koch, Vienna, ca. 1825.

11-key flute, Johann Ziegler, Vienna, ca. 1840.

Ebony; nickel-silver ferrules; decorated in blue checkered pattern on cap head and foot ferrules. Four sections: head, barrel, l.h. joint, r.h. joint-foot. Ivory head, nickel-silver cap, nickel-silver screw-cork indicator. Oval embouchure, eleven pillar-mounted nickel-silver keys, round key heads. The tone holes, head, barrel, and tenon are lined with metal, unstamped silver oval on barrel. E-D trill, C^1, B♭, B♭ (LT), G♯, F (long), F (short), D♯ (long, L4), D♯ (short), C♯ (roller), C (roller). In case. L=720.

Stamped on l.h. joint, r.h. joint-foot: "(Hapsburg eagle) / I.ZIEGLER / WIEN".

2005.13

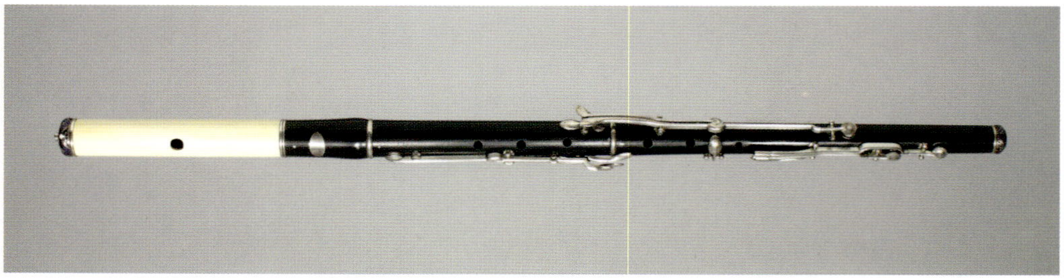

11-key flute, Johann Ziegler, Vienna, ca. 1840.

1-key flute, Johann Wolfgang Hoe, Hof, ca. 1770.

Boxwood; ivory ferrules; multiple beading. Four sections: head, upper joint, lower joint, foot. Oval embouchure, one ring-mounted brass key, square key head. D♯. L=634.

Stamped on head: "I.W. HOE / (star)".

A boxwood 1-key flute by Hoe is in the Miller Collection at the Library of Congress, no. DM977.

Seyfrit 1983, 181.

2005.18

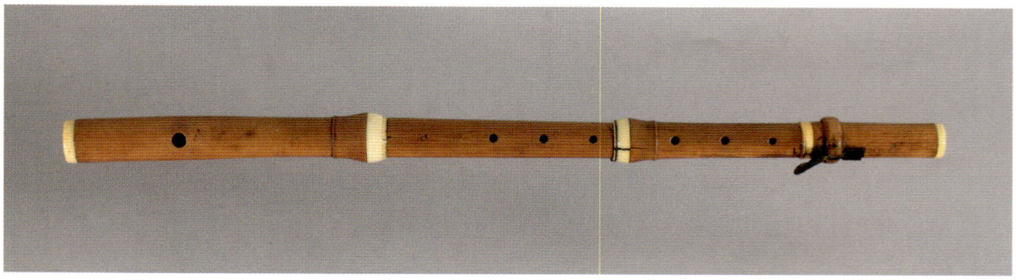

1-key flute, Johann Wolfgang Hoe, Hof, ca. 1770.

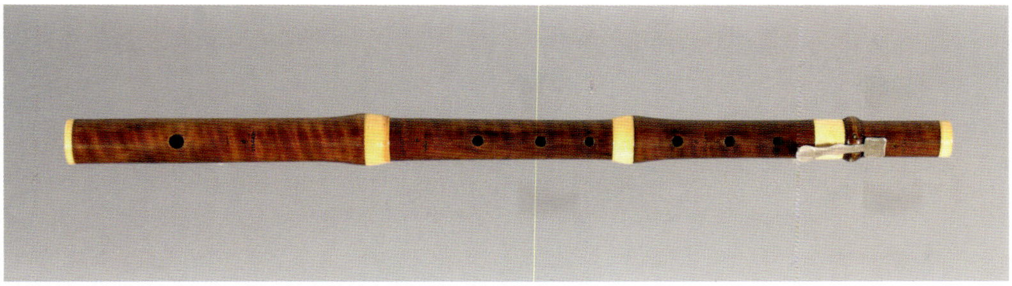

1-key flute, Paul Villars, Paris, ca. 1750.

1-key flute, Paul Villars, Paris, ca. 1750.

Striped boxwood; ivory ferrules; single beading. Four sections: head, upper joint, lower joint, foot. Oval embouchure, one ring-mounted silver key, square key head. D♯. L=518.

Stamped on head, upper joint, foot: "(fleur-de-lis) / VILLARS"; lower joint: "(fleur-de-lis) / VILLARS/ (fleur-de-lis)".

Giannini 1993, 39 (a), 43.

2005.19

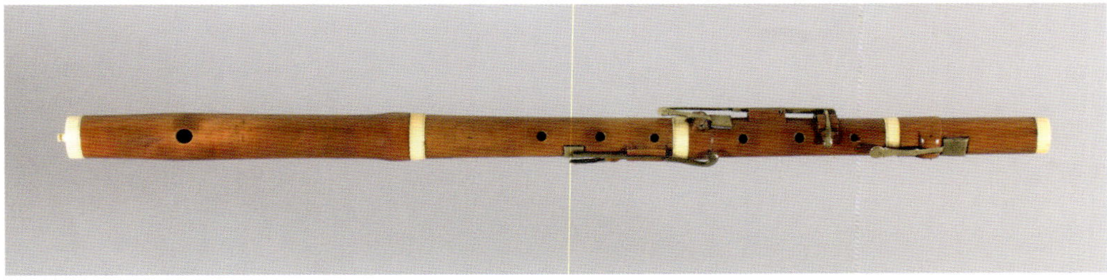

6-key flute, Johann Michael Staudinger, Dresden, ca. 1820.

6-key flute, Johann Michael Staudinger, Dresden, ca. 1820.

Boxwood; ivory ferrules; single beading. Four sections: head, l.h. joint, r.h. joint, foot. Ivory cap, ivory screw-cork indicator. Oval embouchure, six block-mounted brass keys with square key heads. C^1, B♭, G♯, F (long), F (short), D♯. Three l.h. joints. Long and short F keys share the same key head. In wooden case. L=620 (with shortest corps); L of three l.h. joints or corps de rechange=156 (stamped "1"), 152 (stamped "2"), 148 (stamped "3").

Stamped on head: "(crown) / STAUDINGER"; l.h. joint: "1."

2006.03

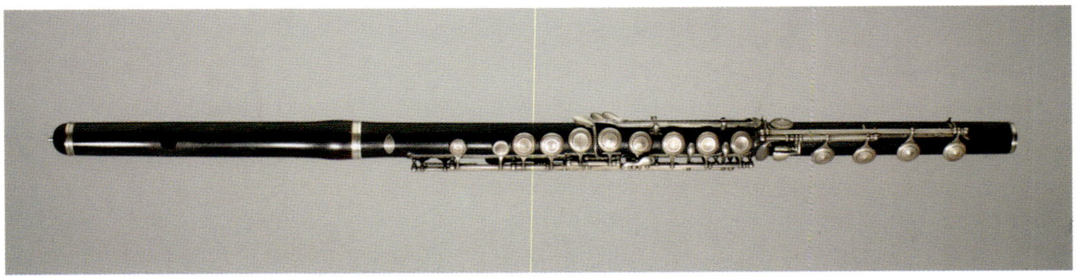

Boehm-system flute, Theodore Berteling, New York, ca. 1870.

Boehm-system flute, Theodore Berteling, New York, ca. 1870.

African black wood; nickel-silver ferrules. Three sections: head, body, foot. African black wood cap, nickel-silver screw-cork indicator. Slightly rectangular embouchure, Boehm-system, plateau keys, low B (L4), B♭ (L4). In case. L=742.

Stamped on nickel-silver plate on body: "BERTELING / NEW YORK (curved)".

2006.04

5-key flute, Joseph Dobner, and Consort, Strasbourg, ca. 1830

Ebony; ivory ferrules. Four sections: head, l.h. joint, r.h. joint, foot. Elongated oval embouchure, five pillar-mounted silver keys. C^1, B♭, G♯, F, D♯. L=613.

Stamped on head, l.h. joint, r.h. joint, foot: "(angel trumpeter) / DOBNER / & / CONSORT / STRASBOURG"; engraved on silver plaque, owner's initials: "JTB".

In original red felt-lined case with a 5-key F flute.

2006.06

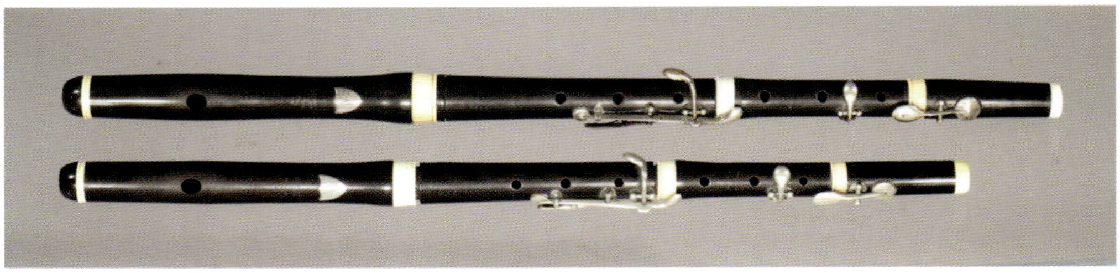

5-key flute, Joseph Dobner and Consort, Strasbourg, ca. 1830 and *5-key flute in F (flute tierce)*, Joseph Dobner, and Consort, Strasbourg, ca. 1830).

5-key flute in F (flute tierce), Joseph Dobner and Consort, Strasbourg, ca. 1830.

Ebony; ivory ferrules. Four sections: head, l.h. joint, r.h. joint, foot. Elongated oval embouchure, five pillar-mounted silver keys. C^1, B♭, G♯, F, D♯. L=530.

Stamped on head, l.h. joint, r.h. joint, foot: "(angel trumpeter) / DOBNER / & / CONSORT / STRASBOURG"; engraved on silver plaque, owner's initials: "JTB".

In original red felt-lined case with a 5-key flute (2006.06).

Pierre 2013, 58.

2006.07

5-key flute in F (flute tierce), Joseph Dobner and Consort, Strasbourg, ca. 1830 and *5-key flute*, Joseph Dobner, and Consort, Strasbourg, ca. 1830) in shared box.

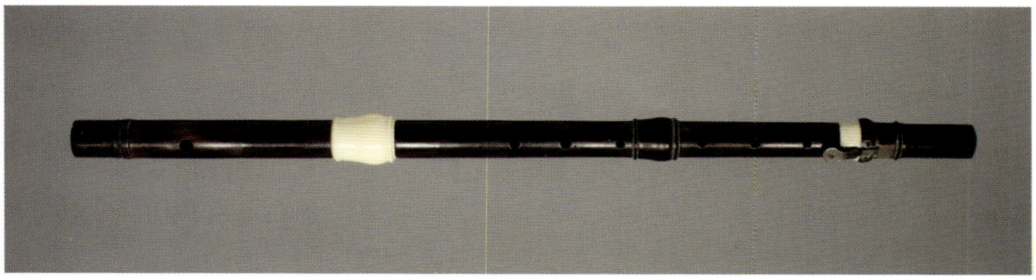

1-key flute, Pierre Naust, Paris, ca. 1710.

1-key flute, Pierre Naust, Paris, ca. 1710.

Stained black wood; ivory and black wood ferrules; multiple beadings and white lines. Four sections: head, upper joint, lower joint, foot. Oval embouchure, one pillar-mounted silver key on a silver oval plate. D♯. L=665.

Stamped on head, lower joint: "NAUST / (striding lion)"; upper joint: "(striding lion) / NAUST / (striding lion)".

Giannini 1993, 4-6; Powell 2002, 67, 74-75, 80.

2006.12

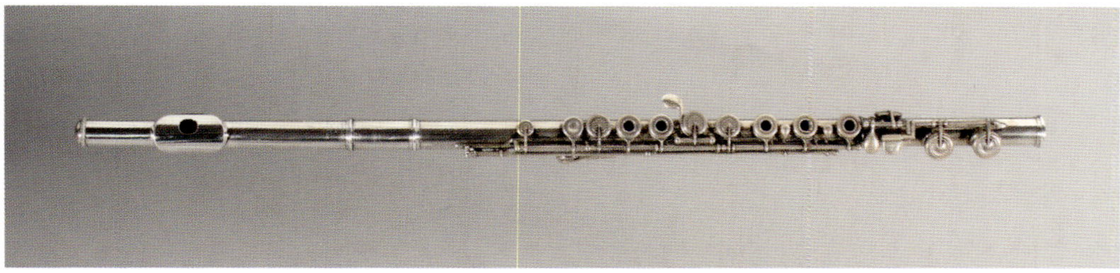

Boehm-system flute, Louis Lot, Paris, ca. 1864.

Boehm-system flute, Louis Lot, Paris, ca. 1864.

Silver-plated; silver-plated ferrules. Four sections: head, barrel, body, foot. Oval embouchure on lip plate. Boehm-system, pillar-mounted silver-plated keys, open plateau keys for L2, L3, R1, R2, R3, low C. Serial no. 885. L=660.

Stamped on head: "L.L. / LOUIS LOT / PARIS / 885 / BREVETÉ"; body: "L.L. / LOUIS LOT / PARIS / BREVETÉ".

Lenski and Ventske (1992), 187.

2006.16

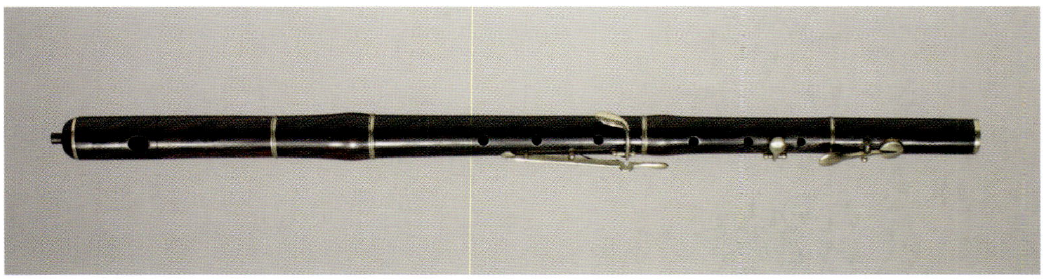

5-key flute, Louis Lot, Paris, ca. 1860.

5-key flute, Louis Lot, Paris, ca. 1860.

Stained black wood; silver ferrules. Five sections: head (cut for tuning?), barrel, l.h. joint, r.h. joint, foot. Black wood cap, brass screw-cork indicator, three l.h. joints. Elongated oval embouchure, four pillar-mounted nickel-silver keys, flat key heads. C[1], B♭, G♯, F, D♯. In wooden case. L of three separate head joints=588, 612, 640.

Stamped on head: "L. LOT"; barrel: "A PARIS"; l.h.joint: "L. LOT".

2006.17

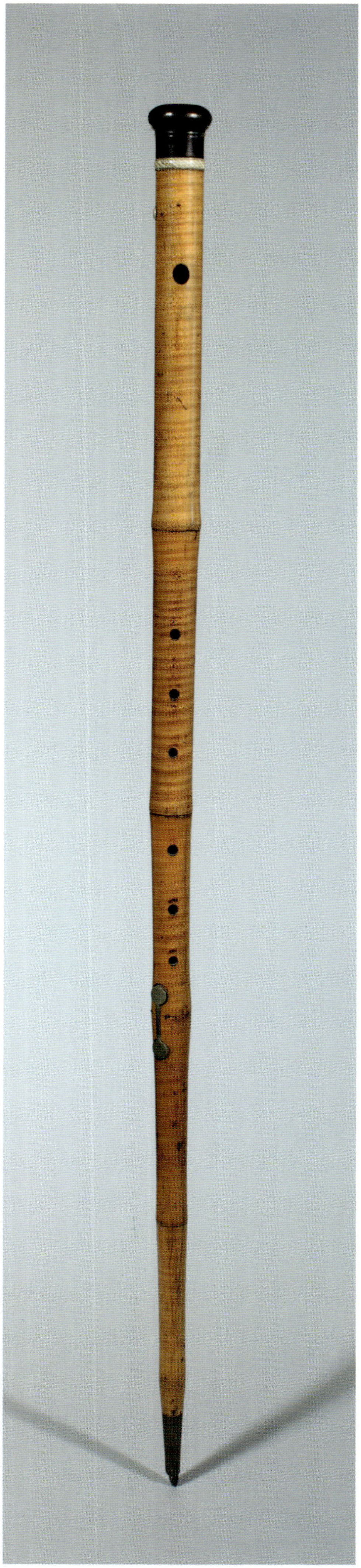

1-key walking-stick flute, Anonymous, of German or Swiss origin, early nineteenth century.

One-piece of striped wood; cuts in the surface indicating l.h. and r.h. joints; a lower extension of brass and tip for use as a cane. Ebony handle, ivory ferrule, diagonal lines, ivory tuning hole below handle, elongated oval embouchure, six finger holes, one brass key mounted by insertion into the outer surface, round, flat touch, round, flat key head. L=865 (with the handle to the end of the brass tip).

No inscription.

2007.10

1-key walking-stick flute, Anonymous, of German or Swiss origin, early nineteenth century.

4-key flute, Meacham & Co., Albany, New York, ca. 1827.

Stained boxwood; ivory ferrules. Four sections: head, l.h. joint, r.h. joint, foot. Oval embouchure, four block and ring-mounted brass keys, salt-spoon key heads. B♭, G♯, F, D♯. L=605.

Stamped on head, l.h. joint: "MEACHAM & CO. / ALBANY".

Eliason (1979-1980), 64.

2007.11

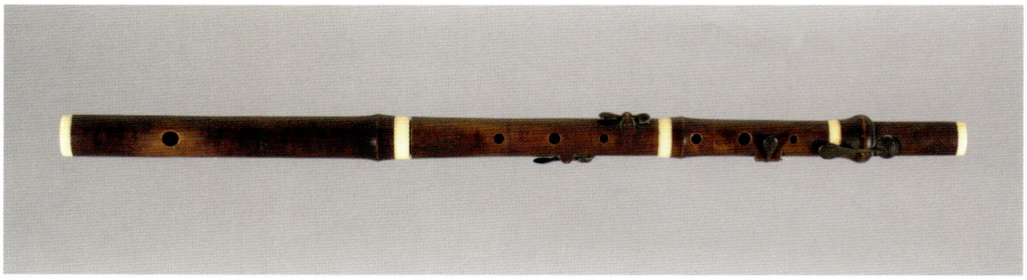

4-key flute, Meacham & Co., Albany, New York, ca. 1827.

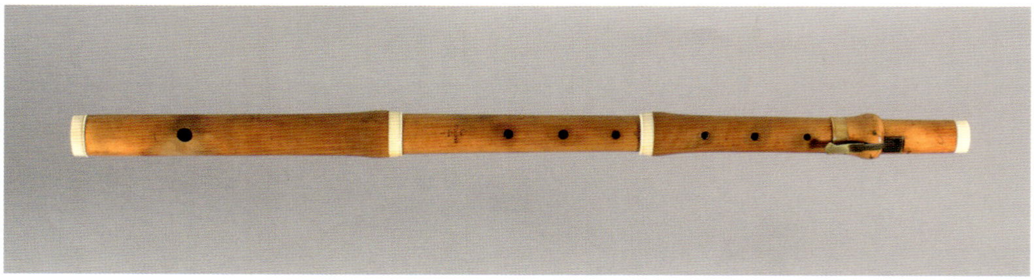

1-key flute, Johann August Crone, Leipzig, ca. 1780.

1-key flute, Johann August Crone, Leipzig, ca. 1780.

Boxwood; ivory and horn ferrules; single beading. Four sections: head, upper joint, lower joint, foot. Oval embouchure, one ring-mounted brass key, square key head. D♯. In wooden case. L of flute with four upper joints or corps de rechange=630 (stamped "1"), 615 (stamped "1"), 610 (stamped "2"), 600 (stamped "3").

Stamped on head, lower joint, foot: "(crown) / I•A• CRONE / (lion rampant with crown)"; upper joint: "1 / (crown) / I•A• CRONE / (lion rampant with crown)".

2007.18

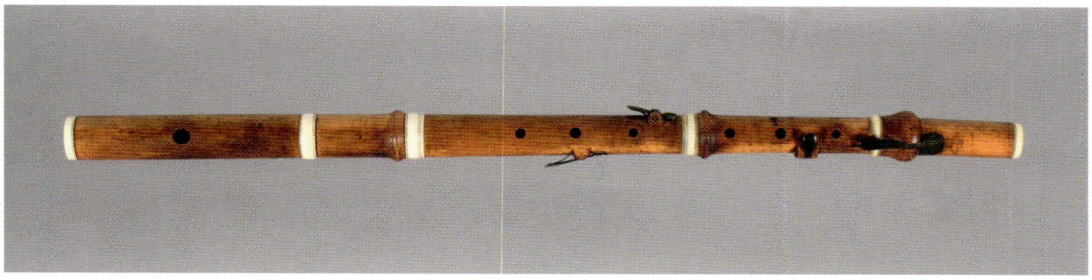

4-key flute, Asa Hopkins, Litchfield, Connecticut, ca. 1830.

4-key flute, Asa Hopkins, Litchfield, Connecticut, ca. 1830.

Boxwood; ivory ferrules; multiple black lines. Five sections: head, barrel, l.h. joint, r.h. joint, foot. Oval embouchure, four block and ring-mounted brass keys, flat, round key heads. B♭, G♯, F, D♯. L=606.

Stamped on head, barrel, foot: "A HOPKINS (curved) / LITCHFIELD / CONN"; l.h. joint, r.h. joint: "A HOPKINS (curved) / LITCHFIELD".

2007.19

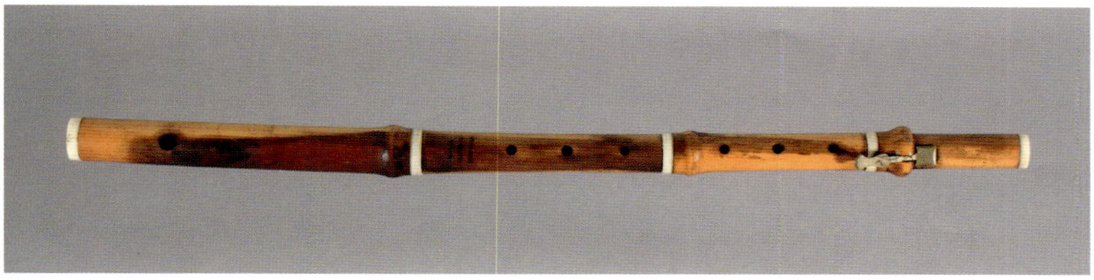

1-key flute, William Geib, New York, ca. 1826.

1-key flute, William Geib, New York, ca. 1826.

Boxwood; ivory ferrules; single beading. Four sections: head, upper joint, lower joint, foot. Oval embouchure, one ring-mounted brass key, square key head. D♯. L=601.

Stamped on l.h. joint: "W. GEIB. / 6th AVENUE / NEW-YORK".

An English imported flute.

Peters (1931), 193.

2007.20

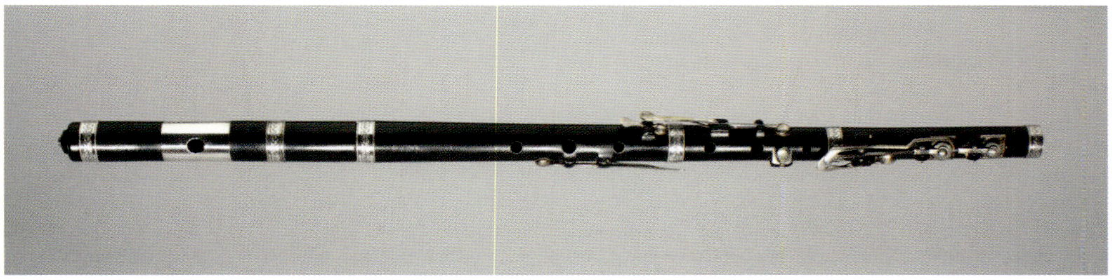

8-key flute, Richard Garrett, London, ca. 1835.

8-key flute, Richard Garrett, London, ca. 1835.

Ebony; floral decorated silver ferrules. Five sections: head, barrel, l.h. joint, r.h. joint, foot. Ebony cap, silver screw-cork indicator. Oval embouchure on wide silver band, eight block-mounted silver keys, salt-spoon and pewter plug key heads (for C♯ and C). Large Nicholson finger holes, L2, R1, R2. C^1 (R1), B♭, G♯, F (L4, long), F (short), D♯, C♯, C (C♯ and C have overlapping touches). L=675.

Stamped on l.h. joint: "(crown) / GARRETT / NO. 2 / KING STREET / WHITEHALL"; foot: "GARRETT / LONDON".

2007.24

1-key flute in F (third flute), Renshaw and Kirkman, London, ca. 1810.

Boxwood; silver ferrules. Four sections: head, upper joint, lower joint, foot. Oval embouchure, one ring-mounted brass key, square key head. D♯. L=515.

Stamped on head: "(unicorn head) / RENSHAW / & KIRKMAN / LONDON / 8"; upper joint: "RENSHAW / & KIRKMAN".

2007.27

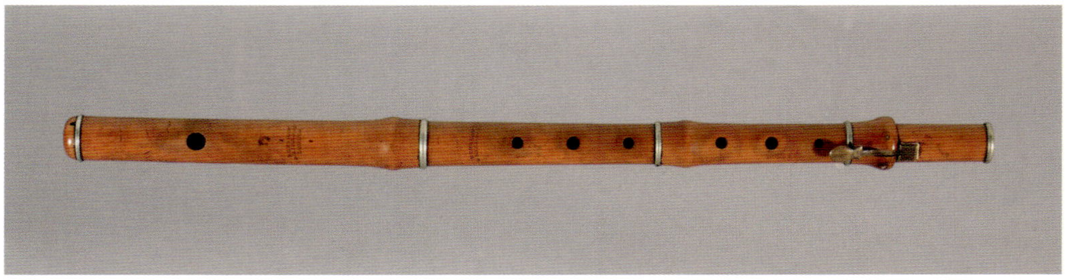

1-key flute in F (third flute), Renshaw and Kirkman, London, ca. 1810.

1-key flute, Martin Lot, Paris, ca. 1760.

Boxwood; ivory ferrules. Five sections: head, upper joint, lower joint, foot, foot register. Oval embouchure, one ring-mounted silver key, square key head. D♯. L=640.

Stamped on head, upper joint, lower joint, foot: "M*LOT / (dolphin)".

Giannini 1993, 22-26, 40.

2007.28

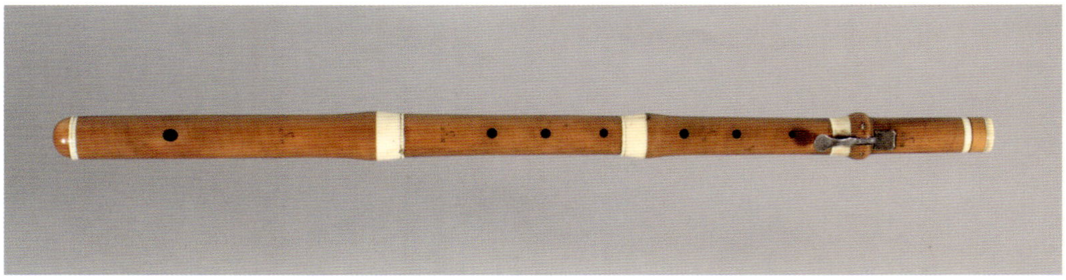

1-key flute, Martin Lot, Paris, ca. 1760.

Boehm-system flute, Clair Godfroy aîné, Paris, ca. 1840.

Stained rosewood; silver ferrules. Three sections: head, body, foot. Oval embouchure, conical body, Boehm-system, pillar-mounted silver keys, rings for L2, L3, R1, R2, R3, low C. Unmarked silver plaque on head. L=660.

Stamped on body: "(head of Medusa) / CLAIR / Godfroy ainé / A PARIS (in oval) / CG (monogram)".

Lenski and Ventske (1992), 168; Giannini (1993), 107 (b).

2008.03

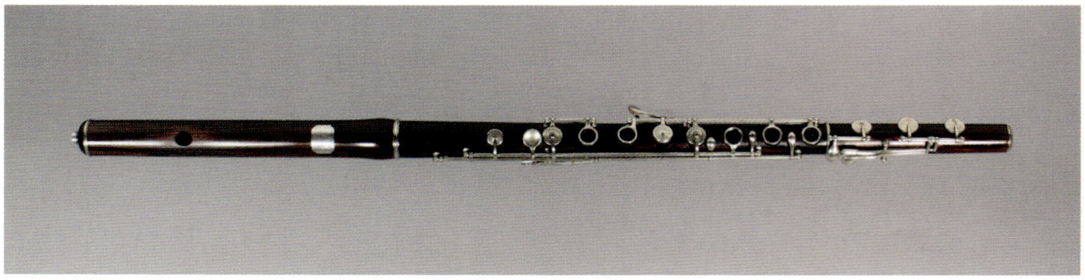

Boehm-system flute, Clair Godfroy aîné, Paris, ca. 1840.

Boehm-system flute, Clair Godfroy aîné, Paris, ca. 1864.

Silver; silver ferrules. Four sections: head, barrel, body, foot. Oval embouchure on lip plate, cylinder body. Boehm-system, rings for L2, L3, R1, R2, R3, low C. Serial no. 965. L=680.

Stamped on head: "CLAIR / GODFROY AINE / Breveté (cursive) / Paris (Gothic) / 965"; body, foot: "CLAIR / GODFROY AINE / Breveté (cursive) / Paris (Gothic)".

Lenski and Ventske (1992), 174; Giannini 1993, 167 (d).

2008.04

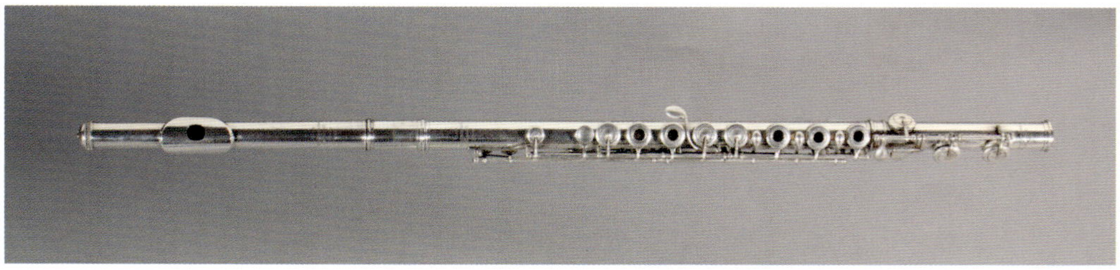

Boehm-system flute, Clair Godfroy aîné, Paris, ca. 1864.

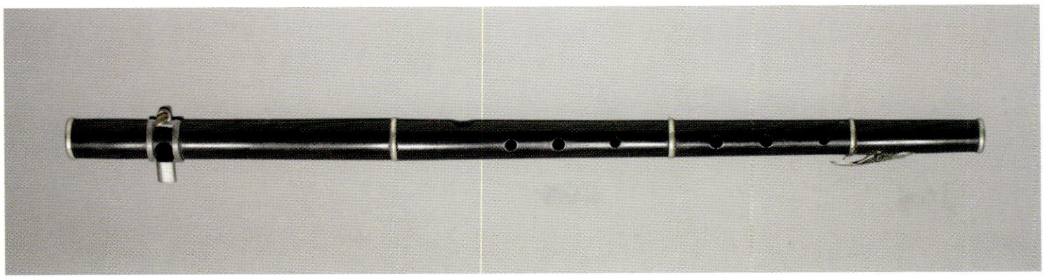

1-key flute, Anonymous, of United States or Great Britain origin, ca. 1850.

1-key flute, Anonymous, of United States or Great Britain origin, ca. 1850.

Stained black cocus wood; nickel-silver ferrules. Four sections, head, upper joint, lower joint, foot. Oval embouchure, one pillar-mounted nickel-silver key, round, flat key head. D♯. Nickel-silver mouthpiece called a "cheater." Groove in upper joint for index finger (L1) to rest. L=585.

No inscription.

2008.07

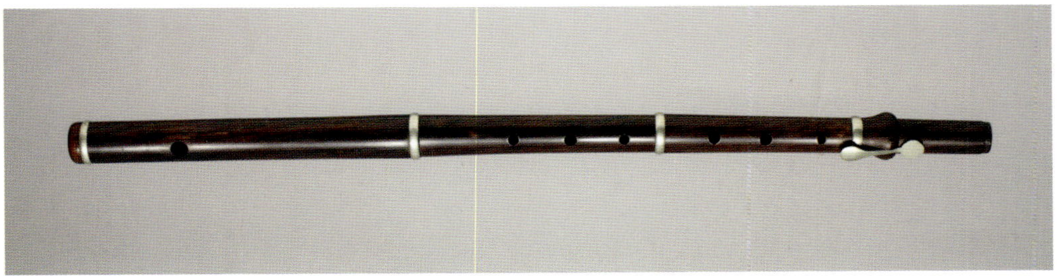

1-key flute, Chabrier Peloubet, New York, ca. 1850.

1-key flute, Chabrier Peloubet, New York, ca. 1850.

Stained cocus wood; nickel-silver ferrules. Four sections: head, upper joint, lower joint, foot (missing ferrule). Oval embouchure, one ring-mounted nickel-silver key, flat, round key head. D♯. L=603.

Stamped on head, upper joint, lower joint: "C. PELOUBET / NEW-YORK / FACTORY AT / BLOOMFIELD / N.J."; foot: "C. PELOUBET / NEW-YORK / FACTORY AT / BLOOMFD / N.J."

2009.02

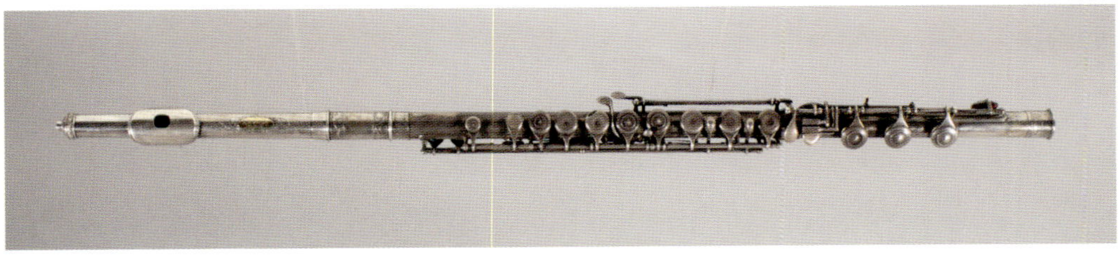

Boehm-system flute, Alfred G. Badger, New York, ca. 1880.

Boehm-system flute, Alfred G. Badger, New York, ca. 1880.

Silver; silver ferrules. Three sections: head, body, foot. Silver engraved cap, engraved foot at end, barrel decorated at both ends, silver screw-cork indicator. Semi-rectangular embouchure hole on lip plate, Boehm-system, pillar-mounted silver keys, plateau keys, low B and B♭. In case. L=743.

Engraved on a gold plated oval, in center of swirls on head: "A.G. Badger (gothic) / N. York (cursive)".

2009.03.

Boehm-system flute, Alfred G. Badger, New York, ca. 1865.

Silver; silver ferrules. Three sections: head, body, foot. Silver engraved cap, silver screw-cork indicator. Oval embouchure on barrel-shaped head decorated with floral engraving. Boehm-system, pillar-mounted silver keys, plateau keys, Dorus G♯, low B. In case. L=720.

Upper part of body has chevron for owner's name, without engraving, floral engraving above and below chevron.

Engraved upside down on a gold-plated oval on head: "A.G. BADGER / NEW-YORK".

Berdahl 1985, vol. 1, 266.

2009.05

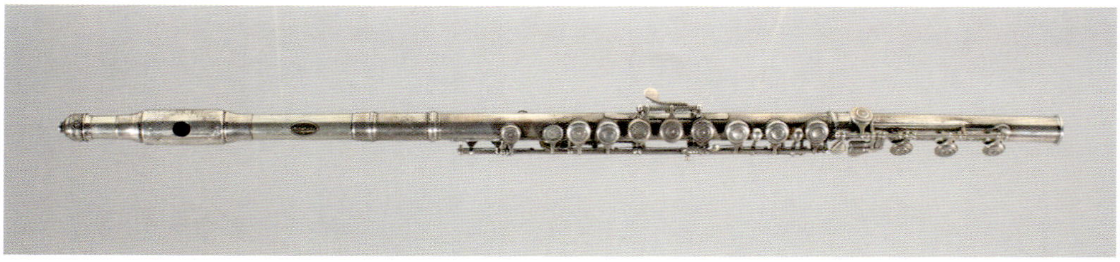

Boehm-system flute, Alfred G. Badger, New York, ca. 1865.

Boehm-system flute, Karl Mendler, Munich, ca. 1895.

Silver; silver ferrules. Four sections: head, barrel, body, foot. Gold-plated head and barrel. Silver cap, silver screw-cork indicator. Semi-rectangular embouchure on silver lip plate, brace for upper part of L1, transparent plastic crutch for LT. Boehm-system, plateau keys with gold-plated circular, raised finger touches, low B. L=670.

Engraved on barrel: "Karl Mendler / München"; owner's gilt engraving on upper part of body: "C.B. King (cursive)".

2009.06

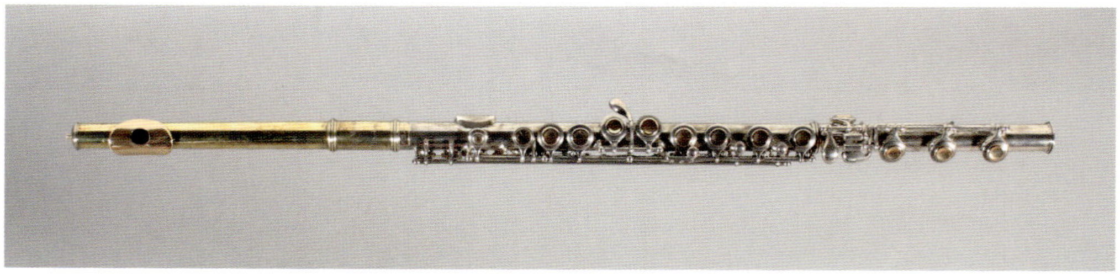

Boehm-system flute, Karl Mendler, Munich, ca. 1895.

1-key flute, James Power, London, ca. 1810.

Boxwood; ivory ferrules; single beading. Four sections: head, upper joint, lower joint, foot. Oval embouchure, one ring-mounted silver key, square key head. D♯. L=625.

Stamped on head: "POWER / 34 STRAND / LONDON"; upper joint, lower joint, foot: "POWER / LONDON".

2010.04

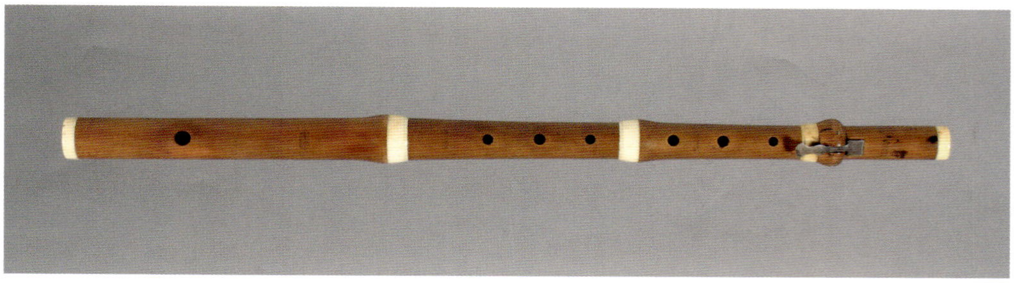

1-key flute, James Power, London, ca. 1810.

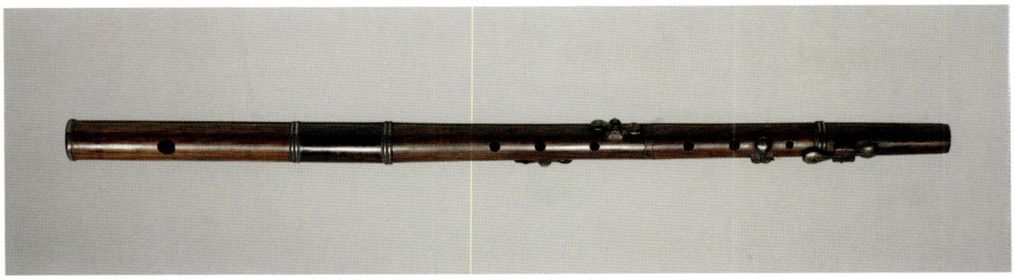

4-key flute, William Rönnberg, New York, ca. 1840.

4-key flute, William Rönnberg, New York, ca. 1840.

Stained cocus wood; nickel-silver ferrules. Five sections: head, barrel, l.h. joint, r.h. joint, foot. Oval embouchure, four block-mounted brass keys, salt-spoon key heads. B♭, G♯, F, D♯. Left-hand joint missing ferrule. L=600.

Stamped on head, l.h. joint: "RÖNNBERG / N.YORK / (star)"; r.h. joint: "(star) / RÖNNBERG / (star)".

2010.05

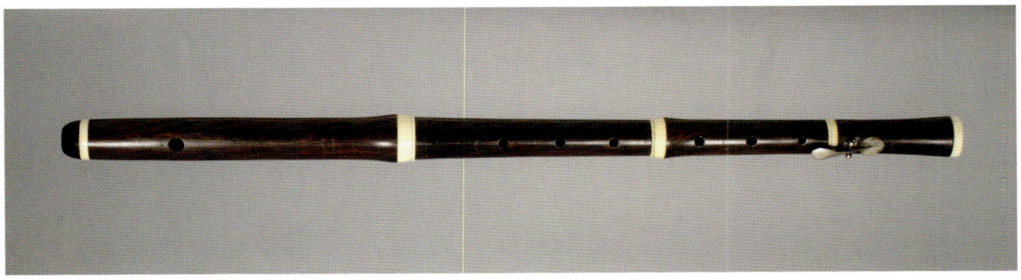

1-key flute, François Jeantet, Lyon, ca. 1825.

1-key flute, François Jeantet, Lyon, ca. 1825.

Stained cocus wood; ivory ferrules; single beading. Four sections: head, upper joint, lower joint, foot. Oval embouchure, one pillar-mounted silver key, flat, round key head, four upper joints. In paper case. D♯. L of flute with four upper joints or corps de rechange=631 (stamped "1"), 628 (stamped "2"), 612 (stamped "3"), 620 (unnumbered).

Stamped on head: "JEANTET (curved) / A LYON"; upper joint: "JEANTET (curved) // 2"; lower joint: "JEANTET (curved)"; foot: "A LYON".

2010.08

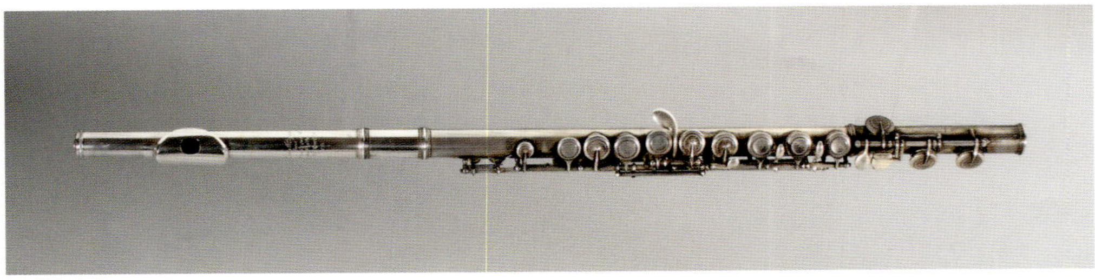

Boehm-system flute, Florentin Barbier, Paris, ca. 1890.

Boehm-system flute, Florentin Barbier, Paris, ca. 1890.

Silver; silver ferrules. Four sections: head, barrel, body, foot. Semi-rectangular embouchure on lip plate, Boehm-system key mechanism, plateau keys, low C. Serial no. 696. L=655.

Engraved on head: "Florent Barbier / Paris / Exposition de Paris / Méd[lle] d'Or / Système Barbier (cursive) / 696".

2011.04

Ocarina, attributed to Max Freyer and Co., Meissen, ca. 1900.

White meissen ware ocarina decorated with flowers and leaves in blue. Eight finger holes, two thumb holes. L=185.

No inscription.

Freyer, ca. 1895.

1996.17

ABOVE: *Ocarina,* attributed to Max Freyer and Co., Meissen, ca. 1900.

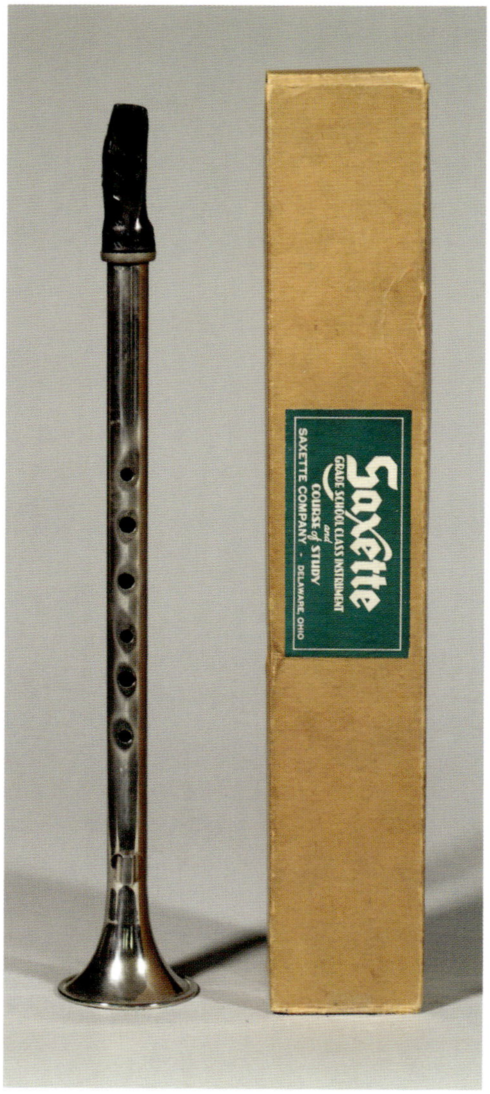

Saxette, Saxette Co., Delaware, Ohio, ca. 1940.

Aluminum; six finger holes; one thumb hole; one vent hole in the bell. Two sections: mouthpiece, body. Black bakelite mouthpiece, pedestal for a music lyre at end of bell. Stored in cardboard box with label: "Saxette / GRADE SCHOOL CLASS INSTRUMENT / and / COURSE of STUDY / SAXETTE COMPANY – DELAWARE, OHIO". L=390 (with mouthpiece).

No inscription.

The saxette, also known as a song flute, was developed in 1929 for young children by Elver Joseph Fitchhorn of Delaware, Ohio; a bakelite mouthpiece was added in 1937.

Waterhouse 1993, 118.

2002.12

Saxette, Saxette Co., Delaware, Ohio, ca. 1940.

Pitch pipe, Anonymous, of Great Britain origin, ca. 1800.

Light brown wood in the shape of a recorder head joint. Dark wood movable stopper, decorative lines in lighter wood; may be extended to 495 mm. Pitch pipe provided a reference note for a church choir. L=335.

No inscription.

2002.16

Pitch pipe, Anonymous, of Great Britain origin, 1772.

Dark brown wood in the shape of a recorder head joint. Light wood movable stopper has an insert of metal or pewter marked with pitch letters; may be extended to 530 mm. Lowest note is "G". L=310.

Stamped: "R•J / 1772".

2004.18

Swanee whistle, Anonymous, of Great Britian origin, ca. 1920.

Wood stained black. Recorder mouthpiece at top; nickel-silver ferrule, ivory end. Nickel-silver handle at 45° angle extends to 220 mm, creating a variable pitch whistling sound when blowing. L=345.

Stamped: "(star) / MODEL deluxe / SWANEE / WHISTLE / OR / LOTUS FLUTE / REGISTERED / MADE IN LONDON / ENGLAND / PRO. / PATENT / REGISTERED / DESIGN / 687087 / REG. U.S. PAT. OFF. / (star)".

A Swanee whistle is in the Metropolitan Museum of Art, no. 1991.349.69.

2004.21.

Pitch pipe, Anonymous, of Great Britain origin, ca. 1800.

Pitch pipe, Anonymous, of Great Britain origin, 1772.

Swanee whistle, Anonymous, of Great Britian origin, ca. 1920.

CHAPTER 3

DOUBLE–REED INSTRUMENTS

2-key oboe, Andrea Fornari, Venice, 1795.

Boxwood; flared ivory ferrules; single beading; vase-shaped top. Three sections: l.h. joint, r.h. joint, bell. Two ring-mounted ivory keys with square key heads, twin third hole, two resonance holes on upper part of bell. E♭[1](spurs), C[1] (spur). L=560.

Stamped on l.h. joint: "(star) / FORNARI / I"; r.h. joint between fourth and fifth holes: "(star) /FORNARI / (star)"; between fifth and sixth holes: "A VENEZIA"; bell: "(star) / FORNARI / 1795 / (star)".

An elegant example of a straight-top oboe with ivory keys and ferrules.

Adkins 2011, 88-156.

1994.02

2-key oboe, Johann August Crone, Leipzig, ca. 1790.

Boxwood; ivory ferrules; single and multiple beading. Three sections: l.h. joint, r.h. joint, bell. Two ring-mounted brass keys, square brass key heads, twin third finger hole, two resonance holes on upper part of bell. E♭[1] (spurs), C[1] (fish-tail touch, spurs). L=570.

Stamped on l.h. joint: "2 / (five-pointed crown) / I•A•CRONE / (star)"; r.h. joint, bell: "(five-pointed crown) / I•A•CRONE / (star)".

1995.04

13-key oboe, Stephan Koch, Sellner system, Vienna, ca. 1825.

Ebony; ivory ferrules; single beading. Four sections: finial tuning slide, l.h. joint, r.h. joint, bell. Thirteen silver keys mounted in silver bushed blocks, round, flat key heads. One bell resonance hole with ivory cover, second bell resonance key a small hole. Lever underneath a large thumb rest, large adjustment screw above thumb rest and ivory ring on r.h. joint. Octave (wraparound), C[2] (R1), B♭[1] (R1), G♯[1], F[1](R3), F♯[1] (cross), F[1] (L4), E♭[1] (cross), E♭[1] (R4, operates the same key head as opened by L4), E♭[1] (L4), C♯[1] (R4), C[1] (R4, roller), B (LT). L=558.

Stamped on l.h. joint, r.h. joint, bell: "(Hapsburg eagle) / S.KOCH / WIEN".

1995.25

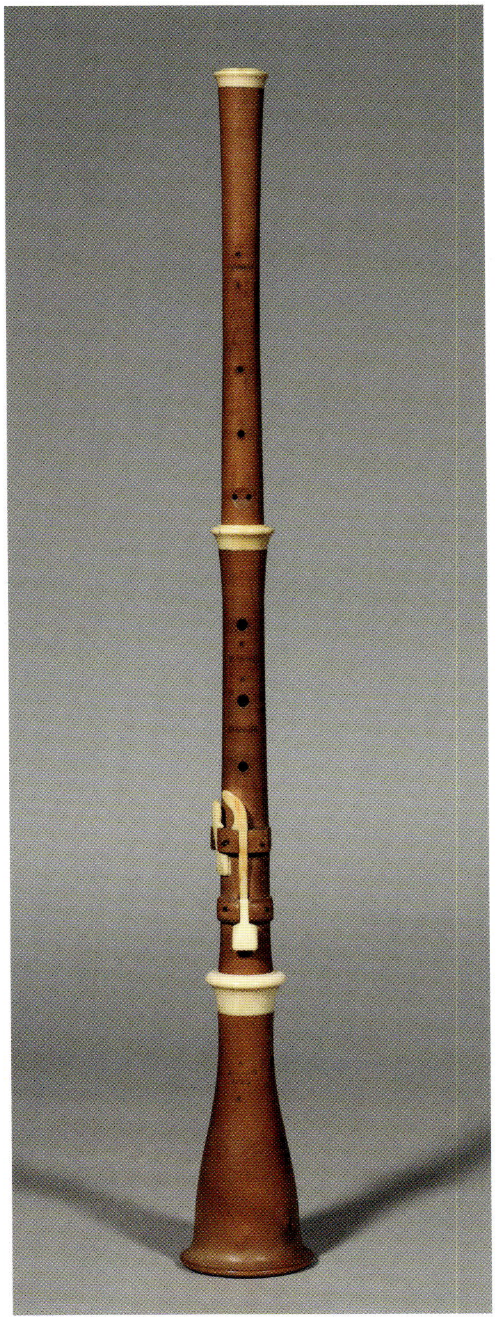

2-key oboe, Andrea Fornari, Venice, 1795.

2-key oboe, Johann August Crone, Leipzig, ca. 1790.

13-key oboe, Stephan Koch, Sellner system, Vienna, ca. 1825.

2-key oboe, Thomas Cahusac senior, London, ca. 1800.

Boxwood; boxwood ferrules; extensive beading. Three sections: l.h. joint, r.h. joint, bell. Two ring-mounted silver keys, round key heads, two resonance holes on upper part of bell, twin third finger hole. E♭[1], C[1] (fish-tail touch, spurs). L=568.

Stamped on l.h. joint, r.h. joint, bell: "CAHUSAC / LONDON".

1995.27

2-key oboe, Carl Augustin Grenser, Dresden, ca. 1760.

Boxwood; boxwood ferrules; single and double beading. Three sections: l.h. joint, r.h. joint, bell. Two ring-mounted brass keys, twin third finger hole, two resonance holes on upper part of bell. E♭[1] (square key head, spurs), C[1] (fish-tail touch, octagonal key head, spurs). L=563.

Stamped on l.h. joint: "B"; bell: "GRENTZER".

This stamp was thought to be used on the earliest examples from August Grenser's shop; see also the large number of "Grentzer" woodwinds in an 1843 auction catalog in Van Kalker and Rice 2014, 233.

Formerly Stradner collection; Stradner 1991, 287, no. 177, 288; Young 1993, 96, Y14.

1996.01

9-key oboe, G. Guglielminetti, Novara, ca. 1850.

Boxwood; horn ferrules; single beading. Three sections: l.h. joint, r.h. joint, bell. Nine block-mounted brass keys with flat, round key heads, large resonance hole in lower part of r.h. joint, twin third finger hole. Octave (wraparound), C[2] (R1), B♭[1] (R1), G♯[1], F[1] (L4), F[1] (cross), E♭[1], C[1], C♯[1] (touch over C[1] touch, curved replaced key head). L=549.

Stamped on l.h. joint, r.h. joint, bell: "GULIELMINETTI (star) NOVARA (star) (in an oval) / (six-petal flower in the center of the oval)".

Carreras 2009, 34.

1996.24

2-key oboe, Thomas Cahusac senior, London, ca. 1800.

2-key oboe, Carl Augustin Grenser, Dresden, ca. 1760.

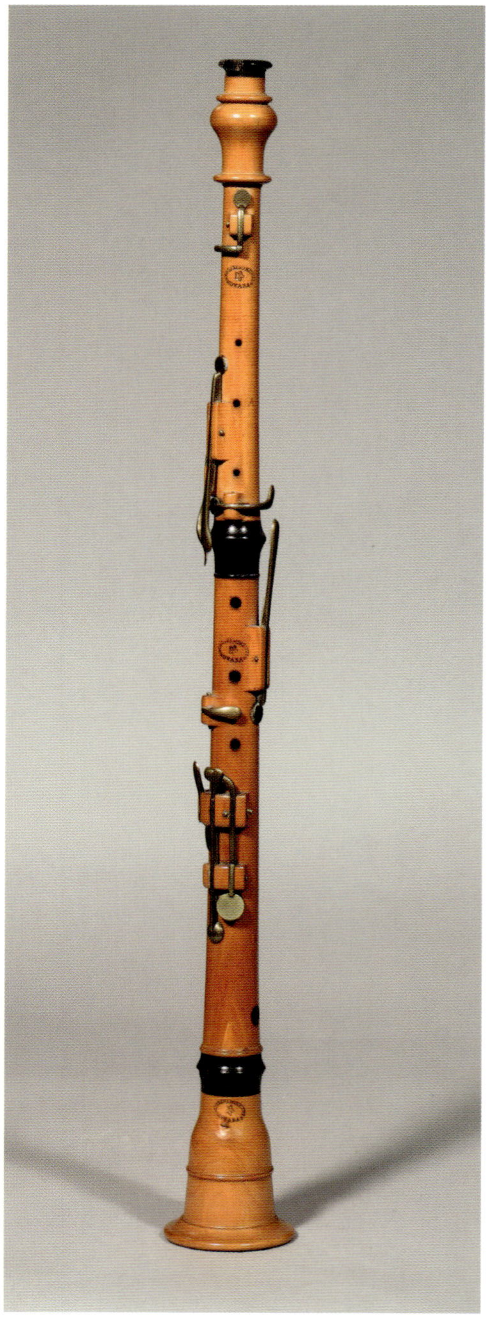

9-key oboe, G. Guglielminetti, Novara, ca. 1850.

3-key oboe, Hendrik Richters, Amsterdam, ca. 1720.

Stained boxwood; boxwood ferrules; multiple beading. Three sections: l.h. joint, r.h. joint, bell. Three ring-mounted brass keys, twin third and fourth finger holes, two resonance holes on upper part of bell. E♭[1] (R4, square key head, spurs), E♭[1] (L4, square key head, spurs), C[1] (fish-tail touch with round, flat, key heads, spurs). L=581.

Stamped on l.h. joint, r.h. joint: "H RICHTERS / (clover leaf stem pointing left)".

Bouterse 2005, 37-38.

1997.05

LEFT: *3-key oboe*, Hendrik Richters, Amsterdam, ca. 1720.

2-key oboe, Carl Augustin Grenser, Dresden, 1778.

Boxwood; boxwood ferrules; single and double beading. Three sections: l.h. joint, r.h. joint, bell. Two ring-mounted brass keys with octagonal key heads, two resonance holes on upper part of bell, twin third finger hole, two bell vent holes. E♭[1] (spurs), C[1] (fish-tail touch, spurs). L=580.

Playing pitch A=422 hertz with a very smooth tone that speaks easily.

Stamped on l.h. joint: "1 / (crossed swords) / A•GRENSER"; r.h. joint: "(crossed swords) / A•GRENSER"; bell: "(crossed swords) / A•GRENSER / DRESDEN / 1778".

Formerly Piguet collection. Piguet 1988, 89, 102, Abb. 10, Nr. 11; Young 1993, 96, Y11.

1997.09

RIGHT: *2-key oboe*, Carl Augustin Grenser, Dresden, 1778.

3-key oboe, Hendrik Richters, Amsterdam, ca. 1720.

Stained ebony; ivory ferrules; ornately carved turning. Three sections: l.h. joint, r.h. joint, bell. Three ring-mounted silver keys, no engraving on key heads, twin third and fourth finger holes, two resonance holes on upper part of bell. E♭[1] (R4, square key head, spurs), E♭[1] (L4, square key head, spurs) C[1] (fish-tail touch, flat, round key head, spurs). L=567.

Playing pitch A=415 hertz with a very clear tone and perfect intonation.

Stamped on l.h. joint, r.h. joint, bell: "H RICHTERS / (clover leaf stem pointing left)".

One of several outstanding oboes by the Richters family demonstrating high-quality carving using special lathes.

Formerly Piguet collection. Piguet 1988, 87, 98, Abb. 6, Nr. 1; Adkins 1990, 41–117; Van Acht, Bouterse, Dhont 1997; Bouterse 2005, 37, no. HR15.

1997.10

LEFT: *3-key oboe*, Hendrik Richters, Amsterdam, ca. 1720.

3-key oboe, Joannes Hyacinthus Rottenburgh I, Brussels, ca. 1720.

Boxwood; boxwood and ivory ferrules; single and multiple beading; decorative lines. Three sections: l.h. joint, r.h. joint, bell. Three ring-mounted brass keys, round key heads, two resonance holes on upper part of bell, twin third finger hole. E♭[1] (L4, spurs), E♭[1] (R4, spurs), C[1] (fish-tail touch, spurs). L=595.

Stamped on l.h. joint, r.h. joint, bell: "I•H• / ROTTENBURGH / (star)".

From the collection of the Marquis de Trouville. Playing pitch=405 hertz, a very good playing instrument with evenness of tone throughout the registers. This instrument was used as the model for the important copies made by Friedrich von Huene of Boston.

Formerly Piguet collection. Piguet 1988, 87, 98, Abb. 7, Nr. 3; Young 1993, 194, Y6.

1997.11

RIGHT: *3-key oboe*, Joannes Hyacinthus Rottenburgh I, Brussels, ca. 1720.

2-key oboe, Carl Wilhelm Sattler, Leipzig, ca. 1770.

Boxwood; boxwood ferrules; single and multiple beading. Three sections: l.h. joint, r.h. joint, bell. Two ring-mounted brass keys, twin third finger hole, two resonance holes on upper part of bell. E♭[1](square key head), C[1] (fish-tail touch, octagonal key head, spurs). L=580.

Playing pitch=425 hertz, has a dark sound with beautiful high notes.

Stamped on l.h. joint: "(crowned two-headed eagle) / CARL / SATTLER / S".

Formerly Piguet collection. Piguet 1988, 88, 102, Abb. 10, Nr. 8; Young 1993, 194, Y9.

1997.12

LEFT: *2-key oboe*, Carl Wilhelm Sattler, Leipzig, ca. 1770.

2-key oboe, Dominique Antony Porthaux, Paris, ca. 1780.

Boxwood; boxwood and ivory ferrules; single and multiple beading; additional turning on all joints. Three sections: l.h. joint, r.h. joint, bell. Two ring-mounted brass keys, octagonal key heads, twin third and fourth finger holes, two resonance holes in upper part of bell. E♭[1] (spurs), C[1] (fish-tail touch, spurs). In a green bag. Reed box covered in leather with five unstamped reeds. L=555 (with no. 3 corp); L of three l.h. joints or corps de rechange=304 (no. 1), 299 (no. 2), 216 (no. 3).

Stamped on l.h. joint: "(star) / PORTHAUX / A PARIS / 3"; r.h. joint, bell: "(star) / PORTHAUX / A PARIS".

1998.02

2-key oboe, Dominique Antony Porthaux, Paris, ca. 1780.

Two corps de rechange in green bag.

Reed box and reeds.

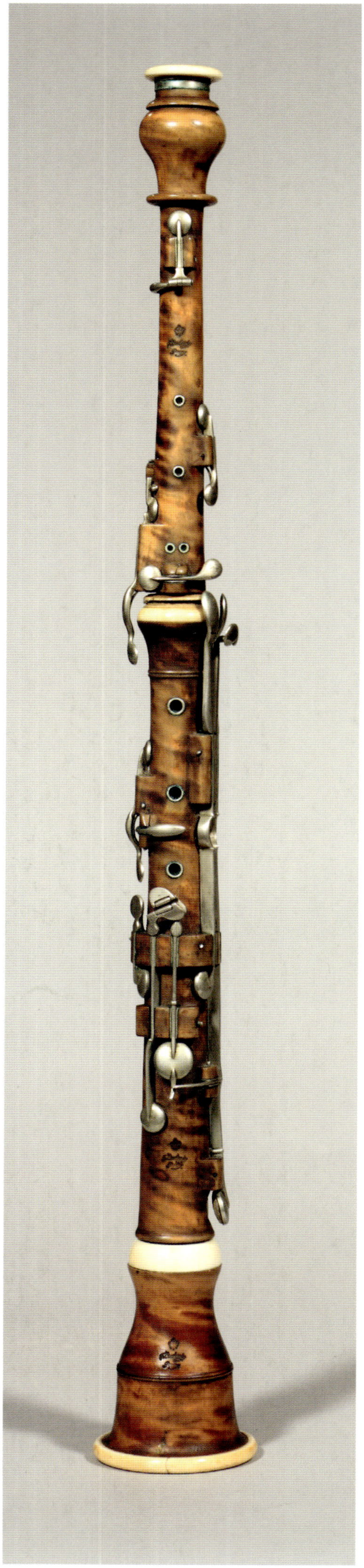

13-key oboe, Franz Ludwig, Prague, ca. 1840.

Boxwood with flame decoration; ivory ferrules; multiple beading. Three sections: l.h. joint, r.h. joint, bell. Twin third finger hole, six nickel-silver tube inlaid finger holes, nickel-silver tube for the left thumb hole, nickel-silver tenons and sockets at each joint. Nickel-silver band below top of finial. Thirteen block-mounted nickel-silver keys, curved key heads. Octave key has two tubular brass axels that move upward, the second axel opening key head on front. Octave (wraparound), C^2 (L3), $B\flat^1$ (LT), $B\flat^1$ (R1, operates the same key head as LT), $G\sharp^1$, F^1 (R3), F^1 (cross), F^1 (L4), $E\flat^1$ (R4), $E\flat^1$ (L4), $C\sharp^1$ (roller, R4, operates the same key head as opened by L4), C^1 (roller, L4), B (L4). L=552.

Stamped on l.h. joint, r.h. joint, bell: "(Hapsburg eagle) / F.Ludwig / Prag (cursive)".

1998.04

LEFT: *13-key oboe*, Franz Ludwig, Prague, ca. 1840.

2-key oboe, George Astor, London, ca. 1795.

Stained boxwood; ivory ferrules; single and double beading. Three sections: l.h. joint, r.h. joint, bell. Two ring-mounted silver keys, octagonal key heads, twin third finger hole, two resonance holes on upper part of bell. $E\flat^1$, C^1 (fish-tail touch, spurs). L=585.

Stamped on l.h. joint, r.h. joint, bell: "ASTOR / LONDON / (unicorn head)".

Straight-top model, pitch=422 hertz, a good playing instrument.

Formerly Piguet collection. Piguet 1988, 89, 104, Abb. 12, Nr. 12; Young 1993, 8, Y1.

1998.05

RIGHT: *2-key oboe*, George Astor, London, ca. 1795.

2-key oboe, Denis Vincent, Paris, ca. 1750.

Boxwood; ivory ferrules; double beading; vase-shaped balluster, two dark lines on upper portion of ivory finial. Three sections: l.h. joint, r.h. joint, bell. Two brass keys, square and round key heads, twin third and fourth finger holes. $E\flat^{1}$ (square key head, spurs) C^{1} (fish-tail touch, round key head, spurs). L=716.

Stamped on l.h. joint, r.h. joint: "VINCENT / (bird)"; bell: "A PARIS / (bird)".

1999.14

2-key oboe, Denis Vincent, Paris, ca. 1750.

11-key oboe, Triebert, Paris, system 3, ca. 1860.

Grenadilla; nickel-silver ferrules. Three sections: l.h.joint, r.h. joint, bell. Eleven pillar-mounted nickel-silver keys, modern key heads, rings for R2 and R3, twin third finger hole. 1st octave (RT), 2nd octave (L1), perforated plate (L1), C^{2} (R1), $B\flat^{1}$ (R1), $G\sharp^{1}$, F^{1} (cross, L3), $E\flat^{1}$ (L4), $E\flat^{1}$ (R4, raises the same key head as L4), C^{1}, $C\sharp^{1}$, B (L4). L=557.

Stamped on r.h. joint: "TRIEBERT (curved) / A PARIS"; bell: "BREVETE / S.G.D.G. / (barbican with three merlons) / TRIEBERT (curved) / A PARIS / 82".

1999.28

11-key oboe, Triebert, Paris, system 3, ca. 1860.

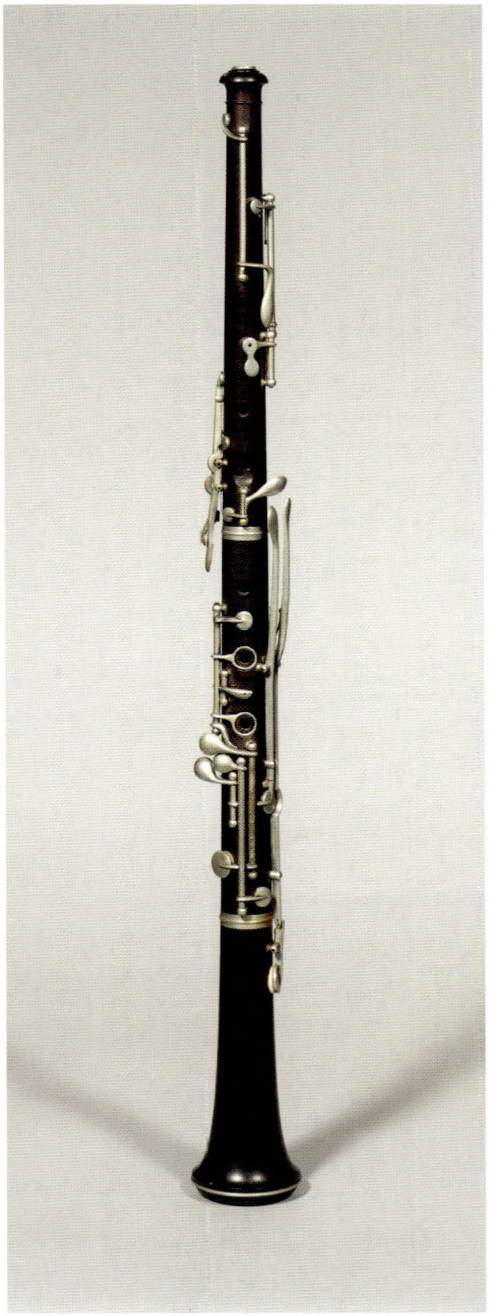

13-key oboe, Carl Theodor Golde, Dresden, ca. 1840.

Boxwood; ivory ferrules; single and double beadings. Three sections: l.h. joint, r.h. joint, bell. Thirteen pillar-mounted brass keys placed on blocks, round, flat key heads, twin third finger hole. Octave (wraparound) (RT), perforated plate (L1), B^{1}-$C\sharp^{2}$ trill (L3), C^{2} (R1), $B\flat^{1}$ (R1), $G\sharp^{1}$, $F\sharp^{1}$ (R3), F^{1} (cross, R3 operates same key head as opened by L4), F^{1} (L4), $E\flat^{1}$ (roller, R4), $E\flat^{1}$ (roller, L4), C^{1} (R4, raises $C\sharp^{1}$ key head when depressed), $C\sharp^{1}$ (R4, roller), B (L4). L=555.

Stamped on r.h. joint: "GOLDE"; bell: "GOLDE / DRESDEN".

2000.01

13-key oboe, Carl Theodor Golde, Dresden, ca. 1840.

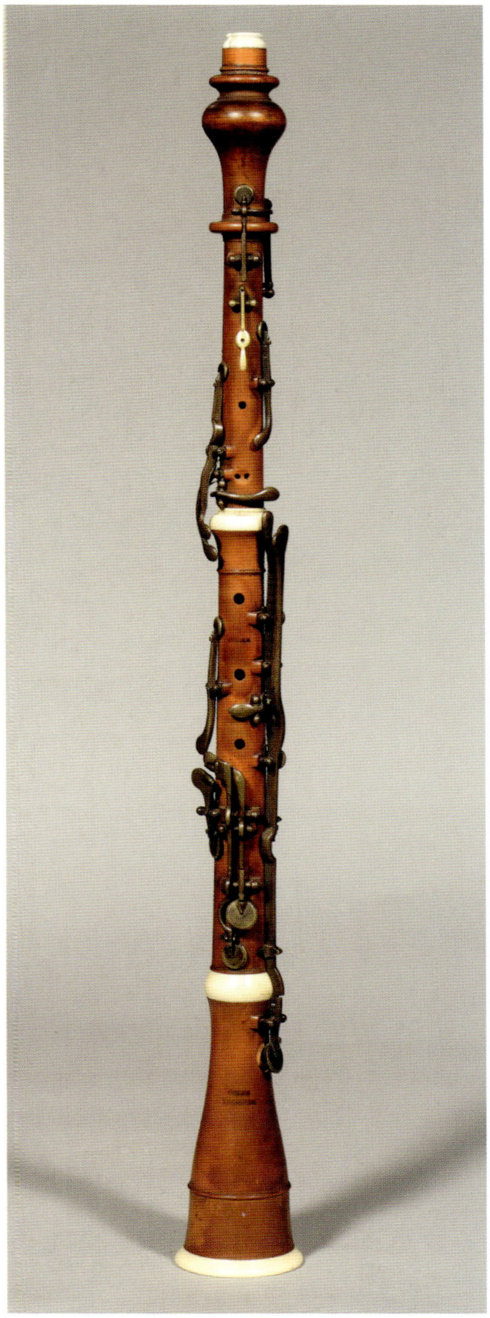

12-key oboe, Wolfgang Küss, Vienna, ca. 1820.

Boxwood; boxwood ferrules; one or two beadings. Three sections: l.h. joint, r.h. joint, bell. Twelve block-mounted brass keys, flat, round key heads, twin third finger hole. Octave (wraparound) (RT), C^2 (L3), $B\flat^1$ (LT), $B\flat^1$ (R1, opens same key head as LT), $G\sharp^1$, $F\sharp^1$ (L3), F^1 (cross, L3), $E\flat^1$ (L4), $E\flat^1$ (R4), C^1, $C\sharp^1$ (closes C^1 key head), B (L4). L=550.

Stamped on l.h. joint, r.h. joint: "(Hapsburg eagle) / Küfs (cursive) / Wien (cursive)"; bell: "(Hapsburg eagle) / Küfs (cursive) / Wien (cursive) / 1".

2001.15

LEFT: *12-key oboe*, Wolfgang Küss, Vienna, ca. 1820.

16-key oboe in B♭, J. Gras, Lille, system 5, ca. 1895.

Nickel-silver plated brass; nickel-silver ferrules. Four sections: bent bocal, l.h. joint, r.h. joint, bell. Plates for LT, R1, R3, perforated plates for L1, R2, rings for L2, L3. Sixteen pillar-mounted nickel-silver keys, modern key heads. 1st octave (automatic, LT), 2nd octave (L1), $C\sharp^2$-D^2 trill (L2, cross), B^1-$C\sharp^2$ trill (L3, cross), C^2 (R1), $B\flat^1$ (R1), $G\sharp^1$ (L4), $G\sharp^1$ (R1 lever), $F\sharp^1$ (R2), F^1 (R3), $E\flat^1$ (R4), $E\flat^1$ (L4), $C\sharp^1$, C^1, B (L4), B♭ (L♯4). L=650.

Stamped on bell: "J. GRAS / Bté S.G.D.G. / LILLE (in an oval)".

2001.18

RIGHT: *16-key* oboe in B♭, J. Gras, Lille, system 5, ca. 1895.

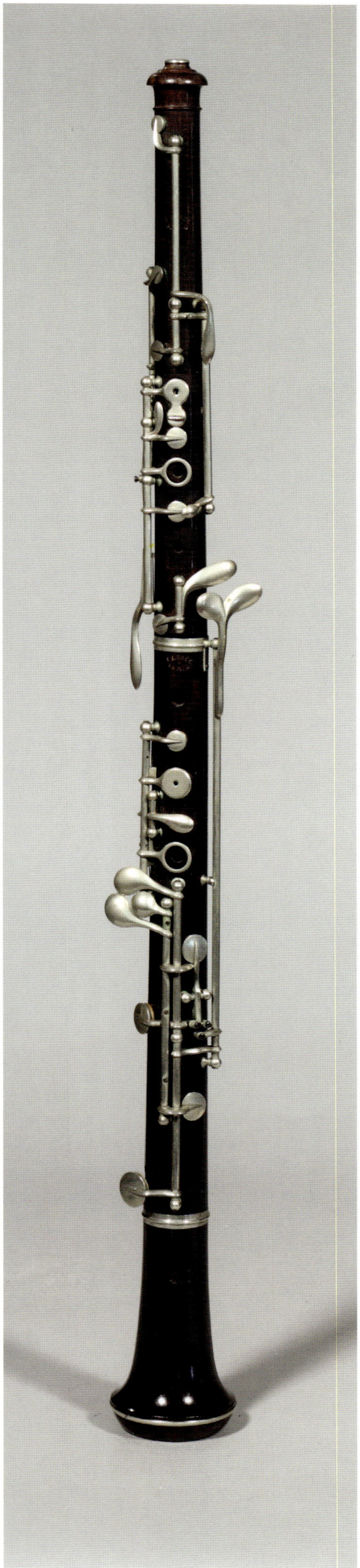

11-key oboe, F. Lorée, Paris, system 4, ca. 1885.

Stained grenadilla; nickel-silver ferrules. Three sections: l.h. joint, r.h. joint, bell. Eleven pillar-mounted nickel-silver keys, modern key heads, ring keys for L2, R3, perforated plates for L1, R2. 1st octave (RT), 2nd octave (L2), C♯²-D² trill (R1), B¹-C♯² trill (L3), G♯¹, F¹ (cross, L3), E♭¹ (R4), E♭¹ (L4), C¹, C♯¹, B (R4). Serial no. B62. In case with Lorée English horn (2001.20). L=567.

Stamped on l.h. joint, r.h. joint, bell: "F. LORÉE (curved) / (five-pointed star) / PARIS (curved)".

2001.19

LEFT: *11-key oboe*, F. Lorée, Paris, system 4, ca. 1885.

11-key oboe, Pierre Louis Gautrot aîné, Paris, system 3, ca. 1870.

Red-stained grenadilla; nickel-silver ferrules. Three sections: l.h. joint, r.h. joint, bell. Eleven pillar-mounted nickel-silver keys, modern key heads, twin third finger hole, perforated plate (L1), rings for R2, R3. Octave (LT), C² (L3), B¹-C♯² trill (R1), B♭¹ (R4) G♯¹, F¹ (cross, L3), E♭¹ (L4), E♭¹ (R4), C¹, C♯¹, B (L4). Serial no. 286. L=558.

Stamped on l.h. joint, r.h joint: "GA (intertwined in an oval) / GAUTROT AINÉ / BREVETÉ / A PARIS"; bell: "GA (intertwined in an oval) / GAUTROT AINÉ / BREVETÉ / A PARIS / 286".

Rousselet and Watel 2012, 77.

2001.21

RIGHT: *11-key oboe*, Pierre Louis Gautrot aîné, Paris, system 3, ca. 1870.

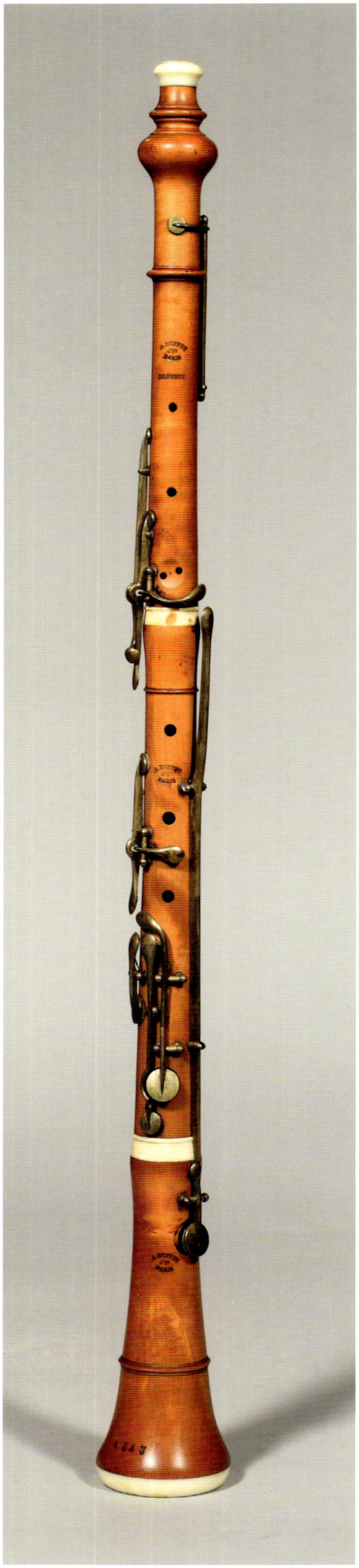

10-key oboe, Louis-Auguste Buffet, Paris, 1843.

Boxwood; ivory ferrules; single beading. Three sections: l.h. joint, r.h. joint, bell. Ten pillar-mounted brass keys, modern key heads, twin third finger hole. Octave (wraparound) (LT), C^2 (R1), B$\flat^1$ (R1), G$\sharp^1$, F$\sharp^1$ (R3), F^1 (cross), E$\flat^1$, C^1, C$\sharp^1$, B (L4). Serial no. 22. L=556.

Stamped on l.h. joint: "A. BUFFET / J$^{\underline{NE}}$ / PARIS / BRÉVETÉ"; r.h. joint: "A. BUFFET / J$^{\underline{NE}}$ / PARIS"; bell: "A. BUFFET / J$^{\underline{NE}}$ / PARIS". Stamped in large numbers on the bell: "22 1843".

This oboe resembles the earliest oboe model, model 1, made by Guillaume Triebert, Paris. The numbers on the bell appear to be serial no. 22 and a date of 1843; Buffet's use of the misspelled word "bréveté" (patented) also appears on clarinets beginning in 1843. The patent referred to is Buffet's French patent (1838, no. 9,380) for the needle spring used on his flutes, clarinets, and oboes.

Howe 2011, 188.

2001.26

LEFT: *10-key oboe*, Louis-Auguste Buffet, Paris, 1843.

9-key oboe, D'Almaine and Co., London, ca. 1840.

Boxwood; ivory ferrules; single and multiple beading. Three sections: l.h. joint, r.h. joint, bell. Nine block-mounted silver keys, round, flat key heads, twin third finger hole, two resonance holes on upper part of bell. Octave (LT), C^2 (L3), B$\flat^1$ (R1), G$\sharp^1$, F$\sharp^1$ (L3), F^1 (cross), E$\flat^1$ (spurs), C^1 (spurs), C$\sharp^1$. L=568.

Stamped on l.h. joint, r.h. joint: "(crown) / D'ALMAINE & C^O"; bell: "(crown between garlands) / D'ALMAINE & C^O / LATE / GOULDING & D'ALMAINE / SOHO SQUARE / LONDON".

2001.27

RIGHT: *9-key oboe*, D'Almaine and Co., London, ca. 1840.

13-key oboe, Gebrüder Alexander, Mainz, ca. 1870

Flame boxwood; ivory and nickel-silver ferrules; single beading. Three sections: l.h. joint, r.h. joint, bell. Thirteen pillar-mounted nickel-silver keys, modern key heads, rings for R2 and R3. 1st octave (wraparound, LT), E^2 (L1), $C\sharp^2$ (L3), C^2 (R1), $B\flat^1$ (R1), $G\sharp^1$, F^1 (cross, R3), F^1 (L4), $E\flat^1$ (R4), $E\flat^1$ (L4), C^1, $C\sharp^1$, B (L4). L=538.

Stamped on l.h. joint, r.h. joint, bell: "ALEXANDER (curved) IN / MAINZ".

2001.28

13-key oboe, Gebrüder Alexander, Mainz, ca. 1830.

Boxwood; ivory ferrules; double beadings. Three sections: l.h. joint, r.h. joint, bell. Thirteen block-mounted silver keys, flat, round key heads, ivory thumb rest, twin third finger hole. 1st octave (wraparound, LT), $C\sharp^2$ (L3), C^2 (R1), $B\flat^1$ (R1), $G\sharp^1$, $F\sharp^1$ (R3), F^1 (pillar-mounted cross, L3), F^1 (L4), $E\flat^1$ (R3), $E\flat^1$ (L4 lifting the same key head as R3), C^1, $C\sharp^1$, B (L4). L=541.

Stamped on l.h. joint, r.h. joint: "(monogram in oval)"; bell: "(monogram in oval) / Alexander (cursive) / IN / MAINZ".

2001.29

10-key oboe, Clair Bélisaire, Paris, model 1, ca. 1850.

Dark-stained boxwood; ivory ferrules; single beading. Three sections: l.h. joint, r.h. joint, bell. Ten pillar-mounted brass keys, round, flat key heads, twin third finger hole. Octave (wraparound, RT), C^2 (R1), $B\flat^1$ (R1), $G\sharp^1$, $F\sharp^1$ (R3), F^1 (cross, R3), $E\flat^1$, C^1, $C\sharp^1$, B (L4). L=563.

Stamped on l.h joint, r.h. joint: "Bélisaire / à Paris (in an oval)".

2001.30

13-key oboe, Gebrüder Alexander, Mainz, ca. 1870.

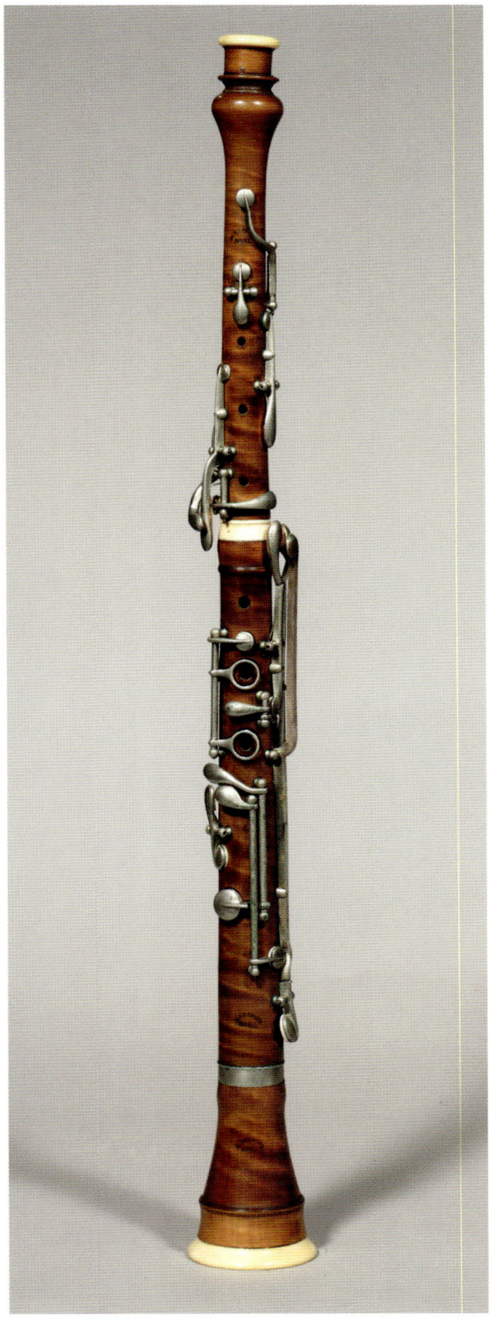

13-key oboe, Gebrüder Alexander, Mainz, ca. 1830.

10-key oboe, Clair Bélisaire, Paris, model 1, ca. 1850.

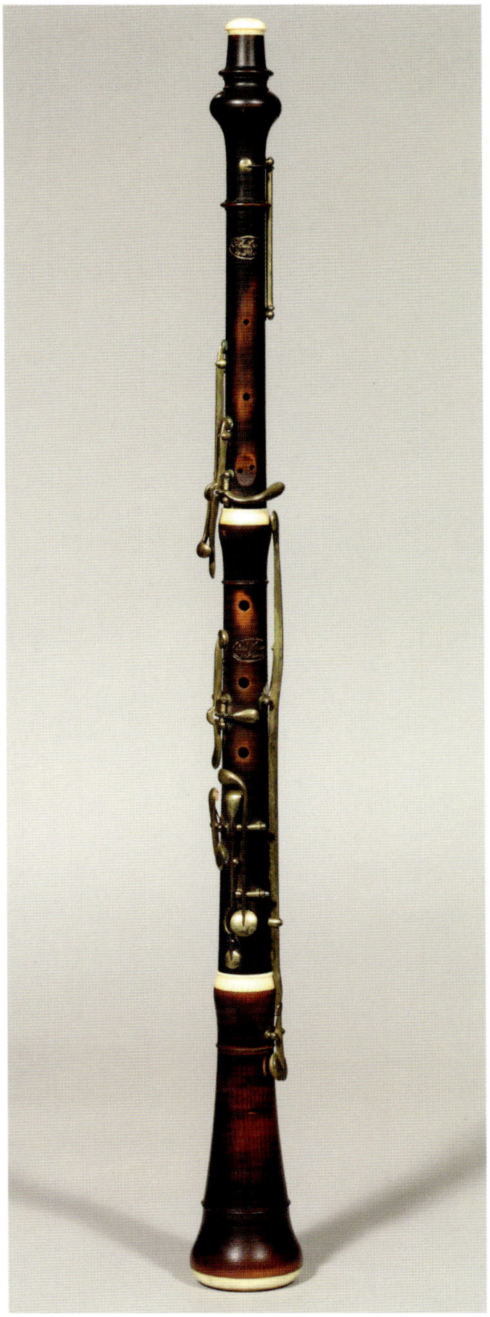

2-key oboe, Savary, Paris, ca. 1800.

Stained boxwood; ivory ferrules; multiple beadings. Three sections: l.h. joint, r.h. joint, bell. Two ring-mounted silver keys, square and octagonal key heads, twin third and fourth finger holes. $E\flat^1$ (square key head, spurs), C^1 (octagonal key head, spurs). L=570.

Stamped on l.h. joint, r.h. joint, bell: "(sunburst) / SAVARY (cursive) / A PARIS / (sunburst)".

2001.35

2-key oboe, Savary, Paris, ca. 1800.

9-key oboe, Guillaume Triebert, Paris, model 1, ca. 1835.

Stained boxwood; ivory ferrules; single beading. Three sections: l.h. joint, r.h. joint, bell. Nine brass pillar-mounted keys, round, flat key heads, perforated plate for L1, two rings for R2 and R3, twin third finger hole. Octave (wraparound, LT), C^2 (R1), $B\flat^1$ (R1), $G\sharp^1$, F^1 (cross, R3), $E\flat^1$ (R4), C^1, $C\sharp^1$, B (L4). L=563.

Stamped on l.h. joint: "TRIEBERT (under perforated key head)"; bell: "(barbican with three merlons) / TRIEBERT (curved) / A PARIS (curved)".

2002.03

9-key oboe, Guillaume Triebert, Paris, model 1, ca. 1835.

10-key oboe, Jean-Louis Tulou, Paris, model 1, ca. 1835.

Stained boxwood; thin boxwood and brass ferrules. Three sections: l.h. joint, r.h. joint, bell. Ten pillar-mounted brass keys with round, flat key heads, twin third finger hole. Octave (wraparound, LT), C^2 (R1), $B\flat^1$ (R1), $G\sharp^1$, $F\sharp^1$ (R3), F^1 (cross, R3) $E\flat^1$ (R4), C^1, $C\sharp^1$, B (L4). L=560.

Stamped on l.h. joint, r.h. joint, bell: "(nightingale) / TULOU / PARIS".

2002.58

10-key oboe, Jean-Louis Tulou, Paris, model 1, ca. 1835.

10-key oboe, Jérôme Thibouville-Lamy, Paris, system 3, ca. 1890.

Stained rosewood; nickel-silver ferrules. Three sections: l.h. joint, r.h. joint, bell. Ten nickel-silver pillar-mounted keys, modern key heads, perforated plate for L1, two rings for R2 and R3, twin third finger hole. 1st octave (LT), 2nd octave (L1), C^2 (R1), $B\flat^1$ (R1), $G\sharp^1$, F^1 (cross, L3), $E\flat^1$ (R4), $C\sharp^1$, C^1, B (L4). L=566.

Stamped on r.h. joint: "J.T.L. / PARIS / A.O / Q^{TE} SUP^{RE}"; bell: "(lyre in auriole) / JTL / (seven medals) / JERÔME / THIBOUVILLE / LAMY / 68 R. Réaumur (cursive) / PARIS / A.O / 1ERE Q$^{TE.}$".

2002.59

15-key oboe, F. Barbier (H. Selmer et Cie), Paris, thumb-plate with Barret action, ca. 1900.

African black wood; nickel-silver ferrules. Three sections: l.h. joint, r.h. joint, bell. Plate for LT, perforated plates for L1, R2, rings for L2, L3, R1, R3. Fifteen pillar-mounted nickel-silver keys, modern key heads. 1st octave (automatic, LT), 2nd octave (L1), $C\sharp^2$-D^2 trill (L2, cross), B^1-$C\sharp^2$ trill (L3, cross), C^2 or $B\flat^1$ (R1), $G\sharp^1$ (L4), $G\sharp^1$ (R1 ring), F^1 (R2), F^1 (R3), $E\flat^1$ (R4), $E\flat^1$ (L4), $C\sharp^1$, C^1, B (L4), B$\flat$ (L4). Serial no. 255. L=594.

Stamped on bell: "F. BARBIER (curved) / PARIS (curved) / FB (monogram)".

2002.65

12-key oboe, F. Lorée, Paris, system 4, ca. 1885.

Rosewood; nickel-silver ferrules. Three sections: l.h. joint, r.h. joint, bell. Twelve pillar-mounted nickel-silver keys, modern key heads, perforated plates for L1, R2, rings for L2, L3, R6. 1st octave (LT), 2nd octave (R1), B^1-$C\sharp^2$ trill (cross, L3), C^2 or $B\flat^1$ (R1), $G\sharp^1$, F^1 (cross, R3), $E\flat^1$ (R4), $E\flat^1$ (L4), $C\sharp^1$, C^1, C^1 (L4), B (L4). L=567.

Stamped on l.h. joint, r.h. joint, bell: "F. LORÉE (curved) / PARIS".

2002.71

10-key oboe, Jérôme Thibouville-Lamy, Paris, system 3, ca. 1890.

15-key oboe, F. Barbier (H. Selmer et Cie), Paris, thumb-plate with Barret action, ca. 1900.

12-key oboe, F. Lorée, Paris, system 4, ca. 1885.

5-key oboe, Goulding and Co., London, ca. 1810.

Boxwood; boxwood ferrules; multiple beading. Three sections: l.h. joint, r.h. joint, bell. Five ring and block-mounted silver keys, hexagonal key heads, twin third and fourth finger holes, two resonance holes on upper part of bell. $E\flat^1$ (R1), $G\sharp^1$, F^1 (cross, R3), $E\flat^1$, C^1 (fish-tail touch, spurs). L=560.

Stamped on l.h. joint, r.h. joint: "GOULDING & C^{O}"; bell: "GOULDING & C^{O} / LONDON".

2002.75

5-key oboe, Goulding and Co., London, ca. 1810.

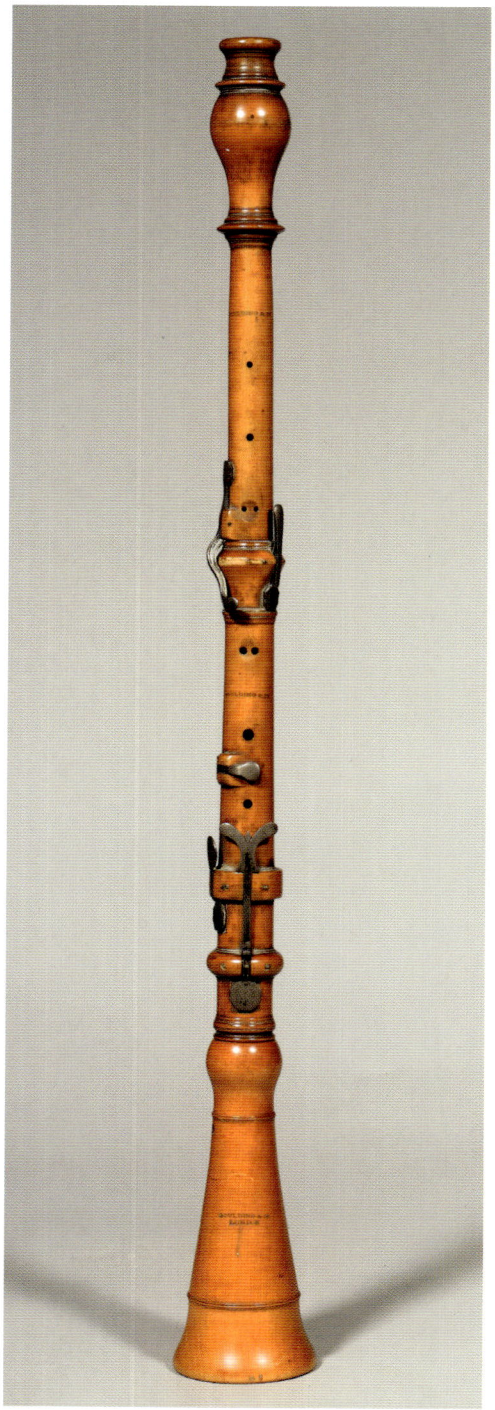

8-key oboe, Johann Ziegler, Vienna, ca. 1840.

Dark-stained boxwood; ivory ferrules; single ferrules with lines. Three sections: l.h. joint, r.h. joint, bell. Eight pillar-mounted brass keys, flat, round key heads, two resonance holes on upper part of bell. Octave (wraparound, LT), $E\flat^1$ (R1), $G\sharp^1$, F^1 (cross, R3), $E\flat^1$ (R4), $E\flat^1$ (L4), C^1 (roller), $C\sharp^1$ (roller). L=560.

Stamped on l.h. joint, r.h. joint, bell: "(Hapsburg eagle) / I:ZIEGLER / WIEN".

2002.81

8-key oboe, Johann Ziegler, Vienna, ca. 1840.

14-key oboe, Buffet-Crampon et Cie, Paris, Half-Boehm system, ca. 1860.

Stained black wood; nickel-silver ferrules. Two sections: body, bell. Fourteen pillar-mounted nickel-silver keys, salt-spoon key heads, plate for L1, rings for L2, R1, R2, R3; twin third finger hole, touch roller for C^1. 1st octave (LT), 2nd octave (R1), C^2-$C\sharp^2$, $C\sharp^2$-D^2 (cross, R1), C^2 (R1), $B\flat^1$ (R1), $G\sharp^1$, $F\sharp^1$ (cross, R2), F^1 (cross, R3), $E\flat^1$ (R4), $E\flat^1$ (L4), $C\sharp^1$ (nickel-silver roller, R4), C^1 (R4), B (L4). L=564.

Stamped on bell: "(lyre) / BUFFET CRAMPON & Cie / A PARIS (in oval) / BC (monogram)".

Kampmann 2007, 4-5.

2002.89

14-key oboe, Buffet-Crampon et Cie, Paris, Half-Boehm system, ca. 1860.

10-key oboe, Lefêvre Frères, Rouen, ca. 1830.

Stained boxwood; ivory rings; single beading. Three sections: l.h. joint, r.h. joint, bell. Ten ring and pillar-mounted brass keys, flat, round and square key heads. Octave (LT), C^2 (R1), $B\flat^1$ (cross, L3), $G\sharp^1$, $F\sharp^1$ (R3), F^1 (cross, R3), $E\flat^1$, C^1, $C\sharp^1$, B (L4, with square key head). L=570.

Stamped on l.h. joint, r.h. joint, bell: "LEFÊVRE F^{ES} / A ROUEN".

2002.90

10-key oboe, Frédéric Guillaume Adler, Paris, ca. 1825.

Boxwood; ivory rings; single beading. Three sections: l.h. joint, r.h. joint, bell. Ten pillar-mounted brass keys, round, flat key heads, twin third and fourth finger holes. Octave (wraparound, LT), C^2 (R1), $B\flat^1$ (R1), $C\sharp^1$, $F\sharp^1$ (R3), F^1 (cross, R3), $E\flat^1$ (R4), C^1, $C\sharp^1$, B (L4). L=550.

Stamped on l.h. joint, r.h. joint: "(crown) / ADLER / A PARIS"; bell: "(crown) / ADLER / RUE MANDAR / A PARIS / (five-pointed star)".

2002.91

12-key oboe, Jean-Baptiste Buffet, Paris, system 3, ca. 1875.

Black wood; nickel-silver rings. Three sections: l.h. joint, r.h. joint, bell. Twelve pillar-mounted nickel-silver keys, modern key heads, perforated plate for L1, rings for L2, R3. 1st octave (LT), 2nd octave (L1), B^1-$C\sharp^2$ trill (L3), C^2 (R1), $B\flat^1$ key (R1), $G\sharp^1$, F^1 (cross, R3), $E\flat^1$ (R4), $E\flat^1$ (L4), C^1, $C\sharp^1$, B (L4). In case. L=543.

Stamped on l.h. joint, r.h. joint: "BUFFET / PARIS (in an oval)".

Rousselet and Watel 2012, 31.

2003.01

10-key oboe, Lefêvre Frères, Rouen, ca. 1830.

10-key oboe, Frédéric Guillaume Adler, Paris, ca. 1825.

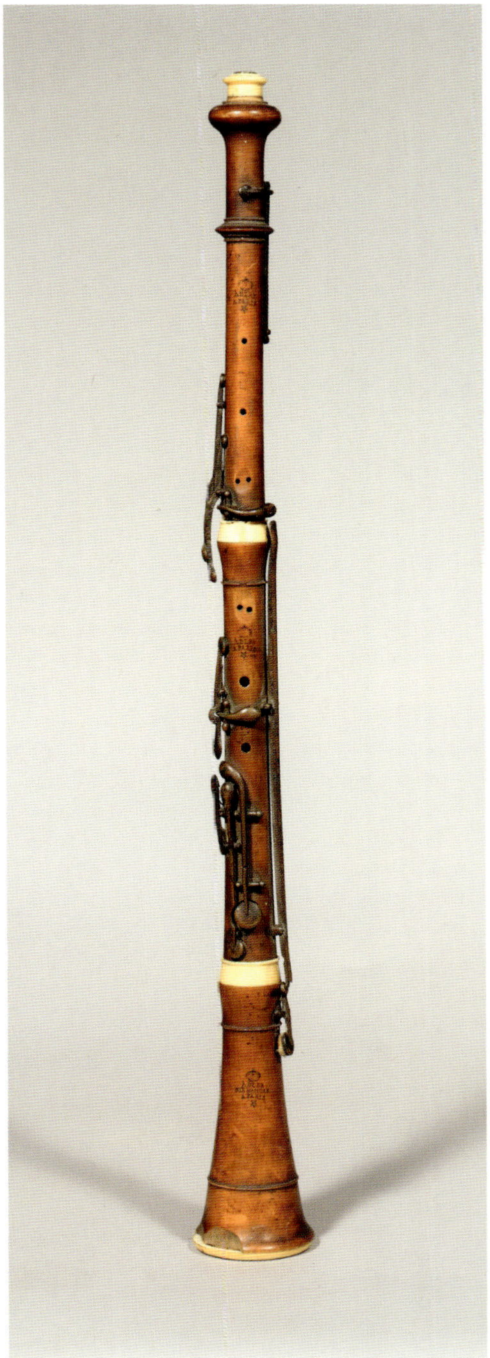

12-key oboe, Jean-Baptiste Buffet, Paris, system 3, ca. 1875.

12-key oboe, Kruspe, Erfurt, ca. 1880.

Boxwood; brass ferrules; beading. Three sections: l.h. joint, r.h. joint, bell. Twelve pillar-mounted brass keys, modern key heads, two ring keys for R2, R3. 1st octave (wraparound, LT), C♯^{1} (L3), C^2 (R1), B♭^{1} (R1), G♯^{1} (removed), F^1 (cross, R3), F^1 (L4), E♭^{1} (R4), E♭^{1} (L4), C^1, C♯^{1}, B (L4). L=570.

Stamped on l.h. joint, r.h. joint, bell: "(lyre) / KRUSPE / ERFURT / (six-spoked wheel)".

2003.05

7-key oboe, William Milhouse, London, ca. 1820.

Boxwood; boxwood ferrules; multiple beadings. Four sections: bocal (replacement), l.h. joint, r.h. joint, bell. Seven ring, block and saddle-mounted silver keys, octagonal and round key heads, twin third finger hole, two resonance holes on upper part of bell. Octave (LT), B♭^{1} (R1, round, flat key head), G♯^{1} (octagonal key head), F♯^{1} (R3, round, flat key head), F^1 (cross, R3), E♭^{1} (octagonal ♯key head, spurs), C^1 (fish-tail touch, octagonal key head, spurs). L=561.

Stamped on l.h. joint, r.h. joint: "W·MILHOUSE (curved) / LONDON (curved)"; bell: "W·MILHOUSE (curved) / LONDON (curved) / 337 OXFORD ST$^{\underline{T}}$".

2003.06

15-key oboe, Margueritat, Paris, thumb-plate and Barret action, system 5, ca. 1900.

African black wood; nickel-silver ferrules. Three sections: l.h. joint, r.h. joint, bell. Plate for RT, perforated plates for L1, R2, rings for L2, L3, R1, R3. Fifteen pillar-mounted nickel-silver keys, modern key heads. 1st octave (automatic, LT), 2nd octave (L1), C♯^{2}-D^2 trill (L2, cross), B^1-C♯^{2} trill (L3, cross), C^2 or B♭^{1} (R1), G♯^{1} (L4), G♯^{1} (R1 lever), F♯^{1} (R2), F^1 (R3), E♭^{1} (R4), E♭^{1} (L4), C^1, C♯^{1}, B (L4), B♭ (L4). L=598.

Stamped on bell: "MARGUERITAT / 21 Bd BONNE NOUVELLE / PARIS (in a dotted oval)".

2003.18

12-key oboe, Kruspe, Erfurt, ca. 1880.

7-key oboe, William Milhouse, London, ca. 1820.

15-key oboe, Margueritat, Paris, thumb-plate and Barret action, system 5, ca. 1900.

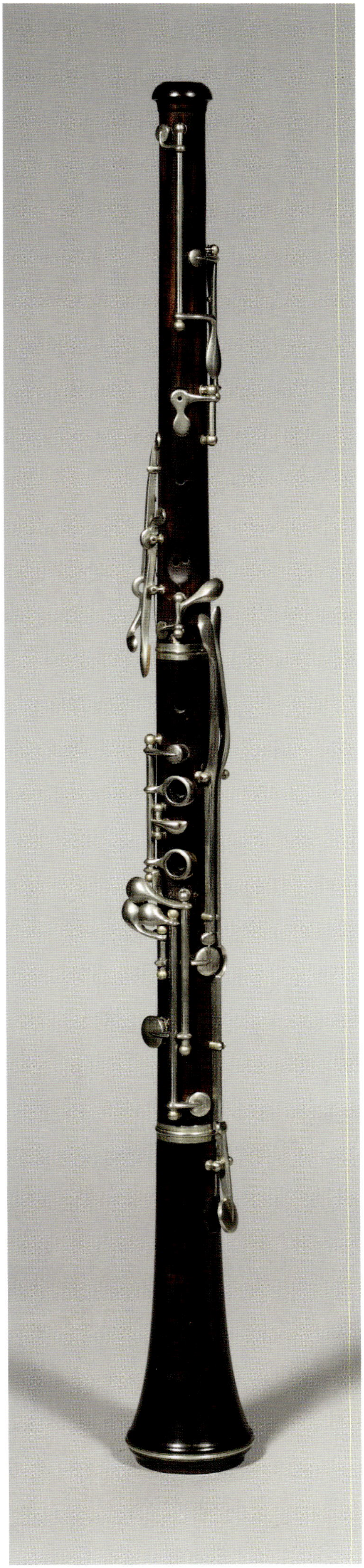

11-key oboe, Halary, Paris, system 3, ca. 1865.

Grenadilla; nickel-silver ferrules. Three sections: l.h. joint. r.h. joint, bell. Eleven pillar-mounted nickel-silver keys, modern key heads, perforated plate for L1, rings for R2 and R3, twin third finger hole. 1st octave (LT), 2nd octave (L1), C² (R1), B♭¹ (R1), G♯¹, F¹ (cross, R3), E♭¹ (R4), E♭¹ (L4, raises the same key head as R4), C¹, C♯¹, B (L4). L=565.

Stamped on l.h. joint, bell: "HALARY (curved) / A PARIS (curved)".

2003.36

LEFT: *11-key oboe*, Halary, Paris, system 3, ca. 1865.

3-key oboe, attributed to François-Adrien Dupuis, Paris, ca. 1700.

Ivory; ivory ferrules decorated with black round inserts. Three sections: l.h. joint, r.h. joint, bell. Three ring-mounted silver keys, square key heads, twin third and fourth finger holes, two resonance holes on lower part of bell. E♭¹ (L4, spurs), E♭¹ (R4, spurs), C¹ (double-wing touch, spurs). L=526.

No inscription.

This oboe is very similar to the Dupuis oboe previously in the Berlin Museum, no. 2933, in its use of black round inserts on baluster, upper ferrule of r.h. joint, and large ferrule on the upper section of bell. A stunning example of an early decorated oboe.

Haynes 2001, 68, photo (a).

2003.43

RIGHT: *3-key oboe,* attributed to François-Adrien Dupuis, Paris, ca. 1700.

2-key oboe, James Power, London, ca. 1810.

Stained boxwood; ivory ferrules; single beading. Three sections: l.h. joint, r.h. joint, bell. Two ring-mounted brass keys, round, flat key heads, twin third finger hole, two resonance holes on upper part of bell. E♭[1] (R4), C[1] (fish-tail touch, spurs). L=578.

Stamped on r.h. joint: "POWER / LONDON".

2003.50

LEFT: *2-key oboe*, James Power, London, ca. 1810.

13-key Boehm-system oboe, Buffet-Crampon et Cie, Paris, ca. 1890.

Stained grenadilla; nickel-silver ferrules. Two sections: body, bell. Thirteen pillar-mounted nickel-silver keys, modern key heads, plate for L1, rings for L2, L3, R1, R2, R3. 1st octave (automatic, R1), 2nd octave (L1), B[1]-C♯[2] trill (L3), C[2] (RT), C[2] (R1), B♭[1] (R1), G♯[1], F[1] (R3, cross), E♭[1] (R4), E♭[1] (L4), C♯[1] (R4), C[1] (R4), B (L4). L=535.

Stamped on body: "(lyre) / BUFFET / Crampon & Cie / A PARIS (in a dotted oval) / BREVETÉS / BC (monogram)"; bell: "(lyre) / BUFFET / Crampon & Cie / A PARIS (in a dotted oval) / BC (monogram)".

2003.61

RIGHT: *13-key Boehm-system oboe*, Buffet-Crampon et Cie, Paris, ca. 1890.

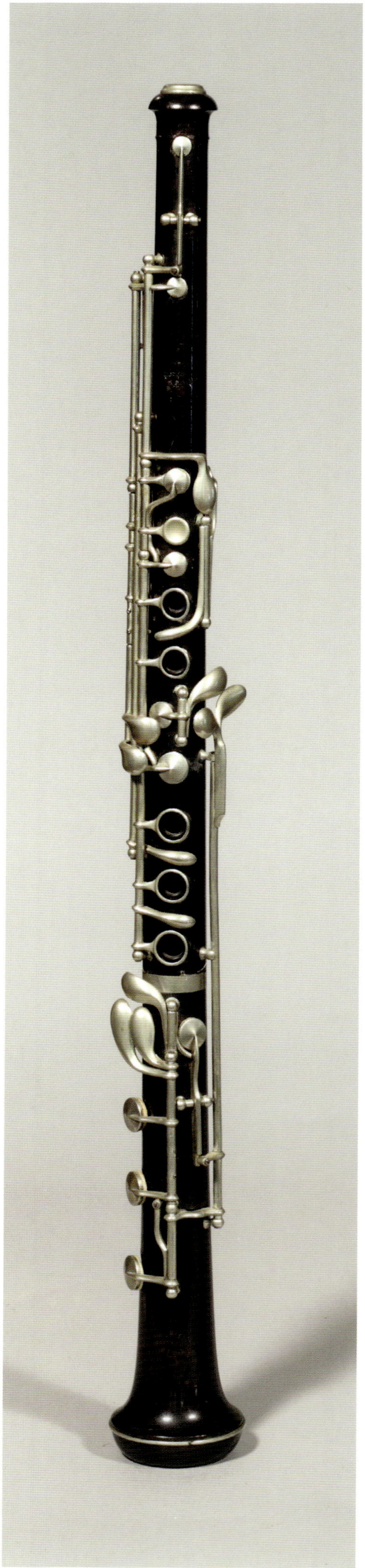

2-key oboe, Charles Joseph Bizey, Paris, ca. 1740.

Stained boxwood; ivory ferrules; multiple beading. Three sections: l.h. joint, r.h. joint, bell. Two ring-mounted brass keys, square key heads, two resonance holes on upper part of bell, twin third and fourth finger holes. $E\flat^1$ (R1, small spurs), C^1 (fish-tail touch, small spurs). L=572.

Stamped on l.h. joint: "(fleur-de-lis) / BIZEY / A PARIS / (sun)"; r.h. joint: "(fleur-de-lis) / BIZEY"

2003.62

LEFT: *2-key oboe*, Charles Joseph Bizey, Paris, ca. 1740.

17-key oboe, V. Kohlert Söhne, Graslitz, system 5, ca. 1910.

Nickel-silver body; nickel-silver ferrules. Two sections: body, bell. Plate for RT, perforated plates for L1, R2, rings for L2, L3, R1, R3. Seventeen pillar-mounted nickel-silver keys, modern key heads. Octave (automatic, LT), $C\sharp^2$-D^2 trill (L2, cross), B^1-$C\sharp^2$ trill (L3, cross), C^2 (R1), $B\flat^1$ (R1), $G\sharp^1$ (L4), $G\sharp^1$ (R1 lever), $F\sharp^1$ (R2), F^1 (cross, R3), F^1 (cross, L4), $E\flat^1$ (R4), $E\flat^1$ (L4), $C\sharp^1$ (R3), C^1 (R4), $C\sharp^1$, B (L4), B♭ (L4). In case. L=620.

Stamped in a flower and leaf motif on bell: "V. KOHLERT / SÖHNE / GRASLITZ".

2005.22

RIGHT: *17-key oboe*, V. Kohlert Söhne, Graslitz, system 5, ca. 1910.

13-key Boehm-system oboe, Gautrot-Marquet, Paris, ca. 1880.

Black wood; nickel-silver ferrules. Two sections: body, bell. Thirteen pillar-mounted nickel-silver keys, round, curved key heads, plate for L1, rings for L2, L3, R1, R2, R3. 1st octave (automatic, LT), 2nd octave (L1), B¹-C♯² trill (L3), C² (R1), B♭¹ (LT), B♭¹ (R1), G♯¹, F¹ (R3, cross), E♭¹ (R4), E♭¹ (L4), C♯¹ (R4), C¹ (R4), B (L4). L=545.

Stamped on upper portion of body: "GA (in stylized oval)"; bell: "GA (in stylized oval) / GAUTROT-MARQUET / BREVETE S.G.D.G. (in oval shape)".

2005.23

14-key oboe, Triebert, Paris, thumb-plate with Barret action, ca. 1890.

Black wood; gold-plated ferrules. Three sections: l.h. joint, r.h. joint, bell. Fourteen pillar-mounted gold-plated keys, modern key heads, leaf touches. Plate for RT, perforated plates for L1, R2, rings for L2, L3, R1, R3. 1st octave (automatic, LT), 2nd octave (L1), C♯²-D² trill or B¹-C♯² trill (L3, cross), C or B♭¹ (R1), G♯¹ (L4), G♯¹ (R1 ring), F♯¹ (cross, R2), F¹ (cross, R3), E♭¹ (R4), E♭¹ (L4), C¹, C♯¹, B (L4), B♭ (L4). L=605.

Stamped on l.h. joint: "BREVETÉ / (barbican with four merlons) / TRIEBERT / A PARIS"; r.h. joint: "TRIEBERT (curved) / A PARIS"; bell: "BREVETÉ / (barbican with four merlons) / TRIEBERT / A PARIS".

2006.19

13-key oboe, Kruspe, Erfurt, ca. 1850.

Boxwood; brass ferrules. Four sections: tuning slide, l.h. joint, r.h. joint, bell. Thirteen pillar-mounted brass keys, round, curved key heads, rings for R2 and R3, tuning slide on upper portion of head adjustable up to 16 mm, twin third finger hole. 1st octave (wraparound, LT), E² (L1), C♯² (L3), C² (R1), B♭¹ (R1), G♯¹, F¹ (cross, R3), F¹ (L4), E♭¹ (R4), E♭¹ (L4), C¹, C♯¹, B (L4). L=542.

Stamped on tuning slide: "(six-spoked wheel) / KRUSPE / ERFURT / (six-spoked wheel) / 1"; l.h. joint: "(six-spoked wheel) / KRUSPE / ERFURT / (six-spoked wheel)"; r.h. joint, bell: "(Schwarzberg eagle) / (six-spoked wheel) / KRUSPE / ERFURT / (six-spoked wheel)".

2007.12

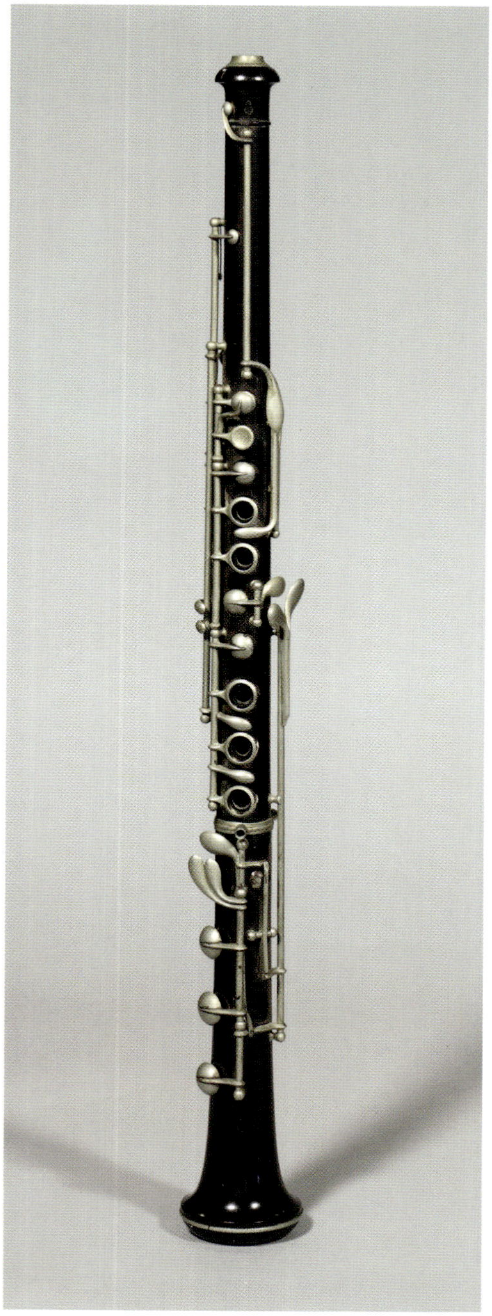

13-key Boehm-system oboe, Gautrot-Marquet, Paris, ca. 1880.

14-key oboe, Triebert, Paris, thumb-plate with Barret action, ca. 1890.

13-key oboe, Kruspe, Erfurt, ca. 1850.

2-key oboe, Joannes Panormo, Naples, ca. 1760.

Ivory; multiple beading. Three sections: l.h. joint, r.h. joint, bell. Two ring-mounted silver keys, octagonal key heads, twin third finger hole, two resonance holes on upper part of bell. E♭^{1} (R4, spurs), C^1 (fish-tail touch, spurs). L=580.

Stamped faintly on l.h. joint, r.h. joint, bell: "PANORM".

2007.25.

LEFT: *2-key oboe,* Joannes Panormo, Naples, ca. 1760.

17-key oboe, August Emil Fischer, Bremen, Barret action, system 5, ca. 1930.

Black wood; nickel-silver ferrules. Three sections: l.h. joint, r.h. joint, bell. Seventeen pillar-mounted nickel-silver keys, modern key heads, plate, LT, perforated plates, L2, R2. 1st octave (automatic, RT), 2nd octave (L1), C♯^{2}-D^2 trill (L2, cross), B^1-C♯^{2} trill (L3, cross), C^2 (R1), B♭^{1} (R1), G♯^{1} (L4), G♯^{1} (R1 lever), F♯^{1} (cross, R2), F^1 (cross, R3), F^1 (L4), E♭^{1} (R4), E♭^{1} (L4), C^1, C♯^{1}, B (L4), B♭ (L4). Serial no. 1827. In case. L=600.

Stamped on l.h. joint: "1827 / A.E. FISCHER"; r.h. joint: "1827 / A.E. FISCHER / BREMEN"; bell: "1827 / A.E. FISCHER / BREMEN / MADE / IN / GERMANY".

2010.02

RIGHT: *17-key oboe,* August Emil Fischer, Bremen, Barret action, system 5, ca. 1930.

2-key oboe da caccia, I. T. Weigel School, Breslau, ca. 1725.

Maple; hexagonal-sided; covered with leather; maple ferrules; multiple beadings. Two sections: curved body, bell, missing bocal. Two block-mounted brass keys with square key heads, two resonance holes on upper part of bell. E♭^{1} (square key head, spurs), C^{1} (fish-tail touch, round key head, spurs). L=825 (for the lower curve).

No inscription.

Identical in shape and design to oboes da caccia by I.T. Weigel, Breslau. Two stamped examples in the Museo Civico of Bologna.

Young 1988 no. 46; Waterhouse 1993, 423.

2001.12

2-key oboe da caccia, I. T. Weigel School, Breslau, ca. 1725.

5-key basse de musette or hautbois d'église, Jeanneret, La Chaux-du-Milieu, ca. 1770.

Maple; ferrules; multiple beadings. Five sections: piroutte (missing), looped bocal, l.h. joint, r.h. joint, bell. Five block-mounted brass keys, round, flat key heads, bell has large resonance hole, l.h. joint damaged. B (L1), G (L3), F (R1), G (R3), C (R4).

Inscription stamped on the lower section of brass, swallowtail key touch, in an octagonal box: "(6-pointed star) (6-pointed star) / IF•R•".

There are thirty-two basse de musettes with an inscription on the lower section of a swallowtail key touch, in a circle: "(inverted fleur-de-lis) / I•IR / (crossed palm branches)." Only two instruments have the "IF•R•" mark.

Young 1988 no. 50; Waterhouse 1993, 193-194; Staehelin 2002, 4-8.

2001.17

5-key basse de musette or hautbois d'église, Jeanneret, La Chaux-du-Milieu, ca. 1770.

Rackett, stamped Bizey, of French origin, eighteenth century.

Maple; two brass ferrules. Three sections: coiled bocal, body, convex bell. On front, six finger holes, two raised metal rings (tentines) inserted in the instrument. On back, a tentine is covered by palm of l.h., two ivory bushed holes are covered with LT and RT, ivory ferrule on bell. H=356; D=98.

Stamped on front of body: "(fleur-de-lis) / BIZEY".

The instrument is awkward to finger and not of the usual high quality by Bizey; it is possible that the stamp was fraudulently added.

2004.05

Rackett, stamped Bizey, of French origin, eighteenth century.

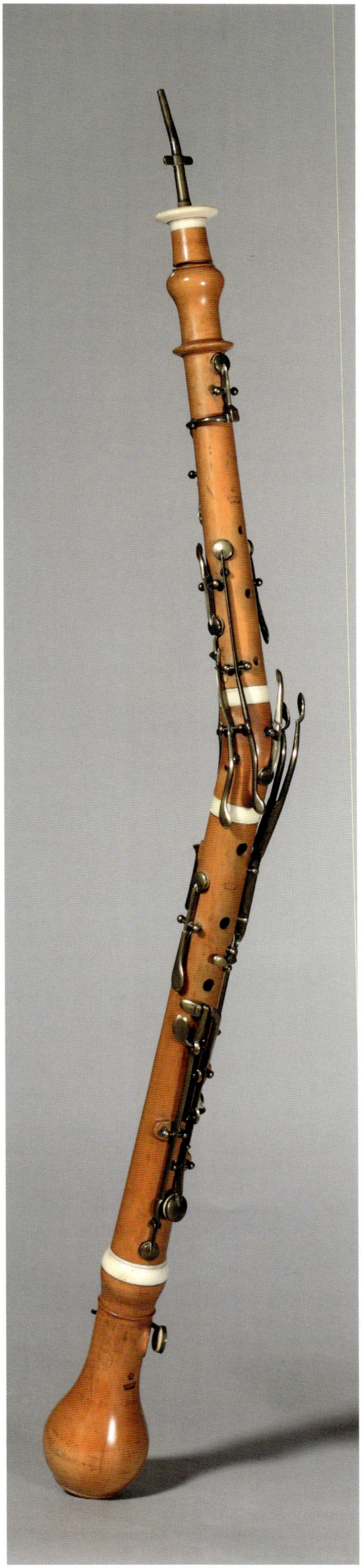

13-key English horn, Stephan Koch, Vienna, ca. 1825.

Boxwood; angular form; ivory ferrules; single beading. Six sections: brass bocal (original or period), tuning slide, l.h. joint, angle joint, r.h. joint, bell (bulb-shaped). Thirteen mounted brass keys, round, flat key heads, large brass thumb rest on back of r.h. joint. Octave (wraparound), C² (L3), C² (R1), B♭¹ (LT), B♭¹ (R1, operates the same key head as opened by LT), G♯¹ (on angle joint), F♯¹ (R3), F¹ (cross), E♭¹ (L4), E♭¹ (R4, brass roller, operates the same keyhead as L4), C¹, C♯¹, B (RT). L=695.

Stamped on l.h. joint, r.h. joint, bell: "(Hapsburg eagle) S.KOCH / WIEN".

1995.03

LEFT: *13-key English horn*, Stephan Koch, Vienna, ca. 1825.

10-key English horn, Triebert, Paris, ca. 1830.

Curved wood covered with black leather; ivory ferrules; single beading. Three sections: l.h. joint, r.h. joint, bell (bulb-shaped). Ends of r.h. and l.h. joints decorated with gilt intertwined leaves and star decorations, ring on back of r.h. joint for strap, bell stained black. Ten pillar-mounted silver keys, flat, round key heads on oval-shaped brass plates, twin third finger-hole. Octave, C² (R1), B♭¹ (R1), G♯¹, F♯¹ (R3), F¹ (cross, R3), E♭¹, C¹, C♯¹, B (RT). L=770 (measured from inside curve).

Stamped on l.h. joint, r.h. joint, bell: "(barbican with three merlons) / TRIEBERT / A PARIS".

2000.09

RIGHT: *10-key English horn*, Triebert, Paris, ca. 1830.

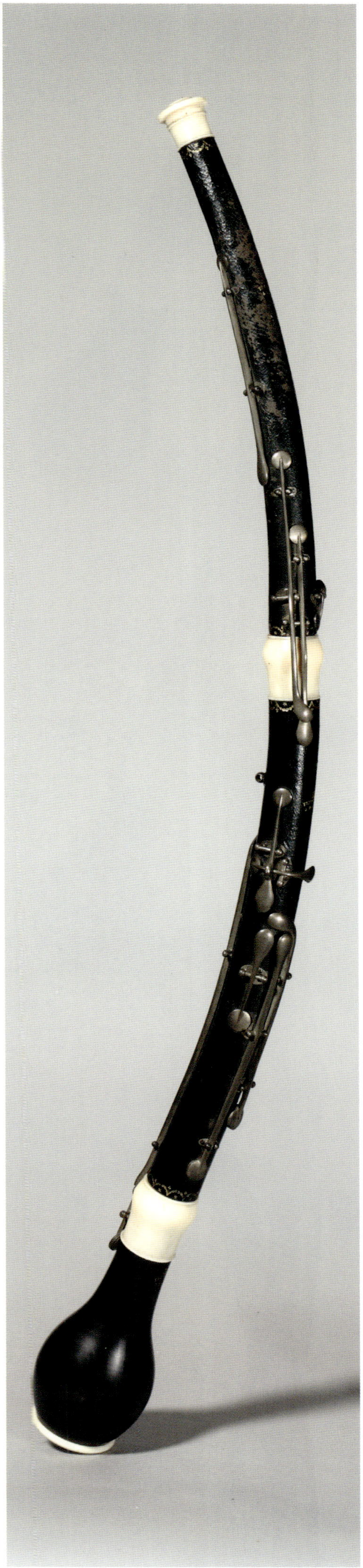

10-key English horn, Anton Nechwalsky, Vienna, ca. 1840.

Stained boxwood; angular form; ivory ferrules; single beading. Six sections: nickel-silver bocal (contemporary), tuning slide, l.h. joint, angle joint, r.h. joint, bell (bulb shaped). Ten block-mounted brass keys, flat, round key heads, twin third finger hole. Ring on back of r.h. joint for sling. Octave (wraparound), B♭^{1} (LT, operates same key head as L1), B♭^{1} (R1, opens the same key head as LT), C^2 (L3), G♯^{1}, F♯^{1}, F^1 (cross), E♭^{1}, C^1, C♯^{1} (overlapping touches for the last two keys). L=788.

Stamped: l.h. joint, r.h joint, bell: "(eagle) / NECHWALSKY / WIEN / (six-pointed star)".

2001.11

LEFT: *10-key English horn*, Anton Nechwalsky, Vienna, ca. 1840.

11-key English horn, F. Lorée, Paris, system 4, 1893.

Stained grenadilla; nickel-silver ferrules. Four sections: bent bocal, l.h. joint, r.h. joint, bell (bulb-shaped). Eleven pillar-mounted nickel-silver keys, modern key heads, thumb rest and ring on back of r.h. joint. Plates for LT, L1, R1, and rings for L2, R2, R3. 1st octave (RT), 2nd octave (L1), C♯^{2}-D^2 trill (R1), B^1-C♯^{2} trill (L3), G♯^{1}, F^1 (cross, L3), E♭^{1} (L4), E♭^{1} (R4), C^1, C♯^{1}, B (L4). Serial no. C42. In case with Lorée oboe (2001.19), two bocals, reed cases, screwdriver, grease pot, and sling. L=800.

Stamped on l.h. joint, r.h. joint, bell: "F. LORÉE (curved) / (star) /PARIS (curved)".

2001.20

RIGHT: *11-key English horn*, F. Lorée, Paris, system 4, 1893.

2-key vox humana or tenor oboe in F, Thomas Key, London, ca. 1810.

Stained boxwood; ivory ferrules; single beading. Two sections: l.h. joint, r.h. joint-bell. Two ring-mounted brass keys, square key heads. E♭^{1}, C^1. L=716.

Stamped on l.h. joint: "KEY / LONDON / (unicorn head)"; r.h. joint-bell: "KEY / LONDON / (unicorn head) // 2. PALL-MALL."

2001.32

LEFT: *2-key vox humana or tenor oboe in F*, Thomas Key, London, ca. 1810.

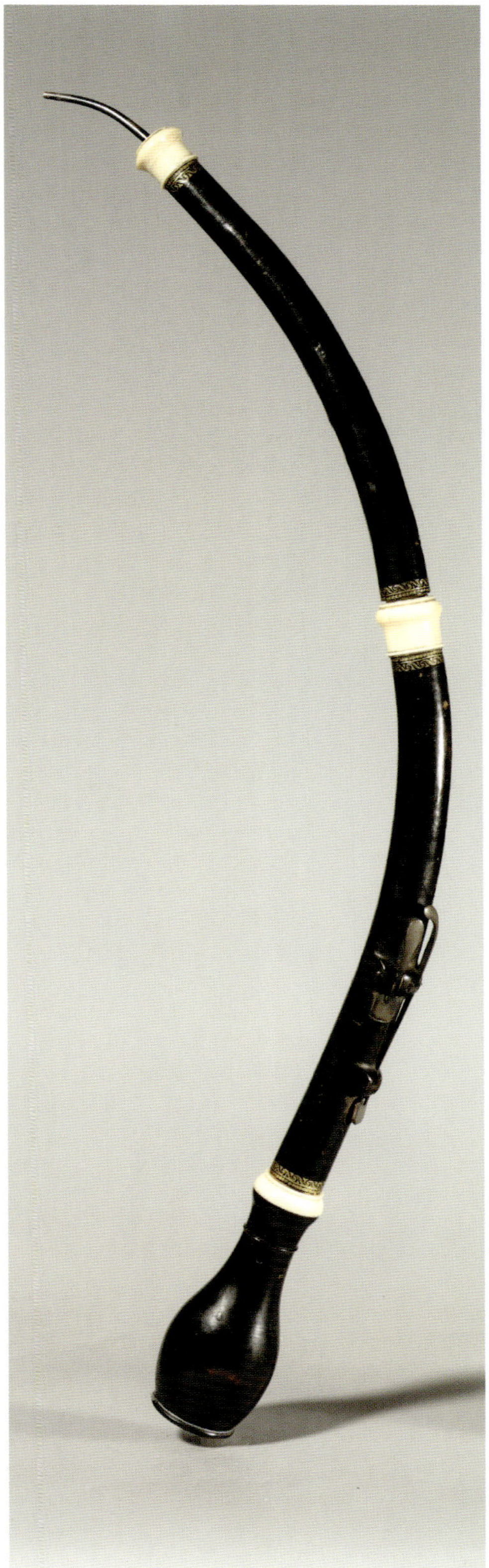

2-key English horn, Frédéric Guillaume Adler, Paris, ca. 1820.

Curved maple covered in leather; decorated at ends of joints with waves in gold leaf; ivory ferrules; single beading. Four sections: bocal (replacement), l.h. joint, r.h. joint, bell. Twin third finger hole, two tuning holes on upper part of bell. Two block-mounted silver keys, square key heads. E♭^{1} (R4), C^1 (R4).

Stamped on l.h. joint, r.h. joint: "(crown) / ADLER / A PARIS (five-pointed star)"; bell: "(crown) / ADLER / RUE MANDAR / A PARIS / (five-pointed star)".

2007.26

RIGHT: *2-key English horn*, Frédéric Guillaume Adler, Paris, ca. 1820.

11-key baritone oboe, Henri Brod, Paris, ca. 1835.

Dark-stained maple; large ivory ferrules; single beading. Six sections: bocal, upper joint, l.h. joint, r.h. joint, boot joint, bell (pear-shaped pointing upward). Twin third and fourth finger holes. Eleven pillar-mounted brass keys, flat, round key heads. Plate for R3, octave key, C^2 (L3), $B\flat^1$ (R1 and LT, removed), $G\sharp^1$ (L4), F^1 (cross, R3), $E\flat^1$ (R3), C♯ (L4), C, B, B♭, A. "22" stamped on back of each section. Serial no. 22. H=100.6.

Stamped on upper joint, l.h. joint, r.h. joint, boot joint, bell: "Brod (cursive) / (cross of Legion of Honor)".

One of the only known examples of Brod's baritone oboe with boot joint and long curved bocal.

Burgess and Haynes 2004, 135.

2013.02

11-key baritone oboe, Henri Brod, Paris, ca. 1835.

Zampogna, Anonymous, of Italian origin, ca. 1800.

Bagpipe with a large chanter; three drone pipes of stained reddish brown wood. Seven sections: mouth pipe (missing), bag (missing), large chanter, small chanter, large drone, small drone, cap. Drones and chanters turned with concentric circles, all enclosed in one large cap of dark brown wood with concentric circles. Bag supplying air to be placed under the arm is missing. Large chanter has three finger holes, one open key for r.h. little finger covered by a barrel or fontanelle with holes. Two resonance holes on upper section of large chanter bell. Small chanter has five holes for l.h., one resonance hole. Two drones have no finger holes. L of large chanter=795; L of small chanter=534; L of large drone=461; L of small drone=285.

No inscription.

Wackernagel 2005, 324-327; Cocks 2013.

2001.13

LEFT: *Zampogna*, Anonymous, of Italian origin, ca. 1800.

7-key musette or oboe pastoral, Michel Rivet, Lyon, ca. 1850.

Stained boxwood; ivory and brass ferrules; single beading. Two sections: body, lower joint-bell. Seven pillar-mounted brass keys on oval brass plates, slightly curved key heads. Octave (LT), $B\flat^{1}$ (R1), $G\sharp^{1}$, F^{1} (R3), C^{1} (R4), $C\sharp^{1}$ (R4), B (L4). L=360.

Stamped on body, lower joint-bell: "(five-pointed star) / RIVET / A LYON (five-pointed star)".

2002.45

RIGHT: *7-key musette or oboe pastoral*, Michel Rivet, Lyon, ca. 1850.

Bombard, Anonymous, of French origin, ca. 1820.

Boxwood; horn ferrules; single beading. Three sections: upper joint, lower joint, bell. Keyless double-reed small shawm traditionally played with the biniou, a bagpipe of Brittany. L=283.

No inscription.

2003.55

LEFT: *Bombard*, Anonymous, of French origin, ca. 1820.

Suona (oboe), Anonymous, of Chinese origin, ca. 1920.

Brown wood. Three sections: brass pirouette, body, bell (brass). Two decoratively pierced brass, hemispherical balls and platform, body has undulating sections, seven finger holes. L=309.

2005.02

Suona (oboe), Anonymous, of Chinese origin, ca. 1920.

Brown wood. Three sections: brass pirouette, body, bell (brass). Two decoratively pierced brass, hemispherical balls and platform, body has undulating sections, seven finger holes. L=327.

2005.03

Suona (oboe), Anonymous, of Chinese origin, ca. 1920.

Brown wood. Three sections: brass pirouette, body, bell (brass). Two decoratively pierced brass, hemispherical balls and platform, body has undulating sections, seven finger holes. L=346.

2005.14

BELOW: *Three suonas (oboes)*, Anonymous, of Chinese origin, ca. 1920.

Musette de cour, Esprit Philippe Chédeville or Nicolas Chédeville, Paris, ca. 1730.

Five sections: bag, two chanters in a common stock, drone pipe, book-shaped bellows. Bag covered with burgundy-colored silk, bordered with metallic fringe. Two ivory chanters in double stock inserted in one end of bag. Large chalumeau: seven finger holes, the seventh hole is doubled, seven ring and block-mounted silver keys, square keys heads. Four on front, A, A (on right side), F♯ (on right side), C♯ (on right side); three on back, E♭, B♭, A♭ or G♯ (on back). Small chalumeau: six block-mounted keys, round, flat key heads. Three on front, D, B, B♭; three on back, C, A, A♭ or G♯. Ivory, cylindrical drone pipe with openings, inserted in middle of bag. Double reeds inside the large chalumeau, and drone, a single reed inside the small chalumeau. Book-shaped red leather bellows connected to silk arm of bag, belt for attaching to arm of player. L of large chalumeau=310; L of small chalumeau=187; L of cylindrical drone=170; L of drone=150.

Inscription on the front of the small chalumeau below the keys: "CHEDEVILLE".

Similar to the musette attributed to Chédeville in the Musée de la Musique, E.571.

Musette chanter illustrations in *Encyclopédie* 1767, vol. 5, pl. 6.

Cocks 2013.

2006.21

Musette de cour, Esprit Philippe Chédeville or Nicolas Chédeville, Paris, ca. 1730.

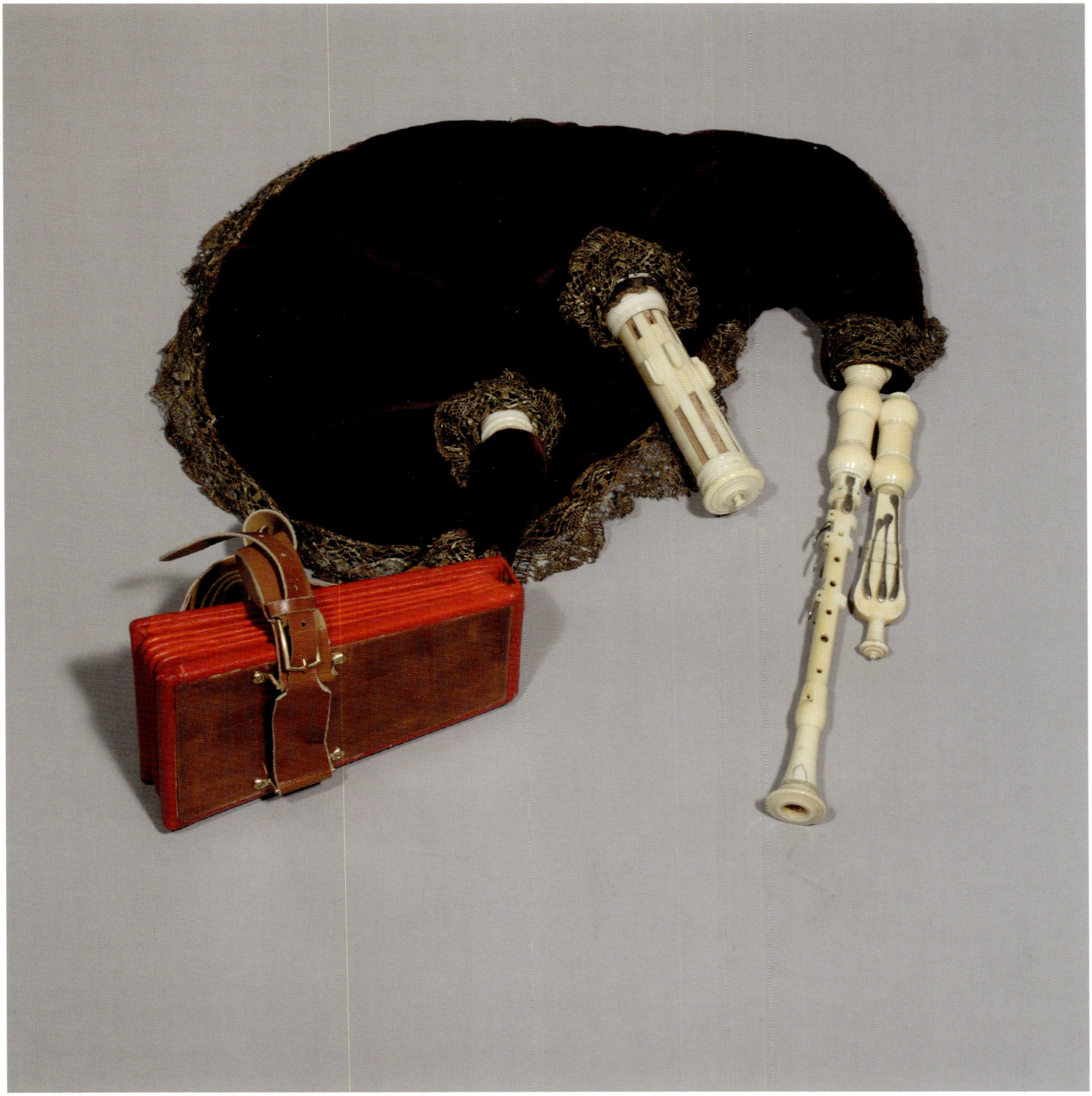

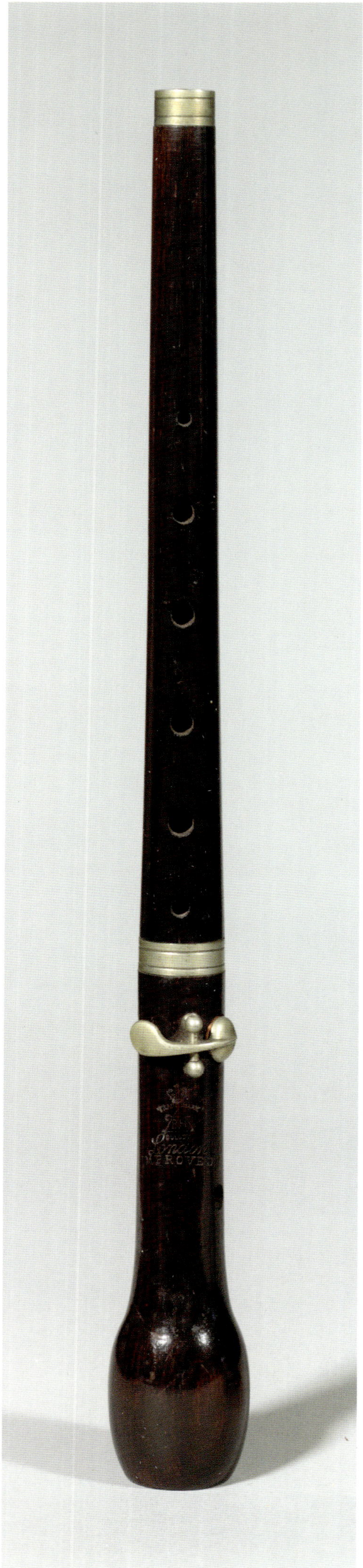

1-key musette (high-pitched oboe), Barnett Samuel, London, ca. 1900.

Stained rosewood; nickel-silver ferrules. Two sections: body, bell (bulbous). Body, six finger holes, bell, one resonance hole, one pillar-mounted nickel-silver key with modern key head for D♯. L=356.

Stamped on bell: "(crown) / TRADEMARK / (triangle with beater, B.S. in frame) / DULCET / LONDON (cursive) / IMPROVED".

2009.10

LEFT: *1-key musette* (high-pitched oboe), Barnett Samuel, London, ca. 1900.

Practice chanter, Peter Henderson, Glasgow, ca. 1880.

Stained rosewood; ivory ferrules; dark line double beading. Two sections: top section, body. Top section holds a double reed inside, body has seven finger holes. L=450.

Stamped on upper portion of body: "HENDERSON / GLASGOW".

Campbell 2001, II.

2011.09

RIGHT: *Practice chanter,* Peter Henderson, Glasgow, ca. 1880.

4-key octave bassoon or fagottino, Godfridus Adrianus Rottenburgh, Brussels, ca. 1760.

Maple; brass ferrules. Five sections: bocal (probably original), wing joint, butt joint, long joint, bell. Four saddle-mounted brass keys, flat, round key heads and spurs. Back: B♭$_1$ (LT), D / front: F (R4, swallowtail touch), G♯.

Stamped on front of bell: "(star) G • A • / ROTTENBURGH / (star)"; long joint: "G • A • / ROTTENBURGH / (star)".

Young 1993, 192, Y1.

1983.13

4-key octave bassoon or fagottino, Godfridus Adrianus Rottenburgh, Brussels, ca. 1760, front and back views.

6-key tenoroon, George Astor and Horwood, London, ca. 1815.

Black-stained maple; brass ferrules. Five sections: bocal, wing joint, butt joint, long joint, bell. No table on the long joint. Six saddle-mounted brass keys, spade and spatula-shaped key heads. Back: B♭$_1$ (LT), D, E♭ (spatula-shaped key head, left of D) / F♯ (RT, spatula-shaped key head) / front: F (R4), G♯ (R4, spatula-shaped key head).

Stamped on back of long joint, butt joint, front of bell: "ASTOR / & / HORWOOD / 79 / CORNHILL / LONDON (unicorn head)".

1995.28

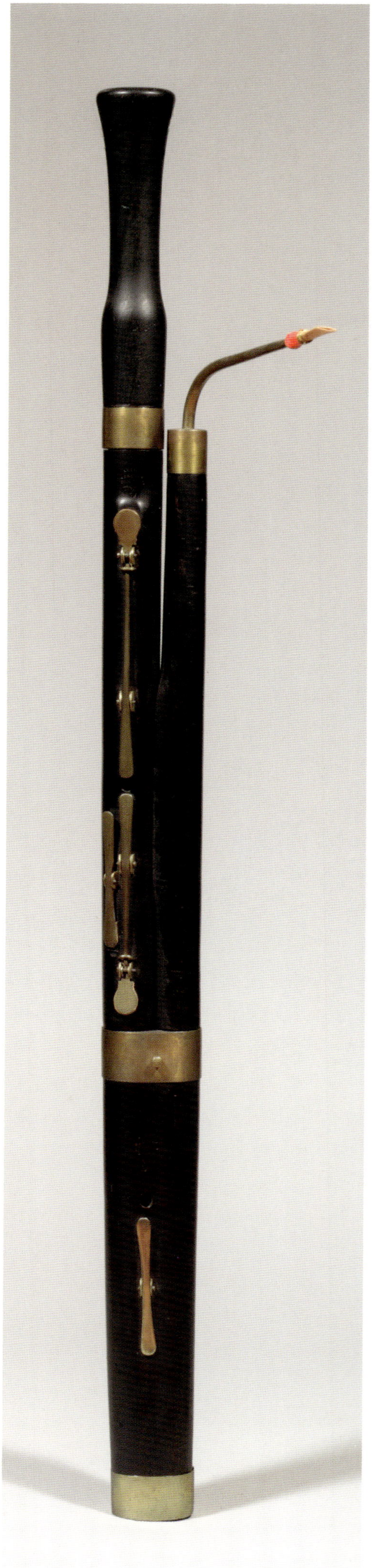

6-key tenoroon, George Astor and Horwood, London, ca. 1815, front and back views.

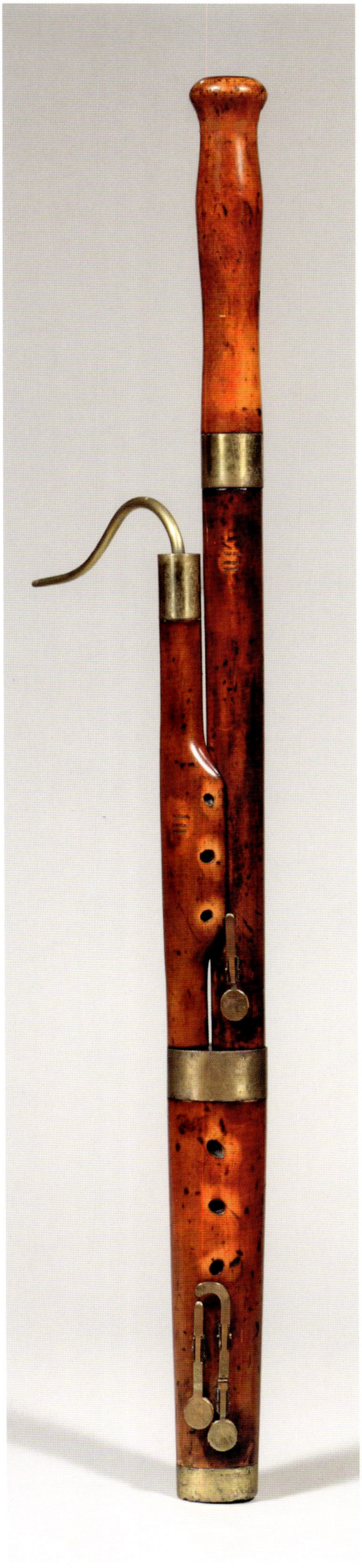

6-key tenoroon, Kaspar Tauber, Vienna, ca. 1815.

Fruitwood; brass ferrules. Five sections: bocal (appears original), wing joint, butt joint, long joint, bell. Six saddle-mounted brass keys, round, flat key heads. Back: B♭[1] (LT), D / F♯ (RT) / front: E♭ (L4) / F (R4), G♯.

Stamped on front of bell, long joint, wing joint, back of butt joint: "KASPAR / TAUBER / WIENN".

2007.15

6-key tenoroon, Kaspar Tauber, Vienna, ca. 1815, front and back views.

8-key bassoon, Richard Milhouse, Newark, ca. 1790.

Fruitwood; brass ferrules. Five sections: bocal (probably original), wing joint, butt joint, long joint, bell. All finger holes on the front lined with ivory inserts. Eight saddle-mounted brass keys, spade and spatula-shaped key heads, two wing keys were later additions, one stamped "IH" for John Hale, London. Back: B♭$_1$ (LT), D (boss with star decoration over key head), E♭ (LT, spatula-shaped key head, right of D touch) / F♯ (RT, spatula-shaped key head) / a^1 (LT, W), c^2 (LT, W2) / front: F (R4, swallowtail touch), G♯ (R4, spatula-shaped key head).

Stamped on front of bell, long joint, butt joint: "MILHOUSE / NEWARK".

Repair or extension on lower end of wing joint.

Young 1993, 159, Y19.

1978.02

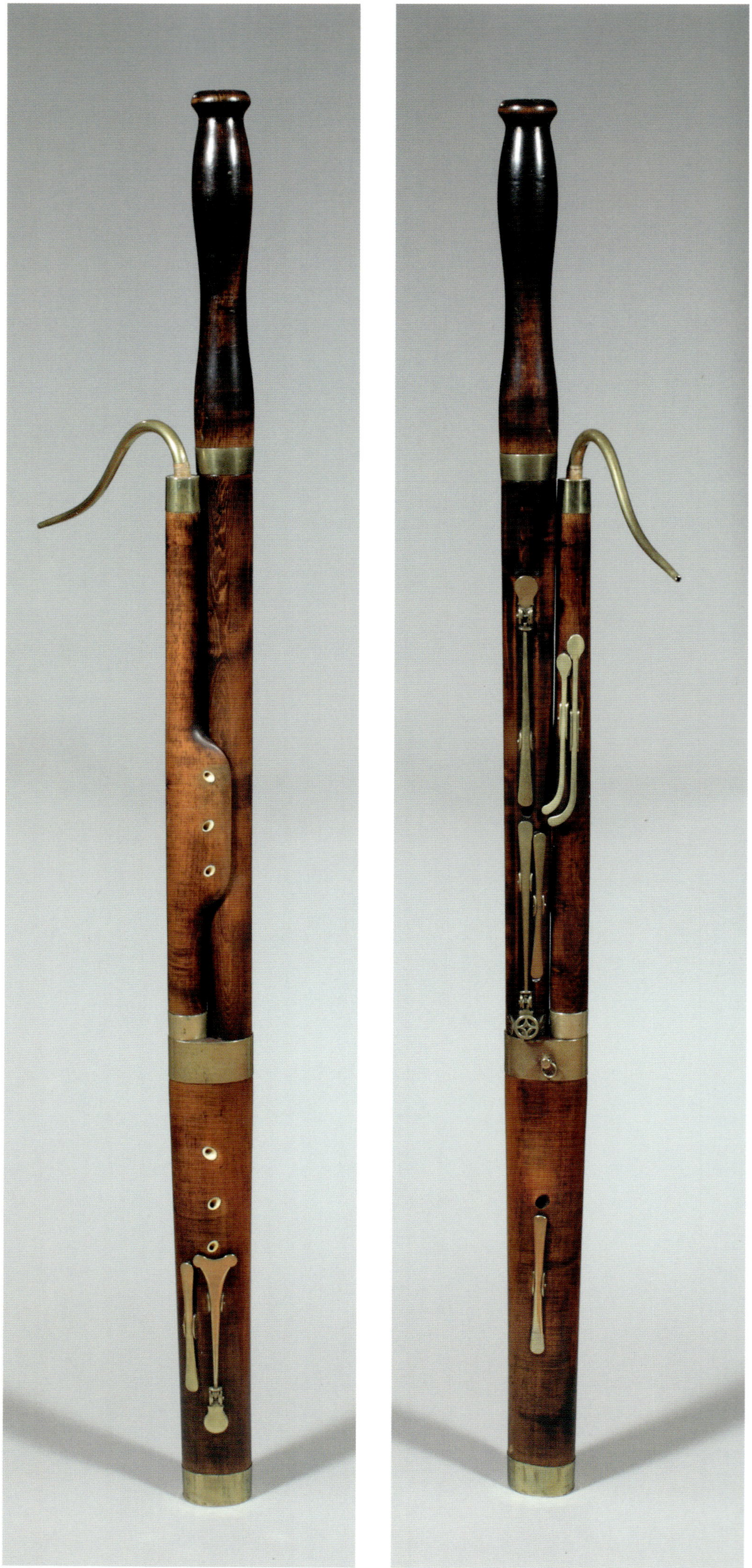

8-key bassoon, Richard Milhouse, Newark, ca. 1790, front and back views.

6-key bassoon, John Hasler, London, ca. 1830.

Maple; brass ferrules. Five sections: bocal (probably original), wing joint, butt joint, long joint, bell. Six saddle-mounted brass keys, spade and spatula-shaped key heads. Back: B♭$_1$ (LT), D, E♭ (spatula-shaped key head, left of D) / F♯ (RT, spatula-shaped key head) / front: F, G♯ (spatula-shaped key head).

Stamped on front of bell: "HASLER / LONDON".

1991.01

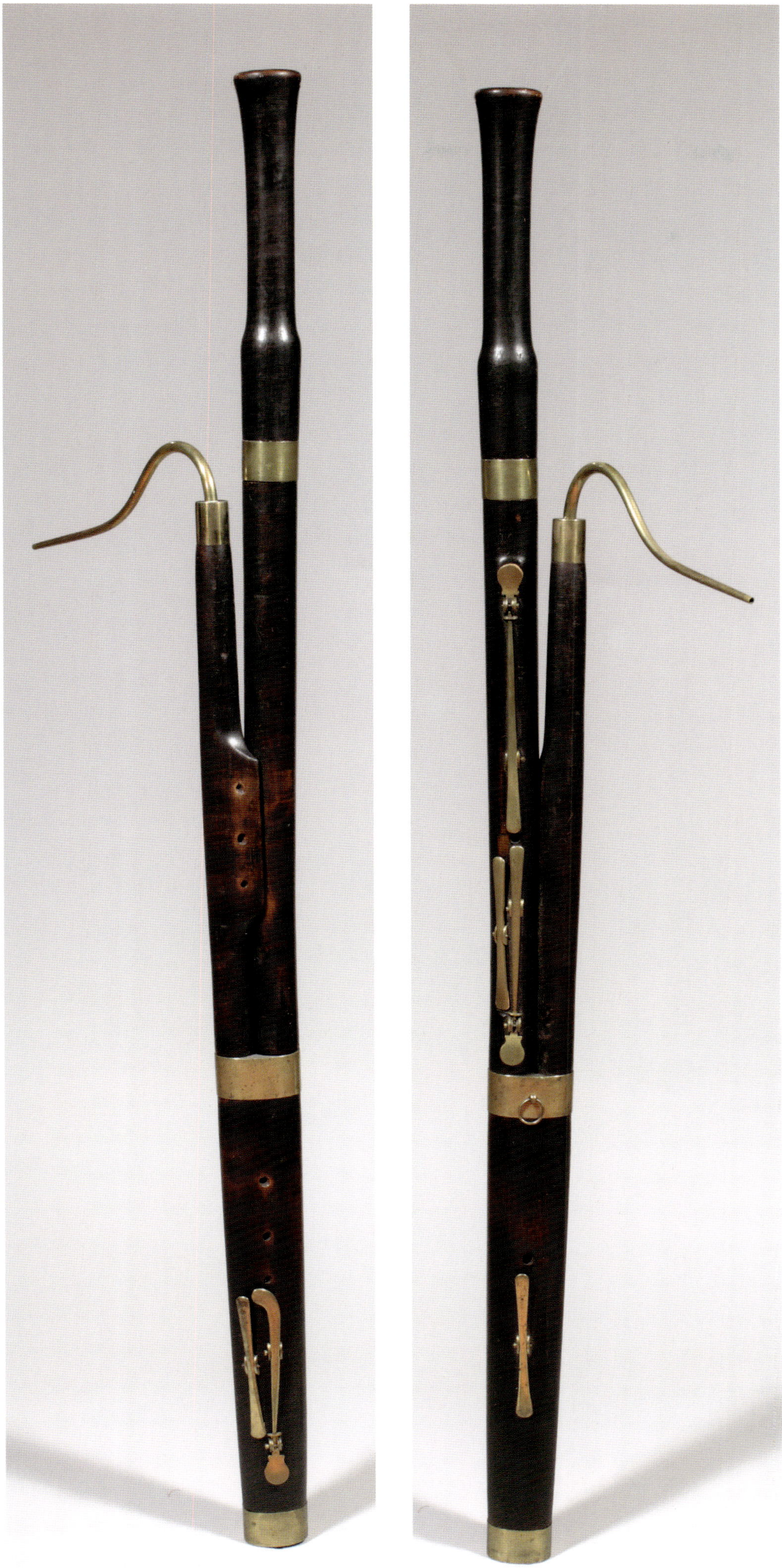

6-key bassoon, John Hasler, London, ca. 1830, front and back views.

4-key bassoon, Carl Augustin Grenser, Dresden, 1773.

Maple; brass ferrules. Five sections: bocal (probably original), wing joint, butt joint, long joint, bell. Four block-mounted brass keys, spade-shaped key heads, brass crown on top of bell. Back: $B\flat_1$, D / front: F (swallowtail touch, protective wood boss below the key head), G♯.

Stamped on front of bell, long joint, wing joint: "(Saxon swords) / A. GRENSER / (star)"; front of butt joint: "(star) /1773 / (star) / (Saxon swords) / A GRENSER / DRESDEN / (star)".

Young 1993, 99, Y17.

1993.02

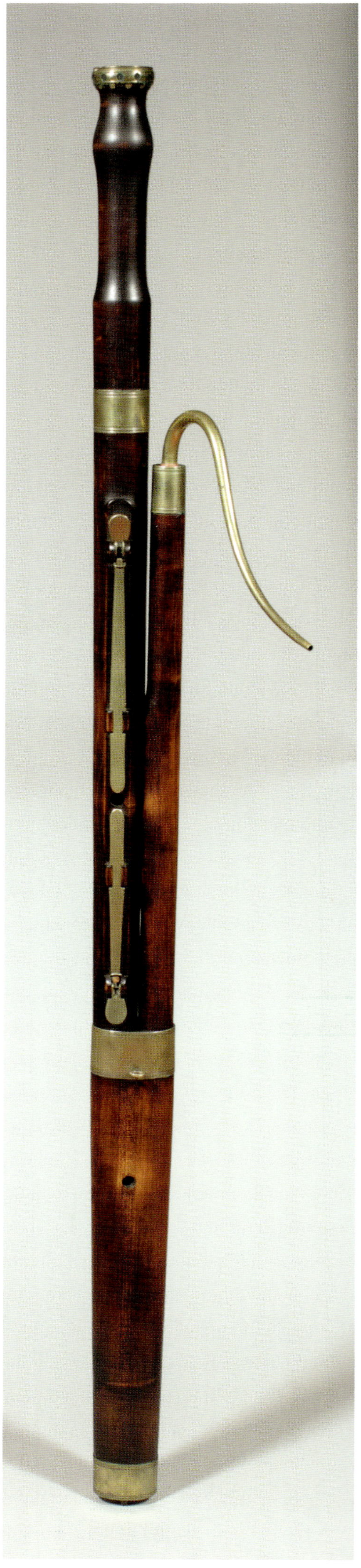

4-key bassoon, Carl Augustin Grenser, Dresden, 1773, front and back views.

5-key bassoon, Prudent Thierriot, Paris, ca. 1770.

Maple; brass ferrules. Five sections: bocal (probably original), wing joint, butt joint, long joint, bell. Five block-mounted brass keys, square key heads. Back: $B\flat_1$ (LT), D, E♭ (right of D) / front: F (swallowtail touch), G♯.

Stamp on front of wing joint, long joint: "(fleur-de-lis) / PRUDENT / A PARIS".

The keys are unusually mounted in blocks on long joint rather than the usual raised table.

Young 1993, 182, Y6; Jeltsch 1997, 129-131, 145.

1993.06

5-key bassoon, Prudent Thierriot, Paris, ca. 1770, front and back views.

8-key bassoon, Clair Godfroy aîné, Paris, ca. 1835.

Maple; brass ferrules. Five sections: bocal, wing joint, butt joint, long joint, bell. Eight saddle-mounted brass keys, round key heads. Back: B♭$_1$ (LT), D (brass guard over key head), E♭ (right of D) / F♯ (RT) / c^2 (W), a^1 (W2) / front: F, G♯.

Stamped on front of bell, butt joint, back of long joint: "(portrait head) / CLAIR / Godfroy aîné / A PARIS (in oval cartouche) / CG (monogram)".

1994.01

8-key bassoon, Clair Godfroy aîné, Paris, ca. 1835, front and back views.

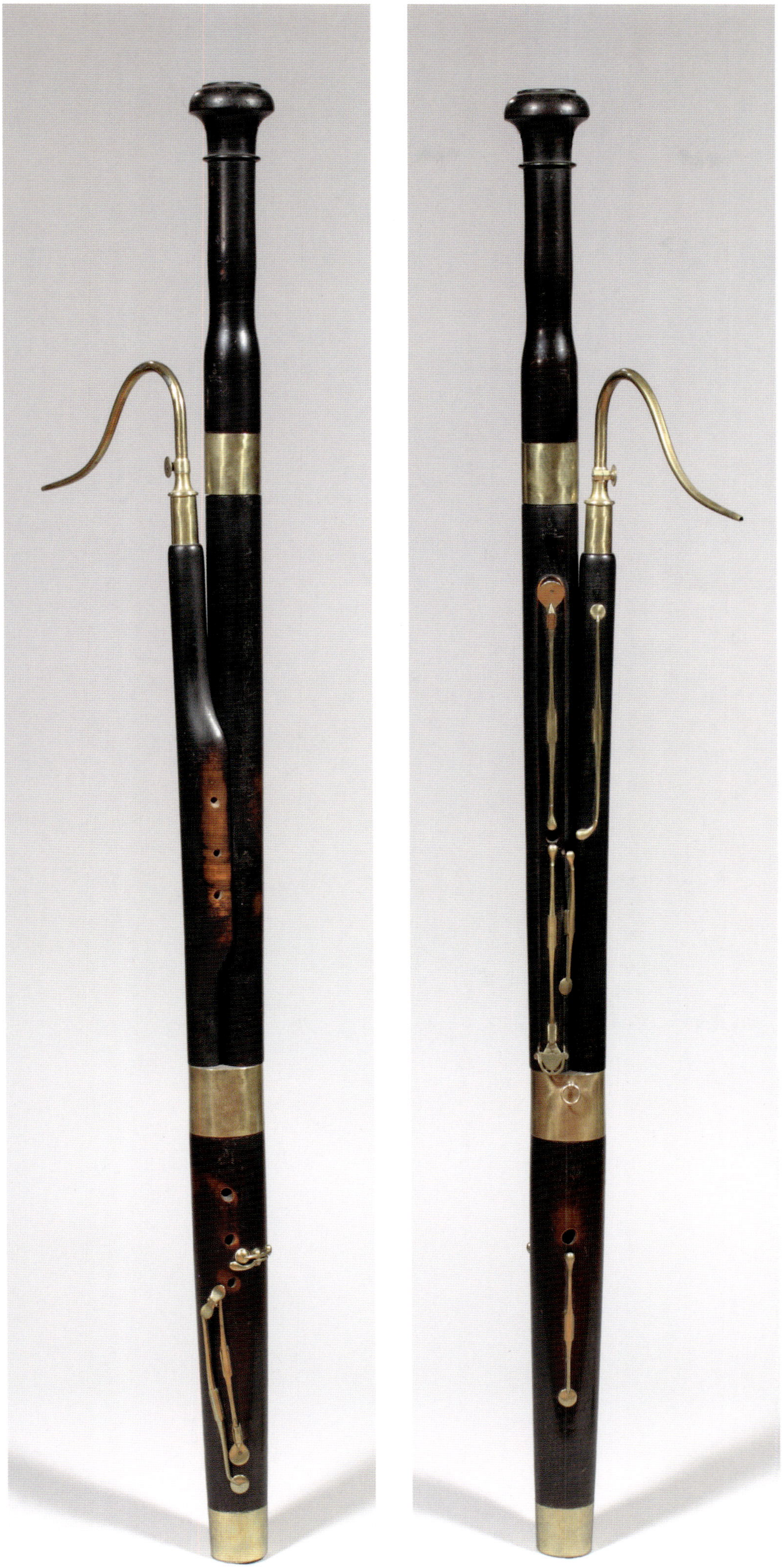

8-key bassoon, Jean Winnen, Paris, ca. 1835.

Dark-stained maple; gold-plated brass ferrules. Five sections: bocal (probably original), wing joint, butt joint, long joint, bell. Eight saddle and pillar mounted gold-plated brass keys, flat, round key heads, screw adjustment of bocal height for tuning. Back: B♭$_1$ (LT), D (decorative brass guard over key head), E♭ (right of D) / F♯ (RT) / c^2 (W) / front: F, G♯ (with one concave touch for both keys), B♭ (pillar-mounted, a primary touch acting on a second lever that lifts a salt-spoon key head). Second wing joint with four keys. L=498.

Stamped on front of bell, butt joint, back of long joint: "(star) / (face in sun) / WINNEN, / A PARIS."; back of wing joint: "(star) / (face in sun) / WINNEN, / A PARIS. / 1".

1994.11

8-key bassoon, Jean Winnen, Paris, ca. 1835, front and back views

8-key bassoon, Ignaz Huittl, Graslitz, ca. 1790.

Maple; brass ferrules. Five sections: bocal (missing), wing joint, butt joint, long joint, bell. Eight block-mounted brass keys, spade and oval-shaped key heads curved to the body. Back: B♭$_1$ (LT), D, E♭ (right of D) / F♯ (RT) / a^1 (W), c^2 (W2) / front: F, G♯.

Stamped on back of butt joint: "•I•HUITTL •".

Unusual mounting of the keys on the long joint, usually made with a raised table.

Young 1993, Y3.

1995.07

8-key bassoon, Ignaz Huittl, Graslitz, ca. 1790, front and back views.

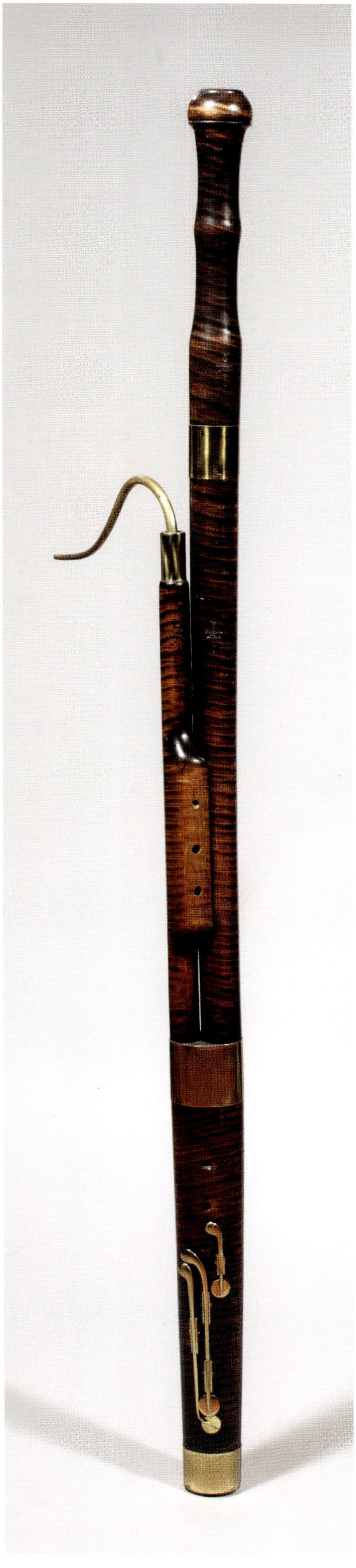

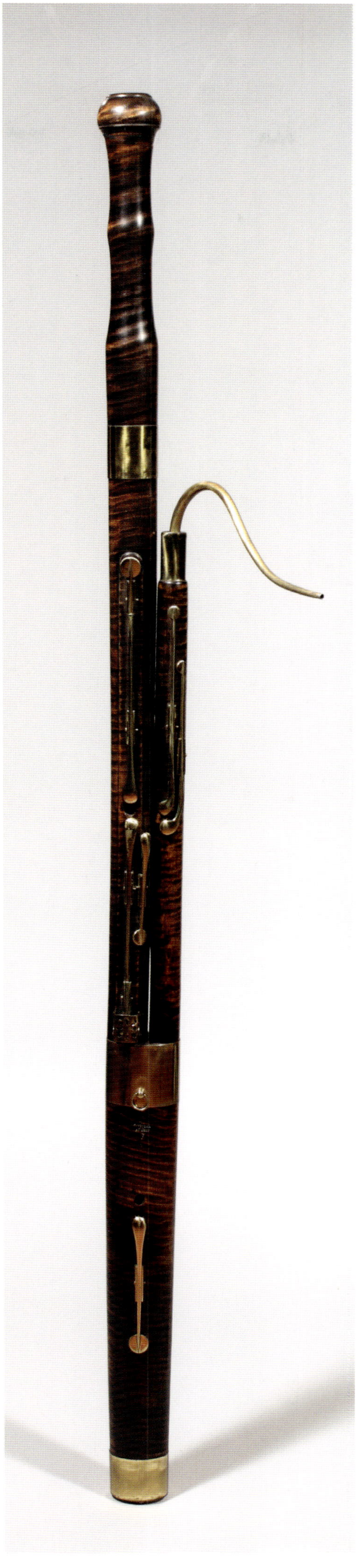

9-key bassoon, Pierre Florent Joseph Cuvillier, St. Omer, ca. 1820.

Maple; brass ferrules. Five sections: bocal, wing joint, butt joint, long joint, bell. Nine saddle-mounted brass keys, round, flat key heads. Back: B♭$_1$ (LT), D (guard with sunburst decoration over key head), E♭ (right of D) / F♯ (RT) / c^2 (W), a^1 (W2) ; front: B♭ (R3) / F (R4), G♯ (R4).

Stamped on back of butt joint, on front of wing joint: "(lyre)/ CUVILLIER / A ST.OMER / (caduceus)"; front of bell, long joint: "(lyre)/ CUVILLIER / A ST.OMER / (caduceus) 2".

Rousselet and Watel 2012, 53.

1995.08

9-key bassoon, Pierre Florent Joseph Cuvillier, St. Omer, ca. 1820, front and back views.

10-key bassoon, Wolfgang Küss, Vienna, ca. 1825.

Maple; brass ferrules. Five sections: bocal (missing), wing joint, butt joint, long joint, bell. Ten block, saddle-mounted brass keys with small brass rod recessed in the wood; flat, round key heads some curved to the body. Ivory insert in thumb hole. Back: B♭$_1$ (LT), D (guard with decoration over key head) / F (RT) F♯ (RT) / a^1 (W), c^2 (W2) / front: E♭ (L4, mounted in a bulge) / B♭ (R3), F (R4), G♯ (R4).

The wing keys are inverted, central European placement. On wing is a bulge or step on front to balance the weight on back.

Stamped on back of butt joint: "(Hapsburg eagle) / Küß (cursive) / Wien (cursive)".

1995.09

10-key bassoon, Wolfgang Küss, Vienna, ca. 1825, front and back views.

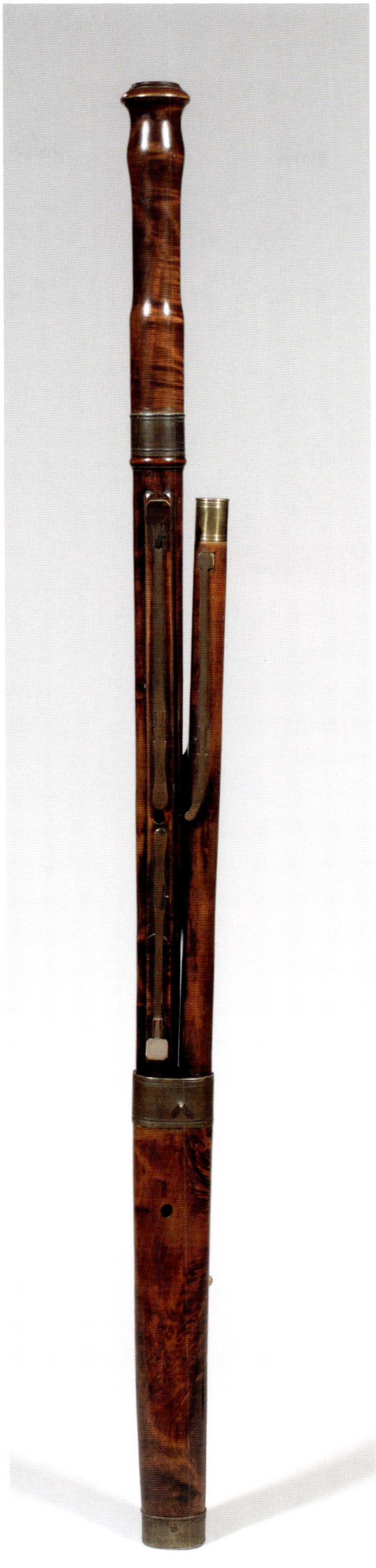

6-key bassoon, Wendelin Schiele, Rottenburg am Neckar, ca. 1800.

Maple; brass ferrules. Five sections: bocal (missing), wing joint, butt joint, long joint, bell. One resonance hole in the bell. Six saddle-mounted brass keys, square key heads. Back: B♭$_1$ (LT), D / c^2 (W) / front: E♭ (L4) / F (R4, swallowtail touch), G♯ (R4).

Stamped on back of long joint, front of butt joint: "Schiele (in cursive) / (fleur-de-lys)".

Formerly Willi Burger collection.

Waterhouse 1993, 353.

1995.10

6-key bassoon, Wendelin Schiele, Rottenburg am Neckar, ca. 1800, front and back views.

4-key bassoon, George Catlin, Hartford, Connecticut, ca. 1805.

Dark-stained maple; brass ferrules. Five sections: bocal (missing), wing joint, butt joint, long joint, bell. Four saddle-mounted keys, spade and spatula-shaped key heads. No table on back of long joint. Back: $B\flat_1$ (LT, "Hartford-spade" key head), D ("Hartford-spade" key head) / F (R4, spade-shaped key head), $G\sharp$ (R4, spatula-shaped key head).

Stamped on back of butt joint: "MADE / By / CATLIN / Hartford / (three marks in circles)".

1995.29

4-key bassoon, George Catlin, Hartford, Connecticut, ca. 1805, front and back views.

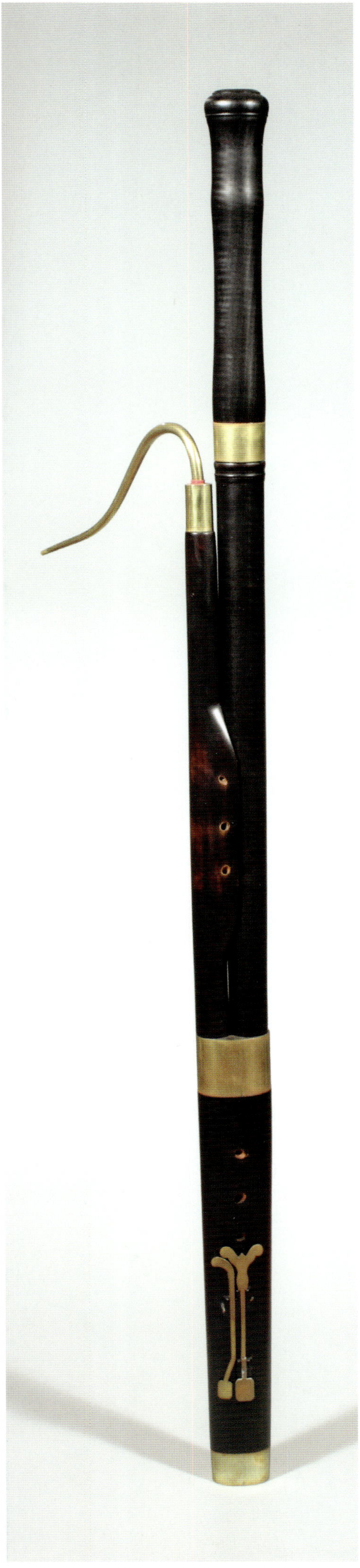

5-key bassoon, Prudent Thierriot, Paris, ca. 1770 (copy), Paul White, Oxford, 1995.

Dark-stained maple; brass ferrules. Five sections: bocal, wing joint, butt joint, long joint, bell. Five block-mounted brass keys with square key heads. Back: B♭$_1$ (LT), D, E♭ (right of D) / front: F (swallowtail touch), G♯.

Engraved on lower bell ferrule: "Paul White / Oxford (cursive)".

1995.30

5-key bassoon, Prudent Thierriot, Paris, ca. 1770 (copy), Paul White, Oxford, 1995, front and back views.

10-key bassoon, Joseph Prowse, London, ca. 1835.

Dark-stained maple; brass ferrules. Five sections: bocal, wing joint, butt joint, long joint, bell. Ten saddle-mounted brass keys, spade and spatula-shaped key heads. Back: B♭$_1$ (LT), D, E♭ (spatula-shaped key head, left of D) / F♯ (RT, spatula-shaped key head) / c (LT), c^2 (W2), a^1 (W) / front: E♭^{1} (L3) / F (R4), G♯ (R4, spatula-shaped key head).

Stamped on back of wing joint, back of butt joint: "J. Prowse / Great Bell Alley / London"; front side of butt joint: "27".

1996.08

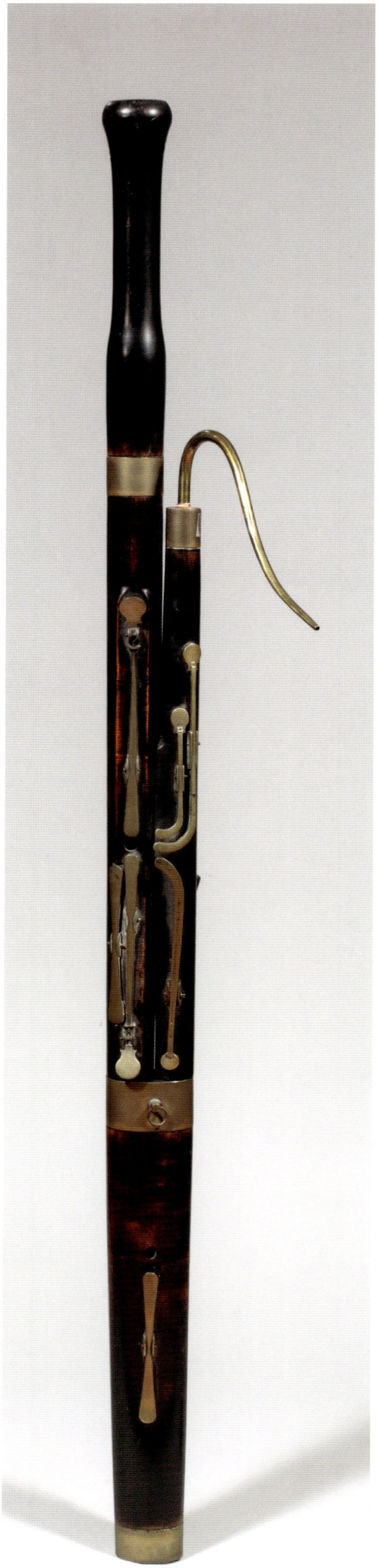

10-key bassoon, Joseph Prowse, London, ca. 1835, front and back views.

5-key bassoon, Klemm and Brother, Philadelphia, attributed to Christian Gottfried Schuster, Markneukirchen, ca. 1820.

Stained maple; brass ferrules. Five sections: bocal, wing joint, butt joint, long joint, bell. Five saddle-mounted brass keys, octagonal-shaped key heads, thumb hole has ivory ring insert. Back: B♭$_1$, D / front: E♭ (L4) / F (R4), G♯ (R4).

Stamped on back side of long joint: "KLEMM&BRO. / PHILD^{A}".

Kopp 2013, 16-18.

1996.20

5-key bassoon, Klemm and Brother, Philadelphia, attributed to Christian Gottfried Schuster, Markneukirchen, ca. 1820, front and back views.

5-key bassoon, Dominique Antony Porthaux, Paris, ca. 1790.

Stained maple; brass ferrules. Five sections: bocal, wing joint, butt joint, long joint, bell. Five saddle-mounted brass keys, flat, spade-shaped key heads. Back: B♭$_1$ (LT), D, E♭ (right of D) / front: G♯ (R4), F (R4). Reed case and four reeds. L of second wing joint=492.

Stamped on front side of bell, long joint, wing joint, butt joint: "(five-pointed star) / PORTHAUX / A PARIS".

1998.01

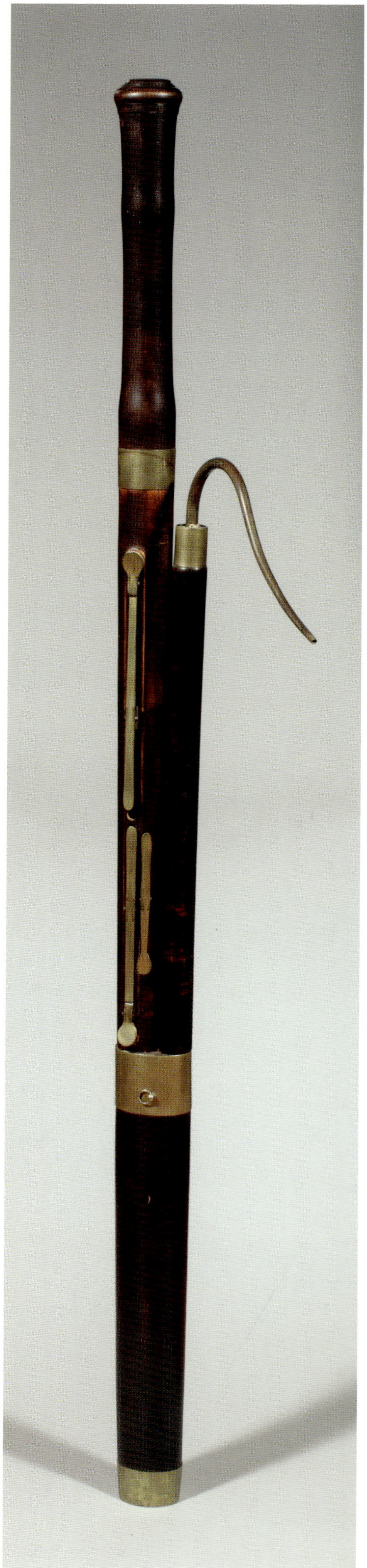

5-key bassoon, Dominique Antony Porthaux, Paris, ca. 1790, front and back views.

8-key bassoon, Hirschbrunner, Sumiswald, ca. 1825.

Tiger-striped maple; brass ferrules. Five sections: bocal (missing), wing joint, butt joint, long joint, bell. Tuning slide on wing joint has boss on back to provide leverage for adjusting. The receiver of the slide is lined, ivory ferrule on top of bell. Eight saddle-mounted brass keys, square key heads, ivory insert for left thumb. Back: B♭$_1$ (LT), D, E♭ (right of D) / F♯ (RT) / front: C♯ (R1), B♭^{1} (R3), F (R4), G♯ (R4).

Stamped on back of long joint: "(five-pointed star) / HIRSCHBRUNNER / SUMISWALD / (five-pointed star)"; front of bell: "(five-pointed star) / (lyre) / HIRSCHBRUNNER / SUMISWALD / (five-pointed star)".

1998.14

8-key bassoon, Hirschbrunner, Sumiswald, ca. 1825, front and back views.

8-key bassoon, Giacomo De Luigi, Milan, ca. 1830.

Maple; brass ferrules. Five sections: bocal (missing), wing joint, butt joint, long joint, bell. Eight saddle-mounted brass keys, round key heads. Back: B♭$_1$ (LT), D, E♭ (right of D) / F♯ (RT) / c^2 (W), a^1 (W2) / front: F (R4), G♯ (R4).

Stamped on back of long joint, wing joint, bell: "(flower) / DE LUIGI / MILANO / (star)".

1998.15

8-key bassoon, Giacomo De Luigi, Milan, ca. 1830, front and back views.

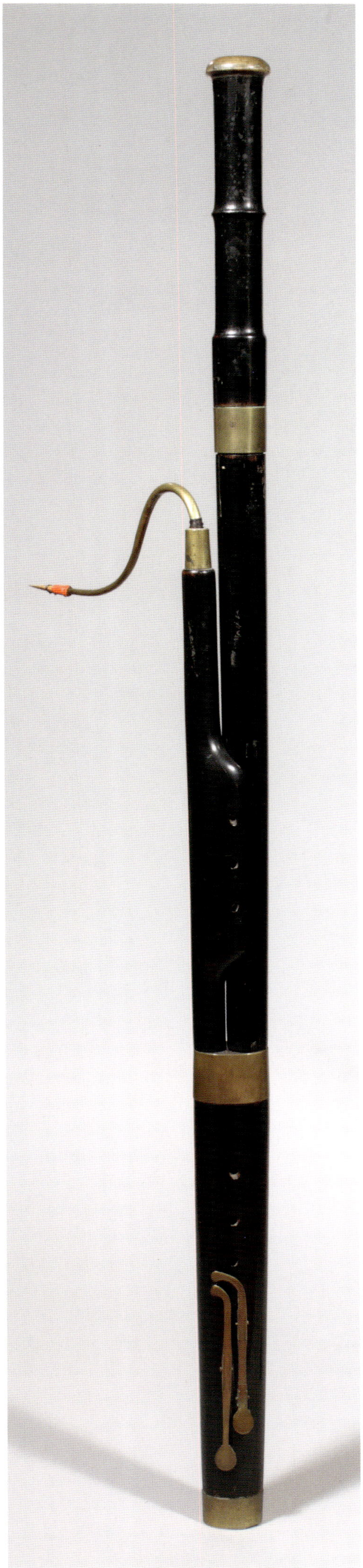

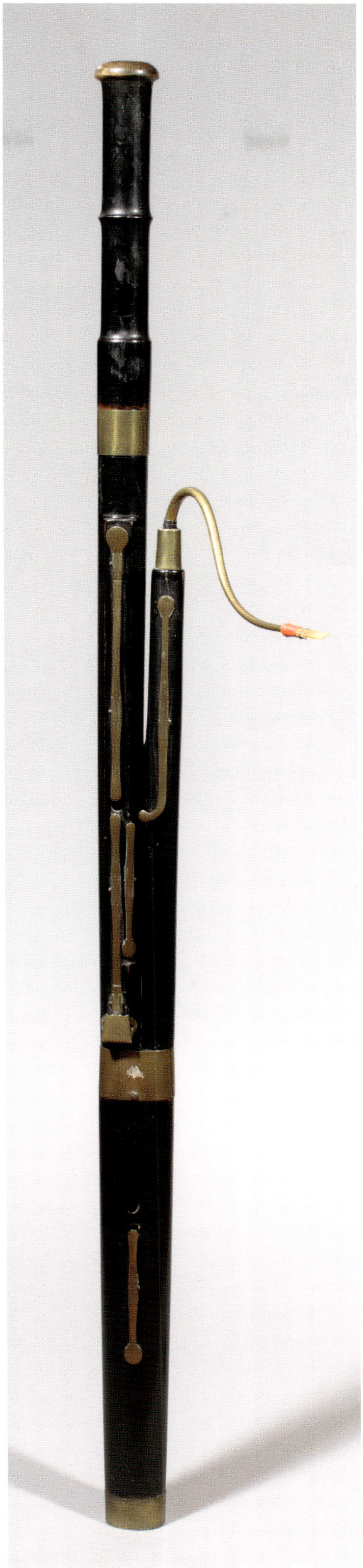

7-key bassoon, Gabriel Bühner and Jean Keller IV, Strasbourg, ca. 1815.

Maple; brass ferrules. Five sections: bocal, wing joint, butt joint, long joint, bell. Seven saddle-mounted brass keys, flat, round key heads. Back: B♭$_1$ (LT), D, E♭ (left of D) / F♯ (RT) / c^2 (W) / front: F, G♯.

Stamped on back of long joint, butt joint, bell: "(angel trumpeter) / Bühner & Keller / à / Strasbourg. (cursive) / (angel trumpeter)".

1999.15

7-key bassoon, Gabriel Bühner and Jean Keller IV, Strasbourg, ca. 1815, front and back views.

7-key bassoon, Jean-Jacques Baumann, Paris, ca. 1800.

Maple; brass ferrules. Five sections: bocal (missing), wing joint, butt joint, long joint, bell. Seven saddle-mounted brass keys, flat, round key heads. Back: $B\flat_1$ (LT), D (brass guard over key head), E♭ (LT, right of D) / F♯ (RT) / c^2 (W) / front: F, G♯.

Stamped on back of long joint, wing joint, butt joint, back of bell: "(five-pointed star) / (lyre) / BAUMANN / A PARIS / (five-pointed star)".

1999.24

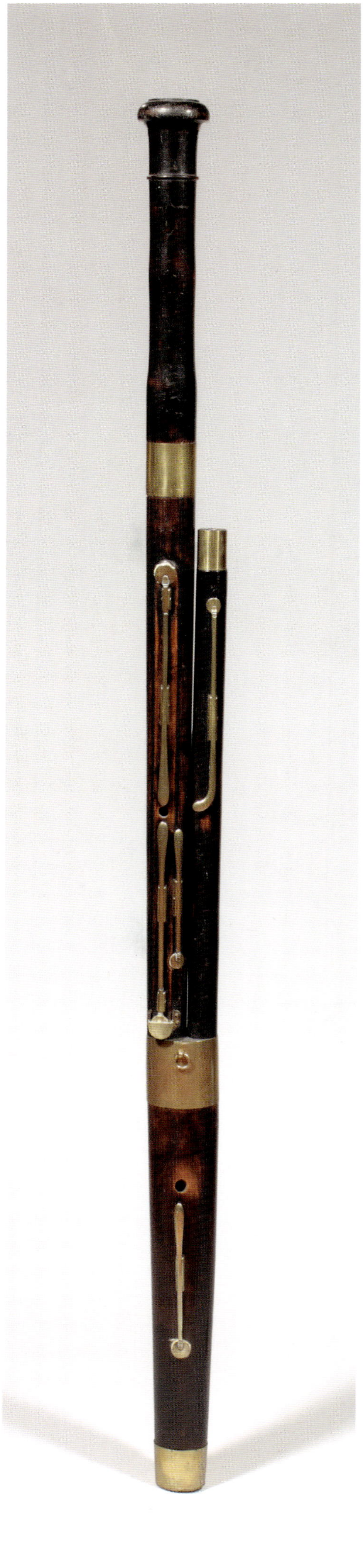

7-key bassoon, Jean-Jacques Baumann, Paris, ca. 1800, front and back views.

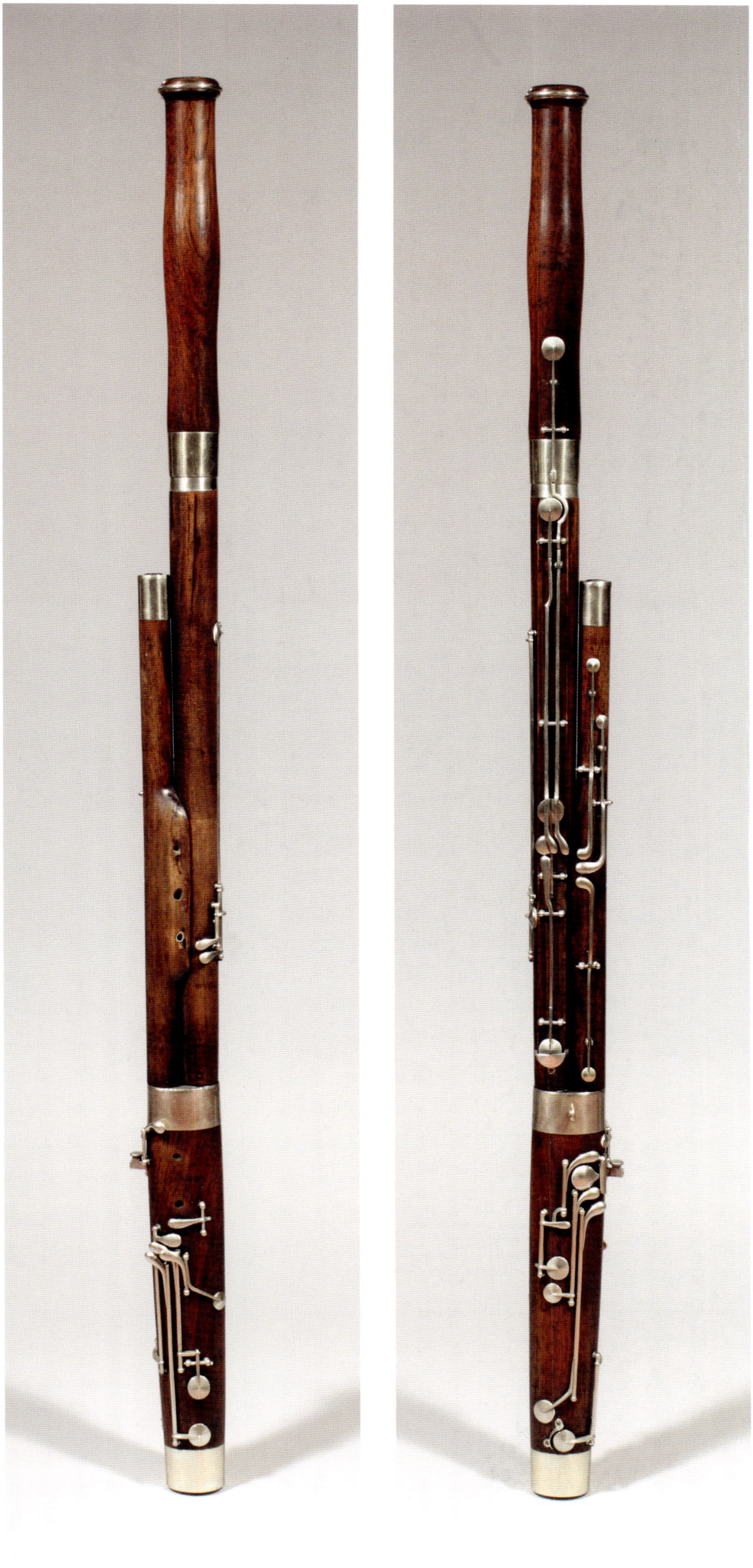

18-key bassoon, Wilhelm Heckel, Biebrich, ca. 1887.

Stained palisander; nickel-silver ferrules. Five sections: bocal, wing joint, butt joint, long joint, bell. On right side of butt joint is a platform for a music lyre. Metal band at the top of the long joint is a crack repair. Eighteen nickel-silver keys mounted on pillars, modern key heads, Heckel system, ivory insert in L3. Back: $B\flat_1$ (LT, farthest right), B_1 (left of $B\flat^1$), C (round plate), D (with partial brass guard over key head) / B♭ (RT), E (round key), F♯, A♭ / c^2 (W), a^1 (W2), C♯ (W3) / front: E♭ (L4), C♯ / c♯ alternate (R1), B♭ (R3, connected by rod to the RT key), lever for R3 tone hole, F (R4), F♯ (R4), A♭ (R4). Serial no. 3486, stamped on U-joint under butt joint cap.

Stamped on back of bell, wing joint: "(crown) / HECKEL / BIEBRICH (crown)".

Baines 1967, 160-161.

2000.15

18-key bassoon, Wilhelm Heckel, Biebrich, ca. 1887, front and back views.

4-key bassoon, N. Curtiss, United States, ca. 1800.

Dark-stained maple; brass ferrules. Five sections: bocal, wing joint, butt joint, long joint, bell. Four saddle-mounted brass keys, spade and spatula-shaped key heads. Back: $B\flat_1$, D / front: F, G♯ (spatula-shaped key head).

Stamped on back of long joint, wing joint: "CURTISS / (flower)"; back of butt joint: "N. CURTISS / (flower) (flower) (flower)".

It is possible that this instrument was made by Nathan Curtiss, Woodbury, Connecticut.

2001.01

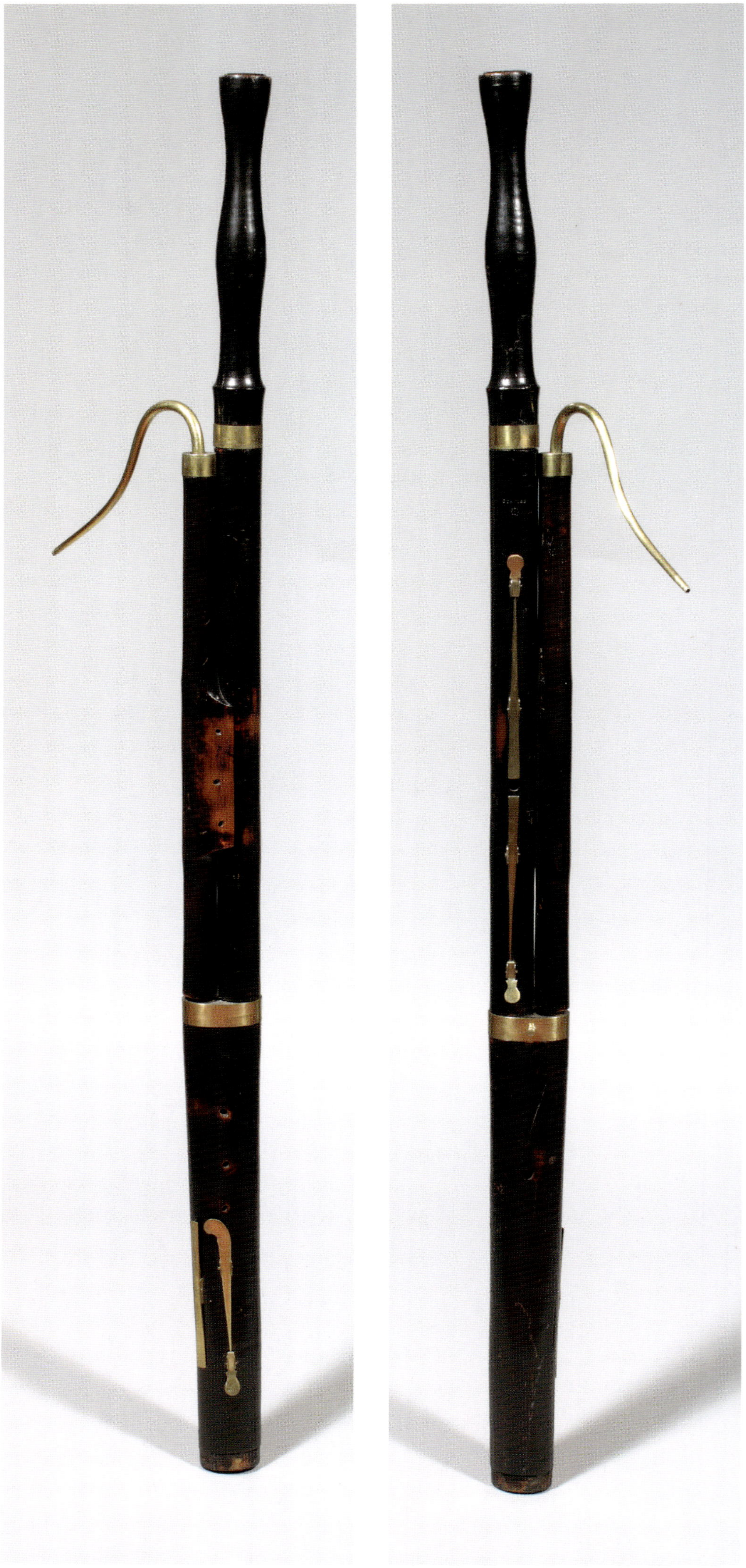

4-key bassoon, N. Curtiss, United States, ca. 1800, front and back views.

9-key bassoon, François Pezé, Paris, ca. 1825.

Stained maple; brass ferrules. Five sections: bocal (missing), wing joint, butt joint, long joint, bell. Nine saddle-mounted brass keys, flat, round key heads. Back: $B\flat_1$ (LT), D (brass guard over key head), $E\flat$ (right of the D key) / $F\sharp$ (RT) / c^2 (W), a^1 (W2) / front: $E\flat^1$ (R3), F, $G\sharp$.

Stamped on front of butt joint: "PEZÉ / A PARIS".

2001.06

9-key bassoon, François Pezé, Paris, ca. 1825, front and back views.

8-key bassoon, Georg Kaspar Lindemann, Strasbourg, ca. 1830.

Stained maple; brass ferrules. Five sections: bocal (missing), wing joint, butt joint, long joint, bell. Eight saddle-mounted brass keys, flat, round key heads. Back: B♭$_1$ (LT), D (brass guard over key head), E♭ (right of the D key) / F♯ (RT) / c^2 (W), a^1 (W2) / front: F, G♯.

Stamped on back of long joint: "(five-pointed star) / LINDEMANN / A STRASBOURG / (five-pointed star)".

2001.14

8-key bassoon, Georg Kaspar Lindemann, Strasbourg, ca. 1830, front and back views.

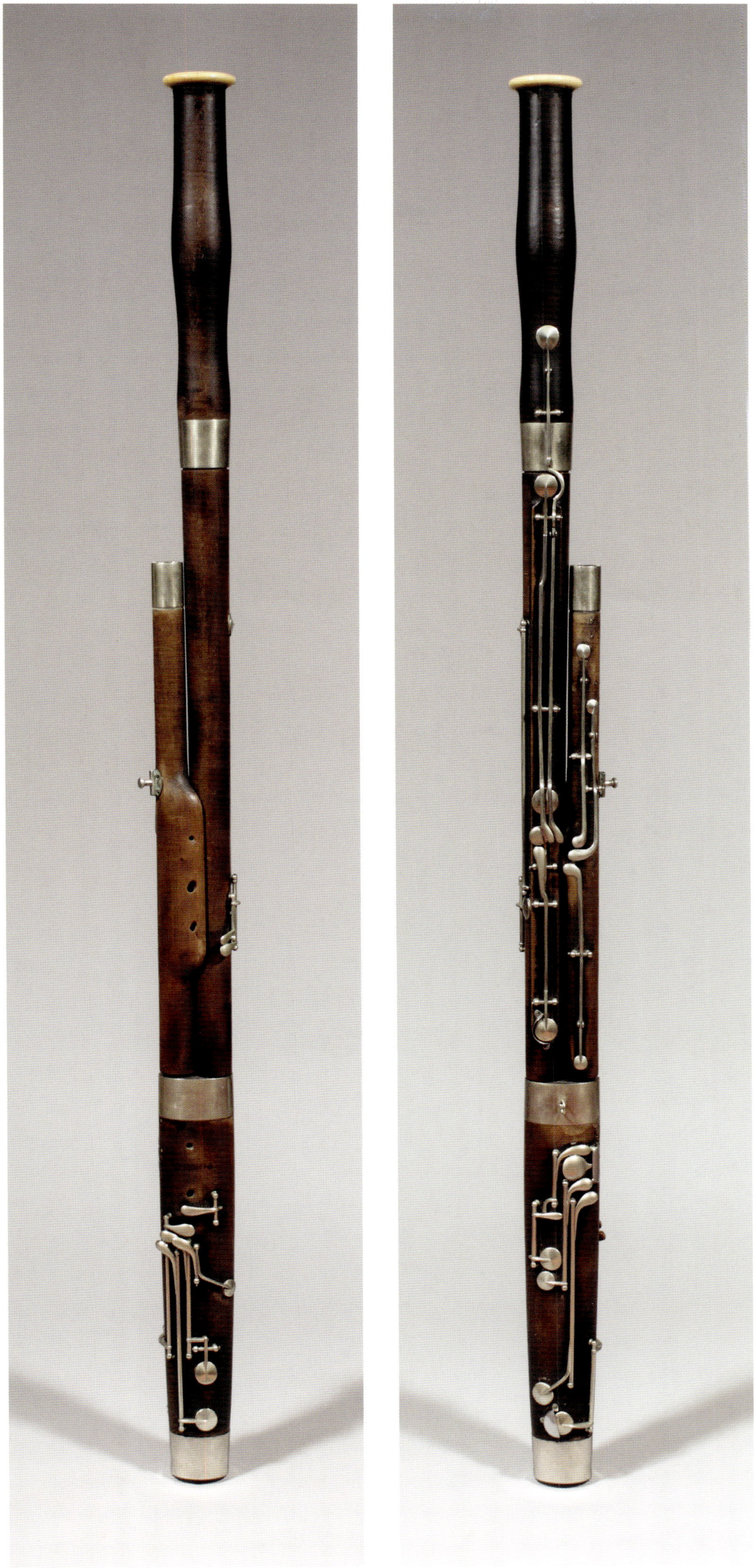

18-key bassoon, Wilhelm Heckel, Biberich, ca. 1887.

Maple; nickel-silver ferrules. Five sections: bocal, wing joint, butt joint, long joint, bell. On right side of wing joint is a platform with screw for a music lyre, ivory bell ring. Eighteen pillar-mounted nickel-silver keys, modern key heads, Heckel system. Back: $B\flat_1$ (LT, farthest right), B_1 (left of $B\flat^1$), C (round key), D (with partial brass guard) / B♭ (RT), E (round key), F♯, A♭ / c^2 (W), a^1 (W2), C♯ (W3) / front: $E\flat^1$ (L4), $c\sharp^2$ (L4) / B♭ (R3, connected by a rod to the LT key), lever for R3 finger hole, F (R4), F♯ (R4), A♭ (R4). Serial no. 3455, stamped on U-joint under butt joint cap.

Stamped on back of wing joint: "HECKEL / BIEBRICH"; front of butt joint: "(crown) / HECKEL / (crown) / BIEBRICH".

Baines 1967, 160-161.

2001.23

18-key bassoon, Wilhelm Heckel, Biberich, ca. 1887, front and back views.

6-key bassoon, John Parker, London, ca. 1810.

Stained maple; brass ferrules. Five sections: bocal (missing), wing joint, butt joint, long joint, bell. Six saddle-mounted brass keys, spade and spatula-shaped, flat key heads. Back: B♭$_1$ (LT), D, E♭ (left of the D key) / F♯ (RT, spatula-shaped key head) / front: F, G♯ (spatula, brass guard over key head).

Stamped on front of butt joint: "PARKER / LONDON".

2001.25

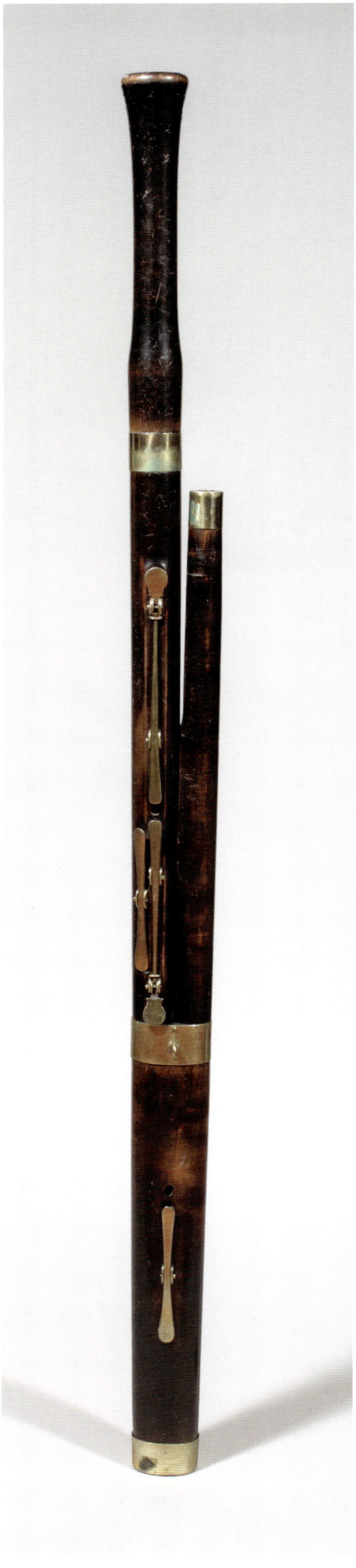

6-key bassoon, John Parker, London, ca. 1810, front and back views.

8-key bassoon, Stephan Koch, Vienna, ca. 1820.

Stained maple; brass ferrules. Five sections: bocal, wing joint, butt joint, long joint, bell. Eight saddle-mounted brass keys, spade-shaped, flat key heads. Back: B♭$_1$ (LT), D (large decorated brass guard over key head), E♭ (right of the D key) / c^2 (W), a^1 (W2, flat, oval key heads) / F♯ (RT) / front: F, G♯ (plastic guard at end of key head).

Stamped on front of butt joint, wing joint, long joint: "(Hapsburg eagle) / S. KOCH / WIEN / 1".

2001.43

8-key bassoon, Stephan Koch, Vienna, ca. 1820, front and back views.

7-key bassoon, Charles Sax, Brussels, ca. 1826.

Stained maple; brass ferrules. Five sections: bocal, wing joint, butt joint, long joint, bell. Seven saddle-mounted brass keys, round, flat key heads, additional saddles for c^2 and $B\flat_1$. Back: $B\flat_1$ (LT), D, E♭ (right of D key) / c^2 (W) / F♯ (RT) / front: F, G♯.

Stamped on back of bell, front of long joint, wing joint, butt joint: "(star) / SAX / FAC^r DU ROI / A BRUXELLES / (star)".

2001.44

7-key bassoon, Charles Sax, Brussels, ca. 1826, front and back views.

16-key bassoon, Samuel Gottfried Wiesner, Dresden, ca. 1840.

Dark-stained maple; nickel-silver ferrules. Five sections: bocal, wing joint, butt joint, long joint, bell. Sixteen saddle and post-mounted nickel-silver keys, round key heads. Back: B♭[1] (LT), B[1], C (round plate), D (decorative nickel-silver guard over key head) / F♯ (RT), E♭ (RT) / d[2] (LT, W), c[2] (W2), a[2] (W3) / front: C♯ (L4), E♭ (L4) / E♭ (L3), c♯ (L4) / B♭ (R3), G♯ (R4), F (R4).

Stamped on front of butt joint, bell: "(crown) / WIESNER / DRESDEN / 2"; front of long joint, wing joint: "(crown) / WIESNER / 2".

2001.45

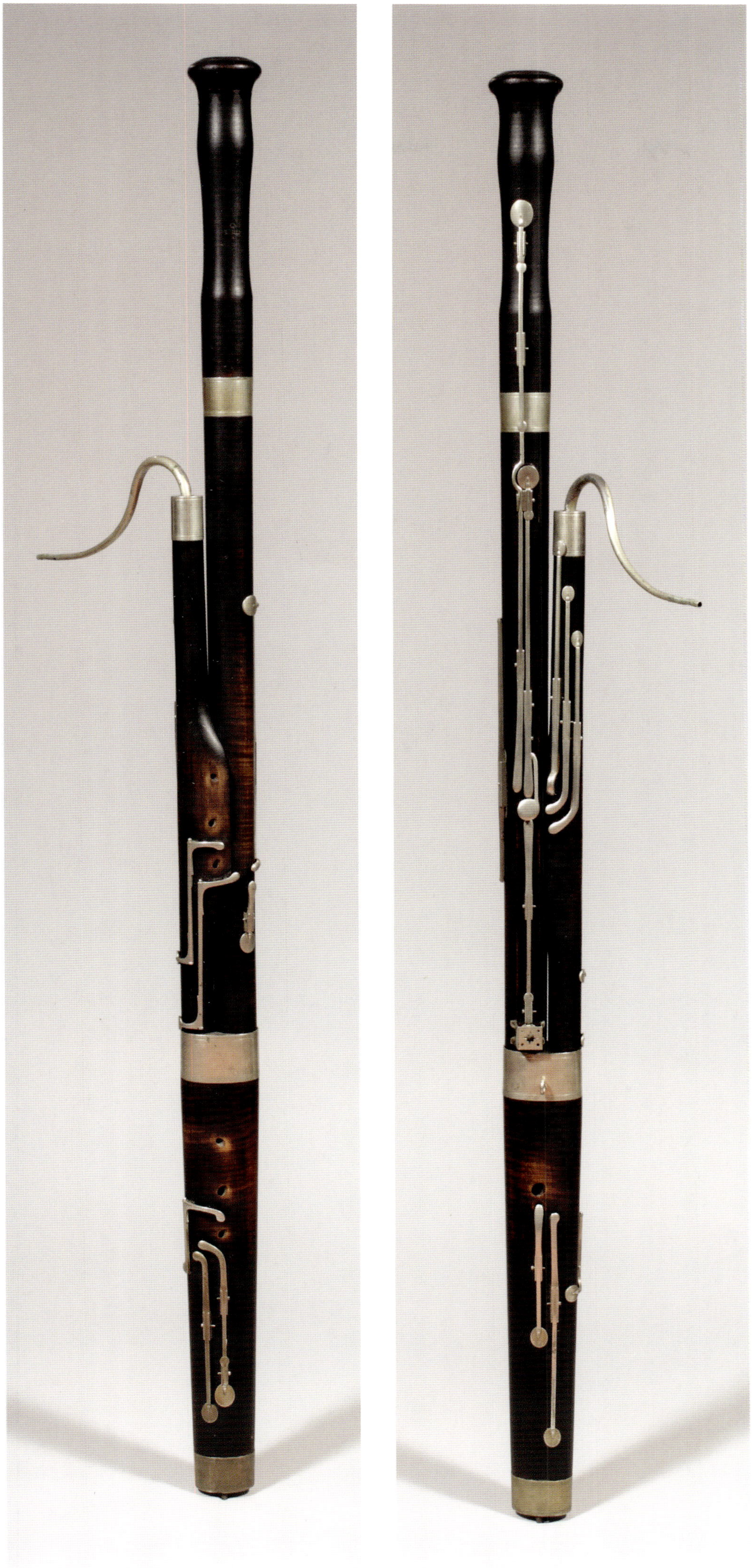

16-key bassoon, Samuel Gottfried Wiesner, Dresden, ca. 1840, front and back views.

20-key bassoon, Mahillon et Cie, Brussels, ca. 1910.

Black-stained maple; nickel-silver ferrules. Five sections: bocal, wing joint, butt joint, long joint, bell. Twenty pillar-mounted keys, modern key heads, two plates, French system. Back: $B\flat_1$ (LT, round plate), B_1 (above the round plate), C (to the left of the B_1 key), D (below the round plate, guard with M design over key head), E♭ (to the left of D) / F♯ (RT) / c^2 (W1) , a^1 (W2), trill key (W3) harmonic key (W4) / front: trill key (L2, above finger hole for L2), 2nd trill key (L3, above finger hole for L3), E♭ (L3), C♯ (L4), bocal key (L4) / g^1-a^1 trill (R2), plate for A (R2), B♭ (R3), plate for G (R3), F (R4 with roller), G♯ (R4 with roller).

Stamped on back of long joint, butt joint, bell: "(star) / C. MAHILLON / A BRUXELLES / (star)".

Baines 1967, 156-158.

2002.36

20-key bassoon, Mahillon et Cie, Brussels, ca. 1910, front and back views.

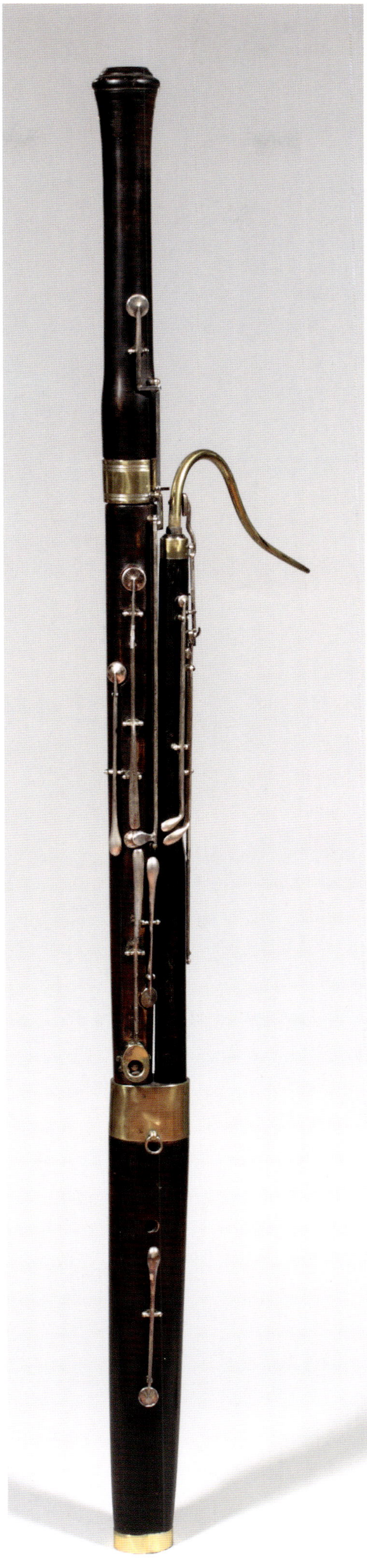

17-key bassoon, Adolphe Sax et Cie, Paris, ca. 1850.

Black-stained maple; brass ferrules. Five sections: bocal, wing joint, butt joint, long joint, bell. Lock provided for wing joint to butt joint, bocal has hole for key. Seventeen pillar-mounted, chrome-plated keys, round key heads, one plate. Back: $B\flat_1$ (overlaying a C_1 plate), C_1 (LT, round plate), B_1 (above the round plate), $C\sharp_1$ (to the left of the B_1 key), D (below the round plate, guard with a hole over key head), E♭ (to the right of D) / F♯ (RT) / d^2 (W1) , a^1 (W2) / front: f^2-g^2 trill or e^2 key (L1), e-f^3 trill or $e\flat^2$ key (L2, above finger hole for L2), d^2-$e\flat^2$ trill (L3, above finger hole for L3), c♯ (L4), bocal key (L4) / B♭ (R3), f (R4), g♯ (R4).

Stamped on front of butt joint, bell: "(cross) / AD. SAX $^{\text{et cie}}$ / PARIS".

The plugs on the back of the wing joint suggest that a d^2 key was removed along with its guide.

Baines 1967, 156-158.

2002.56

17-key bassoon, Adolphe Sax et Cie, Paris, ca. 1850, front and back views.

10-key bassoon, Jean-Nicholas Savary, Paris, 1830.

Flamed maple; brass ferrules. Five sections: bocal, wing joint, butt joint, long joint, bell. Ten saddle-mounted brass keys, round, flat key heads. Back: $B\flat_1$ (LT), B, C (round plate), D (with decorated brass guard), E♭ (to the left of D) / F♯ (RT) / c^2 (W), a^1 (W1) / front: F (R4), G♯.

Stamped on front of bell, long joint, butt joint: "(sun) / Savary (in cursive) / jeune / A PARIS / (sun)"; front of wing joint: "(sun) / Savary (in cursive) / jeune / A PARIS / (sun) /2"; back of butt joint: "1830".

2002.92

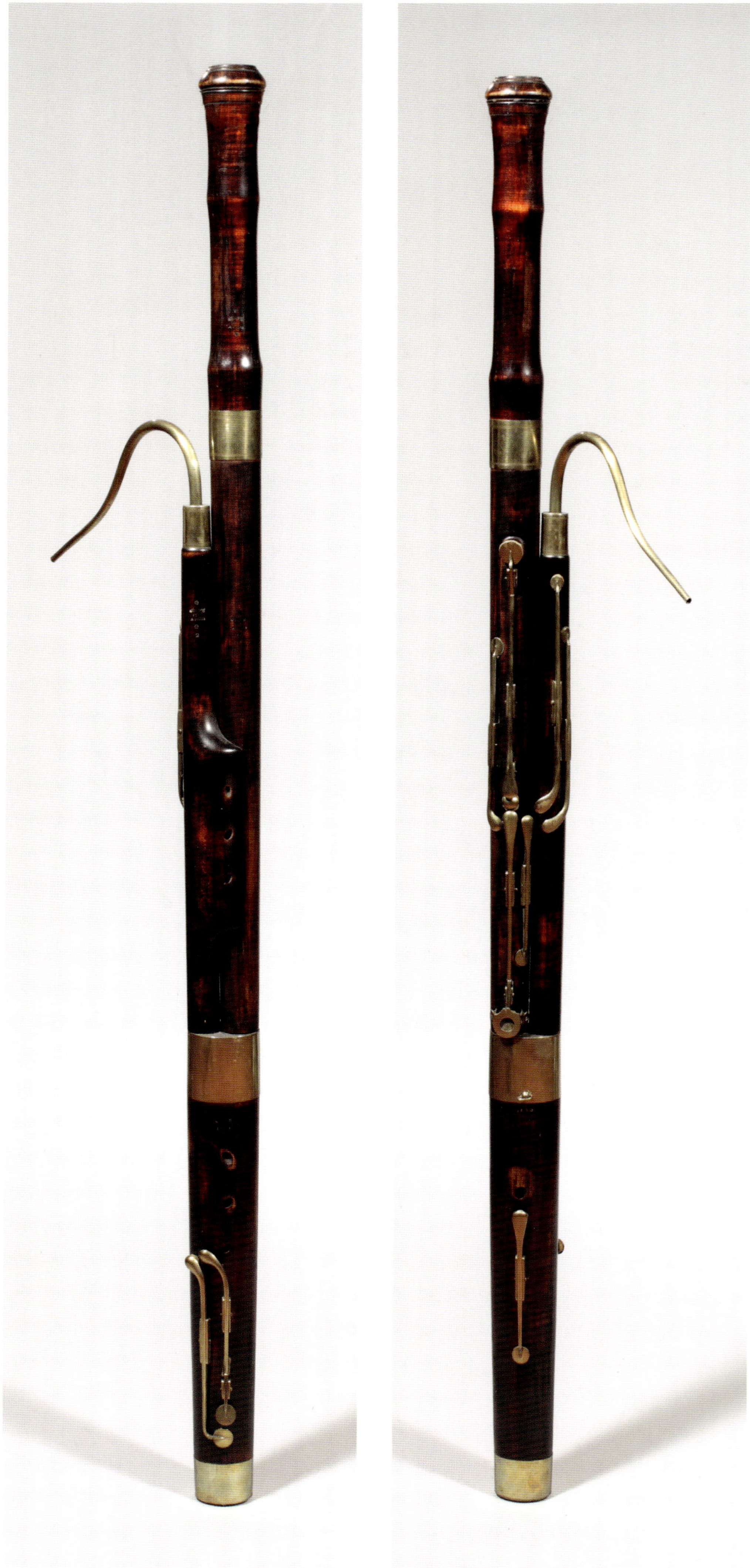

10-key bassoon, Jean-Nicholas Savary, Paris, 1830, front and back views.

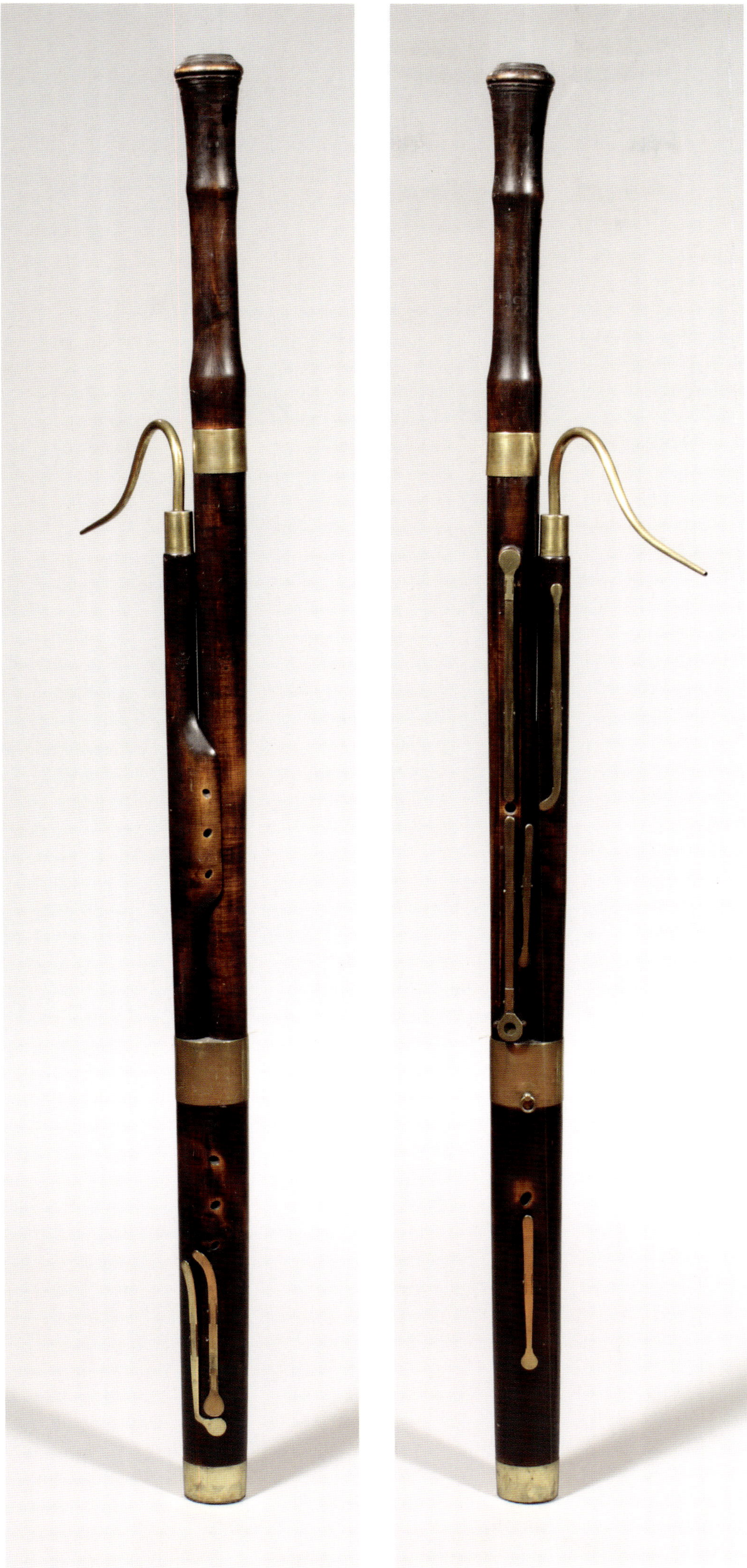

7-key bassoon, Savary, Paris, ca. 1810.

Flamed maple; brass ferrules. Five sections: bocal, wing joint, butt joint, long joint, bell. Seven saddle-mounted brass keys, flat, spade-shaped key heads. Back: B♭$_1$ (LT), D (with decorated brass guard), E♭ (to the left of D) / F♯ (RT) / c^2 (W) / front: F, G♯.

Stamped on front of bell, long joint, butt joint: "(sun) /Savary (in cursive) / A PARIS / (sun)"; front of wing joint: "(sun) /Savary (in cursive) / A PARIS / (sun) /2".

2002.93

7-key bassoon, Savary, Paris, ca. 1810, front and back views.

9-key bassoon, Carl Doke, Linz, ca. 1820.

Dark-stained maple; brass ferrules. Five sections: bocal, wing joint, butt joint, long joint, bell. Brass ferrule on upper part of bell, end of butt joint has two metal posts. Nine saddle-mounted brass keys, flat, round key heads. Back: $B\flat_1$ (LT), D (with decorated brass guard), E♭ (to the right of D) / c♯ (RT), F♯ (RT) / c^2 (W), a^1 (W) / front: F (L4, with a guard below the key head), G♯.

Stamped on front of bell, back of long joint, back of wing joint: "(Hapsburg eagle) / DOKE / LINZ / (flower)"; engraved on butt joint ferrule: "Carl Doke / in Linz (in cursive)".

2007.03

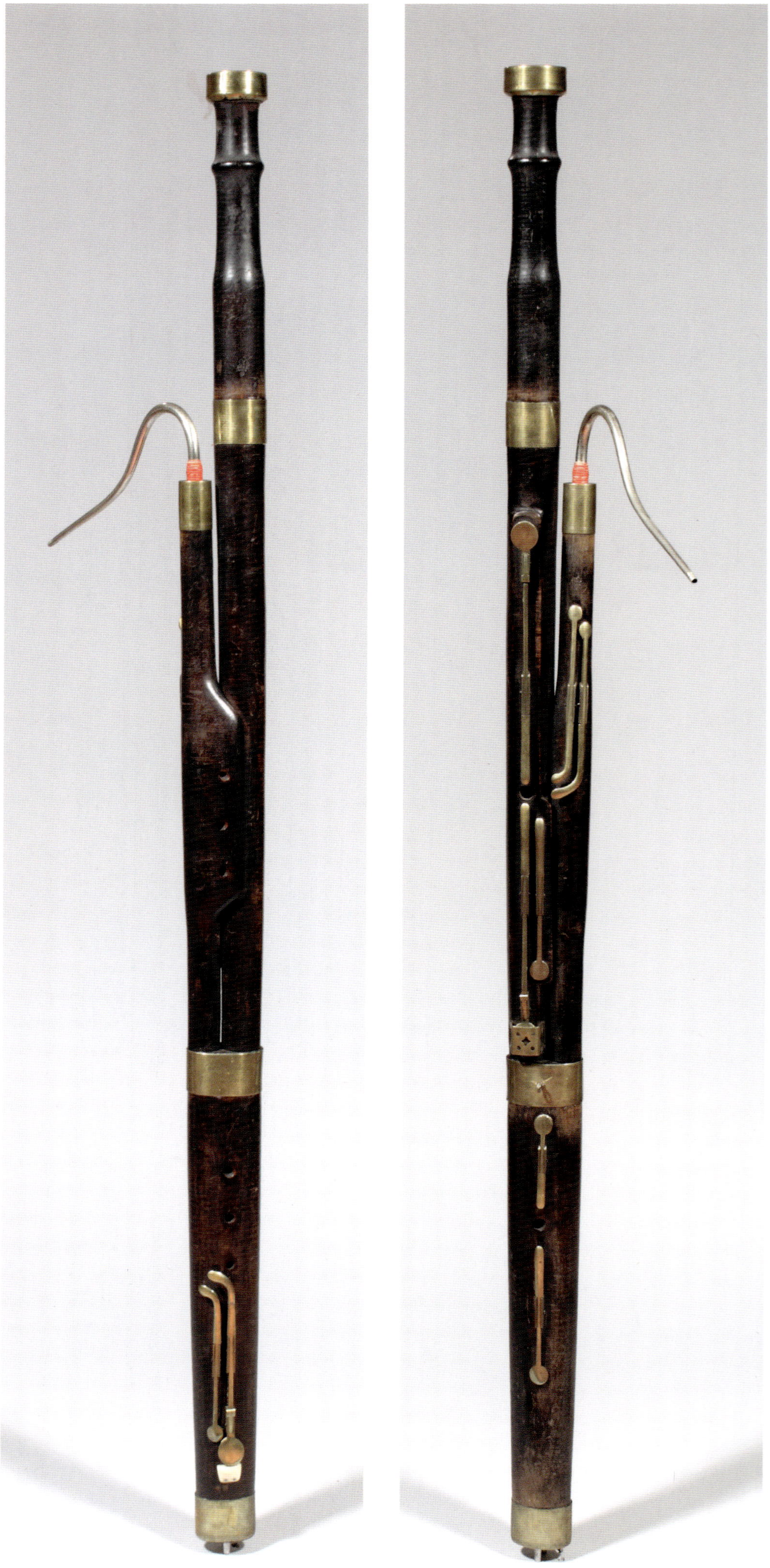

9-key bassoon, Carl Doke, Linz, ca. 1820, front and back views.

13-key bassoon, Alois Doke, Linz, ca. 1830.

Dark-stained maple; brass ferrules. Five sections: bocal (missing), wing joint, butt joint, long joint, bell. Top of bell joint has short brass flare, wing joint has tuning slide. Wing key touches have movable sliders to accommodate a pitch change. Thirteen keys recessed in the wood, round and curved key heads. Back: $B\flat_1$ (LT), C (round key), D (with a decorated key guard) / c♯ (RT), F♯ (RT) / a^1 (W), c^2 (W2) / front: E♭ (L4), E♭ (L3) / B♭ (R3) / f♯ (R4), F (R4), G♯ (R4).

Stamped on back of long joint, front of butt joint: "(Hapsburg eagle) / AL:DOKE / LINZ / (star)".

2007.04

13-key bassoon, Alois Doke, Linz, ca. 1830, front and back views.

8-key bassoon, Johann Baptist Merklein, Vienna, ca. 1810.

Stained striped maple; brass ferrules. Five sections: bocal (missing), wing joint, butt joint, long joint, bell. Eight saddle-mounted brass keys, spade and oval-shaped key heads. Back: $B\flat_1$ (LT), D, E♭ (to the right of the D key) / F♯ (RT), / c^2 (W), a^1 (W2) / front: F (swallowtail touch with support below key head, L4), G♯.

Stamped on front of bell, long joint, wing joint, butt joint: "(Hapsburg eagle) / I:MERKLEIN / WIEN / (six-pointed star)".

2008.01

8-key bassoon, Johann Baptist Merklein, Vienna, ca. 1810, front and back views.

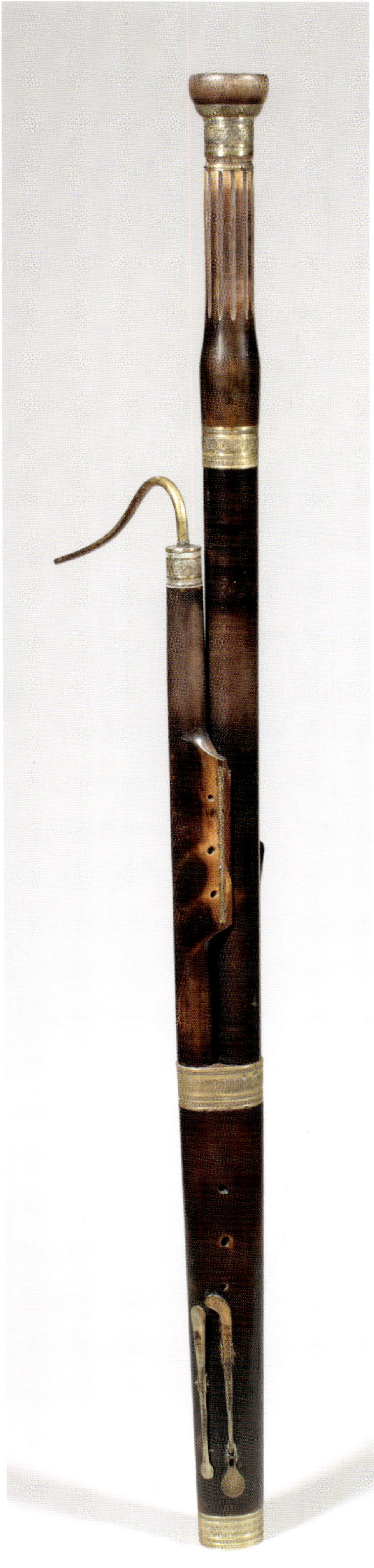

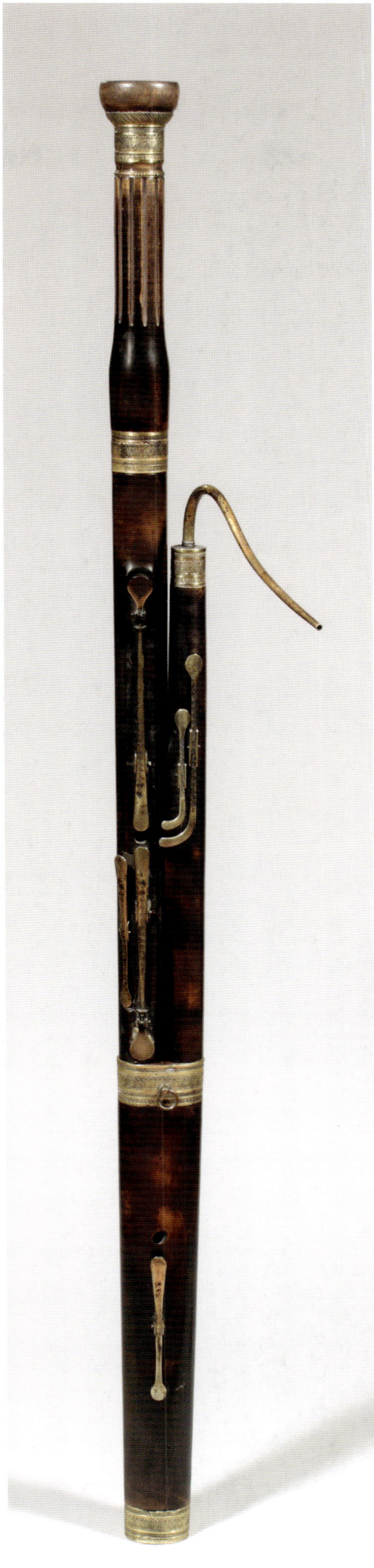

8-key bassoon, Jean Winnen, Paris, ca. 1825.

Stained maple; gold-plated decorated ferrules. Five sections: bocal, wing joint, butt joint, long joint, bell. Front of the wing joint has strip of gold leaf, upper section of bell has parallel grooves, ferrule and lower section of bell have symbols, leaf decorations, and beading. Eight saddle-mounted, gold-plated keys, oval-shaped key heads, lever engraved designs in black. Back: $B\flat_1$ (LT), D, E♭ (to the left of the D key) / F♯ (RT) / a^1 (W), c^2 (W2) / front: F (R4), G♯ (R4).

Stamped on back of wing joint: "(star) / WINNEN / A PARIS".

2008.05

8-key bassoon, Jean Winnen, Paris, ca. 1825, front and back views and bell detail.

6-key bassoon, Astor and Co., London, ca. 1798.

Maple; brass ferrules. Five sections: bocal (missing), wing joint (missing), long joint, butt joint, bell (long, brass). Six saddle-mounted brass keys, spade and spatula-shaped key heads. Bell is probably by John Köhler, London. Back: $B\flat_1$ (LT), D, E♭ (to the left of the D key) / F♯ (RT) / front: F (L4, missing key head), G♯ (to the left of the F key). L of brass bell=455.

Stamped on the back of butt joint: "ASTOR & Cº. / LONDON".

The use of "trumpet tops" or brass bells is documented by John Köhler's trade card of 1795, by a letter written about 1798 explaining that the trumpet tops correspond better visually with the horns, and by an advertisment in an Astor catalog of 1799-1800.

Lasocki 2010, 117, 119.

2010.01

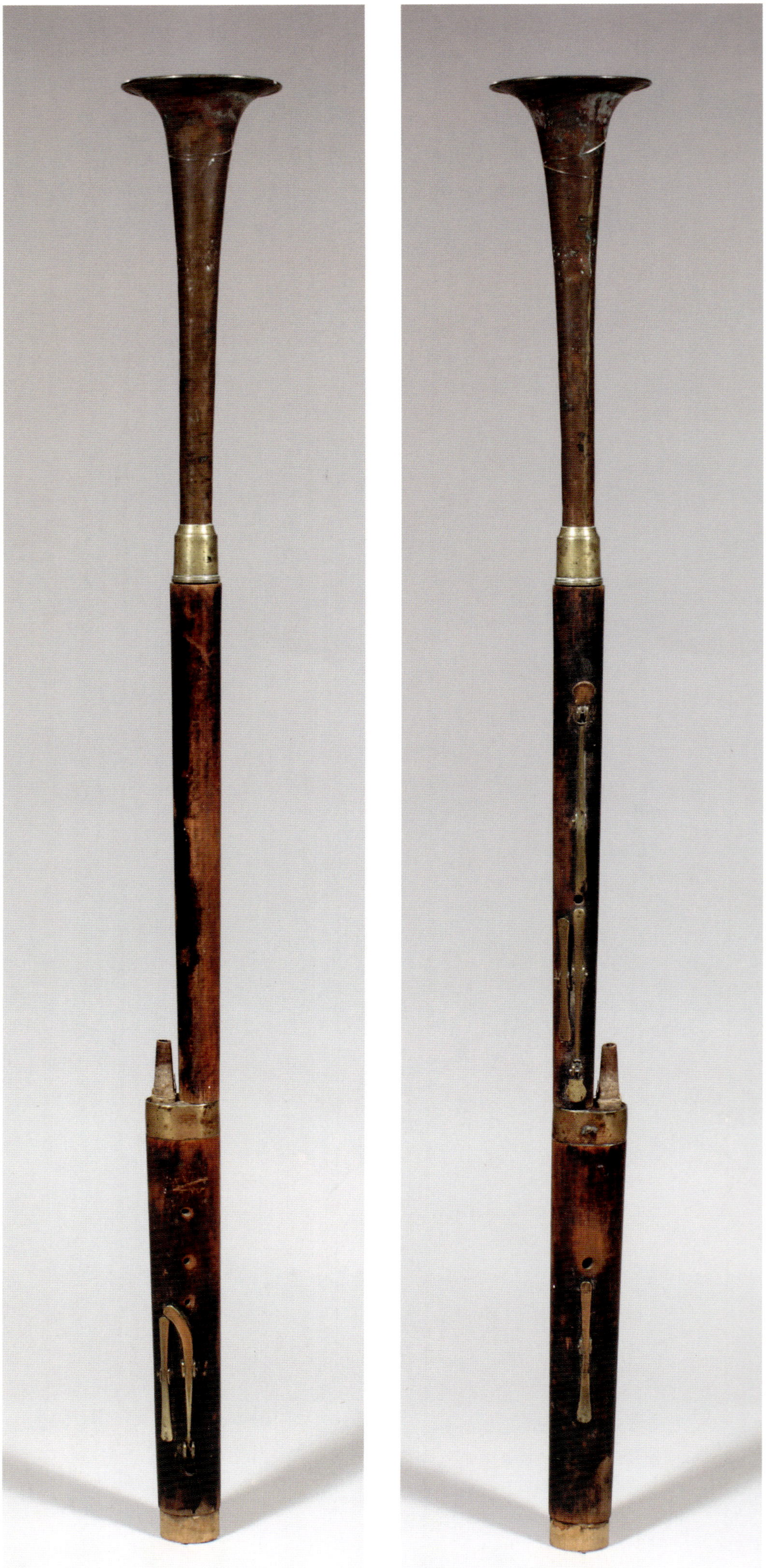

6-key bassoon, Astor and Co., London, ca. 1798, front and back views.

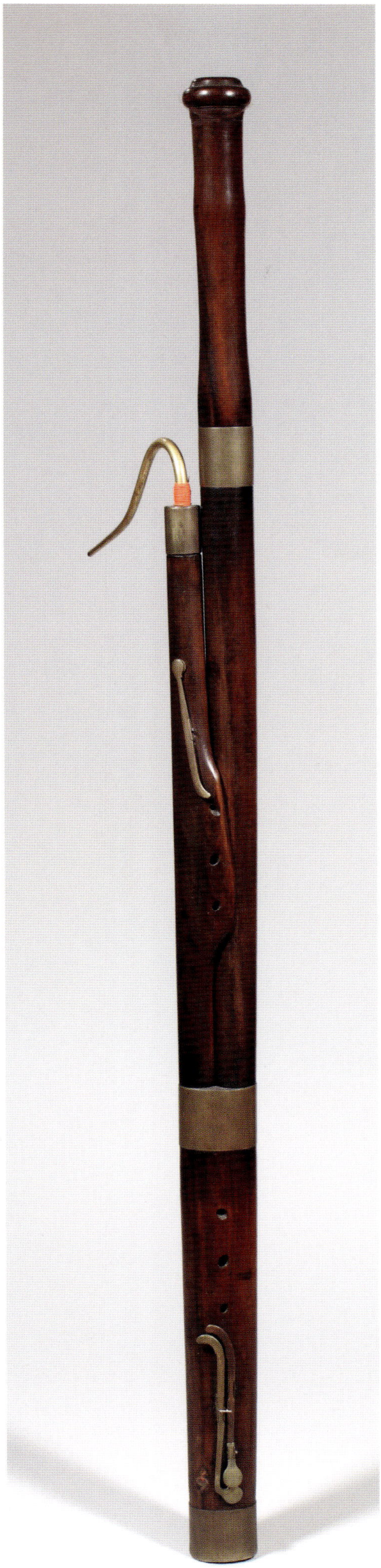

8-key bassoon, D. LeBrun, Brussels, ca. 1830.

Maple; brass ferrules. Five sections: bocal, wing joint, butt joint, long joint, bell. Eight saddle-mounted keys, spade-shaped key heads. Back: $B\flat_1$ (LT), D, E♭ (to the right of the D key) / front: $f\sharp^1$ (L1) / front: F♯ (RT), c^2 (W) / F (L4), G♯.

Stamped on back of long joint, front of upper section of bell: "D. Le Brun / à Bruxelles".

2010.12

8-key bassoon, D. LeBrun, Brussels, ca. 1830, front and back views.

7-key bassoon, Charles Rust, Lyon, ca. 1820.

Maple; brass ferrules. Five sections: bocal (missing), wing joint, butt joint, long joint, bell. Seven saddle-mounted keys, round key heads, saddles concealed under key shafts. Upper section of wing joint is an adjustable tuning slide using two metal clasps, single wing key has an extendable touch. Long and widely flared bell. Back: $B\flat_1$ (LT), D (with brass guard covering three-quarters of key head), E♭ (to right of D key) / F♯ (RT) / c^2 (W) /front: F (L4), G♯.

Stamped on front of bell, long joint: "(five-pointed star) / RUST / A LYON / (five-pointed star) /4"; front upper section of wing joint: "RUST / A LYON / (five-pointed star) /4".

See similarly designed Simiot & Brelet bassoon in Waterhouse 1983, no. 12.

2010.13

7-key bassoon, Charles Rust, Lyon, ca. 1820, front and back views.

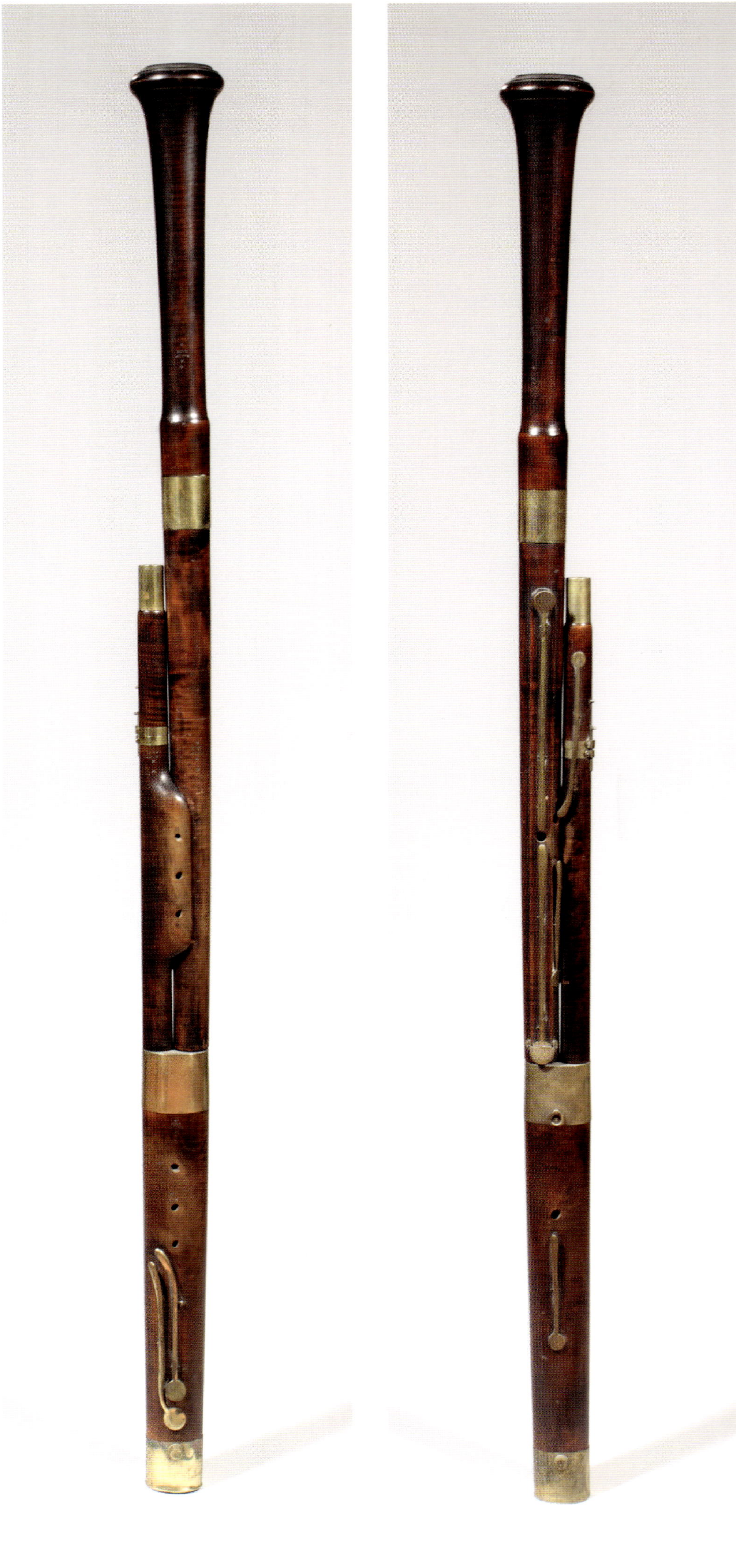

8-key bassoon, Astor and Co., London, ca. 1800.

Stained maple; brass ferrules. Five sections: bocal, wing joint, butt joint, long joint, bell. Eight saddle-mounted keys, spade and spatula-shaped key heads. Back: $B\flat_1$ (LT), D, E♭ (spatula-shaped key head) / F♯ (RT, spatula-shaped key head) / a^1 (W), c^2 (W2) / front: F (L4), G♯.

Stamped on back of butt joint: "ASTOR & Cº. / LONDON".

2011.06

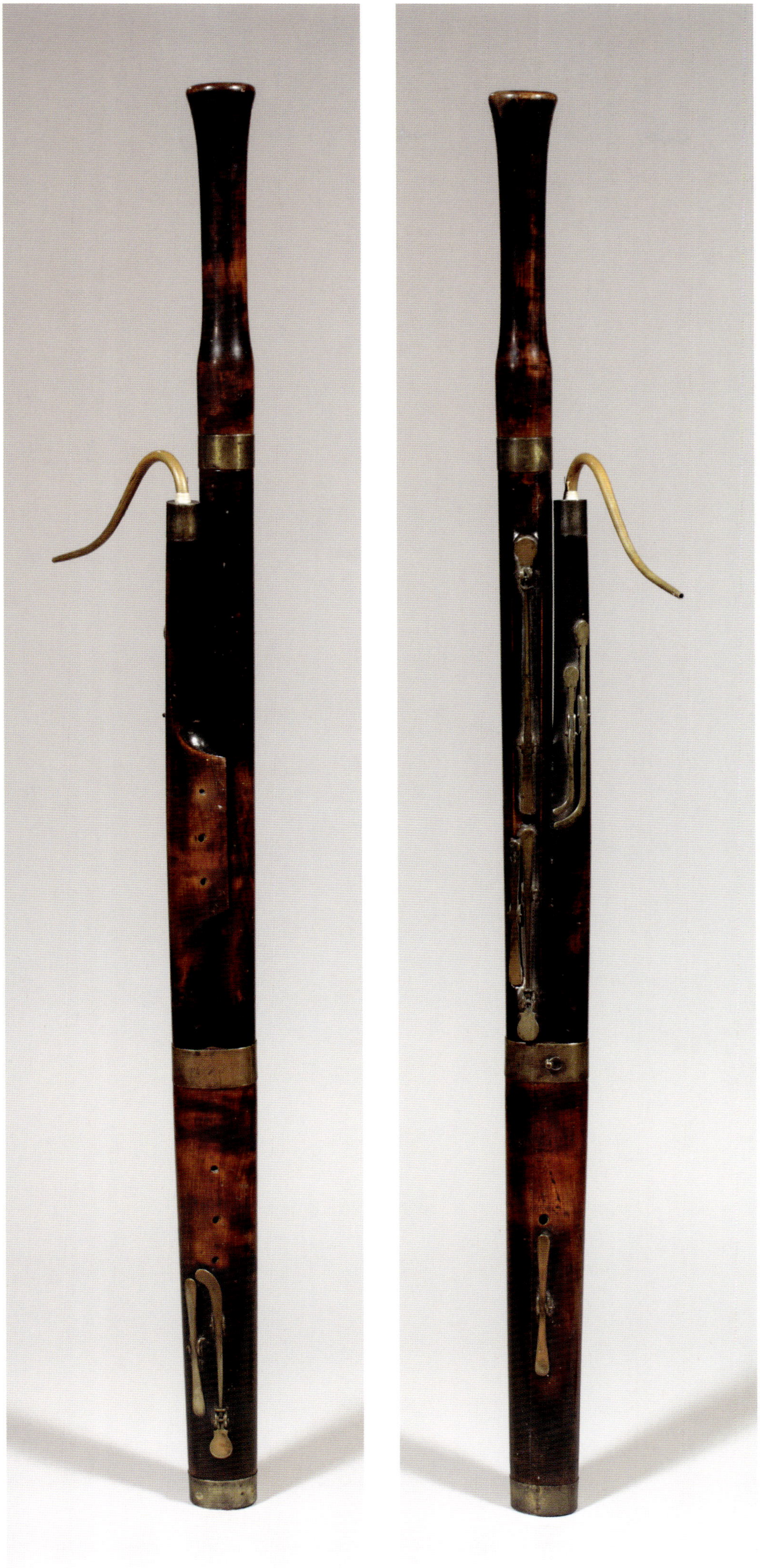

8-key bassoon, Astor and Co., London, ca. 1800, front and back views.

5-key contrabassoon, Franz Schölnast, Pressburg, ca. 1810.

Maple; brass ferrules. Eight sections: bocal (original), lead pipe, inverted butt joint, wing joint, second joint below wing, butt joint, long joint, bell. Bell has two tuning holes on lower section. Five saddle-mounted brass keys, flat, round, or flat, octagonal-shaped key heads. Back: D (LT) / F (RT) / front: E♭ (L4) / F (R4), G♯ (R4).

Stamped on back of wing joint, front of inverted butt joint: "(coat of arms) / F. SCHÖLNAST / PRESSBURG".

1995.24

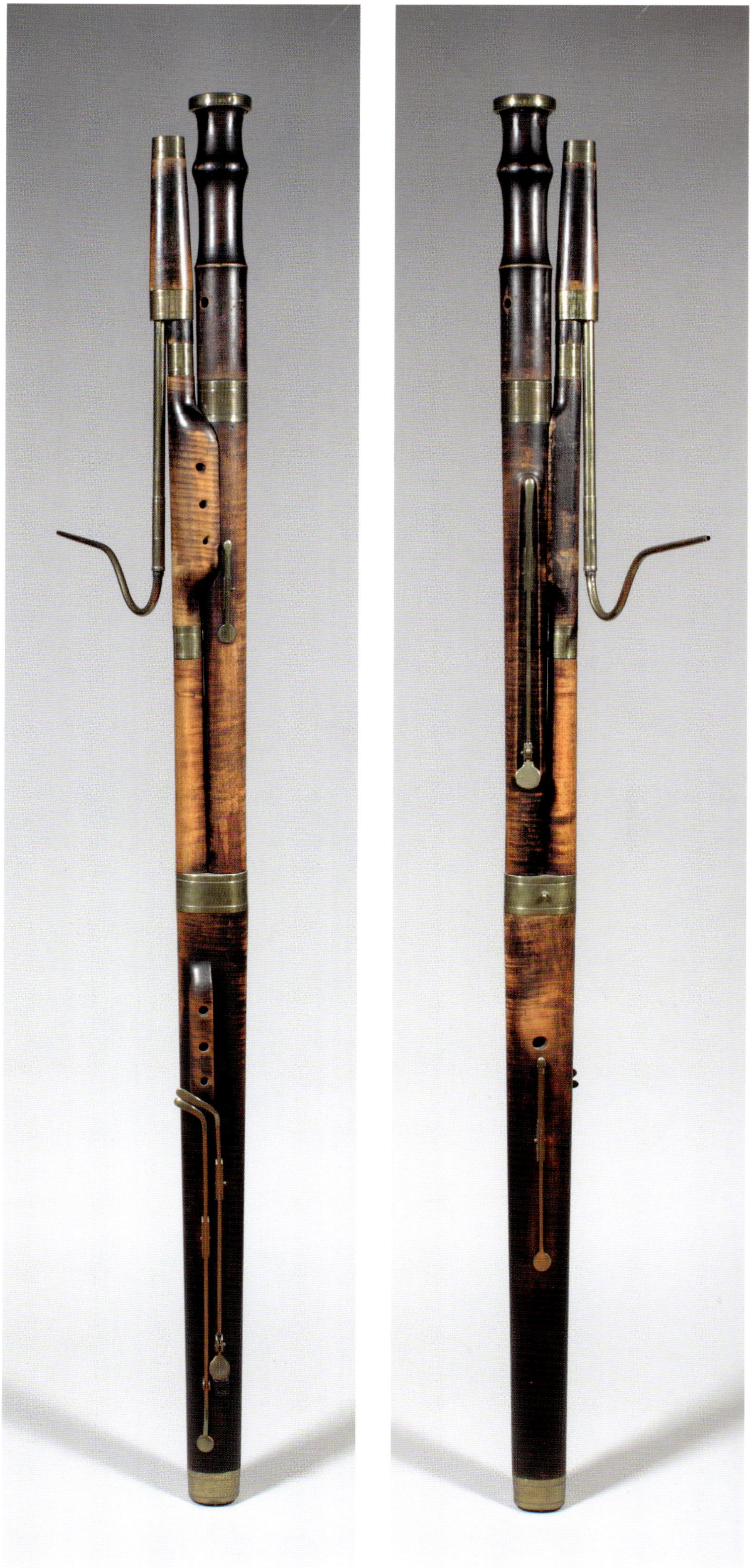

5-key contrabassoon, Franz Schölnast, Pressburg, ca. 1810, front and back views.

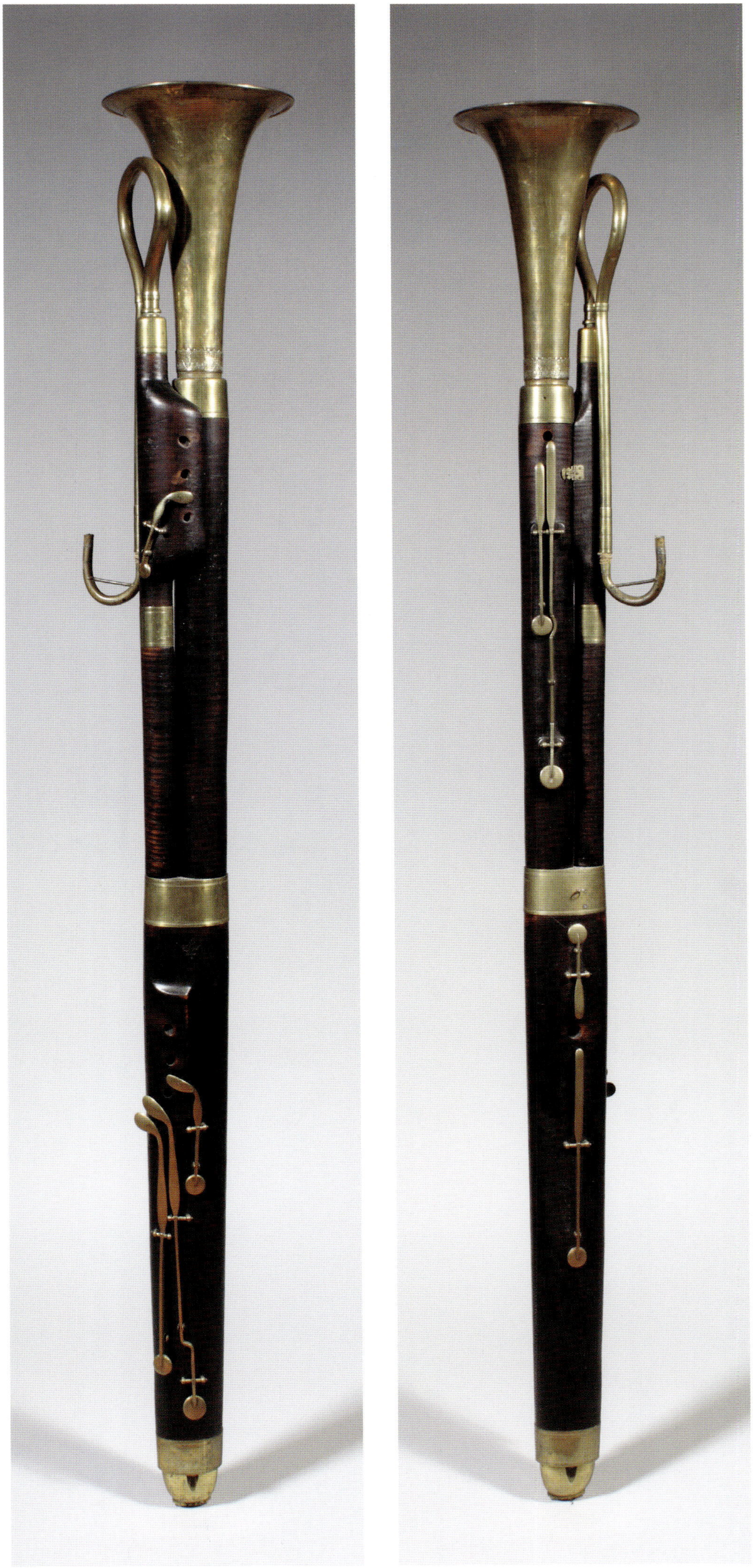

8-key contrabassoon, Martin Schemmel, Vienna, ca. 1830.

Stained maple; brass ferrules. Seven sections: curved bocal, leadpipe (hairpin-shaped), wing joint, joint below wing, butt joint, long joint, bell. Missing bocal. Brass bell with decorative ferrule. Raised shoulder or épaule on front for R1, R2, R3, two raised tables on back for l.h. thumb keys. Metal U-joint at the bottom of the butt joint. Back has clasp holding together wing and long joints, below the F key is a protective wood boss. Eight pillar-mounted brass keys, flat, round key heads. Back: D (LT), E♭ (LT) / c♯ (RT), F♯ (RT) / front: E♭ (L3) / B♭ (R3), F (R4, furthest to the left), G♯ (R4).

Stamped on front side of wing joint, butt joint: "(lyre) / Schemmel / Wien (cursive) / (star)".

1997.01

8-key contrabassoon, Martin Schemmel, Vienna, ca. 1830, front and back views.

15-key contrabassophon, attributed to Heinrich Joseph Haseneier, Koblenz, ca. 1860.

Maple; brass ferrules. Nine sections: bocal, wing joint, brass U-joint, long joint (divided by a brass ferrule), wooden U-joint, first joint (divided by brass ferrule), wooden U-joint, second joint (divided by two brass ferrules), bell. Fifteen keys mounted on pillars and long rods, round, large flat key heads. Front: four touches for L1, L2, L3, L4, and five touches for R1, R2, R3, R4 with two touches for R5. Back: four touches for LT, and two touches for RT. Front: c♯, wing key / c^2, d^2, a^2 and b^2 / E♭, F, F♯, G♯, B♭; back: C, C♯, D♯, D (LT) / E♭, E (RT).

The stamp appears to be removed on back of lower part of first joint.

Heyde 1976, 244; Dibley 2000, plate 3, p. 77.

1998.21

15-key contrabassophon, attributed to Heinrich Joseph Haseneier, Koblenz, ca. 1860, front and back views.

22-key contrabassoon, Buffet-Crampon et Cie, Paris, ca. 1930.

Stained maple; nickel-silver ferrules. Six sections: bocal (missing), wing joint, second wing, third wing, long joint (in two parts), curved bell. Each section is joined together with U-bends of nickel-silver. Two nickel-silver supports on left for r.h., on right for l.h. Platform with screw for insertion of a music lyre on front, bracket secured by a pin on the front holds wing and lower long joint together, water key on the U-bend on back of wing joint. Twenty-two keys: back, seven keys (LT), three keys (RT); front, six keys including plateau keys for L1, L2, L3, six keys including plateau keys for R1, R2, two keys with black rollers on each for L3, and two keys with black rollers on each L4. The lowest note is B♭.

Stamped on back of upper section of long joint: "(lyre) / BUFFET / CRAMPON & C[ie] / A PARIS (in oval) / BC (monogram) / C. Fischer / NEW-YORK"; lower section of long joint, front of bell: "(lyre) / BUFFET / CRAMPON & C[ie] / A PARIS (in oval) / BC (monogram)".

An identical contrabassoon appears in the 1922 Evette & Schaeffer catalog.

Evette & Schaeffer 1922, 9.

2003.32

22-key contrabassoon, Buffet-Crampon et Cie, Paris, ca. 1930, front and back views.

12-key contrabassoon,
Giuseppe Pelitti, Milan, ca. 1880.

Brass; ophicleide shape. Three sections: bocal (coiled), crook (coiled), body. Body has one U-bend, twelve pillar-mounted nickel-silver keys, flat, round key heads. Four levers for l.h., r.h. fingers, two levers for RT and LT. Back: C, C♯ (LT) / front: E♭, E, F, F♯ (R1, R2, R3, R4) / back: G, G♯ (RT) / front: A, B♭, B, C^1 (L1, L2, L3, L4).

Stamped on front of bell on a nickel-silver medallion: "PELITTI / (Great Coat of Arms of the Kingdom of Italy) / MILANO". On back of bell is a nickel-silver medallion of a horse rearing above five three-crenellated towers and an inverted V or emblem.

Pelitti constructed a 12-key contrabassoon in metal (*controfagottone basso in otone a dodici chiavi*) presented at the 1853 Milan Exhibition.

Pelitti 1872, 11 and 1873.

2005.10

12-key contrabassoon, Giuseppe Pelitti, Milan, ca. 1880, back and front views.

15-key tenor sarrusophone in E♭,
Gautrot-Marquet, Paris, ca. 1880.

Brass; ophicleide shape. Two sections: bocal, body. Bocal connected to body, body has U-joint, flaring bell. Large adjustable hand rest for palm of l.h. on back, a platform for a music lyre, ring on back for sling. Fifteen keys, modern key heads: back from top to bottom: 1st octave key (LT), 2nd octave key (LT), B♭ (LT), D (LT); front, l.h. plateau keys for L1, L2, L3, G♯ (L4), C♯ (L4), B (L4); r.h., D (on the left side, R1), C (R1), B♭ (R1), plateau keys for R1, R2, R3, E♭ (R4), C (L4). Serial no. 458.

Engraved on front of bell: "Gautrot Marquet / breveté s.g.d.g. á Paris (cursive) / (GA monogram) / 458".

2002.50

15-key tenor sarrusophone in E♭, Gautrot-Marquet, Paris, ca. 1880, front and back views.

15-key bass sarrusophone in B♭,
Gautrot-Marquet, Paris, ca. 1880.

Silver-plated brass; ophicleide shape. Two sections: bocal, body. Bocal connected to body, three U-joints, flaring bell. Large hand rest for palm of l.h. on back; water key on back of first U-bend; a platform for music lyre; and ring on back for sling. Fifteen keys, modern key heads: back from top to bottom: 1st octave key (LT), 2nd octave key (LT), B♭ (LT), D (LT); front: l.h. plateau keys for L1, L2, L3, G♯ (L4), C♯ (L4), B (L4); r.h. D (on the left side, R1), C (R1), B♭ (R1), plateau keys for R1, R2, R3, E♭ (R4), C (L4).

Engraved on front of bell: "Gautrot Marquet / breveté s.g.d.g. á Paris (cursive) / (GA monogram)".

2003.28

15-key bass sarrusophone in B♭, Gautrot-Marquet, Paris, ca. 1880, front and back views.

17-key alto sarrusophone,
Rampone e Cazzani, Milan, ca. 1920.

Nickel-silver plated brass; ophicleide shape. Two sections: bocal, body. Bocal inserts into body, two U-bends, flaring bell. When lowest key on upper U-bend is closed, air enters the larger U-bend, and lower notes are playable. Adjustable thumb rest for l.h., stationary thumb rest for RT, platform on front with screw for music lyre. Seventeen nickel-silver keys, modern key heads: back: three keys (LT, first two are bocal keys, third for the lowest note); front: fourteen keys, plateau keys for L1, L2, L3, three levers for L4; three touches for R1, plateau keys for R1, R2, R3, two touches for R4; back: three keys, 1st octave key (LT), 2nd octave key (LT), third key for lowest note. In original case.

Stamped on bell: "(star, lyre, wreath) / PREMIA O STABILE / A.RAMPONE / MILANO (in medallion) / ESPORTAZIONE MONDIALE / (five-pointed star) / A. RAMPONE / Ditte Riunite (cursive) / B.CAZZANI&C. (in oval)".

2003.64

17-key alto sarrusophone, Rampone e Cazzani, Milan, ca. 1920, front and back views.

12-key tenor rothphone, A. and M. Bottali Fratelli, Milan, ca. 1915.

Nickel-silver body. Two sections: bocal (curved), body (with upturned bell). Twelve nickel-silver keys, modern key heads, six plateau keys for L1, L2, L3, R1, R2, R3. 1st octave (LT), 2nd octave (LT), E♭ (L1), f (L1), key used with E♭ and f (R1), E♭ (R1), G♯ (L4), E♭ (R4, black roller), C (R4, black roller), C♯ (L4), B (L4).

Stamped on bell: "BREVETTO BOTTALI (in banner) / PRIMARIA / PREMIATA FABBRICA / F^LLI^. A.M. BOTTALI / MILANO / (ITALIA) / MARCA FERD^O^ ROTH (in a cartouche) / 76".

Joppig 1986, 98.

2007.16

12-key tenor rothphone, A. and M. Bottali Fratelli, Milan, ca. 1915.

CHAPTER 4
SINGLE–REED INSTRUMENTS

Metal Boehm-system clarinet in B♭ (skeletal model), Anonymous, of American origin, ca. 1923.

One piece nickel-silver; nickel-silver keys. Boehm-system, seventeen keys, six rings (LT, L1, L2, R1, R2, R3). Speaker, A-B trill, A-B♭ trill, A, G♯, E♭/B♭ (cross), E♭/B♭ (R1), f/c, C♯/G♯, B/F♯ (cross), F/C (L4), F♯/C♯ (L4), E/B (L4), A♭/E♭, F/C (R4), F♯/C♯ (R4), E/B (R4). Serial no. A86865. L=659.

Engraved on bell: "(lyre and foliage) / AMERICAN BEAUTY / U.S.A. / (two diamonds) / (four-pedal shamrock)".

Stamped on front of body below barrel: "A86865".

"American Beauty" is a trade name probably used by an American company such as the Buescher Company in Elkhart, Indiana.

1944.01

6-key clarinet in C, John Firth, William Hall, and Sylvanus Pond, New York, ca. 1840.

Long-tenon rosewood mouthpiece; string ligature; lightly stained boxwood; ivory ferrules; two and three beadings; two and three dark lines. Six sections: mouthpiece, barrel (waisted), l.h. joint, r.h. joint, stock, bell. Six brass keys, block-mounted, square key heads, F/C tone-hole bulge cut straight on the lower side. Speaker, A-B trill (R1) A, A♭/E♭, F♯/C♯ (cranked), E/B. L=536, 595 (with mouthpiece).

Stamped on barrel, l.h. joint, r.h. joint, stock: "FIRTH HALL & POND / N-YORK"; bell: "FIRTH HALL & POND / FRANKLIN SQ^{E} / N-YORK".

1992.03

5-key clarinet in C, Meacham & Co., Albany, New York, ca. 1827.

Rosewood mouthpiece; string ligature; brown-stained wood; ivory ferrules; one and two dark lines; single beading on wood. Five sections: mouthpiece, barrel (waisted), l.h. joint, r.h. joint-stock, bell. Five block-mounted brass keys, square key heads, F/C tone-hole bulge cut straight on the lower side, light wood mouthpiece cap. Speaker, A, A♭/E♭, F♯/C♯ (cranked), E/B. Repair of crack on upper section of r.h. joint, a wide silver band. L=541, 610 (with mouthpiece).

Stamped on barrel, l.h. joint, r.h. joint-stock, bell: "MEACHAM & Co. / ALBANY".

1992.04

Metal Boehm-system clarinet in B♭ (skeletal model), Anonymous, of American origin, ca. 1923.

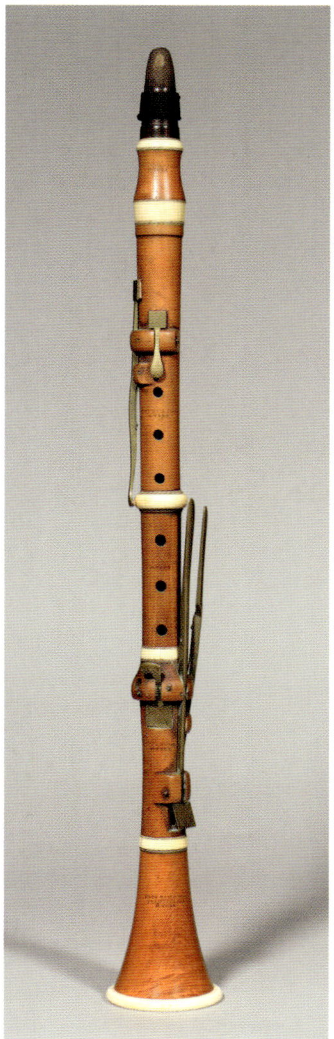

6-key clarinet in C, John Firth, William Hall, and Sylvanus Pond, New York, ca. 1840.

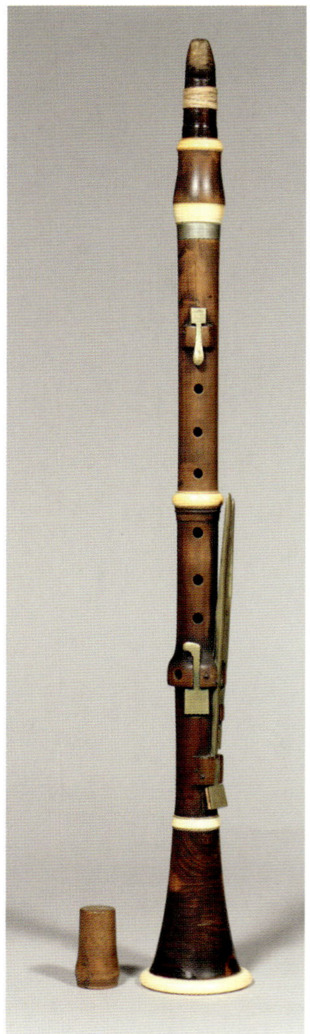

5-key clarinet in C, Meacham & Co., Albany, New York, ca. 1827.

5-key clarinet in B♭, Metzler & Co., London, ca. 1835.

Dark wood mouthpiece; stained boxwood; wide ivory ferrules; single beading; decorative line on bell ferrule. Six sections: mouthpiece, barrel (waisted), l.h. joint, r.h. joint, stock, bell. Five ring-mounted brass keys, square key heads, F/C tone-hole bulge turned out above A♭/E♭ tone hole. Speaker, A, A♭/E♭, F♯/C♯ (cranked), E/B. L=535.

Stamped on barrel, l.h. joint, r.h. joint: "METZLER / LONDON".

1992.05

5-key clarinet in B♭,
Metzler & Co., London, ca. 1835.

5-key clarinet in C, Graves & Co., Winchester, New Hampshire, ca. 1835.

Long-tenon black wood mouthpiece; string ligature; stained boxwood; ivory ferrules; decorated lines and beading. Six sections: mouthpiece, barrel (waisted), l.h. joint, r.h. joint, stock, bell. Five ring-mounted brass keys, round, flat key heads, F/C tone-hole bulge cut straight on the lower side; brown wood mouthpiece cap. Speaker, A, A♭/E♭ (highly curved and decorated touch), F♯/C♯(cranked), E/B. L=533, 590 (with mouthpiece).

Stamped on barrel, l.h. joint, r. h. joint, stock, bell: "GRAVES & Co."

1994.12

5-key clarinet in C, Graves & Co.,
Winchester, New Hampshire, ca. 1835.

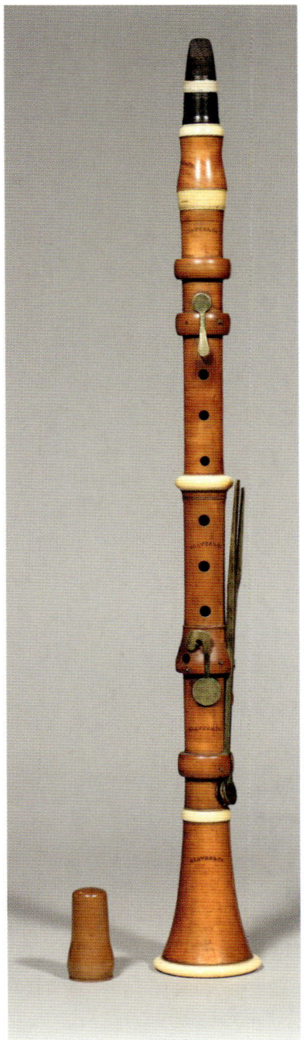

10-key clarinet in C, John Ashton, Boston, ca. 1835.

Long-tenon black wood mouthpiece; stained boxwood; ivory ferrules; single beading. Five sections: mouthpiece, barrel (waisted), l.h. joint, r.h. joint-stock, bell. Ten block-mounted brass keys, round, flat key heads, F/C tone-hole bulge cut straight on the lower side. Speaker, A-B trill, A, E♭/B♭ (cross), C♯G♯, B/F♯ (cross), B♭/F (cross), A♭/E♭, F♯/C♯ (cranked), E/B. L=530, 590 (with mouthpiece).

Stamped on barrel, r.h. joint-stock: "J.ASHTON, / BOSTON."; l.h. joint, bell: "(eagle with spread wings) / J.ASHTON, / BOSTON. / C".

1994.13

10-key clarinet in C,
John Ashton, Boston, ca. 1835.

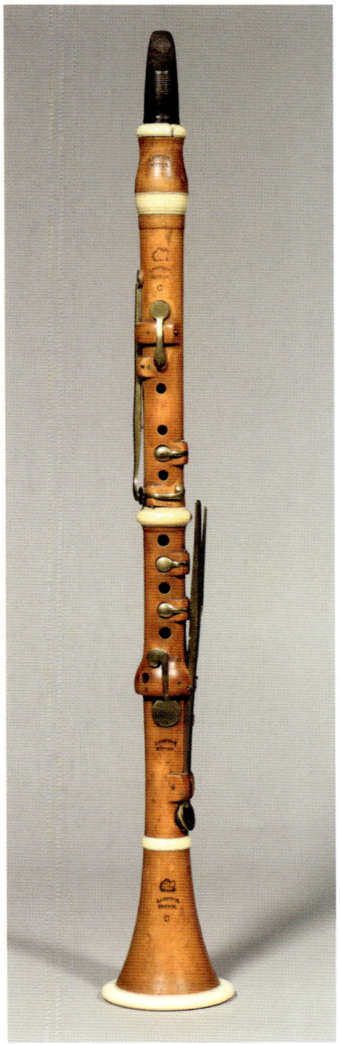

7-key clarinet in B♭, Jean-Jacques Baumann, Paris, ca. 1815.

Dark wood mouthpiece; stained boxwood; ivory ferrules; single beading. Five sections: mouthpiece, barrel, l.h. joint, r.h. joint-stock, bell. Seven gold-plated tubular keys, round key heads slightly curved to fit the contour of body, diamond-shaped posts sunk into the outside wood, inner rods rotate, springs and screws inside tubes. At upper and lower ends of key pivots are brilliants or single stones. All key shanks appear elongated but key heads are placed in correct positions. E/B key lever on back with its key head on right side instead of left. Speaker, A, C♯/G♯, A♭/E♭, F/C, F♯/C♯, E/B. L=600.

Stamped on barrel, l.h. joint, r.h.joint-stock, bell: "(five-pointed star) / (lyre) / BAUMANN, / A PARIS / (five-pointed star) / B".

Similar gold-plated keys were invented by C.H. Felix, Paris, in 1813, used on a seven-key bassoon by Baumann, New York, Metropolitan Museum of Art, 89.4.885. The highest key is inscribed: "INVENTE PAR C.H. FELIX MECANICIEN A PARIS / EN 1813". 7-key bassoon of similar key design by Winnen, Paris inscribed: "INVENTE PAR FELIX MECANICIEN / A PARIS", Paris, Musée de la Musique, E.979.2.14. Probably made as a set of three C, B♭, and A clarinets for a wealthy client.

1995.05

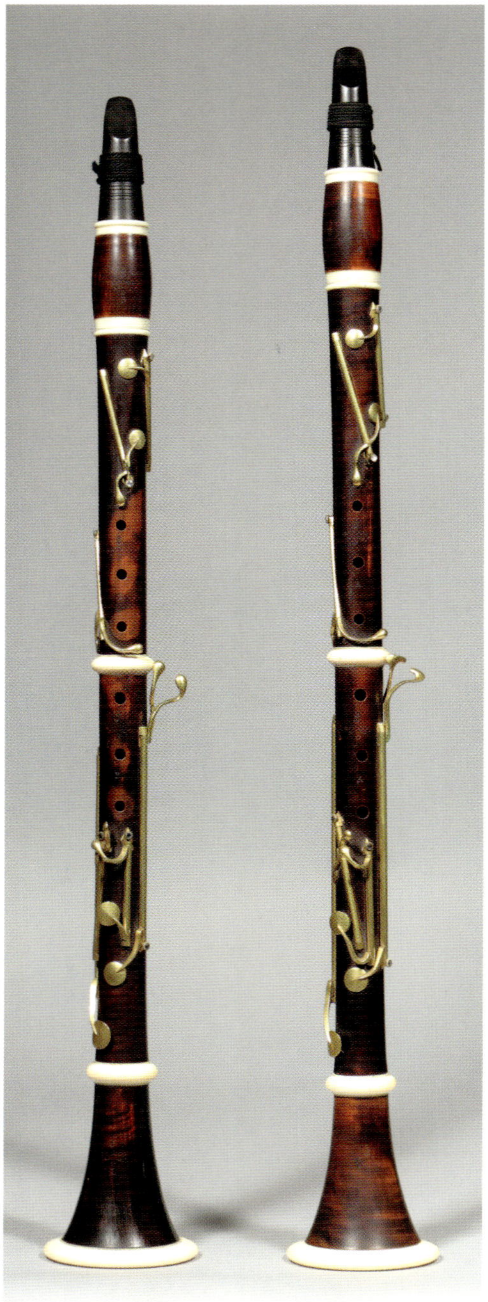

7-key clarinet in B♭, Jean-Jacques Baumann, Paris, ca. 1815, and *7-key clarinet in A*, Jean-Jacques Baumann, Paris, ca. 1815.

7-key clarinet in A, Jean-Jacques Baumann, Paris, ca. 1815.

Dark wood mouthpiece; stained boxwood; ivory ferrules; single beading. Five sections: mouthpiece, barrel, l.h. joint, r.h. joint-stock, bell. Seven gold-plated keys, round key heads slightly curved to fit the contour of the body, diamond-shaped posts sunk into outside wood, inner rods rotate, springs and screws inside tubes. At upper and lower ends of key pivots are brilliants or single stones. All key shanks appear elongated but key heads are placed in correct positions. E/B key lever on back with its key head on right side instead of left. Speaker, A, C♯/G♯, A♭/E♭, F/C, F♯/C♯, E/B. L=628 (with C clarinet bell).

Stamped on barrel, l.h. joint, r.h.joint-stock: "(five-pointed star) / (lyre) / BAUMANN, / A PARIS / (five-pointed star) / A"; bell: "(five-pointed star) / (lyre) / BAUMANN, / A PARIS / (five-pointed star) / C".

Similar gold-plated keys were invented by C.H. Felix, Paris, in 1813, used on a seven-key bassoon by Baumann, New York, Metropolitan Museum of Art, 89.4.885. The highest key is inscribed: "INVENTE PAR C.H. FELIX MECANICIEN A PARIS / EN 1813". Seven-key bassoon of similar key design by Winnen, Paris inscribed: "INVENTE PAR FELIX MECANICIEN / A PARIS", Paris, Musée de la Musique, E.979.2.14.

Probably made as a set of three C, B♭, and A clarinets for a wealthy client.

1995.06

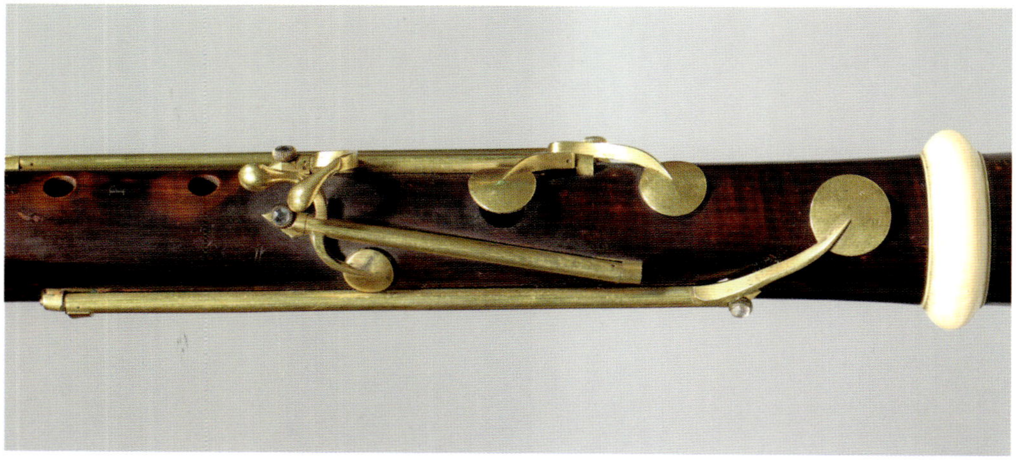

Close-up of r.h. joint-stock on B♭. clarinet

5-key clarinet in C, Hentz Jouve, Paris, ca. 1810.

Stained boxwood; ivory ferrules; beading. Five sections: barrel, l.h. joint, r.h. joint, stock, bell. Barrel darker than other sections and may be a replacement. Five ring-mounted keys, flat, square key heads. Speaker, A, A♭/E♭, F♯/C♯, E/B. L=526.

Stamped on l.h. joint, stock, bell: "(five-pointed star) / JOUVE / A PARIS / C".

1995.11

5-key clarinet in C, Hentz Jouve, Paris, ca. 1810.

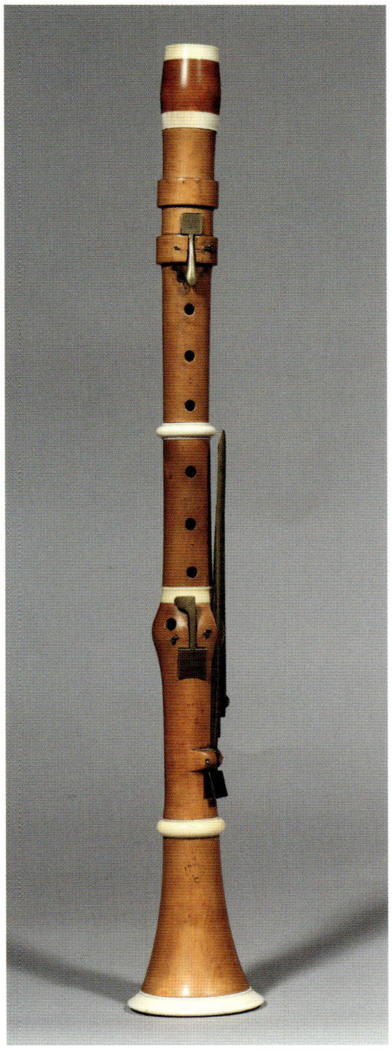

5-key clarinet in D, Jean Arnold Antoine Tuerlinckx, Malines, ca. 1800.

Ivory mouthpiece; stained fruitwood; ivory ferrules; single beading. Six sections: mouthpiece, barrel, l.h. joint, r.h. joint, stock, bell. Outside profile of l.h. joint expands at lower end; outside profile of r.h. joint expands at upper and lower ends. Originally played with an E♭ corps de rechange of two finger hole joints or using D corps de rechange with long touches extended. Five block-mounted brass keys, square, flat key heads. Speaker, A, A♭/E♭, F♯/C♯ (extension on touch), E/B (extension on touch). L=510.

Stamped on barrel: "TUERLINCKX / (fleuron)"; l.h. joint: "TUERLINCX / MALINES / (fleuron)"; r.h. joint: "TUERLINCKX"; stock: "TUERLINCKX / MALINES / (fleuron)".

Formerly Baron Armand Van Zuylen collection, sold at Christie's, London, 16 March 1988; formerly William Maynard collection.

Libin 1994.

1995.13

5-key clarinet in D, Jean Arnold Antoine Tuerlinckx, Malines, ca. 1800.

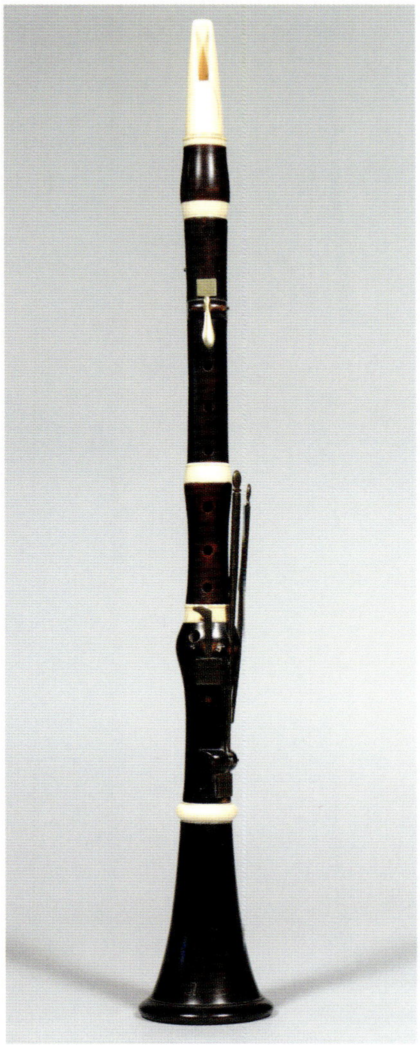

5-key clarinet in F, Jean-Baptiste Tabard, Lyon, ca. 1835.

Stained rosewood mouthpiece; string ligature; stained ebony; ivory ferrules; single beading. Six sections: mouthpiece, barrel, l.h. joint, r.h. joint, stock, bell. Metal tube between barrel and l.h. joint; tuning slide when barrel is pulled; wide ivory bell ring. Five ring and block-mounted silver keys, round, flat key heads. Speaker, A, A♭/E♭ (highly curved touch), F♯/C♯, E/B. L=431 (with mouthpiece).

Stamped on mouthpiece: "Godfroy Ainé"; barrel, l.h. joint, r.h. joint, stock, bell: "(Maltese cross) / TABARD / A LYON / (Maltese cross)".

Formerly William Maynard collection.

Libin 1994.

1995.14

5-key clarinet in F, Jean-Baptiste Tabard, Lyon, ca. 1835.

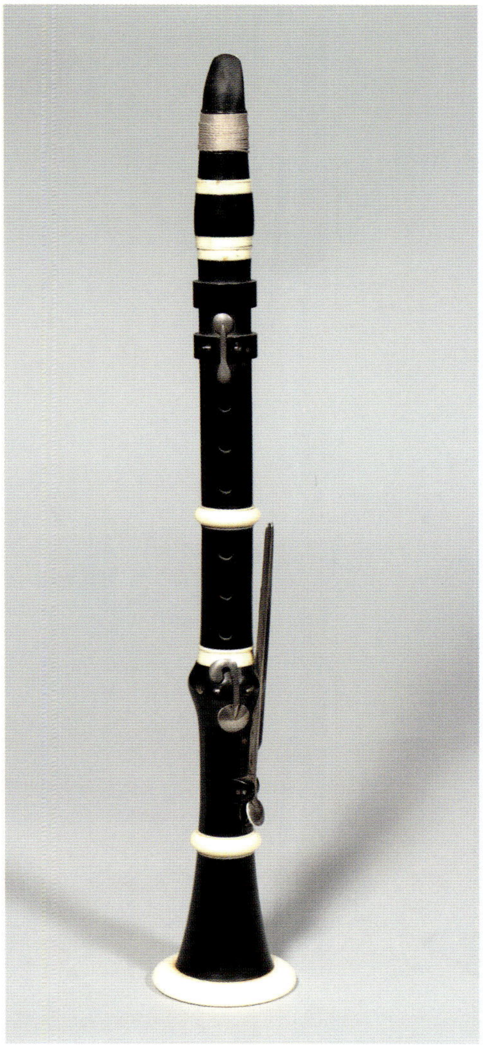

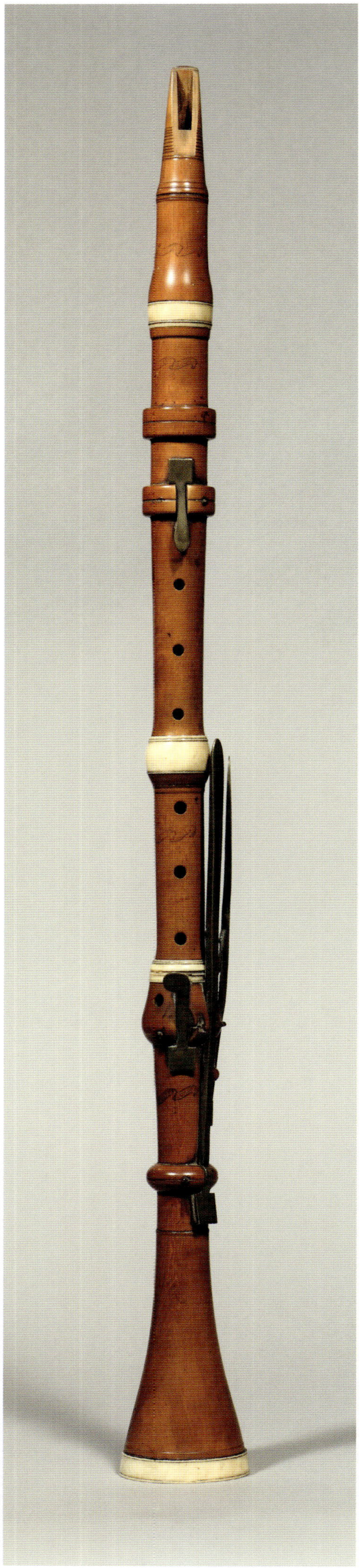

5-key clarinet in B♭, G.C. Payne, London, ca. 1780.

Boxwood; ivory ferrules; multiple decorative lines and beadings. Four sections: mouthpiece-socket, l.h. joint, r.h. joint, stock-bell. Mouthpiece-socket (socket waisted), grooves for cord ligature; wide l.h. joint upper ferrule partly ivory and boxwood. Five ring-mounted brass keys, small square key heads, rings on l.h. joint and stock-bell have center marks; F/C tone-hole bulge is turned out below A♭/E♭ tone hole. Speaker, A, A♭/E♭ (slightly curved touch), F♯/C♯ (short cranked), E/B. L=673.

Stamped on mouthpiece-socket, l.h. joint, r.h. joint: "G.C. PAYNE LONDON (in a banner)"; stock-bell "G.C. PAYNE LONDON (in a banner) / B".

1995.15

LEFT: *5-key clarinet in B♭*, G.C. Payne, London, ca. 1780.

9-key clarinet in B♭, Jacques François Simiot, Lyon, ca. 1815.

Black wood mouthpiece; grooves for cord ligature; boxwood; ivory ferrules with single beading. Six sections: mouthpiece, barrel, l.h. joint, r.h. joint, stock, bell. Metal tuning slide in barrel, twin third finger hole, bell (replaced by Treumann, Lyon). Nine ring, block, and pillar-mounted brass keys, square key heads. Speaker (key head positioned on front with a brass ring), A-B trill, A, C♯/G♯, B/F♯, B♭/F (cross), A♭/E♭ (highly curved touch), F♯/C♯ (extension on touch), E/B (extension on touch). L=592.

Stamped on barrel, r.h. joint: "(sunburst) / • SIMIOT / A LYON / (sunburst) / B♭"; l.h. joint: "B♭ / INNOVEE / PAR / • SIMIOT / A LYON"; stock: "(JS monogram in oval cartouche) / • SIMIOT / A LYON / (sunburst) / B♭"; bell: "(sunburst) TREUMANN (sunburst) / A-LYON / (sunburst) / (sunburst)".

Formerly William Maynard collection. Libin 1994.

1995.16

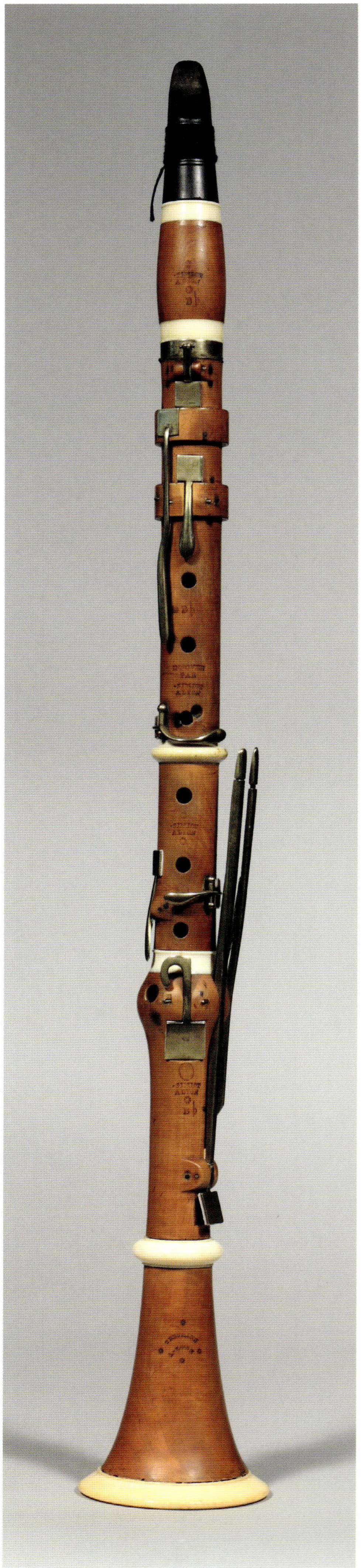

RIGHT: *9-key clarinet in B♭*, Jacques François Simiot, Lyon, ca. 1815.

8-key clarinet in high G, Christian Häussler, Kraców, ca. 1840.

Black wood mouthpiece; red thread ligature; boxwood; black horn ferrules; single beading; two decorative lines on bell. Two rings on l.h. joint have center marks. Six sections: mouthpiece, barrel, l.h. joint, r.h. joint, stock, bell. Eight ring and block-mounted brass keys, square key heads. Speaker, A, G♯, A-B trill, B/F♯, A♭/E♭, F♯/C♯, E/B. L=376 (with mouthpiece).

Stamped on barrel: "(coat of arms on an orb) / Haeufsler. (cursive) / g (cursive)"; l.h. joint, stock, bell: "(coat of arms on an orb) / Haeufsler. (cursive) / (sunburst) / g (cursive)"; r.h. joint: "g (cursive) / (sunburst) / Haeufsler. / (sunburst)".

Formerly William Maynard collection.
Libin 1994.
1995.17

LEFT: *8-key clarinet in high G*, Christian Häussler, Kraców, ca. 1840.

5-key clarinet in C, Asa Hopkins, Litchfield, Connecticut, ca. 1840.

Long-tenon pewter mouthpiece; grooves for a cord ligature; stained boxwood; ivory ferrules; single and double beading. Six sections: mouthpiece, barrel, l.h. joint, r.h. joint, stock, bell. Five ring-mounted brass keys, square key heads, F/C tone-hole bulge cut straight on lower side. Speaker, A, A♭/E♭, F♯/C♯ (cranked), E/B. L=529, 584 (with mouthpiece).

Stamped on barrel, bell: "A. HOPKINS (in semi-circle) / LITCHFIELD / CONN"; l.h. joint, stock: "A. HOPKINS (in semi-circle) / LITCHFIELD / C"; r.h. joint: "A HOPKINS / LITCHFIELD".

Formerly William Maynard collection.
Libin 1994.
1995.18

RIGHT: *5-key clarinet in C* Asa Hopkins, Litchfield, Connecticut, ca. 1840.

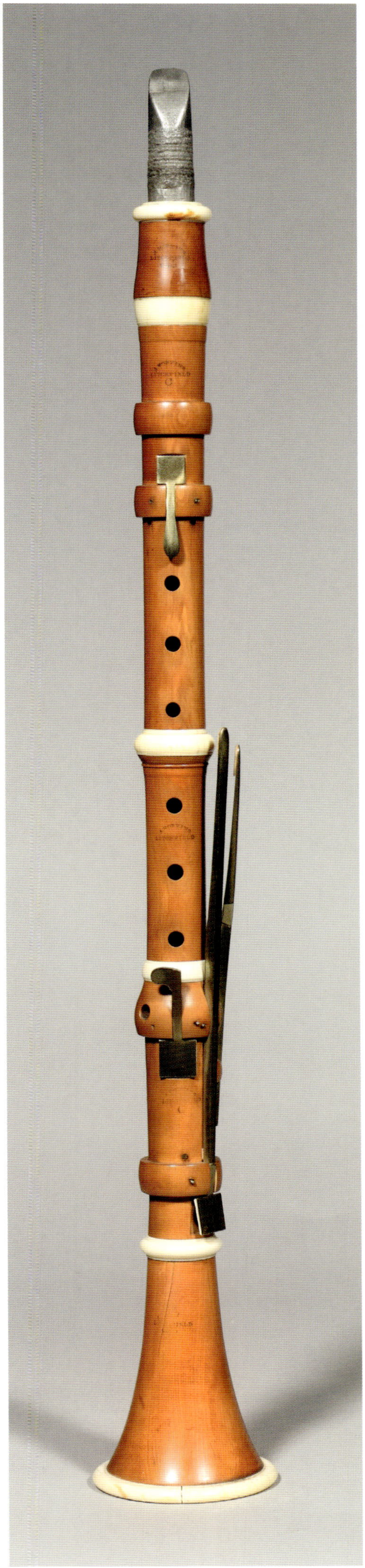

5-key clarinet in B♭, Thomas Cahusac senior, London, ca. 1785.

Black wood mouthpiece; lightly stained boxwood; ivory ferrules; single and multiple beading. Five sections: mouthpiece, barrel, l.h. joint, r.h. joint, stock-bell. Five ring-mounted brass keys with square key heads, F/C tone-hole bulge turned out above A♭/E♭ tone hole. Speaker, A, A♭/E♭ (short touch), F♯/C♯ (cranked), E/B. L=630.

Stamped on mouthpiece: "Brian Ackerman / LONDON"; barrel, l.h. joint, r.h. joint, stock-bell: "B / CAHUSAC / LONDON".

Formerly William Maynard collection.
Libin 1994.
1995.19

5-key clarinet in B♭, Thomas Cahusac senior, London, ca. 1785.

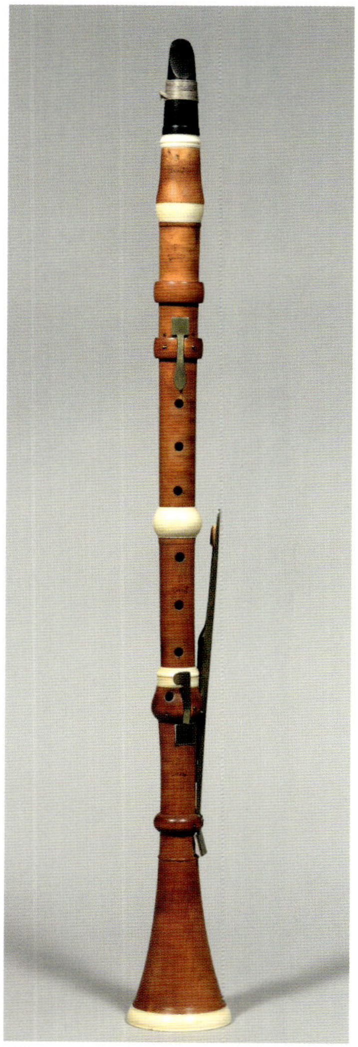

5-key clarinet in C (left-handed), François Pezé, Paris, ca. 1815.

Black wood mouthpiece; boxwood; ivory ferrules; single beading. Six sections: mouthpiece, barrel, l.h. joint, r.h. joint, stock, bell. Five ring and block-mounted brass keys, square key heads mounted for left-handed player. Speaker, A, A♭/E♭, F♯/C♯, E/B. L=538

Stamped on barrel, l.h. joint, r.h. joint, stock, bell: "PEZÉ / A PARIS".

Formerly William Maynard collection.
Libin 1994.
1995.20

5-key clarinet in C (left-handed), François Pezé, Paris, ca. 1815.

12-key clarinet in B♭, Charles Sax, Brussels, ca. 1825.

Black wood mouthpiece; dark-stained boxwood or maple; ivory ferrules; single beading. Six sections: mouthpiece, barrel, l.h. joint, r.h. joint, stock, bell. Metal thumb rest screwed into back. Additional metal braces on levers of A-B trill key and f/c key. F♯/C♯ and E/B touch extensions indicate another corps de rechange in A of a barrel, l.h. and r.h. joints. Twelve ring, block, pillar, and saddle-mounted square brass keys, square key heads (three pillar keys attached to a brass base). Speaker, A-B trill (key head in ring), A, G♯, f/c, E♭/B♭ (cross), C♯/G♯, B/F♯, B♭/F (cross), A♭/E♭, F♯/C♯ (extension on touch), E/B (extension on touch). L=586.

Stamped on back of mouthpiece: "(star)"; front of mouthpiece: "B"; barrel, l.h. joint, r.h. joint, stock, bell: "(star) / SAX / FAC^{T} DU ROI / A BRUXELLES, / (star) / B".

Formerly William Maynard collection.
Libin 1994.
1995.21

12-key clarinet in B♭, Charles Sax, Brussels, ca. 1825.

11-key clarinet in high B♭, Tiercelin, Angers, ca. 1840.

Black wood mouthpiece; grooves for cord ligature; boxwood; ivory ferrules; single beading; gold lines. Five sections: mouthpiece, barrel, l.h. joint, r.h. joint-stock, bell. Eleven nickel-silver pillar and saddle-mounted brass keys, round, flat key heads, F/C attached at lower end, key head close to touch. Speaker, A-B trill, A, G♯, f/c, C♯/G♯, B/F♯, A♭/E♭, F/C, F♯/C♯, E/B. L=327 (with mouthpiece).

Stamped on l.h. joint: "(six-pointed star) / TIERCELIN / À ANGERS / (six-pointed star) / B"; r.h. joint-stock: "TIERCELIN / À ANGERS / B"; bell: "(six-pointed star) / TIERCELIN / A ANGERS /B".

Formerly William Maynard collection.

Libin 1994.

1995.22

5-key clarinet in D, Savary, Paris, ca. 1815.

Black wood mouthpiece; grooves for cord ligature; stained boxwood; ivory ferrules; single beading. Six sections: mouthpiece, barrel, l.h. joint, r.h. joint, stock, bell. Five brass ring and block-mounted keys, square key heads. Speaker, A, A♭/E♭, F♯/C♯, E/B. L=450, 512 (with mouthpiece).

Stamped on barrel, stock: "(sun) / Savary• (cursive) / A PARIS / H.B. / D"; l.h. joint, r.h. joint: "(sun) / Savary• (cursive) / A PARIS / D / H.B."; bell: "(sun) / Savary• (cursive) / A PARIS / H.B."

Formerly William Maynard collection.

Libin 1994; Rousselet and Watel 2012, 157; Waterhouse 1993, 347.

1995.23

12-key clarinet in F, Franz Schöllnast, Pressburg, ca. 1840.

Black wood mouthpiece; stained boxwood; black horn ferrules; single beading. Five sections: mouthpiece, barrel, l.h. joint, r.h. joint-stock, bell. Upper section of l.h joint cut down, indicated by lack of stamp and ill-fitting barrel, raised ring for F/C hole. Twelve block and pillar-mounted nickel-silver keys, flat, round key heads; one resonance hole in bell. Speaker, A-B trill, A, G♯, E♭/B♭, E♭/B♭ (cross), C♯/G♯, B/F♯, B♭/F (cross), A♭/E♭, F♯/C♯ (round and raised touch), E/B (round and raised touch). L=4[illegible]3 (with mouthpiece).

Stamped on barrel, r.h. joint-stock, bell: "(coat of arms) / Schöllnast / (cursive) / Prefsburg / F"; l.h. joint: "Prefsburg / (coat of arms)".

1996.02

11-key clarinet in high B♭, Tiercelin, Angers, ca. 1840.

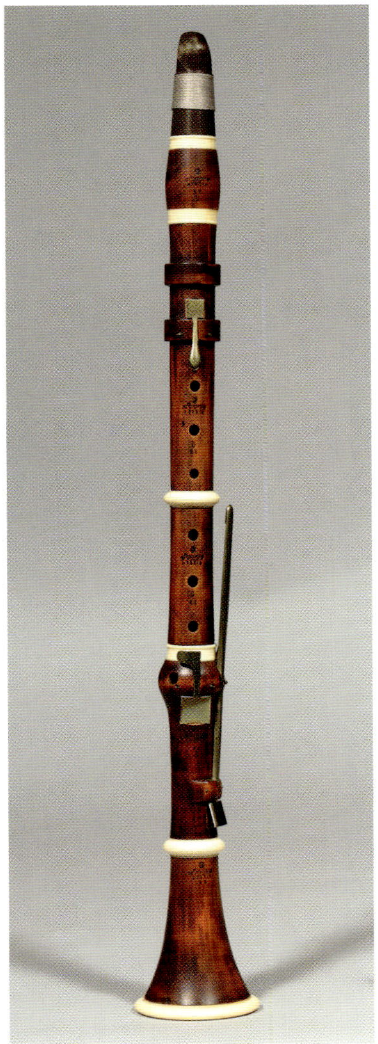

5-key clarinet in D, Savary, Paris, ca. 1815.

12-key clarinet in F, Franz Schöllnast, Pressburg, ca. 1840.

13-key clarinet in A, Kruspe, Erfurt, ca. 1885.

Stained granadilla; nickel-silver ferrules. Five sections: mouthpiece (using B♭ mouthpiece), barrel, l.h. joint, r.h. joint, bell. Thirteen pillar-mounted nickel-silver keys, two ring keys, R2 and R3. Speaker (wraparound to left side), A-B trill, A, G♯ (crossing over A), f/c, E♭/B♭, E♭/B♭ (cross), C♯/G♯, ring (forked B♭/F), B♭/F (cross), A♭/E♭ (nickel-silver roller on touch), F/C (nickel-silver roller on touch), F♯/C♯ (nickel-silver roller on touch), E/B (nickel-silver roller on touch). In case with B♭ and C Kruspe clarinets. L=600.

Stamped on barrel, l.h. joint, r.h. joint, bell: "(crowned eagle) / (Erfurt city crest a six-spoked wheel) / KRUSPE / ERFURT / A".

1996.03

13-key clarinets in C, B♭, A, Kruspe, Erfurt, ca. 1885, in case.

13-key clarinet in B♭, Kruspe, Erfurt, ca. 1885.

Black wood mouthpiece; stained granadilla; nickel-silver ferrules. Five sections: mouthpiece, barrel, l.h. joint, r.h. joint, bell. Thirteen pillar-mounted nickel-silver keys, two ring keys, R2 and R3. Speaker (wraparound to left side), A-B trill, A, G♯ (crossing over A), f/c, E♭/B♭, E♭/B♭ (cross), C♯/G♯, ring (forked B♭/F), B♭/F (cross), A♭/E♭ (nickel-silver roller on touch), F/C (nickel-silver roller on touch), F♯/C♯ (nickel-silver roller on touch), E/B (nickel-silver roller on touch). L=645 (with mouthpiece).

Stamped on mouthpiece, barrel: "B/2/II"; l.h. joint, r.h. joint, bell: "(crowned eagle) / (Erfurt city crest a six-spoked wheel) / KRUSPE / ERFURT / B".

1996.04

13-key clarinet in C, Kruspe, Erfurt, ca. 1885.

Stained granadilla; nickel-silver ferrules. Five sections: mouthpiece (missing), barrel, l.h. joint, r.h. joint, bell. Thirteen pillar-mounted nickel-silver keys, two ring keys, R2 and R3. Speaker (wraparound to left side), A-B trill, A, G♯ (crossing over A), f/c, E♭/B♭, E♭/B♭ (cross), C♯/G♯, ring (forked B♭/F), B♭/F (cross), A♭/E♭ (nickel-silver roller on touch), F/C (nickel-silver roller on touch), F♯/C♯ (nickel-silver roller on touch), E/B (nickel-silver roller on touch). L=540.

Stamped on barrel, l.h. joint, r.h. joint, bell: "(crowned eagle) / (Erfurt city crest a six-spoked wheel) / KRUSPE / ERFURT / C".

1996.05

13-key clarinets in C, B♭, A, Kruspe, Erfurt, ca. 1885.

8-key clarinet in B♭, J. Reilly, Dublin, ca. 1850.

Long-tenon black wood mouthpiece (unreadable stamp); cord ligature; stained boxwood; ivory ferrules; single and double beads; black lines. Five sections: mouthpiece, barrel (waisted), l.h. joint, r.h. joint-stock, bell. Eight block-mounted brass keys, flat, round key heads, cranked F♯/C♯ key, F/C tone-hole bulge cut straight on lower side. Speaker, A-B trill, A, E♭/B♭ (cross), B/F♯ (cross), A♭/E♭ (curved and decorated touch), F♯/C♯ (cranked), E/B. L=652 (with mouthpiece).

Stamped on l.h. joint, r.h. joint-stock, bell: "(trefoil) / J•REILLY / DUBLIN".

1996.11

13-key clarinet in B♭, Thomas Key, London, 1847.

Black wood mouthpiece with socket; cord ligature; ebony; ivory ferrules; double and triple beading. Five sections: mouthpiece, barrel, l.h. joint, r.h. joint-stock, bell. Thirteen block and saddle-mounted silver keys, round, flat key heads, F/C tone-hole bulge turned out above A♭/E♭ tone hole. Speaker, A-B trill, A, G♯ (L2), f/c, E♭/B♭ (cross), C♯/G♯, B/F♯, B/F♯ (cross), B♭/F (cross), A♭/E♭, F♯/C♯ (silver roller on flat touch), E/B (silver roller on flat touch). Hallmarks punched on outside shaft of register, A-B trill key, A and F♯/C♯ keys, and on key heads of A♭/E♭ and E/B keys. Lower ferrules on mouthpiece and barrel marked: "CONFIDO" (Believe). Ornate, ebony mouthpiece cap with ivory ring. L=655 (with mouthpiece).

Stamped on reed side of mouthpiece, barrel, l.h. joint, r.h. joint-stock: "KEY / LONDON / (unicorn head)"; bell: "KEY / LONDON / (unicorn head) / CHARING CROSS".

1996.22

11-key clarinet in D, Heinrich Grenser or Grenser shop, Dresden, ca. 1807.

Black wood mouthpiece; cord ligature; stained boxwood; black horn ferrules; single beading; barrel with ivory ferrules (replacement); twin third finger hole. Six sections: mouthpiece, barrel, l.h. joint, r.h. joint, stock, bell. Eleven block and saddle-mounted brass keys, square key heads. Speaker, A-B trill, A (with spurs), G♯ (with spurs), f/c (L3), E♭/B♭, C♯/G♯, B♭/F (cross), A♭/E♭, F♯/C♯, E/B. L=470, 527 (with mouthpiece).

Stamped on barrel: "(Crown) / (star) 2 (star)"; stock: "(crown) / H•GRENSER / DRESDEN / 1".

1997.02

8-key clarinet in B♭, J. Reilly, Dublin, ca. 1850.

13-key clarinet in B♭, Thomas Key, London, 1847.

11-key clarinet in D, Heinrich Grenser or Grenser shop, Dresden, ca. 1807.

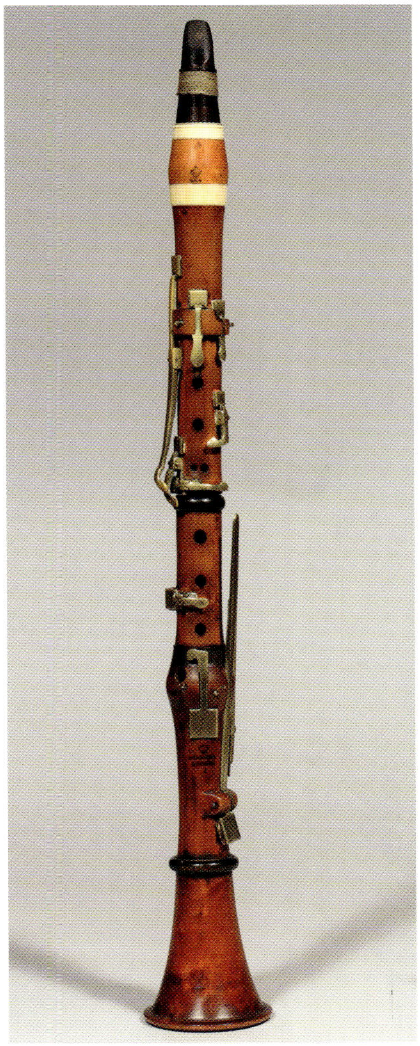

6-key clarinet in C, Charles Wigley, London, ca. 1805.

Black wood long-tenon mouthpiece; grooves for cord ligature; stained boxwood; ivory ferrules; single and double beading; one horn ferrule on stock joint. Six sections: mouthpiece, barrel (waisted), l.h. joint, r.h. joint, stock, bell. Six block-mounted brass keys, square key heads; F/C tone-hole bulge is turned out above A♭/E♭ tone hole. Speaker, A-B trill, A, A♭/E♭, F♯/C♯ (cranked), E/B. L=590 (with mouthpiece).

Stamped on barrel, l.h. joint, r.h. joint, stock, bell: "WIGLEY / 151 STRAND / LONDON".

1997.04

6-key clarinet in C, Charles Wigley, London, ca. 1805.

5-key clarinet in C, Chabrier Peloubet, New York, ca. 1840.

Long tenon black wood mouthpiece; cord ligature; stained boxwood; ivory ferrules; one and two black lines. Six sections: mouthpiece, barrel (waisted), l.h. joint, r.h. joint, stock, bell. Five block-mounted brass keys, square key heads; F/C tone-hole bulge is turned out above A♭/E♭ tone hole. Speaker, A, A♭/E♭, F♯/C♯, E/B. L=522, 581 (with mouthpiece).

Stamped on barrel, r.h. joint, stock: "C. PELOUBET / NEW-YORK"; l.h. joint: "C / C.PELOUBET / NEW-YORK"; bell: "C. PELOUBET / NEW-YORK / FACTORY AT / BLOOMFIELD".

1998.03

5-key clarinet in C, Chabrier Peloubet, New York, ca. 1840.

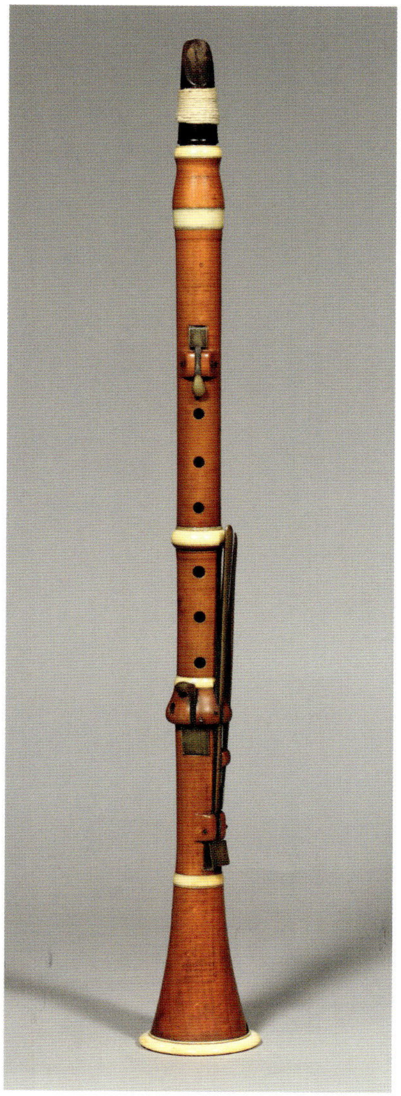

5-key clarinet in F, Johann Tobias Uhlmann, Vienna, ca. 1830.

Black wood mouthpiece; grooves for cord ligature; stained boxwood; horn ferrules; single beading. Six sections: mouthpiece, barrel, l.h. joint, r.h. joint, stock, bell. Five ring and block-mounted brass keys, square key heads, wide rim bell. Speaker, A, A♭/E♭, F♯/C♯, E/B. L=399 (with mouthpiece).

Stamped on barrel, bell: "(Hapsburg eagle) / I.T.UHLMANN / WIEN / (sunburst) / F"; l.h. joint: "(Hapsburg eagle) / I.T.UHLMANN / WIEN / (sunburst) / 3 / F"; r.h. joint: "F / (sunburst) / I.T.UHLMANN / (sunburst) / 3".

1998.08

5-key clarinet in F, Johann Tobias Uhlmann, Vienna, ca. 1830.

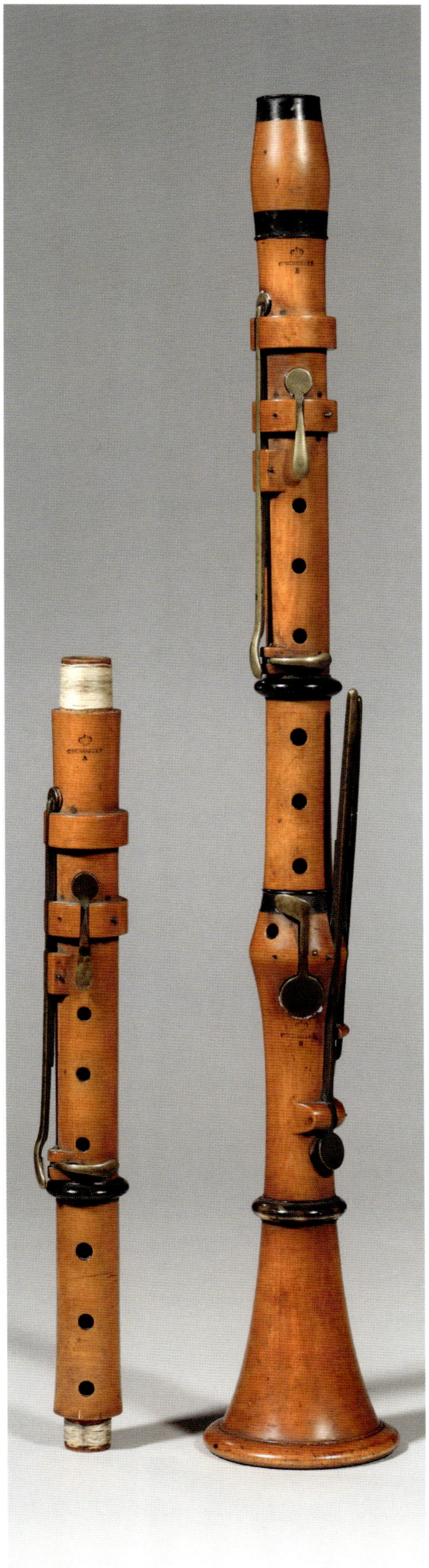

7-key clarinet in B♭ with corps de rechange in A, Christian Gottfried Schuster, Markneukirchen, ca. 1825.

Stained boxwood; black horn ferrules; single beading. Five sections: barrel, l.h. joint, r.h. joint, stock, bell. The corps de rechange in A: l.h. joint and r.h. joint. Seven ring and block-mounted brass keys, flat, round key heads. Speaker, A-B trill, A, C♯/G♯, A♭/E♭, F♯/C♯, E/B. L of B♭ clarinet=580; L of A clarinet=631 (with B♭ barrel and l.h. and r.h. joints in A).

Stamped on l.h. joint, stock: "(crown) / G:SCHUSTER / B"; l.h. joint in A: "(crown) / G:SCHUSTER / A".

Weller 2004, 247.

1998.10

LEFT: *7-key clarinet in B♭ with corps de rechange in* A, Christian Gottfried Schuster, Markneukirchen, ca. 1825.

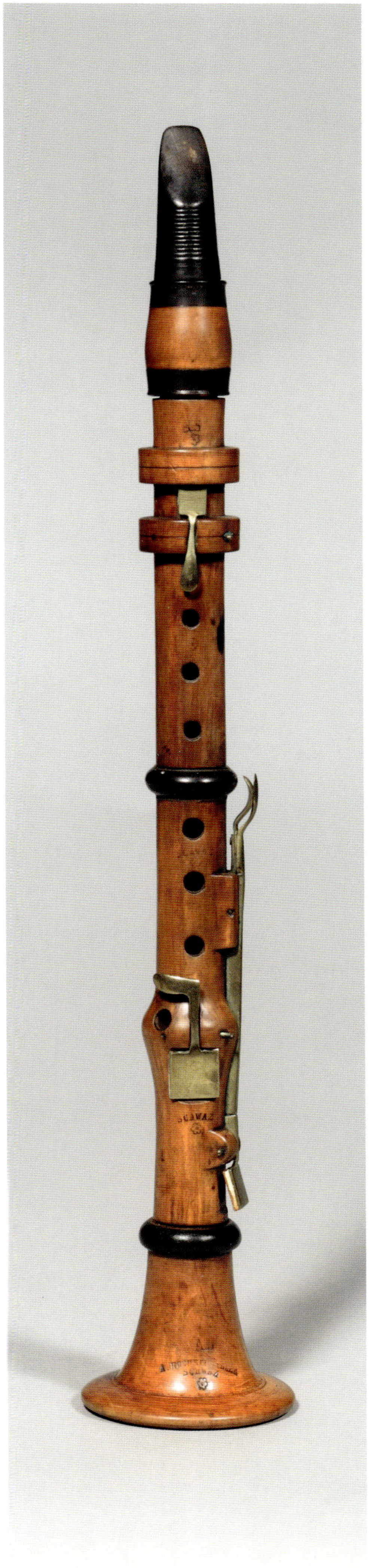

5-key clarinet in A♭, Andrä Hochschwarzer, Schwaz, ca. 1840.

Black wood mouthpiece; grooves for cord ligature; stained boxwood; black horn ferrules; single beading. Five sections: mouthpiece, barrel, l.h. joint, r.h. joint-stock, bell with wide rim, rings on l.h. joint have center marks. Five ring and block-mounted brass keys, square key heads. Speaker, A, A♭/E♭, F♯/C♯ (round and raised touch), E/B (round and raised touch). L=344 (with mouthpiece).

Stamped on l.h. joint: "AS / (flower)"; r.h. joint-stock: "SCHWAZ / (flower)"; bell: "A♭ / A.HOCHSCHWARZER / SCHWAZ / (flower)".

Dullat, 2010a, 216.

1998.13

RIGHT: *5-key clarinet in A♭*, Andrä Hochschwarzer, Schwaz, ca. 1840.

5-key clarinet in B♭, Roustagneq fils, Toulon, ca. 1820.

Stained boxwood; ivory ferrules; single beading; black lines. Five sections: barrel, l.h. joint, r.h. joint, stock, bell. Five ring and block-mounted brass keys, square key heads, rings on l.h. joint have center marks. Speaker, A, A♭/E♭, F♯/C♯, E/B. L=595.

Stamped on barrel: “B / ROUSTAGNEQ / FILS / A TOULON / (sunburst)”; l.h. joint: “ROUSTAGNEQ / FILS / (sunburst) / B”; stock: “ROUSTAGNEQ / FILS / A TOULON / (sunburst) / B”; bell: “A TOULON / (sunburst) / B”.

1998.16

5-key clarinet in B♭,
Roustagneq fils, Toulon, ca. 1820.

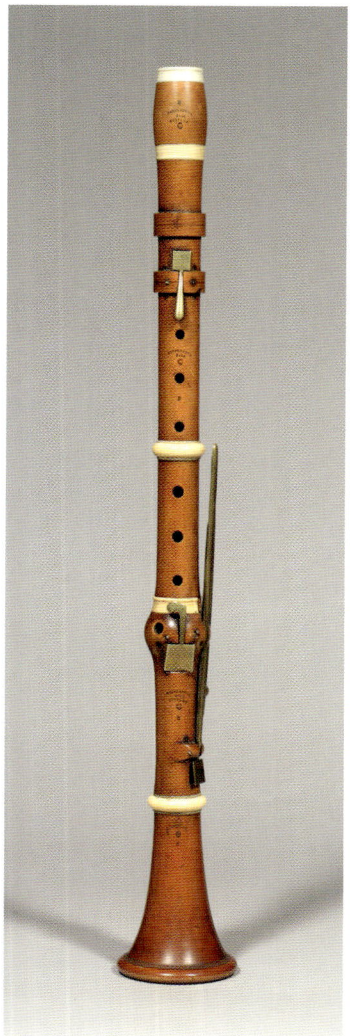

8-key clarinet in B♭, Mikulášek, Žamberk, ca. 1860.

Black wood mouthpiece; boxwood; black horn ferrules, brass ferrules. Five sections: mouthpiece, barrel, l.h. joint, r.h. joint-stock, bell. Eight block-mounted brass keys, round, slightly curved key heads, raised ring for F/C hole. Speaker, A-B trill, A, G♯, C♯/G♯, A♭/E♭, F♯/C♯ (round and raised touch), E/B (round and raised touch). L=575.

Stamped on l.h. joint: “B / MIKULÁSEK / ŽAMBERK. / 1 / 1 / A”; r.h. joint-stock: “B / 1 / B / MIKULÁSEK / ŽAMBERK. / 1”; bell: “1”.

1998.19

8-key clarinet in B♭,
Mikulášek, Žamberk, ca. 1860.

14-key clarinet in B♭, Anonymous, of German or Bohemian origin, ca. 1860.

Black wood mouthpiece; grooves for cord ligature; boxwood; ivory ferrules; single beading. Five sections: mouthpiece, barrel, l.h. joint, r.h. joint-stock, bell. Fourteen pillar-mounted brass keys, round, flat key heads, pointed ends on touches. Speaker, A-B trill, A, G♯, f/c, f/c (cross), E♭/B♭ (cross), C♯/G♯, B/F♯, B♭/F (cross), A♭/E♭, F/C, F♯/C♯ (round and raised touch), E/B. L=585.

No inscription.

1998.20

14-key clarinet in B♭, Anonymous,
of German or Bohemian origin, ca. 1860.

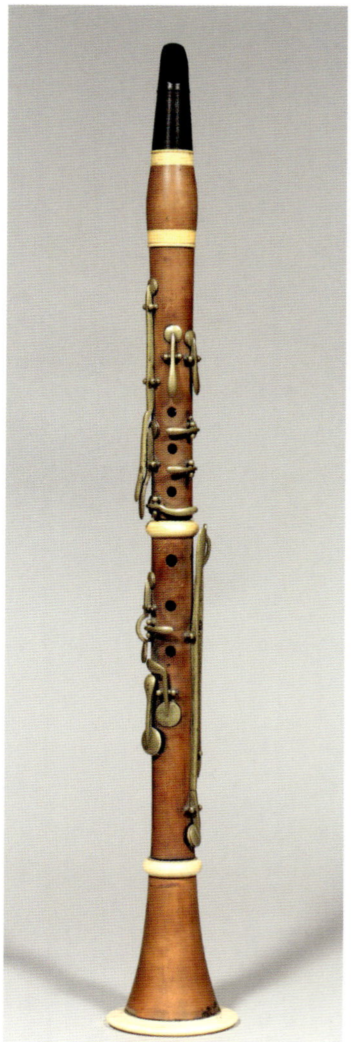

13-key clarinet in B♭, Wilhelm Bellon, Basel, ca. 1910.

Rosewood mouthpiece (damaged); grooves for cord ligature and metal ligature; stained rosewood; nickel-silver ferrules. Five sections: mouthpiece, barrel, l.h. joint, r.h. joint, bell. Thirteen pillar-mounted nickel-silver keys, modern key heads. Speaker (wraparound), A-B trill, A, G♯, f/c, E♭/B♭ (cross), C♯/G♯ (with trill lever for R1), B/F♯, B♭/F (cross), A♭/E♭, F/C, F♯/C♯ (round and raised touch), E/B (round and raised touch). L=592.

Stamped on l.h. joint, r.h. joint: "(ribbon, lyre, ribbon) / Wilhelm Bellon / ° Basel ° (in an oval)".

1999.13

10-key clarinet in E♭, Christian Gottlieb Piering, Graz, ca. 1830.

Black wood mouthpiece; grooves for cord ligature; boxwood, horn ferrules; single beading. Five sections: mouthpiece, barrel, l.h. joint, r.h. joint-stock, bell. Ten block-mounted brass keys, round key heads decorated in shell design, F/C finger hole bulge. Raised F♯/C♯ touch for sliding to E/B touch. Speaker, A-B trill, A, G♯, f/c, C♯/G♯, B/F♯, A♭/E♭, F♯/C♯ (curved touch), E/B. L=444 (with mouthpiece).

Stamped on barrel: "GRATZ / E"; l.h. joint, bell: "(lyre) / PIERING / GRATZ / E"; r.h. joint-stock: "PIERING / GRATZ / E" // "(lyre) / PIERING / GRATZ / E".

2001.07

12-key simple system clarinet in B♭, Charles Borromée Mahillon, Brussels, ca. 1890.

Ebonite mouthpiece; silver-plated metal over dark wood (double-wall); ferrules marked with single line. Five sections: mouthpiece, barrel, l.h. joint, r.h. joint, bell. Twelve pillar-mounted silver-plated keys, modern key heads, patent C♯ mechanism, rings for R2 and R3. Speaker (wraparound), A-B trill (R1), A, G♯ (long tailed, L2), f/c (R1), E♭/B♭ (cross), C♯/G♯, B♭/F (cross, L3), A♭/E♭, F/C (when E/B touch is closed produces F♯/C♯), F♯/C♯, E/B. L=575, 648 (with mouthpiece).

Stamped on barrel: "(star) / C. MAHILLON & Cº / LONDON / (star)"; l.h. joint: "(star) / C.MAHILLON & Cº / LONDON / MADE AT THEIR / BRUSSELS / WORKS / (star)"; r.h. joint, bell: "(star) / C.MAHILLON & Cº / LONDON / (star)".

In 1887, Mahillon patented a C♯ key mechanism for an Albert-system clarinet in Belgian patent no. 79,681.

2001.22

13-key clarinet in B♭, Wilhelm Bellon, Basel, ca. 1910.

10-key clarinet in E♭, Christian Gottlieb Piering, Graz, ca. 1830.

12-key simple system clarinet in B♭, Charles Borromée Mahillon, Brussels, ca. 1890.

13-key clarinet in B♭, Stephan Koch, Vienna, ca. 1830.

Boxwood with diagonal stripes; ivory ferrules; single beading. Five sections: mouthpiece (missing), barrel (missing), l.h. joint, r.h. joint-stock, bell. Thirteen block-mounted brass keys, flat, round key heads. Speaker, A-B trill, A, G♯, f/c (L3), E♭/B♭ (cross), E♭/B♭ (touch for R1 raises key head of cross E♭/B♭ key), C♯/G♯, B/F♯, B♭/F (cross), A♭/E♭, F♯/C♯ (curved touch), E/B (round, raised touch). L=508.

Stamped on l.h. joint: "(Hapsburg eagle) / S:KOCH / WIEN / B"; r.h. joint-stock: "B / (Hapsburg eagle) / S:KOCH / WIEN".

2001.24

6-key clarinet in B♭, Klemm & Brother, Philadelphia, probably Markneukirchen, ca. 1830.

Rosewood mouthpiece; grooves for cord ligature; boxwood; ivory ferrules (missing on bell); single beading. Six sections: mouthpiece, barrel, l.h. joint, r.h. joint, stock, bell. Six ring and block-mounted brass keys, round, flat key heads. Speaker, A, C♯/G♯, A♭/E♭, F♯/C♯, E/B. L=580.

Stamped on upper section of l.h. joint: "KLEMM & BRO / PHILA".

2001.31

13-key clarinet in A, Martin Frères, Paris, ca. 1850.

Black wood mouthpiece; metal ligature; boxwood; ivory ferrules; single beading; dark lines. Five sections: mouthpiece, barrel, l.h. joint, r.h. joint-stock, bell. Thirteen pillar-mounted brass keys, salt-spoon key heads. Wooden mouthpiece cover. Speaker, A-B trill, A, G♯ (over the A), f/c, E♭/B♭ (cross), C♯/G♯, B/F♯, B♭/F (cross), A♭/E♭, F/C, F♯/C♯, E/B. L=615.

Stamped on bell, r.h. joint-stock, bell: "(bee) / MARTIN F$^{\underline{ES}}$ /A PARIS (in oval) / MF (intertwined) / A"; l.h. joint: "(bee) / MARTIN F$^{\underline{ES}}$ /A PARIS (in oval) / MF (intertwined) / 13. A. DE LA / JUSSIENNE / A".

2001.33

13-key clarinet in B♭, Stephan Koch, Vienna, ca. 1830.

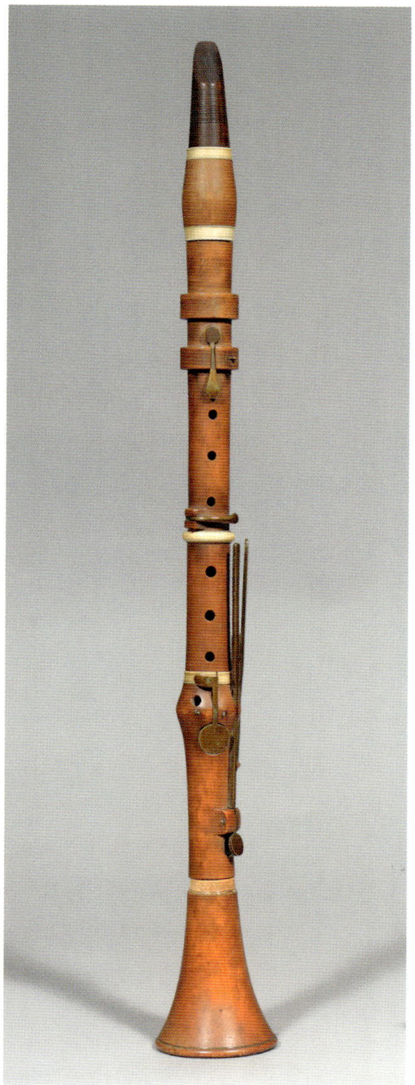

6-key clarinet in B♭, Klemm & Brother, Philadelphia, probably Markneukirchen, ca. 1830.

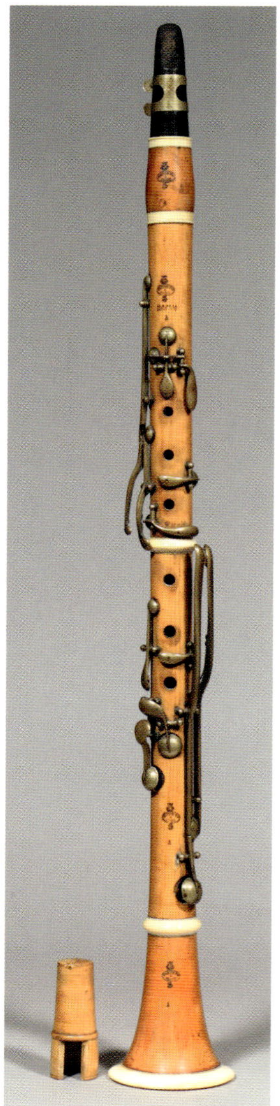

13-key clarinet in A, Martin Frères, Paris, ca. 1850.

6-key clarinet in C, Joseph Karl Felchlin, Berne, ca. 1840.

Black wood mouthpiece (for E♭ clarinet); grooves for cord ligature; boxwood; black horn ferrules; single beading. Six sections: mouthpiece, barrel, l.h. joint, r.h. joint, stock, bell. Six ring and block-mounted brass keys, square key heads. Speaker, A, C♯/G♯ (on pillar), A♭/E♭ (highly curved and decorated touch), F♯/C♯, E/B. L=520.

Stamped on mouthpiece: "S"; barrel, l.h. joint, r.h. joint, stock, bell: "(star) / (lyre) / FELCHLIN, / A BERNE. / (star) / C".

2001.47

6-key clarinet in C,
Joseph Karl Felchlin, Berne, ca. 1840.

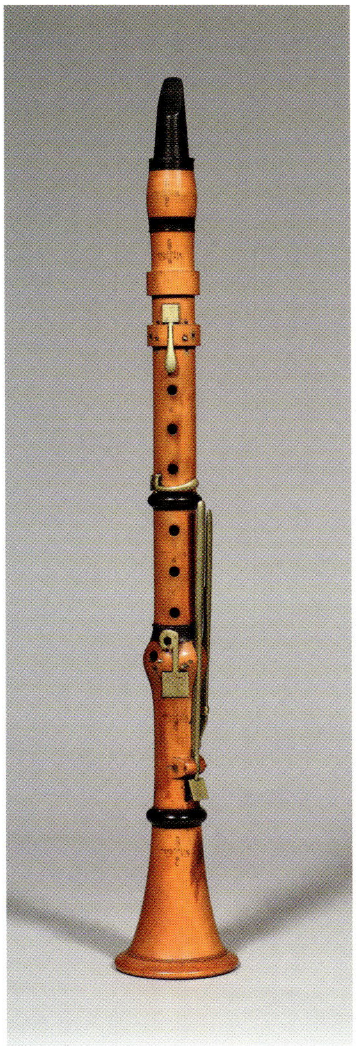

12-key clarinet in B♭, Kruspe, Erfurt, ca. 1875.

Black wood mouthpiece; boxwood; nickel-silver ferrules. Five sections: mouthpiece, barrel, l.h. joint, r.h. joint-stock, bell. Twelve pillar-mounted nickel-silver keys, modern key heads, raised ring for the F/C hole. Speaker (wraparound to the left), A-B trill, A, G♯, f/c, E♭/B♭ (cross), C♯/G♯, B/F♯, B♭/F (cross), A♭/E♭, F♯/C♯ (round and raised touch), E/B (round and raised touch). L=570.

Stamped on barrel, l.h. joint, r.h. joint-stock, bell: "(Butterfly) / C.KRUSPE / ERFURT / B / (star) / (star)".

2002.05

12-key clarinet in B♭, Kruspe, Erfurt, ca. 1875.

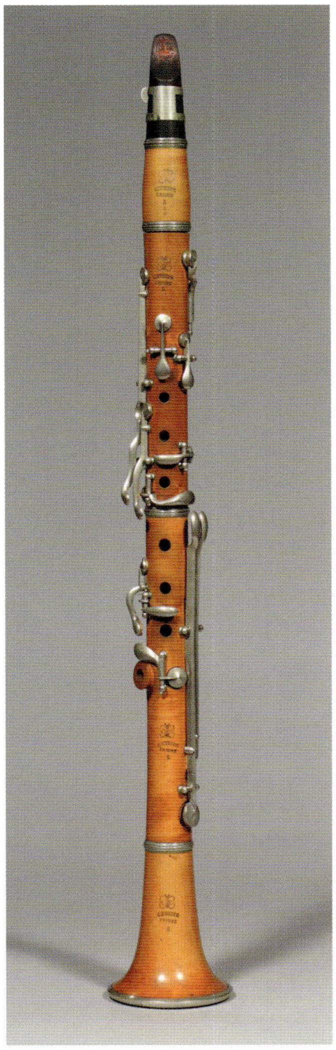

5-key clarinet in C, Klemm & Brother, Philadelphia, probably Markneukirchen, ca. 1830.

Short-tenon black wood mouthpiece; grooves for cord ligature; boxwood; ivory ferrules; single beading. Five sections: mouthpiece, barrel (waisted), l.h. joint, r.h. joint, stock, bell. Five ring-mounted brass keys, flat, round key heads. Speaker, A, A♭/E♭, F♯/C♯, E/B. L=520, 582 (with mouthpiece).

Stamped on l.h.joint: "KLEMM&BRO. / PHILA. / C"; r.h. joint: "C".

2002.09

5-key clarinet in C, Klemm & Brother,
Philadelphia, probably Markneukirchen, ca. 1830.

6-key clarinet in E♭, Goulding and Co., London, ca. 1800.

Black wood long-tenon mouthpiece; grooves for cord ligature; ivory ferrules; single and multiple beading. Six sections: mouthpiece, barrel (waisted), l.h. joint, r.h. joint, stock, bell. Six ring and block-mounted brass keys, square key heads, F/C tone-hole bulge cut straight on the lower side. Speaker, A, A-B trill, A♭/E♭, F♯/C♯ (cranked), E/B. L=432, 490 (with mouthpiece).

Stamped on barrel, l.h. joint, r.h. joint, stock: "GOULDING & CO."; bell: "(Prince of Wales feathers) / GOULDING & CO./ LONDON".

2002.10

6-key clarinet in E♭, Goulding and Co., London, ca. 1800.

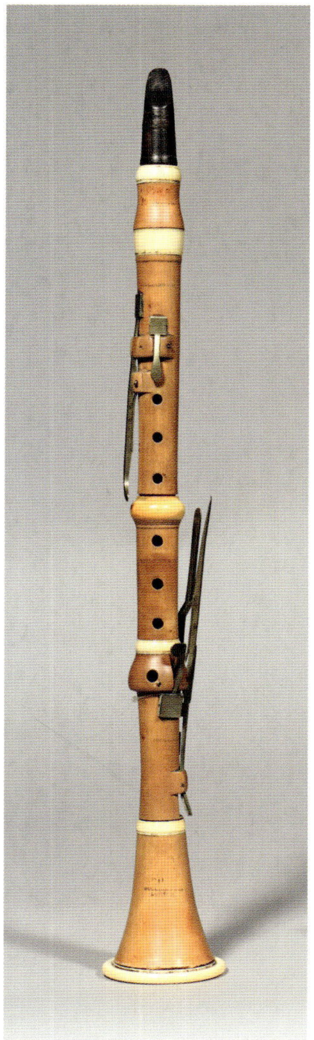

5-key clarinet in B♭, John Firth, William Hall, and Sylvanus Pond, New York, ca. 1840.

Black wood mouthpiece; cord ligature; boxwood; ivory ferrules; single and double beading. Six sections: mouthpiece, barrel (waisted), l.h. joint, r.h. joint, stock, bell. Five block and ring-mounted brass keys, square key heads, F/C tone-hole bulge cut straight on the lower side. Speaker, A, A♭/E♭, F♯/C♯ (cranked), E/B. L=586, 660 (with mouthpiece).

Stamped on barrel, r.h. joint, stock: "FIRTH HALL & POND / N-YORK"; l.h. joint: "FIRTH HALL & POND / FRANKLIN SQE / N-YORK / B"; bell: "FIRTH HALL & POND / FRANKLIN SQE / N-YORK".

2002.13

5-key clarinet in B♭, John Firth, William Hall, and Sylvanus Pond, New York, ca. 1840.

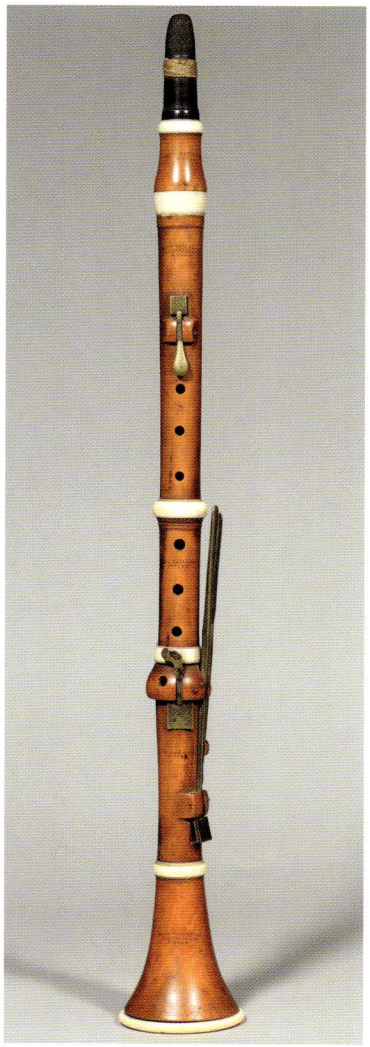

5-key clarinet in C, Wolfgang Küss, Vienna, ca. 1820.

Stained boxwood; black horn ferrules; single beading. Six sections: mouthpiece (missing), barrel, l.h. joint, r.h. joint, stock, bell. Five ring and block-mounted brass keys, round, flat key heads. Missing the upper ferrule of the barrel. Speaker, A, A♭/E♭, F♯/C♯ (cranked), E/B. L=506.

Stamped on l.h. joint: "(Hapsburg eagle) / Küſs (in cursive) / Wien (in cursive) / C"; r.h. joint: "C / Küſs (in cursive)"; stock, bell: "(Hapsburg eagle) / Küſs (in cursive) / Wien (in cursive)".

2002.17

5-key clarinet in C, Wolfgang Küss, Vienna, ca. 1820.

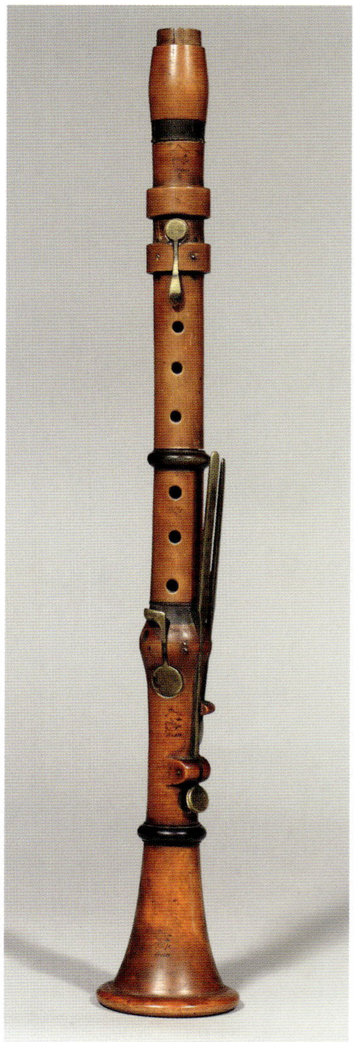

6-key clarinet in B♭, John Firth, William Hall, and Sylvanus Pond, Litchfield, Connecticut, ca. 1845.

Stained boxwood; ivory ferrules; single and double beading; black lines. Six sections: mouthpiece (missing), barrel (waisted), l.h. joint, r.h. joint, stock, bell. Six block-mounted brass keys, round, flat key heads, F/C tone-hole bulge cut straight on lower side, missing ferrule at end of bell. Speaker, A-B trill, A, A♭/E♭, F♯/C♯ (cranked), E/B. L=597.

Stamped on barrel, r.h. joint: "FIRTH HALL & POND / CONN"; l.h. joint: "FIRTH HALL & POND / LITCHFIELD / CONN / B"; stock: "FIRTH HALL & POND / CONN / B"; bell: "FIRTH HALL & POND / LITCHFIELD / CONN". Firth, Hall & Pond woodwinds stamped Litchfield, Connecticut, are rarely found.

Eliason and Rice 2012, 171–174.

2002.18

6-key clarinet in B♭, John Firth, William Hall, and Sylvanus Pond, Litchfield, Connecticut, ca. 1845.

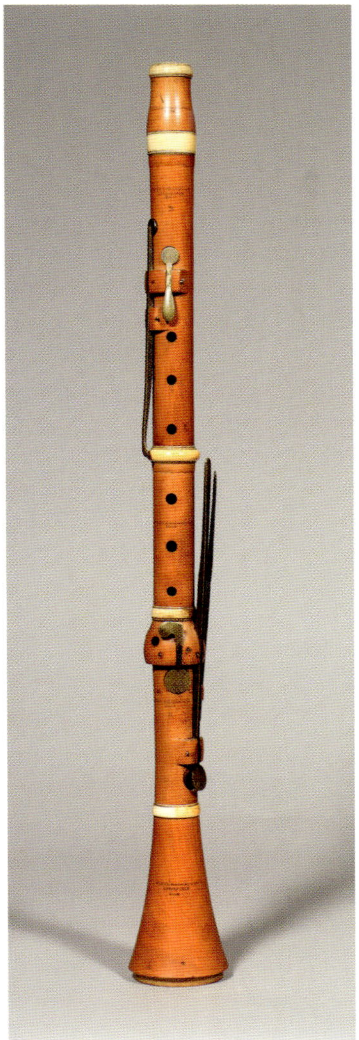

6-key clarinet in C, Christopher Gerock and Robert Wolf, London, ca. 1832.

Long-tenon black wood mouthpiece; grooves for cord ligature; boxwood; ivory ferrules; single and double beading; black lines. Six sections: mouthpiece, barrel (waisted), l.h. joint, r.h. joint, stock, bell. Six block-mounted brass keys, square key heads, F/C tone-hole bulge cut straight on lower side. Speaker, A-B trill, A, A♭/E♭, F♯/C♯ (cranked), E/B. L=530.

Stamped on barrel, r.h. joint, stock: "GEROCK & WOLF / LONDON"; l.h. joint: "(English rose) / GEROCK & WOLF / 79/ CORNHILL / LONDON / (emblem)".

2002.19

6-key clarinet in C, Christopher Gerock and Robert Wolf, London, ca. 1832.

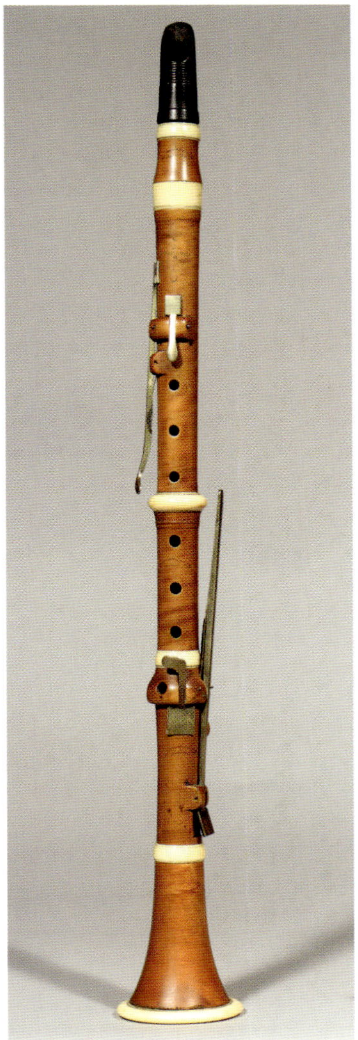

14-key clarinet in B♭, Franz Ott, Würzburg, ca. 1830.

Black wood mouthpiece; boxwood; black horn ferrules (missing on r.h. joint-stock); single beading. Five sections: mouthpiece (damaged), barrel, l.h. joint, r.h. joint-stock, bell. Fourteen block-mounted nickel-silver keys, flat, round key heads. Speaker, A-B trill, A, G♯, f/c, E♭/B♭ (cross, L3), E♭/B♭ (L4, opens key head on cross E♭/B♭), C♯/G♯, B/F♯ (R3), B♭/F (cross, R3), A♭/E♭ (R4), A♭/E♭ (L4), F♯/C♯, E/B. L=570.

Stamped on barrel: "A"; l.h. joint, r.h. joint-stock: "(crown) / F:OTT / WÜRZBURG / B"; bell: "(crown) / F:OTT / WÜRZBURG / A".

2002.23

14-key clarinet in B♭, Franz Ott, Würzburg, ca. 1830.

13-key clarinet in B♭, Triebert (Couesnon), Paris, ca. 1900.

Black wood mouthpiece (damaged); granadilla; nickel-silver ferrules. Five sections: mouthpiece, barrel, l.h. joint, r.h. joint, bell. Thirteen pillar-mounted, nickel-silver keys, two rings for R2 and R3, C♯ mechanism. Speaker (wraparound), A-B trill (R1), A, G♯ (crossing over A), f/c (R1), E♭/B♭ (R1), E♭/B♭ (cross, L3), C♯/G♯, B♭/F (cross, R3), A♭/E♭, F/C, F♯/C♯, E/B. L=571.

Stamped on l.h. joint: "B♭ / H.P."; bell: "B♭ / H.P. / (tower with four merlons) / TRIEBERT / BREVETÉ / A PARIS (in an oval) / (grenade)".

2002.26

13-key clarinet in B♭, Triebert (Couesnon), Paris, ca. 1900.

14-key clarinet in B♭, John Pfaff, Philadelphia, ca. 1865.

Ivory mouthpiece with silver lay; grooves for cord ligature; ivory; silver ferrules. Four sections: mouthpiece, l.h. joint, r.h. joint, bell. Fourteen pillar-mounted silver keys, two rings, R2 and R3, C♯ mechanism. Speaker (wraparound to the left side), A-B trill, A, G♯ (crossing over A), f/c (R1), f/c (cross L2), E♭/B♭ (R1), E♭/B♭ (cross, L3), C♯/G♯ (L4, with lever for R1), B♭/F (cross, R2), A♭/E♭, F/C (patent C♯ key, when E/B touch is closed produces F♯/C♯), F♯/C♯, E/B. L=655.

Stamped on l.h. joint: "J PFAFF / PHILA".

Ivory clarinets were rarely made; this expensive instrument may have been made for an exhibition or a wealthy client.

2002.32

14-key clarinet in B♭, John Pfaff, Philadelphia, ca. 1865.

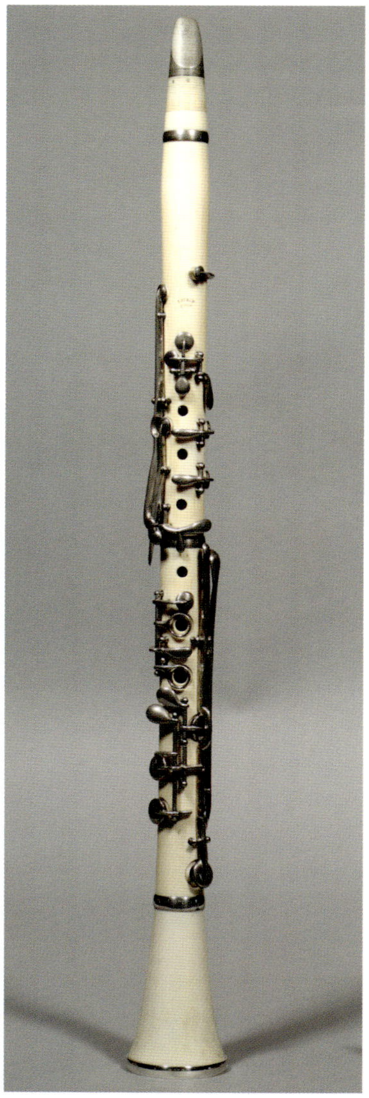

11-key clarinet in C, Gabriel Bühner and Jean Keller IV, Strasbourg, ca. 1815.

Black wood mouthpiece; grooves for cord ligature; boxwood; ivory ferrules; single beading. Six sections: mouthpiece, barrel, l.h. joint, r.h joint, stock, bell. Eleven ring and pillar-mounted brass keys, square key heads. Speaker (wraparound), A, G♯ (brass linings in ring mounting for both key shanks), f/c, E♭/B♭ (cross), C♯/G♯, B/F♯, B♭/F, A♭/E♭ (highly curved touch), F♯/C♯ (extension on touch), E/B (extension on touch). In case with B♭ and A Bühner & Keller clarinets. L=588 (with mouthpiece).

Stamped on barrel, l.h. joint, r.h. joint, bell: "(flying angel trumpeter) / BUHNER & KELLER / (flying angel trumpeter) / C"; stock: "(flying angel trumpeter) / BUHNER & KELLER / A STRASBOURG / (flying angel trumpeter) / C".

2002.37

11-key clarinet in C, Gabriel Bühner and Jean Keller IV, Strasbourg, ca. 1815.

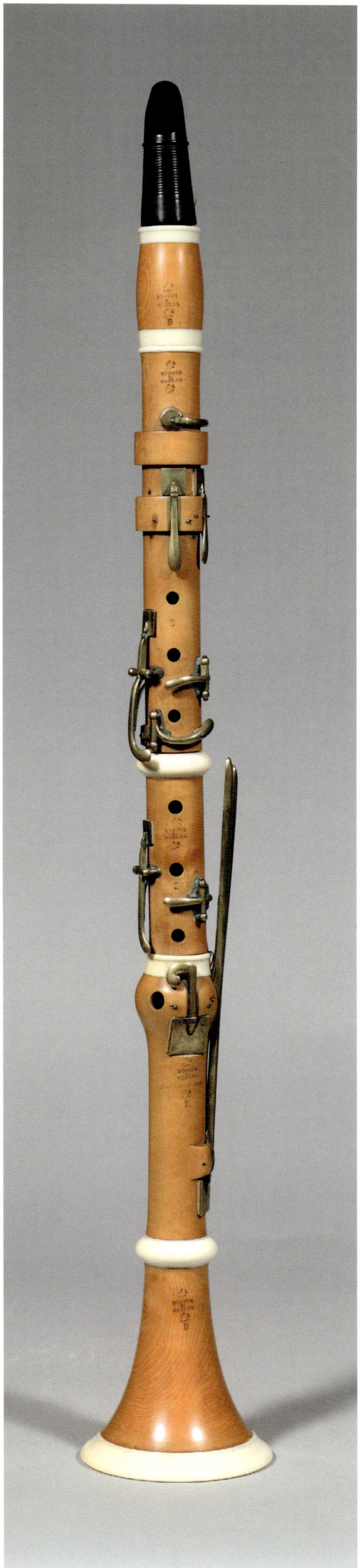

11-key clarinet in B♭, Gabriel Bühner and Jean Keller IV, Strasbourg, ca. 1815.

Black wood mouthpiece; grooves for cord ligature; boxwood; ivory ferrules; single beading. Six sections: mouthpiece, barrel, l.h. joint, r.h. joint, stock, bell. Eleven ring and pillar-mounted brass keys, square key heads. Speaker (wraparound), A, G♯ (brass linings in ring mounting for both key shanks), f/c, E♭/B♭ (cross), C♯/G♯, B/F♯, B♭/F, A♭/E♭ (highly curved touch), F♯/C♯ (extension on touch), E/B (extension on touch). In case with C and A Bühner & Keller clarinets. L=667 (with mouthpiece).

Stamped on barrel, l.h. joint, r.h. joint, bell: "(flying angel trumpeter) / BUHNER & KELLER / (flying angel trumpeter) / B"; stock: "(flying angel trumpeter) / BUHNER & KELLER / A STRASBOURG / (flying angel trumpeter) / B".

2002.38

LEFT: *11-key clarinet in B♭*, Gabriel Bühner and Jean Keller IV, Strasbourg, ca. 1815.

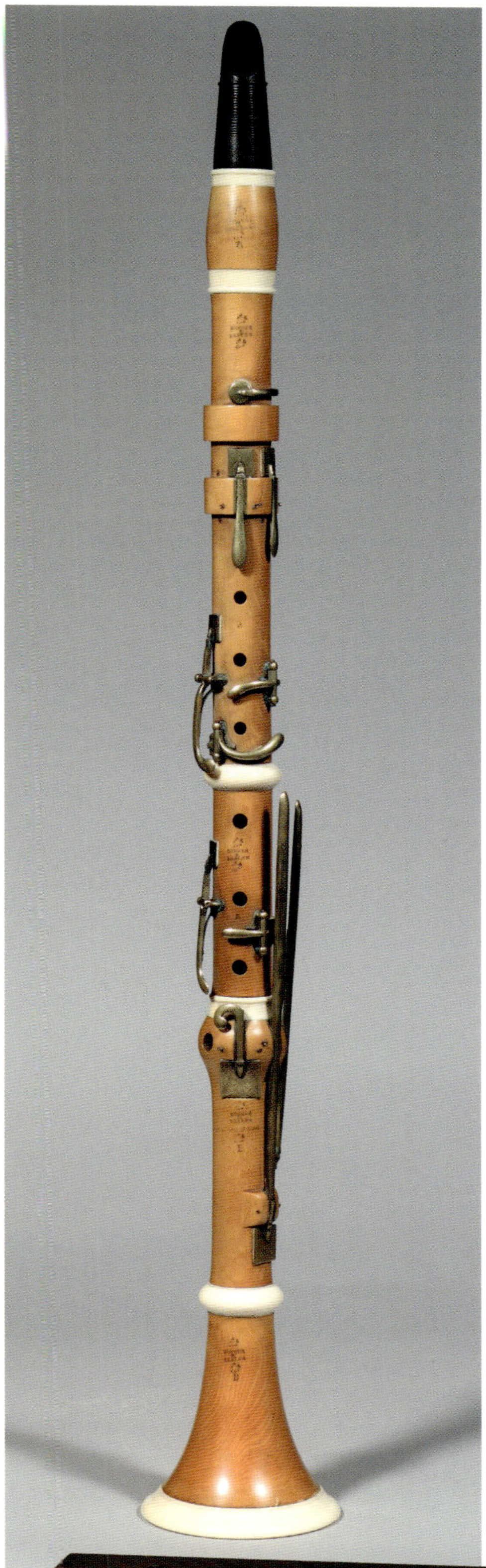

11-key clarinet in A, Gabriel Bühner & Jean Keller IV, Strasbourg, ca. 1815.

Black wood mouthpiece; grooves for cord ligature; boxwood; ivory ferrules; single beading. Six sections: mouthpiece, barrel, l.h. joint, r.h joint, stock, bell. Eleven ring and pillar-mounted brass keys, square key heads. Speaker (wraparound), A, G♯ (brass linings in ring mounting for both key shanks), f/c, E♭/B♭ (cross), C♯/G♯, B/F♯, B♭/F, A♭/E♭ (highly curved touch), F♯/C♯ (extension on touch), E/B (extension on touch). In wooden case with C and B♭ Bühner & Keller clarinets. The A clarinet uses B♭ corps de rechange for stock and bell joints. L=720.

Stamped on barrel, l.h. joint, r.h. joint: "(flying angel trumpeter) / BUHNER & KELLER / (flying angel trumpeter) / A"; stock, bell: "(flying angel trumpeter) / BUHNER & KELLER / A STRASBOURG / (flying angel trumpeter) / B".

2002.39

TOP RIGHT: *11-key clarinet in A*, Gabriel Bühner & Jean Keller IV, Strasbourg, ca. 1815.

RIGHT: *11-key clarinets in C, B♭, A*, Bühner & Keller, Strasbourg, ca. 1815, in case.

12-key clarinet in D, Johann Friedrich Wilhelm Wernicke, Berlin, ca. 1860.

Black wood mouthpiece; grooves for cord ligature; metal ligature; boxwood; ivory ferrules; single beading. Four sections: mouthpiece, barrel, body, bell. Eleven block-mounted brass keys, square key heads, F/C tone-hole bulge turned out above A♭/E♭ tone hole. Speaker, A-B trill (rounded and raised touch, R1), A (spurs on upper and lower lobes of touch), G♯ (spurs on upper and lower lobes of touch), f/c (cross, L2), E♭/B♭ (cross, L3), C♯/G♯, B/F♯ (R3), B♭/F (cross, R3), A♭/E♭, F♯/C♯, E/B. L=440.

Stamped on upper part of body: "HOF-INSTRUMENTENMACHER (curved) / (Prussian eagle) / Wernicke (cursive) / BERLIN / (star)"; lower part of body: "(Prussian eagle) / Wernicke (cursive) / BERLIN / D / (star)"; bell: "HOF-INSTRUMENTENMACHER" / (Prussian eagle) / Wernicke (cursive) / BERLIN / (star)".

2002.43

12-key clarinet in D, Johann Friedrich Wilhelm Wernicke, Berlin, ca. 1860.

Boehm-system clarinet in B♭, F. Barbier (H. Selmer et Cie), Paris, ca. 1920.

Ebonite mouthpiece; nickel-silver ligature; black stained rosewood; nickel-silver ferrules. Five sections: mouthpiece, barrel, l.h. joint, r.h. joint, bell. Seventeen pillar-mounted keys, six ring keys for LT, L1, L2, R1, R2, R3. Speaker, A-B trill (R1), A-B♭ trill (R1), A, G♯, f/c (R1), E♭/B♭ (R1), E♭/B♭ (cross, L3), C♯/G♯, B/F♯ (cross, R3), A♭/E♭ (R4), F/C (L4), F♯/C♯ (L4), E/B (L4), F/C (R4), F♯/C♯ (R4), E/B (R4). Serial no. 2045. L=594.

Stamped on mouthpiece: "Barbier"; l.h. joint, r.h. joint, bell: "F.BARBIER / FB (intertwined) / PARIS".

2002.55

Boehm-system clarinet in B♭, F. Barbier (H. Selmer et Cie), Paris, ca. 1920.

12-key simple system clarinet in B♭, Joseph Wallis and Son, London, ca. 1920.

Rosewood mouthpiece; nickel-silver ligature; rosewood; flat, nickel-silver ferrules. Five sections: mouthpiece, barrel, l.h. joint, r.h. joint, bell. Twelve pillar-mounted keys, six ring keys for L1, L2, L3, R2, R3, C♯ mechanism. Speaker (wraparound), A-B trill, A, G♯, f/c, E♭/B♭ (cross), C♯/G♯, B♭/F♯ (cross), A♭/E♭, F/C (when E/B touch is closed produces F♯/C♯), F♯/C♯, E/B. In case. L=631 (with mouthpiece).

Stamped on barrel, l.h joint, r.h. joint: "J.WALLIS & SON / LONDON"; bell: "J. WALLIS & SON / 135 EUSTON ROAD / LONDON / B♭".

2002.68

12-key simple system clarinet in B♭, Joseph Wallis and Son, London, ca. 1920.

13-key clarinet in C, Carl Theodor Golde, Dresden, ca. 1850.

Black wood mouthpiece; grooves for cord ligature; metal ligature; boxwood; ivory ferrules; single beading. Five sections: mouthpiece, barrel, l.h. joint, r.h. joint-stock, bell. Thirteen pillar-mounted nickel-silver keys, four ring keys for L1, L2, R2, R3. Speaker, A-B trill, A, G♯ (over the A key), f/c (R1), E♭/B♭ (R1), E♭/B♭ (cross, L3), C♯/G♯, B♭/F♯ (cross), A♭/E♭, F/C, F♯/C♯, E/B. L=510.

Stamped on barrel, l.h. joint, r.h. joint-stock, bell: "(star) / (lyre) / C. GOLDE / DRESDEN / C".

Three Golde clarinets in two-tier wooden case, silver plate on top engraved with owner's name: "F.H. Arlitt". B♭ is on top, C and A are on bottom. Two tuning forks marked: "Philharmonic Pitch" both giving the same A; pads; screwdrivers; two wooden safety pins for playing music outdoors; three metal mouthpiece caps; curved metal lever used for attaching needle springs to the underside of keys.

Stamped on l.h. joint: "(star) / (lyre) / C.GOLDE / DRESDEN / C"; r.h. joint-stock, bell: "(lyre) / C. GOLDE, DRESDEN. / C".

2002.72

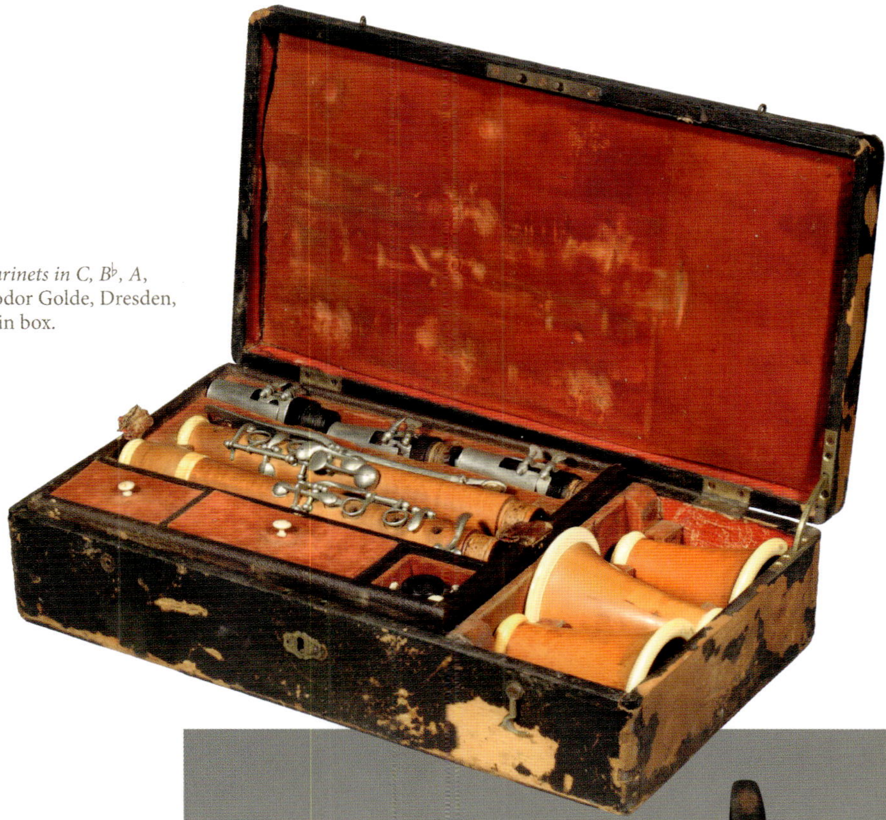

13-key clarinets in C, B♭, A, Carl Theodor Golde, Dresden, ca. 1850, in box.

13-key clarinet in B♭, Carl Theodor Golde, Dresden, ca. 1850.

Black wood mouthpiece; grooves for cord ligature; metal ligature; boxwood; ivory ferrules; single beading. Five sections: mouthpiece, barrel, l.h. joint, r.h. joint-stock, bell. Thirteen pillar-mounted nickel-silver keys, four ring keys for L1, L2, R2, R3. Speaker, A-B trill, A, G♯ (over the A key), f/c (R1), E♭/B♭ (R1), E♭/B♭ (cross, L3), C♯/G♯, B♭/F♯ (cross), A♭/E♭, F/C, F♯/C♯, E/B. L=581.

Stamped on l.h. joint, r.h. joint-stock, bell: "(lyre) / C. GOLDE / DRESDEN / B".

2002.73

13-key clarinet in A, Carl Theodor Golde, Dresden, ca. 1850.

Black wood mouthpiece; grooves for cord ligature; metal ligature; boxwood; ivory ferrules; single beading. Five sections: mouthpiece, barrel, l.h. joint, r.h. joint-stock, bell. Thirteen pillar-mounted nickel-silver keys, four ring keys for L1, L2, R2, R3. Speaker, A-B trill, A, G♯ (over the A key), f/c (R1), E♭/B♭ (R1), E♭♯/B♭ (cross, L3), C♯/G♯, B♭/F♯ (cross), A♭/E♭, F/C, F♯/C♯, E/B. L=615.

Stamped on l.h. joint, r.h. joint-stock, bell: "(lyre) / C. GOLDE / DRESDEN / A".

2002.74

13-key clarinets in C, B♭, A, Carl Theodor Golde, Dresden, ca. 1850.

11-key clarinet in F, Johann Stehle, Vienna, ca. 1850.

Black wood mouthpiece; string ligature; boxwood; black horn ferrules; single beading. Five sections: mouthpiece, barrel, l.h. joint, r.h. joint-stock, bell. Eleven block-mounted keys with round, flat key heads, raised ring for F/C hole, wide rim bell. Speaker, A-B trill (R1), A, G♯, E♭/B♭ (R1), C♯/G♯, B/F♯ (R3), B♭/F (cross, R3), A♭/E♭, F♯/C♯, E/B (the last two keys have raised touches). L=413 (with mouthpiece).

Stamped on barrel: "Stehle (cursive) / (star)"; l.h. joint: "Stehle (cursive) / Wien (cursive) / (star) /F"; r.h. joint-stock: "F / Stehle (cursive) / Wien (cursive) / (star)"; bell: "(Hapsburg crowned eagle) / Stehle (cursive) / Wien (cursive) / (star)".

2002.80

LEFT: *11-key clarinet in F*, Johann Stehle, Vienna, ca. 1850.

13-key simple system clarinet in B♭ with Barret action, Eugène Albert, Brussels, ca. 1890.

Ebonite mouthpiece; brass ligature; black wood; flat, nickel-silver ferrules. Five sections: mouthpiece, barrel, l.h. joint. r.h. joint, bell. Thirteen pillar-mounted nickel-silver keys, rings for L2, L3, R2, R3, C♯ mechanism, nickel-silver mouthpiece cap. Speaker (wraparound), A-B trill, A, G♯ (long tailed, L2), f/c (R1), E♭/B♭ (R1), E♭/B♭ (cross, L3), C♯/G♯, B♭/F (cross), A♭/E♭, F/C (when E/B touch is closed produces F♯/C♯), F♯/C♯, E/B. L=680.

Stamped on mouthpiece: "E.J. ALBERT / J.R.LAFLEUR & SON"; F♯/C♯ key head: "BREVETÉ"; l.h. joint: "(star) / A. CHAPPELL / E. ALBERT / 50 NEW BOND STREET / LONDON / (star)"; r.h. joint: "E. ALBERT / A BRUXELLES / (star)"; bell: "(star) / APPROVED BY / M^R. LAZARUS / (star)".

Henry Lazarus (1815-1895) was one of the most important English clarinetists of the nineteenth century. He owned several clarinets by Albert and knew the oboist Apollon Barret (1804-1879) when they both played at the Italian Opera in London. Samuel Arthur Chappell (1834-1904) was Albert's sole agent in London, and many Albert clarinets include the stamp: "Approved by Mr. Lazarus". The Breveté designation on F♯/C♯ key head refers to Albert's use of the "C♯ mechanism" in his 1866 clarinet model adopted at the Brussels Conservatory. Samuel Arthur Chappell bought James Tyler's 1862 English C♯ patent (no. 1,308), licensing it to Eugène Albert when he worked for Boosey & Co. in London from 1879 to 1885.

Baines 1967, 138-140; Weston 1974-1975; Waterhouse 1993, 4; Kelly and Myers 2004, 70-71; Weston 2008, 112-119.

2002.82

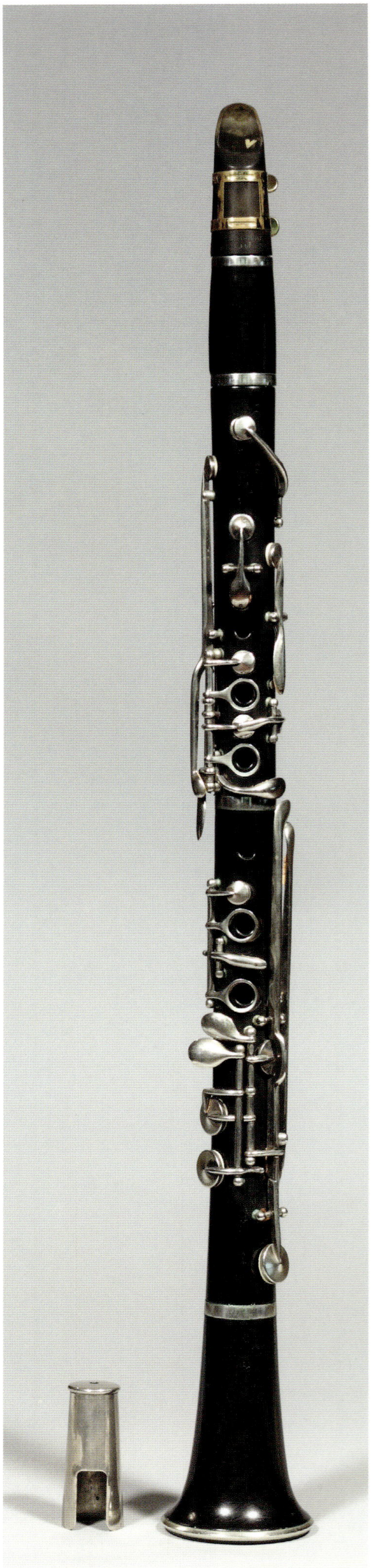

RIGHT: *13-key simple system clarinet in B♭ with Barret action*, Eugène Albert, Brussels, ca. 1890.

13-key simple system clarinet in A with Barret action, Eugène Albert, Brussels, ca. 1890.

Stained black wood; flat, nickel-silver ferrules. Five sections: mouthpiece, barrel, l.h. joint, r.h. joint, bell. Thirteen pillar-mounted nickel-silver keys, rings for L2, L3, R2, R3, C♯ mechanism. Speaker (wraparound), A-B trill, A, G♯ (long tailed, L2), f/c (R1), E♭/B♭ (R1), E♭/B♭ (cross, L3), C♯/G♯, B♭/F (cross), A♭/E♭, F/C (when E/B touch is closed produces F♯/C♯), F♯/C♯, E/B. L=608.

Stamped on barrel, bell: "(six-pointed star) / S.A.CHAPPELL / (six-pointed star)"; l.h. joint: "(six-pointed star) / S.A.CHAPPELL / SOLE AGENT / 52 / NEW BOND STREET / LONDON / (six-pointed star)"; r.h. joint: "(six-pointed star) / MANUFACTURED / BY / E.ALBERT / BRUSSELS / (six-pointed star)".

Baines 1967, 138-140.

2002.83

5-key clarinet in C, Dominique Antony Porthaux, Paris, ca. 1790.

Black wood mouthpiece (reproduction); boxwood; ivory ferrules; single beading. Five sections: mouthpiece, barrel, l.h. joint, r.h. joint, stock-bell. Five ring-mounted brass keys, square key heads. Speaker, A, A♭/E♭, F♯/C♯, E/B. L=542.

Stamped on barrel, l.h.joint, r.h joint, stock-bell: "(crown) / PORTHAUX / A PARIS".

2002.94

15-key clarinet in E♭, Charles Borromée Mahillon, Brussels, ca. 1890.

Ebonite mouthpiece; black wood; flat nickel-silver ferrules. Four sections: mouthpiece, barrel, body, bell. Fifteen pillar-mounted nickel-silver keys, four rings for L1, L2, R2, R3, C♯ mechanism. Speaker (wraparound), C-B♭ trill (R1), A-B trill (R1), A, G♯ (L2), f/c (R1), f/c (L3), E♭/B♭ (R1), E♭/B♭ (cross, L3), C♯/G♯, B♭/F (cross), A♭/E♭ (nickel-silver roller), F/C (nickel-silver roller; when closed with the E/B key produces F♯/C♯), F♯/C♯ (nickel-silver roller), E/B (nickel-silver roller). L=480 (with mouthpiece).

Stamped on barrel: "(star)"; body: "MEDAILLE D'OR / PARIS 1878 (star) / (star) C. MAHILLON / BRUXELLES / (star)"; bell: "(star) / MEDAILLE D'OR / PARIS 1878 / (crest with lion of Brabant) / C. MAHILLON / BRUXELLES / (star)".

2002.97

13-key simple system clarinet in A with Barret action, Eugène Albert, Brussels, ca. 1890.

5-key clarinet in C, Dominique Antony Porthaux, Paris, ca. 1790.

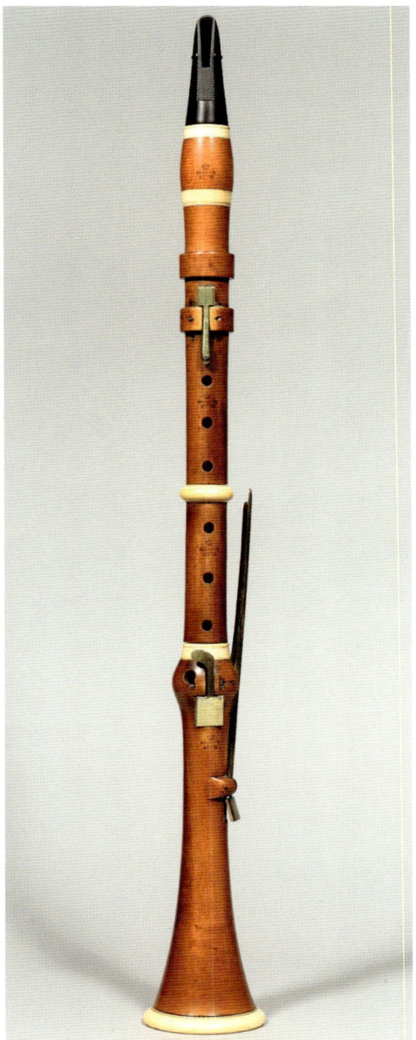

15-key clarinet in E♭, Charles Borromée Mahillon, Brussels, ca. 1890.

5-key clarinet in C, Keller Frères, Strasbourg, France, ca. 1791-1794.

Black wood mouthpiece; boxwood; ivory ferrules; single beading. Five sections: mouthpiece, barrel, l.h. joint, r.h. joint, stock-bell. Five ring-mounted brass keys, F/C tone-hole bulge. Speaker, A, A♭/E♭, F♯/C♯, E/B. L=623.

Stamped on barrel: "C / 1"; l.h. joint, r.h. joint: "(angel with two trumpets) / FRÉRES / KELLER / 1 C"; stock-bell: "(angel with two trumpets) / KELLER / A STRASBOURG / (angel with two trumpets) / 1 / C".

Rousellet and Watel 2012, 95.

2002.98

10-key clarinet in C, Ferdinand Zogbaum, New York, ca. 1860.

Black wood mouthpiece; brass ligature; boxwood; ivory ferrules; single beading. Six sections: mouthpiece, barrel, l.h. joint, r.h. joint, stock, bell. Ten pillar and ring-mounted brass keys, salt-spoon key heads. Speaker, A, G♯, f/c, E♭/B♭, C♯/G♯, B♭/F, A♭/E♭, F♯/C♯, E/B. L=485.

Stamped on l.h. joint: "F. ZOGBAUM (curved) / IN / NEW-YORK (curved)"; r.h. joint: "C"; stock, bell: "F. ZOGBAUM (curved) / IN / NEW-YORK (curved) / C".

2003.03

8-key clarinet in C, William Milhouse, London, ca. 1820.

Black wood mouthpiece; string ligature; boxwood; ivory ferrules; single and double beading. Five sections: mouthpiece, barrel (waisted), l.h. joint, r.h. joint-stock, bell. Eight block-mounted brass keys, square key heads, F/C tone-hole bulge cut straight on lower side. Speaker, A-B trill, A, E♭/B♭, B/F♯, A♭/E♭, F♯/C♯, E/B. L=528.

Stamped on barrel, l.h joint, r.h. joint-stock: "W•MILHOUSE / LONDON / C"; bell: "W•MILHOUSE / LONDON / C / 337 OXFORD ST"

2003.07

5-key clarinet in C, Keller Frères, Strasbourg, France, ca. 1791-1794.

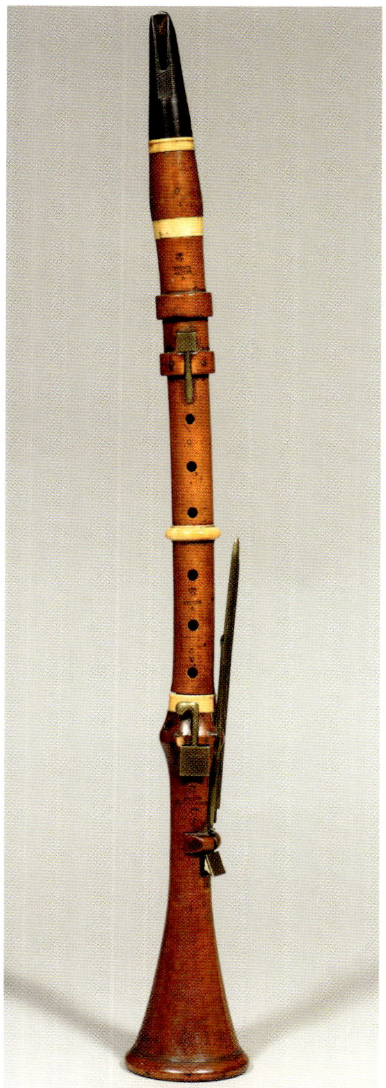

10-key clarinet in C, Ferdinand Zogbaum, New York, ca. 1860.

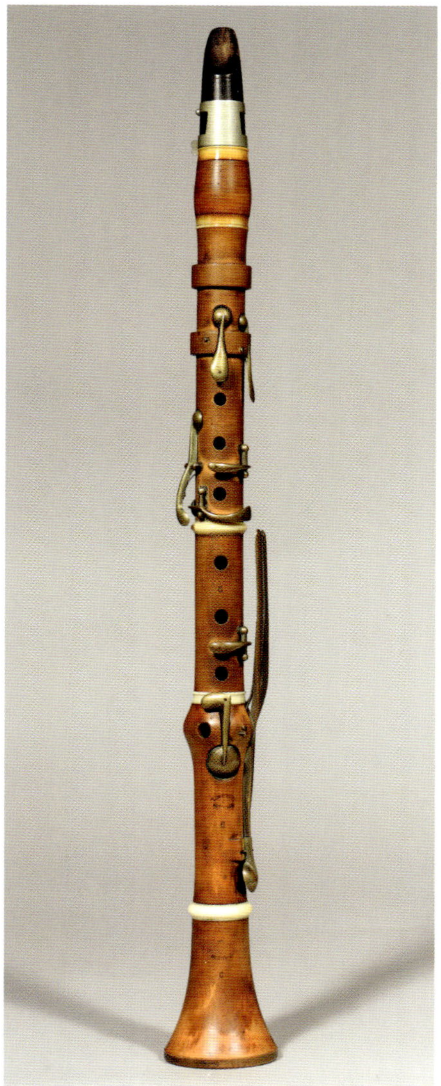

8-key clarinet in C, William Milhouse, London, ca. 1820.

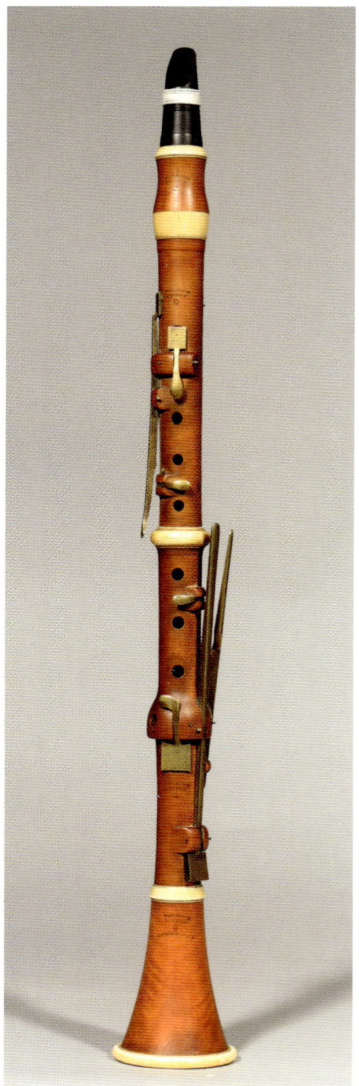

12-key simple system clarinet in A, Jacques Émile Albert, Brussels, ca. 1880.

Ebonite mouthpiece; nickel-silver ligature; stained rosewood; flat, nickel-silver ferrules. Five sections: mouthpiece, barrel (one wood, one nickel-silver tuning rings on upper portion), l.h. joint, r.h. joint (with a wide nickel-silver repaired ferrule), bell. Mouthpiece has long metal tenon. Twelve pillar-mounted nickel-silver keys, two rings for R2 and R3, C♯ mechanism. Speaker (wraparound), A-B trill (R1), A, G♯ (long tailed, L2), f/c (R1), E♭/B♭ (cross, L3), C♯/G♯, B♭/F (cross), A♭/E♭ (nickel-silver roller), F/C (nickel-silver roller; when E/B touch is closed it produces F♯/C♯), F♯/C♯, E/B. L=680 (with mouthpiece unextended).

Stamped on barrel: "(sunburst) / JACQUES ALBERT / (sunburst)"; l.h. joint: "(sunburst) / JACQUES ALBERT / A BRUXELLES / (sunburst)"; r.h. joint: "A / (sunburst) / JACQUES ALBERT / A BRUXELLES / (sunburst)"; bell: "(sunburst) / W.D. CUBITT / SON & C^O / 3 G^T MARLBORO' S^T / LONDON / (sunburst)".

2003.11

8-key clarinet in E♭, Martin Frères, Paris, ca. 1865.

Black wood mouthpiece (damaged); grooves for cord ligature; boxwood; ivory ferrules; single and double beading. Six sections: mouthpiece, barrel, l.h. joint, r.h. joint, stock, bell. Eight pillar and ring-mounted nickel-silver brass keys, flat, round key heads. Speaker, A, G♯, E♭/B♭ (cross), C♯/G♯, A♭/E♭, F♯/C♯, E/B. L=495 (with mouthpiece).

Stamped on back of mouthpiece: "MARTIN"; l.h. joint: "MARTIN (curved) / Frères (cursive) / A PARIS"; r.h. joint: "MF (monogram)"; stock: "(bee) / MARTIN (curved) / Frères (cursive) / A PARIS / MF (monogram)", bell: "(bee) / MARTIN / A PARIS/ MF (monogram)".

2003.08

5-key clarinet in B♭, William Whiteley, Utica, New York, ca. 1825.

Rosewood mouthpiece; grooves for cord ligature; boxwood; ivory ferrules; single beading. Five sections: mouthpiece, barrel (convex shape), l.h. joint, r.h. joint-stock, bell. Five ring and block-mounted brass keys, flat, round key heads, F/C tone-hole bulge cut out above A♭/E♭ tone hole. Speaker, A, A♭/E♭, F♯/C♯, E/B. L=600.

Stamped on l.h. joint, r.h. joint-stock, bell: "W^M WHITELEY / UTICA".

Made in "German" style; that is, with a short-tenon mouthpiece, convex barrel, and a straight F♯/C♯ lever.

2003.09

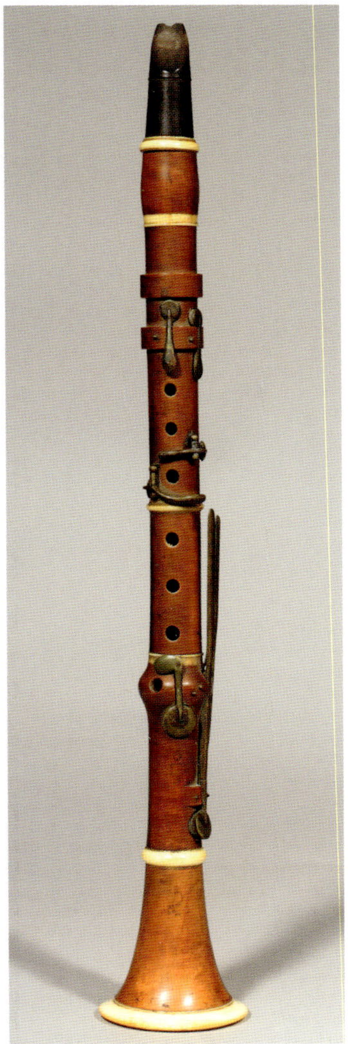

8-key clarinet in E♭, Martin Frères, Paris, ca. 1865.

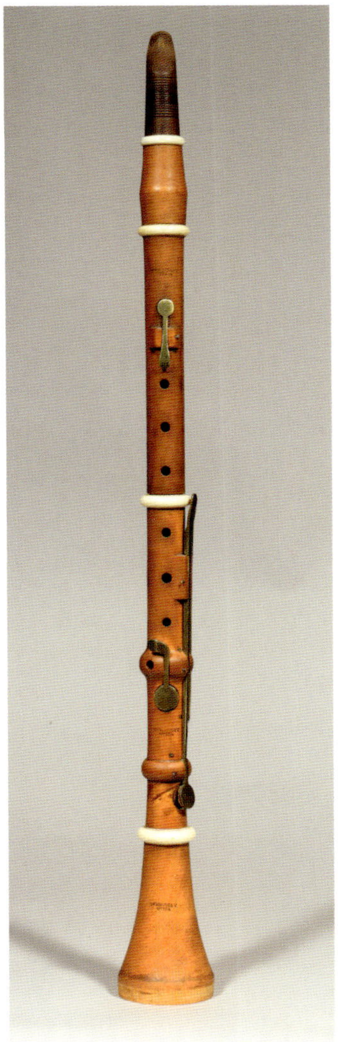

5-key clarinet in B♭, William Whiteley, Utica, New York, ca. 1825.

12-key simple system clarinet in A, Jacques Émile Albert, Brussels, ca. 1880.

12-key simple system clarinet in B♭, Q. Cecconi and Son, Portsmouth, ca. 1875.

Rosewood mouthpiece (damaged); nickel-silver ligature; stained rosewood; nickel-silver ferrules. Five sections: mouthpiece, barrel, l.h. joint, r.h. joint, bell. Twelve pillar-mounted nickel-silver keys, two rings for R2 and R3, C♯ mechanism. Speaker (wraparound), A-B trill (R1), A, G♯ (long tailed, L2), f/c (R1), E♭/B♭ (cross, L3), C♯/G♯, B♭/F (cross), A♭/E♭, F/C (when E/B touch is closed it produces F♯/C♯), F♯/C♯, E/B. L=567.

Stamped on barrel, l.h. joint, r.h. joint, bell: "Q. CECCONI (curved) / PORTSMOUTH (curved)".

2003.16

12-key simple system clarinet in B♭, Q. Cecconi and Son, Portsmouth, ca. 1875.

12-key simple system clarinet in B♭, Charles Gerard Conn, Elkhart and New York, ca. 1900.

Ebonite mouthpiece; nickel-silver ligature; black wood; gold-plated ferrules, keys, pillar mounts. Five sections: mouthpiece, barrel, l.h. joint, r.h. joint, bell. Thirteen pillar-mounted keys, two gold-plated rings for R2 and R3, C♯ mechanism. Speaker (wraparound), A-B trill (R1), A, G♯, f/c (R1), E♭/B♭ (cross, L3), C♯/G♯ (L4, with lever for R1), B♭/F (cross), A♭/E♭ (roller) F/C (roller; when E/B touch is closed it produces F♯/C♯) F♯/C♯ (roller), E/B (roller). No serial number. In case. L=660 (with mouthpiece).

Stamped on back of mouthpiece: "TRADE (lyre and eagle) MARK"; barrel: "CONN (in cursive)"; bell: "(decorative marquee) / MADE BY / C.G. CONN / ELKHART, IND. / NEW YORK."

2003.17

12-key simple system clarinet in B♭, Charles Gerard Conn, Elkhart and New York, ca. 1900.

12-key simple system clarinet in B♭, Metzler & Co., London, ca. 1900.

Ebonite mouthpiece; nickel-silver ligature; rosewood; flat, nickel-silver ferrules. Five sections: mouthpiece, barrel, l.h. joint, r.h. joint, bell. Twelve pillar-mounted nickel-silver keys, modern key heads, two rings for R2 and R3. Speaker (wraparound), A-B trill (R1), A, G♯ (long-tailed), f/c (R1), E♭/B♭ (cross, L3), C♯/G♯, B♭/F (cross), A♭/E♭, F/C, F♯/C♯, E/B. In case. L=676 (with mouthpiece).

Stamped on l.h. joint, bell: "METZLER & CO. / LONDON".

2003.27

12-key simple system clarinet in B♭, Metzler & Co., London, ca. 1900.

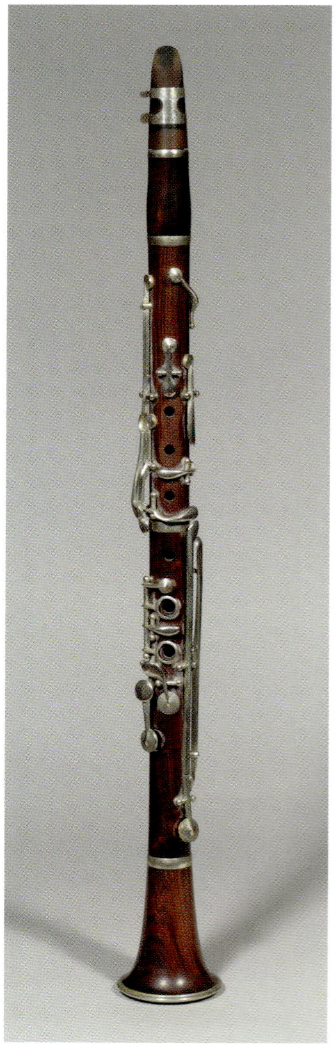

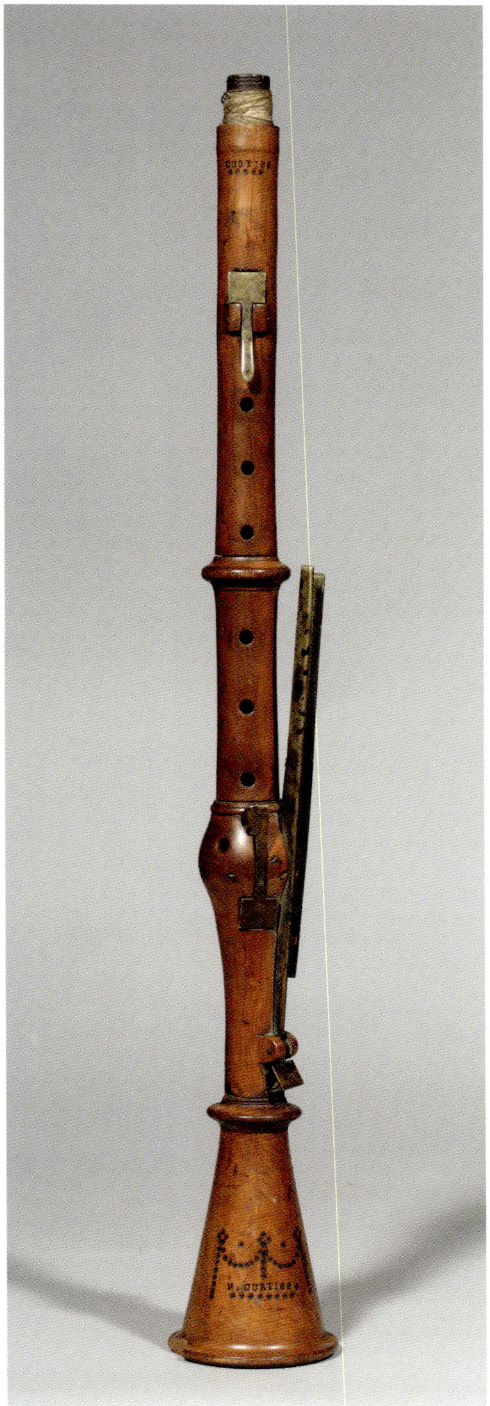

5-key clarinet in C, N. Curtiss, United States, ca. 1800.

Fruitwood; fruitwood ferrules; single and double turning. Four sections: l.h. joint, r.h. joint, stock, bell. Missing barrel and mouthpiece. Five block-mounted brass keys, square key heads, F/C tone-hole bulge. Speaker, A, A♭/E♭ (very short touch), F♯/C♯, E/B. The thin edges of the F♯/C♯ and E/B levers are placed upward creating an awkward feel for the l.h. little finger. Made by an amateur maker. L=490.

Stamped on l.h. joint: "CURTISS / (five stars)"; bell: "(stars arranged in two posts on either side of thirteen stars, one post in the center of eight stars with two links between posts of nine stars, and two stars in the sky) / N. CURTISS (star) / (nine stars)".

It is possible that this instrument was made by Nathan Curtiss, Woodbury, Connecticut.

2003.44

LEFT: *5-key clarinet in C,* N. Curtiss, United States, ca. 1800, and detail of bell stamp.

5-key clarinet in C, William Whiteley, Utica, New York, ca. 1820.

Black wood mouthpiece; string ligature; boxwood; ivory and horn ferrules; single beading. Six sections: mouthpiece, barrel (waisted), l.h. section, r.h. section, stock, bell. Five ring-mounted brass keys, square key heads, F/C tone-hole bulge turned out above A♭/E♭ tone hole. Speaker, A, A♭/E♭, F♯/C♯ (cranked), E/B. L=530 (with mouthpiece).

Stamped on l.h. joint, stock, bell: "(sunburst) / WHITELEY / UTICA"; r.h. joint: "(sunburst)".

2003.48

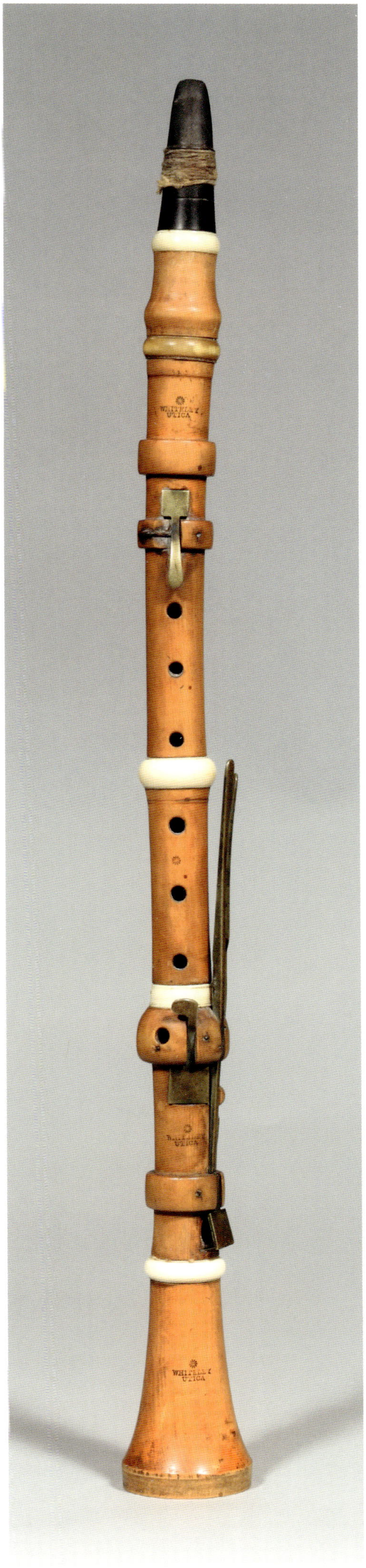

RIGHT: *5-key clarinet in C,* William Whiteley, Utica, New York, ca. 1820.

Boehm-system clarinet in B♭ with Mazzeo mechanism, Selmer, Signet 100 model, Elkhart, Indiana, ca. 1960.

Ebonite mouthpiece; nickel-silver ligature; black wood; nickel-silver ferrules. Five sections: mouthpiece, barrel, l.h. section, r.h. section, bell (without ferrule). Seventeen pillar-mounted nickel-silver keys, modern keyheads, six rings for LT, L1, L2, R1, R2, R3. Optional B♭ mechanism opens A-B trill key head with any ring keys for l.h. or r.h. Speaker, A-B trill (R1), A-B♭ trill (R1), A, G♯, f/c (R1), E♭/B♭ (R1), E♭/B♭ (cross, L3), C♯/G♯, B/F♯ (cross), A♭/E♭, F/C (L4), F/C (R4), F♯/C♯ (L4), F♯/C♯ (R4), E/B (L4) E/B (R4). In Signet case. Serial no. 110773. L=600, 673 (with mouthpiece).

Stamped on mouthpiece: "SELMER / HS (five-pointed star) / MADE IN FRANCE"; l.h. joint: "MAZZEO / ® / MODEL / 100 / Signet (cursive in a circle) / ® / Selmer / U.S.A."; r.h. joint: "Signet (cursive in a circle) / ® / Selmer / U.S.A."; bell: "100 / Signet (cursive in a circle) / ® / Selmer / U.S.A."

In 1959, Rosario Mazzeo patented an optional device to raise the A-B♭ trill key head by pressing any of the rings for R1, R2, or R3, US patent no. 3,035,473.

2003.49

LEFT: *Boehm-system clarinet in B♭ with Mazzeo mechanism*, Selmer, Signet 100 model, Elkhart, Indiana, ca. 1960.

Boehm-system clarinet in B♭, Grafton (John E. Dallas & Sons, Ltd.), London, 1953.

Ebonite mouthpiece; yellow plastic; nickel-silver ferrules. Five sections: mouthpiece, barrel, l.h. joint, r.h. joint, bell. Seventeen pillar-mounted nickel-silver keys with six rings for LT, L1, L2, R1, R2, R3. Speaker, A-B trill (R1), A-B♭ trill (R1), A, G♯, f/c (R1), E♭/B♭ (R1), E♭/B♭ (cross, L3), C♯/G♯, B/F♯ (cross), A♭/E♭ (R4), F/C (L4), F/C (R4), F♯/C♯(L4), F♯/C♯(R4), E/B (L4), E/B (R4). L=588.

Stamped on l.h.joint: "Grafton (cursive)".

Hector Sommaruga (1904-1985) developed a plastic saxophone after World War II when metal was scarce. In 1946, he applied for two British patents (nos. 604,407 and 605,418) that were approved in 1948. Sommaruga and John E. Dallas in London started producing alto saxophones in 1950. They were not successful, Sommaruga left the Dallas Company in 1953. The Dallas Company made some plastic clarinets in 1953, but these were also unsuccessful.

Cottrell 2012, 89-91, 356.

2004.11

RIGHT: *Boehm-system clarinet in B♭*, Grafton (John E. Dallas & Sons, Ltd.), London, 1953.

6-key clarinet in C, Claire Bélisaire, Paris, ca. 1850.

Boxwood; ivory ferrules; single beading. Six sections: mouthpiece (missing), barrel, l.h. joint, r.h. joint, stock, bell. Six block, ring, and pillar-mounted brass keys, round, flat key heads. Speaker, A, C♯/G♯ (mounted on pillar), A♭/E♭, F♯/C♯, E/B. L=518.

Stamped on barrel, l.h. joint (twice), r.h. joint, stock, bell: "CLAIR / Bélisaire / A PARIS. (in an oval)".

2005.06

6-key clarinet in C, Claire Bélisaire, Paris, ca. 1850.

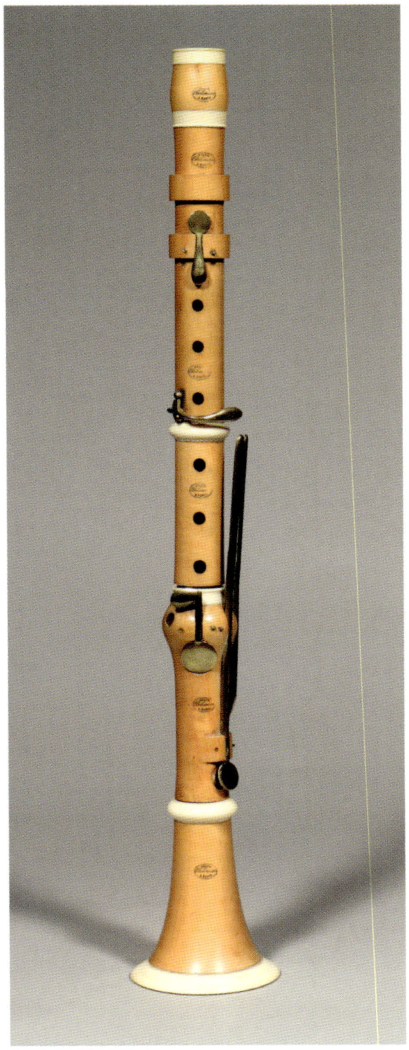

12-key clarinet in C, Adolphe Sax et Cie, Paris, ca. 1850.

Rosewood mouthpiece; rosewood; nickel-silver ferrules. Four sections: mouthpiece, l.h. joint, r.h. joint, bell. Twelve pillar-mounted nickel-silver keys, round, curved key heads decorated with flower designs. Speaker, A-B trill (R1), A, G♯ (cross over A), f/c (R1), E♭/B♭ (cross, L3), C♯/G♯, B♭/F (cross), A♭/E♭ (R4), F/C (R4), F♯/C♯(L4), E/B (L4). L=573.

Stamped on back of mouthpiece: "(flower) / AD SAX et cie"; l.h. joint, r.h. joint, bell: "(flower) / AD. SAX et cie / PARIS".

Reil 2012, 106.

2005.07

12-key clarinet in C, Adolphe Sax et Cie, Paris, ca. 1850.

12-key clarinet in A, Adolphe Sax et Cie, Paris, ca. 1850.

Stained rosewood mouthpiece; grooves for cord ligature; rosewood; nickel-silver ferrules. Four sections: mouthpiece, l.h. joint, r.h. joint, bell. Twelve pillar-mounted nickel-silver keys, round, curved key heads with flower designs. Speaker, A-B trill (R1), A, G♯ (cross over), f/c (R4), E♭/B♭ (cross, L3), C♯/G♯, B♭/F (cross), A♭/E♭ (R4), F/C (R4), F♯/C♯ (L4), E/B (L4). L=690.

Stamped on l.h. joint, r.h. joint, bell: "(flower) / AD. SAX et cie / PARIS".

Reil 2012, 106.

2005.08

12-key clarinet in A, Adolphe Sax et Cie, Paris, ca. 1850.

11-key clarinet in B♭ with corps de rechange in A, Heinrich Grenser, Dresden, ca. 1810.

Black wood mouthpiece (reproduction); grooves for a cord ligature; boxwood; ivory ferrules; single beading. Six sections: mouthpiece, barrel, l.h. joint, r.h. joint, stock, bell. Eleven ring and saddle-mounted brass keys, square key heads; F/C tone-hole bulge. Corps de rechange in A in three sections: barrel, r.h. joint, l.h. joint; eight ring and saddle-mounted brass keys, square key heads. Speaker, A-B trill, A, G♯, f/c (cross), E♭/B♭ (cross), C♯/G♯ (cross), B♭/F (cross), A♭/E♭, F♯/C♯ (extension on E/B touch), E/B. L of B♭ clarinet=595; L of A clarinet=631.

B♭ clarinet stamped on barrel: "2 / (crown)"; l.h. joint, r.h. joint: "(crown) / H•GRENSER"; stock: "(crown) / H•GRENSER / DRESDEN"; A clarinet stamped on barrel: "1 / (crown)"; l.h. joint, r.h. joint: "(crown) / H•GRENSER"; stock: "(crown) / H•GRENSER / DRESDEN".

2005.11

14-key clarinet in E♭, Lebrecht Fischer, Markneukirchen, ca. 1920.

Wooden mouthpiece; grooves for cord ligature; brass ligature; stained black wood; nickel-silver ferrules. Five sections: mouthpiece, barrel, l.h. joint, r.h. joint, bell. Fourteen pillar-mounted nickel-silver keys, modern key heads, four rings for L1, L2, R2, R3. Speaker (wraparound to the left side), A-B trill (R1), A, G♯, f/c (R1), E♭/B♭ (R1), E♭/B♭ (cross, L3) C♯/G♯ (L4, with lever for R1), B♭/F (cross), A♭/E♭, A♭/E♭ (L4, ebonite roller), F/C (ebonite roller, R4), F♯/C♯ (ebonite roller, L4), E/B (ebonite roller, L4). In case. L=490 (with mouthpiece).

Stamped on barrel, bell: "LEBRECHT FISCHER / MARKNEUKIRCHEN 1/S".

2005.20

13-key clarinet in C, Buffet-Crampon & Cie, Paris, 1860.

Black wood mouthpiece; boxwood; brass ferrules. Four sections: mouthpiece, l.h. joint, r.h. joint, bell. Thirteen pillar-mounted brass keys, salt-spoon key heads, ferrule replaced on upper part of l.h. joint. Speaker, A-B trill (R1), A, G♯ (over A), f/c (R1), E♭/B♭ (cross, L3), C♯/G♯, B/F♯ (R3), B♭/F (cross, R3), A♭/E♭, F/C, F♯/C♯, E/B. No serial number. L=531.

Stamped on l.h. joint: "(lyre) / BUFFET / Crampon & Cie (in cursive) / A PARIS (in oval) / BC (intertwined) / BREVETÉS / S.G.D.G."; r.h. joint, bell: "(lyre) / BUFFET / Crampon & Cie (in cursive) / A PARIS (in oval) / BC (intertwined)".

2005.21

11-key clarinet in B♭ with corps de rechange in A, Heinrich Grenser, Dresden, ca. 1810.

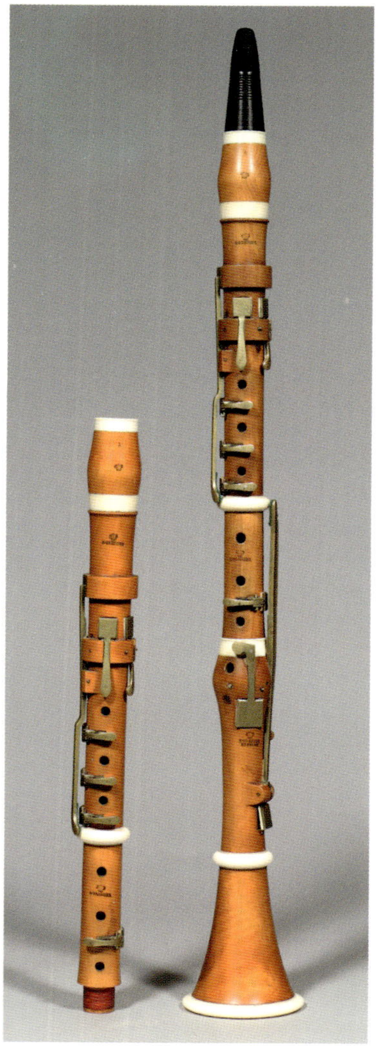

14-key clarinet in E♭, Lebrecht Fischer, Markneukirchen, ca. 1920.

13-key clarinet in C, Buffet-Crampon & Cie, Paris, 1860.

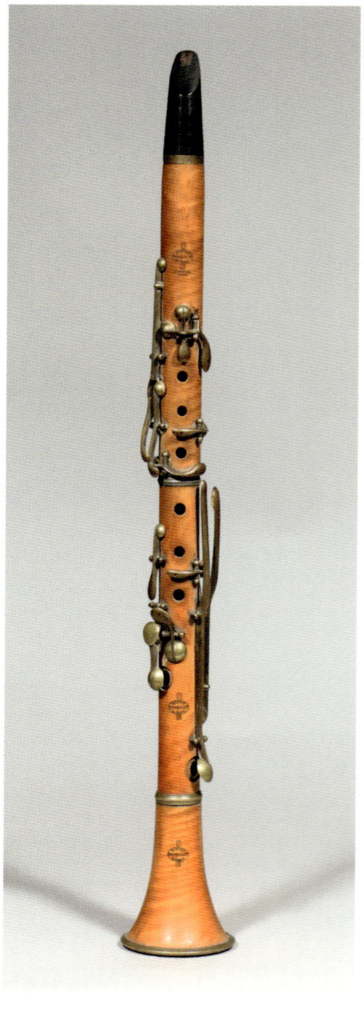

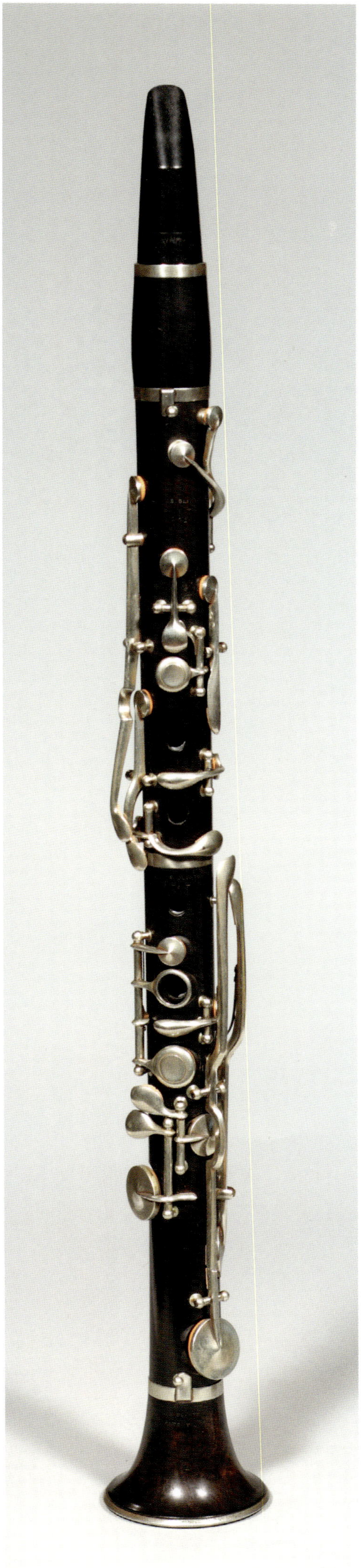

13-key combination clarinet in B♭ or A, James Clinton, London (Jacques Albert, Brussels), ca. 1892.

Wooden mouthpiece; black wood; nickel silver ferrules. Five sections: mouthpiece, barrel, l.h. joint, r.h. joint, bell. Thirteen pillar-mounted nickel-silver keys; modern key heads. Two plates for L1 and R3, 1st speaker (LT for B♭ clarinet), 2nd speaker (LT for A clarinet), A-B trill (R1), A, G♯ (long tailed, L2), f/c (R1), E♭/B♭ (cross, L3), C♯/G♯, B♭/F (cross), A♭/E♭, F/C, F♯/C♯, E/B. Serial no. 101. L of A clarinet=625; L of B♭ clarinet=593.

Stamped on mouthpiece: "BUFFET / Crampon & Cie / A PARIS (in dotted oval)"; l.h. joint: "JAMES CLINTON / PATENT / 101"; r.h. joint: "JAMES CLINTON / PATENT".

In 1892, James Clinton was granted a British patent (no. 3,686) for a combination C-B♭ or B♭-A clarinet. Parts are connected by a coaxial rotating metal tube. Outer wooden tube carries the whole mechanism and the tone holes. Inner metal tube has the same series of tone holes in duplicate, arranged on opposite sides of the tube, one series for the B♭ clarinet and one for A. When the bell is twisted through about 120°, pulled out, and latched, the A clarinet series of holes comes under the keys. The upper section is then slid out, the barrel slides in a helical guide; the bell is also pulled out and latched. The instrument was made for Clinton by Jacques Albert in Brussels.

Joseph 2012, 76-78.

2006.02

LEFT: *13-key combination clarinet in B♭*, James Clinton, London (Jacques Albert, Brussels), ca. 1892.

RIGHT: *13-key combination clarinet in A*, James Clinton, London (Jacques Albert, Brussels), ca. 1892.

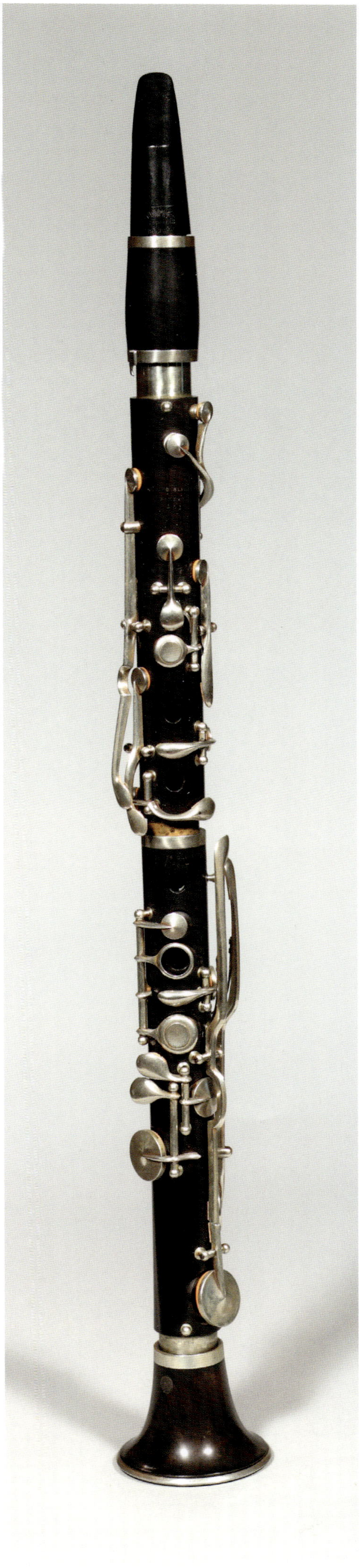

19-key Oehler-system clarinet in B♭,
Oskar Oehler, Berlin, ca. 1910.

Metal-lined wooden mouthpiece; grooves for cord ligature; stained black wood; nickel-silver ferrules. Five sections: mouthpiece, barrel, l.h. joint, r.h. joint, bell. Seventeen pillar-mounted nickel-silver keys, five ring keys for L1, L2, L3, R1, R3, one plate key (R2), a high E correction key, C♯ mechanism. 1st speaker (wraparound to the left); 2nd speaker corresponding with L1, C-D trill (R1), B♭-C trill (R1), A, G♯, High E correction key (a ring and vent for R1 with the A♭/E♭ key), f/c (R1), f/c (cross, L2), E♭/B♭ (R1), E♭/B♭ (cross, L3), C♯/G♯ (L4, with lever for R1), B♭/F (L4), B♭/F (cross, R3), A♭/E♭ (L4), A♭/E♭ (ebonite roller, R4), F/C (ebonite roller, R4; when F/C and E/B touches are closed produces F♯/C♯), F♯/C♯ (ebonite roller, L4), E/B (ebonite roller, L4). L=665 (with mouthpiece).

Stamped on l.h. joint, r.h. joint: "(lyre) /O. Oehler / Berlin (in oval) / (design) / B"; bell: "O. Oehler / Berlin (in oval) / (design) / A (scratched in)".

Reil and Weller 2008.

2006.08

19-key Oehler-system clarinet in B♭,
Oskar Oehler, Berlin, ca. 1910.

19-key Oehler-system clarinet in A,
Oskar Oehler, Berlin, ca. 1930.

Stained black wood; nickel-silver plated ferrules. Five sections: mouthpiece (missing), barrel, l.h. joint, r.h. joint, bell. Seventeen pillar-mounted nickel-silver keys, six ring keys for L1, L2, L3, R1, R2, R3, high E correction key, C♯ mechanism. 1st speaker (wraparound to the left); 2nd speaker corresponding with L1, C-D trill (R1), B♭-C trill (R1), A, G♯, High E correction key (a ring and vent for R1 with the A♭/E♭ key), f/c (R1), f/c (cross, L2), E♭/B♭ (R1), E♭/B♭ (cross, L3), C♯/G♯ (L4, with lever for R1), B♭/F (L4), B♭/F (cross, R3), A♭/E♭ (L4), A♭/E♭ (ebonite roller, R4), F/C (ebonite roller, R4; when F/C and E/B touches are closed produces F♯/C♯), F♯/C♯ (ebonite roller, L4), E/B (ebonite roller, L4). L=623.

Stamped on l.h. joint, bell: "(lyre) /O. Oehler / Berlin (in oval) / (design) / A"; r.h. joint: "O. Oehler / Berlin (in oval) / (design) / A".

Left-hand joint is similar to Ottensteiner's design in its placement of touch and axle of cross E♭/B♭ key and satellite key of L1 ring.

Voorhees 2000, 170; Reil and Weller 2008.

2006.09

19-key Oehler-system clarinet in B♭,
Oskar Oehler, Berlin, ca. 1910.

Stained black wood; nickel-silver ferrules. Five sections: mouthpiece (missing), barrel, l.h. joint, r.h. joint, bell. Seventeen nickel-silver keys mounted on pillars, six ring keys for L1, L2, L3, R1, R2, R3, high E correction key, C mechanism. 1st speaker (wraparound to the left); 2nd speaker corresponding with L1, C-D trill (R1), B♭-C trill (R1), A, G♯, high E correction key (a ring and vent for R1 with the A♭/E♭ key), f/c (r1), f/c (cross, L2), E♭/B♭ (R1), E♭/B♭ (cross, L3), C♯/G♯ (L4, with lever for R1), B♭/F (L4), B♭/F (cross, R3), A♭/E♭ (L4), A♭/E♭ (ebonite roller, R4), F/C (ebonite roller, R4; when F/C and E/B touches are closed produces F♯/C♯), F♯/C♯(ebonite roller, L4), E/B (ebonite roller, L4). In case with Oehler A clarinet. L=580.

Stamped on l.h. joint, bell: "(lyre) /O. Oehler / Berlin (in oval) / (design) / B"; r.h. joint: "O. Oehler / Berlin (in oval) / (design) / B".

Left-hand joint is similar to Ottensteiner's design in its placement of touch and axle of cross E♭/B♭ key and satellite key of L1 ring.

Reil and Weller 2008.

2006.10

19-key Oehler-system clarinet in A, 19-key clarinet in Oehler-system B♭, Oskar Oehler, Berlin, ca. 1910.

12-key clarinet in E♭, Heinrich Joseph Haseneier, Koblenz, ca. 1860.

Black wood mouthpiece; boxwood; nickel-silver ferrules. Five sections: mouthpiece, barrel, l.h. joint, r.h. joint, bell. Twelve pillar-mounted nickel-silver keys, raised finger hole for F/C. Speaker, A-B trill (R1), A, G♯, f/c (R1), E♭/B♭ (cross, L3), C♯/G♯, B/F♯(L3), B♭/F (cross, L3), A♭/E♭ (mounted diagonally), F♯/C♯, E/B. L=414.

Stamped on l.h. joint: "Haseneier / Coblenz."

2006.11

6-key clarinet in B♭, Clair Godfroy aîné, Paris, ca. 1865.

Rosewood mouthpiece; boxwood; ivory ferrules; single beading. Six sections: mouthpiece, barrel, l.h. joint, r.h. joint, stock, bell. Six block-mounted brass keys, flat, round key heads. Speaker, A, C♯/G♯, A♭/E♭, F♯/C♯, E/B. Serial no. 4045. L=598.

Stamped on barrel, l.h. joint, r.h. joint, stock: "(portrait head) / CLAIR / Godfroy aîné / A PARIS (in an oval) / CG (monogram) / B"; bell: "(portrait head) / CLAIR / Godfroy aîné / A PARIS (in an oval) / CG (monogram) / B / 4045".

2006.13

Boehm-system clarinet in B♭, Millereau, Paris, ca. 1890.

Rosewood mouthpiece; nickel-silver ligature; rosewood; nickel-silver ferrules. Five sections: mouthpiece, barrel, l.h. joint, r.h. joint, bell. Seventeen pillar-mounted keys, modern key heads, six rings for LT, L1, L2, R1, R2, R3. Nickel-silver mouthpiece cap. Speaker (wraparound), A-B trill (R1), A-B♭ trill (R1), A, G♯ (long tailed, L2), f/c (R1), E♭/B♭ (R1), E♭/B♭ (cross, L3), C♯/G♯, B♭/F (cross), A♭/E♭ (R4), F/C (L4), F/C (R4), F♯/C♯ (L4), F♯/C♯ (R4), E/B (L4), E/B (R4). L=576.

Stamped on barrel: "(treble clef with music staff and the notes C, E, G)"; l.h. joint, r.h. joint, bell: "(treble clef with music staff and the notes C, E, G) / MILLEREAU / BREVETÉ / 66.RUE D'ANGOULÊME / PARIS".

2006.15

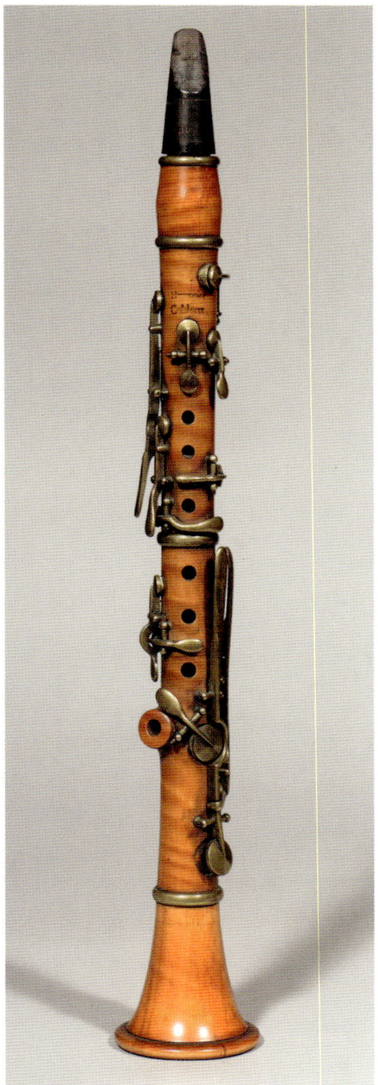

12-key clarinet in E♭, Heinrich Joseph Haseneier, Koblenz, ca. 1860.

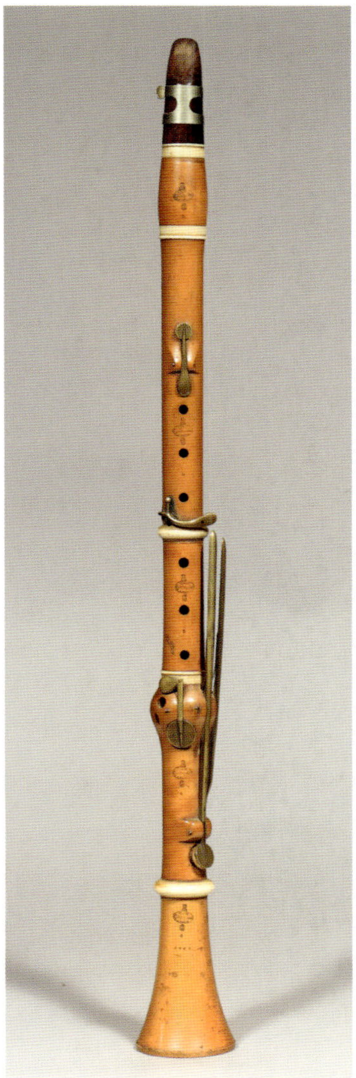

6-key clarinet in B♭, Clair Godfroy aîné, Paris, ca. 1865.

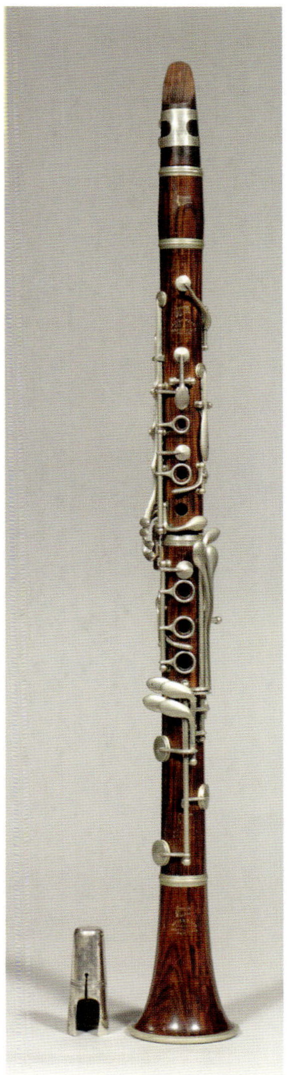

Boehm-system clarinet in B♭, Millereau, Paris, ca. 1890.

5-key clarinet in F, François-Michel Amelingue, Paris, ca. 1820.

Black wood mouthpiece; cord ligature; boxwood; boxwood ferrules; single beading. Five sections: mouthpiece, barrel, l.h. joint, r.h. joint, stock-bell. Five ring and block-mounted brass keys, square key heads. Speaker, A, A♭/E♭, F♯/C♯, E/B. L=430 (without mouthpiece).

Stamped on barrel, l.h. joint, r.h. joint, stock-bell: "(five-pointed star) / AMELINGUE / A PARIS / F".

Rousellet and Watel 2012, 7.

2006. 22

12-key clarinet in C, James Welsh Pepper, Philadelphia, ca. 1890.

Rosewood mouthpiece; nickel-silver ligature; stained black wood; nickel-silver ferrules. Five sections: mouthpiece, barrel, l.h. joint, r.h. joint, bell. Twelve pillar-mounted nickel-silver keys, round, flat key heads, rings for R2 and R3. Speaker (wraparound), A-B trill (R1), A, G♯ (over A), f/c (R1), E♭/B♭ (cross, L3), C♯/G♯, B♭/F (cross), A♭/E♭, F/C, F♯/C♯, E/B. L=492.

Stamped on l.h. joint, r.h. joint: "C"; bell: "J.W. PEPPER / PHILADELPHIA / CHICAGO".

2007.13

3-key clarinet in C, Porthaux, Paris, probably twentieth century.

Fruitwood; fruitwood ferrules; single beading. Four sections: barrel, l.h. joint, r.h. joint, stock-bell. Three ring and block-mounted brass keys, square key heads. The rings on the l.h. joint have center marks. Speaker, A, E/B. L=582.

Stamped on barrel, l.h. joint, r.h. joint: "(star) / PORTHAUX"; stock-bell: "(star) / PORTHAUX / PARIS".

This clarinet was constructed to appear to have been made in the eighteenth century. The inaccurate proportions of the joints, poor quality of wood, keys, gouge marks on the l.h. joint and bell, and amateur quality of the stamps indicate a probable fake.

2007.14

5-key clarinet in F, François-Michel Amelingue, Paris, ca. 1820.

12-key clarinet in C, James Welsh Pepper, Philadelphia, ca. 1890.

3-key clarinet in C, Porthaux, Paris, probably twentieth century.

6-key clarinet in B♭, François Sautermeister and Louis Müller, Lyon, ca. 1835.

Black wood mouthpiece; boxwood; ivory ferrules; single beading. Six sections: mouthpiece (broken tip), barrel, l.h. joint, r.h. joint, stock, bell. Six ring, block and pillar-mounted brass keys, square key heads. Speaker, A, C♯/G♯ (mounted on pillar), A♭/E♭ (with highly curved touch), F♯/C♯, E/B. L=572.

Stamped on barrel, l.h. joint, r.h. joint, stock, bell: "(bird) / V^{e}. Sautermeister / & / Müller / (bird) a Lyon (bird) / (bird)".

2007.22

6-key clarinet in B♭, François Sautermeister and Louis Müller, Lyon, ca. 1835.

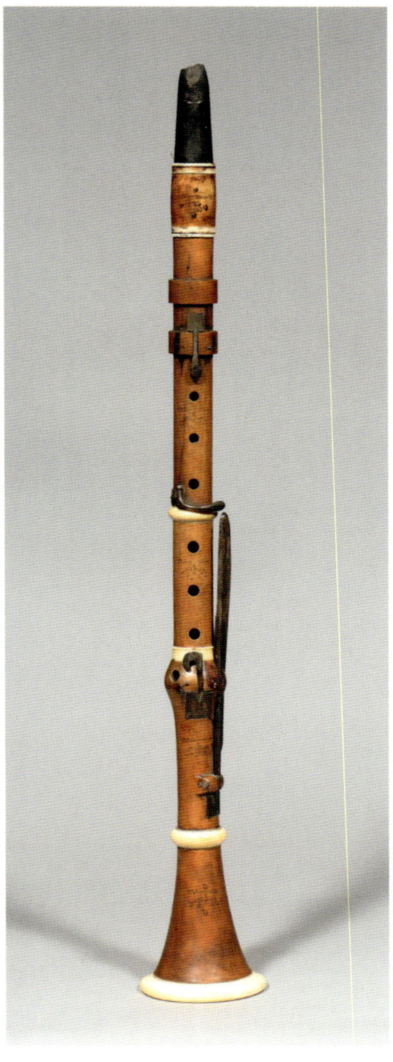

13-key clarinet in C, Walter Crosby, Boston, ca. 1850.

Black wood mouthpiece(replacement); brass ligature; boxwood; ivory ferrules; single and double beading. Five sections: mouthpiece, barrel (waisted), l.h. joint, r.h. joint-stock, bell. Thirteen ring and block-mounted brass keys, flat, round key heads, F/C tone-hole bulge turned out above A♭/E♭ tone hole. Speaker, A-B trill (R1), A, G♯ (L2, long-tailed), f/c (R1), E♭/B♭ (cross, L3), C♯/G♯, B/F♯ (cross, R2), B/F♯ (R3), B♭/F (cross, R3), A♭/E♭, F♯/C♯, E/B (metal rollers are on the touches of the F♯/C♯ and E/B keys). L=520.

Stamped on mouthpiece: "FRANCE"; barrel, l.h. joint, r.h. joint-stock, bell: "W. CROSBY / BOSTON".

2008.06

13-key clarinet in C, Walter Crosby, Boston, ca. 1850.

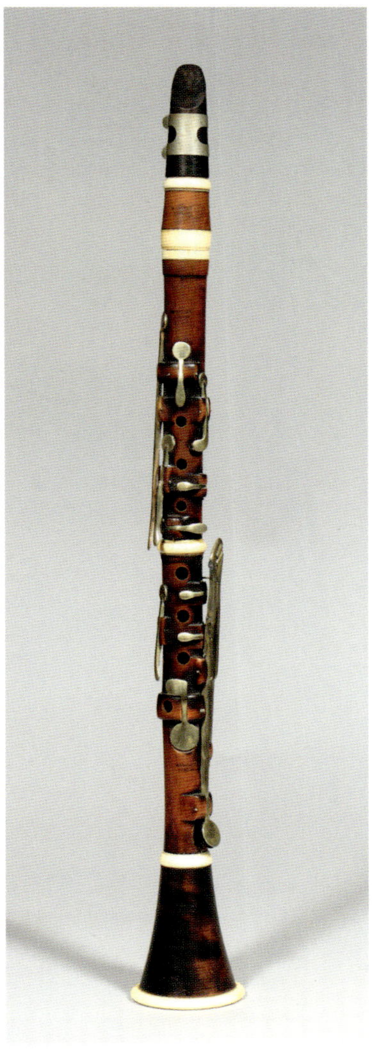

11-key clarinet in D, Heinrich Friedrich Kayser, Hamburg, ca.1850.

Rosewood mouthpiece; grooves for cord ligature; boxwood; ivory ferrules; single beading. Five sections: mouthpiece, barrel, l.h. joint, r.h. joint-stock, bell. Eleven saddle and pillar-mounted nickel-silver keys, salt-spoon key heads, raised knob for F/C tone hole, two rings for R2 and R3. Speaker, A-B trill (R1), A, G♯, f/c (R1), E♭/B♭ (cross), C♯/G♯, B♭/F (cross), A♭/E♭, F♯/C♯ (metal roller), E/B (metal roller). L=435.

Stamped on barrel, bell: "H. KAYSER. / D"; l.h. joint, r.h. joint-stock: "H. KAYSER. / HAMBURG. / D".

2008.09

11-key clarinet in D, Heinrich Friedrich Kayser, Hamburg, ca.1850.

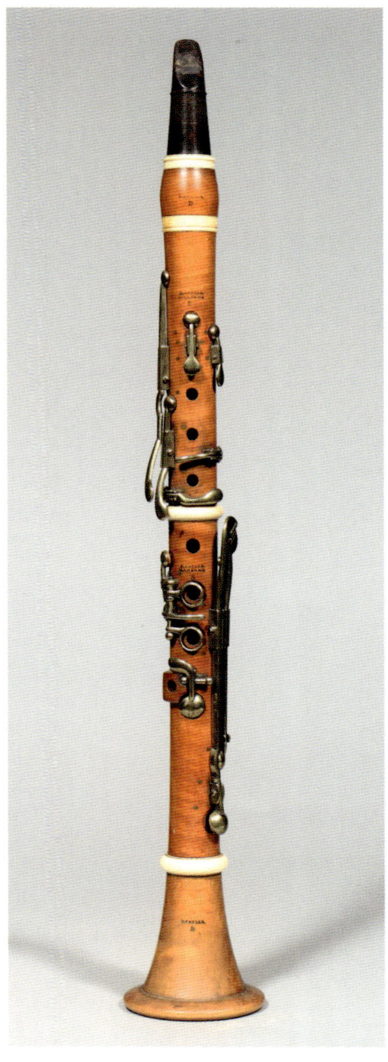

12-key clarinet in B♭, Heinrich Friedrich Kayser, Hamburg, ca.1850.

Stained rosewood mouthpiece; grooves for cord ligature; boxwood; ivory ferrules; single beading. Five sections: mouthpiece, barrel, l.h. joint, r.h. joint-stock, bell. Twelve saddle and pillar-mounted nickel-silver keys, salt-spoon key heads, F/C finger hole bulge. Speaker, A-B trill (R1), A, G♯, f/c (R1), E♭/B♭ (cross), C♯/G♯, B/F♯, B♭/F (cross), A♭/E♭, F♯/C♯ (metal roller), E/B (metal roller). L=581.

Stamped on barrel, bell: "H. KAYSER / B"; l.h. joint, r.h. joint-stock: "H. KAYSER / HAMBURG / B".

2008.10

12-key clarinet in B♭, Heinrich Friedrich Kayser, Hamburg, ca.1850.

12-key clarinet in E♭, Heinrich Friedrich Kayser, Hamburg, ca. 1850.

Rosewood mouthpiece; grooves for cord ligature; boxwood; ivory ferrules; single beading. Five sections: mouthpiece, barrel, l.h. joint, r.h. joint-stock, bell. Twelve saddle and pillar-mounted brass keys, salt-spoon key heads, raised knob for F/C tone-hole, heavily pinned on the l.h. and r.h. joints. Speaker, A-B trill (R1), A, G♯, f/c (R1), E♭/B♭ (cross, L3), C♯/G♯, B/F♯ (R3), B♭/F (cross, R3), A♭/E♭, F♯/C♯ (metal roller, L4), E/B (metal roller, L4). In case. L=487.

Stamped on barrel, bell: "H. KAYSER / Es"; l.h. joint, r.h. joint-stock: "H. KAYSER / HAMBURG / Es".

2008.11

12-key clarinet in E♭, Heinrich Friedrich Kayser, Hamburg, ca. 1850.

13-key clarinet in A, Ferdinand Zogbaum, New York, ca. 1870.

Stained rosewood mouthpiece; metal band and screw covering back of mouthpiece from teeth marks; rosewood; nickel-silver ferrules. Five sections: mouthpiece, barrel, l.h. joint, r.h. joint, bell. Twelve pillar-mounted nickel-silver keys, salt-spoon key heads, missing bell ring. Speaker, A-B trill (R1), A, G♯ (over A), f/c (R1), E♭/B♭ (cross), C♯/G♯, B/F♯ (R3), B♭/F (cross, R3), A♭/E♭, F/C, F♯/C♯, E/B. L=617, 693 (with mouthpiece).

Stamped on mouthpiece: "F. ZOGBAUM (curved) / IN / NEW YORK (curved)"; barrel, l.h. joint, bell: "F. ZOGBAUM (curved) / IN / NEW YORK (curved) / A".

2009.07

13-key clarinet in A, Ferdinand Zogbaum, New York, ca. 1870.

5-key clarinet in F, Alexis Michel Bernard, Lyon, ca. 1800.

Black wood mouthpiece; grooves for cord ligature; boxwood; ivory ferrules; single beading. Four sections: mouthpiece (damaged), barrel, body, stock-bell. Five ring-mounted brass keys, square key heads, two rings on upper part of body have center marks. Speaker, A, A♭/E♭, F♯/C♯, E/B. L=390.

Stamped on body: "(five-pointed star) / BERNARD / A LYON / F. // I"; stock-bell: "(five-pointed star) / BERNARD / A LYON / F. I".

2010.09

5-key clarinet in F, Alexis Michel Bernard, Lyon, ca. 1800.

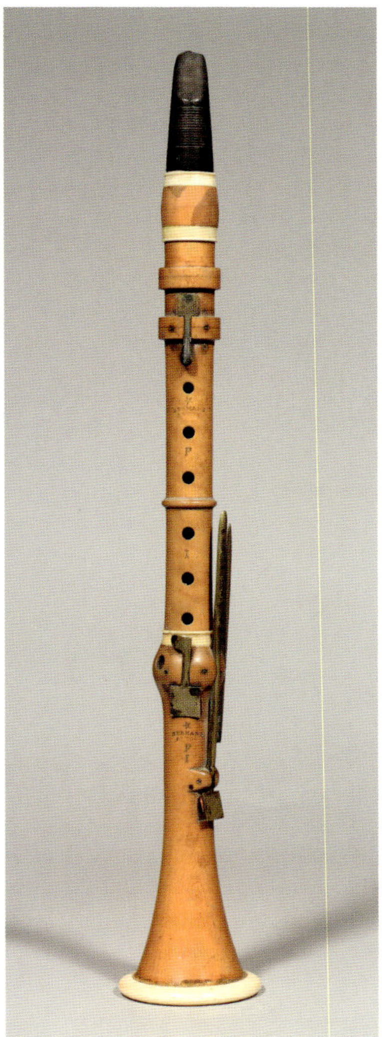

9-key clarinet in high A♭, Martin Schemmel, Vienna, ca. 1840.

Black wood mouthpiece; grooves for cord ligature; boxwood; black horn ferrules; single beading. Four sections: mouthpiece (damaged), barrel, body, bell. Nine ring, block and pillar-mounted brass keys, round key heads, raised knob for F/C finger hole. Speaker, A-B trill, A, E♭/B♭ (cross), C♯/G♯, B♭/F, A♭/E♭, F♯/C♯ (round and raised touch), E/B (round and raised touch). L=350.

Stamped on body: "(lyre and wreath) / Wien (cursive) / (star) // As // Schem̄el (star)"; bell: "(lyre and wreath) / Schem̄el / Wien (cursive) / (star)".

2010.10

9-key clarinet in high A♭, Martin Schemmel, Vienna, ca. 1840.

5-key clarinet in B♭, Carl Augustin Grenser, Dresden, 1796.

Black wood mouthpiece; grooves for cord ligature; boxwood; boxwood ferrules; double beading. Five sections: mouthpiece, barrel, l.h. joint, r.h.joint, stock-bell. Five ring and block-mounted keys, square key heads, twin third finger hole. Repair to top of barrel is a wide brass ferrule. Speaker, A, A♭/E♭, F♯/C♯, E/B. L=630.

Stamped on l.h. joint, r.h. joint: "(crossed swords) / A•GRENSER"; bell: "(crossed swords) / A•GRENSER / DRESDEN / 1796".

One of three dated A. Grenser clarinets.

Christie's New York Fine Musical Instruments auction, 2012, 18, no. 41.

2012.01

5-key clarinet in B♭, Carl Augustin Grenser, Dresden, 1796.

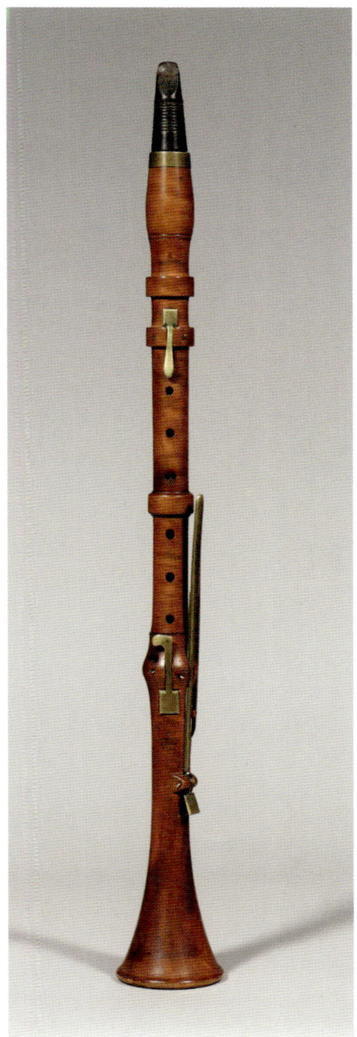

Clar-O-Sax, C.G. Conn Ltd., Elkhart, Indiana, ca. 1930.

Nickel-silver single-reed mouthpiece; nickel-silver ligature; nickel-silver conical tube. Two sections: mouthpiece, body (with short bell). Six irregular sized finger holes, nickel-silver mouthpiece cap. Storage box marked "The CONN CLAR-O-SAX. A Real Musical Instrument----Not a Toy! The first step to Saxophone and clarinet playing. Plays and sounds like a Saxophone. Excellent musical training for children." L=375 (with mouthpiece).

Stamped on front of body above bell: "CLAR-O-SAX / MANUFACTURED BY / C.G. CONN LTD. / ELKHART, IND / PAT. PENDING".

2004.08

Clar-O-Sax, C.G. Conn Ltd., Elkhart, Indiana, ca. 1930.

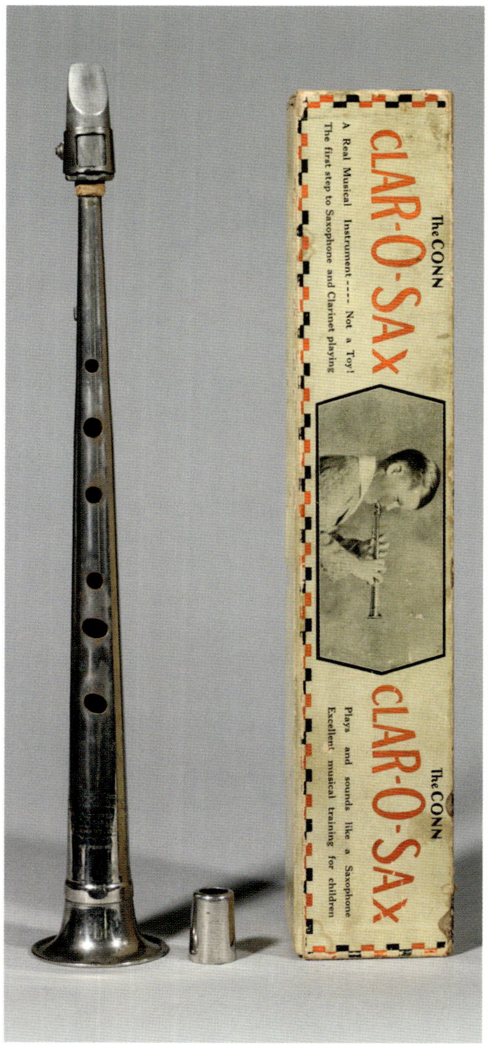

13-key clarinet in C, Couesnon et Cie, Paris, saxo-clarinet model, ca. 1935.

Ebonite mouthpiece; nickel-silver ligature; black wood; nickel-silver keys. Five sections: mouthpiece, curved nickel-silver neck, l.h. joint, r.h. joint, bell. Thirteen pillar-mounted keys, modern key heads, four rings for L1, L2, R2, R3, and C♯ mechanism. Speaker (wraparound), A-B trill (R1), A, G♯ (over A), f/c (R1), E♭/B♭ (R1), E♭/B♭ (cross, L3), C♯/G♯, B♭/F (cross), A♭/E♭ (ebonite roller), F/C (ebonite roller), F♯/C♯ (ebonite roller), E/B (ebonite roller). Flat touch design for key touches with rollers; the bell is gold plated. L= 620 (with mouthpiece).

A novelty instrument.

Stamped on l.h. joint: "SUPERTONE".

The trade name Supertone was used by Couesnon and sold in the United States by Sears Roebuck & Co.

Waterhouse 1993, 392.

2010.11

13-key clarinet in C, Couesnon et Cie, Paris, saxo-clarinet model, ca. 1935.

9-key clarinet in C, Graham Lyons, London, ca. 1990.

Black ABS plastic E♭ mouthpiece; black plastic ligature; ABS black plastic body; ABS plastic bell. Black acetal keys, body is molded in two halves. Mouthpiece and bell are separate castings but not detachable. Keys are mounted along ridges on sides, some hinged at both sides. Keys are molded with clips that snap into recesses molded into the ridges. Key pads are silicone rubber, metal springs, black ABS plastic mouthpiece cover. Nine keys, four rings for L1, R1, R2, R3. Speaker, A, G♯, f/c, C♯/G♯, A♭/E♭, F/C, F♯/C♯ (plastic roller), E/B (plastic roller). L=583 (with mouthpiece).

Stamped on body: "L (on a five-lined staff in an oval)"; bell: "Lyons".

These instruments are built for the small span of children's hands; the earliest versions of Lyons' plastic clarinets were called "Clarineo".

Designed by Ted Planas, keys by Ian Dampney.

Lawson 1991, 2b.

2011.10

9-key clarinet in C, Graham Lyons, London, ca. 1990.

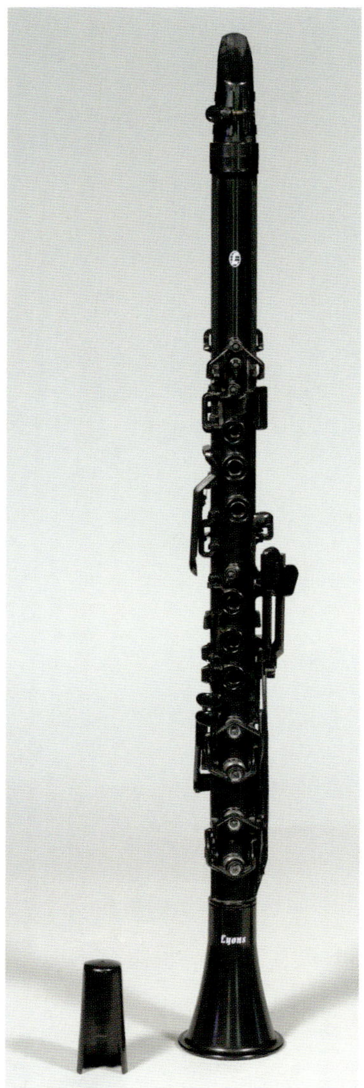

6-key clarinet d'amour, Hippolyte Collin, Paris, ca. 1810.

Black wood mouthpiece; maple; light and dark horn ferrules; single beading. Seven sections: mouthpiece, barrel, curved brass neck, l.h. joint, r.h. joint, stock, bell (bulb-shaped). Six ring and block-mounted brass keys, flat, round key heads. Speaker, A, C♯/G♯ (mounted on pillar), A♭/E♭, F♯/C♯, E/B. L=716.

Stamped on barrel, l.h. joint, r.h. joint: "(sunburst)/ COLLIN, / A PARIS / (sunburst) / B"; bell: "(sunburst)/ COLLIN".

Two finger hole joints stamped "B" indicating a B♭ clarinet. Although both fingerhole sections are from a B♭ clarinet, Collin appears to have made a clarinet d'amour in G.

Rice 2009a, 47.

2003.45

6-key clarinet d'amour, Hippolyte Collin, Paris, ca. 1810.

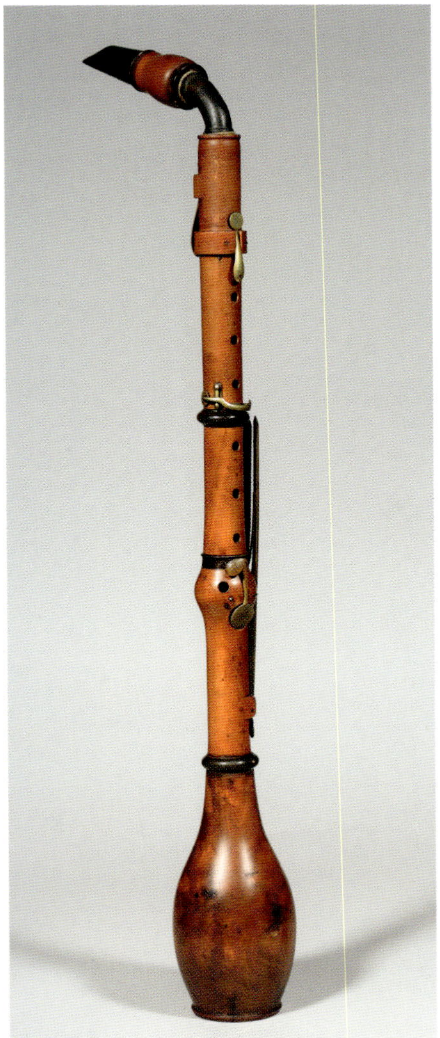

13-key clarinet d'amour in G, Wilhelm Heckel, Biebrich, ca. 1880.

Rosewood mouthpiece; stained rosewood; stained wood ferrules; single beading. Five sections: mouthpiece, long curved barrel, l.h. joint, r.h. joint, bell (bulb-shaped). Thirteen pillar-mounted nickel-silver keys, modern key heads. Two ring keys for R2 and R3. Metal thumb rest. Speaker (wraparound to the left), C♯-D♯ trill (R1), A, G♯, f/c (R1), E♭/B♭ (R1), E♭/B♭ (cross, L3), C♯/G♯, B♭/F (cross), A♭/E♭, F/C, F♯/C♯, E/B. L=670.

Stamped on barrel, l.h. joint, bell: "HECKEL / BIEBRICH"; r.h. joint: "BIEBRICH".

During the twentieth century, Heckel continued to make clarinets d'amour in A♭ and G. Their 1906 catalog lists them as "Heckel-Klarinette d'amore in G oder As mit Fis-Brillen am Ober- u. Unterstück, H-Cis, Cis-Dis-Triller" [Heckel clarinet d'amour in G or A♭ with F♯ rings on the upper and lower joints, B-C♯, C♯, and E♭ trill keys].

Heckel 1906, 4, no. 18m.

2006.14

13-key clarinet d'amour in G, Wilhelm Heckel, Biebrich, ca. 1880.

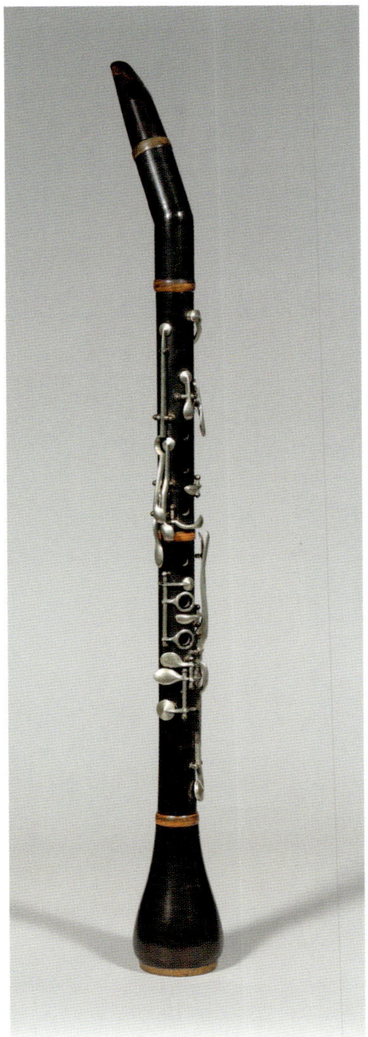

13-key alto clarinet in F, Jacques François Simiot and François Brelet, Lyon, ca. 1840.

Black wood mouthpiece; stained maple; ivory ferrules; single beading. Five sections: mouthpiece, curved barrel, l.h. joint, r.h. joint-stock, bell. Thirteen pillar-mounted gold-plated brass keys soldered to oval plates, round, flat key heads, plates for LT, closing key head, R3; ring key for R2. F♯/C♯ and E/B levers are raised with large supports providing room for A♭/E♭ key head. Gilded thumb rest. Speaker, A-B trill (R1), A, G♯ (straight), f/c (R1), E♭/B♭ (cross, L3), C♯/G♯, B/F♯ (R3), B♭/F (L3), A♭/E♭, F/C, F♯/C♯, E/B. L=785, 850 (with mouthpiece).

Stamped on barrel, l.h. joint, r.h. joint-stock, bell: "(sunburst) / SIMIOT / ET / BRELET / A LYON / (sunburst) / FA".

Three other altos by Simiot and Brelet are known.

Rice 2009a, 59-60.

2007.29

13-key alto clarinet in F, Jacques François Simiot and François Brelet, Lyon, ca. 1840.

13-key basset horn in F, Franz Harrach, Vienna, ca. 1815.

Black wood mouthpiece; stained boxwood; ivory ferrules; single beading. Seven sections: mouthpiece (reproduction), barrel, l.h. joint, ivory knee, r.h. joint, box (with chimney), brass bell (reproduction). Thirteen ring, block, and saddle-mounted brass keys, square key heads. Speaker, A-B trill, A, G♯, E♭/B♭, C♯/G♯, B♭/F, A♭/E♭, F/C, F♯/C♯, E/B, D (RT), C (RT).

One of three known Harrach basset horns.

Stamped on l.h. joint, r.h. joint, right side of box: "(Hapsburg eagle) / HARRACH / WIENN".

Rice 2009a, 135.

2013.03

13-key basset horn in F, Franz Harrach, Vienna, ca. 1815.

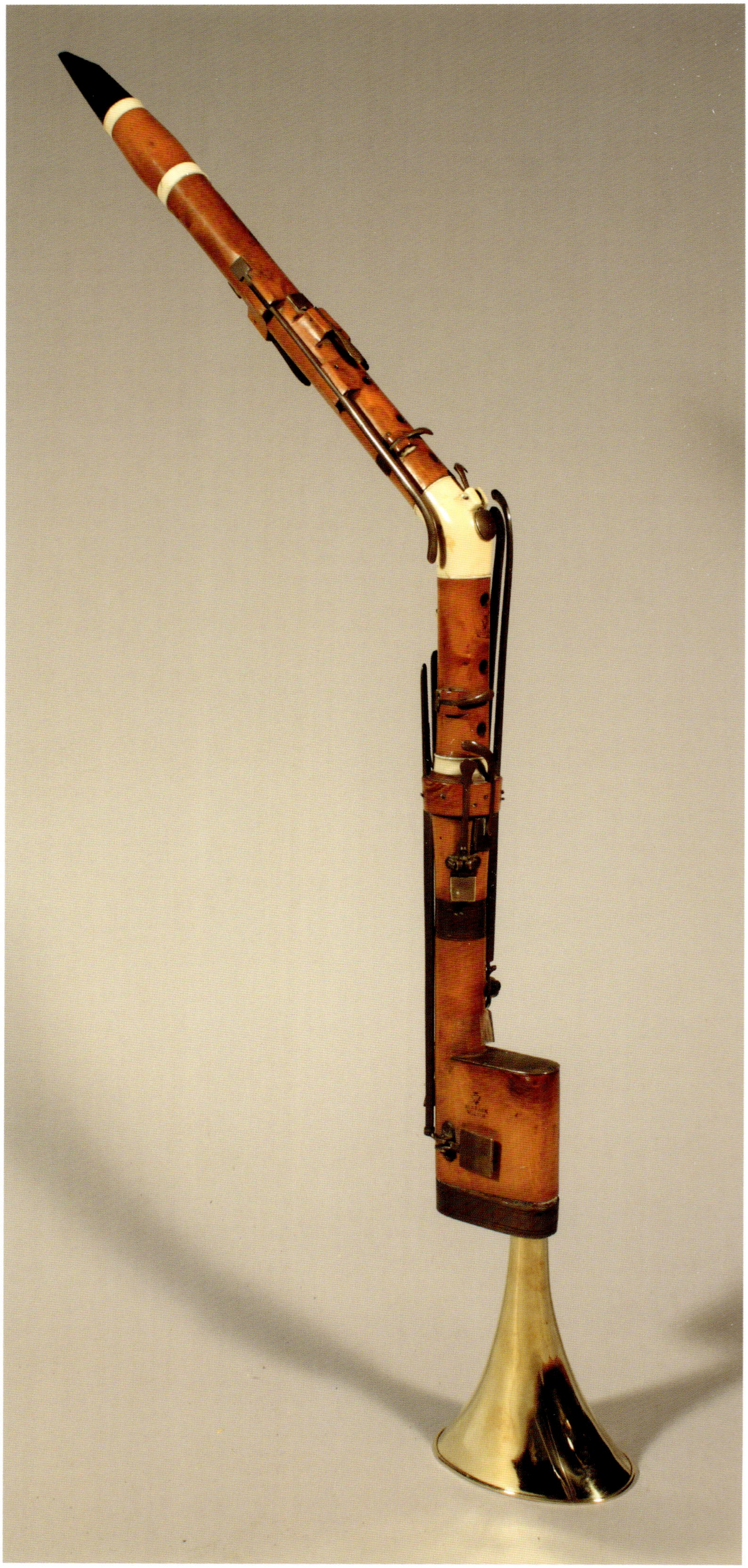

Boehm-system bass clarinet in B♭,
F. Barbier (H. Selmer et Cie),
Paris, ca. 1900.

Wooden mouthpiece; brass ligature; nickel-silver neck; granadilla; nickel-silver ferrules; nickel-silver upright bell. Five sections: mouthpiece, neck (curved), l.h. joint, r.h. joint, bell. Eighteen pillar-mounted nickel-silver keys, seven plateau keys. 1st speaker (on body), 2nd speaker (on neck), A-B trill, A-B♭ trill, A, G♯, f/c, E♭/B♭, E♭/B♭ (cross), C♯/G♯, B♭/F (cross), A♭/E♭, F/C (L4), F♯/C♯ (L4), E/B (L4), F/C (R4), F♯/C♯ (R4), E/B (R4).

Stamped on l.h. joint, r.h. joint, bell: "F.BARBIER / FB (intertwined) / PARIS".

2002.66

Boehm-system bass clarinet in B♭,
F. Barbier (H. Selmer et Cie), Paris, ca. 1900.

14-key bass clarinet in B♭,
Fernand Chapelain,
La Couture-Boussey, ca. 1900.

Wooden mouthpiece; black wood; gold-plated ferrules. Five sections: mouthpiece, gold-plated curved neck, l.h. joint, r.h. joint, curved gold-plated bell. Fourteen pillar-mounted gold-plated keys; modern key heads, plateau keys for thumb and six fingers. Curved thumb rest and ring on back of r.h. joint, ring on back of l.h. joint. 1st speaker (on body), 2nd speaker (on the neck), A-B trill (R1), A, G♯ (over A), f/c (R1), E♭/B♭ (R1), E♭/B♭ (cross, L3), C♯/G♯, B♭/F (cross), A♭/E♭, F/C, F♯/C♯, E/B.

Stamped on l.h. joint: "B♭ / HP / 'FRANCE'/ (rooster) FERNAND Chapelain (cursive) / & Cie (in an oval) / CF (monogram) / Bté S.G.D.G."

2003.31

14-key bass clarinet in B♭, Fernand Chapelain,
La Couture-Boussey, ca. 1900.

14-key bass clarinet in B♭,
Adolphe Sax et Cie, Paris, ca. 1870.

Black wood mouthpiece; nickel-silver ligature, stained black wood; silver plated ferrules. Five sections: mouthpiece, silver plated curved neck, l.h. joint, r.h. joint, curved silver plated bell. Fourteen pillar-mounted keys, flat, round decorated key heads, centers are worn showing the brass, seven plateau keys for LT, L1, L2, L3, R1, R2, R3, curved thumb rest on r.h. joint, ring on ferrule. 1st speaker (on body), 2nd speaker (on neck), A-B trill (R1), A, G♯ (over A), f/c (R1), E♭/B♭ (R1), E♭/B♭ (cross, L3), C♯/G♯, B♭/F (cross), A♭/E♭, F/C, F♯/C♯, E/B.

Stamped on mouthpiece: "Buffet-Crampon et Cie"; l.h. joint: "AD.SAX$^{et\ cie}$ / PARIS"; engraved on bell: "Clarinette basse en si ♭ / Adolphe Sax, à Paris / F^{teur} de la M^{son} Mil^{re} de l'Empereur".

One of eleven bass clarinets by Adolphe Sax. It is possible that this bass clarinet was made by a subcontractor, since it is the only example with an engraved bell, and the key system differs from the other Sax bass clarinets.

Rice 2012, 95-96, 99.

2006.18

14-key bass clarinet in B♭, Adolphe Sax et Cie,
Paris, ca. 1870.

13-key bass clarinet in B♭, Carl Wilhelm Moritz, Berlin, ca. 1850.

Ebonite mouthpiece; stained rosewood; brass ferrules. Five sections: mouthpiece, curved brass neck (replacement), l.h. joint, r.h. joint, curved brass bell. Flat touches, rollers, r.h. plate mechanism has two key heads, lowest has a broken lever. Seven plateau keys for LT, L1, L2, L3, R1, R2, R3; curved thumb rest, ring attached on back of r.h. joint. Thirteen pillar-mounted copper keys, highly rounded cupped key heads. Speaker, A-B trill (R1), A, G♯ (over A), f/c (R1), E♭/B♭ (R1), E♭/B♭ (cross, L3), C♯/G♯ (lever broken off), B♭/F (cross), A♭/E♭ (brown horn roller), F/C (ebonite roller), F♯/C♯(brown horn roller), E/B (brown horn roller).

Stamped on l.h. joint, r.h. joint: "Moritz / Berlin (cursive)"; bell: "C. W. Moritz / Berlin (cursive)".

Possibly made in Paris for Moritz.

2010.16

LEFT: *13-key bass clarinet in B♭*, Carl Wilhelm Moritz, Berlin, ca. 1850.

13-key bass clarinet in C, Louis-Auguste Buffet, Paris, ca. 1845.

Rosewood mouthpiece; ligature; stained maple; large nickel-silver ferrules; brass neck; flat touch pieces with rollers. Five sections: mouthpiece, curved brass neck, l.h. joint, r.h. joint, wooden bell. Fourteen pillar and saddle-mounted nickel-silver keys, round key heads. Plateau keys for L3 (roller), and R1. Speaker, A-B trill, A, G♯ (over A), f/c (R1), E♭/B♭ (roller), C♯/G♯, B/F♯ (R3), B♭/F (cross, roller), A♭/E♭ (roller), F/C (roller), F♯/C♯(roller), E/B (roller).

Stamped on mouthpiece: "Buffet-Crampon & Cie"; l.h. joint, r.h. joint, bell: "(face in a sunburst) / A. BUFFET / J$^{\underline{NE}}$/ A PARIS (in an oval) / (cross of Legion of Honor) / C".

One of four early L.A. Buffet bass clarinets.

Rice 2009a, 288-289.

2013.01

RIGHT: *13-key bass clarinet in C*, Louis-Auguste Buffet, Paris, ca. 1845.

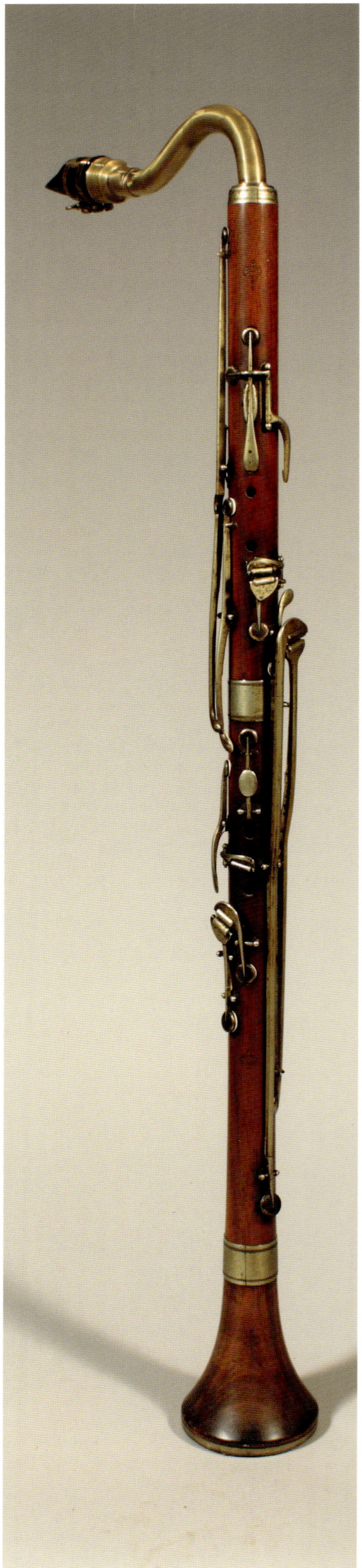

18-key tenor saxophone in B♭, Buescher Co., Elkhart, Indiana, 1939.

Ebonite mouthpiece; nickel-silver ligature; brass gold lacquer. Three sections: mouthpiece, neck, body. Eighteen keys: fifteen touches, ten plateau keys, mother-of-pearl touch covers. Plateau keys, L1, L2, L3, R1, R2, R3, alternate key for f^3 (R1, mother-of-pearl touch cover), "bis" touch B♭-B trill (L2, mother-of-pearl touch cover), touch G♯-G trill (R2). Octave (LT, automatic), f^2 (L1), d^2 (L1), E♭^{2} (L1), G♯ (L4), B♭ (L4), C (L4), B (L4), C♯ (L4), e^2 (R1), C (R1), B♭ (R1), F♯ (R3, mother-of-pearl key cover), E♭ (R4), C (R4). Four red plastic rollers between B♭, C, B and C♯ (L4), two rollers between E♭ (R4) and C (R4). Serial no. 290811.

Engraved on bell: "BUESCHER / ARISTOCRAT / ELKHART-IND-USA".

1943.01

17-key tenor (C-Melody) saxophone in C, Buescher Co., Elkhart, Indiana, 1922.

Ebonite mouthpiece; nickel-silver ligature; silver-plated satin finish brass. Three sections: mouthpiece, neck, body. Seventeen keys: fifteen touches, eight plateau keys, mother-of-pearl touch covers. Plateau keys, L1, L2, L3, R1, R2, R3, "bis" touch B♭-B trill (L2, mother-of-pearl touch cover), touch G♯-G trill (R2). Octave (LT, automatic), f^2 (L1), d^2 (L1), E♭^{2} (L1), G♯ (L4), B♭ (L4), C (L4), B (L4), C♯ (L4), e^2 (R1), C (R1), B♭ (R1), F♯ (R3), E♭ (R4), C (R4). Four black plastic rollers between B♭, C, B and C♯ (L4), two rollers between E♭ and C (R4). Serial no. 107843.

Engraved on bell: "BUESCHER / ELKHART IND."

1987.03

14-key baritone saxophone in E♭, C.G. Conn Ltd., Elkhart, Indiana, ca. 1914.

Ebonite mouthpiece; ligature; silver-plated brass. Three sections: mouthpiece, neck, body. Fourteen keys: twelve touches, seven plateau keys, mother-of-pearl touch covers. Plateau keys, L1, L2, L3, R1, R2, R3, "bis" touch B♭-B trill (L2, mother-of-pearl touch cover). Octave (LT, automatic), d^2 (L1), E♭^{2} (L1), G♯ (L4), B♭ (L4), C (L4), B (L4), C♯ (L4), C (R1), B♭ (R1), F♯ (R3), E♭ (R4), C (R4). Four black plastic rollers between B♭, C, B, and C♯ (L4), two rollers between E♭ and C (R4). Serial no. 30375.

Engraved on bell: "MADE BY / C.G. CONN / ELKHART, IND."

1994.06

18-key tenor saxophone in B♭, Buescher Co., Elkhart, Indiana, 1939.

17-key tenor (C-Melody) saxophone in C, Buescher Co., Elkhart, Indiana, 1922.

14-key baritone saxophone in E♭, C.G. Conn Ltd., Elkhart, Indiana, ca. 1914.

17-key alto saxophone in E♭, Grand Rapids Band Instrument Co., Grand Rapids, Minnesota, ca. 1930.

Ebonite mouthpiece; sliver plated ligature; brass. Three sections: mouthpiece, neck, body. Seventeen keys: fifteen touches, eight plateau keys, mother-of-pearl touch covers. Plateau keys, L1, L2, L3, R1, R2, R3; "bis" touch B♭-B trill (L2, with a mother-of-pearl touch cover), touch G♯-G trill (R2). Octave (LT, automatic), f^2 (L1), d^2 (L1), E♭^{2} (L1), G♯ (L4), B♭ (L4), C (L4), B (L4), C♯ (L4), e^2 (R1), C (R1), B♭ (R1), F♯ (R3), E♭ (R4), C (R4). Four black plastic rollers between B♭, C, B and C♯ (L4), two black rollers between E♭ and C (R4). Serial no. 75287.

Engraved on bell: "(flower) / GRAND RAPIDS / BAND INST. CO. / Grand Rapids / Mich. / (flower)."

1994.08.

17-key alto saxophone in E♭, Grand Rapids Band Instrument Co., Grand Rapids, Minnesota, ca. 1930.

11-key alto saxophone in E♭, Adolphe Sax et Cie, Paris, ca. 1860.

Wooden mouthpiece; ligature; brass. Three sections: mouthpiece, neck, body. Eleven brass keys: eleven touches, six plateau keys, L1, L2, L3, R1, R2, R3. Octave 1 (LT), Octave 2, d^2 (L1), E♭^{2} (L1), G♯ (L4), B (L4), C♯ (L4), C (R1), B♭ (R1), E♭ (R4), C (R4). Serial no. 20572.

Engraved on bell: "No. 20572 / Saxophone alto en mi. b♭. Breveté / Adophe Sax à Paris / F^{teur} de la M^{son} M^{ilre} de l'Empereur / 50, Rue S^{t}. Georges à Paris/ AS (intertwined)".

Young 1993, 203; Howe 2003b, 173.

1999.01

11-key alto saxophone in E♭, Adolphe Sax et Cie, Paris, ca. 1860.

11-key tenor saxophone in B♭, Adolphe Sax et Cie, Paris, ca. 1865.

Ebonite mouthpiece; ligature; brass. Three sections: mouthpiece, neck, body. Eleven brass keys: eleven touches, six plateau keys, L1, L2, L3, R1, R2, R3. Octave 1 (LT), Octave 2, d^2 (L1), E♭^{2} (L1), G♯ (L4), B (L4), C♯ (L4), C (R1), B♭ (R1), E♭ (R4), C (R4). Serial no. 27340.

Stamped on mouthpiece: "Johnston-Selmer, New York"; engraved on bell: "No. 27340 / Saxophone tenor en Si. –♭ Breveté / Adolphe Sax F^{teur} Breveté / de la M^{son} M^{ilre} de l'Empereur / 50, Rue S^{t}. Georges à Paris / AS (intertwined)".

Young 1993, 204; Howe 2003b, 175.

1999.02

11-key tenor saxophone in B♭, Adolphe Sax et Cie, Paris, ca. 1865.

10-key soprano saxophone in B♭, Adolphe Sax et Cie, Paris, ca. 1859.

Wooden mouthpiece; ligature; brass. Two sections: mouthpiece, body. Ten brass keys: ten touches, six plateau keys, L1, L2, L3, R1, R2, R3. Octave 1 (LT), Octave 2, d^2 (L1), E♭^{2} (L1), G♯ (L4), B (L4), C♯ (L4), B♭ (R1), E♭ (R4), C (R4). Serial no. 18672.

Stamped on mouthpiece: "A. Lelandais / France"; engraved on bell: "No. 18672 / Saxophone soprano en Si ♭ Breveté / Adolphe Sax à Paris / F^{teur} de la M^{son} M^{ilre} de l'Empereur" / AS (intertwined)"; stamped on bell: "53 / L & I".

Young 1993, 201–203; Howe 2003b, 173.

1999.03

LEFT: *10-key soprano saxophone in B♭*, Adolphe Sax et Cie, Paris, ca. 1859.

10-key bass saxophone in B♭, Adolphe Sax et Cie, Paris, ca. 1870.

Wooden mouthpiece; ligature; brass. Three sections: mouthpiece, neck, body. Ten brass keys: ten touches, six plateau keys, L1, L2, L3, R1, R2, R3. Octave 1 (LT), Octave 2, d^2 (L1), E♭^{2} (L1), G♯ (L4), B (L4), C♯ (L4), B♭ (R1), E♭ (R4), C (R4).

Engraved on bell: "no. 34287 / Saxophone basse en Si. ♭. breveté / Adolphe Sax à Paris / F^{teur} de la M^{son} Mil^{re} de l'Empereur / 50 Rue St. Georges à Paris" / AS (intertwined)".

Young 1993, 205; Howe 2003b, 176.

1999.05

RIGHT: *10-key bass saxophone in B♭*, Adolphe Sax et Cie, Paris, ca. 1870.

10-key baritone saxophone in E♭,
Adolphe Sax et Cie, Paris, ca. 1864.

Wooden mouthpiece; ligature; brass. Three sections: mouthpiece, neck, body. Ten pillar-mounted brass keys: ten touches, six plateau keys, L1, L2, L3, R1, R2, R3, B key positioned behind the bell. Octave 1 (LT), Octave 2, d^2 (L1), E♭^{2} (L1), G♯ (L4), B (L4), C♯ (L4), B♭ (R1), E♭ (R4), C (R4). Serial no. 26063.

Stamped on mouthpiece: "Dolnet Lefèvre & Cie, PARIS"; engraved on bell: "No. 26063 / Saxophone baryton en mi ♭ breveté / Adolphe Sax à Paris / F^{teur} de la M^{son} Mil^{re} de l'Empereur" / AS (intertwined)".

Young 1993, 205.

2000.03

10-key baritone saxophone in E♭, Adolphe Sax et Cie, Paris, ca. 1864.

16-key alto saxophone in E♭,
Leblanc, Paris, Semi-Rationnel model, ca. 1935.

Ebonite mouthpiece; ligature; silver-plated brass. Three sections: mouthpiece, neck, body. Sixteen keys: seventeen touches, eight plateau keys, mother-of-pearl touch covers. Plateau keys, L1, L2, L3, R1, R2, R3, "bis" touch B♭-B trill (L2, mother-of-pearl touch cover). Octave (LT, automatic), f♯^{2} (L1, to the right) f^2 (L1, to the right), d^2 (L1 to the left), E♭^{2} (L1 to the left), G♯ (L4), B♭ (L4), C (L4), B (L4), C♯ (L4), e^2 (R1), C (R1), B♭ (R1), F♯ (R3, black plastic touch cover), E♭ (R4), C (R4). Four black plastic rollers between B♭, C, B, and C♯ (L4), two rollers between E♭ and C (R4). Serial no. 80.

Stamped on mouthpiece: "LEBLANC / PARIS"; ferrule above U-bend of bell: "SRB-80"; bell, engraved above chevron: "80"; engraved in chevron: "G. LEBLANC / 90 Rue des Rigoles (cursive) / PARIS". "SRB" [semi-rationnel] above an engraving of a banner.

The Rationnel system introduced by Charles Houvenaghel in 1931 aided fingering and trills; the Semi-Rationnel system was a simplified version introduced at the same time. Although both versions were well designed, they were not popular and few instruments were made. A very similar Leblanc alto Semi-Rationnel model is in the Musée de la Musique, E.996.2.1, serial no. 15, made at 90 Rue des Rigoles. Other examples are seen on the web site http://thesax.info/gallery3/index.php/Leblanc/Semi-Rationnel--SRB, accessed Dec. 8, 2013.

MacGillivray 1959, 68-70; Voorhees 2000, 219; Kampman 2005, 110; Cottrell 2012, 88.

2001.41

LEFT: *16-key alto saxophone in E♭*, Leblanc, Paris, Semi-Rationnel model, ca. 1935.

10-key sopranino saxophone in E♭,
Adolphe Sax fils, Paris, ca. 1910.

Cut-down wooden soprano saxophone mouthpiece; ligature; silver-plated brass. Two sections: mouthpiece, body. Ten silver-plated brass keys: ten touches, six plateau keys, L1, L2, L3, R1, R2, R3. Octave 1 (LT), Octave 2, d^2 (L1), E♭^{2} (L1), G♯ (L4), B (L4), C♯ (L4), B♭ (R1), E♭ (R4), C (R4). L=477.7 (with mouthpiece).

Stamped on mouthpiece: "A Lelandais / France"; back of bell: "(AS monogram; FILS on letter S) / MÉDAILLE D'OR 1900 (in frame) / Adolphe SAX / 84, RUE MYRHA / PARIS".

This is one of the earliest surviving sopranino saxophones.

2002.49

LEFT: *10-key sopranino saxophone in E♭,* Adolphe Sax fils, Paris, ca. 1910.

11-key soprano saxophone in B♭,
François Sudre, Paris, ca. 1890.

Wooden mouthpiece; ligature; brass. Two sections: mouthpiece, body. Eleven brass keys: eleven touches, six plateau keys, L1, L2, L3, R1, R2, R3, platform for insertion of music lyre. Octave 1 (LT), Octave 2, d^2 (L1), E♭^{2} (L1), G♯ (L4), B (L4), C♯ (L4), C (R1), B♭ (R1), E♭ (R4), C (R4). In case. L=643 (with mouthpiece).

Engraved on bell: "FS (in monogram) / 83 MÉDAILLES & BREVETÉ (in banner) / Halari (in cursive) / DIPLÔME D'HONNEUR / F. SUDRE / SEUL FORN[R] DE LA MARINE / A PARIS".

2002.60

RIGHT: *11-key soprano saxophone in B♭,* François Sudre, Paris, ca. 1890.

10-key soprano saxophone (curved) in B♭, Henri Sax, Paris, ca. 1905.

Brass. Two sections: mouthpiece (missing), body (with upturned bell). Ten keys: ten levers, six plateau keys, L1, L2, L3, R1, R2, R3, music lyre inserted in platform in center of body. Octave 1 (LT), Octave 2 (LT), B (L4), C (R4), C♯ (L4), E♭ (R4), G♯ (L4), B♭ (R1), d^2 (L2), E♭^{2} (L1).

Engraved on bell: "Henri Sax / Paris (cursive)".

2004.02

LEFT: *10-key soprano saxophone (curved) in B♭*, Henri Sax, Paris, ca. 1905.

15-key alto saxophone in E♭, Grafton (John E. Dallas & Sons, Ltd., London), ca. 1955.

White plastic mouthpiece; ligature; cream-colored acrylic plastic. Three sections: mouthpiece, brass neck, body (with upturned bell). Fifteen keys: seventeen touches, nine plateau keys, mother-of-pearl touch covers. Plateau keys, L1, L2, L3, R1, R2, R3; "bis" touch B♭-B trill (L2), F♯ (R3) touch. Octave (LT, automatic), f^2 (L1), d^2 (L1), E♭^{2} (L1), G♯ (L4), B♭ (L4), C (L4), B (L4), C♯ (L4), e^2 (R1), C (R1), B♭ (R1), F♯ (R3, with a mother-of-pearl touch), E♭ (R4), C (R4). Four cream plastic rollers between B♭, C, B, and C♯ (L4), two rollers between E♭ and C (R4).

Stamped on bell: "Grafton (cursive)"; name molded on transparent plastic above C pad: "Grafton (cursive)".

Hector Sommaruga applied for British patents (nos. 604,407 and 604,418) in 1945 and 1946, granted in 1948; received a US patent (no. 2,471,290) in 1949. The name "Grafton" was adopted from a street in north London where Sommaruga initially established his company.

Dullat 1999, 69-71; Dullat 2010b, 122, 153-154, 282–283, 297; Cottrell 2012, 89-91, 356.

2004.04

RIGHT: *15-key alto saxophone in E♭*, Grafton (John E. Dallas & Sons, Ltd., London), ca. 1955.

13-key octavin in C, Oscar Adler, Markneukirchen, ca. 1900.

Black wood mouthpiece; ligature; rosewood. Four sections: mouthpiece, neck, body (in bassoon shape), bell (nickel-silver pointing outward). Thirteen pillar-mounted nickel-silver keys, rings for R2, R3, nickel-silver ferrules. Octave, half-hole key (L1), C^1 (R1), B♭ (L2), B♭ (R1), G♯ (L3), F♯ (L4), F (L4), E♭ (R3), C♯ (R4), C (R4), B (L1 lower phalange), B♭ (L1 lower phalange), A (L1 lower phalange).

Stamped on body: "C / OSCAR ADLER / D.R.P. [Deutsches Reichspatent] 83005".

The German patent for the octavin was awarded to Oscar Adler and Hermann Jordan on Sept. 17, 1895 (no. 83,005).

Dullat 2010a, 55; Dullat 2010b, 52.

1999.21

LEFT: *13-key octavin in C*, Oscar Adler, Markneukirchen, ca. 1900.

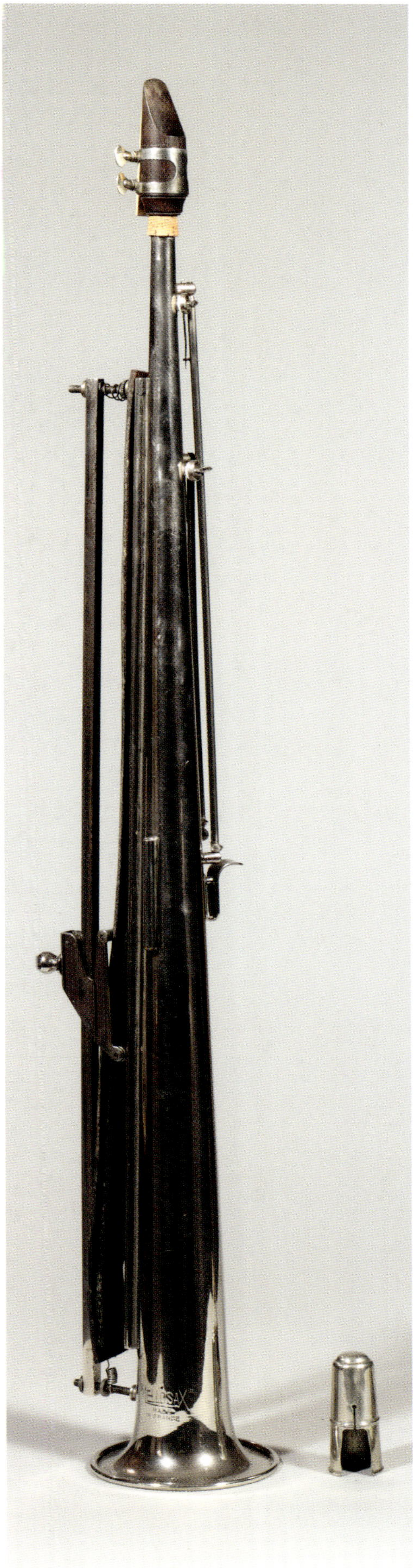

Slide saxophone or Mellowsax, Anonymous, of French origin, ca. 1930.

Wooden mouthpiece; ligature; nickel-silver. Two sections: mouthpiece, body. Knob attached above body for slide, two octave keys, nickel-silver clarinet mouthpiece cap. L=680 (with mouthpiece).

Stamped on body above bell: "MELLOWSAX: / MADE / IN FRANCE".

René Émile Lazare of Paris and William Clapham of Chantilly patented a slide saxophone in 1928 in France; in 1929 in Germany (no. 485,234); and in the US (no. 1,722,249).

Cohen 1994, 8; Van Oostrom 2009, 121, 125; Dullat 2010b, 39, 59, 116, 143-144.

1999.22

RIGHT: *Slide saxophone or Mellowsax*, Anonymous, of French origin, ca. 1930.

Slide saxophone or Swanee-sax, Anonymous, of English origin, ca. 1930.

Ebonite mouthpiece; ligature; nickel-silver. Three sections: mouthpiece, curved brass neck, body, (knob for slide). Pitch letters stamped on left of handle, nickel-silver clarinet mouthpiece cap. L=495 (with mouthpiece).

Stamped on back of body: "PATENT № 277221/27 / FOREIGN PATENTS APPLIED FOR".

The 1927 British patent (no. 277,221) was taken out by Samuel Bowley Barnes, London, illustrated with both a straight body and a saxophone-shaped body.

Cohen, 1994, 6-8; Van Oostroom, 2009, 121, 127; Dullat, 2010b, 281, 295.

1999.23

Slide saxophone or Swanee-sax, Anonymous, of English origin, ca. 1930.

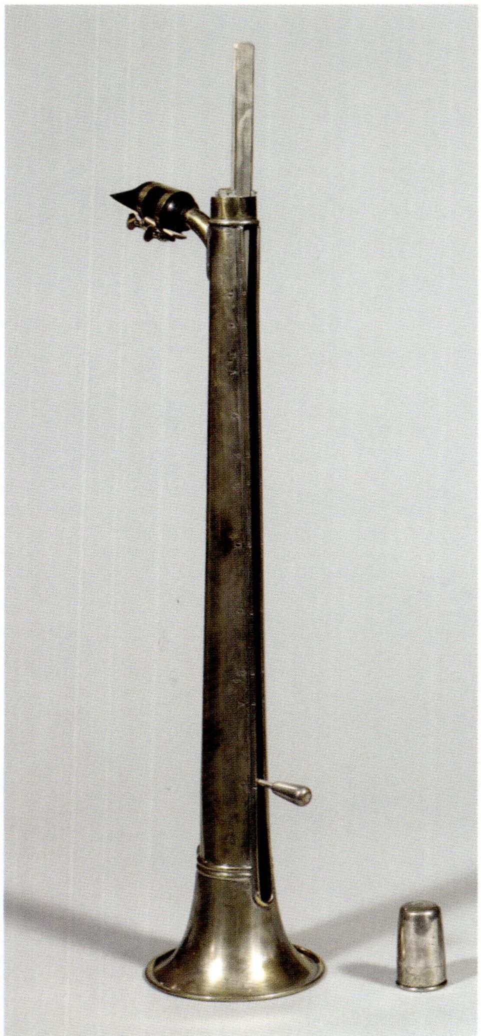

2-key saxie, Couesnon & Cie, Paris, ca. 1925.

Ebonite mouthpiece; ligature; nickel-silver. Two sections: mouthpiece, body (saxophone-shaped with large resonance hole). Two nickel-silver keys: register, key for f♯^{1}, d♯^{2} or f♯^{2}. Instrument half the size of alto saxophone. L=730 (with mouthpiece).

Stamped on bell: "COUESNON & CIE / -PARIS- / CHATEAU-THIERRY / FRANCE / =SAXIE= / U.S. PATENT JUNE 3^{d} 1924 / -B^{TÉ} S.G.D.G.-"

In 1924, Frederick B. Hammann of Baltimore, Maryland, took out US patent (no. 1,496,535) for the instrument as a toy.

Dullat 1999; Rycroft 1999, 195-201; Van Oostrom, 2009, 119, 123.

1999.29

2-key saxie, Couesnon & Cie, Paris, ca. 1925.

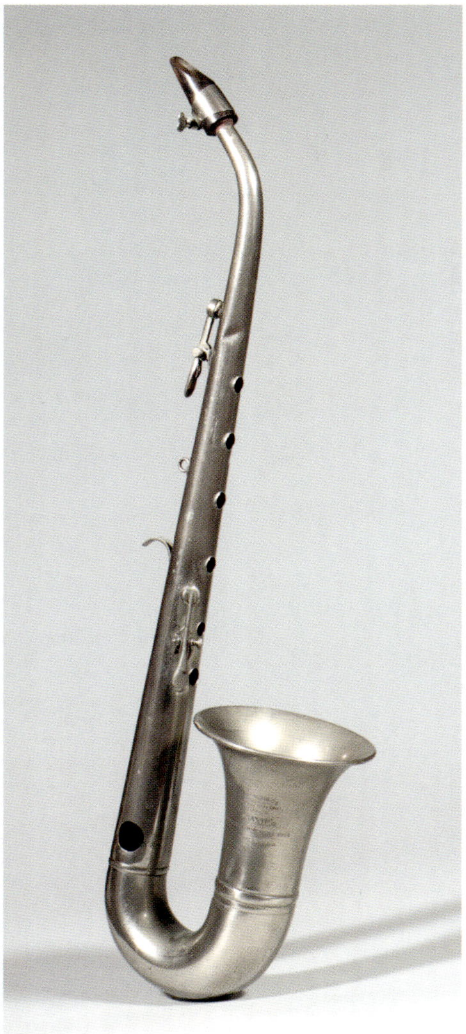

15-key soprano saxello in B♭, H. N. White Co., Cleveland, Ohio, ca. 1925.

Ebonite mouthpiece; ligature; silver-plated brass. Three sections: mouthpiece, (curved) neck, body (with bell pointing forward and gold wash inside of bell). Fifteen keys: fourteen touches, seven plateau keys, L1, L2, L3, R1, R2, R3, mother-of-pearl touch covers. "Bis" touch B♭-B trill (L2, mother-of-pearl touch cover). Octave (LT, automatic), d^2 (L1), E♭^{2} (L1), G♯ (L4), B♭ (L4), C (L4), B (L4), C♯ (L4), e^2 (R1), C (R1), B♭ (R1), F♯ (R3), E♭ (R4), C (R4). Three black plastic rollers between B♭, C, B, and C♯ (L4), two rollers between E♭ and C (R4).

Stamped on mouthpiece: "H. N. White"; engraved on bell: "KING / Saxello / MADE BY / The H.N. WHITE CO. / CLEVD.O".

In 1926, a US patent (no. 1,605,101) was approved for Henry E. Dreves on behalf of H.N. White Company for a soprano saxophone with bell pointing forward.

Cohen 1985, 7; Dullat 1999, 71–73; Rice 2004, 1, 5.

2001.05

15-key soprano saxello in B♭, H. N. White Co., Cleveland, Ohio, ca. 1925.

2-key saxie, Couesnon & Cie, Paris, ca. 1925.

Ebonite mouthpiece; ligature; brass. Two sections: mouthpiece, body (saxophone-shaped with large resonance hole). Two nickel-silver keys: register, key for f♯^{1}, d♯^{2}, or f♯^{2}. Instrument half the size of alto saxophone. L=620.

Stamped on bell: "COUESNON & CIE / -PARIS- / CHATEAU-THIERRY / FRANCE / =SAXIE= / U.S. PATENT JUNE 3^d 1924 / -B^{TÉ} S.G.D.G.-".

In 1924, Frederick B. Hammann of Baltimore, Maryland, took out US patent (no. 1,496,535) for the instrument as a toy.

Dullat 1999, 76-77; Rycroft, 1999, 195-201; Van Oostrom, 2009, 119, 123.

2002.28

Slide saxophone or bass Swanee-Sax, Anonymous, of English origin, ca. 1930.

Ebonite mouthpiece; nickel-silver body. Two sections: mouthpiece, body. The body has an opening in the front for a knob, curved brass neck, upward-pointing bell. H=505.

Stamped on side of bell: "SWANEE-SAX / REGISTERED / PATENT N^o / 277221/ 27 / BRITISH MADE".

The 1927 British patent (no. 277,221) was taken out by Samuel Bowley Barnes, London, and illustrated with a straight body and a saxophone-shaped body. Designated as model D, advertised with range of two octaves, e♭ to e♭^{2}.

Cohen, 1994, 6-8; Dullat 1999, 77; Van Oostroom 2009, 121, 127; Dullat 2010b, 281, 295.

2004.10

13-key tarogato in B♭, Armin Sternberg, Budapest, ca. 1895.

Black wood mouthpiece; maple body; brass ferrules. Four sections: mouthpiece, l.h. joint, r.h. joint, bell. Thirteen pillar-mounted keys, Octave (LT), c♯ (L1), c (R1), E♭ (R1), B♭ (L3), G♯ (L4), F♯ (R3), F (R3), E♮ (R4), C (R4), C♯ (L4), B (L4), low B♭ (RT). L=726.

Stamp partially effaced on l.h. joint, bell: "STERNBERG ARMIN / CS. ESKIR. UDV / HANGSVER-GYAR / BUDAPEST".

2006.23

2-key saxie, Couesnon & Cie, Paris, ca. 1925.

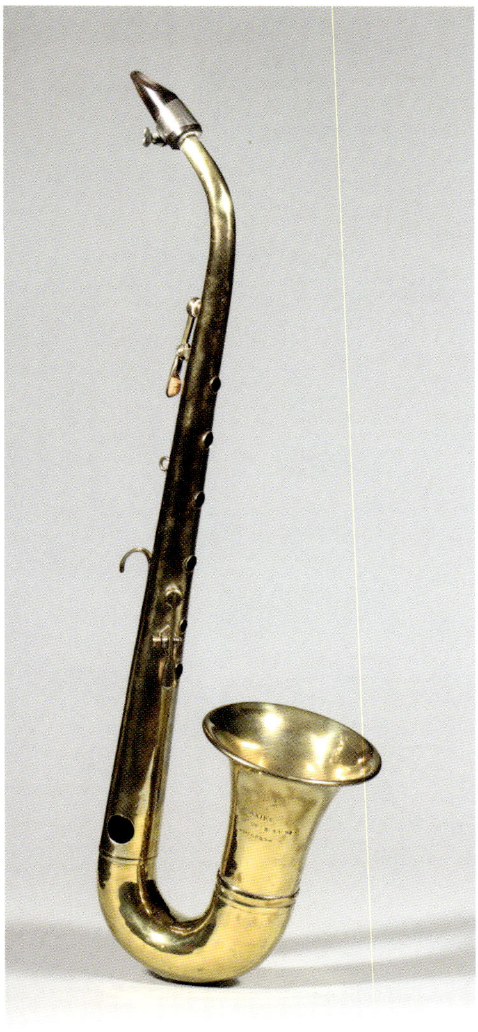

Slide saxophone or bass Swanee-Sax, Anonymous, of English origin, ca. 1930.

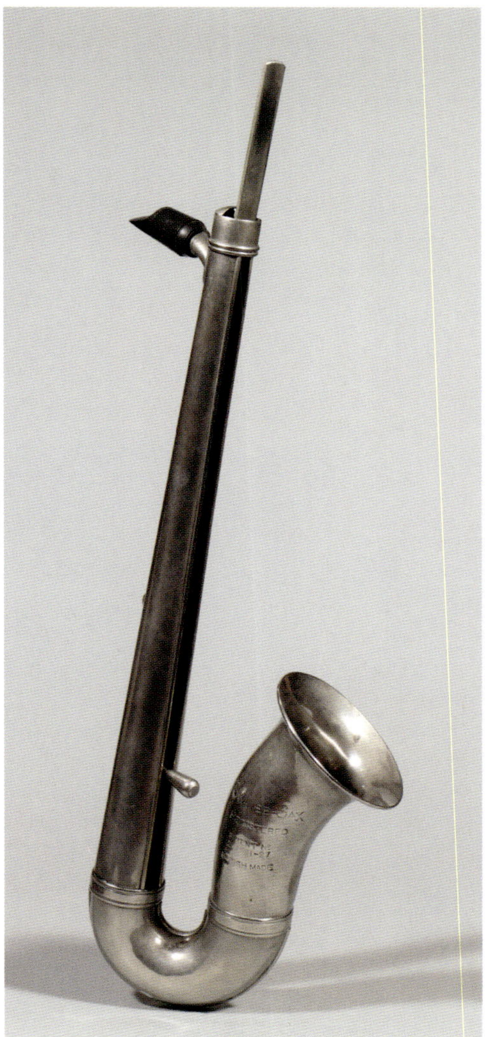

13-key tarogato in B♭, Armin Sternberg, Budapest, ca. 1895.

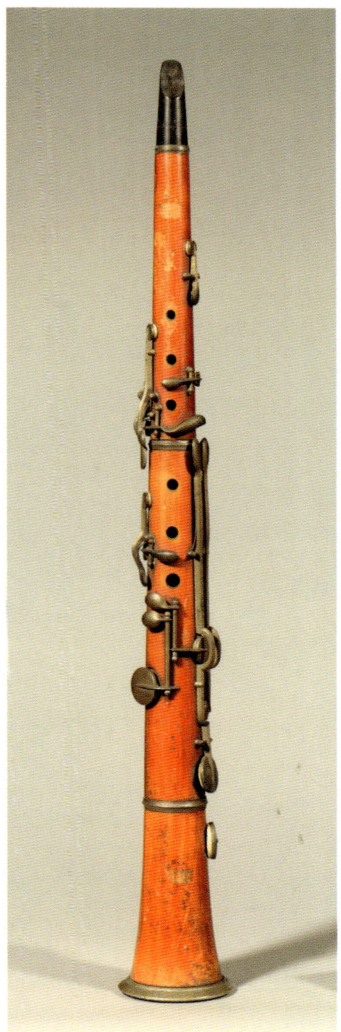

Two Double Hornpipes, Anonymous, North Africa, ca. 1920.

Two similar hornpipes. Three sections: two idioglot reeds, two bodies, two bells. Two idioglott reeds are inserted into two bamboo pipes lashed and glued together, five finger holes on each pipe, two animal horns are lashed to the pipes. L for 2005.04a=220; L for 2005.04b=266.

Both reeds are taken into the mouth while blowing, both of the first three finger holes are covered by the finger and second phalange of L1, L2, L3, the last two by the finger and second phalange of R1, R2.

No inscription.

2005.04a-b

BELOW & RIGHT: *Two Double Hornpipes*, Anonymous, North Africa, ca. 1920.

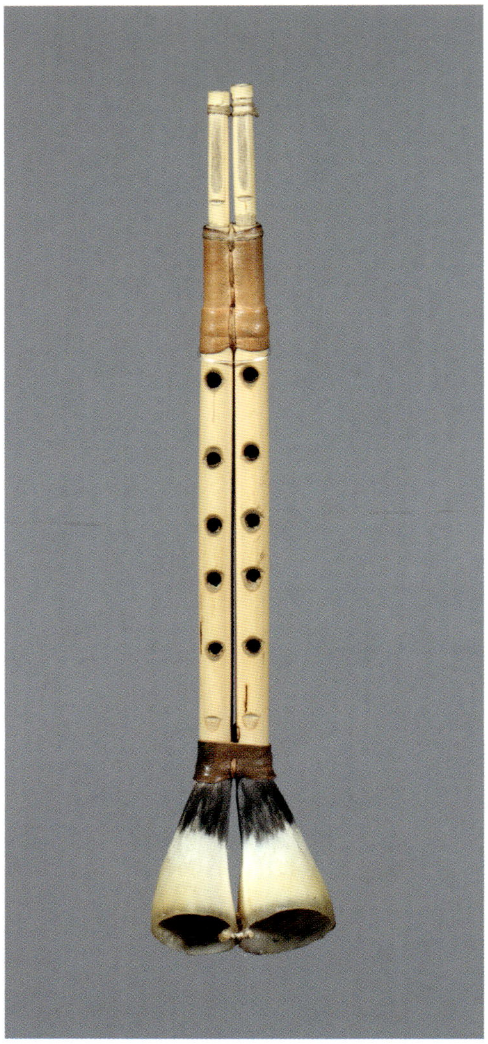

Dudelsack (bagpipe), Anonymous, near Pilsen, Bohemia, ca. 1850.

Brown wood chanter; brass ferrule; bag. Four sections: brown cloth bag, bellows with handle, chanter with bell, drone with bell. Chanter: seven holes, LT, L1, L2, L3, R1, R2, R3, resonance hole, brass elbow joint, connected to curved animal horn, connected to oval decorated brass bell. Drone: turned brown wood, large brass ferrules, brass elbow joint, connected to curved cow horn, connected to large oval decorated brass bell. Chanter and drone have single, heteroglott reeds. Large, pear-shaped carved and decorated bellows, large brass handle, connected to bag with carved and decorated brown wood at 45 degree angle.

L of drone on longest side=1,041; L of chanter on longest side=609.

No inscription.

Cwach 2012.

2007.05

BELOW: *Dudelsack* (bagpipe), Anonymous, near Pilsen, Bohemia, ca. 1850.

CHAPTER 5
FREE-REED INSTRUMENTS

Reed organ, Estey Cottage Organ Manufactory, Brattleboro, Vermont, 1877.

Mahogany veneered; fretwork upper section; red cloth backing; ledge for music. Two rounded sides opposite the nameboard continued in lower section by rounded legs attached to base. Fallboard covers keyboard, two oval-shaped fretwork sections below keyboard, on either side, red cloth backing. Serial no. 69403. Compass: 5 octaves, FF to f^3; nine stops above the keyboard operate: Diapason 8'; Melodia 8'; Viola; II Forte; Vox Humana; Forte; Vox Jubilante; Violetta; and Flute 4'. Three-measure length=488; natural coverings: ivory, no scribe lines; sharps: wood stained black; key fronts: ivory. L=1,055; W=585; H=1,010.

Inscription on nameboard in gilt letters: "J.Estey & Co. // Brattleboro, Vt."

1960.01

Reed organ, Estey Cottage Organ Manufactory, Brattleboro, Vermont, 1877, and detail of pull stops.

Rocking melodeon (melodion), Abraham Prescott, Concord, New Hampshire, 1845.

Rosewood; buttons for chromatic scale; metal reeds in individual slots; bellows. Compass: 3 octaves + 4, F to a^2; ivory button keyboard staggered in two rows; accidentals marked with black circle inlaid on top. "Forte-piano" shutter opened by white pearl button on left, opens bellows by springs under top. One circular bone decoration around holes on top is missing. Inside case in pen marked "9.4.45", stamped "568". L=484.

Engraved on brass plate holding damper button: "A PRESCOTT / MANUFACTURER / CONCORD N.H."

Libin 1985, 193-194; Gellerman 1998, 192.

1987.05

Rocking melodeon (melodion), Abraham Prescott, Concord, New Hampshire, 1845.

Symphonium, Charles Wheatstone, London, ca. 1830.

Rectangular; nickel-silver; four out-turned legs. Back engraved with foliate wreath. Oval embouchure hole placed over an ivory bushing. Fifteen ivory-tipped buttons (eight on the right and seven on the left) open valves for reeds when pressed. The right buttons are for C, F, B, E, A, D, G, and F♯; the left buttons for G, C, F, B, E, A, and F♯. Diatonic tones distributed alternately between the right and left fingers, similar to Wheatstone's later design of the concertina. Compass is g^1 to c^3 in a diatonic scale, a sounding pitch of 425 Herz. H=54; D=23; W=55.

Engraved on blow hole side: "BY HIS MAJESTY'S LETTERS PATENT. / C. WHEATSTONE, INVENTOR, / 20, Conduit St. Regent Str.^{t} / LONDON."

No serial number.

Another Symphonium is at the Museum of Fine Arts, Boston, 1996.115.

Neil 1991, 123.

1993.04

Symphonium, Charles Wheatstone, London, ca. 1830.

Bible reed organ, Metzler and Co., London, ca. 1900, and inscription.

Portable reed organ, Estey Organ Co., Brattleboro, Vermont, ca. 1943.

Folding case; black stained wood; keyboard, compass: 4 octaves, C-c^3; two pedals attached with green and yellow stripped straps to bellows underneath keyboard. Three-octave measure, 483; natural coverings: ivory, contiguous heads and tails; sharps: wood stained black; key fronts: plastic. L=741; W=418; H=737.

No name board inscription; printed paper label pasted inside: "ESTEY ORGAN CORPORATION / Manufacturer / BRATTLEBORO, VERMONT, U.S.A. / No. 475581 / Assembled___________ / Tested__________ / Corrected__________ / Inspected___________".

Gellerman 1998, 69.

2000.04

Bible reed organ, Metzler and Co., London, ca. 1900.

Oak; folding music desk; two book-shaped bellows above keyboard; two hooks on front below keyboard. To be placed on table and played with right hand. Compass: 3½ octaves, C-c^3; three-octave measure: 426; natural coverings: ivory, contiguous heads and tails; sharps: wood stained black, key fronts: plastic. L=607; D=205; H=123.

Inscription in black rectangle with decorated border on inside of lid, in gilt: "Metzler & Co. / 42, GREAT MARLBOROUGH STREET, LONDON."

2002.79

Reed organ, George A. Prince, Albany, New York, ca. 1870.

Stained mahogany; dark wood lid and fallboard; folding carved music desk; four rosewood, octagonal-sided, bulbous legs; wide, carved wooden skirt below keyboard; carved lyre-shaped pedal stand; two metal pedals: bellows, swell; two metal hand stops on each side above keyboard. Compass: 5 octaves, FF-f^3. Three-octave measure: 426; natural coverings: ivory, no scribe lines, rounded fronts; sharps: ebony; key fronts: wood. L=607; D=205; H=123.

Inscription on nameboard on brass plaque with raised letters: "GEO.A.PRINCE & CO. / BUFFALO, N.Y."

2007.08

Portable reed organ, Estey Organ Co., Brattleboro, Vermont, ca. 1943.

Reed organ, George A. Prince, Albany, New York, ca. 1870, and inscription.

Harmonium, Anonymous, of French origin, ca. 1890.

Rosewood; rectangular shape, two butterfly-shaped openings above decorative grained brown-wood; two ornamental supports on each side of front, left damaged; top decorated with circular and curved openings, with white material backing. Compass: 3 octaves, F to f^3; three pull stops in front of case. Three-octave measure: 390; natural coverings: plastic, no scribe line; sharps: wood stained black; key fronts: none. L=454; W=204; D=157.

No Inscription.

2009.09

Harmonium, Anonymous, of French origin, ca. 1890.

Rocking melodeon (melodion), Abraham Prescott and Son, Concord, New Hampshire, ca. 1850.

Rosewood; buttons for chromatic scale; metal reeds in individual slots; bellows. Compass: 3 octaves +4, F to a^2; ivory button keyboard staggered in two rows; accidentals marked with black circle inlaid on top. "Forte-piano" shutter opened by brown horn button on left; bellows kept open by springs under top. L=483. Instrument in box with large blue label inside: "ABRAHAM PRESCOTT & SON, / MANUFACTURERS OF / SERAPHINES AND MELODIONS / PREMIUM BASS AND DOUBLE BASS VIOLS". Illustrations are of keyed bugle, two over-the-shoulder trombones, trumpet, accordion, clarinet bell, flute head joint, violin scroll, two reed organs, rocking melodeon.

Engraved on brass plate holding damper button: "A PRESCOTT / MANUFACTURER / CONCORD N.H."

Gellerman 1998, 192.

2011.01

Rocking melodeon (melodion), Abraham Prescott and Son, Concord, New Hampshire, ca. 1850.

Accordion, Anonymous, of French origin, ca. 1850.

Rosewood; satinwood inlay with floral pattern on both sides. Bellows covered with white paper decorated in red and blue. Top, right, two rows of eight and seven mother-of-pearl keys, round touches, staggered in two rows. Touches connected to metal lever that opens round key head. Each touch controls two metal reeds attached to a block, one speaking on the press, the other on the draw of the bellows, pressed by the left arm. Brass register key, right; brass key, left side; air key played by thumb or palm, used to fill or empty bellows without sounding a note. L=290.

No inscription.

Baines 1992, 1; Harrington and Kubik 2013.

1992.06

Accordion, Anonymous, of French origin, ca. 1850.

Accordion, Anonymous, of French origin, ca. 1840.

Rosewood; gold, red, and green inlays in floral pattern on both sides. Bellows covered with white paper decorated in green and gold diamond shapes. Top, right, two rows of eight and seven mother-of-pearl keys, square and rectangular touches staggered in two rows. Touches connected to metal lever that opens round key head. Each touch controls two metal reeds attached to a block, one speaking on the press, the other on the draw of the bellows, pressed by the left arm. Two brass register keys, right; brass air key, left. L=315.

No inscription.

Baines 1992, 1; Harrington and Kubik 2013.

1992.11

Accordion, Anonymous, of French origin, ca. 1840.

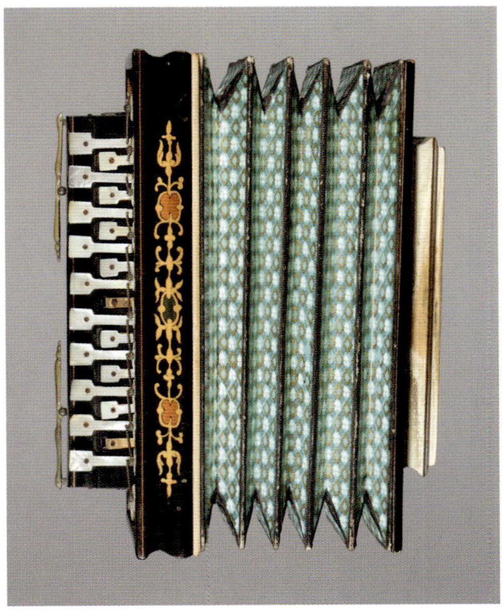

Roll harmonica, Rolmonica Music Co., Baltimore, ca. 1925.

Red and black plastic case, mouthpiece on front; lower crank with yellow plastic handle advances roll; upper crank rerolls the roll. When air is blown in the instrument, and lower crank is moved, paper roll advances so that holes are opened to allow air to enter against metal reeds in the case. Compass: about one octave. L=120; W=95.

The box with additional paper rolls reads: "ROLMONICA / TRADE MARK / MUSIC ROLL / MANUFACTURED ONLY BY / THE ROLMONICA MUSIC CO. / BALTIMORE, MD."

1994.05

Roll harmonica, Rolmonica Music Co., Baltimore, ca. 1925.

Accordion, Anonymous, of French origin, ca. 1870.

Wooden case stained black. Bellows are covered with light gray paper ornamented with red and white flowers, blue leaves, and smiling faces. Top, right, two rows of twelve mother-of-pearl keys, square and rectangular touches staggered in two rows, six missing mother-of-pearl. Touches connected to metal lever that opens key head inside case. Each touch controls two metal reeds attached to a block, one speaking on the press, the other on the draw of the bellows, pressed by the left arm. Left side has two pull stops and three brass air keys. In cardboard box. L=384.

No inscription.

Bowers 1973, 739, 741; Baines 1992, 1; Harrington and Kubik 2013.

1995.26

Accordion, Anonymous, of French origin, ca. 1870.

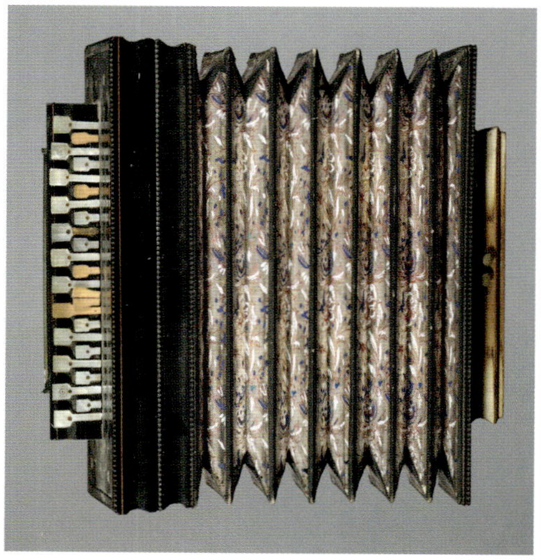

Accordion, Anonymous, of French origin, ca. 1836.

Rosewood; satinwood stringing. Bellows are covered with white paper decorated with red and green leaves. Top, right, two rows of eight and seven mother-of-pearl keys, rectangular touches, staggered in two rows. Touches connected to metal lever that opens round key head. Each touch controls two metal reeds attached to a block, one speaking on the press, the other on the draw of the bellows, pressed by the left arm. Register key on right side; left side, two brass air keys. L=279.

Instrument is accompanied by a tutor entitled *Preceptor for the French Accordion containing all the requisite Instruction & a selection of simple & pleasing AIRS arranged Expressly for the Instrument*, Boston: Joseph L. Bates, 1836, 19 pages.

No inscription

1999.04

Accordion, Anonymous, of French origin, ca. 1836.

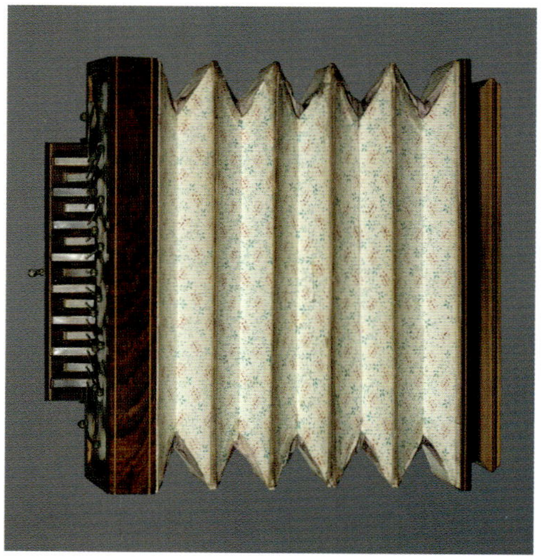

Play-A-Sax, Q-R-S De Vry Corporation, Chicago, ca. 1935.

Gold-painted nickel-silver; organette in saxophone shape; sixteen-note paper roll. When player blows and handle is moved, roll pattern opens pallets allowing air to play reeds, creating a tune. L=400.

Red label marked in black: "Q-R-S / PLAYASAX / Q-R-S De Vry / Corp."

Bowers 1973, 727, 741, 776; Van Oostrom 2009, 121, 124.

2000.05

Play-A-Sax, Q-R-S De Vry Corporation, Chicago, ca. 1935.

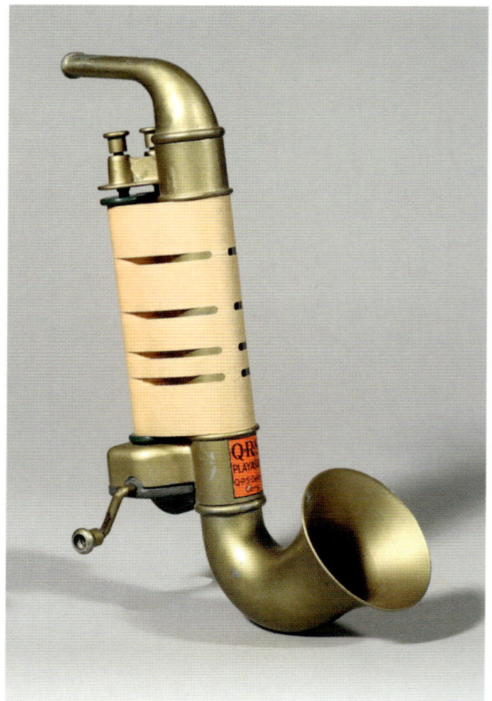

Hohner-Sax, M. Hohner, Trossingen, ca. 1922.

Brass harmonica in saxophone shape; six touches for treble reeds; four touches, blow and draw reeds; two bass reeds, lower end. Three sections: neck, body, bell. Mouthpiece and one key missing. Serial no. 233. L=695.

Engraved on bell in oval-shaped medallion: "Hohner Sax / M. HOHNER / TROSSIGEN".

Advertisement in *The Music Trade Review* (May 6, 1922), 24, offers these instruments for $5.00.

2001.09

Hohner-Sax, M. Hohner, Trossingen, ca. 1922.

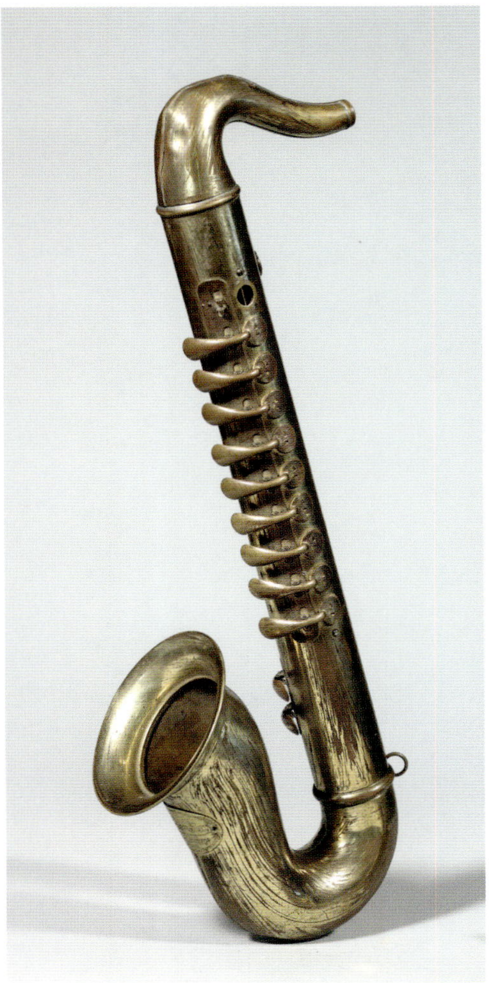

Accordion, Anonymous, of French origin, ca. 1850.

Wood; gold, gray, white, black inlays, rosewood, and light wood. Bellows covered with white paper decorated with green, red flowers, leaves. Top, right, two rows of eight mother-of-pearl keys, square and rectangular touches, staggered in two rows, one mother-of-pearl touch missing. Touches connected to metal lever that opens round key head. Each touch controls two metal reeds attached to a block, one speaking on the press, the other on the draw of the bellows, pressed by the left arm. Two brass register keys, right; three brass air keys, left. Wooden case. L=299.

No inscription.

2002.06

Accordion, Anonymous, of French origin, ca. 1850.

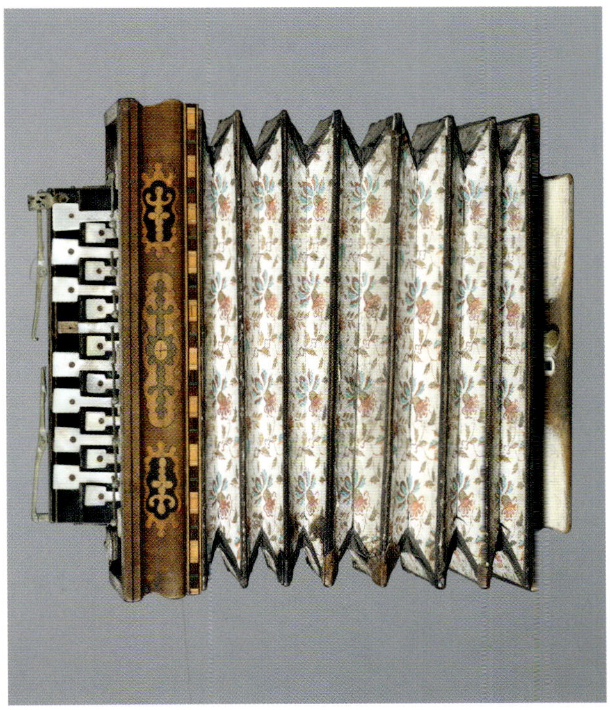

Blow accordion, Anonymous, of United States origin, ca. 1880.

Black stained wood; mouthpiece; ten round, ivory keys, right hand; connected by nickel-silver lever to round key heads; two nickel-silver air keys, left hand. L=345.

No inscription.

John F. Stratton, ca. 1878, 21: "blow accordions with ten keys, net wholesale, $.90; catalogue, $1.75."

No inscription.

2002.54

Blow accordion, Anonymous, of United States origin, ca. 1880.

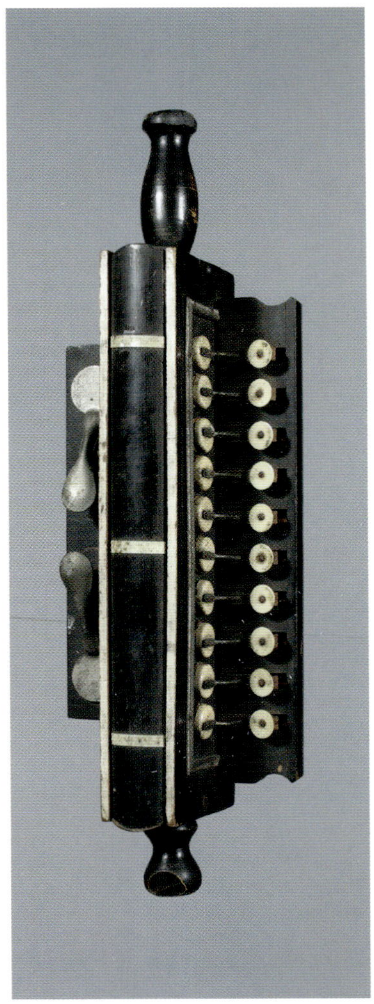

CHAPTER 6
CUP–MOUTHPIECE INSTRUMENTS

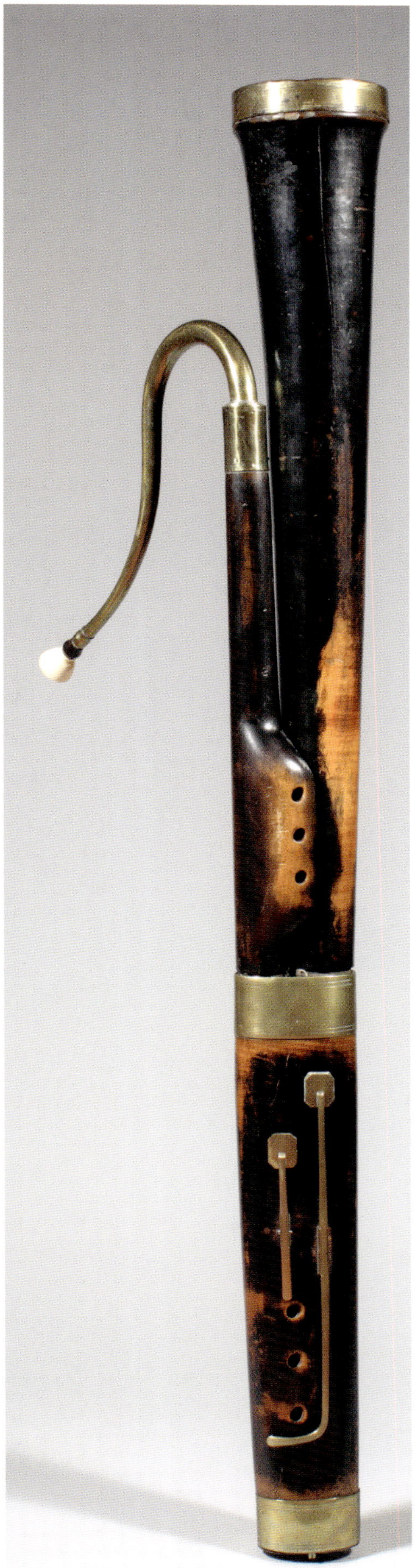

3-key bass horn, Max Stiegler, Munich, ca. 1810.

Maple; brass ferrules. Five sections: ivory mouthpiece, crook (probably original), wing joint, long joint, butt joint. Two brass keys on front of butt joint, mounted in saddles with square key heads; brass key with a large octagonal key head on back of bell.

Stamped on back of butt joint: "(lion rampant) / STIEGLER / MÜNCHEN / (five-pointed star) (five-pointed star)."

1994.03

3-key bass horn, Max Stiegler, Munich, ca. 1810.

3-key Russian bassoon, Pierre Paul Ghislain Joseph Dupré, Tournai, ca. 1820.

Maple; brass ferrules. Six sections: ivory mouthpiece, coiled crook, wing joint, long joint, butt joint, brass bell. Three saddle-mounted brass keys with round, flat key heads on long joint, wing joint, and butt joint.

Stamped on front of butt joint: "(five-pointed star) / DUPRE / A / TOURNAY / (five-pointed star)".

2009.08

3-key Russian bassoon, Pierre Paul Ghislain Joseph Dupré, Tournai, ca. 1820.

CHAPTER 7 PLUCKED & BOWED STRINGED INSTRUMENTS

Tenor banjo, Anonymous, of United States origin, ca. 1940.

Four strings; four sagittal pegs with nickel-silver plated tuners; white plastic tuner buttons. Dark wood fingerboard; seventeen metal frets. Twenty screw tightening brackets around rim; dot mother-of-pearl inlay behind fourth, sixth, ninth, eleventh frets. Broken calf head. String L=552; D of resonator=286.

No stamp on wooden rod.

1970.00

LEFT: *Tenor banjo*, Anonymous, of United States origin, ca. 1940.

Mandora, Antonio Monzino, Milano, ca. 1790.

Vaulted body constructed of separate ribs; ivory escutcheon on head; twelve ebony pegs; mother-of-pearl inlay on peg head; soundboard has intricately carved rosette inserted into sound hole. Ivory binding; soundboard decorated with painted green and brown leaves; decorative mark below rose. Ivory bound, some ivory missing; ebony fingerboard; replacement bridge for six strings; eight ivory frets on fingerboard; four ivory frets on body; mother-of-pearl inlay behind first, fifth, eighth, ninth frets. String L=615.

Printed paper label inside body: "ANtonio Monzani Fabri- / catore Iftrumenti che / abbita in Milano nella con / trada della Dogana."

1972.03

RIGHT: *Mandora*, Antonio Monzino, Milano, ca. 1790.

Guitar, with label of Francesco Stradivari, Cremona, 1740.

Six-string guitar; originally ten strings; six sagittal pegs, two missing; ebony fingerboard; nine metal frets; ivory nut; sound hole decorated with concentric rings; mustache bridge; ivory saddle. Similar body outline to guitars by Delaplanque, Lille. String L=575; L of upper bout=220; L of lower bout=275.

Printed paper label inside body: "Francifcus Stradivararius Cremonenfis / filius Antonii faciebat Anno 1*740*" (last two digits added by hand).

According to a recently found letter, Francesco Stradivari (1671–1743) worked with an individual in Cremona named Della Noce for two years supplying guitars. Sketches or forms matching this type of guitar are not found at the Museo Stradivariano in Cremona. The instrument, however, could have been made or brought to Stradivari's shop in 1740, or was made in France during the late eighteenth century, the label taken from a violin. It was possibly made by Gerard Delaplanque, Lille, ca. 1770.

Gregori 1997, 22–23.

1972.05

LEFT: *Guitar*, with label of Francesco Stradivari, Cremona, 1740.

Guitar, Anonymous, of French origin, ca. 1750.

Six-string guitar; six sagittal tuners; ebony fingerboard; boxwood nut; eleven metal frets; six metal frets on body. Double white inlay purfling; four concentric white rings around soundhole; mustache bridge added later. String L=633; L of lower bout=250.

No inscription.

1972.06

RIGHT: *Guitar*, Anonymous, of French origin, ca. 1750.

Harp-guitar, G. Jenkins, Montreal, ca. 1900.

Double-neck; black-finished top, rosewood sides and back. Guitar neck: six strings; slotted brown wood peghead; six sagittal plastic tuner buttons, mechanical tuners; ebony neck, mother-of-pearl diamond-shaped inlays; eighteen metal frets. Ivory nut, four white plastic rings around oval sound hole; decorated with four inlays of brown wood. Bass neck: twelve bass strings on separate ebony neck; without frets; tuning pins on brown wood head. Dark wood bridge for both necks; two ivory saddles. String L=650; L of upper bout=370; L of lower bout=490.

Inscription on a business card: "HARP GUITAR // MONTREAL, CANADA / G. Jenkins / MAKER / UPTOWN 1412 // 746 UNION AVE."

1986.03

Harp-guitar, G. Jenkins, Montreal, ca. 1900.

Mandolin, C.F. Martin and Co., Nazareth, Pennsylvania, Style 2, 1919.

Eighteen rosewood ribs; rosewood peg head stamped on back: "C.F. MARTIN / NAZARETH, PA."; eight white plastic, horizontal pegs; tortoiseshell pickguard; ebony bridge; ivory nut; twenty metal frets on ebony fingerboard; dot inlay on fingerboard behind fifth, seventh, tenth metal frets; oval sound hole, chevron inlay. Serial no. 7056. String L= 335.

Paper label: "C.F. MARTIN & CO. / NAZARETH, PA. / 7056".

Gruhn and Carter 1999, 460.

1987.02

LEFT: *Mandolin*, C.F. Martin and Co., Nazareth, Pennsylvania, Style 2, 1919.

Banjo, Gilbert O. Kibbe, Hartford, Connecticut, ca. 1885.

Left-handed; five-string banjo; four sagitally placed pegs; fifth peg on left side of fingerboard below fourth fret; ebony fingerboard; dot inlay behind third, fifth, seventh, tenth, thirteenth, seventeenth frets; eighteen screw-tightening brackets. Serial no. 216. String L=517; D of resonator=214.

Stamp on pole: "G.O. KIBBE 261".

Holmes 2004.

1991.09

RIGHT: *Banjo*, Gilbert O. Kibbe, Hartford, Connecticut, ca. 1885.

Guitar, Christian Friedrich Martin, Nazareth, Pennsylvania, ca. 1870.

Spruce top; rosewood back, sides; ivory, rosewood binding; ebony fingerboard; ivory nut; eighteen metal frets; ebony bridge; ivory saddle; four rosewood soundhole rings with green and white rope pattern purfling in center of rings; slotted peghead, three on a side ivory tuners. Style 2½-17. String L=615; L of upper bout=210; L of lower bout=290.

Stamped inside body: "C.F. MARTIN / NAZARETH, PA."; back of peg head "C.F. MARTIN / NEW-YORK".

Gruhn and Carter 1999, 435.

1992.08

LEFT: *Guitar*, Christian Friedrich Martin, Nazareth, Pennsylvania, ca. 1870.

Portuguese Guitar, José Vieira Maciel, San Jorge Island, Azores, ca. 1890.

Twelve-string, double strung; dark brown wood veneered head; sagittal wooden pegs, three missing; ebony fingerboard; two heart-shaped soundholes, rosewood inlay beneath soundholes; two cracks on top; single rosewood inlay on top; six-string bridge, replacement; wooden saddle; inlay of light and dark brown woods below bridge. String L=551; L of upper bout=208; L of lower bout=260.

Label inscription: "José Vieira Maciel / Oferece-se para fazer Violas / Rabecas Guitarras mais / alguns Instrumentos d'esta / Classe. Morador nos Degraus / S. Jorge. / Maciel (in pen)".

Caldeira Cabral 2007.

1994.04

RIGHT: *Portuguese Guitar*, José Vieira Maciel, San Jorge Island, Azores, ca 1890.

Guitar, John C. Haynes and Co., Boston, ca. 1870.

Six-strings; six sagittal ivory tuner buttons, brass mechanical tuners; rosewood slotted peghead; ebony fingerboard, eighteen metal frets, light wood and dark wood binding; silver medallion mounted on a wooden spar (patented dowel) in sound hole that extends from heel to end; rosewood bridge with holes; floating silver tailpiece.

Inscription on medallion in sound hole: "W^{m}. B. TILTON'S / IMPROVEMENT. / NEW YORK. / Patented (cursive) MARCH 4 1856 / ZOGBAUM & FAIRCHILD / NEW YORK."; tailpiece: "JOHN C. HAYNES & CO. / MAKERS, / BOSTON"; upper medallion: "(within a wreath) AWARDED TO / ZOGBAUM & FAIRCHILD / For / the best / Guitars. (cursive) / 'Tilton's Patent' / 1865"; medallion on tailpiece: "AMERICAN INSTITUTE / (a woman with a wreath in one hand and a flag in the other hand, next to a union shield, bald eagle, caduceus, and horn of plenty) / NEW YORK." String L=610; L of upper bout=220; L of lower bout=300.

William B. Tilton's US patent (no. 14,378) for his bridge was granted March 4, 1856. By about 1860, Ferdinand Zogbaum and Rufus Fairchild bought the rights to Tilton's patent, made guitars with it, using their label and Tilton's patent. During the late 1860s, John C. Haynes bought the rights to Tilton's patent, made guitars with it, using his label, Zogbaum and Fairchild's name, and Tilton's patent.

Gura 2003, 127-134, pl. 4-13.

1996.14

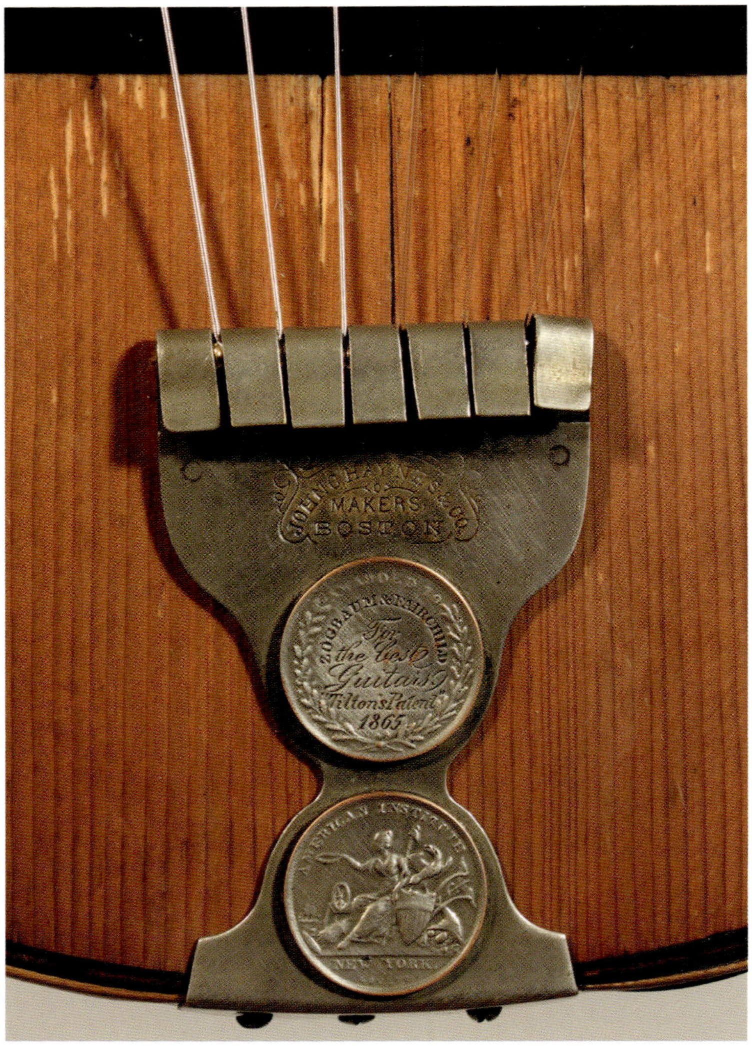

Guitar, John C. Haynes and Co., Boston, ca. 1870, medallion in sound hole, and medallion on tailpiece.

Guitar, James Lang Hewitt and Co., Boston, probably of German origin, ca. 1830.

Slotted peg head with decorated ivory button; sagittal ebony tuner buttons, brass mechanical tuners; ebony fingerboard, twelve frets, eight frets on ebony placed on body; rosewood double line binding, rosewood soundhole, five soundhole rings with mother-of-peal diamonds set in black mastic. Mustache bridge; ivory saddle; circle with ornamental decoration below bridge. String L=610.

Label inside body: "Manufactured for / JAMES L. HEWITT & C^{O}. / No. 34 & 36 Market St. / Boston."

1998.17

LEFT: *Guitar*, James Lang Hewitt and Co., Boston, probably of German origin, ca. 1830.

English guitar, attributed to James Longman and Francis Broderip, London, ca. 1780s.

Pear-shaped outline, flat front, wide grain; four lines of purfling edged with red-painted purfling; four rings of purfling; red painting in center of rings around dome rosette sound hole, in form of twelve-pointed star, each ray veneered in ebony and ivory, linked by maple flame-like shapes. Six course, wire-strung; twelve frets. Ebony-veneered convex fingerboard; twelve metal frets, four holes for capo tasto behind first four frets. Tuning head with hook finial decorated with painted square. Ten watch-key tuners; nut, bridge are missing. String L=426; D of body=275.

No inscription.

Poulopoulos, 2011.

1998.18

RIGHT: *English guitar*, attributed to James Longman and Francis Broderip, London, ca. 1780s.

Guitar, Gennaro Fabricatore, Naples, 1826.

Spruce soundboard; ebony binding, five ivory and ebony rings with mother-of-pearl ring in black mastic in center of rings, continuing around ebony fingerboard to top of peg head. Six nickel-silver horizontal tuner buttons with mechanical tuners; ebony sound hole ring with six ebony and ivory rings; decorative mother-of-pearl ring in black mastic ring. Black-stained wood moustaches cover lower bout; wooden bridge. Ebony nut; twelve nickel-silver frets on ebony neck with altered positions; seven nickel-silver frets (one missing) on body. Rosewood and ebony sides. String L=641; L of upper bout=231; L of lower bout=300.

Printed paper label in a decorated oval below a depiction of a man playing the guitar: "GENNARO FABRICATORE / Anno 18*26* (added in pen) / Strada Toledo N 297. / Napoli".

A guitar by Gennaro Fabricatore dated 1830 with similar inlay on the body and neck is in the collection of James Westbrook.

Westbrook 2005, 106.

2000.07

LEFT: *Guitar*, Gennaro Fabricatore, Naples, 1826.

Guitar, Dubois, Brussels, ca. 1840.

Spruce soundboard; ivory binding; six ebony rings with mother-of-pearl inlay and floral decorations in center of rings; ebony sound hole, nine ivory and ebony rings, mother-of-pearl inlay with floral decorations in center of rings, around sound hole. Slotted peg head veneered in ebony, decorated with mother-of-pearl banner and flowers; sagittal ivory tuners, mechanical tuners. Fingerboard veneered with mother-of-pearl, lightly engraved with buildings and scenes; seventeen metal frets; ivory nut. Rosewood rectangular bridge with curved ends and two mother-of-pearl dots; ivory saddle; mother-of-pearl, florally engraved lower section; rosewood back and sides. String L=650; L of upper bout=220; L of lower bout=300.

Stamped on inside of back "DUBOIS / A BRUXELLES". Printed paper label of dealer: "HINE & SON / Pianoforte, Harps & Music / WAREHOUSE. / LONDON."

A plain guitar by Dubois of Paris is in the University of Edinburgh collection, no. 285.

2000.10

RIGHT: *Guitar,* Dubois, Brussels, ca. 1840.

English guitar, John Preston, London, ca. 1770.

Pear-shaped outline, flat front, wide grain; two lines of dark wood purfling; gilt sound hole, three ivory rings, three dark wood rings around sound hole. Sound hole with dome cast metal rose depicting the sun in the center, attached by its rays to a garland of instruments, some tied together: oboe, English guitar, horn, recorder, viola da gamba, horn, recorder, English guitar, horn, recorder, viola da gamba, horn. Two lowest strings are single and four double courses. Ebony-veneered convex fingerboard; twelve frets; five holes for capo tasto behind first five frets. Tuning head with hook finial decorated with large ivory square. Ten watch-key tuners with key tied to neck with piece of white material. Pitches are inscribed on watch-key mechanism: G, E, G, C, E, and on fingerboard behind the fifth, seventh, ninth, tenth frets; wooden bridge, ivory string retainer at end of body. String L=430; W of body=290.

Stamped on back of peg head: "(GR both letters crowned) [George Rex] / PRESTON · MAKER. / LONDON".

Poulopoulas 2011, 349-350, note 611.

2002.62

LEFT: *English guitar*, John Preston, London, ca. 1770.

Mandolin, William A. Pond and Co., New York, ca. 1910.

Spruce soundboard; ivory bound top with three rosewood rings, two rings of alternating white and black inlay, and one ring of various color inlays among the rings. Oval sound hole bound by ivory, four rosewood rings, two rings of alternating white and black inlay; one ring of various color inlays, among the rings. Rosewood head with four horizontal ivory tuner buttons on both sides; two nickel-silver plates covering the mechanism. Ebony fingerboard with pearl inlay behind the first, third, fifth, seventh, tenth, twelfth, and fifteenth fret. Rosewood pick guard with ivory inlay of lyre and two figures of angels entwined with leaves. Rosewood bridge with ivory saddle, engraved nickel-silver string retainer. String L=375.

Paper label: "WM. A. POND & CO. / 124 FIFTH AVE. / NEW YORK".

2002.67

RIGHT: *Mandolin*, William A. Pond and Co., New York, ca. 1910.

Viola d'amour, Jacques Pierre Michelot, Paris, ca. 1775.

Sloping shoulders; flame tone holes; carved scroll of woman's head. Seven bowed strings, five sympathetic strings, five holes for sympathetic strings in bridge. Ebony fingerboard; double light wood purfling. Five brass tuning pins at the bottom end for sympathetic strings. String L=330; L of body=365; L of upper bout=175; L of lower bout=217.

Stamped on bottom: "MICHELOT".

1972.04

Viola d'amour, Jacques Pierre Michelot, Paris, ca. 1775.

Vielle à roue, Anonymous,
of United States or French origin,
nineteenth century.

Brown wood top; viol-shape; wide F holes, thirteen black wood keys on right side. Ivory and ebony checkered binding on handle cover and key mechanism cover; large scroll head; six pegs (one missing); rose inlay on wheel handle cover; brown wood wheel handle. Missing strings, wheel cover. Overall L=755; L without head=515; L of upper bout=230; L of lower bout=280; D at handle end=138.

No inscription.

1982.01

LEFT: *Vielle à roue,* Anonymous, of United States or French origin, nineteenth century.

Vielle à roue, Claude Bas,
Chaveyriat, ca. 1860.

Lute-shaped body; two wooden pegs (four missing); alternating ivory and black wood purfling; two small C-holes on lower belly. Carved man's head scroll; metal wheel hand crank, ivory handle. Missing key cover and wooden wheel cover. L without pegbox and head=515.

Inscription on label: "(five-pointed star) / BAS / (five-pointed star)".

1986.01

RIGHT: *Vielle à roue,* Claude Bas, Chaveyriat, ca. 1860.

Violin, Anonymous, with a Hornsteiner label, nineteenth century.

Double purfling; two F holes. Scroll deeply cut.

String L=325; L of upper bout=161; L of lower bout=183.

Inscription on reproduced label: "Mathias Hornsteiner, Geigenmacher / (unreadable) / Anno 1803".

1987.01

LEFT: *Violin*, Anonymous, with a Hornsteiner label, nineteenth century.

Pochette, attributed to Mathias Wörle, Augsburg, 1686.

Sides and fingerboard veneered in tortoise shell; ivory neck; stained black wood pegbox; double line purfling; heart on body; round escutcheon; mother-of-pearl dot; C-holes. Overall L=410; string L=275; L of bow with ivory screw handle=498.

Label difficult to read.

Similar pochette by George Wörle, Augsburg, 1669, in the Musée de la Musique, Paris, no. D. OA.421.

1997.06

BELOW: *Pochette*, attributed to Mathias Wörle, Augsburg, 1686, front and side views.

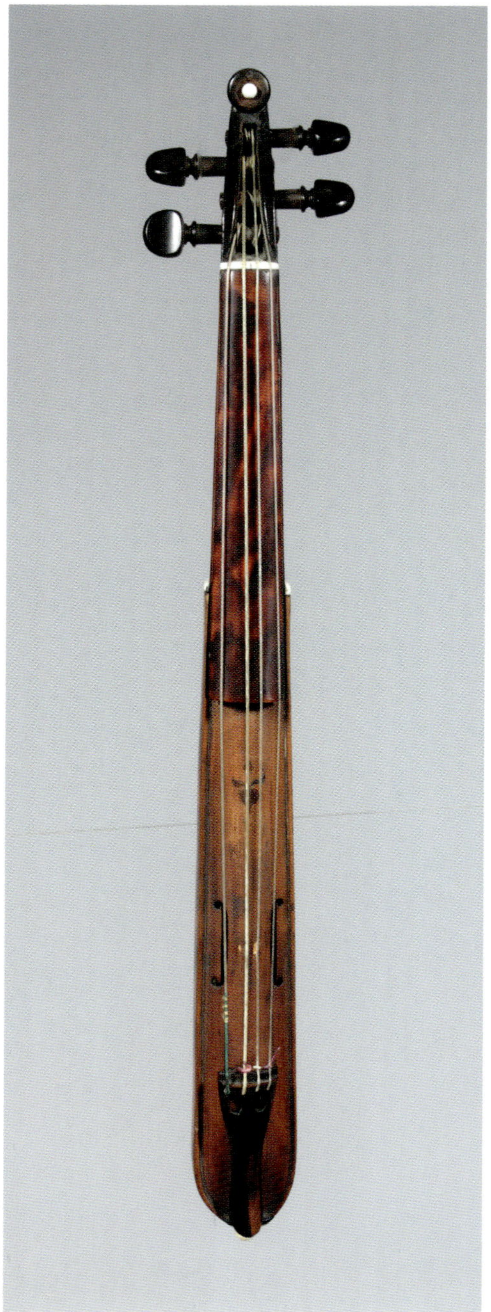

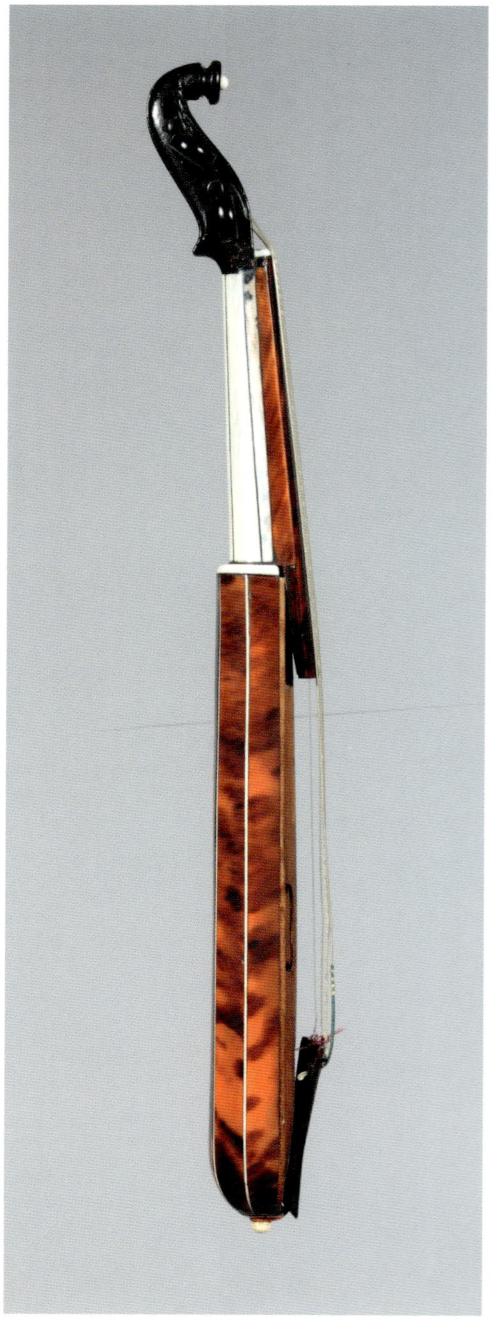

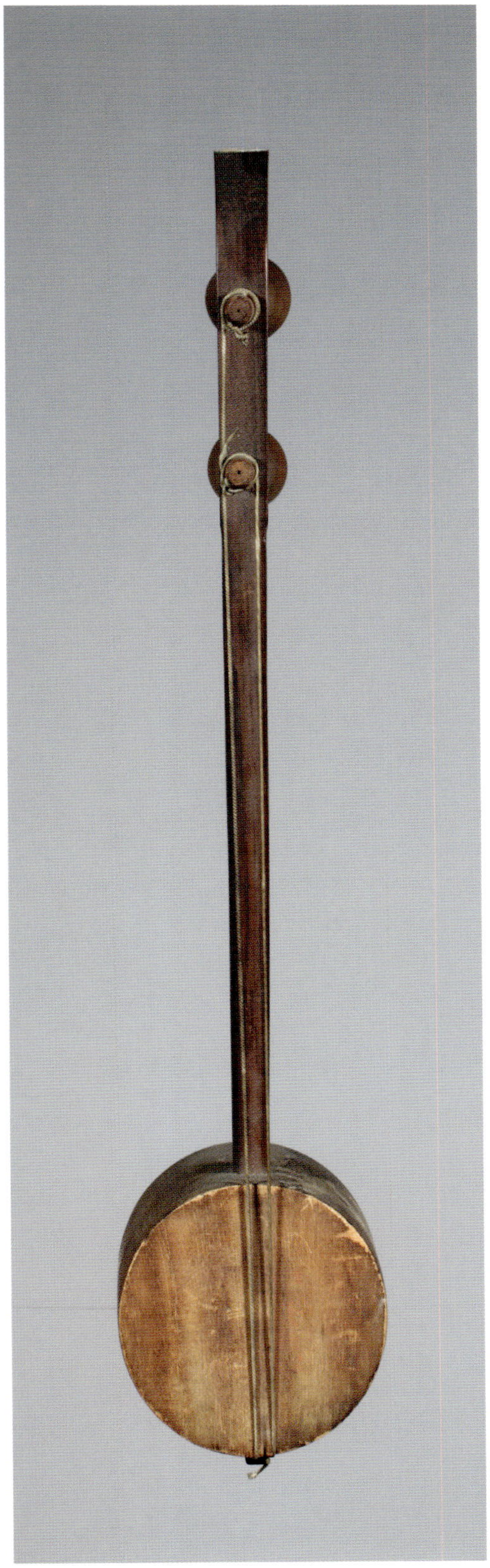

Erhu, Anonymous,
of Chinese origin, ca. 1930.

Two-string bowed spike lute; two large light wood horizontal pegs; rosewood fingerboard; bowl-shaped body. L=590.

No inscription.

1983.05

Sanxian, Anonymous,
of Chinese origin, ca. 1920.

Three-string plucked long-neck lute; three rosewood horizontal pegs; circular python-skin resonator. L=903; D of head=103.

No inscription.

1983.06

LEFT & BELOW: *Erhu*, Anonymous, of Chinese origin, ca. 1930, front and side views.

BELOW: *Sanxian*, Anonymous, of Chinese origin, ca. 1920.

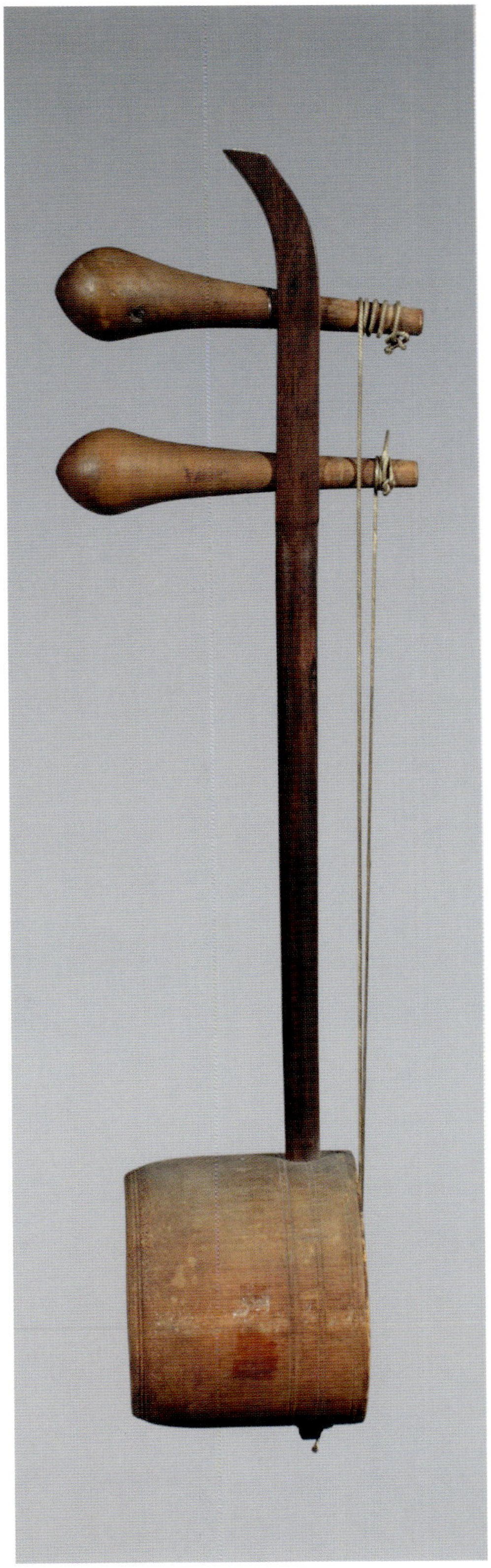

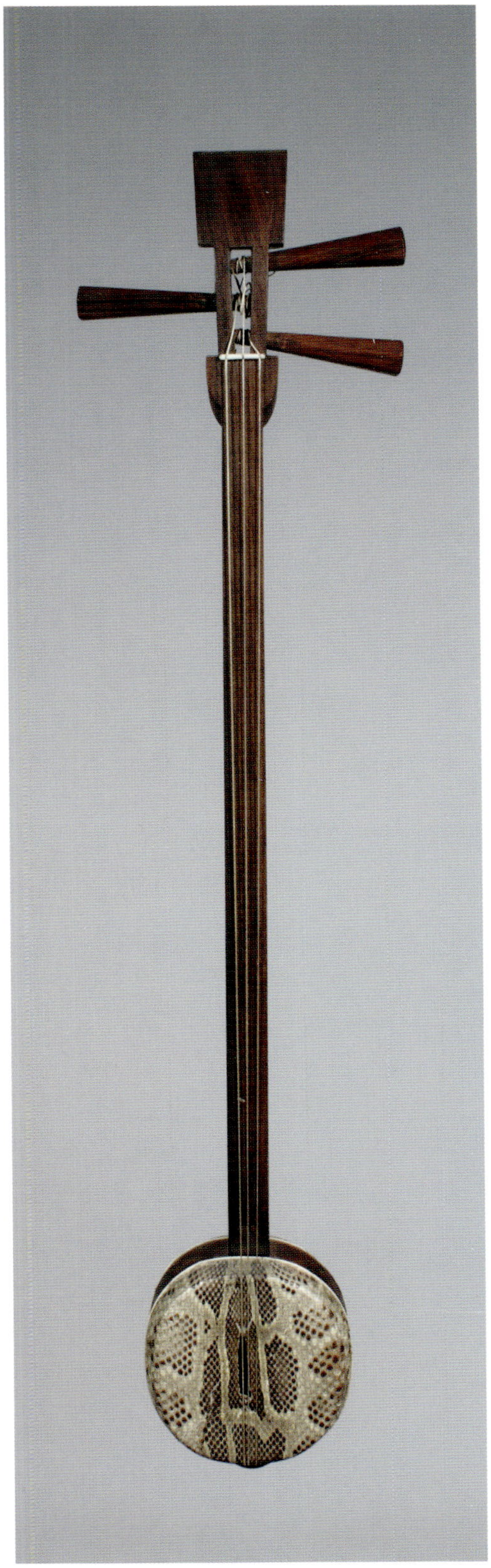

Gekkin, Anonymous,
of Japanese origin, ca. 1920.

Four-string plucked, round bodied lute; four carved dark wood horizontal pegs; flower-petal escutcheon; sixteen ivory frets. L=585; D of body=330.

No inscription.

1983.07

BELOW: *Gekkin*, Anonymous, of Japanese origin, ca. 1920.

Gusle, Anonymous,
of Yugoslavian origin, ca. 1930.

One-string bowed lute; hollow pear-shaped resonator covered with skin; four dots in cross pattern. Wood neck carved with a double-head crowned eagle (coat of arms of Yugoslavia), with two snakes bordering colored images of Maria of Yugoslavia (reigned 1921–1934) marked "IBB / KM"; Alexander I (Alexander Karađorđevič, reigned 1921-1934) marked "Ђ / K; B / A"; and Nikola P. Pašič, Prime Minister of Yugoslavia, 1921-1934) marked "H / K, B / Π". Symbolic figures on the neck above the resonator are St. George on a horse slaying a dragon with a spear and the inscription: "CB.ħ.YPħe". L=845.

No inscription.

1983.08

RIGHT: *Gusle*, Anonymous, of Yugoslavian origin, ca. 1930.

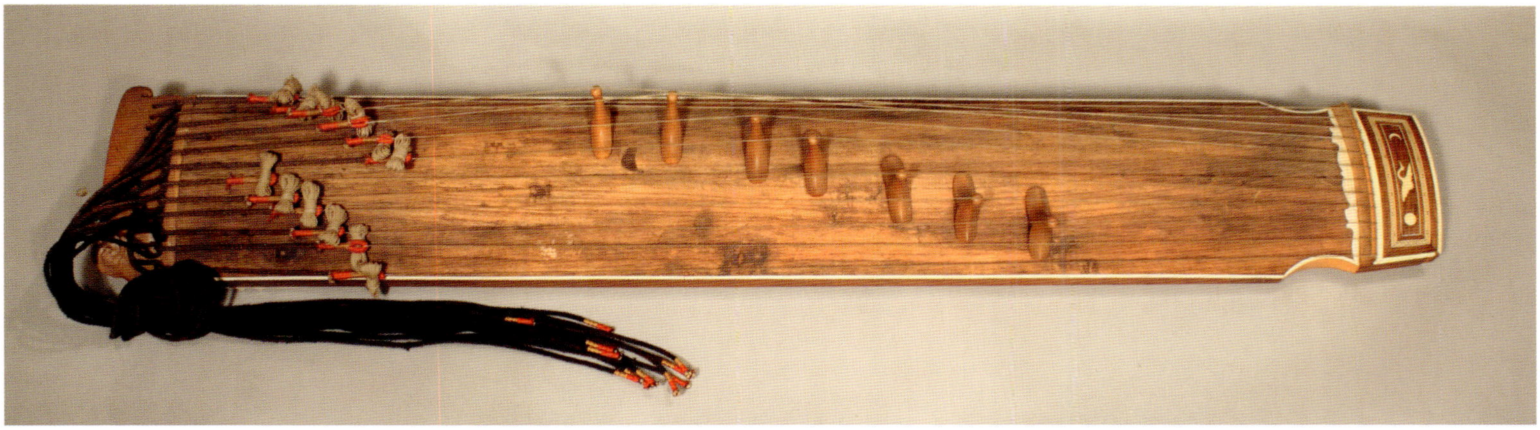

Kayagum, Anonymous,
of Korean origin, twentieth century.

Paulownia wood; gently curving front; partially hollowed out from rear. Stylized carved ram's horns carved at left end. Twelve strings connected to pegs under right end through small holes, over curved, fixed bridge, across twelve moveable bridges (five missing), across fixed bridge to looped moorings, where extra string is kept in coils.

L=839.

No inscription.

1983.09

ABOVE: *Kayagum*, Anonymous, of Korean origin, twentieth century.

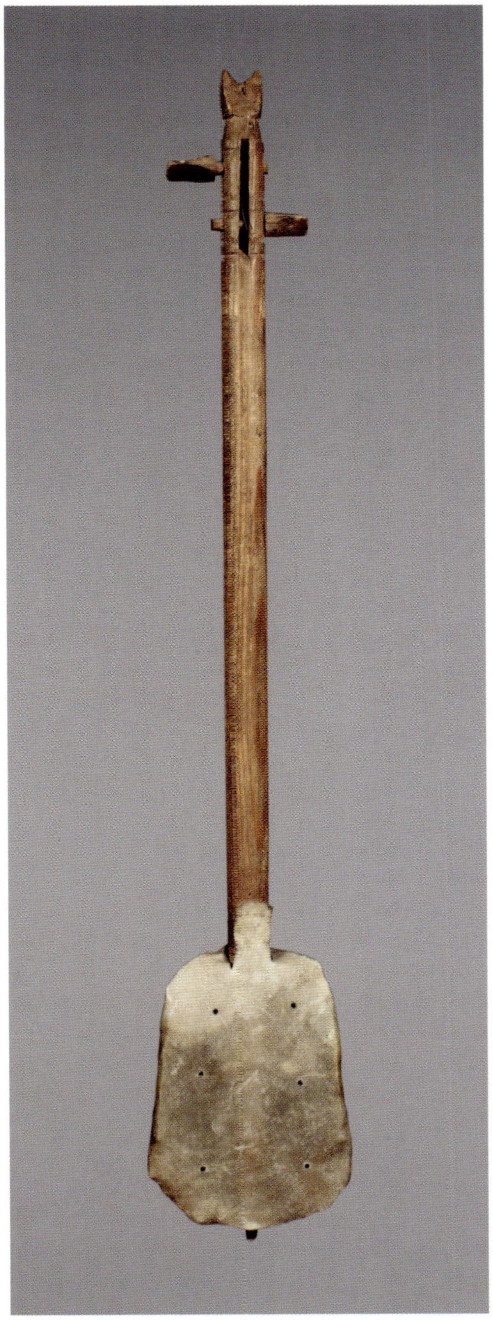

Rebab, Anonymous,
of Algerian origin, ca. 1920.

Two-string fiddle; turtle-shell resonator covered with skin; six holes. Two horizontal pegs; brown wood; decorated head. L=740.

No inscription.

1983.11

RIGHT: *Rebab*, Anonymous, of Algerian origin, ca. 1920, front and back views.

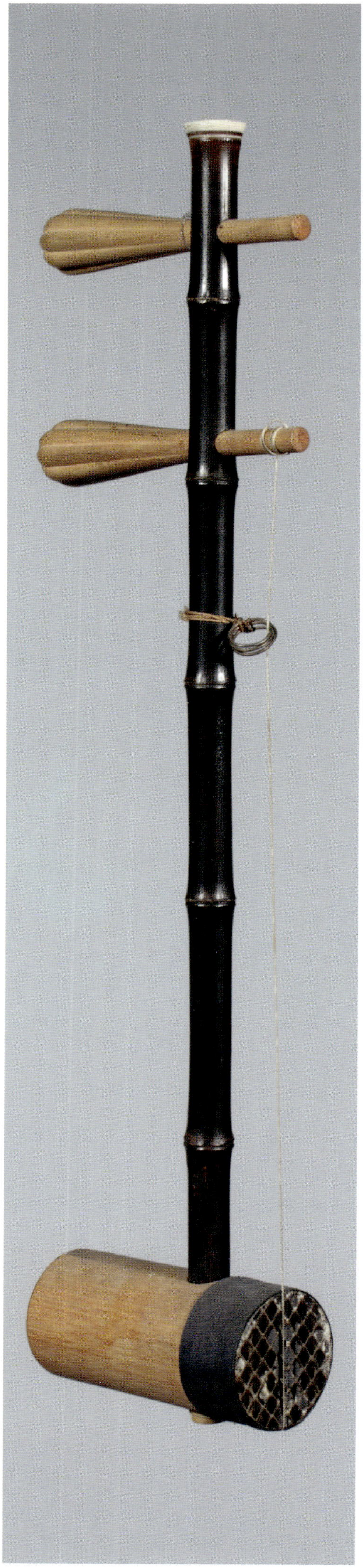

Huqin, Anonymous,
of Chinese origin, ca. 1920.

Two-string fiddle; stained black bamboo; two lightwood, carved horizontal pegs; round resonator, python skin; bow fits between two strings. L=487; D of body=56.

No inscription.

1983.12a

LEFT: *Huqin*, Anonymous, of Chinese origin, ca. 1920.

Huqin, Anonymous,
of Chinese origin, ca. 1920.

Two-string fiddle; bamboo, two light wood, carved horizontal pegs, round resonator; black material around end of resonator, dark python skin; bow fits between strings.

No inscription.

1983.12b

RIGHT: *Huqin*, Anonymous, of Chinese origin, ca. 1920.

Huqin (Sihu), Anonymous, of northern Chinese origin, ca. 1920

Four-string fiddle; four-sided rosewood, four lightwood, carved horizontal pegs, six-sided resonator, python skin. The four strings are tuned in pairs a fifth apart (such as, d^1-a^1-d^1-a^1); the bow hair of the sihu is divided into two strands, one of which sounds one of each pair of strings.

Thrasher and Stock, 2013.

1983.12c

Huqin (Sihu), Anonymous, of northern Chinese origin, ca. 1920.

Ukelin, International Musical Corporation, Hoboken, New Jersey, ca. 1930.

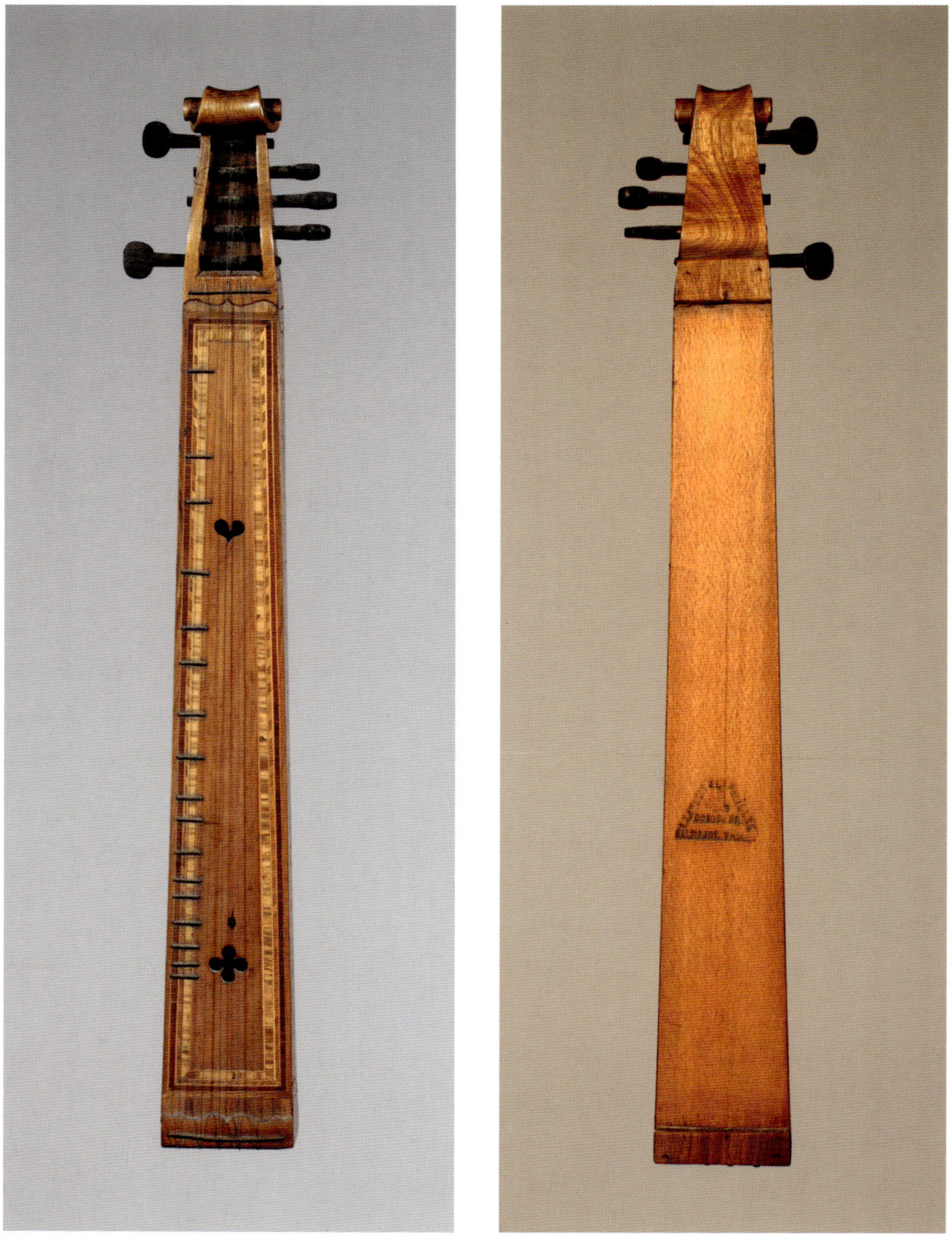

Epinettes des Vosges, Amé Lambert, Val-d'Ajol, ca. 1890, front and back views.

Ukelin, International Musical Corporation, Hoboken, New Jersey, ca. 1930.

Wooden body, rectangular form with lower section slightly curved. Two sets of strings; one group of sixteen, compass: two octaves, from c^1 to c^3; four groups of four strings, each group tuned to a chord. Eight metal hooks on each side act as saddles to direct strings to hooks. Placed on table, larger end toward performer, while right hand plays a melody on treble strings with violin bow, accompanying chords are played on bass strings with left hand using either fingers or pick. Each string and chord group is numbered; sheet music is written in numerical system intended to assist people unable to read standard musical notation. L=700.

Label: "Distributed By / International Musical / Corporation / 14th and Bloomfield St. / HOBOKEN, N.J."

Paul F. Richter's US patent of the ukelin on December 3, 1923, awarded on April 6, 1926; assigned to the Phonoharp Company of Boston. In 1926, the Phonoharp Company merged with Oscar Schmidt International, Inc. Ukelins were sold by Schmidt and its subsidiaries, including The International Musical Corporation of Hoboken, New Jersey.

"The Ukelin and Related Instruments" 2013.

1992.14

Epinettes des Vosges, Amé Lambert, Val-d'Ajol, ca. 1890.

Zither; curved head scroll; five horizontal wooden pegs; heart-shaped sound hole; clover-shaped sound hole; seventeen metal frets. L=590.

Stamped about two-thirds of the way down the back: "LAMBERT A LA FEUILLÉE / (rooster) / NOROTHER / VALDALJOL VOSGES".

Amé Lambert's (1843-1908) firm is estimated to have produced up to five hundred examples per year. Épinette des Vosges by A. Lambert are found in several museums. www.mimo-international.com.

1998.11

Pianoette (bowed zither), Pianolin Co., Mt. Pleasant, Iowa, made by Henry C. Marx, New Troy, Michigan, 1939.

Rectangular stained piece of wood with sunburst finish, stencils indicate pitch names. Right side has twenty-five strings double and triple strung, two octaves from c to c^2 played with bow; left section has twenty double strings for five chords played with thumb or pick: C major, G major, F major, D major, A major. Metal projection on right supports the side making it easier to bow. Bow is simple white stick with head attached at one end, and black frog at other end. L=570; W=206.

Inscription in red on label inside: "$28.50 / PIANOETTE / PIANOLIN Co. / Mt. Pleasant, Iowa / Serial No. 1842".

www.fretlesszithers.net/ QuickIdentiferPages/Pianolin.htm.

2002.33

Zither, Georg Tieffenbrunner, Munich, ca. 1885.

Rosewood body; five melody strings, thirty-two chord strings; tuning pins on right. Two gilt inlayed wood rings around circular body and sound hole; one gilt inlay ring around tuning pins; ebony fingerboard, thirty metal frets; mother-of-pearl dots behind sixth, tenth, thirteenth, eighteenth fret. L=495; W=310.

Label: "GEORG TIEFFENBRUNNER / Hof-Saiteninstrumenten-und Saitenfabrik / S.I. (Hoheit des Herzog Maximilian in Bayern / und J.K.Hoheit der Kronprinzeſsin Alexandra) / von England / MÜNCHEN Petersplatz 8/1 / Preisegekrönt zu London, München, Paris, Philadelphia, Nürnberg. / Groſse goldene Ehrenmedaille des Herzog Maximilian in Bayern / Gegründet 1842." / Signed: "Chas. Botz". Two stamps of the Bavarian coat of arms and the United Kingdom coat of arms on either side of the text. On lower label: "Preisgekrönt / München, Paris, / Wien, Philadelphia, Graz, Sidney / u. Melbourne." Red stamp above label: "JOSEPH KELLER / IMPORTER, MILWAUKEE, WIS." Stamped on top of fingerboard: "G. TIEFENBRUNNER / StPETERSBURG".

2002.42

Concert zither, Eduard Heidegger, Linz, ca. 1880.

Rosewood; ivory binding; four rings of lightwood and rosewood inlay around body; tuning pins with engraved nickel-silver plate on right. Five melody strings, five ivory tuning pegs; thirty-one chord strings; carved stained black wood lion above top of turned black wood column. Ebony fingerboard with thirty metal frets; mother-of-pearl dots behind sixth, tenth, thirteenth, sixteenth fret. L=586; W=327.

Label: "EDUARD HEIDEGGER / LINZ. / (medals won at exhibitions)".

Stamped on top of nickel-silver plate: "E. HEIDEGGER / LINZ".

2002.61

Pianoette (bowed zither), Pianolin Co., Mt. Pleasant, Iowa, made by Henry C. Marx, New Troy, Michigan, 1939.

Zither, Georg Tieffenbrunner, Munich, ca. 1885.

Concert zither, Eduard Heidegger, Linz, ca. 1880.

CHAPTER 8

PERCUSSION INSTRUMENTS, CROMAMETRO

Small double-headed cylindrical drum, Anonymous, of African origin, twentieth century.

Cord-and-peg construction. Placed on the floor and played with both hands; skin resonators attached to each end with pegs. On one side, a depiction of an elephant. W=244; D of head=202.

1983.03

Small double-headed cylindrical drum, Anonymous, of African origin, twentieth century.

Double-headed drum, Anonymous, of Chinese origin, twentieth century.

Skin resonators tacked to each end. Held on the lap and played with one or both hands. Wood shell is unadorned. W between two heads=80; D of two heads=about 200.

1983.04a

Double-headed drum, Anonymous, of Chinese origin, twentieth century.

Two small double-headed drums, Anonymous, of Chinese origin, twentieth century.

Skin resonators tacked to each end. One has a rope with black, white, and red threads attached to allow player to hold it on the shoulder while playing. Sides decorated with images of flowers and shapes in various colors; heads decorated around the rim with four sections having lozenges in various colors, and a tri-color (black, red, and orange) circle in the center. For both drums: W=179; D of head=300.

1983.04b-c

Two small double-headed drums, Anonymous, of Chinese origin, twentieth century.

Long drum, Anonymous,
of Haitian origin, twentieth century.

Skin resonator attached by large pegs at wide end. Small end decorated with carving. H=820; D of head=216.

1983.10

LEFT: *Long drum*, Anonymous, of Haitian origin, twentieth century.

Cromametro (piano tuning device),
Giovanni Ricordi, Milan, ca. 1828.

Mahogany; sides curved and turned at bottom; single string attached to knurled metal ring at bottom, placed over bridge, under metal capo tasto, and tied to screw with wide fingerplate on top. Upper section has metal plate with twelve notches on right side; left side marked in pen with letters indicating twelve notes in half steps from C to B. When the capo tasto is moved to the notch, lever at base may be pushed to operate hammer that strikes the string through the sound hole. H=824.

Marked in pen on front: "Cromametro / Presso Gio Ricordi / in Milano".

Identical in construction and appearance to a Chromamètre by Jean Roller & Pierre Blanchet, Paris, 1828, in Musée de la Musique, E.2247. This instrument was marketed and sold in Italy by the Ricordi company. Ricordi's cromametro is advertised in *I Teatri* 1827, vol. 1, pt. 2, 593.

Sotheby's 1998.

1999.20

RIGHT: *Cromametro* (piano tuning device), Giovanni Ricordi, Milan, ca. 1828.

BIBLIOGRAPHY

Adams, Peter. 2009. *An Annotated Index to Selected Articles from The Musical Courier, 1880–1940.* Lanham: Scarecrow Press.

Adkins, Cecil. 1990. "Oboes beyond Compare: The Instruments of Hendrik and Fredrik Richters," *Journal of American Musical Instrument Society* 16 (1990), 42–117.

Adkins, Cecil. 2001. "The German Oboe in the Eighteenth Century," *Journal of American Instrument Society* 27 (2001), 5–47.

Adkins, Cecil. 2011. "Why Straight Tops?" *Journal of American Instrument Society* 37 (2011), 88–156.

Baines, Anthony. 1967. *Woodwind Instruments and their History.* 3rd ed. London: Faber and Faber.

Baines, Anthony. 1992. *The Oxford Companion to Musical Instruments.* Oxford: Oxford University Press.

Bär, Frank. 2003. *Verzeichnis der Europäischen Musikinstrumente im Germanischen Nationalmuseum Nürnberg.* Band 4: Klarinetten normaler und höherer Stimmlage mit 2 bis 9 Klappen, Beschreibender Katalog. Wilhelmshaven: F. Noetzel.

Bate, Philip. 1975. *The Oboe.* 3rd ed. New York: W.W. Norton.

Berdahl, Susan. M. 1986. "The First Hundred Years of the Boehm Flute in the United States, 1845–1945: A Biographical Dictionary of American Boehm flutemakers," PhD diss., University of Minnesota, 3 vols.

"Berteling's Concert Flutes," 1893. In *Catalogue K. 1894–'95 August Pollmann, importer and manufacturer of Musical Mercandise.* New York: A. Pollmann.

Bigio, Robert. 2011. *Rudall, Rose & Carte: The Art of the Flute in Britain.* London: T. Bingham.

Birsak, Kurt. 1973. *Die Holzblasinstrumente im Salzburger Museum Carolino Augusteum.* Salzburg: Salzburger Museum Carolino Augusteum.

Boalch, Donald H. 1995. Ed. Charles Mould, *Makers of the Harpsichord and Clavichord 1440–1840.* 3rd ed., Oxford: Clarendon Press.

Bouterse, Jan. 2005. *Dutch Woodwind Instruments and Their Makers, 1660–1760.* Utrecht: Koninklijke Vereniging voor Nederlandse Muziekgeschiedenis.

Bowers, Q. David. 1973. *Encyclopedia of Automatic Musical Instruments.* Vestal, New York: The Vestal Press.

Brauchli, Bernard. 1998. *The Clavichord.* Cambridge: Cambridge University Press.

Burgess, Geoffrey, and Bruce Haynes. 2004. *The Oboe.* New Haven: Yale University Press.

Burgess, Geoffrey. 2009. "Pedagogic Material for the Oboe from the Nineteenth Century." In *Celebrating Double Reeds: A Festschrift for William Waterhouse and Philip Bate.* Ed. T. B. Ewell. Baltimore: International Double Reed Society.

Caldeira Cabral, Pedro. 2007. "Costrutores da Guitarra Portuguesa." www.guitarraportuguesa.org.

Campbell, Jeannie. 2001. *Highland Bagpipe Makers.* Edinburgh: Magnus Orr Publishing.

Carreras, Francesco. 2009. *Il Flauto Traverso in Italia: Tre secoli di storia nella collezione Carreras/Flute-making in Italy: Three centuries of History in the Carreras Collection.* Rome: Museo degli strumenti musicali dell'Accademia Nazionale di Santa Cecilia.

Christie's London. Works of Art from the Collection of The Barons Nathaniel and Albert von Rothschild, 8 July 1999. London: Christie's.

Christie's New York Fine Musical Instruments. 2012. Auction catalog, 26 April 2012. New York: Christie's.

Clinkscale, Martha. 1993. *Makers of the Piano 1700–1820.* Oxford: Clarendon Press.

Clinkscale, Martha. 1999. *Makers of the Piano Volume 2 1820–1860.* Oxford: Clarendon Press.

Clinkscale Online: http:// earlypianos.org.

Cocks, William A. et al. 2013. "Bapgpipe," *Oxford Music Online,* www. oxfordmusiconline.com.

Cohen, Paul. 1985. "Vintage Saxophones Revisited," *Saxophone Journal* 10, no. 2 (Summer 1985), 5–7.

Cohen, Paul. 1994. "Vintage Saxophones Revisited: Voices of the Slide Saxophone, Part II," *Saxophone Journal* 19, no. 2 (Sept.-Oct. 1994), 6–8.

Cole, Michael. 1998. *The Pianoforte in the Classical Era.* Oxford: Clarendon Press.

Cole, Michael. 2005. *Broadwood Square Pianos: Their Historical Context, and Technical Development.* Cheltenham: Tatchley Books.

Cottrell, Stephen. 2012. *The Saxophone.* New Haven: Yale University Press.

Cranmer, Margaret. et. al. 2013. "Geib," *Oxford Music Online,* www. oxfordmusiconline.com.

Cwach, Michael. 2012. "The *Pukl* in Chodsko: The Development and Establishment of the Bellows-blown *Bock* in a Corner of Western Bohemia," *Journal of American Instrument Society* 38 (2012), 47–77.

Da Silva, Jose. 1992. "Contribution aux tentatives de reperage chronologique des hautbois Triebert Fils (Frederic), periode d'activite: 1830 à 1870 environ," *Larigot* 10, 8–16.

Da Silva, Jose. 1993. "Catalogue de la collection d'instruments de musique à vent," *Larigot Spécial,* no. 2.

Diagram Group. 1976. *Musical Instruments of the World: An Illustrated Encyclopedia.* New York: Facts on File.

Dibley, Tom. 2000. "A Contrabassophone by Alfred Morton," *Galpin Society Journal* 53 (2000), 60–77.

Dike, Catherine. 1983. *Cane Curiosa from Gun to Gadget.* Geneva: Les Editions de l'Amateur.

Dowd, William. 1984. "The Surviving Instruments of the Blanchet Workshop," in *The Historical Harpsichord. A Monograph Series in Honor of Frank Hubbard.* Vol. 1, ed. H. Schott, 17–107. New York: Pendragon Press

Dullat, Günter. 1999. *Saxophone: Erfindung und Entwicklung einer Musikinstrumenten-Familie und ihre bedeutenden Hersteller.* 3rd ed. Nauheim: The Author.

Dullat, Günter. 2010a. *Verzeichnis der Holz-und Metallblasinstrumentenmacher auf Deutschsprachigem Gebiet von 1500 bis Mitte des 20. Jahrhunderts*. Tutzing: H. Schneider.

Dullat, Günter. 2010b. *200 Jahre Patente, Privilegien und Gebrauchmuster im internationalen Holz- und Metallblasinstrumentenbau.* Wilhelmshaven: F. Noetzel.

Eliason, Robert E. 1975. *Graves & Company: Musical Instrument Makers.* Dearborn, Michigan: The Edison Institute.

Eliason, Robert E. 1979–1980. "The Meachams, Musical Instrument Makers of Hartford and Albany," *Journal of American Instrument Society* 5–6 (1979–1980), 54–73.

Eliason, Robert E. 2001. "Charles G. Christman, Musical Instrument Maker in Nineteenth-Century New York," *Journal of American Instrument Society* 27 (2001), 84–119.

Eliason, Robert E. and Frederick R. Selch. 2010. "William Whiteley, Utica, New York, Musical Instrument Maker," *Journal of American Instrument Society* 36 (2010), 5–57.

Eliason, Robert E. with Albert R. Rice. 2012. "The Continuation of Phillip T. Young's Research: A New Article about Asa Hopkins, Jabez M. Camp, and Firth, Hall & Pond Woodwind Making," *Journal of American Instrument Society* 37 (2012), 170–175.

Encyclopédie. Recueil de planches. 1767. Paris, 1767; reprint ed., 1986. Grimbergen, Belgium: Continental Printing.

Evette & Schaeffer. 1922. *Manufacture Spéciale d'Instruments de Musique Buffet, Crampon & Cie. A Paris. Evette & Schaeffer Successeurs. Extrait du Catalogue 1922.* Paris: Evette & Schaeffer.

Farrar, Lloyd. 1995. "Pat Cooperman: Friend to Fifers and Bastion against Losing our Martial Music Heritage," *The Woodwind Quarterly* no. 10 (August 1995), 92–99.

Freyer. ca. 1895. *Neueste Preisliste von Freyer & Co., Meißen i. Sa.:* Freyer.

Gellerman, Robert F. 1998. *Gellerman's International Reed Organ Atlas.* 2nd ed. Lanham: Vestal Press.

Germann, Sheridan. 2002. "Harpsichord Decoration – A Conspectus," *The Historical Harpsichord. A Monograph in Honor of Frank Hubbard.* Vol. 4, ed. H Schott, 1-213. Hillsdale, NY: Pendragon Press.

Giannini, Tula. 1993. *Great Flute Makers of France: The Lot & Godfroy Families 1650–1900.* London: T. Bingham.

Giannini, Tula. 2005. "Frédéric Triebert (1813–1878), Designer of the Modern Oboe: Newly Found Archival Documents Featuring the Inventory and Auction of His Musical Instrument Enterprise," in *Liber americorum Isabelle Cazeaux: Symbols, Parallels and Discoveries in Her Honor.* Ed. P.A. Bempéchat, 49–90. Hillsdale, NY: Pendragon Press.

Good, Edwin M. 2001. *Giraffes, Black Dragons, and Other Pianos: A Technological History from Cristofori to the Modern Concert Grand*, 2nd ed. Stanford: Stanford University Press.

Gregori, Gianpaolo. 1997. "La harpe et les guitares d'Antonio Stradivari," *Musique-Images-Instruments* 3 (1997), 8–31.

Groce, Nancy. 1991. *Musical Instrument Makers of New York: A Directory of Eighteenth and Nineteenth Century Urban Craftsmen.* Stuyvesant, NY: Pendragon.

Gruhn, George, and Walter Carter. 1999. *Gruhn's Guide to Vintage Guitars: An Identification Guide for American Fretted Instruments.* 2nd ed. San Francisco: Miller Freeman.

Gura, Philip F. 2013. *C.F. Martin and His Guitars 1796–1873.* Chapel Hill: University of North Carolina Press.

Harding, Rosamond E.M. 1933. *The Piano-forte Its History Traced to the Great Exhibition of 1851*, Cambridge: Cambridge University Press; reprint, 1973, New York: Da Capo Press.

Harrington, Helmi Strahl, and Gerhard Kubik. 2013. "Accordion," *Oxford Music Online*, www.oxfordmusiconline.com.

Heckel, Wilhelm.1906. *Fabrik seiner Blas-Instrumente von Wilhelm Heckel. Preisliste über seine Instrumente.* Ausgabe 202.

Haupert, Mary Ellen Patnaude. 1989. "The Square Pianos of Jonas Chickering", PhD diss., Washington University.

Haynes, Bruce. 2001. *The Eloquent Oboe: A History of the Hautboy from 1640 to 1760.* Oxford Early Music Series. Oxford: Oxford University Press.

Heyde, Herbert. 1976. *Historische Musikinstrumente im Bachhaus Eisenach.* Eisenach: Bachhaus.

"History of Oliver Ditson Company." 1915. *The Musical Courier* 70, no. 8 (Feb. 24, 1915), 8; www.peteradams.com/history_of_oliver_ditson_company.htm_ftn1.

Holmes, Michael I. 2011. "American Fretted Musical Instrument Makers, pre-Civil War to WWII" (2011); http://www.mugwumps.com/AmerInstMkr.html.

Horwood, Wally. 1985. "The Grafton Story: Hector Sommaruga and His Revolutionary Saxophone," *Clarinet and Saxophone* 10, no. 4. (December 1985).

Hôtel des ventes de Vichy. 2005. Auction catalog, 9–10 December 2005. Paris: B. Kampmann.

Howe, Robert. 2003a. "The Boehm System Oboe and Its Role in the Development of the Modern Oboe," *Galpin Society Journal* 56 (2003), 27–60.

Howe, Robert. 2003b. "The Invention and Early Development of the Saxophone, 1840–55," *Journal of American Instrument Society* 29 (2003), 97–180.

Howe, Robert. 2011. "Nineteenth-Century French Oboe Making Revealed: a Translation and Analysis of the Treibert et Cie '1855' *Nouveau Prix-Courant*," *Galpin Society Journal* 64 (2011), 79–116, 188–194.

I Teatri: Giornale Drammatico, Musicale e Coregrafico 1827. Vol. 1 (1827), pt. 2, 593.

International Inventions Exhibition 1885. Official Catalogue. London: W. Clowes and Sons.

Jeltsch, Jean. 1997. "'Prudent à Paris': vie et carrière d'un maître faiseur d'instruments à vent," *Musiques-Image-Instruments* 3 (1997), 128–152.

Joppig, Gunther. 1986. "Sarrusophone, Rothphone (Saxorusophone) and Reed Contrabass," *Journal of American Instrument Society* 12 (1986), 68–107.

Joseph, James. 2012. "Clarinets of the Clinton Family," *Proceedings of the Clarinet and Woodwind Colloquium 2007 Celebrating the Collection of Sir Nicholas Shackleton: Papers presented at the meeting organised by the Edinburgh University Collection of Historic Musical Instruments, Edinburgh, 22–24 June 2007.* Eds. A. Myers, E. Smith, and H. Fricke, 73–78. Edinburgh: Edinburgh University Collection of Historic Musical Instruments.

Jourdain, Margaret. 1922. *English Decoration and Furniture of the Later XVIIIth Century (1760–1820).* London: B.T. Batsford.

Kampmann, Bruno. 2006. "Catalogue de la collection d'instruments de musique à vent, tome 5," *Larigot* no. Speciale XVII (Feb. 2006).

Kampmann, Bruno. 2007. "Un hautbois Buffet-Crampon très particulier," *Larigot* 40, 4–5.

Kenyon de Pascual, Beryl. 1991. "Two Features of Early Spanish Keyboard Instruments," *Galpin Society Journal* 44 (March 1991), 94–102.

Kenyon de Pascual, Beryl. 2002. "18th-19th Century Spanish Clavichords with Fretting Variants" in *Fundament aller Clavirten Instrumenten-Das Clavichord. Symposium im Rahmen der 26. Tage Alter Musik in Herne 2001.* Eds. C. Ahrens and G. Klinke, 139–154. Munich: Katzbichler.

Kiefer, Thomas. 2010. "Tiefstimmige Doppelrohrblatt-Instrumente von der Harmoniemusik bis in das Blasorchester des 19. Jahrhunderts: Zu ihrer Entwicklung im Berich der Donaumonarchie und den Auswirkungen auf den Instrumentenbau in Berlin und Mailand," in *Wissenschaftliches Jahrbuch der Tiroler Landesmuseen 2010*, 46–99.

Kirnbauer, Martin. 1994. *Verzeichnis der Europäischen Musikinstrumente im Germanischen Nationalmuseum Nürnberg. Band 2. Flöten-und Rohrblattinstrumente bis 1750. Beschreibender Katalog.* Wilhelmshaven: F. Noetzel.

Kopp, James B. 2013. "Two Bassoons Marked 'KLEMM / PHILADA,'" *Newsletter of the American Musical Instrument Society* 42, no. 2 (Fall 2013), 16–18.

Koster, John. 1994. *Keyboard Musical Instruments in the Museum of Fine Arts, Boston.* Boston: Museum of Fine Arts.

Kottick, Edward L. 2003. *A History of the Harpsichord.* Bloomington: Indiana University Press.

Kuronen, Darcy. 1992. "The Musical Instruments of Benjamin Crehore," *Journal of the Museum of Fine Arts* 4 (1992), 52–79.

Lambert, Barbara. 1985. *Music in Colonial Massachusetts.* Boston: University Press of Virginia, 2 vols.

Latcham, Michael. 1998. "Mozart and the Pianos of Johann Andreas Stein," *Galpin Society Journal* LI (1998), 114–153.

Lasocki, David. 2010. "New Light on Eighteenth-Century English Woodwind Makers from Newspaper Advertisements," *Galpin Society Journal* 63 (May 2010), 73–142.

Lawson, Colin. 1991. "The Lyons C Clarinet, a review," *The Clarinet* 18, no. 3 (May-June 1990), 26–27.

Lenski, Karl, and Karl Ventske. 1992. *Das goldene Zeitalter der Flöte: Die Boehmflöte in Frankreich 1832–1932, Durchsetzung, Gestaltung, Wirkung.* Celle: Moeck.

Libin, Laurence. 1985. *American Musical Instruments in The Metropolitan Museum of Art.* New York: W.E. Norton.

[Libin, Laurence.] 1994. *Clarinets from the collection of William J. Maynard.* New York: The Metropolitan Museum of Art, brochure.

Libin, Laurence and Sabine K. Klaus. 2000. "Two Spanish Clavichords in Private U.S. Collections," in *De Clavicordio IV: Proceedings of the IV International Clavichord Symposium.* Eds. B. Brauchli, S. Brauchli, A. Galazzo, 127–138. Magnano: Musica Antica a Magnano.

MacGillivray, James A. 1959. "Recent Advances in Woodwind Fingering Systems," *Galpin Society Journal* 12 (May 1959), 68–72.

Maclagan, Susan J. 2009. *A Dictionary for the Modern Flutist.* Lanham, Maryland: Scarecrow Press.

MacMillan, Douglas Middleton. 2013. "The Flageolet in England 1800–1900: The Instrument, Its Music and Social Context," Doctor of Music diss., Royal College of Music.

Maniguet, Thierry. 2009. "Le piano en forme de clavecin Erard," *Musique-Images-Instruments* no 11 (2009), 82–97.

Mann, Walter Edward. 1977. "Piano Making in Philadelphia Before 1825," Ph.D. diss., The University of Iowa.

Michel, Guy-Jean. 1978. "La Bûche à Musique: Epinette des Vosges," in *Arts et traditions de la Vallée des lacs*, eds., S. Rattaire, et al., Ingersheim: Éditions SAEP, 1978, 141–148

Montagu, Jeremy. 2002. *Timpani & Percussion.* New Haven: Yale University Press.

Nahm, Dorothea A. and Robert E. Sheldon. 1996. "The Virgil Practice Clavier," in *Encyclopedia of the Piano.* Eds. R. Palmieri and M. W. Palmieri, 439–442, New York: Garland.

Neil, Wayne. 1991. "The Wheatstone English Concertina," *Galpin Society Journal* 44 (March 1991), 117–149.

Patents for Inventions. 1984. *Patents for Inventions. Abridgments of Specifications relating to music and musical instruments. A.D. 1694–1866.* 2nd ed. London, 1871, reprint, London: T. Bingham.

Palmer, Francis. 1985. "Merlin and Music," in *John Joseph Merlin: The Ingenious Mechanic*, London: Greater London Council, 103–105.

Pelitti, Giuseppe. 1872. *Catalogo della Fabbrica-Strumenti Musicali di Giuseppe Pelitti.* Milan: Stabilimento Sonzogno.

Pelitti, Giuseppe. 1873. *Disegni della Fabbrica-Strumenti Musicali di Giuseppe Pelitti.* Milan: G. Brambilla.

Peters, Harry T. 1976. *America on Stone: The Other Printmakers to the American People.* 1931, reprint: New York: Arno Press.

Pierre, René. 2013. *Collection René Pierre.* Paris: Larigo, no. XXV spécial.

Piguet, Michel. 1988. "Die Oboe im 18. Jahrhundert: Versuch einer Chronologie verschiedener Oboentypen anhand von Messungen und Betrachtungen von neunzehn Instrumenten aus der Sammlung M. Piguet," *Basler Jahrbuch für Historische Musikpraxis* 12 (1988), 81–107.

Poulopoulos, Panagiotis. 2011. "The Guittar in the British Isles, 1750–1810," PhD diss., The University of Edinburgh.

Powell, Ardal. Dated historic flutes; www.flutehistory.com/Resources/Lists/Dated_Instruments.php3.

Powell, Ardal. 2002. *The Flute.* New Haven: Yale University Press.

Ravenel, Bernard. 1992. "Pierre-la-Treiche et le monocorde de Joseph Poussot," *Conférence donnée à Toul, le 13 octobre 1992*, 3–14; accessible from www.etudes-touloise.com/articles/66/art1.pdf.

Reil, Thomas. 2012. "Extant soprano clarinets by Adolphe Sax," *Proceedings of the Clarinet and Woodwind Colloquium 2007 Celebrating the Collection of Sir Nicholas Shackleton: Papers presented at the meeting organised by the Edinburgh University Collection of Historic Musical Instruments Edinburgh, 22–24 June 2007.* Eds. A. Myers, E. Smith, and H. Fricke, 100–113. Edinburgh: Edinburgh University Collection of Historic Musical Instruments.

Reil, Thomas and Enrico Weller. 2008. *Der Klarinettenbauer Oskar Oehler.* Markneukirchen: Verein der Freunde und Förderer der Musikinstrumentenmuseum-Museums Markneukirchen e.V.

Rice, Albert R. 2004. "Buried Treasure-An H.N. White Saxello at the Fiske Museum," *Newsletter of the American Musical Instrument Society* 33, no. 3 (Fall 2004), 1, 5.

Rice, Albert R. 2009a. *From the Clarinet d'Amour to the Contra Bass: A History of Large Size Clarinets, 1740–1860*. New York: Oxford University Press.

Rice, Albert R. 2009b. "Making and Improving the Nineteenth-Century Saxophone," *Journal of American Instrument Society* 35 (2009), 81–122.

Rice, Albert R. 2012. "The Bass Clarinets of Adolphe Sax and Their Historical Importance," *Proceedings of the Clarinet and Woodwind Colloquium 2007 Celebrating the Collection of Sir Nicholas Shackleton: Papers presented at the meeting organised by the Edinburgh University Collection of Historic Musical Instruments, Edinburgh, 22–24 June 2007*. Eds. A. Myers, E. Smith, and H. Fricke, 84–99. Edinburgh: Edinburgh University Collection of Historic Musical Instruments.

Ripin, Edwin, and John Koster. 2013. "Orphica," *Oxford Music Online;* www.oxfordmusiconline.com.

Rousselet, William, and Denis Watel. 2012. *Le Livre d'Or de la Clarinette Française: Index des facteurs et des marques illustré par les instruments de l'ancienne collection Rousselet*. Paris: ACIMV, *Larigo* no. special 24.

Rycroft, David. 1999. "A Six-Finger Hole Saxophone: The *Saxie*," *Galpin Society Journal* 52 (April 1999), 195–201.

Seyfrit, Michael. 1982. *Musical Instruments in the Dayton C. Miller Flute Collection at the Library of Congress: A Catalog. Volume I: Recorders, Fifes, and Simple System Transverse Flutes of One Key*. Washington, DC: Library of Congress.

Sotheby's Musical Instruments, London. 1992. Auction catalog, 26 November 1992, London: Sotheby's.

Sotheby's Early Musical Instruments, New York. 1992. Auction catalog, November 4, 1998. New York: Sotheby's.

Staehelin, Martin. 2002. "Wer war der Holzblasinstrumentenbauer 'I.IR'"? *Glareana* 51, 4–8

Stradner, Gerhard. 1991. *Die Klangwelt Mozarts: 28. April bis 27. Oktober 1991 Wien, Neue Burg, Sammlung Alter Musikinstrumente. Eine Austellung des Kunsthistorischen Museums,* Vienna: Kunsthistorische Museum.

Stratton, John F. ca. 1878. *Manufacturer, Importer and Wholesale Dealer in All Kinds of Musical Merchandise*. New York: Stratton, wholesale price list and catalog.

Thrasher, Alan R. and Jonathan P.J. Stock, "Hugin," *Oxford Music Online*.

Tsalka, Michael. 2013. *Türk, Easy Keyboard Sonatas Collection I and II*. 2 CDs, Germany: HNH International Ltd.

"The Ukelin and Related Instruments." 2013. *Encyclopedia Smithsonian:* www.si.edu/Encyclopedia_SI/nmah/ukelin.htm.

Van Act, Rob, Vincent van den Ende, and Hans Schimmel. 1991. *Niederländische Blockflöten des 18. Jahrhunderts/Dutch Recorders of the 18th Century*. Celle: Moeck.

Van Acht, Rob, Jan Bouterse, and Piet Dhont. 1997. *Niederländische Doppelrohrblattinstrumente des 17. und 18. Jahrhunderts/Dutch Double Reed Instruments of the17th and 18th Centuries*. Laaber: Laaber Verlag.

Van Kalker, Johan, and Albert R. Rice. 2014. "The Musical Instruments in Lodewijk Plattner's Auction (1843)" *Galpin Society Journal* 67 (2014), 217–230.

Van Oostrom, Leo. 2009. *100+1 Saxen De Collectie van Leo Van Oostroom/The Collection of Leo Van Oostroom*. [Netherlands]: Edition Sax.

Vichy Enchères. 2011. Auction catalog, 18 June 2011, [Saint-Chartier}: D. et F. Sinnier de Ridder.

Voorhees, Jerry L. 2000. *The Development of Woodwind Fingering Systems in the Nineteenth and Twentieth Centuries*. Hammond, LA: The Author.

Wackernagel, Bettina. 2005. *Bayerisches Nationalmuseum München. Holzblasinstrumente*. Tutzing: H. Schneider.

Waterhouse, William. 1983. *The Proud Bassoon: An Exhibition Showing the Development of the Bassoon over the Centuries*. Edinburgh: Edinburgh University Collection of Historic Musical Instruments.

Waterhouse, William. 1993. *The New Langwill Index: A Dictionary of Musical Wind-Instrument Makers and Inventors*. London: T. Bingham.

Waterhouse, William. 1999. "The Double Flageolet-made in England," *Galpin Society Journal* 52 (1999), 172–182.

Weller, Enrico. 2004. *Der Blasinstrumentenbau im Vogtland von den Anfängen bis zum Beginn des 20. Jahrhunderts: Untersuchungen und Dokumentationen zur Geschichte eines Gewerbezweiges der Musikinstrumenteninsdustrie*. Markneukirchen: Stiftung der Sparkasse Vogtland.

Wells, Elizabeth, and Christopher Nobbs. 2007. *European Stringed Instruments. Royal College of Music Museum of Instrument Catalogue Part III*. London: Royal College of Music.

Westbrook, James. 2005. *The Century That Shaped the Guitar (From the Birth of the Six-String Guitar to the Death of Tárrega)*. [Hove, East Sussex]: The Author.

Weston, Pamela. 1974–1975. "Lazarus's Instrument Collection," *NACWPI Journal* 23, no. 2, 3–7; republished in Weston, Pamela. 2008. *Heroes & Heroines of Clarinettistry: A Selection of Writings*. Victoria, BC: Trafford.

White, Kelly, and Arnold Myers. 2004. "Woodwind Instruments of Boosey & Company," *Galpin Society Journal* 57 (May 2004), 62–80.

White, Paul. 1990. "Early Bassoon Fingering Charts," *Galpin Society Journal* 43 (1990), 68–111.

Wilson, Michael. 1968. *The English Chamber Organ: History and Development 1650–1850*. Columbia, SC: University of South Carolina Press.

Wilson, Richard. 2013. "19th Century Boehm Flutes": http://www.oldflutes.com/boehm.htmspr.

Yorke, James. 1986. *Keyboard Instruments at the Victoria and Albert Museum*. London: Victoria and Albert Museum.

Young, Phillip T. 1988. *Loan Exhibition of Historic Double Reed Instruments*. Vancouver: University of Victoria.

Young, Phillip T. 1993. *4900 Historical Woodwind Instruments: An Inventory of 200 Makers in International Collections*. London: T. Bingham.

MAKER'S INDEX

Chapter 1: Keyboard Instruments

Chapter 2: Flute & Whistle Instruments

Chapter 3: Double-Reed Instruments

Chapter 4: Single-Reed Instruments

Chapter 5: Free-Reed Instruments

Chapter 6: Cup-Mouthpiece Instruments

Chapter 7: Plucked & Bowed Stringed Instruments

Chapter 8: Percussion Instruments

CITY & COUNTRY INDEX